Lecture Notes in Computer Science 8870

Commenced Publication in 1973
Founding and Former Series Editors:
Gerhard Goos, Juris Hartmanis, and Jan van Leeuwen

Azizah Jaafar   Nazlena Mohamad Ali
Shahrul Azman Mohd Noah   Alan F. Smeaton
Peter Bruza   Zainab Abu Bakar
Nursuriati Jamil
Tengku Mohd Tengku Sembok (Eds.)

Information Retrieval Technology

10th Asia Information Retrieval Societies Conference
AIRS 2014
Kuching, Malaysia, December 3-5, 2014
Proceedings

Springer

Volume Editors

Azizah Jaafar, Malaysia; E-mail: azizah@ivi.ukm.edu.my

Nazlena Mohamad Ali, Malaysia; E-mail: nazlena.ali@ukm.edu.my

Shahrul Azman Mohd Noah, Malaysia; E-mail:shahrul@ukm.edu.my

Alan F. Smeaton, Ireland; E-mail: alan.smeaton@dcu.ie

Peter Bruza, Australia; E-mail: p.bruza@qut.edu.au

Zainab Abu Bakar, Malaysia; E-mail: zainab@tmsk.uitm.edu.my

Nursuriati Jamil, Malaysia; E-mail: liza@tmsk.uitm.edu.my

Tengku Mohd Tengku Sembok, Malaysia; E-mail: tmts@upnm.edu.my

ISSN 0302-9743   e-ISSN 1611-3349
ISBN 978-3-319-12843-6   e-ISBN 978-3-319-12844-3
DOI 10.1007/978-3-319-12844-3
Springer Cham Heidelberg New York Dordrecht London

Library of Congress Control Number: 2014952692

LNCS Sublibrary: SL 3 – Information Systems and Application, incl. Internet/Web and HCI

Typesetting: Camera-ready by author, data conversion by Scientific Publishing Services, Chennai, India

Printed on acid-free paper

Springer is part of Springer Science+Business Media (www.springer.com)

Preface

The Asian Information Retrieval Societies Conference, 2014 (AIRS 2014), was is a continuation of the conference series initiated from the Information Retrieval with Asian Languages (IRAL) workshop series back in 1996 in Korea. The objective of AIRS is to bring together international researchers and developers to exchange new ideas and the latest development in information retrieval (IR). The scope of the conference encompasses the theory and practice of all aspects of IR in text, audio, image, video, and multimedia data. This year, the tenth series of the AIRS conference was organized by the Malaysian Society of Information Retrieval and Knowledge Management (PECAMP) in collaboration with seven universities in Malaysia including Universiti Kebangsaan Malaysia (UKM), Universiti Teknologi MARA (UiTM), Universiti Putra Malaysia (UPM), Universiti Pertahanan Nasional Malaysia (UPNM), Kolej Universiti Islam Antarabangsa Selangor (KUIS), Universiti Malaysia Sarawak (UNIMAS), and the International Islamic University Malaysia (IIUM). The conference was held in Kuching, Sarawak, Malaysia, during December 3-5, 2014.

Seven tracks were the focus of AIR 2014: IR Models and Theories; IR Evaluation, User Study and Interactive IR; Web IR, Scalability and IR in Social Media; Multimedia IR; Natural Language Processing for IR; Machine Learning and Data Mining for IR; and IR Applications. This year, the Organizing Committee acknowledged an overwhelming response with submissions from academics and practitioners from 23 countries from Asia, Australia, Europe, Africa, and North America. All the submitted papers were reviewed and scrutinized by experts representing more than 123 Program Committee members from Asia, Europe, Oceania, and the USA. Each paper was reviewed by at least three reviewers. Due to the stringent reviewing process, the acceptance rate of the papers was 41%. Only 45 papers were accepted to be published in this year's proceedings. The LNCS proceedings are a compilation of the successful papers selected for the AIRS 2014 conference.

The editorial board of AIRS 2014 extends our sincere gratitude to all authors and contributors to this year's conference. Special thanks goes to the AIRS Steering Committee for choosing PECAMP to organize AIRS 2014. A special thank you is also extended to all conference sponsors, especially to Sarawak Convention Bureau (SCB), Perbadanan Nasional Berhad (PNB), Majlis Profesor Negara (MPN), Institute of Visual Informatics (IVI), and FTSM Knowledge Technology Research Group, UKM. Lastly, the editorial board would like to acknowledge the members of the Organizing Committee, Program Committee, support committee, and all the individuals who gave their invaluable support in making the conference a success.

December 2014

Azizah Jaafar
Nazlena Mohamad Ali
Shahrul Azman Mohd Noah
Alan F. Smeaton
Peter Bruza
Zainab Abu Bakar
Nursuriati Jamil
Tengku Mohd Tengku Sembok

Organization

The 10th Asian Information Retrieval Societies Conference (AIRS 2014) was organized by the Malaysian Society of Information Retrieval and Knowledge Management (PECAMP) in collaboration with seven universities in Malaysia including Universiti Kebangsaan Malaysia (UKM), Universiti Teknologi MARA (UiTM), Universiti Putra Malaysia (UPM), Universiti Pertahanan Nasional Malaysia (UPNM), Kolej Universiti Islam Antarabangsa Selangor (KUIS), Universiti Malaysia Sarawak (UNIMAS), and the International Islamic University Malaysia (IIUM).

Conference Chairs

Zainab Abu Bakar	Universiti Teknologi MARA, Malaysia
Nursuriati Jamil	Universiti Teknologi MARA, Malaysia
Tengku Mohd	Tengku Sembok Universiti Pertahanan Nasional Malaysia, Malaysia

Secretary Chairs

Shyamala Doraisamy	Universiti Putra Malaysia, Malaysia
Norhaslinda Kamaruddin	Universiti Teknologi MARA, Malaysia
Rabiah Abdul Kadir	Universiti Kebangsaan Malaysia, Malaysia

Finance Chairs

Azreen Azman	Universiti Putra Malaysia, Malaysia
Ibrahim Mohamed	Universiti Kebangsaan Malaysia, Malaysia

Publication Chairs

Azizah Jaafar	Universiti Kebangsaan Malaysia, Malaysia
Nazlena Mohamad Ali	Universiti Kebangsaan Malaysia, Malaysia
Shahrul Azman Mohd	Noah Universiti Kebangsaan Malaysia, Malaysia

Publicity Chairs

Shereena Mohd Arif	Universiti Kebangsaan Malaysia, Malaysia
Khirulnizam Abd Rahman	Kolej Universiti Islam Antarabangsa Selangor, Malaysia
Amzari Abu Bakar	Universiti Teknologi MARA, Malaysia
Norshita Mat Nayan	Universiti Kebangsaan Malaysia, Malaysia

Local Organizing Committee

Narayanan Kulathuramaiyer   Universiti Malaysia Sarawak, Malaysia
Shlomo Geva   Queensland University of Technology, Brisbane, Australia

AIRS Steering Committee

Alistair Moffat   The University of Melbourne, Australia
Dawei Song   The Robert Gordon University, UK
Gary Geunbae Lee   Pohang University of Science and Technology, Korea
Hsin-Hsi Chen   National Taiwan University, Taiwan
Hwee Tou Ng   National University of Singapore, Singapore
Masaharu Yoshioka   Hokkaido University, Japan
Wai Lam   The Chinese University of Hong Kong, Hong Kong, SAR China
Zhicheng Dou   Microsoft Research Asia, China

Program Chairs

Alan F. Smeaton   Dublin City University, Ireland
Peter Bruza   Queensland University of Technology, Australia

Area Chairs

(A) IR Applications

Kazunari Sugiyama   National University of Singapore, Singapore
Shahrul Azman Mohd Noah   Universiti Kebangsaan Malaysia, Malaysia

(B) IR Evaluation, User Study and Interactive IR

Fabio Crestani   University of Lugano, Switzerland
Azizah Jaafar   Universiti Kebangsaan Malaysia, Malaysia
Masnizah Mohd   Universiti Kebangsaan Malaysia, Malaysia

(C) Multimedia IR

Joemon Jose   University of Glasgow, UK
Fatimah Dato' Ahmad   Universiti Pertahanan Nasional Malaysia, Malaysia

(D) IR Models and Theories

Peter Bruza	Queensland University of Technology, Australia
Zainab Abu Bakar	Universiti Teknologi MARA, Malaysia

(E) Web IR, Scalability and IR in Social Media

Alistair Moffat	University of Melbourne, Australia
Azreen Azman	Universiti Putra Malaysia, Malaysia

(F) Natural Language Processing for IR

Atsushi Fujii	University of Tsukuba, Japan
Rabiah Abdul Kadir	Universiti Kebangsaan Malaysia, Malaysia

(G) Machine Learning and Data Mining for IR

Alan F. Smeaton	Dublin City University, Ireland
Muthukarrupan Annamalai	Universiti Teknologi MARA, Malaysia

Technical Program Committee

Abdul Razak Hamdan	Universiti Kebangsaan Malaysia, Malaysia
Abdulaziz Almaktoom	Wichita State University, USA
Adam Bermingham	Dublin City University, Ireland
Aida Mustapha	Universiti Putra Malaysia, Malaysia
Aixin Sun	Nanyang Technological University, Singapore
Alan F. Smeaton	Dublin City University, Ireland
Alistair Moffat	University of Melbourne, Australia
Andrew MacFarlane	City University, UK
Andrew Trotman	University of Otago, New Zealand
Azizah Jaafar	Universiti Kebangsaan Malaysia, Malaysia
Azreen Azman	Universiti Putra Malaysia, Malaysia
Ben He	University of Chinese Academy of Sciences, China
Changsheng Chen	Hong Kong University of Science and Technology, Hong Kong, SAR China
Charles Clarke	University of Waterloo, Canada
Chenliang Li	Wuhan University, China
Chintan Bhatt	Charotar University of Science and Technology, India
Chiung Ching Ho	Multimedia University, Malaysia

Deyi Xiong	Institute for Infocomm Research, Singapore
Faaizah Shahbodin	Universiti Teknikal Malaysia Melaka, Malaysia
Fabio Crestani	University of Lugano, Switzerland
Fadzilah Siraj	Universiti Utara Malaysia, Malaysia
Fatimah Dato' Ahmad	Universiti Pertahanan Nasional Malaysia, Malaysia
Fatimah Khalid	Universiti Putra Malaysia, Malaysia
Gabriella Pasi	Università degli Studi di Milano-Bicocca, Italy
Hamid Jalab	Universiti Malaya, Malaysia
Hamido Fujita	Iwate Prefectural University, Japan
Hyowon Lee	Singapore University of Technology and Design, Singapore
Iadh Ounis	University of Glasgow, UK
Ian Ruthven	University of Strathclyde, UK
Ibrahim Mohamed	Universiti Kebangsaan Malaysia, Malaysia
Ichiro Ide	Nagoya University, Japan
In-Su Kang	Kyungsung University, South Korea
James Thom	RMIT University, Australia
Jianyun Nie	Université de Montréal, Canada
Jun Xu	Huawei Technologies, China
Justin Zobel	University of Melbourne, Australia
Kasturi Dewi	Universiti Malaya, Malaysia
Kazuhiro Seki	Konan University, Japan
Kazunari Sugiyama	National University of Singapore, Singapore
Kenji Hatano	Doshisha University, Japan
Kiran Kaur a/p Gurmit Singh	Universiti Malaya, Malaysia
Lailatulqadri Zakaria	Universiti Kebangsaan Malaysia, Malaysia
Laure Soulier	IRIT- Paul Sabatier University, France
Leong Kew	National University of Singapore, Singapore
Liangchai Gao	Peking University, China
Lilly Suriani Affendey	Universiti Putra Malaysia, Malaysia
Luis Barreto	Instituto Politécnico de Viana do, Portugal
Maizatul Akmar Ismail	Universiti Malaya, Malaysia
Marcos Cintra	Federal Territorial University of the Semi-Arid, Brazil
Mark Sanderson	RMIT University, Australia
Mas Rina Mustaffa	Universiti Putra Malaysia, Malaysia
Masnizah Mohd	Universiti Kebangsaan Malaysia, Malaysia
Masrah Azrifah Azmi Murad	Universiti Putra Malaysia, Malaysia
Matthias Hagen	Bauhaus-Universität Weimar, Germany
Mazidah Puteh	Universiti Teknologi MARA, Malaysia
Miao Chen	Indiana University Bloomington, USA
Mike Joy	University of Warwick, UK

Rabiah Abdul Kadir	Universiti Kebangsaan Malaysia, Malaysia
Rita Zaharah Wan Chik	Universiti Kuala Lumpur, Malaysia
Roslina Othman	International Islamic University Malaysia, Malaysia
Saidah Saad	Universiti Kebangsaan Malaysia, Malaysia
Sazilah Salam	Universiti Teknikal Malaysia Melaka, Malaysia
Shahrul Azman Mohd Noah	Universiti Kebangsaan Malaysia, Malaysia
Sharifah Yasin	Universiti Putra Malaysia, Malaysia
Shereena Mohd Arif	Universiti Kebangsaan Malaysia, Malaysia
Shuzlina Abdul Rahman	Universiti Teknologi MARA, Malaysia
Shyamala Doraisamy	Universiti Putra Malaysia, Malaysia
Siti Khaotijah Mohammad	Universiti Sains Malaysia, Malaysia
Siti Norul Huda Sheikh Abdullah	Universiti Kebangsaan Malaysia, Malaysia
Siti Salwa Salleh	Universiti Teknologi MARA, Malaysia
Sri Devi Ravana	Universiti Malaya, Malaysia
Sujeeth Bharadwaj	University of Illinois at Urbana-Champaign, USA
Syed Abdul Rahman Al-Haddad Syed Mohamed	Universiti Putra Malaysia, Malaysia
Tan Tien Ping	Universiti Sains Malaysia, Malaysia
Tengku Mohd Tengku Sembok	Universiti Pertahanan Nasional Malaysia, Malaysia
Tetsuya Sakai	Microsoft Research Asia, China
Timothy Baldwin	University of Melbourne, Australia
Waidah Ismail	Universiti Sains Islam Malaysia, Malaysia
Wan Fatimah Wan Ahmad	Universiti Teknologi Petronas, Malaysia
Wenyu Liu	Huazhong University of Science and Technology, China
Xiaozhong Liu	Indiana University Bloomington, USA
Yi Guo	East China University of Science and Technology, China
Yi Yu	National University of Singapore,Singapore
Yin Zhang	Zhejiang University, China
Yiqun Liu	Tsinghua University, China
Yu Suzuki	Nagoya University, Japan
Yu-N Cheah	Universiti Sains Malaysia, Malaysia
Yun Huoy Choo	Universiti Teknikal Malaysia Melaka,Malaysia
Yunqing Xia	Tsinghua University, China
Zainab Abu Bakar	Universiti Teknologi MARA, Malaysia
Zalinda Othman	Universiti Kebangsaan Malaysia, Malaysia

Sponsoring Institutions

Universiti Kebangsaan Malaysia, Malaysia (UKM)
Universiti Teknologi MARA, Malaysia (UiTM)
Universiti Putra Malaysia, Malaysia (UPM)
Universiti Malaysia Sarawak, Malaysia (UNIMAS)
Universiti Pertahanan Nasional Malaysia, Malaysia (UPNM)
Kolej Universiti Islam Antarabangsa Selangor, Malaysia (KUIS)
Sarawak Convention Bureau, Malaysia (SCB)
Permodalan Nasional Berhad, Malaysia (PNB)
Majlis Profesor Negara (MPN)

Table of Contents

IR Applications

IR Evaluation, User Study and Interactive IR

Multimedia IR

IR Models and Theories

Web IR, Scalability and IR in Social Media

Natural Language Processing for IR

Machine Learning and Data Mining for IR

Leveraging Deletion Neighborhoods and Trie
for Efficient String Similarity Search and Join

Jia Cui[1,3], Dan Meng[2], and Zhong-Tao Chen[1,3]

[1]Institute of Computing Technology, Chinese Academy of Sciences, Beijing, China
[2]Institute of Information Engineering, Chinese Academy of Sciences, Beijing, China
[3]University of Chinese Academy of Sciences, Beijing, China
{cuijia,chenzhongtao}@ncic.ac.cn, {mengdan}@iie.ac.cn

Abstract. String similarity search and joins are primitive operations in database and information retrieval to address the poor data quality problem. Due to the high complexity of deletion neighborhoods, existing methods resort to hashing schemes to achieve reduction in space requirement of the index. However the introduced hash collisions need to be verified by the costly edit distance computation. In this paper, we focus on achieving a faster query speed with affordable memory consumptions. We propose a novel method that leverages the power of deletion neighborhoods and trie to answer the edit distance based string similarity query efficiently. We utilize the trie to share common prefixes of deletion neighborhoods and propose subtree merging optimization to reduce the index size. Then the index partition strategies are discussed and bit vector based verification method is proposed to speed up the query. The experimental results show that our method outperforms state-of-art methods on real dataset.

Keywords: similarity search, similarity join, deletion neighborhoods, edits distance, trie.

1   Introduction and Related Work

The development of network technology has greatly promoted the growth of textual data volume. With the advent of WEB 2.0 era, many novel applications appeared, such as social-networking websites (e.g. Facebook, Google+, etc) and micro-blogging websites (e.g. Twitters, Jaiku, etc), which further boost textual data volume at an exponentially rate. Conducting queries on such large amounts of textual data encapsulates several problems. One of the major concerns is poor data quality problem, such as typos, abbreviations etc, which is prevalent and brings us the need for efficient string similarity query methods. The string similarity query has involved many application scenarios, such as data cleaning [1], record linkage [9], query auto-completion [2], approximate named entity extraction [4,5] and bio-informatics. The ability to perform fast string similarity query is a prime requirement for these applications. Given a dataset with N strings, naively computing edit distance for $N(N-1)/2$ pairs is rather costly. Therefore many studies have been devoted to developing techniques for answering edit distance based string similarity queries with features of fast, scalable

A. Jaafar et al. (Eds.): AIRS 2014, LNCS 8870, pp. 1–13, 2014.

and memory efficient. Most of modern strategies adopt preprocessing to index dataset for facilitating the fast evaluation of queries.

One widely adopted technique employs a filter-and-verify framework [8],[13,14] which includes two steps: (1) filter step: devising effective filtering algorithms to prune a large number of dissimilar strings and generating a set of candidates; and (2) verification step: verifying candidates by computing their real similarity and comparing to the threshold. Most of existing filter-and-verify framework based algorithms employ a signature scheme to extract substrings as signatures, such that if two strings are similar, their signatures must have overlaps. Existing signature schemes include: fixed-length signatures (e.g., q-gram [8], q-chunk [18]) and variable-length signatures (e.g., vgram [10], vchunk [12] and partitions [11]). Many efficient filtering algorithms are proposed, e.g., length filtering [13], position filtering [13], count filtering [13] and prefix filtering [1], etc. By exploiting signature schemes and filtering algorithms, the filter-and-verify framework performs the string similarity query efficiently. However it is still inefficient for short strings since the difficulties in the extraction of high quality signatures, which leads to a large number of candidates that need to be verified. Thus algorithm TrieJoin [15] is devised to solve similarity join on short string dataset over a trie index by computing active node set during the query time and the verification step can be avoided.

Another powerful scheme suitable for short strings is based on neighborhoods generation which enumerates the similar strings (neighbors) of dataset within a certain threshold, such that transforms string similarity search to exactly matching of their neighbors. Assume the edit distance threshold is τ, an alphabet size is $|\Sigma|$, a dataset with n strings and the average string length is l. In [20] the authors has theoretically proved the space requirement for the neighbors is $O(nl^{\tau}|\Sigma|^{\tau})$. The large space requirement makes it impractical for real world applications. In [17] the authors developed the algorithm FastSS based on deletion neighborhoods scheme which enumerates neighbors by deleting characters no more than τ. It reduces the space requirement to $O(nl^{\tau})$ which is insensitive to the alphabet size. In [19] the authors proved the selectivity of deletion neighborhoods scheme is higher than that of the popular q-gram. In [16] the author proposed an improved deletion neighborhood generation method base on divide-and-conquer strategy. In [4] the authors proposed a prefix based reduction method to decrease the space requirement to $O(l_p\tau^2)$ (l_p being a parameter: prefix length). Inspired by [4], [19] developed an index reduction method which indexes the suffix of the neighborhoods. The main idea in [4], [19] is to index part of neighborhoods instead of entire ones and makes their filter conditions weaker than the original one in [17]. Notice that the reduction in space requirement is on the cost of admitting more false positives in candidates and requires more time for verification.

In this paper, we focus on achieving a faster query speed with affordable memory consumptions. Our contributions are the following:

- We present a novel method which leverages the power of deletion neighborhoods and trie to answer the edit distance based string similarity queries.
- Index partition and optimization strategies are proposed to further reduce index size. The bit vector based verification method is proposed to speed up verification.

- We implement our method on both similarity search and join and compare our method with the state-of-the arts methods. The experimental results report a significant promotion on the performance of methods based on deletion neighborhoods.

The remainder of this paper is organized as follows: Section 2 presents preliminaries. Section 3 describes the indexing and verification method. Section 4 presents implementation details on similarity search and join. Experimental study is given in Section 5. Section 6 concludes this paper.

2   Preliminaries

There are two types of functions for quantifying the similarity of strings. One is called token-based similarity, which tokenizes strings as token sets (bag of words or grams) and then quantifies similarity by computing the overlaps between token sets, e.g, *Jaccard Similarity* and *Cosine Similarity*. The other is called character-based similarity and the most widely-used function is *Edit Distance*. Its formal definition is the minimum number of single character edit operations (i.e., *insertion, deletion* and *substitution*) needed to transform from one string to another. Let $ed(r,s)$ denote the edit distance between r and s. The classical algorithm for computing edit distance is dynamic programming and its time complexity is $O(|r| \times |s|)$ [6]. An improved algorithm reduces the computation in $O(\tau \cdot \min(|r|,|s|))$ time [3].

The string similarity query can be classified into similarity search and similarity join. Consider a dataset D with a large number of strings and each string has a unique identifier, i.e., with the form $<id_i, s_i>$. Their definitions based on edit distance are:

Definition 1. Similarity search *Given a dataset D and a query instance Q as a tuple $<q,\tau>$, where q is a query string and τ is an edit distance threshold, returns all the strings $\{id_i \mid ed(s_i,q) \leq \tau, <id_i, s_i> \in D\}$.*

Definition 2. Similarity join *Given two datasets R and S, an edit distance threshold τ, the similarity join returns all the string pairs $R \bowtie_\tau S = \{<id_i, id_j> \mid ed(r_i, s_j) \leq \tau, <id_i, r_i> \in R, <id_j, s_j> \in S\}$. If $R=S$, it is called self similarity join.*

Let Σ be a finite alphabet of symbols, each symbol is called a character. A string s is an ordered sequence of symbols drawn from Σ. Let $|s|$ denote the length of s and $s[i]$ denote its i-th character (from left to right). $s[i,...,j]$ is the sub-sequence between position i and j in s. Assume we are to delete one character $s[i]$ in s, the concatenation of residual strings $s[1,...,i-1,i+1,...,|s|]$ is called a 1-deletion neighbor of s, denoted by $d(s,i)$. E.g., $d(\text{AIRS},2)=\text{ARS}$. $D(s,1)$ is the set of all possible 1-deletion neighbors of s. Given a edit distance threshold τ, deleting τ characters in s will result in a residual string s' which is called τ-deletion neighbor and the set of all possible s' is denoted by $D(s,\tau)$. We now define the τ-variant family.

Definition 3. τ-variant family *Given a string s and an edit distance threshold τ, the τ-variant family is all deletion neighbors of s by deleting no more than τ characters, denoted by $F(s,\tau)$, $F(s,\tau)=\{s' \mid s' \in D(s,k), 0 \leq k \leq \tau\}$.*

Lemma 1 [17]. *Given two strings s_1 and s_2, if $ed(s_1,s_2) \leq \tau$, then $F(s_1,\tau) \cap F(s_2,\tau) \neq \Phi$.*

The underlying idea of lemma 1 is if the total number of single character edit operations required to transform s_1 to s_2 is no larger than τ, then two strings must be reducible to a common pattern after deleting no more than τ characters. Notice that the filtering condition in lemma 1 is a necessary condition. Even the strings meet this condition, their edit distance may not be within τ. E.g., $F(abcd,1) \cap F(abdf,1) = \{abd\}$, but $ed(abcd,abdf) = 2$. As the deletions is applied recursively, we define a deletion neighbor pair with the form $<s',\mathcal{L}(s')>$, where s' is the neighbor and $\mathcal{L}(s')$ is the deletion list which records the deleted position to transform s to s'.

Lemma 2 [4]. *Given two string s_1 and s_2 that satisfy $ed(s_1,s_2) \leq \tau$, if and only if there exist $<s_1',\mathcal{L}(s_1')> \in F(s_1,\tau)$ and $<s_2',\mathcal{L}(s_2')> \in F(s_2,\tau)$, such that $s_1'=s_2'$ and $|\mathcal{L}(s_1') \cap \mathcal{L}(s_2')| \leq \tau$.*

Lemma 2 extends lemma 1 with a verification method by computing cardinality of the union of two deletion lists. E.g., $<abd,[3]> \in F(abcd,1)$ and $<abd,[4]> \in F(abdf,1)$, $|[3,4]|=2>1$, thus $ed(abcd, abdf)>1$.

3   Indexing

3.1   Basic Structure and Verification

The τ-variant family is generated recursively by deleting characters in order. To avoid the generation of duplicated deletion neighbors, we stipulate that the position of deleted character in the i-th recursion should not be smaller than that of in the $(i-1)$-th recursion. Algorithm 1 shows the pseudocode of τ-variant family generation process in our work. Notice that the parameter τ' controls the remaining recursion depth that needs to be processed and is decreased by 1 at each recursion level. After the τ-variant family of strings is generated, we insert them in a trie with some extensions. Generally a trie node stores a single character and the path from root node to leaf node represents a string. On leaf nodes, we store a list with the form $<id, del-list>$, where id is the string identifier and $del-list$ is the deletion list corresponding to the neighbor on the leaf node.

Algorithm 1. DNF-Gen(s, p, τ, τ', v)
Input: string s, position p, edit-distance τ, remaining recursion depth τ', bit vector v.
Output: τ-variant family of s, $F(s,\tau)$.

```
1. p←1, l←|s|, τ'←τ;
2. for i = p to l do
3.    temp←s;
4.    delete temp[i];
5.    new a bit-vector bv and bv[i]←1;
6.    bv←(bv≪(τ−τ'))&v;
7.    F(s,τ)←<temp, bv>;
8.    if (τ-1)>0 and |temp|>τ-1   then
9.       DNF-Gen(temp, i, τ, τ-1,v);
```

The deletion lists in FastSS [17] and other related studies are ordered integer arrays, i.e., they store the position of deleted character in the current recursion in order. Generally an integer occupies 4 bytes in a 32-bits computer and it takes $4k$ bytes to store a deletion-list for any k-deletion neighbor. For a string with length l, it takes $4\times \sum_{i=0}^{\tau} C_l^i$ bytes to store all deletion lists for its τ-variant family. In order to reduce the space requirement for these deletion lists, we adopt a bit vector to record the positions of deleted character. The deletion list is generated along with deletion neighbors in the recursive procedure and computed based on the deletion list in the last recursion step. Suppose the i-th character is deleted, a bit vector bv is initialized by setting $bv[i]=1$. Then we left shift bv for number of remaining recursions depth and apply bitwise operator 'AND' between bv and deletion list from the last recursion level (algorithm 1, line 4-6). Suppose the maximum string length of a dataset is L and then we only need $\lceil L/8 \rceil$ bytes to store a deletion-list. For the short strings whose length is no larger than 32, given an edit distance threshold $\tau \geq 1$ such that $L \not\geq 32\times\tau$. Therefore the bit vector format deletion list definitely saves the index space. Different from the integer array deletion list which stores the *relative* deleted positions at each recursion step, the bit vector format deletion list stores the absolute deleted positions in original string. In the bit vector, the bit "1" indicates the positions of deleted characters in original string. We observe that if the number of overlapped "1" in two deletion lists is x, then it needs x edit operations for transformation, and if the number of non-overlapped "1" is y, then it needs $2y$ edit operations for transformation. If two strings are within edit distance τ, then $x+2y\leq\tau$ is always true. Based on this observation, we propose a fast verification method using bit vector format deletion list. First we define a function *count_bit()* that returns the total number of "1" in a bit vector. Algorithm 2 shows the description.

Algorithm 2. $BV(<s_1',\mathcal{L}(s_1')>,<s_2',\mathcal{L}(s_2')>)$
Input: two deletion neighbor pair $<s_1',\mathcal{L}(s_1')>,<s_2',\mathcal{L}(s_2')>$;edit distance threshold τ.
Output: true: $ed(s_1,s_2)\leq\tau$, false: otherwise.
1. **if** $s_1' \neq s_2'$ **then**
2.   return false;
3. **else** $\rho \leftarrow count\_bit\,(\mathcal{L}(s_1')$ 'OR' $\mathcal{L}(s_2'))$;
4. **if** $\rho\leq\tau$ **then**
5.   return true;
6. **else**
7.   return false;

For example, assume the maximum string length is 8, edit distance threshold is 2, given the strings $s_1=steven$, $s_2=stevems$, $s_3=sewden$.
$F(s_1,2) \cap F(s_2,2)=<steve,\mathcal{L}_1=00100000>,<steve,\mathcal{L}_2=01100000>;$
$F(s_1,2) \cap F(s_3,2)=<seen,\mathcal{L}_3=00001010),<seen,\mathcal{L}_4=00001100>.$
$count\_bit(\mathcal{L}_1$ 'OR' $\mathcal{L}_2)=2 \Longrightarrow ed(s_1,s_2)\leq2; count\_bit(\mathcal{L}_3$ 'OR' $\mathcal{L}_4)=3 \Longrightarrow ed(s_1,s_3)>2.$

Given a dataset D, we generate the τ-variant family for every string in D and insert them in a trie with the bit vector format deletion list, see Fig. 1(a). For convenience of narration, we call it S-DNT (Single Deletion Neighborhoods Trie). Obviously, S-DNT is huge and complex in structure. The drawback of S-DNT is that such centralized index should be loaded into memory when the query is issued. If the dataset is scalable, S-DNT may be too large for small memory computers. So we adopt some partition strategies to index the τ-variant families separately in tries, named P-DNT (Partition based Deletion Neighborhoods Trie). Following are the partition strategies.

Length based partition (LP). The motivation comes from the fact that if two strings are within the edit distance threshold τ, their length difference should be within [-τ,τ]. Let Ŧ denote a partition of the P-DNT index, i.e. a trie. The partition strategy can be classified into non-overlapping strategy and overlapping strategy. According to the length range of a dataset $[a:b]$, the non-overlapping strategy divides the range into N even partitions and the length of a partition is $\lceil (b-a)/N \rceil$. Thus each Ŧ stores the τ-variant family whose original string length belongs to the specified range. The over-lapping strategy also divides the range into N even partitions, but with 2τ overlaps between the adjacent partitions. Given a query string q, for overlapping strategy, it only needs to look up in $Ŧ_{[m,n]}$ that $|q|\pm\tau\in[m,n]$. For non-overlapping strategy, it needs to look up in several index partitions that cover the range $[|q|-\tau, |q|+\tau]$.

Deletion number based partition (DNP). Given an edit distance threshold τ and generate the τ-variant family of all strings in a dataset. Each i-deletion neighbors was inserted into the partition $Ŧ_i$, so the index P-DNT is a set of $\{Ŧ_0,...,Ŧ_i,... ,Ŧ_\tau\}$. The benefits are that it supports any edit distance threshold no large than τ and the candi-date size is small as for some certain index partitions, the verification can be skipped. For example, assume a query q with the threshold is $\alpha\leq\tau$. For the strings in α-variant family $F(q,\alpha)$, we need to visit $Ŧ_\gamma\in\{Ŧ_0,...,Ŧ_\alpha\}$. For the deletion neighbor $q'\in D(q,\beta)$ $(\beta\in[0,\alpha])$, if $\beta+\gamma<\alpha$, the verification can be skipped.

For P-DNT, the index partitions for a query to lookup are clearly specified. It aims to reduce the candidate size but on the cost of additional space requirement. Because storing τ-variant family separately in tries may slightly contradict to the purpose of sharing prefix. As we can preprocess the dataset and retrieve the partitions of P-DNT from disk whenever the query needs, it saves in-memory index space.

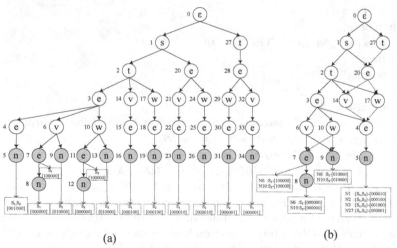

(a)   (b)

Fig. 1. (a) An example of DNT index. (b) DNT index after subtree merging

3.2   Subtree Merging

From the Fig. 1(a) we see that τ-variant enumeration generates a large number of similar strings and indexing them in a trie costs redundant space. In order to remove the duplicate paths in the trie, we propose to compress index by merging common subtrees which are identical or isomorphic. Many techniques are devoted to compress a trie, e.g., double array trie which achieves 17 per cent smaller than the list based trie but the insertion is quite time consuming [7]. From Fig. 1(a) we can see that merging common subtrees (duplicate path) may achieve a remarkable reduction on index size. We notice three cases of common subtrees can be merged.

Case 1. Two nodes are with the same label (character) and their subtrees are literally identical, including the string ids in the list of leaf nodes. E.g. node 20 and 28 in Fig. 1(a), we merge the deletion list pairs on the same labeled leaf nodes (26 and 31, 19 and 34), then divert the incoming edge of node 28 to node 20 and delete node 28 and all its subtrees. Finally we obtain the node 5 in Fig. 1(b) with the merged list item $N27:\{S_1,S_2\}$-[000001].

Case 2. Two nodes are with the different labels but their subtrees are literally identical, including the string ids in the list of leaf nodes. E.g. node 2 and 20 in Fig. 1(a), we divert the incoming edge of node 21 and 24 to node 14 and 17, merge the deletion list pair on the leaf nodes with routing information for the deletion list, then delete the node 21 and 24 and their subtrees. Finally we obtain the node 5 in Fig. 1(b) with the merged list item $N2:\{S_1,S_2\}$-[000010].

Case 3. Two nodes with the different characters and their subtree are isophmoic but the string ids on the leaf nodes are different. E.g., the node 6 and 10 in Fig. 1(a), their substrees are isophmoic and different ids on the leaf nodes. We divert the outgoing edges of node 10 to the children of node 6, and merge their inverted list on the leaf nodes, specify the routing information for the string ids. As shown in Fig. 1(b), the node 7 contains the list $\{N6:S_1,N10:S_2\}$, this means the path from node 6 ('v') is corresponding to the string s_1 and node 10 ('w') is corresponding to the string s_2.

The total number of nodes in Fig. 1(a) and (b) is 34 and 14, we can see that merging common subtree definitely achieves a reduction in size of trie index.

4   Implementation

4.1   Similarity Search

First, we prove that the deletion neighborhoods based string similarity search retrieves duplicate results. Then we give the algorithm of similarity search.

Lemma 3. Given an edit distance threshold τ, we consider τ-variant family as a universal set. If there exists a string r that satisfies $ed(r,q)=\tau'<\tau$ with the query string q, then the set difference of $F(r,\tau')$ and $F(q,\tau')$ concerning their respective universal set have overlap, i.e., $\{F(r,\tau)-F(r,\tau')\}\cap\{F(s,\tau)-F(s,\tau')\}\neq\Phi$.

Proof. According to Lemma 1, $F(r,\tau')\cap F(s,\tau')\neq\Phi$. Without loss of generality, let $p \in F(r,\tau')\cap F(s,\tau')$, such that $p\in D(r,m)$ and $p\in D(s,n)$ $(m, n\in[0,\tau'])$. Continue to generate 1-deletion neighborhoods set for p ($|p|>1$) and obtain $D(p,1)$, $D(p,1)\subset D(r,m+1)$ and

$D(p,1) \subset D(s,n+1)$,   i.e., $D(p,1) \subset \{F(r,\tau'+1)-F(r,\tau')\} \cap \{F(s,\tau'+1)-F(s,\tau')\}$.Extending $D(p,1)$ to $D(p,x)$, so $D(p,x) \subset \{F(r,\tau'+x)-F(r,\tau')\} \cap \{F(s,\tau'+x)-F(s,\tau')\}$, $(x \in [1,\tau-\tau'])$. Let $x=k-k'$, $\{F(r,\tau)-F(r,\tau')\} \cap \{F(s,\tau)-F(s,\tau')\} \neq \Phi$.

Lemma 3 proves that the deletion neighborhoods scheme causes duplicate results.

In order to remove the duplicate results in retrieval process, we adopt a minimum-heap data structure to store the string *ids* that has passed the verification step. When a string *id* is inserted into the heap, it calls for a binary search to check if it has already existed. Finally it pops elements from heap as results. Algorithm 3 shows the pseudo-code of similarity search on S-DNT index. Note that the function *exactly_search(s,*Ŧ*)* searches *s* on the index Ŧ and then returns the list on the leaf node as candidates which exactly matches *s*.

Algorithm 3. SimilaritySearch-DNT(R,q,τ)

Input: dataset R, a query string q, edit distance threshold τ.

Output: $\{r| ed(r,q) \leq \tau, r \in R\}$.

1. $Ŧ(R,\tau) \leftarrow DNF\_GEN(r,1,\tau,\tau,u)$;
2. $F(q,\tau) \leftarrow DNF\_GEN(q,1,\tau,\tau,v)$;
3. **foreach** $q' \in F(q,\tau)$ **do**
4.   Candidates$\leftarrow$exactly_search(q',Ŧ(R,τ));
5.   Min-Heap $H \leftarrow$ BV($\mathcal{L}(q')$, $\mathcal{L}(c,c \in$Candidates));
6. pop H
7. **end**

4.2   Similarity Join

An intuitive way to perform similarity join for two datasets is to index their τ-variant family in S-DNT, then apply depth-first or breadth-first traversal algorithm to retrieve the candidates on the leaf nodes and verify the candidates pairwisely (referred as SJ-SDNT). However it is inefficient since the traverse cannot start until the index is constructed, and for two large datasets, it may fail due to the limited memory space. To address this problem, we proposed an incremental similarity join algorithm called ISJ-DNT. We describe the case of self similarity join as example. First, the dataset R is ordered by the increasing order of string length and lexicographic order, i.e., $|r_i| \leq |r_j|$, $i \leq j$, $r_i, r_j \in R$. To minimize the space requirement, we adopt the non-overlapping length based partition strategy. Given a threshold τ, we generate τ-variant family $F(r_i,\tau)$ for string r_i in R sequentially and enumerate neighbors in $F(r_i,\tau)$ to search $\{Ŧ_{|r_i|-\tau},...,Ŧ_{|r_i|}\}$ and verify the candidates. Finally, we insert $F(r_i,\tau)$ into $Ŧ_{|r_i|}$ and remove the $Ŧ_{|r_i|-\tau}$ in order to save the memory space if meeting the strings with length $|r_i|+1$. The pseudo-code is shown in algorithm 4.

Algorithm 4. ISJ-DNT(R,τ)

Input: dataset R, edit distance threshold τ.

Output: similarity pairs $\{<r_i,r_j>| ed(r_i,r_j) \leq \tau, r_i, r_j \in R\}$.

1. Sort R in ascending order of string length and lexicographic order;
2. **for** each $r \in R$ **do**
3. $F(r,\tau) \leftarrow DNF\_Gen(r,1,\tau,\tau,v)$;
4.   **for** each $r' \in F(r,\tau)$ **do**

5.   **for** each $\mathbb{F}_i \in \{\mathbb{F}_{|r|-\tau}, \ldots, \mathbb{F}_{|r|}\} \neq$ NULL **do**
6.   Candidates=exactly_search(r',$\mathbb{F}_i$);
7.   Min-Heap $H \leftarrow$ BV($\mathcal{L}(r')$, $\mathcal{L}(c, c \in$ Candidates));
8. pop H
9. end

5   Experiments

In this section, we compare our method with the state-of-art methods. All programs are implemented in C++ and complied in GCC 4.1.2 with the –O3 flag. To guarantee even comparison, all programs are running in single thread. We ran programs on a machine with AMD Opteron 4×8 cores, 800MHz and 32GB Memory running Red Hat Enterprise Linux Server 5.5 with kernel 2.6.18. The experiments are conducted on a publicly available dataset: ENGLISH-DICT[1]. It has 150K records and the average length is 9, $|\Sigma|$ is 27. We compared our method with following methods:

- The naïve method that directly indexes deletion neighbors with integer deletion arrays, denoted by HashTable(Ori-Nohash). The candidates are verified by comparing two deletion lists.
- In [17], it indexes the hash value of deletion neighbors and along with integer deletion list, denoted by HashTable(Ori-BKDR). The hash function is BKDR designed specifically for strings. The candidates are verified by comparing two deletion lists.
- In [4], it indexes the prefix of deletion neighbors and verifies candidate strings by computing the edit distance using algorithm in [3], denoted by HashTable(pre-l_p).
- In [19], it indexes the suffix of deletion neighbors and verifies candidate strings by computing the edit distance using algorithm in [3], denoted by HashTable(suf-s_p).

5.1   Evaluating Index Construction

We compare the construction performance of the indices mentioned above, including S-DNT, P-DNT with non-overlapping length based partition (LP-NO), P-DNT with overlapping length based partition (LP-O), P-DNT with deletion number based partition

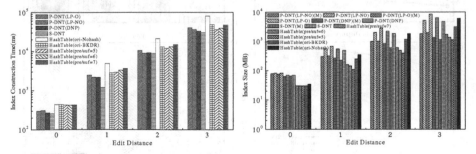

Fig. 2. Index construction time and size versus edit distance threshold

[1] http://dbgroup.cs.tsinghua.edu.cn/wangjn/data/word.format.tar.gz

(DNP). Since the max length of English-Dict is 30, we divide the length partition based P-DNT into 4 even partitions. Since the average length of dataset is 9, we choose the length of prefix or suffix from 5 to 7. All hash tables are implemented with C++ STL Map. Fig. 2 reports the index construction time without compression and index size after compression. We can see that construction time of DNT index (without compression) is faster than hashtables. Then we apply the subtree merging strategy on DNT to compress the index, and (M) means the index after subtree merging. We can see that the reduction is not obvious when τ=0 because these are not many similarity strings on the path and the size of hashtable is smaller than DNT. From τ=1 to 3, the subtree merging reduce the DNT index by 2.5 to 4 times and achieves the same level with the HashTable(ori-BKDR) index. But the size of compressed DNT index is still little bigger the prefix or suffix based hash table as the latter does not store any deletion lists. The time cost of subtree merging is shown in Table 1. We see that the subtree merging costs about 3 times as construction time.

Table 1. The time cost of merging subtrees on English-Dict

τ	S-DNT	P-DNT(LP-NO)	P-DNT(LP-O)	P-DNT(DNP)
1	3.2s	6.1s	6.7s	6.2s
2	16.6s	17.1s	22.9s	18.1s
3	40.9s	47.2s	60.6s	43.3s

5.2 Evaluating Similarity Search

We study similarity search performance on different indexing schemes. Firstly, we fix edit distance threshold from to 0 to 3 uniformly with a query file of 1000 queries.

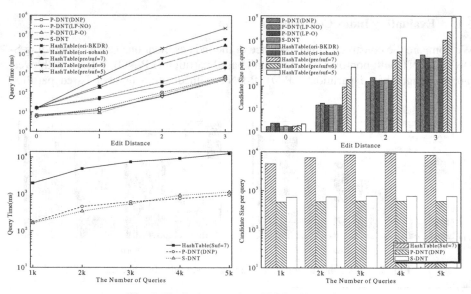

Fig. 3. Similarity search on ENGLISH-DICT

Then we fix the maximum edit distance threshold to 3, vary the query file with 1000-5000 queries with edit distance threshold from 0 to 3 randomly. The total query time and average candidate size are shown in Fig. 3. We can see in the first experiment, our method outperform the prefix/suffix based hash index because our method obtains smaller candidates size and our verification algorithm performs faster. Then we select the best two of our method and the best of prefix/suffix hash based method for the second experiment as they require smaller index space than HashTable(ori-BKDR) for τ=3. We can see that for the random threshold query, our method performs up to 10 times faster and generate smaller candidate size per query. The results proved that our method achieves a faster query speed with affordable memory consumptions.

5.3 Evaluating Similarity Join

We study the performance of similarity join by varying the edit distance threshold. To the best of our known, there isn't any experimental evaluation of similarity join using the deletion neighborhoods scheme. We compare our method with the state-of-art algorithm Trie-Join [15]. Fig. 4 reports the total execution time (including the indexing time and the joining time) and the status of memory usage during the processing.

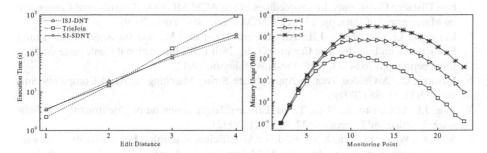

Fig. 4. Self similarity joins on ENGLISH-DICT

We see that for τ=1, Trie-Join is 1.6 times faster than our method; for τ=2, our method is very close to Trie-Join; for τ>2, our method outperforms Trie-Join. The main reason is that for a small edit distance threshold, the active node set for computing in Trie-Join is small, but τ-variant family generation costs more time. As the threshold increases, the active node sets become huge and the time for computing active node set becomes larger than that of τ-variant family generation and search. For instance, for τ=4, ISJ-DNT is 3.5 times faster than Trie-Join. The memory usage during the processing indicates that ISJ-DNT is related to length distribution of the dataset.

6   Conclusion

Deletion neighborhoods scheme is efficient for string similarity query but requires a huge space requirement for indexing. In this paper, we leverage trie to reduce the space requirement for deletion neighborhoods and propose subtree merging to further reduce the index size, we propose the bit vector format deletion list while keeps the power of deletion neighborhoods. Experimental results show our method is more efficiently than the state-of-art method based on deletion neighborhoods.

Acknowledgements. This work is partly supported by China National 863 High Technology Program (No.2013AA13204, 2012AA01A401), China National Natural Science Funds (No. 60903047, 61272361).

References

1. Chaudhuri, S., Ganti, V., Kaushik, R.: A Primitive Operator for Similarity Joins in Data Cleaning. In: 22nd IEEE International Conference on Data Engineering, p. 5. IEEE Press, New York (2006)
2. Chaudhuri, S., Kaushik, R.: Extending Auto-completion to Tolerate Errors. In: Proceedings of the ACM SIGMOD International Conference on Management of Data, pp. 707–718. ACM Press, New York (2009)
3. Ukkonen, E.: Algorithm for Approximate String Matching. J. Information and Control 64(1-3), 100–118 (1985)
4. Wang, W., Xiao, C., Lin, X.M., Zhang, C.: Efficient Approximate Entity Extraction with Edit Distance Constraints. In: Proceedings of the ACM SIGMOD International Conference on Management of Data, pp. 759–770. ACM Press, New York (2009)
5. Deng, D., Li, G.L., Feng, J.H.: An Efficient Trie-based Method for Approximate Entity Extraction with Edit-distance Constraints. In: 28th IEEE International Conference on Data Engineering, pp. 762–773. IEEE Press, Washington (2012)
6. Navarro, G.: A Guided Tour to Approximate String Matching. J. ACM Computing Surveys 33(1), 31–88 (2001)
7. Aoe, J.I., Morimoto, K., Sato, T.: An Efficient Implementation of TrieStructures. J. Software: Practice and Experience 22, 695–721 (1992)
8. Xiao, C., Wang, W., Lin, X.M.: Ed-Join: An Efficient Algorithm For Similarity Joins with Edit Distance Constraints. In: 34th ACM International Conference on Very Large Data Bases, pp. 933–944. ACM Press, New York (2008)
9. Koudas, N., Sarawagi, S., Srivastava, D.: Record Linkage: Similarity Measures and Algorithms. In: Proceedings of the ACM SIGMOD International Conference on Management of Data, pp. 802–803. ACM Press, New York (2006)
10. Li, C., Wang, B., Yang, X.: VGRAM: Improving Performance of Approximate Queries on String Collections Using Variable-length Grams. Journal Proc of VLDB Endowment, 303–314 (2007)
11. Li, G.L., Deng, D., Wang, J.N., Feng, J.H.: Pass-join: A Partition-based Method for Similarity Joins. Journal Proc of VLDB Endowment 5(3), 253–264 (2011)
12. Wang, W., Qin, J.B., Chuan, X.M., Shen, H.T.: VChunkJoin: An Efficient Algorithm for Edit Similarity Joins. IEEE Transactionson Knowledge and Data Engineering 25(8), 1916–1929 (2012)
13. Gravano, L., Ipeirotis, P.G., Jagadish, H.V., Koudas, N.: Approximate String Joins in a Database (almost) for Free. In: 34th International Conference on Very Large Data Bases, pp. 491–500. ACM Press, New York (2001)
14. Bayardo, R.J., Ma, Y., Srikant, R.: Scaling up all pairs similarity search. In: 16th International World Wide Web Conference, pp. 131–140. ACM Press, New York (2007)

15. Wang, J.N., Feng, J.H., Li, G.L.: Trie-join: Efficient Trie-based String Similarity Joins with Edit-distance Constraints. Journal Proc of VLDB Endowment 3(1-2), 1219–1230 (2010)
16. Karch, D., Luxen, D., Sanders, P.: Improved Fast Similarity Search in Dictionaries. In: Chavez, E., Lonardi, S. (eds.) SPIRE 2010. LNCS, vol. 6393, pp. 173–178. Springer, Heidelberg (2010)
17. Bocek, T., Hunt, E., Stiller, B.: Fast Similarity Search in Large Dictionaries. Technique report, Zurich: University of Zurich (2007)
18. Qin, J.B., Wang, W., Lu, Y.F., Xiao, C., Lin, X.M.: Efficient Exact Edit Similarity Query Processing with the Asymmetric Signature Scheme. In: Proceedings of the ACM SIGMOD International Conference on Management of Data, pp. 1033–1044. ACM Press, New York (2011)
19. Mishra, S., Gandhi, T., Arora, A., Bhattachayrya, A.: Efficient Edit Distance based String Similarity Search Using Deletion Neighborhoods. In: Proceeding of the Joint EDBT/ICDT Workshops, pp. 375–383. ACM Press, New York (2013)
20. Ukkonen, E.: Finding Approximate Patterns in Strings. Journal of Algorithms 1, 132–137 (1985)

Content-Based Medical Image Retrieval System for Infections and Fluids in Chest Radiographs

Wan Siti Halimatul Munirah Wan Ahmad[1], W Mimi Diyana W Zaki[2],
Mohammad Faizal Ahmad Fauzi[1], and Tan Wooi Haw[1]

[1]Faculty of Engineering, Multimedia University, Malaysia
{siti.halimatul,faizal1,twhaw}@mmu.edu.my
[2]Faculty of Engineering and Built Environment, Universiti Kebangsaan Malaysia, Malaysia
wmdiyana@eng.ukm.my

Abstract. This paper presents a retrieval system based on the image's content for the application in medical domain. This system is aimed to assist the radiologists in healthcare by providing pertinent supporting evidence from previous cases. It is also useful for the junior radiologists and medical students as teaching aid and training mechanism. The system is tested to retrieve the infections and fluid cases in chest radiographs. We explored several feature extraction techniques to see their effectiveness in describing the low-level property of the radiographs in our dataset. These features are Gabor transform, Discrete Wavelet Frame and Grey Level Histogram. The retrieval of these cases was also experimented with a number of distance metrics to observe their performances. Promising measures based on recognition rate are reported.

Keywords: Content-based medical image retrieval, chest x-ray, lung infection, lung fluid, Gabor transforms, Discrete Wavelet Frame, Grey Level Histogram.

1 Introduction

Numerous advancements have been seen in the area of medical image retrieval since the past few years. Current medical image retrieval techniques can be classified according to the type and nature of the features used for indexing. They are text-based, content-based and semantic-based approaches. The PACS system is widely used in medical institutions where it is dedicated to the storage, retrieval, distribution and presentation of medical images. Images in PACS are annotated manually by medical officers and indexed by text keywords, hence limiting its features to textual descriptions only, besides unable to sufficiently describe the visual features of the images. In TBIR, information is either extracted from a DICOM image header or annotated manually by an expert and stored in a traditional relational or object-relational database. This type of retrieval has very limited ability to represent all the possible descriptions of anatomical information, complex image contents, and it is also unable to capture the visual content such as colour, texture or shape. The method is considered 'traditional' and limited, thus the research focus in medical image retrieval has shifted to the content-based approach.

A. Jaafar et al. (Eds.): AIRS 2014, LNCS 8870, pp. 14–23, 2014.
© Springer International Publishing Switzerland 2014

Diagnostic radiology requires accurate interpretation of complex signals in medical images. CBIR techniques could be valuable to radiologists in assessing medical images by identifying similar images in large archives that could assist with decision support. Many advances have occurred in CBIR, and a variety of systems have appeared in the medical domains. Although CBIR has frequently been proposed for use in medical image management, only a few CBMIR systems have been developed and using various image types with different project goals. The most popular CBMIR systems found in the literature are ASSERT (HRCT of the lung), FICBOS (functional PET), CBIR2 (spine X-Ray), MIMS (CT of the head), APKS (mammographics of breasts), IRMA (varied images), medGIFT (varied images), SPIRS (spine X-Ray), CervigramFinder (cervicographic images for cervix cancer), ILife (MRI brain), MIRS (spine X-Ray) and SPIRS-IRMA (spine X-Ray). Some of the systems were reviewed intensively in these literatures [1,2,3,4,5].

Each designed system will address the imaging modality used in their dataset. The modality defines the type of information that can be extracted from medical images. This limits usable image representation and features. Consequently, the modality targeted by a medical CBIR system is important. Only few medical CBIR systems support multimodality [6,7] and tested with more than one datasets [8,9]. Several systems were targeted to retrieve different body parts from the same modality, particularly radiographs of various body parts from ImageCLEF[10,11,12] and IRMA [13], as well as ultrasound of liver, kidney and pelvis [14]. The remaining systems were design to retrieve specific modality and body part. It is important to note that, if the CBIR techniques are focused on the analysis of certain pathology, high level features can be achieved for processing certain types of images. It is also very interesting to note that, to the best of our knowledge, no work has been done in CBMIR for the retrieval of chest radiographs, specifically to retrieve the similar lung diseases.

Image descriptors or features are one of the main components in a CBIR system, which represents the visual information contained in image pixels. They are derived from visual cues of an image and their representations are designed to encode colour and texture properties of the image, the spatial layout of objects and various geometric shape characteristics of perceptually coherent structures within the image. The colour and texture cues are derived directly from raw pixel intensities, while the shape cues are deduced directly from the image, such as point sets, contours or curves, surfaces and regions. For colour features, a global characterization of the image can be obtained by binning pixel colour components into a histogram, or by dividing the image into sub-blocks, and compute the average colour component vector of each block. However, since most of the medical images are in grey scale, the characterization is only applicable in intensity scales such as grey level histogram and grey level co-occurrence matrix [9], [14,15,16].

In medical domain, texture-based descriptors have become very important because they may potentially reveal the fine details contained within an image structure. Cysts and solid nodules for instance, normally have uniform characteristics of internal and signal density, while more complex lesions and infiltrative diseases have heterogeneous characteristics. Texture features encode the spatial organization of pixel values of image region. Generally, it is obtained by invoking the standard transform domain analysis tools such as Fourier transforms, wavelets or Gabor filters [8], [13,14], [16] on local image blocks. Some texture features may be unperceivable by humans, and computers may be able to extract important texture and pattern information that is not readily visible.

Previous works on the lung analyses prove that the best feature extraction techniques in analysing lung diseases specifically the infections in chest X-Ray (CXR) are texture and intensity-based features. In [17], van Ginneken et al. used the subdivision of the lung fields and applied a multiscale filter bank to extract texture features based on Gaussian derivatives for detection of tuberculosis cases and other abnormalities of a diffuse textural nature in CXR. Other work in [18]used an intensity histogram signatures characterising the intensities for detection of pulmonary infections and in [19], they used the Grey Level Histograms together with Gabor texture features for detection of consolidations. For detection of pneumonia cases in [20], a few of wavelets features were used, namely the Discrete Wavelet Transform (DWT), Wavelet Frame Transform (WFT) and Wavelet Packet Transform (WPT).

In this paper, we present a CBMIR system to retrieve the infections and fluids cases from chest radiographs. Both intensity and texture features are tested and the retrieval accuracies are compared and discussed in order to find the best technique to be used in further application. The features are based on Gabor Transform, Discrete Wavelet Frame and Grey Level Histogram. This system is aimed to assist the radiologists in healthcare by providing pertinent supporting evidence from previous cases. It is also useful as teaching aid and training mechanism for junior radiologists and medical students.

This paper is organized as follows. The next section briefly describes the methodology of the system, including the review of medical images, feature extraction techniques and the retrieval procedure used in the experiment. The results will be presented and discussed in Section 3, followed by the conclusions and future work in Section 4.

2   Methodology

2.1   Medical Images

Medical images in our collection consist of chest radiographs from both public and private datasets. The public dataset is provided by Japanese Society of Thoracic Radiology (JSRT) and the private dataset is obtained from collaborating hospital, Serdang Hospital (SH), Malaysia. The JSRT dataset comprises of 247 standard posterior-anterior (PA) chest radiographs with no infection or fluid case, and the SH dataset contains both PA and anterior-posterior (AP) radiographs, with a total of 125 images: 18 with infection, 17 with fluid cases, and the rest are normal. The image format is DICOM with varying resolutions. For the abnormal cases, 32 infection regions are manually extracted from the 18 images, and 24 fluid regions from the 17 images. Some examples of the images for both infection and fluid cases are shown in Fig. 1.

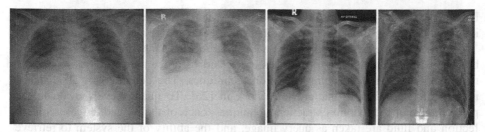

Fig. 1. Examples of chest radiographs with fluids (two from left) and infections (two from right) cases

2.2   Feature Extraction Techniques

The feature extraction techniques that have been used in the system are texture and intensity based features. The first technique used is a two-dimensional Gabor transform proposed by Manjunath and Ma [21],which extracts texture information from an image. Based on our observation during experimental work, the total number of scales, S=4 and total number of orientations, K=6 are found to be the best parameters. There are SxK output images produced by the Gabor transform, resulting in a total of 24-dimensional features for each radiograph.

In addition, Discrete Wavelet Frame (DWF) is applied to produce four wavelet co-efficient images that are the same size as the input image due to an over complete wavelet decomposition [22]. It is called an over complete decomposition because the filtered images are not sub-sampled. The coefficient images produced are from these channels: low-low (LL), low-high (LH), high-low (HL), and high-high (HH). For the next decompositions, it is done on the LL channels just as normal wavelet transform. In this paper, we use a three level decomposition with the Daubechies 4-tap wavelet basis, resulting in 10-dimensional feature vector.

The last technique is the basic intensity-based Grey Level Histogram (GLH), where the intensity of grey level colour map is described by a set of bins. Each bin represents a few levels of grey intensity by counting the number of pixels that fall into the bins. We tested with no of bin, n=64 and 128, yielding 64 and 128 features respectively.

As a comparison, we also tested the retrieval with combinations of these features, to see if the combined features will give better results and if it is significant or not.

2.3   Retrieval Procedure

The retrieval system comprises of 2 stages: offline feature extraction stage and online retrieval stage. The methodology of the proposed retrieval system is illustrated in Fig. 2. The features of the images are extracted using the three feature extraction techniques during the offline stage. Each of the technique produces different length of feature vectors (FVs), as previously described in Section 2.2. The FVs are stored in the FV database, separated for each technique. Throughout the online retrieval stage, the features of the query region are computed using one of the techniques and compared to all FVs in the FV database of the selected technique. The similarity index between the

FVs of the database image is computed using several distance metrics. Small distance indicates that the resultant image is similar to the query image and vice versa.

The distance metrics used in this work are Euclidean, Manhattan, the normalized of both and Mahalanobis. Several metrics are tested in order to get the most suitable metric for each of the feature extraction techniques. The equations of all distance metrics are described in our previous work in [23]. To quantitatively evaluate the performance of the feature extraction techniques, each of the 32 and 24 cases for infection and fluid are taken as query image, and the ability of the system to retrieve images from the same case to the query images indicates the accuracy of the feature extraction techniques. The ground truths of the relevant cases were prepared with the help of radiologists from Serdang Hospital. The retrieved images are then automatically compared using a simple algorithm to check if they are relevant or not.

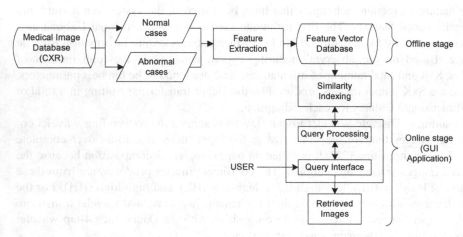

Fig. 2. Methodology of the proposed retrieval system

3   Results and Discussions

The retrieval accuracies for the techniques in the proposed system are evaluated using a measure called recognition rate, which is defined in equation (1). The recognition rate is well known as recall rate (and normally used with precision rate), but when used alone, it is suitable to measure the progress of the retrieval rate against the number of retrieved images. Table 1 summarises the recognition rates for all tested techniques using all distance metrics for the retrieval of each infection and fluid cases. Since the number of infection cases is 32 and fluid cases is 24, we initially analyse them as the top 35 and 25 retrieved images respectively, then followed by the top 50 for both. As the number of retrieved images increased, the recognition rates will also increase to indicate that more relevant images are found.

$$Recognition\ rate = \frac{number\ of\ relevant\ images\ retrieved}{total\ number\ of\ relevant\ images\ in\ the\ database} \tag{1}$$

For the infection cases, among all the techniques tested, the intensity-based technique gives the highest retrieval accuracy, where the rates are almost identical to the two decimal points for both GLH64 and GLH128 of all distance metrics, except Mahalanobis metric. The highest rate is given by Euclidean metric with 0.761 for top 35 of both intensity techniques, and 0.957 and 0.961 for top 50 of GLH64 and GLH128. This is followed by texture-based technique of DWF, with the retrieval accuracies of 0.693 and 0.888 for both top 35 and 50, using Normalized Manhattan distance metric. The lowest among the tested techniques is using Gabor transform, where the top 35 and 50 give only 0.297 and 0.319 recognition rates.

For the fluid cases, similar results to the infection cases were obtained, where the highest accuracies are from the GLH technique, followed by DWF and lastly Gabor. However, there are differences in the results for GLH64 and GLH128 which are quite significant, where the top 25 retrieved images gives an accuracy of 0.554 for GLH64, and 0.602 for GLH128, both obtained by Mahalanobis distance metric. For the top 50 results, GLH128 produced the highest rate with 0.986, then DWF (0.957), GLH64 (0.932) and Gabor (0.328). Different distance metrics were observed in providing good results for the fluid cases, especially the GLH technique. By taking the majority performance, we can see that the Gabor transform works best with Euclidean and DWF with Normalized Manhattan for both infection and fluid cases. The GLH however performs excellently with Euclidean for infection cases, and Mahalanobis for fluid cases. Based on these results, next we will discuss the performances of combined techniques, which are presented in Table 2.

Table 1. Recognition rates for all techniques using all distance metrics

		Infection Cases		Fluid Cases	
		Top 35	Top 50	Top 25	Top 50
Gabor	E	**0.297**	**0.319**	**0.293**	0.323
	NE	0.279	0.300	0.290	**0.328**
	M	0.229	0.250	0.184	0.224
	NM	0.228	0.254	0.194	0.248
	ML	0.049	0.052	0.061	0.063
DWF	E	0.182	0.226	0.165	0.253
	NE	0.202	0.242	0.182	0.243
	M	0.687	0.885	**0.540**	0.953
	NM	**0.693**	**0.888**	0.526	**0.957**
	ML	0.417	0.473	0.474	0.622
GLH64	E	**0.761**	**0.957**	0.424	0.835
	NE	0.738	0.930	0.464	0.880
	M	0.725	0.923	0.464	0.899
	NM	0.719	0.914	0.509	**0.932**
	ML	0.613	0.878	**0.554**	0.929
GLH128	E	**0.761**	**0.961**	0.418	0.835
	NE	0.738	0.930	0.462	0.880
	M	0.724	0.919	0.464	0.906
	NM	0.715	0.912	0.509	0.936
	ML	0.546	0.832	**0.602**	**0.986**

E=Euclidean, NE=Normalized Euclidean, M=Manhattan,
NM=Normalized Manhattan, ML=Mahalanobis

Table 2. Recognition rates for combined techniques using all distance metrics

		Infection Cases		Fluid Cases	
		Top 35	Top 50	Top 25	Top 50
Gabor + DWF	E	0.289	0.313	0.266	0.314
	NE	0.272	0.304	0.271	0.316
	M	0.488	0.546	0.566	0.771
	NM	**0.542**	**0.662**	**0.580**	**0.842**
	ML	0.052	0.052	0.071	0.076
Gabor + DWF + GLH64	E	0.665	0.865	0.490	0.946
	NE	**0.665**	**0.900**	0.545	0.960
	M	0.591	0.811	0.573	0.988
	NM	0.592	0.846	**0.606**	**0.993**
	ML	0.113	0.129	0.158	0.201
Gabor + DWF + GLH128	E	0.643	0.841	0.493	0.898
	NE	**0.665**	**0.900**	0.545	0.958
	M	0.598	0.831	0.576	0.993
	NM	0.604	0.853	**0.604**	**0.993**
	ML	0.262	0.292	0.345	0.427
DWF + GLH128	E	0.731	0.922	0.446	0.910
	NE	**0.739**	**0.927**	0.470	0.896
	M	0.702	0.886	0.505	**0.972**
	NM	0.718	0.899	0.536	0.953
	ML	0.571	0.862	**0.564**	0.962

E=Euclidean, NE=Normalized Euclidean, M=Manhattan,
NM=Normalized Manhattan, ML=Mahalanobis

From Table 2, it is observed that generally techniques that are fused with intensity features give better recognition rate compared to combination of texture features alone. For the case of infection, the best accuracies are achieved with combination of DWF and GLH128 for both top 35 and 50 retrieved images with the rates of 0.739 and 0.927. These are followed by similar results obtained by Gabor, DWF and GLH64 or GLH128: 0.665 and 0.900 respectively for top 35 and 50. The lowest rates are given by Gabor and DWF, with accuracies of only 0.542 and 0.662.For the techniques that are fused with intensity features, Normalized Euclidean offers the best rates, whilst for texture features, it is Normalized Manhattan, caused by the bias of DWF alone.

The fluid cases give slightly different results, where the combination of all texture and intensity features produce the best rates, similar effect either with GLH64 or GLH128 for the top 25 and 50 retrieved images. These were obtained by using Normalized Manhattan distance metric, with rounded measure of 0.61 and 0.99. The next combined techniques that give higher results are depends on the number of retrieved images. For the top 25, it is given by Gabor and DWF (0.580 using Normalized Manhattan) and then DWF and GLH128 (0.564 using Mahalanobis). Whereas the top 50 results show the opposite performance; second highest is DWF and GLH128 (0.972 with Manhattan metric) and then Gabor with DWF (0.842 by Normalized Manhattan metric). From the overall results, we can see that any technique fused with Gabor will not perform well using Mahalanobis distance, and combinations of all three techniques achieve high recognition rates with Normalized Euclidean for infection cases and Normalized Manhattan for fluid cases. For DWF and GLH128, the most suitable metric to retrieve infection cases is Normalized Euclidean. Since the difference of rates given by Mahalanobis and Manhattan is very minimal for the top 50 of fluid cases, we conclude that Mahalanobis is better in retrieving fluid cases for this combined technique.

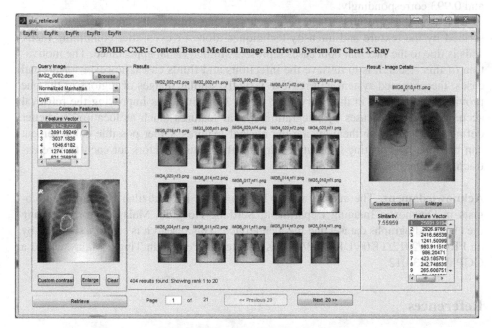

Fig. 3. GUI of the CBMIR system

For the purpose of testing and analysing the retrieval performances, we develop a graphical user interface (GUI) for the proposed CBMIR system, as shown in Fig. 3. The left panel contains the query information: query image name, selected distance metric, selected feature extraction technique, the FV list and the query image itself with user-selected region shown in the image. The middle panel shows the retrieved results, with 20 images per page. When the user selected one of the image's result, the details of that particular image will be shown in the right panel, consists of the image itself with the similar region highlighted, the FV list, and the similarity measure using the selected distance metric.

4   Conclusions

In this paper, we presented a content-based medical image retrieval (CBMIR) system for the purpose of retrieving infection and fluid cases in chest radiographs. Several feature extraction techniques and distance metrics have been tested to get the best retrieval accuracies. We also experimented with a few combinations of those techniques to see if higher rates can be achieved. For the infection cases, the best method to describe the features is the GLH128, with Euclidean as the best distance metric for the retrieval. The recognition rates are 0.761 and 0.961 respectively for top 35 and 50 retrieved images. As for the fluid cases, the highest accuracy was achieved by fusing the Gabor, DWF and GLH64 techniques with Normalized Manhattan as the most suitable distance metric. The measures for both top 25 and top 50 images were 0.606 and 0.993 correspondingly.

Based on these results, it can be concluded that fluid cases are harder to be described by the texture and intensity techniques alone or even after combining them. This is due to the fact that both cases represent similar visual appearance. The motivation of this research is to retrieve the infections and fluids cases, however for normal cases, the proposed system will retrieve visually similar images or regions to the one provided by the user in the query. Our future work includes improving the retrieval accuracies for both cases by integrating spatial features (such as location) to better define and distinguish them among the normal features. Other possible enhancement can be done by selecting the features among the feature vectors for each feature extraction technique.

Acknowledgment. The authors would like to thank Dr. Fadzilah Hashim, Radiologists in Diagnostic Imaging Department, Serdang Hospital, Malaysia, for providing the chest radiographs dataset and medical advice. This research is supported in part by an FRGS/1/2012/TK06/UKM/03/2 by Kementerian Pengajian Tinggi Malaysia and a GGPM-2013-012.

References

1. Akgul, C.B., Rubin, D.L., Napel, S., Beaulieu, C.F., Greenspan, H., Acar, B.: Content-Based Image Retrieval in Radiology: Current Status and Future Directions. J. Digit Imaging 24, 208–222 (2011)
2. Avni, U., Greenspan, H., Konen, E., Sharon, M., Goldberger, J.: X-Ray Categorization and Retrieval on the Organ and Pathology Level, Using Patch-Based Visual Words. IEEE Trans. Med. Imaging 30, 733–746 (2011)
3. Bugatti, P.H., Ponciano-Silva, M., Traina, A.J.M., Traina, A.J.M., Marques, P.: Content-Based Retrieval of Medical Images: From Context to Perception. In: 22nd IEEE International Symposium on Computer-Based Medical System, pp. 1–8 (2009)
4. Castellanos, A., Benavent, X., García-Serrano, A., Cigarrán, J.: Multimedia Retrieval in a Medical Image Collection: Results Using Modality Classes. In: Greenspan, H., Müller, H., Syeda-Mahmood, T. (eds.) MCBR-CDS 2012. LNCS, vol. 7723, pp. 133–144. Springer, Heidelberg (2013)
5. Dimitrovski, I., Guguljanov, P., Loskovska, S.: Implementation of Web-Based Medical Image Retrieval System in Oracle. In: 2nd International Conference on Adaptive Science & Technology, pp. 192–197 (2009)
6. Ergen, B., Baykara, M.: Content Based Medical Image Retrieval Feature Extraction of Using Statistical Spatial Methods for Content Based Medical Image Retrieval. In: 18th IEEE on Signal Processing and Communications Applications Conference, pp. 692–695 (2010)
7. Iakovidis, D.K., Pelekis, N., Kotsifakos, E.E., Kopanakis, I., Karanikas, H., Theodoridis, Y.: A Pattern Similarity Scheme for Medical Image Retrieval. IEEE Trans. Inf. Technol. Biomed. 13, 442–450 (2009)

8. Jiangli, L., Ke, C., Yuanwen, Z., Guangfu, Y.: Content-Based Medical Ultrasound Image Retrieval Using a Hierarchical Method. In: 2nd International Congress on Image and Signal Processing, pp. 1–4 (2009)
9. Khapli, V.R., Bhalachandra, A.S.: Cbir System for Biomedical Images: Challenges and Open Issues. In: IET International Conference on Wireless, Mobile and Multimedia Networks, pp. 85–88 (2008)
10. Lehmann, T.M., Guld, M.O., Thies, C., Fischer, B., Spitzer, K., Keysers, D., Ney, H., Kohnen, M., Schubert, H., Wein, B.B.: Content-Based Image Retrieval in Medical Applications. Methods Inf. Med. 43, 354–361 (2004)
11. Long, L.R., Antani, S., Deserno, T.M., Thoma, G.R.: Content-Based Image Retrieval in Medicine: Retrospective Assessment, State of the Art, and Future Directions. Int. J. Healthc. Inf. Syst. Inform. 4, 1–16 (2009)
12. Manjunath, B.S., Ma, W.Y.: Texture Features for Browsing and Retrieval of Image Data. Pattern Analysis and Machine Intelligence 18, 837–842 (1996)
13. Müller, H., Michoux, N., Bandon, D., Geissbuhler, A.: A Review of Content-Based Image Retrieval Systems in Medical Applications - Clinical Benefits and Future Directions. International Journal of Medical Informatic 73, 1–23 (2004)
14. Parveen, N.R.S., Sathik, M.M.: Detection of Pneumonia in Chest X-Ray Images (2011)
15. Quellec, G., Lamard, M., Cazuguel, G., Cochener, B., Roux, C.: Wavelet Optimization for Content-Based Image Retrieval in Medical Databases. Med. Image Anal. 14, 227–241 (2010)
16. Rahman, M.M., Antani, S.K., Thoma, G.R.: A Learning-Based Similarity Fusion and Filtering Approach for Biomedical Image Retrieval Using Svm Classification and Relevance Feedback. IEEE Transactions on Information Technology in Biomedicine, 640–646 (2011)
17. Tsevas, S., Iakovidis, D.K.: Patient Specific Normalization of Chest Radiographs and Hierarchical Classification of Bacterial Infection Patterns. In: IEEE International Conference on Imaging Systems and Techniques, pp. 156–160 (2010)
18. Tsevas, S., Iakovidis, D.K., Papamichalis, G.: Mining Patterns of Lung Infections in Chest Radiographs. In: Iliadis, Maglogiann, Tsoumakasis, Vlahavas, Brame (eds.) Artificial Intelligence Applications and Innovations III. IFIP, vol. 296, pp. 205–213. Springer, Boston (2009)
19. Unser, M.: Texture Classification and Segmentation Using Wavelet Frames. IEEE Transactions on Image Processing, 1549–160 (1995)
20. van Ginneken, B., Katsuragawa, S., ter Haar Romeny, B.M., Doi, K., Viergever, M.A.: Automatic Detection of Abnormalities in Chest Radiographs Using Local Texture Analysis. IEEE Trans. Med. Imaging 21, 139–149 (2002)
21. Wu, M., Sun, Q., Wang, J.: Medical Image Retrieval Based on Combination of Visual Semantic and Local Features. International Journal of Signal Processing, Image Processing and Pattern Recognition 5, 43–56 (2012)
22. Yang, L., Jin, R., Mummert, L., Sukthankar, R., Goode, A., Zheng, B., Hoi, S.C., Satyanarayanan, M.: A Boosting Framework for Visuality-Preserving Distance Metric Learning and Its Application to Medical Image Retrieval. IEEE Trans. Pattern Anal. Mach. Intell. 32, 30–44 (2010)
23. Mimi Diyana, W., Zaki, W., Faizal, M., Fauzi, A., Besar, R.: Retrieval of Intracranial Hemorrhages in Computed Tomography Brain Images Using Binary Coherent Vector. Journal of Electronic Imaging 19 (2010)

Topic-Focused Summarization of News Events Based on Biased Snippet Extraction and Selection

Pingping Lin, Shize Xu, and Yan Zhang

Department of Machine Intelligence, Peking University, Beijing 100871, China
Key Laboratory on Machine Perception, Ministry of Education, Beijing 100871, China
linpingping12@pku.edu.cn, xszsmail@gmail.com, zhy@cis.pku.edu.cn

Abstract. In this paper, we propose a framework to produce topic-focused summarization of news events, based on biased snippet extraction and selection. Through our approach, a summarization only retaining information related to a predefined topic (e.g. economy or politics) can be generated for a given news event to satisfy users with specific interests. To better balance coherence and coverage of the summarization, snippets rather than sentences or paragraphs are used as textual components. Topic signature is employed in snippet extraction and selection in order to emphasize the topic-biased information. Experiments conducted on real data demonstrate a good coverage, topic-relevancy, and content coherence of the summaries generated by our approach.

Keywords: Topic-focused summarization, Snippet, Topic signature.

1 Introduction

When surfing the Web, especially browsing news reports, we are eager for quick access to the most important information with least time. Luckily, researchers have paid much effort to the extraction of a brief and to-the-point summary. News summarization has undergone development from monolingual to multilingual, from text summarization to cross-media summarization, from single-point summarization to timeline.

Meanwhile, topic-focusing or even personalization is a growing trend of all kinds of Internet applications, such as recommendation systems, searching results, apps, and so on. As we know, a news event usually involves several topics of information, for instance, economy, politics, military and history. Users from a specific field may show interests in only some specific topics. Therefore, a summary which is focused on a predefined topic can help to satisfy users' interests in this topic. Luhn [10] proposes that we can take a particular sphere of interest into consideration for personalization. Paice and Jones [12] also find that users would consider an abstract a "good" one as it includes the detail they are interested in.

Although previous studies have addressed the problem how to extract the topic-biased contents for a topic-focused summary, they seldom discuss coverage, topic bias and content coherence at the same time. In this paper, we propose a framework to produce topic-focused summarization for a given news event, based on topic-biased snippet extraction and selection. Our method exhibits excellent performance in all of these three aspects.

A. Jaafar et al. (Eds.): AIRS 2014, LNCS 8870, pp. 24–35, 2014.

The contributions of our work can be summarized as follows:

1. We present a framework to produce topic-focused summarization by retaining information related to a specific topic, which can satisfy users with special interests.
2. We employ snippets, each of which is composed of several consecutive sentences, rather than sentences or paragraphs to compose the summary in order to improve content coherence as well as the coverage.
3. We select snippets based on topic-relevancy as well as content-relevancy, and hence guarantee the quality of the summarization.

2 Related Work

2.1 Keyphrase Extraction

Keyphrase extraction is the basis for further knowledge discovery and data mining. Sakai and Masuyama [14] assign large weights to nouns appearing locationally and chronologically front. Frank *et al.* [6] and Turney [15] determine whether a given n-gram is a keyphrase or not using a model trained with annotated data beforehand. Boudin *et al.* [2], Mihalcea and Tarau [11], Wan and Xiao [16] focus on graph-based ranking. Lin and Hovy [9] propose topic signatures which are identified by a log-likelihood ratio test based on their relative frequencies in relevant and irrelevant document sets.

2.2 Snippet Extraction

In our previous study [17], we propose snippet, which is composed of several consecutive sentences, to describe an entity. Starting from a head sentence, a snippet grows up by adding relevant neighboring sentences into itself. Most studies on summarization so far are based on sentences or paragraphs, while the proposition of snippets can provide a new idea for more coherent and informative summarization.

2.3 Personalized Summarization

Personalization is a growing trend of all kinds of Internet applications, such as recommendation systems and searching results. Sakai and Masuyama [14] let a user choose keywords which he/she is interested in and increase the weight of the chosen words. Díaz and Gervás [5] ask a user for words to describe his interest and model it. Yan *et al.* [18] support user interaction of clicking into the summary sentences and examining source contexts, which implicitly indicates what readers are interested in. Qu and Chen [13] combine collaborative filtering and summarization, making use of the information that users with similar interests tagged. Hu *et al.* [7] make use of social websites and bookmarking sites to personalize summarization.

3   Methodology

To make a topic-focused summary for a given event, we first construct corresponding topic signature using the method in [9], and then we extract biased snippets based on the topic signature. In our method, snippets rather than sentences and paragraphs are used as textual components of the summary for both content coherence and coverage. After extracting snippets, we cluster them for the consideration of redundancy elimination, deciding the number of clusters through an optimization problem involving inner-cluster coherence and inter-cluster diversity. We select one representative snippet from each cluster according to content-relevancy as well as topic-relevancy. After that, we order the selected snippets chronologically and hence we get the final result.

Fig. 1 shows the whole process of our method. We will explain each step as follows, and use s to denote a sentence and S to denote a snippet.

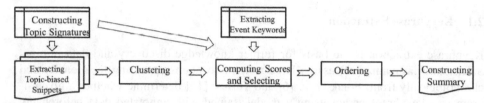

Fig. 1. Framework of our method

3.1   Topic-Biased Snippet Extraction

In our previous study [17], we propose the concept *snippet* and a snippet growth model. Starting from a head-sentence, a snippet grows up by adding relevant neighboring sentences into itself, while the relevancy is decided by text similarity, distance function and influence function. In this paper, we expand our model to emphasize information related to a given topic, as shown in Algorithm 1. Let us describe the functions used in Algorithm 1 one by one.

Given some topics and preclassified document sets focused on different topics respectively, we can construct different topic signature from the corresponding preclassified document set using $-2log\lambda$, which is computed by Lin and Hovy's method [9]. λ is likelihood ratio and more appropriate than χ^2 test for sparse data, and the quantity $-2log\lambda$ is asymptotically χ^2 distributed.

To choose appropriate topic-biased head sentences, we compute $-2log\lambda$ for each word w in each sentence, and then we get hs value for s, as shown in Equation 1.

$$hs(s) = \frac{\sum\limits_{w \in s} -2\log \lambda(w)}{|s|} \qquad (1)$$

Text similarity is computed by Equation 2, where $s^{expanded}$ is the expanded word set of sentence s. With the help of WordNet, we expand sentence s with the synonyms, hypernyms and hyponyms of each noun and verb in s.

$$sim(s_i, s_j) = |s_i{}^{expanded} \cap s_j{}^{expanded}| \qquad (2)$$

Algorithm 1. Topic-biased snippet growth model

```
procedure MAIN ALGORITHM(texts)
   Initialize snippet S = ∅
   while hs(s) < thres_head do
      Scan texts
   end while
   Select s as head-sentence
   S = {s}
   while R_before ≥ thres_expanding or R_after ≥ thres_expanding do
      if R_before ≥ thres_expanding then
         s_j ← the nearest sentence before current snippet
         R_before ← ComputeRelation(s_j, S)
         if R_before ≥ thres_expanding then
            S ← S ∪ s_j
         end if
      end if
      if R_after ≥ thres_expanding then
         s_j ← the nearest sentence after current snippet
         R_after ← ComputeRelation(s_j, S)
         if R_after ≥ thres_expanding then
            S ← S ∪ s_j
         end if
      end if
   end while
   return S
end procedure
procedure COMPUTERELATION(s, S)
   Expand s using WordNet
   for s_i ∈ S do
      R ← R + sim(s, s_i) * dis(s, s_i) * infl(x_i, μ, δ)
                     ▷ sim(s, s_i) denotes text similarity between s and s_i
          ▷ dis(s, s_i) denotes the influence of distance between s and s_i
              ▷ infl(x_i, μ, δ) denotes relevancy of s_i to head-sentence
   end for
   R ← R/|S|
   return R
end procedure
```

In distance function (see Equation 3), d_{ij} is the number of sentences between s_i and s_j and θ is a coefficient.

$$dis(s_i, s_j) = \log \frac{\theta}{d_{ij}} \qquad (3)$$

In influence function (see Equation 4), x_0 is the coordinate of head-sentence, d_{0i} is the distance between head-sentence and s_i, β is a coefficient deciding the length of a snippet to some extent. μ and δ are the mean and standard deviation of the variables natural logarithm.

$$infl(x_i, \mu, \delta) = \frac{1}{x_i \delta \sqrt{2\pi}} e^{-\frac{(\ln x_i - \mu)^2}{2\delta^2}}$$

$$x_i = \begin{cases} x_0 - \beta d_{0i}, if \ s_i \ is \ before \ head\text{-}sentence \\ x_0 + \beta d_{0i}, if \ s_i \ is \ after \ head\text{-}sentence \end{cases} \tag{4}$$

3.2 Snippet Clustering

Snippets we get in Section 3.1 may share similar information with each other. To reduce information redundancy, we use LDA method to cluster the extracted snippets, and then select one representative snippet from each cluster.

To decide the number of clusters for each topic (denoted as K), we design an algorithm (Algorithm 2) which can achieve both high inner-cluster coherence and inter-cluster diversity.

We first define coherence and diversity for the clustering result under K as Equation 5 and 6. C denotes the set of K clusters $\{c_1, c_2, ..., c_K\}$. Coherence is computed as the reciprocal of average inner-cluster semantic distances of all clusters, and diversity is the average inter-cluster semantic distances of every two clusters. Semantic distance between two snippets $KL(S_i, S_j)$ is computed as Kullback-Leibler Divergence.

$$Coh(C) = 1/(\frac{1}{K} \sum_{1 \leq k \leq K} \frac{\sum_{1 \leq i \leq |c_k|, 1 \leq j \leq |c_k|, i \neq j} KL(S_i, S_j)}{|c_k|(|c_k| - 1)}) \tag{5}$$

$$Div(C) = \frac{1}{K(K-1)} \sum_{1 \leq k_1 \leq K, 1 \leq k_2 \leq K, k_1 \neq k_2} \frac{\sum_{s_i \in c_{k_1}, s_j \in c_{k_2}} KL(S_i, S_j)}{|c_{k_1}||c_{k_2}|} \tag{6}$$

Kullback-Leibler Divergence is given as Equation 7, based on semantic probability distribution of words in a snippet $p(w_l|S)$.

$$KL(S_i, S_j) = \sum_w p(w|S_i) log \frac{p(w|S_i)}{p(w|S_j)} \tag{7}$$

Semantic probability distribution is given as Equation 8, estimated by word frequency.

$$p(w_l|S) = \frac{TF(w_l)}{\sum_{w \in S} TF(w)} \tag{8}$$

In Equation 9, $tf(w_l, S)$ is the frequency of word w_l in snippet S, and $w^{expanded}$ is the expanded word set of w. It assigns lower frequency to a word that is expanded out with more words.

$$TF(w_l) = \sum_{w \in S} \frac{e(w_l, w^{expanded})}{|w^{expanded}|} + tf(w_l, S)$$

$$e(w_l, w^{expanded}) = \begin{cases} 1, if \ w_l \in w^{expanded} \\ 0, if \ w_l \notin w^{expanded} \end{cases} \tag{9}$$

Actually the problem of snippet clustering can be transformed into the following optimization problem:

$$\forall c \in C, |c| \geq thres_{len}$$
$$Coh(C) \geq thres_{Coh}$$
$$Div\,(C) \ \ is \ maximized. \tag{10}$$

An approximate solution is given in Algorithm 2.

Algorithm 2. Decision of K based on coherence and diversity

---

procedure (*initialK, topic-biased snippets, $K_{upperbound}$*)
   Initialize $K_{lowerbound} = 1$
   while $K_{lowerbound} \leq K_{upperbound}$ **do**
      $K \leftarrow (K_{lowerbound} + K_{upperbound})/2$
      $C \leftarrow LDA(K)$ ▷ Cluster snippets into K clusters using LDA method
      Compute $Coh(C)$ and $Div(C)$
      if $\forall c \in C, |c| \geq thres_{len}$ **and** $Coh(C) \geq thres_{Coh}$ **then**
         if $Div(C) \geq maxDiv$ **then**
            $maxDiv \leftarrow Div(C)$
            $C_{final} \leftarrow C$
         end if
         $K_{lowerbound} \leftarrow K + 1$
      else
         $K_{upperbound} \leftarrow K - 1$
      end if
   end while
   return C_{final}
end procedure

3.3 Snippet Selection

After clustering, we select one snippet with highest score from each cluster as candidates to form the final summary. Score is made up of both content-relevancy and topic-relevancy, which are respectively evaluated by news event keywords and topic signature.

We extract event keywords according to Equation 11, where d denotes news event document set and D denotes Google Ngram corpus. The final score of a snippet is computed according to Equation 12. Content-relevancy is computed according to the part before plus sign ("+"), and topic-relevancy is after the plus sign. α denotes the weight of content-relevancy and $|S|$ is the number of sentences in S.

$$weight(w_l) = \frac{tf(w_l, d)}{\log tf(w_l, D)} \tag{11}$$

$$score(S) = \frac{\sum_{s \in S}(\sum_{w_l \in s}\left(\alpha\frac{-2\log\lambda(w_l)}{max_w - 2\log\lambda(w)} + (1 - \alpha)\frac{weight(w_l)}{max_w weight(w)}\right)/|s|)}{|S|} \tag{12}$$

According to [1], chronological ordering, including publication date of a document and sentence position in the document, plays a major role in arranging sentences. Thus we arrange selected snippets in a chronological order to achieve the final summary.

4   Experiments

4.1   Datasets

We illustrate four topics, i.e. economy, politics, military and history, in our experiments. To extract the topic signatures, we construct four document sets, which emphasize on economy, politics, military and history respectively. These documents are collected from seven selected sources, as shown in Table 1. $\#Sents$ denotes the total number of sentences in a document set.

Table 1. Datasets used to extract topic signatures

Topic	Economy	Politics	Military	History
#Docs	194	231	206	194
#Sents	4150	3334	3782	9528
Sources	CNN, Xinhua	Xinhua, WhiteHouse	MND[1], DOD[2]	CASS[3], History(UK)[4]

In order to get news documents that contain information about all of the four topics, we collect a document set rather than using an existing one. As shown in Table 2 and Table 3, we use "Diaoyu Islands", "Edward Snowden", "2013 US Government Shutdown" and "Syria Crisis" as queries and collect documents from five influential international news websites. $\#RS$ denotes the number of reference summaries, and $\#AvgLen(RS)$ is the average number of sentences of reference summaries.

Table 2. News sources

News Source	Region	News Source	Region
CNN	US	SCMP	Hong Kong
BBC	UK	Xinhua	China
Japan Daily Press	Japan		

Table 3. News event datasets

News Subject	Diaoyu Islands	Edward Snowden	2013 US government shutdown	Syria crisis
Docs	502	993	630	884
#Sents	9405	24687	21851	21851
#RS	2	2	3	2
#AvgLen(RS)	20	15	16	18
Sources	Oct, 2013 - Dec, 2013	Jun, 2013 - Aug, 2013	Sep, 2013 - Nov, 2013	Sep, 2013 - Dec, 2013

---

[1] The Ministry of National Defense, PRC.
[2] U.S. Defense Ministry.
[3] http://jds.cass.cn/
[4] http://www.history.co.uk/

We perform anaphora resolution of person pronouns and nouns of time with Stanford CoreNLP, word stemming with Porter Stemmer, as well as stop-word removing on these news event document sets.

4.2 Evaluation Metrics

The coverage of important information in a summary is of significance to the overall quality of the summary. Most recent researches focus on the $ROUGE$ evaluation [4], [8]. In our experiments, we compute $ROUGE$-1 for each method according to Equation 13, where $Count_{match}(gram_n)$ is the maximum number of n-grams co-occurring in a candidate summary and a set of reference summaries.

$$ROUGE - N = \frac{\sum_{summary \in ReferenceSummaries} \sum_{gram_n \in summary} Count_{match}(gram_n)}{\sum_{summary \in ReferenceSummaries} \sum_{gram_n \in summary} Count(gram_n)} \quad (13)$$

Since there is not much previous work, we employ a novel manual approach to evaluate our contributions, topic-biased information and content coherence.

Firstly, we evaluate topic bias. We split the 4 summaries of different topics into sentences, disorganize them, and then present them to evaluators. They are requested to classify these sentences into four groups, focusing on economy, politics, military and history respectively. We compute the $F1$-$Measure$ according to Equation 14 to evaluate the outcome of topic bias. P is the precision while R is the recall of classification.

Next, we focus on content coherence. We consider a summary to be coherent and logical if its order of sentences corresponds to manual ordering. On the promise of a certain coverage of important information, we disorder sentences in a summary and request evaluators to reorder them. We employ $nDCG$ index (given in Equation 15) used in Information Retrieval to evaluate the consistence of ordering between reordered summary and candidate summary. $IDCG$ is DCG value of the corresponding summary reordered by evaluators. $score_i$ is the score of the ith sentence, and a higher score is assigned to a sentence with an earlier position in reordered summary.

$$F1 = \frac{2PR}{P+R} \quad (14)$$

$$nDCG\,(summary) = \frac{DCG}{IDCG}$$
$$(I)\,DCG = score_1 + \sum_{1 \le i \le |(Reordered)summary|} \frac{score_i}{\log i} \quad (15)$$

We compare our method with several baselines, listed as follows.

1. Random: It selects sentences and orders them randomly.
2. REF: Manual summary.
3. SUI: Sakai and Masuyama's method [14]. Its relevant keywords (selected by users) are given as the top 20 topic signatures we extract.

4. SP: Our proposed method, extracting topic-biased snippets to form a topic-focused summary.
5. SL: Our method without topic-focusing. It selects head-sentences randomly and extracts unbiased snippets to form a generic summary.
6. PL: Our method without snippet extraction. It extracts topic-biased sentences to form a summary.

4.3 Overall Performance Comparison

We set $thres_{head}$ as 4.2, $thres_{expanding}$ as 100, θ as 10, μ as 0, δ as 0.25, β as 0.17, $thres_{len}$ as 20, $thres_{Coh}$ as 3.5, and $K_{upperbound}$ as 20.

Table 4 shows the top 8 signature terms for 4 topics. We can see that these terms describe each topic properly and distinguish from others. Table 5 shows the average

Table 4. Top 8 signature terms for 4 topics

	Signature Terms
Economy	billion, dollar, market, growth, bank, investor, percent, euro
Politics	congress, cpc, pete, committe, communist, elect, legislatur
Military	defens, armi, militari, pla, command, liber, navi, mission, gen
History	imperi, histori, war, qing, period, emperor, origin, diplomat

$ROUGE - 1$ value of 4 news events of each method. We can find that our proposed method performs well. The reason why SL gets poor scores may be that a reference summary includes information of a specific topic which the result of SL does not include.

Table 6 shows the average $F1\text{-}score$ of 4 news events of each method. We find that both PL and SP achieve good $F1\text{-}scores$, that is, topic-biased information is well retained. All scores of historical topic are less than other topics. The reason may be that the signature terms we extract for this topic are relatively imprecise. Besides, news documents themselves contain little historical information.

Table 7 shows the average $nDCG$ value of 4 news events of each method. We are aware that methods based on snippets (SL and SP) perform much better than others.

Table 5. $ROUGE - 1$ values of different methods

	Random	SUI	PL	SL	SP
Economy	0.202	0.560	0.512	0.391	0.553
Politics	0.187	0.503	0.402	0.351	0.510
Military	0.210	0.520	0.497	0.386	0.531
History	0.175	0.521	0.398	0.346	0.501

Table 8 shows the summaries of "Diaoyu Islands" produced by our method. We do not show the history-focused summary since it includes some sensitive information. We can find that different topic-focused summaries have distinct information from others although they share some common information.

In order to show the topic bias between summaries produced by different methods, we provide Word Storm using Castella and Sutton's method [3]. From Fig. 2, we can

Table 6. $F1 - scores$ of different methods

	Random	SUI	PL	SL	SP
Economy	0.112	0.639	0.650	0.320	0.645
Politics	0.092	0.606	0.608	0.345	0.600
Military	0.128	0.622	0.630	0.298	0.628
History	0.090	0.511	0.540	0.313	0.530

Table 7. $nDCG$ of different methods

	Random	SUI	PL	SL	SP	REF
Economy	0.304	0.819	0.812	0.866	0.906	0.942
Politics	0.298	0.778	0.765	0.843	0.865	0.967
Military	0.435	0.868	0.836	0.915	0.920	0.941
History	0.367	0.790	0.781	0.895	0.877	0.955

Table 8. Topic-focused summaries of "Diaoyu Islands" produced by SP

Economy	Sales at Dongfeng Peugeot Citroen Automobile Company Ltd. in the first three quarters also hit a record high of 312,728 units, up 7.1 percent from 2012-10-10. The boost in sales is seen as a result of the Diaoyu Islands issue. Anger towards Japan grew in China after the Japanese government's purchase" of part of the Diaoyu Islands on 2013-09-11. Speaking on the island conflict with IMF Chief Economist Olivier Blanchard on 2013-10-09, he said it was too early to tell if there will be any macro-economic effects from the conflict. It's clear the Eurozone crisis is starting to have effects in the slowdown of China and the emerging world. The worsening of exports reflected both the global slowdown and anti-Japan protests in China, said Naoki Lizuka, from Citigroup Global Markets in Tokyo. Japanese-brand car makers will not give up on the Chinese market despite tumbling sales amid Beijing and Tokyo's dispute over the Diaoyu Islands. China's state-run media Xinhua revealed on Monday(2013-12-09) that the country's government-owned banks have withdrawn from the International Monetary Fund (IMF) and World Bank meetings held in Tokyo starting on Tuesday (2013-12-09). This last-minute cancellation can only be seen as another relation to the ongoing dispute over the Senkaku/Diaoyu Islands and the strained relations between Japan and China. You would expect the banking sector to remain immune from political dispute between China and Japan with regards to the Senkaku Islands.
Politics	Top diplomats from China and Japan met to discuss the territorial dispute over the uninhabited Diaoyu Islands in the East China Sea, Tokyo said on 2013-10-24, signalling mutual willingness to ease tension ahead of a key communist party congress. Lin Xiaoguang, a professor of international relations at the Central Party School, said any rise in tension with Japan ahead of the congress could trigger unease among Chinese leaders. In a group interview on the sidelines of the 18th National Congress of the Communist Party of China, which opened Thursday (2013-11-10), Chen said China's exports to Japan and Japan's exports to China both fell to different extents after the illegal purchase of Diaoyu Islands by Japanese government. For the United States and its regional allies, the disputes are a case study in containing a rising power, for china, it is also a test run to accomplish its newly declared ambition of becoming a "maritime power, as stated by President Hu Jintao in a keynote policy document at the recent 18th party congress. Japan's Kyodo News reported that the Senate's decision was intended to keep China's moves to assert its claim in check. Richard Hu, an associate professor in the University of Hong Kong's politics and public administration department, said china still had time to lobby against the amendment. "China has enough time to use its political influence by putting pressure on the White House, lobbying US congressmen and using other measures to stop it from being passed," Hu said.
Military	The US and Japan have begun joint military exercises, amid simmering tensions with China over disputed islands in the East China Sea. China is conducting naval exercises in the East China Sea, state media report, amid heightened tensions with Japan over islands both claim. The exercises are aimed at "sharpening response to emergencies in missions to safeguard territorial sovereignty". Japan's Liberal Democratic Party on 2013-11-26 announced the Japanese campaign platform, proposing an increase of military spending and a tough stance toward China on the Diaoyu Islands issue. President of the Liberal Democratic Party of Japan Shinzo Abe said that China's growing military spending and attitude on the Diaoyu Islands issue is the reason for regional tension and strained China-Japan relations. China has always followed the principle of not worsening its internal and peripheral situations when handling the issues and safeguarding its territorial sovereignty. On the Huangyan Islands issue, China has always been restrained and does not advocate the use of force. In the Diaoyu Islands waters, China has only deployed surveillance ships and aircraft. The Diaoyu Islands has been and will be further proved that China's marine strategy is for peaceful development. In the South China Sea, China established the city of Sansha to administer the Xisha, Zhongsha and Nansha Islands and surrounding waters to counter the provocations. China sent marine surveillance ships to patrol the waters surrounding the Diaoyu Islands.

see that summaries generated by REF, SP, PL and SUI contain some topic-biased words, such as "economy", "bank", "sales", and so on. The sizes of these words demonstrate their different importance in different summaries.

5 Conclusion

In this paper, we propose a framework to produce topic-focused summarization for a given news event, based on topic-biased snippet extraction and selection. Experiments conducted on real data demonstrate a good coverage, topic-relevancy, and content coherence of the summaries generated by our approach. As our future work, more robust evaluations will be conducted. Furthermore, we will try to produce personalized summarization by replacing "topic signature" with "person signature".

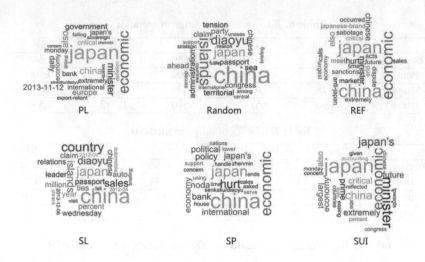

Fig. 2. Word storm for economy-focused summaries of "Diaoyu Islands"

Acknowledgments. We sincerely thank all the anonymous reviewers for their valuable comments, which have helped a lot to improve this paper. This work is supported by NSFC with Grant No. 61370054 and 973 Program with Grant No. 2014CB340405.

References

1. Bollegala, D., Okazaki, N., Ishizuka, M.: A bottom-up approach to sentence ordering for multi-document summarization. Information Processing & Management 46(1), 89–109 (2010)
2. Boudin, F., Morin, E., et al.: Keyphrase extraction for n-best reranking in multi-sentence compression. In: Proccedings of the NAACL HLT 2013 Conference (2013)
3. Castella, Q., Sutton, C.: Word storms: Multiples of word clouds for visual comparison of documents. arXiv preprint arXiv:1301.0503 (2013)
4. Christensen, J., Mausam, S.S., Etzioni, O.: Towards coherent multi-document summarization. In: Proceedings of NAACL-HLT, pp. 1163–1173 (2013)
5. Díaz, A., Gervás, P.: User-model based personalized summarization. Information Processing & Management 43(6), 1715–1734 (2007)
6. Frank, E., Paynter, G.W., Witten, I.H., Gutwin, C., Nevill Manning, C.G.: Domain-specific keyphrase extraction (1999)
7. Hu, P., Ji, D.H., Teng, C., Guo, Y.: Context-enhanced personalized social summarization. In: COLING, pp. 1223–1238 (2012)
8. Lin, C.Y.: Rouge: A package for automatic evaluation of summaries. In: Text Summarization Branches Out: Proceedings of the ACL 2004 Workshop, pp. 74–81 (2004)
9. Lin, C.Y., Hovy, E.: The automated acquisition of topic signatures for text summarization. In: Proceedings of the 18th Conference on Computational Linguistics, vol. 1, pp. 495–501. Association for Computational Linguistics (2000)
10. Luhn, H.P.: The automatic creation of literature abstracts. IBM Journal of Research and Development 2(2), 159–165 (1958)

11. Mihalcea, R., Tarau, P.: Textrank: Bringing order into texts. In: Proceedings of EMNLP, Barcelona, Spain, vol. 4, p. 275 (2004)
12. Paice, C.D., Jones, P.A.: The identification of important concepts in highly structured technical papers. In: Proceedings of the 16th Annual International ACM SIGIR Conference on Research and Development in Information Retrieval, pp. 69–78. ACM (1993)
13. Qu, Y., Chen, Q.: Collaborative summarization: When collaborative filtering meets document summarization. In: PACLIC, pp. 474–483 (2009)
14. Sakai, H., Masuyama, S.: A multiple-document summarization system with user interaction. In: Proceedings of the 20th International Conference on Computational Linguistics, p. 1001. Association for Computational Linguistics (2004)
15. Turney, P.D.: Learning algorithms for keyphrase extraction. Information Retrieval 2(4), 303–336 (2000)
16. Wan, X., Xiao, J.: Collabrank: towards a collaborative approach to single-document keyphrase extraction. In: Proceedings of the 22nd International Conference on Computational Linguistics, Association for Computational Linguistics, vol. 1, pp. 969–976 (2008)
17. Wang, Y., Zhao, L., Zhang, Y.: Magiccube: choosing the best snippet for each aspect of an entity. In: Proceedings of the 18th ACM Conference on Information and Knowledge Management, pp. 1705–1708. ACM (2009)
18. Yan, R., Nie, J.Y., Li, X.: Summarize what you are interested in: an optimization framework for interactive personalized summarization. In: Proceedings of the Conference on Empirical Methods in Natural Language Processing, pp. 1342–1351. Association for Computational Linguistics (2011)

Query Ambiguity Identification Based on User Behavior Information

Cheng Luo, Yiqun Liu, Min Zhang, and Shaoping Ma

State Key Laboratory of Intelligent Technology and Systems
Tsinghua National Laboratory for Information Science and Technology
Department of Computer Science and Technology, Tsinghua University
Beijing 100084, China
c-luo12@mails.tsinghua.edu.cn,
{yiqunliu,z-m,msp}@tsinghua.edu.cn

Abstract. Query ambiguity identification is of vital importance for Web search related studies such as personalized search or diversified ranking. Different from existing solutions which usually require a supervised topic classification process, we propose a query ambiguity identification framework which takes user behavior features collected from click-through logs into consideration. Especially, besides the features collected from query level, we focus on how to tell the differences between clear and ambiguous queries via features extracted from multi-query sessions. Inspired by recent progresses in word representation researches, we propose a query representation approach named *"query2vec"* which constructs representations from the distributions of queries in query log context. Experiment results based on large scale commercial search engine logs show effectiveness of the proposed framework as well as the corresponding representation approach.

1 Introduction

Traditional search engines usually focus on satisfying elaborative information needs. However, research [1] shows that queries often come out ambiguous or underspecified, especially with the increase of mobile device usage in recent years.

When a search engine receives an ambiguous/broad query from a user and it knows little about this user, the best it can do is to present a diversified result list that covers several interpretations/subtopics of the query (see Fig. 1 for an example). On the contrary, if the search engine knows much about the user, it can generate a personalized search result list according to the user's profile [2]. Compared with traditional search tasks, diversified search and personalized search tasks require more computational resources. Meanwhile, diversification may lack effectiveness, and may even hurt the performance of clear queries. Therefore, query ambiguity identification is essential for assessing whether search engine should introduce a diversified ranking or personalized search process. However, identifying a query's ambiguity manually is laborious and complicated. When judging a query, a human annotator usually makes a decision based on

A. Jaafar et al. (Eds.): AIRS 2014, LNCS 8870, pp. 36–47, 2014.

his/her personal experience. In such case, the annotator might not be able to make the correct judgment until he/she invests enough time in researching on a specific query. It is thus of vital importance for Web search engines to identify query ambiguity automatically.

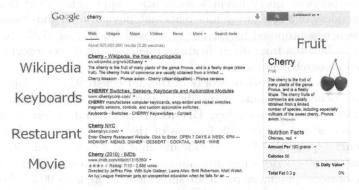

Fig. 1. Search result page for an ambiguous query *"cherry"*

To identify ambiguous queries automatically, there have been a number of works such as [3,4]. They classified queries into 3 categories: *Ambiguous*, *Broad* and *Clear*. Based on this taxonomy, they proposed a supervised learning model to classify queries to Type A (Ambiguous) and Type $\overline{A}$ (Broad and Clear). The top retrieved documents are crawled as a description of the query. Each document is classified into predefined categories and modeled as a possibility distribution on different topics. Further, they estimate the distances between documents and train a binary classifier with Support Vector Machine.

We can see that, to a great extent, most existing query ambiguity identification frameworks depend on a process of supervised document topic classification. It is an ambitious move to construct a high-quality training corpus for document classification. More importantly, the training corpus should be updated with the rapid changes of Web content, which is both time/labor consuming and almost impossible for practical Web search applications.

In this work, we try to address the problem of query ambiguity identification without topic-based classification. We propose a query ambiguity identification framework which adopts a supervised learning approach to automatically identify query ambiguity based on the features extracted from a number of evidences, i.e., query logs, SERPs and query sessions. Inspired by recent word representation approach *"word2vec"* [5], we adopt the algorithm on large scale of search sessions to present queries as vectors and then extract features for ambiguity identification.

Our main contribution includes: (1) we proposed a query ambiguity identification framework without a content classification; (2) we proposed a novel query ambiguity description method based on query representation, to the best of our knowledge, this is the first approach that adopts *"word2vec"* methods in the context of Web search user behavior; (3) we construct a dataset for query ambiguity identification with information collected from a practical search engines.

2   Related Work

2.1   Query Ambiguity Taxonomy

Most of the previous query intent identification approaches were based on a famous taxonomy of 3 categories: informational, navigational and transactional; this approach was proposed by Border *et al.* and Rose *et al.* [7,8]. To judge if search results benefits from diversification, query ambiguity categories is more instructive for search engines.

Song *et al.* reviewed previous works [9,10] and constructed the taxonomy of queries from being ambiguous to specific in three types: **Ambiguous**: a query that has more than one meaning; **Broad**: a query that covers a variety of subtopics, and a user might look for one of the subtopics by issuing another query; **Clear**: a query that has a specific meaning and covers a narrow topic [3]. A user study on 60 queries which five human subjects involved in indicates that human annotators' judgment reach an agreement as high as 90% when classifying queries into Type A and Type $\overline{A}$ (Type B and Type C), while it is more difficult for the annotators to discriminate whether a query falls under Type B or Type C.

Another taxonomy about query ambiguity differentiate queries by how *"narrow"* or *"general"* the intent of the query reflects [11]. Narrow queries usually means users submit queries for specific answers, such as *"how to configure java"*, while general queries means that users attempt to visit some relevant web resources like the query *"New York"*.

2.2   Query Classification

Web queries can be classified according to different taxonomies, such as search task type (Navigational, Informational and Transactional), query topics (KDD-Cup 2005) [12] and query ambiguity (Ambiguity vs Broad vs Clear, or Narrow vs General).

The search result lists returned by search engines are often regarded as a pseudo-relevance feedback [13]. The KDD-CUP participants started the trend of using the search engine directory services and the categories of the open directory project (ODP) to classify queries to predefined categories [14]. Document content, anchor links, hyperlinks and URLs have been considerably used in classifications. The importance of inlinks, authorities, hubs and anchors in web query classification were compared by Westerveld et.al [15].

Several previous works included user behavior as a functional feature in query classification [16,17]. Liu *et al.* proposed a method to differentiate navigational queries from informational/transactional queries with features extracted from user click histories [18]. Wang *et al.* [19] proposed an ambiguous query identification method with user entropy.

Song *et al.* have proposed a SVM classifier to solve the query ambiguity classification problem [3]. In their approach, each query is represented by possibility distributions on content categories of its top retrieved documents. Features are extracted from the distances between the possibility vectors. In a following work, they included user clicks which may affect the weights of document [4], and improves the classification performance.

However, as stated earlier, document classification is a great challenge on web environment because the construction and update of training corpus is complex and time-consuming. It must be pointed out that there is a significant difference between Song *et al.*'s approach and ours in the way of query session information utilization. They scrawled the top 20 snippets of follow up queries for content classification while we attempt to analyze the distributions of vectors whose queries are in session context.

Hafernik *et al.* proposed a less expensive method to classify queries into narrow or general using only part of speech (POS) information and query length as features [11]. It could be argued they did not utilize any user behavior information for classification.

2.3 Distributional Representation

Distributional representation has been successfully used for a wide variety of tasks in natural language processing and information retrieval, such as synonym detection, concept categorization and sentiment analysis. Mikolov *et al.* proposed a skip-gram based method significantly improved the training speed and vector quality by subsampling of frequent words [5,6]. The linearity of skip-gram model make it very suitable on process large amount of documents.

3   Methods

To assess diversification or personalization opportunities, we are focusing on differentiating queries that reflect clear user intents between the ones that needs diversification. We adopt the taxonomy and ambiguity definitions proposed by Song *et al.*, however, we attempt to classify query into Type C (Clear) and Type $\overline{C}$ (Ambiguous and Broad). This is because ambiguous queries and broad queries need diversified search or personalized search while clear queries need not, which means we have to take broad queries into account while deciding whether diversification or personalization is needed. Thus, from this perspective, classification between Type C and Type $\overline{C}$ is more instructive for search engines.

3.1   Problem Formulation and Framework Overview

The problem of query ambiguity identification can be formulated as a classification process:

$$f : Q \vdash \{C, \overline{C}\} \tag{1}$$

f is the identification function which indicates whether the query is clear or not and $Q = \{q_1, q_2, q_3, \ldots\}$, which denotes the query space,

The framework is shown in Fig. 2. It is constructed on three levels: data, feature and application.

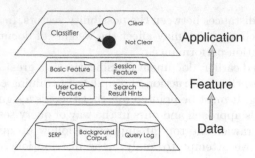

Fig. 2. Query ambiguity identification framework

On the data level, given a query q_i, we first enrich the information on q_i with various evidence resources. By scrawling search result pages of the query, we can get the most relevant documents about the query. From user click-through data, we can learn the interaction pattern of specific users. By collecting large scale of user sessions, we can adopt query representation algorithm on the dataset to present every query as a vector for further analysis.

On the feature level, we extract features from both the query q_i itself (for example, the query length, if the query contains stopwords etc.) and the information enriched before. In this work, we investigate the effectiveness of **Basic Features (BF)**, **User Click Behaviors (UCB)**, **Search Result Hints (SRH)** and **Session Features (SF)**.

On the application level, we construct a training set by sampling some queries from search logs and labeling them by ambiguity. Each query and its label can be presented as (q_i, l_i) where q_i is a query and the label $l_i \in \{-1, +1\}$. We apply Support Vector Machine (SVM) to learning a classifier that minimizes the generalization error, or at least an upper bound on it. We select the nonlinear SVM with RBF (Radial Basis Function) kernel as our setting because it performs well on our dataset.

3.2 Query Enrichment and Feature Extraction

In this section, we describe how to use user clicks, sessions and SERPs to enrich a query and extract features that are designed to distinguish query ambiguity.

Basic Features. There are three basic features that may be useful in identifying query ambiguity: (1) *QueryLength*: the length of the query; (2) *IfContainStopword*: if the query contains a stopword; (3) *IfContainQuestion*: if the query contains a question or interrogative. All of the three features can be extracted without any other web resource. It is notable that *QueryLength* is assumed to be very helpful because usually the longer the query is, the more intent information it may carry. If a query contains a stopword or appears to be a question, it usually describes the user's intent specifically. Thus , *IfContainStopword* and *IfContainQuestion* are supposed to be functional.

User Click Features. Previous works shows that user click features are very helpful in query intent classification and they might be functional to our query ambiguity identification task, because query intent in some degree suggests the ambiguity of query. For example, a navigational query usually reflects clear intent to visit the homepage of a website.

Liu *et al.* proposed two assumptions in [18]: *Less Effort Assumption* (user tends to click a small number of URLs when performing a navigational type search) and *Cover Page Assumption* (user tends to click only the first few URLs when performing a navigational type search).

Based on these two assumptions, they proposed two features *nClickSatisfied(nCS)* and *nResultSatisfied(nRS)*for query intent classification as follows :

$$nCS = \frac{\#\left(Sessions\ of\ q\ that\ involves\ less\ than\ n\ clicks\right)}{\#\left(Sessions\ of\ q\right)} \quad (2)$$

$$nRS = \frac{\#\left(Sessions\ of\ q\ where\ only\ top\ n\ results\ are\ clicked\right)}{\#\left(Sessions\ of\ q\right)} \quad (3)$$

Click distribution proposed by Lee [20] is believed to be functional. We calculate the percentage of clicks on the top-n clicked results (*nTCP*).

$$nTCP = \frac{\sum_{i=1}^{N} \#\left(Clicks\ on\ i^{th}\ most\ freq\ clicked\ result\right)}{\#\left(Clicks\ in\ session\ of\ q\right)} \quad (4)$$

Besides these features, we are introducing two features which indicates the types of user clicked result, *RecommClickedPercentage(RCP)* and *CommonResultClickedPercentage(CRCP)* defined as follows:

$$RCP/CRCP = \frac{\#\left(Clicks\ on\ recommendation/common\ results\ on\ SERP\ of\ q\right)}{\#\left(Clicks\ in\ session\ of\ q\right)} \quad (5)$$

The type distribution of user-clicked results might suggest some characteristics of the query specificity. For example, if many users submit a query and then click its query recommendation on the SERP, this process of actions may suggests that it is very possible that the query is ambiguous and user needs to narrow down to a subtopic with the help of recommendations.

Search Result Hints. Modern search engines usually incorporate search results from multiple vertical search engines into SERP (See an example in the Fig. 3). These vertical search engines usually focus on some categories of web resource such as videos, images, maps and dramas etc. When the search engine receives a query, it might activate some vertical search engines, and vertical search results might be incorporated into the SERP according the result of ranking algorithm. This way, we can try to figure out what the queries are talking about by digging into the specific types of results presented on the SERP. Further more, it may help us identify query ambiguity. By reviewing the content types of vertical

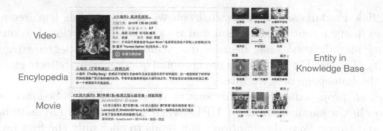

Fig. 3. Search result page(query:*Big Bang*) with results from vertical search engines

results on SERPs, we extract 13 features by counting if a certain type of vertical result appears on the SERP, for instance, video, image, music, drama, news and etc. Each of them may describe a particular aspect of the queries, for example, if the there are direction results on the SERP, that may suggest that the query contains a name of a location.

3.3   Session Features

Query2vec. Query session context may contain some information about the query ambiguity. By reviewing the session corpus, we intuitively find that for a clear query, the queries in session context usually focus on a specific topic while ambiguous queries are often surrounded by queries which covers many subtopics. For example, take the queries in Table 1 for example, the query *"wind"* is ambiguous, its preceding queries and following queries cover several domains or topics: *Operating System* (windows, wind7 download), *Music* (bboxwind, nobody knows, Dad I'm back), *Weather* (windy, wind speed) and *Wind Information Co., Ltd* (wind information, wind dataset, wind stock expert), which is a famous integrated service provider of financial data, information and software. Another query *"high-resolution map of China"* is clear and its context queries are mainly focused on the map of China, with differences in the details.

Table 1. Query context of query *"wind"* and *"high-resolution map of China"*

Query: wind (Ambiguous)		Query: high-resolution map of China (Clear)	
Pre. Queries(Freq)	Fol. Queries(Freq)	Pre. Queries(Freq)	Fol. Queries(Freq)
bbox wind (2389)	windows(2432)	China map(4362)	China map(4783)
wind info.(1897)	thunder(1701)	entire China map(1541)	entire China map(1857)
windows(1765)	wind info.(1623)	China map high-reso(273)	pic of China map(365)
wind dataset(1282)	wind dataset(1452)	China map search(210)	map(286)
nobodyknows(453)	wind speed(432)	World map(110)	world map(215)
Dad Im back(323)	win7 download(321)	entire world map(106)	Chinese province map(210)
win(301)	win(286)	Chinese China map(95)	search on China map(187)
telephone(211)	wind stock expert(178)	China map copy(85)	China map download(158)
windy(153)	bboxwind(21)	pic of China map(81)	China map high-reso.(153)

Inspired by recent distributional word representation approach [5], we attempt to present every query as a vector and extract features from both the original query and its *"neighbors"* vectors. We call it *"query2vec"* to shadow, as an application of *"word2vec"*.

We further assume that context queries of a specific query, which carry vague intent, may scatter in the query vector space. If we treat a user *search session* as a *document, queries* in the sessions are just like *words* in the documents. We can learn a vector presentation for every query by training on large scale of user sessions. Formally, we can describe this the training process as the following

First, we collect a large scale of user sessions as a document $D = \{s_1, s_2, s_3 \ldots\}$, where s_i denotes the user sessions, each session contains a sequence of individual queries. Similar to [5], skip-gram model is adopted on this problem, the training objective is to learn query vector representations that are good at predicting the nearby queries. We chose a computationally efficient approximation of the full softmax, the hierarchical softmax, which will improve both the quality of the vectors and the training speed. One of applications with the vectors is to calculate similarities between any two items. For words in documents, the similarities means the possibility that the two words have similar meanings or share common properties, or propose the same connotation. For queries in sessions, the similarities between queries usually indicates the similarity of user intents, which the two queries reflect.

Features Extraction. As stated before, each query can be presented as a vector with *query2vec* algorithm. For query q_i, we can pick out its top-k frequently occurred preceding and following queries separately as $P(\overrightarrow{q_i}, k)$ and $F(\overrightarrow{q_i}, k)$. each query can be presented by its vector, We can get two vector sets P^V and F^V by replacing queries by vectors,

$$P^V(\overrightarrow{v_i}, k) = \{\overrightarrow{v_{i,1}}, \overrightarrow{v_{i,2}}, \overrightarrow{v_{i,3}}, \ldots \overrightarrow{v_{i,k}}\} \quad F^V(\overrightarrow{v_j}, k) = \{\overrightarrow{v_{j,1}}, \overrightarrow{v_{j,2}}, \overrightarrow{v_{j,3}}, \ldots \overrightarrow{v_{j,k}}\} \quad (6)$$

where the queries is sorted by times of co-occurance in descending order.

We calculate *Diameter, Mean* and *Standard Deviation* (SD) on similarities between queries from both $P^V(\overrightarrow{v_i}, k)$ and $F^V(\overrightarrow{v_i}, k)$ to quantify the distribution of Preceding and Following queries. Click entropy is also chosen to describe the distribution of the two sets. The vector similarity is measured by cosine similarity. We utilize the open source toolkit *word2vec*[1] to train the query representations. The length of top co-occurred preceding and following queries is a parameter can be tuned.

4   Experiments

4.1   Experiment Setup

With the help of a famous Chinese commercial search engine, we collect query logs from April 1, 2012 to April 30, 2012. We extract the information of the query,

---

[1] code.google.com/p/word2vec/

clicked URL, timestamp and anonymized user-id. Private information is removed as much as possible to avoid the leak of privacy information. The click-through log contains 2,625,029 unique queries, 4,699,150 unique URLs, 72,106,874 query-URL pairs, and 717,916,107 individual clicks.

Search sessions are divided according to the time interval between two queries issued by a user. We separate two consecutive queries into two sessions if the interval exceeds 30 minutes. After removing all the single-query sessions, there are 160,526,561 sessions left on which the *"query2vec"* algorithm is conducted.

To construct a training set, we randomly sample 1,000 queries from query logs. After removing the pornographic ones, there are 810 queries left. With the help of 2 professional assessors, we label each query as clear or not-clear according to the following labeling criteria:

Clear: the query reflects a clear user intent.

Not Clear: the query may have different interpretations (Ambiguous) or covers several subtopics (Broad) of an entity.

After the annotators double-checked the annotations, the query-set contains 485 *Clear* queries and 325 *Not clear* queries in total. The κ value of annotation between three assessors is 0.756, which denotes the accessors reach agreements on most of the instances.

4.2 Classification Performance

By adopting the proposed query enrichment and feature extraction methods, several groups of features are extracted to describe the corresponding queries including: Basic Features (BF), User Click Features (UCF), Session Features (SF) and Search Result Hints (SRH). We train a SVM classifier to combine these features. Intuitively, we choose Precision, Recall and F1-Score for evaluation purposes just as other query ambiguity identification works[3,4]. All the evaluation results are obtained with 5-folded cross validation. The length of top co-occurred preceding and following queries, parameters of SVM(cost and γ) are tuned to gain its best performance for comparison.

Table 2. Performance comparison with different features combinations

#	Feature	Precision	Recall	F_1 Score	F_1 Score Improvement Compared with Baseline
1	BF	0.756	0.747	0.748	-2.09%
2	UCF	0.624	0.619	0.568	-25.65%
3	SF	0.710	0.711	0.710	-7.07%
4	SRH	0.715	0.702	0.682	-10.73%
5	BF+UCF	0.789	0.789	0.789	3.27%
6	BF+SF	0.766	0.766	0.766	0.26%
7	BF+SRH	0.767	0.767	0.764	0.00%
8	BF+UCF+SRH	0.813	0.813	0.811	6.15%
9	BF+UCF+SF	0.798	0.798	0.797	4.32%
10	BF+SF+SRH	0.788	0.788	0.785	2.75%
11	**BF+UCF+SF+SRH**	**0.821**	**0.820**	**0.819**	**7.20%**
12	Hafernik *et al.* (Baseline)	0.769	0.763	0.764	N/A

From Table 2, we can see that the *Basic Features* plays an important role in query ambiguity identification. Feature combinations 1 to 4 show the performance of classifiers with only one group of features. Since Basic Features get the best performance, we focus on the improvement brought by User Click Features, Session Features and Search Result Hints with the existence of Basic Features. With the number of involved feature groups increases, the classification performance also improves. Feature combinations No. 7 and No. 11 illustrates that Session Features help improve the performance (compared with Feature combinations No.1 and No. 9 respectively), which show the effectiveness of the proposed *'query2vec"* method. **BF+UCF+SF+SRH** outperforms other feature combinations and archives Precision 0.821, Recall 0.820 and F-Score 0.819. Comparing with other combinations, we find that Basic Features is the most helpful for the query ambiguity problem and Search Result Hints, User Click Features and Session Features, also contribute to the classification performance.

The taxonomy of Narrow/General queries proposed by Hafernik *et al.* is quite similar with our Clear/Not-Clear from the ambiguity identification's perspective. Therefore, we also implemented their classification method as a baseline to compare with. As shown in Table 2, several of our feature combinations (including Combinations No. 5, 6, 8, 9, 10 and 11) outperforms this baseline method.

The classifier sometimes makes mistakes when predicting ambiguous queries. For example, the query *'5566'*, it is the name of a famous boy band which was very active ten years ago, it is also the name of a well-known Chinese navigational website . However, most users select the results for navigation website, making the user behavior features (UCF, SF) bring negative influence to the classifier.

We divide the the queries into two group: low&medium frequency group(0-1000 clicks) and high frequency group(1000+ clicks) and compare algorithm performance with all features on different queries groups.

Table 3. Performance comparison on different query groups

Groups	Precision	Recall	F_1 Score
low & medium frequency queries	0.855	0.860	0.857
high frequency queries	0.806	0.799	0.802

Results from Table 3 show that our algorithm is of most help for low&medium frequency queries. It would be promising because the vast majority of queries processed by search engines is made up by low and medium frequency queries.

4.3   Comparison of Feature Contributions

Experiment is also conducted to evaluate the contributions of individual features. First, we train a model with **BF+UCF+SF+SRH** features, and the parameters are tuned to gain its optimal performance.

After that, we remove each feature from the above model with all features and calculate the performance loss caused by the feature removal. We use accuracy

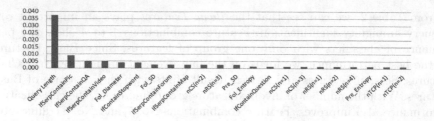

Fig. 4. Feature contribution comparison

(the proportion of both true positive and true negative examples) to evaluate the differences with the original model. We can see that a larger performance loss represents a larger contribution of the corresponding feature to the classification framework.

According to the results shown in Fig. 4, *Query Length* contributes the most to this task. This effect can be explained by the fact that most ambiguous queries are relatively short, which accords with the conclusions given by [4], [11].

5   Conclusion and Future Work

Nowadays, a typical short query submitted to a search engine usually cannot offer enough information for the ranking algorithm to give a high quality result list. Therefore, the best a search engine can do is to provide a diversified or personalized search results. In this work, to identify query ambiguity, we propose a 3-level framework which takes user behavior features collected from click-through logs into consideration. Especially, besides the features collected from queries, we focus on how to tell the differences between clear and ambiguous queries via features extracted from multi-query sessions. Inspired by recent progresses in word representation, we propose a query representation approach named *"query2vec"* which constructs representations from the distributions of contexts in query logs. Experiments based on large scale commercial search engine logs show effectiveness of the proposed framework as well as the corresponding representation approach. In the future, we plan to adopt the ambiguity identification algorithm in practical search environment to guide the diversified or personalized ranking process.

Acknowledgment. This work was supported by Natural Science Foundation (61073071) and a Research Fund FY14-RES-SPONSOR-111 from Microsoft Research Asia.

References

1. Clarke, C.L.A., Kolla, M., Vechtomova, O.: An Effectiveness Measure for Ambiguous and Underspecified Queries. In: Azzopardi, L., Kazai, G., Robertson, S., Rüger, S., Shokouhi, M., Song, D., Yilmaz, E. (eds.) ICTIR 2009. LNCS, vol. 5766, pp. 188–199. Springer, Heidelberg (2009)

2. Mirco, S., Gauch S.: Personalized Search based on User Search Histories. In: The 2005 IEEE/WIC/ACM International Conference on IEEE, Web Intelligence, pp. 622–628 (2005)
3. Song, R., et al.: Identification of Ambiguous Queries in Web Search. Information Processing & Management 45(2), 216–229 (2009)
4. Song, R., et al.: Learning Query Ambiguity Models by using Search Logs. Journal of Computer Science and Technology 25(4), 728–738 (2010)
5. Mikolov, T., et al.: Distributed Representations of Words and Phrases and their Compositionality. Advances in Neural Information Processing Systems (2013)
6. Mikolov, T., et al.: Efficient Estimation of Word Representations in Vector Space. arXiv preprint arXiv:1301.3781 (2013)
7. Broder, A.: A Taxonomy of Web Search. SIGIR Forum 36(2) (2002)
8. Rose, D.E., Levinson, D.: Understanding User Goals in Web Search. In: Proceedings of the 13th International Conference on World Wide Web, pp. 13–19. ACM (2004)
9. Zhai, C.X., Cohen, W.W., Lafferty, J.: Beyond Independent Relevance: Methods and Evaluation Metrics for Subtopic Retrieval. In: Proceedings of SIGIR 2013, pp. 10–17. ACM (2003)
10. Chirita, P.A., et al.: Using ODP Metadata to Personalize Search. In: Proceedings of the 28th Annual International ACM SIGIR Conference on Research and Development in Information Retrieval, pp. 178–185. ACM (2005)
11. Carolyn Theresa, H., Jansen, B.J.: Understanding the Specificity of Web Search Queries. In: CHI 2013 Extended Abstracts on Human Factors in Computing Systems, pp. 1827–1832. ACM (2013)
12. Li, Y., Zheng, Z., Dai, H.K.: KDD CUP-2005 report: Facing a Great Challenge. ACM SIGKDD Explorations Newsletter 7(2), 91–99 (2005)
13. Shen, D., et al.: Building Bridges for Web Query Classification. In: Proceedings of SIGIR 2006, pp. 131–138. ACM (2006)
14. Beitzel, S.M., et al.: Varying Approaches to Topical Web Query Classification. In: Proceedings of the 30th Annual International ACM SIGIR Conference on Research and Development in Information Retrieval, pp. 783–784. ACM (2007)
15. Westerveld, T., Kraaij, W., Hiemstra, D.: Retrieving Web Pages using Content, Links, Urls and Anchors, pp. 663–672 (2002)
16. Brenes, D.J., Gayo-Avello, D.: Automatic Detection of Navigational Queries according to Behavioural Characteristics, pp. 41–48. LWA (2008)
17. Agichtein, E., Zheng, Z.: Identifying Best Bet Web Search Results by Mining Past User Behavior. In: Proceedings of the 12th ACM SIGKDD International Conference on Knowledge Discovery and Data Mining, pp. 902–908. ACM (2006)
18. Liu, Y., Zhang, M., Ru, L., Ma, S.: Automatic Query Type Identification based on Click through Information. In: Ng, H.T., Leong, M.-K., Kan, M.-Y., Ji, D. (eds.) AIRS 2006. LNCS, vol. 4182, pp. 593–600. Springer, Heidelberg (2006)
19. Wang, Y., Agichtein, E.: Query Ambiguity Revisited: Clickthrough Measures for Distinguishing Informational and Ambiguous Queries. In: Human Language Technologies: The 2010 Annual Conference of the North American Chapter of the Association for Computational Linguistics. ACL (2010)
20. Lee, U., Liu, Z., Cho, J.: Automatic Identification of User Goals in Web Search. In: Proceedings of the 14th International Conference on World Wide Web, pp. 391–400. ACM (2005)

Revisiting the Evaluation of Diversified Search Evaluation Metrics with User Preferences

Fei Chen[1], Yiqun Liu[1], Zhicheng Dou[2,*], Keyang Xu[1], Yujie Cao[1], Min Zhang[1], and Shaoping Ma[1]

[1] Tsinghua University, Beijing, China
[2] Renmin University of China, Beijing, China
chenfei27@gmail.com

Abstract. To validate the credibility of diversity evaluation metrics, a number of methods that "evaluate evaluation metrics" are adopted in diversified search evaluation studies, such as Kendall's τ, Discriminative Power, and the Intuitiveness Test. These methods have been widely adopted and have aided us in gaining much insight into the effectiveness of evaluation metrics. However, they also follow certain types of user behaviors or statistical assumptions and do not take the information of users' actual search preferences into consideration. With multi-grade user preference judgments collected for diversified search result lists displayed parallel, we take user preferences as the ground truth to investigate the evaluation of diversity metrics. We find that user preference at the subtopic level gain similar results with those at the topic level, which means we can use user preference at the topic level with much less human efforts in future experiments. We further find that most existing evaluation metrics correlate with user preferences well for result lists with large performance differences, no matter the differences is detected by the metric or the users. According to these findings, we then propose a preference-weighted correlation, the *Multi-grade User Preference* (*MUP*) method, to evaluate the diversity metrics based on user preferences. The experimental results reveal that *MUP* evaluates diversity metrics from real users' perspective that may differ from other methods. In addition, we find the relevance of the search result is more important than the diversity of the search result in the diversified search evaluation of our experiments.

1 Introduction

Evaluation metrics have always been one of the most important and challenging topics in information retrieval research because of the part they play in tuning and optimizing retrieval systems [3]. For diversified search tasks, many evaluation methods, such as $\alpha - nDCG$ [7] and $D\# - measures$ [14], have been proposed. These metrics more or less simplify the assumptions about user behaviors. For example, with the assumption that users always view search results from top

---

* The work was done when Zhicheng Dou was working at Microsoft Research.

A. Jaafar et al. (Eds.): AIRS 2014, LNCS 8870, pp. 48–59, 2014.
© Springer International Publishing Switzerland 2014

to bottom, most metrics leverage a ranking-based discount. These assumptions may help to simplify the evaluation process but also make the evaluation deviate from user's actual experience and satisfaction [17].

In this paper, we propose to take user preferences as the ground truth to evaluate diversity metrics. We first compare user preferences collected at the subtopic level, user preferences at the topic level, and the weighted user preferences with each other. Diversity metrics are then discussed in terms of the performance differences of run pairs detected by the metric, which is similar with Sanderson's work [16] (more recent than Turpin's work [18,19]) except that we involve more diversity metrics. Other differences between Sanderson's work and ours are that we collect user preferences in a graded strategy and leverage τ_b to evaluate the correlations between diversity metrics and the graded user preferences, whereas Sanderson *et al.* use agreement/disagreement between metrics and binary user preferences to discuss metrics' properties. And on the other hand, we further discuss the same metrics in terms of the performance differences of run pairs detected by the users. Based on the graded user preferences, we then propose a preference-weighted correlation, namely Multi-grade User Preference (MUP), to evaluate the diversity metrics. Finally, three widely-used methods for evaluating diversity metrics, namely Kendall's τ, Discriminative Power and the Intuitiveness Test are compared with MUP.

The major contributions of this paper are as follows:

1. We construct a test collection that contains 6,000 graded preferences collected at both the topic and subtopic levels (50 queries with 3 subtopics per query) on 10 run pairs. We investigate the consistency between the graded user preferences collected at the subtopic level and the preferences at the topic level for a better strategy to collect user preferences efficiently.

2. The correlations (τ_b) between a large number of diversity metrics and the graded user preferences are studied in two dimensions. The one is in terms of performance differences of run pairs detected by the metric and the other is in terms of the differences detected by the user.

3. We propose a preference-weighted correlation, namely Multi-grade User Preference (MUP), to evaluate the diversity metrics based on user preferences. Discussions between MUP and Kendall's τ, Discriminative Power and the Intuitiveness Test are performed in details.

The remainder of this paper is organized as follows. In Section 2, we review related work regarding the ways to evaluate diversity metrics. Section 3 compares the user preferences collected at the subtopic level with the user preferences at the topic level. Next, in Section 4 we compare the correlations between several widely-used diversity metrics and user preferences. Section 5 presents the proposed method to evaluate diversity metrics. In Section 6, we provide our experiments and corresponding analyses. Finally, Section 7 presents our conclusions and directions for future work.

2   Related Work

It is difficult to evaluate a diversity metric because different metrics make different assumptions to simplify the process of diversity evaluation. To present the possible effectiveness of a diversity metric, several methods have been developed.

Sakai et al. [15] propose to leverage Discriminative Power [11] to assess the effectiveness of diversity metrics. The method computes a significance test between every pair of the system runs and reports the percentage of pairs that a metric can significantly distinguish at some fixed significance level.

Kendall's τ [9] is another method used to compare different metrics. It is defined as the value proportional to the number of pairwise adjacent swaps needed to convert one ranking into the other ranking. Many previous works related to evaluation leverage it to compare their proposed metrics with other widely-used metrics [4,5].

The Intuitiveness Test [12] is developed by Sakai to compare the intuitiveness of different diversity metrics. In this method, a metric that is simple but can effectively represent the intuitiveness, e.g., the most important property that the diversity metrics should satisfy, is taken as the gold standard metric. The relative intuitiveness of two diversity metrics is measured in terms of preference agreement with its gold standard metric.

Moffat [10] proposes to characterize metrics by seven numeric properties, i.e. boundedness, monotonicity, convergence, top-weightedness, localization, completeness, and realizability. These properties are used to partition the evaluation metrics and help the metrics to be better understood.

Amigó et al. [2] propose reliability and sensitivity to compare evaluation metrics. Reliability is the probability of finding the document relationships of a system run in a chosen gold standard run, whereas sensitivity is the probability of finding the document relationships of a chosen gold standard run in a system run.

In general, these methods are lack of consideration about user preferences. After all, the ultimate aim of diversified search is satisfying the diverse information needs of users. In this paper, we highlight the possible effectiveness of user preferences in the evaluation of diversity metrics.

3   User Preferences Discussion

We first select 5 of the 12 runs created by different methods in NTCIR 10 Intent-2 task [13] (Table 1). Each two of the 5 runs are then presented to users in a paralleled way to collect user preference. To decrease the total work of preference collection, we only choose 50 of the 200 queries that contain as fewer (but at least 3) subtopics as possible. This is because in the experiments, only the top 3 subtopics ordered by weight are reserved for every query (for small workloads). We need to possibly decrease the bias of the subtopic reservation. The weights of the three reserved subtopics are then re-normalized by their sum.

3.1   Graded User Preferences Collection

Because in diversified search a query topic is considered to contain several subtopics, we collect user preferences at both the subtopic and the topic levels. We present a subtopic with search results from two different runs to collect user preference at the subtopic level, whereas simultaneously present all the three subtopics underlying a query with the search results to collect user preference at the topic level. The annotator is required to assess his preference by a number between 0 and 4. Because we have selected 50 queries with 150 subtopics, there are 200 presentations for each run pair. Considering 5 runs can generate 10 run pairs and each is confirmed to be presented to 3 annotators in the experiment, 110 annotators participate in this experiment with one person finishing 60 annotations. 10 annotators are filtered because the number of their decisions made within 10 seconds are larger than 30. Therefore, we collect 6,000 user preferences.

3.2   Graded User Preferences Comparisons

User preferences at the subtopic level are collected by presenting one subtopic at a time without giving the subtopic weight. However, the weights of subtopics underlying a query may always differ from each other. To compare the bias, we linearly combine the user preferences at the subtopic level with corresponding subtopic weights to form the weighted preferences at topic level. We can then compare the preferences at the topic level with the weighted preferences and even with the user preferences at the subtopic level.

We average the user preferences and present results in Table 1. The average preferences for each run pair at the subtopic level are computed based on the 150 subtopics, whereas the average weighted preferences and the average preferences at the topic level are based on the 50 queries. Table 1 shows that in our experiment no matter what type of user preferences is considered, the relative orders between each pair are identical. For example, users prefer BASELINE-D-C-1 to THUIR-D-C-1A in terms of all the three types of preferences according to the first row of Table 1.

Table 1 shows that the three types of user preferences have the same assess results for all the run pairs, although the significant results at the subtopic level contain the most items, which completely includes all of the significant results of the other two types of user preferences. This may be caused by a larger number of instances at the subtopic level considered in the significance test. Because user preferences at the subtopic level are collected without giving subtopic weights, it is more reasonable to consider the results of weighted preferences or the use preferences at the topic level. On the other hand, Table 1 shows that both the assess results and the significant results of weighted preferences are similar with the results of user preferences at the topic level. If we only collect user preferences at the topic level, 1,500 rather than 6,000 user preferences need to be collected. The corresponding cost would decrease to one-fourth. In the following sections of this paper, we only consider the user preferences at the topic level.

Table 1. User preference comparison. ">" in column PF indicates the left system is on average better than the right, whereas "<" indicates the right system is better than the left. The checkmarks in the columns SSL, SWS, and STL indicate the significance of user preferences at the subtopic level, the weighted level and the topic level, respectively.

Left	Right	PF	SSL	SWS	STL
BASELINE-D-C-1	THUIR-D-C-1A	<	✓	✓	✓
KECIR-D-C-3B	THUIR-D-C-1A	<	✓	✓	✓
KECIR-D-C-2B	THUIR-D-C-1A	<	✓	✓	✓
THUIR-D-C-1A	THUIR-D-C-4A	>			
BASELINE-D-C-1	THUIR-D-C-4A	<			
KECIR-D-C-3B	THUIR-D-C-4A	<	✓		
KECIR-D-C-2B	THUIR-D-C-4A	<	✓	✓	✓
BASELINE-D-C-1	KECIR-D-C-3B	>	✓		
KECIR-D-C-2B	KECIR-D-C-3B	<	✓	✓	✓
BASELINE-D-C-1	KECIR-D-C-2B	>	✓		✓

4 Correlation between Diversity Metrics and User Preferences

There are many works about methods to evaluate a diversified search result. These works have proposed diversity metrics such as $\alpha - nDCG$, $IA - measures$, $D\# - measures$. These metrics more or less simplify the assumptions about user behaviors, which prevent the metrics from reflecting aspects of the search processes that are experienced by the user. In this section, we take user preferences collected in Section 3 as the ground truth to present the user behavior related properties of diversity metrics in details. We consider a large range of diversity metrics such as $IA - nDCG$ [1], $IA - ERR$ [6], $\alpha - nDCG$ [7], $NRBP$ [8], $I - rec$ [11], $D - nDCG$, $D\# - nDCG$, $D - Q$, $D\# - Q$ [14], $DIN\# - nDCG$, $DIN\# - Q$, $P + Q$, $P + Q\#$ [12].

4.1 Comparing Correlations on Run Pairs with Different Performance

For a certain query, we leverage diversity metrics to evaluate the retrieval results of every two different runs. According to the evaluation score, we can obtains the run preferred by the metric within each pair. On the other hand, we have also collected user preferences on the same pairs. The correlation between the metric and user preferences can then be computed for these pairs. Since there may be a tie in both the evaluation scores and the user preferences, we compute the τ_b coefficient. τ_b is similar with the Kendall's τ [9] except that the former explicitly excludes the influences of the tie in the rankings.

We first demonstrate the changes of correlations from run pairs with small differences to run pairs with large differences by classifying the run pairs into two bins. The run pairs whose difference in terms of a metric is greater than the average difference of all the pairs are assigned into a large Δ bin and the other pairs are into a small Δ bin. The correlations between metrics and user preferences are computed within each bin, respectively. From another dimension, we also classify the run pairs into different categories according to user preferences. As described in Section 3, we collect user preferences in a graded strategy(between 0 and 4). We equally split this range into 4 different subranges. Within each subrange, we compute the correlations between the metrics and user preferences.

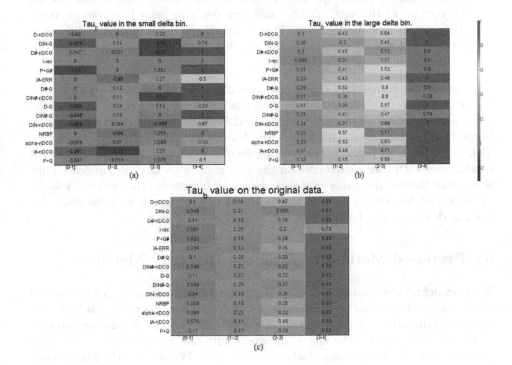

Fig. 1. The τ_b values between diversity metrics and user preferences. The x axis is the subranges of user preferences. Warmer color indicates stronger correlation with user preference. (a) presents the τ_b values computed on run pairs of the small Δ bin. (b) presents the τ_b values computed on run pairs of the large Δ bin. (c) presents the τ_b values on all the run pairs.

Fig. 1 presents all the results. In these heatmaps, a rectangle with color near the red indicates a strong positive correlation, whereas a rectangle with color near the blue indicates a strong negative correlation. From these heatmaps, we can find:

1. Comparing Fig. 1(a) with Fig. 1(b), we can find τ_b values in the large Δ bin are larger than the corresponding τ_b values in the small Δ bin. This means when the differences of two systems detected by metrics become larger, the metrics may agree with user preferences better.

2. From the dimension of user preferences (x axis), we also find that the metrics agree with user preferences better when the differences of run pairs detected by users are larger, whereas it is difficult for diversity metrics to agree with user preferences on the run pairs with small differences.
3. The τ_b values of $DIN\# - Q$, $DIN\# - nDCG$, $D\# - Q$, $P + Q\#$, and $D\# - nDCG$ in subrange (3-4] of the small Δ bin are larger than the corresponding τ_b values in the same subrange of the big Δ bin. By investigating the data, we find these metric only contain one system pair in subrange (3-4] of the small Δ bin, in which case the τ_b value includes much bias. In fact, for all the metrics in the small Δ bin there are few run pairs (on average, 0.9% of the total) in subrange (3-4]. This means if the users think the difference between two runs is small, then the metric is likely to think the difference is small as well.

The discussions above show that when the differences of run pairs are large, the metrics are more likely to achieve agreements with user preferences, whereas the agreements are difficult to achieve when the differences are small. This conclusion keeps true no matter the differences are detected by the metrics or the users. This inspires us to penalize the metric more in evaluating diversity metrics if it disagrees with user preferences on the run pairs with large differences. That is because the metric makes mistakes on run pairs where other metrics seldom make a mistake. The τ_b itself is not aware of this, although we have discussed the metrics based on the τ_b value.

5   Proposed Method to Evaluate Diversity Metrics

We first define some symbols in use. We denote a run pair as c. All of the 500 run pairs mentioned above compose a pair set C. Then, we define an indicator $J(c)$ satisfying $J(c) = 1$ if the metric agrees with the user preference on run pair c, whereas $J(c) = -1$ if the metric disagrees with the user preference. The user preference of c is denoted as u_c (where $0 \le u_c \le 4$). We propose the Multi-grade User Preference (MUP) to evaluate diversity metrics as follows:

$$MUP = \frac{sum_{c \in C}(u_c \times J(c))}{sum_{c \in C} u_c} \tag{1}$$

In Formula 1, if the metric agrees with the user preference on a pair c, then both the numerator and the denominator increase by u_c. However, if the metric disagrees with the user preference, then $J(c) = -1$ and the sum of the corresponding $u_c \times J(c)$ in the numerator is indeed equal to subtracting the user preference u_c from the sum. In contrast, the denominator always increases by u_c. This is taken as the penalization of the disagreement. If u_c is larger, MUP punishes the disagreement more. This is meaningful because the experiments and corresponding discussions in Section 4 show that the metrics achieve a better agreement with user preferences when the differences of run pairs are larger, whereas they perform worse on the run pairs with smaller differences. If a metric makes a mistake (which means the metric disagrees with the user preference) on a run pair whose difference can be easily detected, it should be heavily penalized when we evaluate the metric. However, if the mistake is made on the run pair whose differences are small and difficult to detect, the corresponding punishment may be slight. Especially, MUP does not consider the run pairs with $u_c = 0$.

We can also discuss Formula 1 from the user's perspective. A large user preference means the user considers the difference between the run pair to be large. It is reasonable to consider that the user can, on average, detect a large difference with more confidence than when detecting a small difference. Therefore, if a metric makes a mistake on the run pair whose difference is detected by the user with much confidence, the metric should be penalized more. In contrast, a small u_c indicates a small difference detected by the user. We can also consider that the user is more confused when he is required to decide which one of two similar runs is better. Therefore, a smaller u_c would indicate less user confidence on the user's preference decision. If a metric makes a mistake on the run pair with a small u_c, the penalization may be slight.

5.1 Relationships between MUP and Kendall's τ

The MUP defined in Formula 1 is similar with the τ value. The difference is that MUP leverages the user preference u_c to weight the agreements and the disagreements considered in τ. As we discussed above, this weighted agreements (disagreements) would make MUP to penalize the mistakes more on the run pairs with large differences while to weaken the penalization to the mistakes on the run pairs with small differences.

We also can define MUP_b based on MUP, just like the extension from τ to τ_b.

$$MUP_b = sum_{c \in C}(u_c \times J(c)) \times \frac{1}{\sqrt{sum_{c \in C}(u_c + u_c \times T_0(c))}} \times \frac{1}{\sqrt{sum_{c \in C}(u_c + u_c \times T_0'(c))}} \quad (2)$$

Where $T_0(c)$ is an indicator satisfying $T_0(c) = 1$ when the run pair c is tied only in terms of the metric, otherwise $T_0(c) = 0$. $T_0'(c)$ is a similar indicator satisfying $T_0'(c) = 1$ when the run pair c is tied only in terms of user preferences, otherwise $T_0'(c) = 0$. Note that if $T_0'(c) = 1$, then we obtain $u_c = 0$ according to the definition of $T_0'(c)$. This means $u_c \times T_0'(c)$ is always equal to 0. Formula 2 can then be simplified as:

$$MUP_b = \frac{sum_{c \in C}(u_c \times J(c))}{\sqrt{sum_{c \in C}(u_c \times (1 + T_0(c))) \times sum_{c \in C} u_c}} \quad (3)$$

6 Experimental Comparisons

As discussed in Section 5, MUP (MUP_b) is a weighted τ (τ_b). In this section, we first construct experiments to discuss the consistency of them. As most of the existing studies in the literature usually leverage Discriminative Power and the Intuitiveness Test to investigate the different aspects of the diversity metric, the discussions about them are also included in the experiments.

We compute the MUP, MUP_b, τ, τ_b, and Discriminative Power values on the selected 500 run pairs, respectively. We leverage the two-tailed paired boot-strap test with 1,000 bootstrap samples [11] for the Discriminative Power. The significance level in use is $\alpha = 0.05$. The results are presented in Fig. 2.

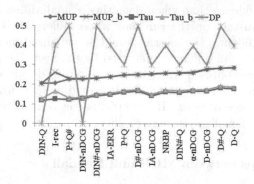

Fig. 2. The values of MUP, MUP_b, τ, τ_b and Discriminative Power. The metrics are ordered by their MUP values in an ascending order.

Fig. 2 shows:

1. D-Q gets higher MUP value than $\alpha - nDCG$, $NRBP$, and $IA - ERR$. This means D-Q simulates the user behaviors better in terms of the weighted correlation. From the definition of D-Q metric, we know that D-Q considers users browser search results from top to bottom until his information need is satisfied. the results indicate this assumption may be useful in the diversity evaluation. After adding other features, such as user information type or subtopic recall, $D\# - Q$, $DIN - Q$ and $DIN\# - Q$ become worse. This can also be observed from $D - nDCG$ to $D\# - nDCG$, $DIN - nDCG$, and $DIN\# - nDCG$.

2. The MUP_b values of most metrics are nearly the same with (indeed, slightly different from) the MUP values of the corresponding metrics, except for the values of $I - rec$. Note that there is an additional factor $\sqrt{1 + T_0(c)}$ in the denominator of MUP_b comparing to MUP. According to the definitions of $J(c)$ and $T_0(c)$, the value of $\sqrt{1 + T_0(c)}$ is equal to either 1 or 2 (its value equals to 2 when the run pair c is tied only in terms of the metric). The larger MUP_b value of $I - rec$ indicates there are a lot of run pairs on which the score of $I - rec$ is tied, whereas the user preference is not tied. This may result from the fact that $I - rec$ is a set-based metric, and only considers a binary relevance. In contrast, the slight difference between the MUP_b and MUP values of the other metrics indicates that there exist few run pairs which are tied only in terms of the corresponding metric.

3. The τ (τ_b) value decreases from $I-rec$ to $P+Q\#$ while The MUP (MUP_b) value increases, which shows the main difference between MUP (MUP_b) and τ (τ_b). This is caused by the weighted agreement/disagreement in MUP. Fig. 1(c) shows that in the subranges (0-1] and (1-2], the τ_b values of $I-rec$ are larger than the corresponding values of $P+Q\#$ while in the subrange (3-4], the τ_b value of $I-rec$ is smaller than the τ_b value of $P+Q\#$. Considering that MUP leverages the user preferences to weight the agreement/disagreement, the user preferences lying in subrange (3-4] cause the increment of MUP value. Similar reasons can be found in the decrements of $IA-nDCG$ and $D-Q$.

4. The Discriminative Power is not correlative with the MUP or MUP_b. Metrics with large discriminative power may not have large MUP or MUP_b values, whereas metrics with small discriminative power may not indicate small MUP or MUP_b values. This means the aspects evaluating by Discriminative Power may differ from those aspects evaluating by MUP or MUP_b. We only have 10 run pairs to compute the discriminative power here, which may cause some bias in the experiment.

Table 2. Intuitiveness based on preference agreements with the gold standard metric. The number of disagreements is shown in parentheses. We **highlight** the item if the relative order of the corresponding two metrics in this table agrees with their relative order in terms of MUP values.

Metric	$D-Q$	$D\#-Q$	$DIN\#-Q$	$DIN\#$ $-nDCG$	$P+Q$	$P+Q\#$	$NRBP$
The gold standard metric: $I-rec$							
$\alpha-nDCG$	0.936/0.489 (94)	**0.618/0.971** (68)	0.573/0.987 (75)	0.545/1 (77)	**0.933/0.472** (89)	**0.480/1.000** (75)	**0.741/0.667** (27)
$D-Q$	-	0.000/1.000 (66)	0.180/1.000 (89)	0.306/1.000 (111)	0.695/0.712 (59)	0.229/1.000 (105)	0.483/0.933 (89)
$D\#-Q$	-	-	0.696/1.000 (23)	0.745/0.979 (47)	0.989/0.267 (90)	0.600/0.975 (40)	**0.970/0.582** (67)
$DIN\#-Q$	-	-	-	0.808/0.962 (26)	0.989/0.215 (93)	0.690/0.966 (29)	**0.987/0.553** (76)
$DIN\#-nDCG$	-	-	-	-	0.991/0.287 (108)	0.861/0.972 (36)	**0.988/0.537** (82)
$P+Q$	-	-	-	-	-	0.000/1 (80)	**0.500/0.906** (96)
$P+Q\#$	-	-	-	-	-	-	0.988/0.488 (82)
The gold standard metric: $Ef-P$							
$\alpha-nDCG$	**0.287/0.894** (94)	**0.441/0.765** (68)	0.427/0.827 (75)	0.506/0.740 (77)	0.438/0.775 (89)	0.547/0.680 (75)	0.630/0.630 (27)
$D-Q$	-	0.864/0.333 (66)	0.787/0.483 (89)	0.811/0.459 (111)	0.881/0.434 (59)	0.848/0.400 (105)	0.899/0.258 (89)
$D\#-Q$	-	-	0.565/0.913 (23)	0.745/0.660 (47)	0.578/0.667 (90)	0.800/0.500 (40)	0.776/0.448 (67)
$DIN\#-Q$	-	-	-	0.923/0.462 (26)	0.624/0.624 (93)	1.000/0.310 (29)	0.829/0.434 (76)
$DIN\#-nDCG$	-	-	-	-	0.574/0.685 (108)	0.833/0.611 (36)	0.732/0.512 (82)
$P+Q$	-	-	-	-	-	0.713/0.463 (80)	0.760/0.448 (96)
$P+Q\#$	-	-	-	-	-	-	0.671/0.549 (82)

6.1 Comparison between MUP and the Intuitiveness Test

The Intuitiveness Test is proposed by Sakai [12] to quantify the intuitiveness of a metric. It requires a gold standard metric to represent the intuitiveness that the diversity metric should satisfy. Following the work of Sakai, we take $I-rec$ and $Ef-P$ as the gold standard metrics and list the intuitiveness computed in Table 2. The metrics considered here are distributed in the top, middle and bottom positions of the ranking ordered by the MUP value.

From Table 2, we can find: When $Ef - P$ is taken as the gold standard, the Intuitiveness Test agrees better with MUP than it does when $I - rec$ is taken as the gold standard. The τ_b value between MUP and the Intuitiveness Test in the former case is 0.333, whereas the τ_b value in the latter case is -0.407. Since both $I - rec$ and $Ef - P$ are set-based metrics based on binary relevance, the possible bias of this type may be weakened. Considering that $I - rec$ is the gold standard of the diversity property and $Ef - P$ is the gold standard of the relevance property, the larger τ_b value in the former case indicates in the user's opinion, the relevance of the search result is more important than the diversity of the search result in the diversified search evaluation of our experiments. This result may direct the design of new diversity metrics and help us tune the trade-off parameters between relevance and diversity in diversity metrics such as $D\# - nDCG$. We will do a further research for this in future work.

7   Conclusions and Future Work

It is difficult to evaluate the effectiveness of diversity metrics. Most of the existing studies leverage Discriminative Power, Kendall's τ, or the Intuitiveness Test to evaluate the possible effectiveness of a diversity metric. However, they are lack consideration about the behaviors of user preferences. In this paper, we first collect 6,000 effective user preferences for 500 difference run pairs. A comparison between the weighted user preferences and the user preferences collected at the topic level shows they share similar characters, which means we only need to collect user preferences at the topic level with much less efforts. Then we investigate the correlations between the diversity metrics and user preferences. We find that diversity metrics agree better with user preferences when the difference of a run pair is larger, no matter the difference is detected in terms of the metric or user preferences. Based on these findings, we propose a preference-weighted correlation, namely MUP to evaluate diversity metrics. In the experiments, we first present the effort of the "preference-weighted" correlation by comparing MUP (MUP_b) with τ (τ_b). The results also show that MUP method evaluates diversity metrics from the aspects that may differ from Discriminative Power. In addition, we construct experiments to compare MUP with the Intuitiveness Test and find that when $Ef - P$ is taken as the gold standard of relevance evaluation, the Intuitiveness Test agrees better with MUP than it does when $I - rec$ is taken as the gold standard of diversity evaluation. Since the MUP method evaluates diversity metrics from real users' perspective, then this larger agreement reveals that in the user's opinion, the relevance of the search result is more important than the diversity of the search result in the diversified search evaluation of our experiments. This result may direct the design of new diversity metrics and help us tune the trade-off parameters between relevance and diversity in diversity metrics. In future work, we will base on the conclusions in this paper to develop new diversity metrics. We will also do a further research for tuning trade-off parameters in diversity metrics such as $D\# - nDCG$.

Acknowledgement. This work was supported by Natural Science Foundation (61073071) and a Research Fund FY14-RES-SPONSOR-111 from Microsoft Research Asia.

References

1. Agrawal, R., Gollapudi, S., Halverson, A., Leong, S.: Diversifying search results. In: Proc. of ACM WSDM 2009, pp. 1043–1052. ACM, Barcelona (2009)
2. Amigó, E., Gonzalo, J., Verdejo, F.: A general evaluation measure for document organization tasks. In: Proc. of SIGIR 2013, pp. 643–652. ACM, Ireland (2013)
3. Ashkan, A., Clarke, C.L.A.: On the informativeness of cascade and intent-aware effectiveness measures. In: Proc. of ACM, Hyderabad, India, pp. 407–416 (2011)
4. Aslam, J.A., Pavlu, V., Savell, R.: A unified model for metasearch, pooling, and system evaluation. In: Proc. of ACM CIKM 2003, pp. 484–491. ACM, New Orleans (2003)
5. Buckley, C., Voorhees, E.M.: Retrieval evaluation with incomplete information. In: Proc. of ACM SIGIR 2004, pp. 25–32. ACM, New York (2001)
6. Chapelle, O., Metlzer, D., Zhang, Y., Grinspan, P.: Expected reciprocal rank for graded relevance. In: Proc. of ACM CIKM 2009, pp. 621–630. ACM, New York (2009)
7. Clarke, C.L.A., Kolla, M., Cormack, G.V., Vechtomova, O.: Novelty and diversity in information retrieval evaluation. In: Proc. of ACM SIGIR 2008, pp. 659–666. ACM, Singapore (2008)
8. Clarke, C.L.A., Kolla, M., Vechtomova, O.: An effectiveness measure for ambiguous and underspecified queries. In: Azzopardi, L., Kazai, G., Robertson, S., Rüger, S., Shokouhi, M., Song, D., Yilmaz, E. (eds.) ICTIR 2009. LNCS, vol. 5766, pp. 188–199. Springer, Heidelberg (2009)
9. Kendall, M.: A new measure of rank correlation. Biometrica 30, 81–89 (1938)
10. Moffat, A.: Seven numeric properties of effectiveness metrics. In: Banchs, R.E., Silvestri, F., Liu, T.-Y., Zhang, M., Gao, S., Lang, J. (eds.) AIRS 2013. LNCS, vol. 8281, pp. 1–12. Springer, Heidelberg (2013)
11. Sakai, T.: Evaluating evaluation metrics based on the bootstrap. In: Proc. of ACM SIGIR 2006, pp. 525–532. ACM, Seattle (2006)
12. Sakai, T.: Evaluation with informational and navigational intents. In: Proc.s of ACM WWW 2012, pp. 499–508. ACM, Lyon (2012)
13. Sakai, T., Dou, Z., Yamamoto, T., Liu, Y., Zhang, M., Song, R.: Overview of the ntcir-10 intent-2 task. In: Proc. of NTCIR 2010, Tokyo, Japan (2011)
14. Sakai, T., Song, R.: Evaluating diversified search results using per-intent graded relevance. In: Proc. of SIGIR 2011, pp. 1043–1052. ACM, Beijing (2011)
15. Sakai, T., Song, R.: Diversified search evaluation: Lessons from the ntcir-9 intent task. Journal of Information Retrieval 16, 504–529 (2013)
16. Sanderson, M., Paramita, M.L., Clough, P., Kanoulas, E.: Do user preferences and evaluation measures line up? In: Proc. of ACM SIGIR 2010, pp. 555–562. ACM, Geneva (2010)
17. Smucker, M.D., Clarke, C.L.A.: Time-based calibration of effectiveness measures. In: Proc. of ACM SIGIR 2012, pp. 95–104. ACM, Portland (2012)
18. Turpin, A., Scholer, F.: User performance versus precision measures for simple search tasks. In: Proc. of SIGIR 2006, pp. 11–18. ACM, Seattle (2006)
19. Turpin, A.H., Hersh, W.: Why batch and user evaluations do not give the same results. In: Proc. of SIGIR 2001, pp. 225–231. ACM, New Orleans (2001)

Hybrid Crowd-Machine Methods as Alternatives to Pooling and Expert Judgments

Christopher G. Harris[1] and Padmini Srinivasan[2]

[1] Department of Computer Science, SUNY Oswego, Oswego, NY 13126
christopher.harris@oswego.edu
[2] Department of Computer Science, University of Iowa, Iowa City, IA 52242
padmini-srinivasan@uiowa.edu

Abstract. Pooling is a document sampling strategy commonly used to collect relevance judgments when multiple retrieval/ranking algorithms are involved. A fixed number of top ranking documents from each algorithm form a pool. Traditionally, expensive experts judge the pool of documents for relevance. We propose and test two hybrid algorithms as alternatives that reduce assessment costs and are effective. The machine part selects documents to judge from the full set of retrieved documents. The human part uses inexpensive crowd workers to make judgments. We present a clustered and a non-clustered approach for document selection and two experiments testing our algorithms. The first is designed to be statistically robust, controlling for variations across crowd workers, collections, domains and topics. The second is designed along natural lines and investigates more topics. Our results demonstrate high quality can be achieved and at low cost. Moreover, this can be done by judging far fewer documents than with pooling. Precision, recall, F-scores and LAM are very strong, indicating that our algorithms with crowd sourcing offer viable alternatives to collecting judgments via pooling with expert assessments.

Keywords: Pooling, Crowdsourcing, Retrieval evaluation, Relevance judgment.

1   Introduction

Collecting relevance judgments is crucial for Information Retrieval research. Batch mode algorithm evaluation requires that we know the correct answers, i.e., which documents in a collection are relevant to a query. A standard approach to obtain relevance judgments when multiple algorithms are involved is by a process called 'pooling' [24], first introduced in the 1992 TREC initiative [7]. In pooling a fixed number N of documents are taken from each algorithm's output to form a pool. Pooling combined with TREC assessor judgments has generated many valuable collections of relevance judgments. Recognizing the expense of assessor judgments the TREC Crowdsourcing track (since 2011) spearheaded research on alternative mechanisms for collecting relevance judgments [12]. Continuing in the same spirit we propose two hybrid crowd/machine approaches for collecting judgments. In each an algorithm (clustered or non-clustered) selects documents for judgment (in contrast to pooling) and crowd workers provide judgments.

A. Jaafar et al. (Eds.): AIRS 2014, LNCS 8870, pp. 60–72, 2014.

Our first goal is to test the effectiveness of our two approaches (clustered versus non-clustered) for collecting relevance judgments in a *statistically robust* manner addressing domain differences (News versus Biomedicine) and controlling for worker variations. Previous crowdsourcing work has not addressed the effect of domain. TREC Crowdsourcing has focused on news and web data. Perhaps it is easier for a crowd worker to judge relevance for a query related to news and general web information than for a query related to more technical chemical patents or in biomedicine. Work quality may differ due to differences in background, expertise, level of commitment to the task etc. We know that multiple judgments are needed [14], but the typical approach is to obtain just 3 judgments on a document – query pair. We address this goal with an ANOVA design experiment. The ANOVA power calculation for medium power specifies a minimum of 24 workers to judge for each algorithm–collection combination. Moreover, each worker must judge all topics in a given combination. For practical reasons (e.g., to avoid worker fatigue), we limit this experiment to three topics. *Note that this is still sufficient to make statistically valid conclusions.* As required by ANOVA design we ensure that the two domains are comparable in topics (prevalence of relevant information) and documents (e.g., word complexity, number of sentences). We study both main and interaction effects.

Our second goal is to conduct another experiment (with News) using typical settings seen in crowdsourcing papers. Also we use full documents and more topics (20). We use a majority vote from three judgments for each decision. We compare our approaches with each other and with pooling in efficiency, effectiveness and cost.

As highlights of our results: in our first experiment we find, for example, that the clustered approach achieves significantly better recall while the non-clustered one achieves better precision, F-score and LAM. In the second experiment, the non-clustered approach achieves F-score of 0.73 while the clustered approach is just short of 0.8. LAM (Logistic Average Misclassification rate) scores are around 0.05. Though not strictly comparable these results appear competitive with the best TREC 2012 results. When compared to pooling, our methods are more efficient and cost far less. Thus despite wide concerns about quality of work done by crowdsourcing (e.g., [11], [28]), our methods provide results of high quality at much lower cost. Moreover, our methods are scalable and easy to extend to other relevance assessment campaigns.

2   Related Research

In IR experiments research groups have obtained relevance judgments from many types of sources including students, librarians, subject specialists and TREC assessors. Using individuals external to the research group almost always requires payment usually in the form of money. Besides cost there is the impracticality of getting judgments for every document retrieved. Thus we see wide usage of sampling strategies such as pooling. In recent years crowdsourcing is being tested as a source for relevance judgments (and other kinds of decisions). Utilizing non-experts through crowdsourcing platforms has proven to be cost-effective (e.g.,[2],[11],[14]). However, two key challenges are the variability of assessors' judging abilities and the aggregation of noisy labels into a single consensus label. Even within the TREC/NIST framework, considerable variability across trained assessors still exists (e.g., [4],

[26]); this is shown to increase when non-experts are used [21]. To address noise, typically a majority vote is obtained across several judgments [18].

Several others have recognized the challenges of relevance assessment that are not met by pooling, and have introduced some new approaches. Soboroff et. al. examined some methods that could approximate pooling, including using a shallower pooling depth and identification of the duplicate documents normally removed by pooling, improving upon standard pooling methods [20]. We build on their methods, using the amount of duplication as an important input into our ranking algorithm. Sanderson and Joho sidestep pooling by using existing TREC judgments as inputs to a relevance feedback algorithm [23], which provides valuable information to identify which documents to investigate further. Carterette et. al. algorithmically determined the smallest test collection size to judge using a variation of MAP [3]. Their method uses ranked lists to choose documents for judgment, which is one aspect we use in our own methods. Yilmaz et. al. used stratified sampling with pooling at different k-depths in [30], providing good results, but the focus in their study was primarily on improving existing IR evaluation measures.

In 2011, the TREC Crowdsourcing track was begun to examine the crowd's ability to provide quality relevance assessments while addressing the above challenges [12]; this continued with the TRAT sub-track in 2012 [22] and 2013. A number of approaches using the crowd were examined. The top-performing BUPT-Wildcat [29] used an elaborate multi-stage prescreening process for crowd workers and an E-M Gaussian process to determine a consensus label among these workers. The complexity in their method, requiring the development, evaluation, and testing of prescreening tools suggests that it might have difficulty in scaling. Likewise, in 2012, Skierarchy, a top-performer requires an impressive but complex hierarchy of experts and crowd workers [16]; this approach too might have problems with increasing scale due to the requirement of more subject-matter experts, which are often in limited supply. In contrast we use a hybrid machine-human approach involving fusion of ranks across submitted lists of retrieved documents, optional text-feature based clustering, document batching and selection, and criteria to stop the relevance judgment process. The power of our approach is in its simplicity and in its effectiveness. The approach is an extension of our earlier work in TREC [8]; significant differences include our use of full submissions versus pooling and more refined document selection strategies. In addition, we present more extensive experiments in multiple domains compared to the TREC TRAT effort.

3   Algorithms

We propose two algorithms (clustered and non-clustered) to select documents for relevance judgments. Consider a typical TREC ad hoc retrieval task with a set of M runs submitted by competing systems for a topic T. Each run is an ordering of documents ranked by system estimated relevance to T. Both algorithms start with the union (U) of *all* documents in these M runs. This contrasts with pooling which only takes a limited number (e.g., 100) of the top ranked documents. Our advantage is that we need not use an artificial cutoff. We then calculate a score CW for each document in U with respect to topic T. Documents in U are ranked by their CW scores. $CS_T(d)$ is a *simple count* of the number of submitted runs that retrieved document d. $CB_T(d)$ is the *Borda count* which takes into account document rank [6].

$$CW_T(d) = \propto CS_T(d) + (1-\propto)CB_T(d)$$

$$CB_T(d) = \sum_{i=1}^{M} N - r_{id}$$

Here r_{id} is d's rank in run i. N is a fixed number equal to or larger than the maximum number of documents that may be submitted in a run. For runs not retrieving d, rank is equal to N. The TREC campaigns generally allow a maximum of 1000 submitted documents per run per topic. In training runs using 10 separate topics we tested α from 0 to 1 in increments of 0.05. For each α we assessed the resulting ranking of U using RS_α.

$$RS_\alpha = \frac{\sum_{n=1}^{|U|} \text{rel}_T(n) * CW_T(n)_\alpha}{\sum_{n=1}^{|U|} \text{rel}_T(n)}$$

Here $rel_T(n)$ is 1 if document n is relevant to topic T and 0 otherwise. RS_α is highest when all relevant documents occupy top ranks. Averaging RS_α across all ten training topics for each dataset the best results were at $\alpha = 0.8$. We therefore use this value in our experiments. At this point our two algorithms deviate as described next.

3.1 Algorithm 1 – Non-clustered Approach

Documents in U ranked by their CW_T score are partitioned into batches of equal size. Starting with the top ranking batch, crowd workers judge documents till a batch with no relevant documents is reached. Judgment then stops with all remaining documents marked as "not relevant". Again using our training set we determined that the best batch size is 20. For this training step and for later training steps we run the approach using the gold standard data to simulate crowd relevance assessment. This best-case scenario places a ceiling in the effectiveness of our algorithms.

3.2 Algorithm 2 – Clustered Approach

The motive is to involve text features in the document selection process. The well-known cluster hypothesis [13] indicates textually similar documents are more likely to be co-relevant (or co-non-relevant) to a given topic than dissimilar documents. We first cluster documents in U using k-means representing each document with a word-based unigram feature vector. We then rank documents in each cluster by CW and partition them into batches. Documents of the top-ranking batch of each cluster are automatically selected for judgment followed by the next ranked batch. If a batch yields zero relevant documents then the remaining batches of its cluster are marked non relevant. Thus at least k batches are judged, one for each cluster. This is to accommodate documents retrieved by possibly distinct retrieval algorithms.

We establish k for k-means using standard approaches (e.g., [4], [16]). We evaluate k=5 through 20 in increments of 3 and calculate the variance in the number of relevant documents appearing in each cluster. Greater variance implies an increasing tendency for relevant documents to concentrate in fewer clusters, which is desirable. We then explore values of k one unit away on either side of the best value. As a result, we set k=11 for both collections in our experiments. Batch size remains 20 documents as in algorithm 1.

4   Datasets And Topics

4.1   Datasets and Documents

General Domain: News Dataset. This is the TREC-8 ad hoc task (TREC disks 4 and 5, less the Congressional Record). We use the document set corresponding to the TREC-8 ad hoc task [27] and topics 401-443. *Specialized Domain*: OHSUMED Dataset. This is the TREC-9 filtering track dataset, topics 1 – 43 [19].

Table 1. Domain characteristics. M: mean, sd: standard deviation

Text Statistic	OHSUMED		News	
	M	SD	M	SD
No. of sentences	6.97	1.04	6.99	0.04
No. of words	149.24	18.48	140.63	21.07
No. of complex words	32.04	3.96	24.90	10.63
% of complex words (>= 3 syllables)	22.19%	0.02	17.71%	0.03
Average words/sentence	21.13	1.39	20.12	0.48
Average syllables/word	1.76	0.09	1.68	0.11

OHSUMED has only titles, abstracts and metadata whereas the News documents are full text. Since length differences can bias results we use only the headline and first 7 sentences for News; for OHSUMED, we use the title and the abstract. These reduced News documents are shown to crowd workers and they are used when clustering (section 3.2). Collection features (after this step is completed) are provided in Table 1. Rows 3 to 6 of Table 1 illustrate differences intrinsic to the domains.

4.2   Topics, Runs, Gold Standard Data

To prevent topic differences from biasing results, we identified three comparable topics (in prevalence of relevant documents) from each collection. Intuitively prevalence, the percentage of submitted documents that is relevant, may indicate topic difficulty. Prevalence for News topics ranges from (0.03, 2.46) and for OHSUMED

(0.04, 4.62). We ranked the OHSUMED topics that fall in the overlapping region (0.04, 2.46) and divided them into 3 groups of roughly equal size. Randomly selecting one OHSUMED topic from each group we then identified 3 News topics that most closely matched in prevalence (see Table 2). For each selected topic all documents in submitted runs of past TREC participants are collected.

Table 2. Characteristics of selected OHSUMED topics

	OHSUMED				News		
Topic ID	No of Submitted Docs	No of Relevant Docs	Percentage Relevant	Topic ID	No of Submitted Docs	No of Relevant Docs	Percentage Relevant
12	5291	7	0.132%	403	15636	21	0.134%
1	5784	44	0.761%	421	11090	83	0.748%
13	5841	77	1.318%	436	13940	180	1.291%

For News the TREC-8 ad hoc task obtained binary relevance assessments using pooling and TREC experts. For OHSUMED the TREC-9 filtering task provides assessments in one of three relevance states ("not relevant", "partially relevant", or "definitely relevant"). Following [2] we group "partially relevant" and "definitely relevant" documents as "relevant". It should be noted that OHSUMED relevance judgments were obtained in earlier studies [9, 10] and not via TREC expert assessors and pooling. We simulate pooling (selecting top 100 documents) with OHSUMED.

4.3   Participants

Crowd participants were from Amazon Mechanical Turk (MTurk). Participants were assigned randomly to either the non-clustered or clustered algorithm and were only permitted to participate once (as tracked by IP address and MTurk ID). They were compensated $0.20/batch of 20 documents assessed. For each algorithm–collection combination we used 24 participants; each participant evaluated all 3 topics for that collection. Participants not completing the full assessment of 3 topics had their assessments removed and the task given to other crowd participants. Judgments were collected via a web interface.

5   Results

Table 3 provides the means and standard deviations across our four metrics: recall, precision, F-score and LAM. Statistically significant differences are marked by * (p < 0.05) and ** (p < 0.002). Examining main effects we find that the non-clustered algorithm gives significantly superior precision, F-score and LAM compared to the clustered algorithm. However, the clustered algorithm is significantly superior in recall. In main effects we also find that the biomedical domain provides significantly superior results on all 4 measures compared to News. We discuss these surprising results later. Post-hoc analyses were conducted on all statistically significant pairings

66

C.G. Harris and P. Srinivasan

between algorithm and domain for each measure. All pairs tested were also found to be statistically significant (p < .05) using Fisher's LSD post-hoc test. These results reject all main effects null hypotheses claiming no difference between algorithms or between domains on these measures. The two-way, algorithm × domain interaction results are similar in precision and F-score; combinations involving the non-clustered algorithm and either domain are significantly superior to combinations involving the clustered approach. For LAM this pattern is seen only for OHSUMED. For recall, combinations involving the clustered approach provide significantly superior results. We reject all but one of the two-way interaction null hypotheses.

Table 2. Means and standard deviations for the measures (n = 96)

Condition	Precision		Recall		F-score		LAM		N
	M	SD	M	SD	M	SD	M	SD	
Algorithm type									
Non-clustered	0.610*	0.089	0.543	0.102	0.551*	0.101	0.043*	0.007	48
Clustered	0.323	0.040	0.740*	0.055	0.430	0.044	0.062	0.004	48
Domain type									
News	0.451	0.137	0.584	0.137	0.449	0050	0.056	0.007	48
OHSUMED	0.482*	0.180	0.699*	0.087	0.532*	0.117	0.050*	0.013	48
Algorithm × Domain									
Non-cluster, News	0.572**	0.078	0.452	0.029	0.467*	0.049	0.049	0.005	24
Non-cluster, OHSUMED	0.648**	0.084	0.635	0.054	0.635**	0.062	0.037*	0.004	24
Cluster, News	0.331	0.043	0.717**	0.035	0.431	0.045	0.062	0.003	24
Cluster, OHSUMED	0.315	0.036	0.764**	0.062	0.430	0.044	0.062	0.005	24

6   Analysis

The relative performance of the two algorithms is consistent across collections. The non-clustered algorithm provides better precision, F-score, and LAM while the clustered algorithm provides better recall. The former relies on the weighted score *(CW)* while the latter also exploits textual features via document clustering. The improvement in recall is consistent with the cluster hypothesis. However, this is at the expense of precision; non-relevant documents are also attracted towards relevant documents through similarity. In the combined F-score, the simpler non-clustered algorithm wins over clustering.

Another aspect that might have caused lower precision for the clustered approach is that at least 1 batch (the top ranking one) is judged from each cluster (see Section 3.2). Given 11 clusters/topic and 20 documents/batch we have a minimum of 220 judgments. Retrospectively we feel precision might improve if we are more selective in clusters to judge. We chose to judge at least 1 batch/cluster to capture different subthemes of relevance and because unique retrieval strategies may retrieve distinctive relevant documents. We address this in Section 7.1.

Surprisingly the performance for OHSUMED is better than for News on all measures. We expected familiarity with the domain to favour general news stories and not biomedicine. A possible explanation is that with News we had to limit our document to the first 7 sentences of text in order to possible length-based bias across domains. It may be that the text necessary for relevance judgments appears outside of these initial 7 sentences for News. OHSUMED have focused abstracts which may have enabled more accurate judgments. We address this in the next experiment.

Finally though not strictly comparable, our best LAM score for News (0.049) is better than the best scores obtained in TREC (also for News). Importantly, this is achieved while maintaining reasonable scores for the other three measures.

6.1   Comparing the Algorithms and Pooling: Efficiency and Effectiveness

We compare the algorithms with each other and with pooling in efficiency balanced against effectiveness. Pooling starts with the union of top N (typically set to 100 in TREC) ranked documents from each run. In contrast our algorithms start with the union of all retrieved documents submitted by all runs (this is typically set to 1000 in TREC runs). Thus we run the risk of judging a large number of documents; most are likely to be non-relevant.

Pooling for the 3 OHSUMED topics with N=100 would have judged 50% to 62% of the submitted documents; for News 6.7 to 16%. In contrast the clustered approach judged 8 to 14% for OHSUMED and 5 to 9.4% for News. The non-clustered approach judged 1% to 5% for OHSUMED and 0.6% to 3% for News. The savings in our methods are clear. Overall, our percentages are quite reassuring given that we start with the full set of submitted documents. The clustered approach is less efficient than the non-clustered again because at least 1 batch is judged from each of the 11 clusters (220 documents). The non-clustered approach has no such minimum.

Efficiency is only interesting if the strategies are effective at finding the relevant documents. Although the means presented earlier indicate effectiveness, we can look at the results in more detail. On average across the topics, the non-clustered algorithm evaluated 3.1% of the submitted OHSUMED documents, to find 68.0% of the relevant documents; the clustered algorithm evaluated 11.0% finding 77.5%. For News the non-clustered algorithm only evaluated 1.8% of the collection finding 46.8% of the relevant documents. The percentages were low for topics 421 and 436. With clustering 7.6% of the News submissions were evaluated, with 73.2% of the relevant documents found. While these are good results, we will strive to improve effectiveness of our strategies in future work.

Particularly noteworthy is our algorithm's success even when there are only a few relevant documents – for example, the non-clustered algorithm only evaluated 0.6% of the 15,636 documents retrieved for topic 403, but was able to find nearly all of the 21 relevant documents.

6.2   Comparing Methods on Cost

Relevance judgments costs are important given budgetary constraints. The 2007 TREC Legal track overview document is one in which TREC relevance assessment costs are indicated. Also they note that human assessors evaluate on average 20 documents per hour. Their relevance assessment cost was estimated at $150 an hour, or $7.50 per document [25]. A total of 9442 judgments would have been made with pooling setting $N = 100$ for OHSUMED and 4758 judgments were made for News. This is assuming a single judgment for a query document pair. This gives a total of $70,815 and $35,685 for OHSUMED and News respectively. Admittedly assessment for TREC Legal would have been amongst the costliest. However, even if we were to reduce the TREC cost drastically to $1/judgment, the TREC pooling process for the 3 topics in OHSUMED and News would be $9,442 and $4,758 respectively. In comparison, our cost was $0.22/batch of 20 documents, including Amazon Mechanical Turk overhead fees; this is slightly more than $0.01/document. The cost for all 24 participants to evaluate the same 3 News topics was $792.00 for the clustered algorithm and $179.52 for the non-clustered algorithm. For OHSUMED these costs are $496 and $143 respectively. Using only 3 crowd workers and the majority decision, as discussed in [1, 2], we can reduce these costs further by 87.5%.

6.3   Detecting Potentially Relevant Documents

Another aspect of our approach is that since we start with all submitted documents there is the possibility of discovering relevant documents missed by the pooling process. Limiting our attention to News and only those document – query pairs that were judged by at least 12 participants we find that there are 9 potentially relevant documents that were not included in the TREC pool and so were not judged and assumed non relevant. There were also four documents that our participants thought were relevant that were declared non relevant by TREC assessors and 10 documents in the reverse direction. These numbers may appear to be minor and yet they could in a different context make an appreciable difference.

7   Experiment 2: More Topics, Natural Design

We present results from a second experiment with the News dataset. We use only 3 judges for a document–query pair, a typical number in crowd sourcing tasks relying on a majority vote. We selected 17 additional topics randomly from the News dataset and added these to our 3 topics from experiment 1 (topics 403, 421, and 436). Also we use the full text of News items rather than just the first 7 sentences plus headline. This full text is used during clustering and is also shown to the participant judging the document. Similar to the earlier experiment, each participant is expected to evaluate 3 randomly assigned (out of 20) topics. If this was not done for any reason, then a substitute participant was solicited.

The mean precision, recall, F-score, and LAM scores are strong: 0.8826, 0.6282, 0.7270, and 0.0499 respectively for the non-clustered algorithm, and 0.8174, 0.7645,

0.7861 and 0.0524 respectively for the clustered algorithm. Wilcoxon Signed-Rank tests found that the non-clustered approach is better than the clustered approach in precision and in LAM (both at p< 0.0005). The clustered algorithm is better than the non-clustered one in recall and F-score (both a p < 0.0005). With the exception of F-score, these results are consistent with our findings in the first experiment, where we had used a larger number of participants for statistical robustness but fewer topics. The F-score results indicate that the difference in recall between the two algorithms more than adequately makes up for the difference in precision in this second experiment. In general, scores obtained in experiment 2 (20 topics) are higher than in experiment 1 (3 topics) with some differences being quite remarkable (e.g., in precision). Focusing only on the 3 News topics common to both experiments there are 19 of 24 measurements (2 algorithms × 4 measures × 3 topics) where experiment 2 gives better results and only 5 where experiment 1 is better. The key design difference is that experiment 2 uses the full text of the news items as opposed to just the first 7 sentences. It appears that this aspect makes a crucial difference.

7.1   Reducing the Number of Clusters Evaluated

In our clustered algorithm, at least one batch from each of 11 clusters is judged. This may be why this algorithm has lower precision compared to the non-clustered algorithm. If we can be more selective about clusters we might improve the performance overall. We explore a strategy based on the *CW* score. For each topic we rank the 11 clusters by their mean *CW* score. We remove clusters, one at a time, lowest to highest mean evaluating performance each time. Results are in Fig. 1.

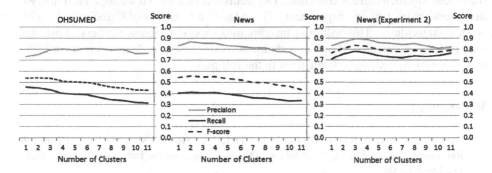

Fig. 1. Performance as the number of clusters increases for OHSUMED (left), news (center) in experiment 1 and for news in experiment 2 (right)

When all 11 clusters are evaluated, our F-score (middle line) is at its lowest. For News the best F-score is obtained using only the top 2 clusters while for OHSUMED it is with the top 3 clusters. These numbers are considerably smaller than 11. Experiment 2 yields similar results; the optimal number of clusters is approximately 3. These emphasize that it would be useful to select clusters to judge. In future research we will also explore functions of mean *CW* score as a cutoff.

8   Conclusion

We presented alternatives to pooling that use an algorithm to select documents for judgment and crowd workers to make the judgments. Our best algorithm is able to locate a majority of the relevant documents in two types of collections at a fraction of the cost of pooling. In both experiments we obtain LAM scores for News that are competitive with the best 2012 TREC Crowdsourcing results [22] (though the experiments are not strictly comparable). We find that contrary to some predictions [15] and our own expectations, results in OHSUMED (e.g., LAM is 0.037), a more challenging domain, are also strong. Overall we have demonstrated that our hybrid approach using rank fusion, optional clustering, document batching with intuitive stopping criteria, though simple in design is both effective and cost efficient. This backs up the earlier findings by Soboroff et. al. [23], Carterette et. al. [3], and Sanderson and Joho [20]; it builds on aspects of their methods with a clustering technique that is simple yet effective. We have presented results using statistically robust design considering carefully potential variations across crowd workers.

There are a number of ways in which we can improve our approach and extend this study. First we will further explore strategies for being selective in the clusters chosen for judgment. Second we would like to know if the relative ranking of the participating systems changes if we were to use just the judgments provided by our methods. This will parallel efforts such as [23]. Third we would like to conduct topic level analysis of our data. Some topics are likely more challenging for crowd workers than others. A follow up goal would be to see if we can predict which topics are likely to be challenging. A fourth direction is to analyze the crowd judgments to see the extent to which there is consensus. Our dataset is rich in that we have each query–document pair (as in experiment 1) judged by up to 48 individuals (24 workers/algorithm). This will offer insights into variations across workers. Last, we plan to look at stratified sampling techniques as discussed by Yilmaz et. al. in [30], and how system rankings coordinate with the full pool.

References

1. Alonso, O., Mizzaro, S.: Can We Get Rid of TREC Assessors? Using Mechanical Turk for Relevance Assessment. In: Proc. SIGIR 2009 Workshop on the Future of IR Evaluation, pp. 15–16 (2009)
2. Alonso, O., Mizzaro, S.: Using Crowdsourcing for TREC Relevance Assessment. Information Processing & Management 48(6), 1053–1066 (2012)
3. Carterette, B., Allan, J., Sitaraman, R.: Minimal Test Collections for Retrieval Evaluation. In: SIGIR 2006, pp. 268–275. ACM (2006)
4. Carterette, B., Soboroff, I.: The Effect of Assessor Error on IR System Evaluation. In: SIGIR 2010, pp. 539–546. ACM (2010)
5. Duda, R.O., Hart, P.E.: Pattern Classification and Scene Analysis, vol. 3. Wiley, New York (1973)
6. Emerson, P.: The Original BordaCount and Partial Voting. Social Choice and Welfare 40(2), 353–358 (2013)

7. Harman, D.K.: The First Text Retrieval Conference (TREC-1), Rockville, MD, USA, November 4-6 (1992); Information Processing & Management 29(4), 411–414 (1993)
8. Harris, C., Srinivasan, P.: Using Hybrid Methods for Relevance Assessment. In: TREC Crowd 2012, TREC Notebook Paper (2012)
9. Hersh, W., Buckley, C., Leone, T.J., Hickam, D.: OHSUMED: An Interactive Retrieval Evaluation and New Large Test Collection for Research. In: SIGIR 1994, pp. 192–201. ACM (1994)
10. Hersh, W., Hickam, D.: Use of a Multi-Application Computer Workstation in a Clinical Setting. Bulletin of the Medical Library Association 82(4), 382 (1994)
11. Kazai, G., Milic-Frayling, N.: On the Evaluation of the Quality of Relevance Assessments Collected through Crowdsourcing. In: SIGIR 2009 Workshop on the Future of IR Evaluation, p. 21 (2009)
12. Lease, M., Kazai, G.: Overview of the TREC 2011 Crowdsourcing Track. TREC Notebook Paper (2011)
13. Manning, C.D., Raghavan, P., Schütze, H.: Introduction to Information Retrieval. Cambridge University Press, Cambridge (2008)
14. McCreadie, R., Macdonald, C., Ounis, I.: Identifying Top News using Crowdsourcing. Information Retrieval, 1–31 (2013)
15. Meilă, M., Heckerman, D.: An Experimental Comparison of Several Clustering and Initialization Methods. In: Proc. of the 14th Conference on Uncertainty in Artificial Intelligence, pp. 386–395. Morgan Kaufmann (1998)
16. Nallapati, R., Peerreddy, S., Singhal, P.: Skierarchy: Extending the Power of Crowdsourcing using a Hierarchy of Domain Experts, Crowd and Machine Learning. TREC Notebook Paper (2012)
17. Qi, H., Yang, M., He, X., Li, S.: Re-examination on Lam% in Spam Filtering. In: SIGIR 2010, pp. 757–758. ACM (2010)
18. Raykar, V.C., Yu, S., Zhao, L.H., Valadez, G.H., Florin, C., Bogoni, L., Moy, L.: Learning from Crowds. Journal of Machine Learning Research 99, 1297–1322 (2010)
19. Robertson, S.E., Hull, D.A.: The TREC-9 Filtering Track Final Report. In: Online Proc. of TREC (2000)
20. Sanderson, M., Joho, H.: Forming Test Collections with no System Pooling. In: SIGIR 2004, pp. 33–40. ACM (2004)
21. Smucker, M.D., Jethani, C.P.: Human Performance and Retrieval Precision Revisited. In: SIGIR 2010, pp. 595–602. ACM (2010)
22. Smucker, M.D., Kazai, G., Lease, M.: Overview of the TREC 2012 Crowdsourcing Track. TREC Notebook Paper (2012)
23. Soboroff, I., Nicholas, C., Cahan, P.: Ranking Retrieval Systems without Relevance Judgments. In: SIGIR 2001, pp. 66–73. ACM (2001)
24. Sparck Jones, K., van Rijsbergen, C.: Report on the Need for and Provision of an "Ideal" Information Retrieval Test Collection, British Library Research and Development Report 5266, Computer Laboratory, Univ. of Cambridge (1975)
25. Tomlinson, S., Oard, D.W., Baron, J.R., Thompson, P.: Overview of the TREC 2007 Legal Track. In: Online Proceedings of TREC (2007)
26. Voorhees, E.M.: Variations in relevance judgments and the measurement of retrieval effectiveness. Information Processing & Management 36(5), 697–716 (2000)
27. Voorhees, E.M., Harman, D.: Overview of the Fifth Text REtrieval Conference (TREC-5). TREC (97), 1–28 (1996)

28. Vuurens, J., de Vries, A.P., Eickhoff, C.: How Much Spam Can You Take? An Analysis of Crowdsourcing Results to Increase Accuracy. In: Proc. ACM SIGIR Workshop on Crowdsourcing for Information Retrieval, pp. 21–26 (2011)
29. Xia, T., Zhang, C., Li, T., Xie, J.: BUPT_WILDCAT at TREC Crowdsourcing Track. TREC Notebook Paper (2012)
30. Yilmaz, E., Kanoulas, E., Aslam, J.A.: A Simple and Efficient Sampling Method for Estimating AP and NDCG. In: SIGIR 2008, pp. 603–610. ACM (2008)

How Do Sponsored Search Results Affect User Behavior in Web Search?

Zeyang Liu, Yiqun Liu, Min Zhang, and Shaoping Ma

State Key Laboratory of Intelligent Technology and Systems,
Tsinghua National Laboratory for Information Science and Technology,
Department of Computer Science and Technology, Tsinghua University, Beijing, 100084,
China P.R.
{zy-liu13,yiqunliu,z-m,msp}@tsinghua.edu.cn

Abstract. Sponsored search has gained considerable attention in Web search-related studies. In this paper, we investigate into the user interaction process on search engine result pages (SERPs) considering the influence of sponsored search results. We integrate different styles of sponsored links into SERPs to systematically study how they affect users' behavioral preferences. Based on an analysis into users' eye movements and click-through behavior, we showed that different presentation styles among sponsored links might lead to different behavior biases, not only for the sponsored search results but also for the organic ones. We also showed that search task type might influence the click-through of sponsored links, whereas this factor has little effect on the visual attention that users devote to top sponsored results. Interestingly, it seems that user satisfaction, which was intuitively measured by participants, was unaffected by the different sponsored search result appearances. These results help us better understand how users interact with search engines and how we can improve the placement of sponsored search results on SERPs.

Keywords: User behavior, sponsored search, eye tracking, click-through.

1 Introduction

Web search has revolutionized the way users obtain Web information by providing large quantities of information efficiently and freely. Because of the differences between users' needs and advertisers' desires in search engines, it is difficult to achieve the perfect balance between sponsored and organic search results given the fact that sponsored search is a major source of revenue for commercial search engines. It is therefore important to gain a good understanding of how people interact with search engine result pages (SERPs), especially with sponsored links.

Eye tracking devices, which are designed to record participants' eye gaze information, have been widely adopted to explore search users' examination behavior. Due to the behavior of examination is closely related to the decision whether users would click the results [4], [14], eye-tracking studies have been a major way to improve relevance feedback performance based on click-through behavior logs. In

A. Jaafar et al. (Eds.): AIRS 2014, LNCS 8870, pp. 73–85, 2014.

this paper, we perform an eye-tracking analysis to explore the potential impact of sponsored search results on users' examination behavior and study the user's decision process on the SERPs that contain sponsored search results.

There are already a number of existing eye-tracking studies which looked into user's interaction with sponsored search results. For example, [11] indicated that quality of sponsored search results (i.e. relevance to user queries) affect users' visual attention allocation. [2] showed people behave differently on a same sponsored search result when it is displayed in different devices. Although these studies revealed a number of important findings, the results are based on a specific presentation style. Most of them only concentrated on the content-based influence and rarely considered the presentation biases on sponsored links.

Essentially, there is a large difference in sponsored result styles among different search engines. By considering the users' online experience, most commercial search engines usually adopt their own special layouts for sponsored links, and several of them even provide two different appearances of the same advertisement at different times. Fig. 1 shows examples of sponsored results from Google and Baidu (China's most popular search engine). Since existing studies have demonstrated that a presentation bias widely exists in search results [3] and especially in vertical results [4], it is reasonable to presume that the diversity in advertisement presentation styles may also lead to different user behaviors in a web search. Taking it one step further, we seek to understand how user behavior (e.g., examination, click preference) is affected by different presentation of the sponsored search results and why certain existing factors do not suffer from the impact of these differences.

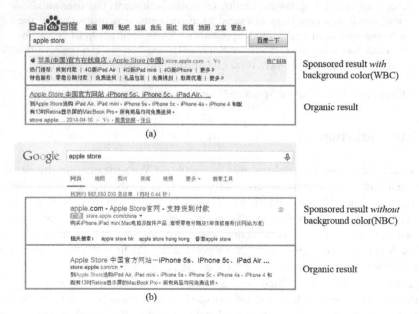

Fig. 1. Different presentation styles of sponsored results on SERPs (Baidu and Google)

Due to the existence of banner blindness [1], sponsored links may only have limited effects on user behaviors. However, according to our findings, the different types of sponsored links, which are displayed on the top position of SERPs, might inevitably capture users' visual attention during the search task. We believe that this phenomena may not only affect the users' behavior on organic results but also have an additional influence on search efficiency. For example, do users still skip banner ads if there is no difference between the sponsored and organic results? How do users change their behavior if we manually vary the sponsored link's style? Taking this case into account, we also analyze the effects of users' examination and click behavior on the organic results to completely analyze the decision process with different presentation forms of sponsored links.

The rest of the paper is organized as follows: we first present an overview of the related work. Then, we introduce the experimental design for collecting user behavior information through the use of eye tracking. After analyzing the user behavior data based on the eye-tracking experiment, we provide several conclusions in Section 4. A summary of the experiment results is presented in Section 5.

2   Related Work

2.1   Web Search Behavior

Because eye-tracking technology was first applied in reading research [5, 6], it has become increasingly popular in many domains associated with user behavior research, such as human-computer interaction interface design and autism diagnoses. In 2004, [7] proposed an eye-tracking approach to analyze user behavior on SERPs and to infer the relevancy of documents in the Web search. Comparing the implicit feedback versus the explicit feedback, [8, 9] indicated that the users' decision processes are influenced not only by the relevance of the results but also by the *trust* and *quality* of the result set. [10] showed that cursor movements are particularly correlated to the viewing position based on the eye-tracking analysis. [3] studied presentation biases and indicated that users tend to choose one of the top results on the SERPs. They also proposed a site reputation bias in their research. [4] found that the existence of presentation bias may also lead to different behavioral biases on federated searches. Most of these studies were concerned about the user behavior from the 10 organic results.

2.2   Studies on Sponsored Search Results

Because sponsored search results are becoming essential and important components of the SERPs in current commercial search engines, considerable work has focused on this regard. [11] reported that the users' visual attention devoted to SERPs depends on both the task type and ad quality, and the order in which ads of different quality were presented also influence the user behavior. [12] integrated sponsored and organic links into a single listing on SERPs. They showed that the combination of these results does not appear to increase the clicks on sponsored listings. Even though they made no difference between sponsored and organic links on SERPs, the ranking and mixture of these results, which depends on the built-in algorithm of meta-search engines, might not be widely representative of the web search. Essentially, the position of the sponsored and organic results is relatively fixed and are separated rather than mixed in the major search engines. [1] proposed text advertising blindness, which may cause a user to skip ads on a web page. Further, [2] focused on the user's behavior on mobile devices. They conducted a study in which users had to interact with the SERPs that contained advertisements on mobile phones. Interestingly, they found that Generation Y did not exhibit banner blindness on mobile screens when most of them viewed both the advertisements and organic results.

Overall, most prior studies on sponsored links adopted a controlled experimental approach to characterize the visual attention or mouse movements on SERPs. Nevertheless, to the best of our knowledge, previous work rarely considered the presentation effects of sponsored results and strictly analyzed the influence, which might cause different users' examination and clicks on SERPs, especially on the organic results. Considering the existence of presentation biases on result lists (shown in Section 2.1), we are curious about whether the presentation forms of sponsored links could also lead to different user behavior. In this paper, we analyze the influence of presentation forms on the users' examination as well as the click preference when different styles of sponsored links are presented in random order. We also attempt to determine how sponsored result styles affect user satisfaction to provide a reasonable strategy on the presentation of sponsored results.

3   Collecting User Behavior Information

3.1   Participants

Thirty-three participants, all of whom were undergraduate students from a major university in China, were recruited using cash compensation. The students range in age from 17 to 20 with a mean age of 18.5 and have various majors in this university. The gender distribution is split between 14 males and 19 females. Because of the precision limitation of the eye tracker, not all of their eye movement data were available. As a result, 30 of the students that went through the calibration of correctness were finally taken into account. Particularly, all but two participants self-reported that the search engine we provided in this experimentation was their primary search instrument in their daily life, and they were very familiar with its operation.

3.2   Tasks

Participants had to complete the same set of 24 search tasks by using the same search engine, which we assigned. Each of these participants was required to solve these tasks in random order, which could eliminate the effects of trust bias [8, 9]. To make the initial result page comparable, we assigned an initial query for each task. All of these queries were selected from real-world commercial search logs so that they could reflect the users' search intention realistically. We extracted 810 medium frequency queries automatically from the raw search logs[1],which were supplied by a major commercial search engine in China. Then, the original SERPs related to these queries were examined one by one, and the SERPs that contained more than three sponsored links could be selected into the initial SERP set. Finally, there were seven navigational queries (i.e., to reach a particular web site) and 17 informational/transactional queries (i.e., to acquire specific information) in our experimentation. Moreover, we also provided a short description for each query to avoid possible ambiguities. Several examples of the initial queries are shown in Table 1.

We transferred the search sever that stored the static set of SERPs captured from the original search engine. This allowed us to have a consistent initial SERP for each query and to strictly control the experimental factor, which may affect the user's behavior. After the initial SERP was presented, there were no restrictions on users' behavior on the search result pages. Thus, participants could be free to behave on the SERP as usual in ways, such as clicking the related search links, jumping to the next page of results, and reconstructing the query. The aim of this design is to achieve the real user appearances on search results in a laboratory environment.

Table 1. Examples of search queries adopted in the eye-tracking experimentation

Query	Translation	Intent Type
中国移动网上营业厅	China Mobile Online Service	Navigational
悦达起亚k2报价	Price of KIA K2	Informational
多动症的表现	The symptoms of ADHD	Informational

Unlike previous work that only concentrated on user behavior, we also consider the user's online experience. In this study, user satisfaction on SERPs was collected in our system. Participants were required to evaluate his/her satisfaction intuitively on the initial result page after completing a task session. They could score their evaluation ranging from 1 to 5: a score of 1 represents user disappointment on this page, while a score of 5 stands for the highest level of user satisfaction. To some extent, these scores could reflect the relative level of users' online experience across these tasks.

3.3   SERP Generation

As we described in section 1, the appearance of sponsored links may be largely different among different search engines. Even though this may lead to a wide variety of sponsored styles, there is still commonality among them. After observing the layout of major search engines such as Google, Bing, Baidu and Yahoo!, we classify the presentation styles of sponsored search results into two categories:

- With background color (WBC): this style of sponsored links ordinarily contains a particular color background, which makes the sponsored ads more special and outstanding than the other elements on the page. As a traditional style, it is the most widely used in contemporary search engines, such as Yahoo! and Bing.

---

[1] http://www.sogou.com/labs/dl/q.html

- No background color (NBC): Compared with the WBC, sponsored links with this style seem to be more similar to the organic results. Intuitively, there is no difference between the sponsored links and organic results except for several unobvious sponsored tags or brands. A good example of this is Google sponsored results.

Depending on the analysis above, we focus on the influence of these two types of sponsored link styles in this paper, which could cover the majority of the application area for the existing sponsored search results. Furthermore, because the negative effects might be caused by the different layouts of SERPs, it is important to provide a uniform interface for each initial result page. For this reason, we finally generate our result lists based on the layout of Baidu SERPs, which could display two types of sponsored links (WBC and NBC style) as a realistic component of the SERPs.

In the study, each of the initially fixed SERPs mainly consists of three top sponsored links and ten organic results. All of the result lists, including the sponsored links and organic results, were captured from the same original search engines so that the initial SERPs for all components could look as natural as possible. Particularly, while the sponsored search results were shown in different styles, both the content of the sponsored results (e.g., link title, snippet etc.) and the order of sponsored results remained consistent for the same query. Fig. 2 shows an example of the interface for the SERPs, which has a different sponsored link style.

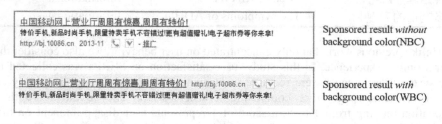

Fig. 2. Examples of sponsored results with and without background color for the same query

In addition, based on the conclusion of [4], organic results need to be tackled by removing the vertical results (e.g., images, videos, etc.)to eliminate the influence of other elements on the SERPs that we do not expect.

Following the pre-procedure steps above, we implemented 48 initially fixed SERPs in total. Half of them contain WBC sponsored links, and the rest contain NBC sponsored links. The 24 tasks were equally split between these two types of styles. For each of the participants, these two types of sponsored link styles were selected randomly and were shown alternatively for a specific query.

3.4 Measurements

The main goal of this paper is to study how users distribute their visual attention and clicks on different components of the result lists when sponsored links are presented on SERPs. For this reason, both the users' eye movements and clicks are collected in our experimentation.

We use the Tobii X2-30 eye tracker, which is able to record the main indicators of ocular behavior (e.g., fixations, saccades, pupil dilation etc.) and to capture the participants' eye movements. Because fixations are the most relevant metric for evaluating information processing in an online search [8], we detect fixations by using built-in algorithms from Tobii Studio. In these algorithms, a fixation is defined as a gaze duration above 100ms around a specific location. Additionally, to analyze the differences among the various parts of the SERP, we labeled each result document boundary manually and recorded the fixation duration per result document.

Because users' click and scroll behavior is another important metric in our study, we also capture and analyze users' mouse movements during the search tasks, including the click time, scroll time, and clicked URL. For example, we count the number of clicks on sponsored links and organic results, respectively. Moreover, user satisfaction regarding the sponsored SERP is taken into account as well, which has been discussed in the previous section.

4   Analysis of User Behavior

Our study focuses on the potential influence of sponsored search results. We look into the users' actual examination and click behavior on sponsored and organic results and attempt to explore several potential impacts of sponsored links on SERPs. The following sections present this work in detail.

4.1   How do Users Examine/Click on Sponsored Search Results with Different Styles?

First, we study the influence of different styles on sponsored search results. Fig. 3 compares the average fixation duration on sponsored links that are displayed in WBC and NBC style.

It is clear that the fixation duration on the NBC sponsored results (μ =2197.667 σ = 131.783) was consistently higher than that on the WBC sponsored results (μ = 1095.667 σ = 59.219), which means that it took substantially more time for participants to view the sponsored results when the NBC style was presented. From this bar chart, we can see the visual attention devoted to the sponsored links that were displayed in the NBC style is approximately twice as much as that displayed in the WBC style. To some extent, this result reflects that participants might tend to spend more time distinguishing the real organic results from the whole result lists because of the extremely similar appearances between the sponsored and organic results.

Similarly, this behavior bias also causes significant differences in the average click numbers, which are shown in Fig. 4. We can find that the average click number on the NBC style (μ = 0.165 σ = 0.027) is almost three times greater than that of the WBC counterparts ($\mu = 0.048$ $\sigma = 0.013$). Interestingly, for each specific style, while the third-ranked result receives the lowest click-through among the three sponsored links, it accounts for the highest proportion from the total amount of visual attention. It can be observed that participants might more easily recognize the search advertisements and avoid clicking them when they spend more time examining these links.

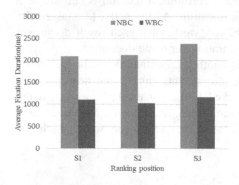
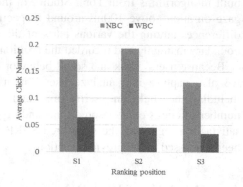

Fig. 3. Comparison of the average fixation duration on sponsored links that were displayed in WBC and NBC style

Fig. 4. Average number of clicks on the sponsored links that were displayed in WBC and NBC style

In conclusion, the presentation forms of the sponsored links had a noticeable influence on users' performance, including user examination and click behavior. When the appearances of sponsored links were similar to the organic links, it seemed that these sponsored results might be more likely to attract additional attention and click-through. In addition, we found that additional examination on sponsored results did not absolutely increase the corresponding click-through or even reverse the click-through on them.

4.2 How do Users Examine/Click on Organic Results on A SERP with Sponsored Results?

Following the analysis in Section 4.2, we are also curious about the effects of the organic results on the SERP containing sponsored results. Fig. 5 illustrates an average fixation duration for organic links that are broken down separately for the sponsored links, which were presented in the WBC and NBC styles. Compared with the influence on the sponsored results, there is a smaller difference in the examination of organic results in general. Interestingly, for the NBC style, the visual attention that participants distributed to the third ranked sponsored result (mean time = 2383.958msσ = 904.634) was very close to that of the first organic result (mean time = 2623.667msσ = 827.776). To a certain extent, this reflects the fact that participants were more likely to be confused by the hidden appearance of sponsored links and devote more time to the examination to these links to eliminate misleading clicks.

Furthermore, unlike the performance on the NBC style, we can see that participants tended to overlook the WBC sponsored links and focused more on the first organic results. Based on this analysis, we can infer that the presentation forms might be an important factor that can cause users' banner blindness differently.

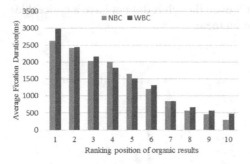
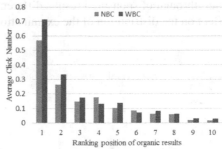

Fig. 5. Average fixation duration on organic results split between the NBC and WBC styles of the sponsored links

Fig. 6. Average number of clicks on the organic results split between the NBC and WBC styles of the sponsored links

Conversely, we found that the sponsored links' presentation affected the distribution of clicks on organic results. Because the NBC style attracts more visual attention and clicks, the average click number for the organic results in the NBC style ($\mu = 0.150$) is less than that in the WBC style ($\mu = 0.177$). Because of the considerable distraction from the sponsored links, especially those whose appearances are similar to the organic results, it might be easier for users to lose patience when examining and clicking the links on the organic result lists.

To summarize the organic results, the presentation of sponsored links has significant effects on the distribution of clicks but not on the examination behavior. Additionally, we found that users' banner blindness might be influenced by the appearances of sponsored results to some extent.

4.3   How does the Task Type Affect Users' Examination/Click-Through Behavior?

It can be observed from Fig. 7 that most of the organic results attracted more examination for informational tasks than navigational tasks, whereas the distribution of visual attention was unaffected on the sponsored results. These results are consistent with the prior studies concerning the effects of the task type, such as [11], [13,14].

To take a further step, we analyze the corresponding click-through behavior regardless of the presentation bias of the sponsored links, which is shown in Fig. 8. We can see that the distribution of click-throughs on the organic results (organic 2 to 9)also reflected this bias in which users allocated more clicks on the links in the informational tasks rather than in the navigational tasks. However, the distribution of click-throughs on the sponsored links was not in line with this rule even though the visual attention on these click-through was almost the same. For example, the click-through of the third ranked link accounted for the highest proportion among the top three sponsored results in navigational tasks, while it made up the lowest proportion in the informational tasks. This indicated that the task type bias might also lead to the click-through of sponsored results differently even though it did not have a noticeable effect on the distribution of the examination on them.

Fig. 7. Average fixation duration on the sponsored and organic results split between the different task types (navigational/informational and transactional)

Fig. 8. Average click-through of the sponsored and organic results split by different task type (navigational/informational and transactional)

4.4   How does the Sponsored Result Style Affect User Satisfaction?

Because the sponsored result style causes a different influence on both the sponsored and organic results, we are also concerned about how users feel about the SERPs when the different sponsored link style was displayed. Fig. 9 shows the average score for the initial SERPs of 24 tasks, which contained the NBC or WBC style.

The average satisfaction score for the NBC style is 4.098 ($\sigma = 0.275$), while the score for the WBC style is 4.188 ($\sigma = 0.259$). Interestingly, user satisfaction seemed to be unaffected by the varied style of sponsored links in our experimentation. In other words, there was nearly no difference between the users' online experience on SERPs when the sponsored links were presented in the WBC or NBC style ($r = 0.798$ $p < 0.01$). We deduced that part of the reason for this is that participants might not really discover the existence of sponsored links if their presentation styles were similar to the organic results. This means that participants might regard these hidden advertisements as organic results and might be more tolerant toward the misleading clicks on SERPs. Thus, the presentation forms, which are similar to the organic style, may provide better strategies for improving the placement of sponsored search results on SERPs.

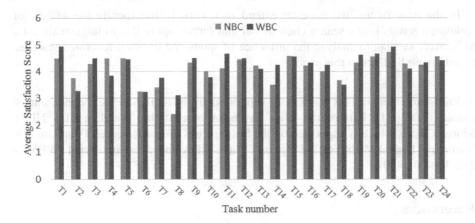

Fig. 9. Average satisfaction score for the initial SERPs of 24 tasks that contained the NBC or WBC style

5   Conclusions and Future Work

We presented a study using eye-tracking techniques to explore the effects of sponsored search results on user decision strategies for web searches. Different from most previous approaches that focused on a specific presentation form of sponsored links, we systematically investigate how variations in the appearance of sponsored results affect user behavior on SERPs.

First, we found that the presentation styles of sponsored links have a significant influence on users' examination and clicks, where participants contributed to both the sponsored and organic results. There is a shape difference in the result for the examination and click-through behavior when the different sponsored styles were presented. In particular, we found that users' examination and clicks were not strictly correlated with each other on the same sponsored link style. In other words, the more visual attention that users devoted to the sponsored results might not result in more click-through to them.

Second, our study showed that the organic result entries capture more visual attention from users in informational tasks than in navigational tasks as opposed to task biases against sponsored links, which is consistent with previous studies [11]. However, the users' examination behaviors on sponsored results are not influenced by this factor, and there is still a real difference in click-through for the different types of tasks.

Finally, based on the analysis into users' satisfaction on different interfaces of the SERPs, it is interesting to find that the organic-like sponsored results, which are similar to the real organic result entries, did not significantly decrease the users' online experience even though these results might more easily lead to users' distraction on the SERPs.

In the near future, we hope to extend this work to incorporate the effects of sponsored results into a search click model and further apply this to large-scale data. Moreover, we plan to analyze the influence of sponsored links on federated searches based on our findings in this paper.

Acknowledgements. This work was supported by Natural Science Foundation of China (61073071). Part of the work has been done at the Tsinghua-NUS NExT Search Centre, which is supported by the Singapore National Research Foundation & Interactive Digital Media R&D Program Office, MDA under research grant (WBS:R-252-300-001-490).

References

1. Owens, J.W., Chaparro, B.S., Palmer, E.M.: Text Advertising Blindness: The New Banner Blindness? Journal of Usability Studies 6(3), 172–197 (2011)
2. Djamasbi, S., Hall-Phillips, A., Yang, R(R.): SERPs and ads on mobile devices: An eye tracking study for generation Y. In: Stephanidis, C., Antona, M. (eds.) UAHCI 2013, Part II. LNCS, vol. 8010, pp. 259–268. Springer, Heidelberg (2013)
3. Bar-Ilan, J., Keenoy, K., Levene, M., Yaari, E.: Presentation Bias is Significant in Determining User Preference for Search Results - A user study. Journal of the American Society for Information Science and Technology 60(1), 135–149 (2009)
4. Wang, C., Liu, Y., Zhang, M., Ma, S., Zheng, M., Qian, J., Zhang, K.: Incorporating Vertical Results into Search Click Models. In: Proceedings of the 36th International ACM SIGIR Conference on Research and Development in Information Retrieval, pp. 503–512. ACM (2013)
5. Jacob, R.J., Karn, K.S.: Eye Tracking in Human-Computer Interaction and Usability Research: Ready to deliver the promises. Mind 2(3), 573–605 (2003)
6. Reichle, E.D., Rayner, K., Pollatsek, A.: Eye Movement Control in Reading: Accounting for Initial Fixation Locations and Refixations within the EZ Reader Model. Vision Research 39(26), 4403–4411 (1999)
7. Granka, L.A., Joachims, T., Gay, G.: Eye-Tracking Analysis of User Behavior in WWW Search. In: Proceedings of the 27th Annual International ACM SIGIR Conference on Research and Development in Information Retrieval, pp. 478–479. ACM (2004)
8. Joachims, T., Granka, L., Pan, B., Hembrooke, H., Gay, G.: Accurately Interpreting Click Through Data as Implicit Feedback. In: Proceedings of the 28th Annual International ACM SIGIR Conference on Research and Development in Information Retrieval, pp. 154–161. ACM (2005)
9. Joachims, T., Granka, L., Pan, B., Hembrooke, H., Radlinski, F., Gay, G.: Evaluating the Accuracy of Implicit Feedback from Clicks and Query Reformulations in Web Search. ACM Transactions on Information Systems (TOIS) 25(2), 7–32 (2007)
10. Huang, J., White, R.W., Dumais, S.: No Clicks, No Problem: Using Cursor Movements to Understand and Improve Search. In: Proceedings of the SIGCHI Conference on Human Factors in Computing Systems, pp. 1225–1234. ACM (2011)
11. Buscher, G., Dumais, S.T., Cutrell, E.: The Good, the Bad, and the Random: An Eye-Tracking Study of Ad Quality in Web Search. In: Proceedings of the 33rd International ACM SIGIR Conference on Research and Development in Information Retrieval, pp. 42–49. ACM (2010)

12. Jansen, B.J., Spink, A.: Investigating Customer Click Through Behaviour with Integrated Sponsored and Nonsponsored Results. International Journal of Internet Marketing and Advertising 5(1), 74–94 (2009)
13. Broder, A.: A Taxonomy of Web Search. ACM Sigir Forum 36(2), 3–10 (2002)
14. Cutrell, E., Guan, Z.: What Are You Looking For?: An Eye-Tracking Study of Information Usage in Web Search. In: Proceedings of the SIGCHI Conference on Human Factors in Computing Systems, pp. 407–416. ACM (2007)

Is the First Query the Most Important: An Evaluation of Query Aggregation Schemes in Session Search

Dongyi Guan[1],[*] and Hui Yang[2]

[1] Microsoft, 1 Microsoft Way, Redmond, WA 98025
[2] Department of Computer Science, Georgetown University, 37th and O Street NW,
Washington, DC 20057
doguan@microsoft.com, huiyang@cs.georgetown.edu

Abstract. Web users often issue a series of related queries, which form a search session, to fulfill complicated information needs. Query aggregation utilizes and combines multiple queries for session search. Prior research has demonstrated that query aggregation is an effective technique for session search. Consequently, how to effectively weight queries in a session becomes an interesting problem. This paper evaluates various query aggregation schemes and proposes a new three-step query aggregation method. Evaluation on TREC 2011 and 2012 Session tracks shows that the proposed scheme works very well and significantly outperforms the best TREC systems.

1 Introduction

Complicated search tasks often require multiple queries. These queries form a search session and work as a whole to fulfill an information need. Session search [3], [6,7], [11], [13], [18], [23] is the Information Retrieval (IR) task that retrieves documents for a session.

Session search happens frequently on the social media and the Web, such as planning a trip, consulting for medical choices, or looking for a good kindergarten. In a typical session, a user starts from an initial query and then goes through the returned search results and chooses some documents to examine. The user may find the search results satisfying the information need or insufficient. This motivates the user to modify the query and examine the newly returned documents. This process continues until user's information need is fulfilled.

The TREC (Text REtrieval Conference) 2010-2012 Session tracks [15,16,17] have strongly promoted research in session search in academia. TREC Session tracks simulated a typical interactive search scenario: a user keeps refining queries to achieve a specific information need. This simulating task covered large scope in topics like daily life, technology, and literal arts. Meanwhile, the queries were created by assessors who were not necessarily specialists of the given topic. Therefore, these sessions closely reflected real search behaviors. All queries and intermediate search results, including user behavior like click and time spent on every result, are provided to participants so

---

* This work was done when the first author studied at Georgetown University.

A. Jaafar et al. (Eds.): AIRS 2014, LNCS 8870, pp. 86–99, 2014.
© Springer International Publishing Switzerland 2014

that they can design effective search models. Table 3 shows an example from the TREC 2012 Session track [16].

Although TREC Session task focuses on retrieval for the last query, TREC participants [1], [6], [11] have demonstrated that using all queries in a session is an effective technique for session search. Particularly, using all queries can generally achieve a 15% ~ 20% nDCG@10 [5] improvement over only using the last query. We term the technique of utilizing and combining multiple queries in a session *"query aggregation"*. In TREC 2012 Session track, 17 out of 21 submissions which applied query aggregation gained improvements of search accuracy (measured by nDCG@10).

In this paper, we investigate this promising technique, *query aggregation*, and its impact on session search. The most frequently used query aggregation scheme for session search is uniform aggregation which treats every query in a session equally. In many cases, however, some queries are more interesting to the user; hence it is reasonable to treat them differently. We argue that a query's importance could be related to its position in the session. One possible and intuitive assumption is that a query nearing to the last query is more important than others since it motivates the last query. We answer the research question of *"what is the best query aggregation scheme for session search"* in this work. We propose a three-step aggregation scheme, which is inspired by U-shape query weight curves learned from training data. Through experimenting the new query aggregation scheme in combination with two state-of-the-art retrieval models, we find that the proposed three-step aggregation scheme achieves the best search accuracy for TREC 2012 with a 4.69% gain in nDCG@10 over the TREC 2012 best system.

The remainder of this paper is organized as follows. Section 2 discusses the related work. Section 3 states the problem definition and section 4 presents the experimental setup. Section 5 describes how we learn the query weight curve by SVM ranking and section 6 proposes the new three-step query aggregation scheme. Section 7 evaluates various aggregation schemes in combination with different retrieval models. Section 8 concludes the paper.

2   Related Work

Session search is challenging since it involves multiple queries in search. Existing query aggregation schemes can be grouped into *explicit aggregation* that assigns explicit weights to each query and separates aggregation from the retrieval models and *implicit aggregation* that merges query weighs in the retrieval models.

2.1   Explicit Query Aggregation

We summarize the explicit query aggregation schemes as the following. Let λ_i represents the weight for each query q_i in a session. Below are commonly used query aggregation schemes:

Uniform: All queries are weighted equally with the same weight 1.

Previous vs. current (PvC): All queries before the last query share a same lower weight while the last query employs a higher weight: $\lambda_i = 1$ if $i = n$, otherwise $\lambda_i = \lambda_p$. where $\lambda_p < 1$. Two top TREC 2012 systems [6], [11] both used this aggregation scheme. [11] set a discounted weight for the previous queries when computing

Table 1. Dataset statistics for TREC 2011 and TREC 2012 Session tracks

Year	#topic	#session	#query	Session length
2011	62	76	280	3.68
2012	48	98	297	3.03

Table 2. Training datasets with different session lengths

Session length	#session	#training instance
2	59	960,485
3	48	840,777
4	20	356,979
5	11	184,359

the Maximum Likelihood Estimation (MLE) of features such as single terms, ordered, and unordered phrases. [6] directly applied the discounted weights when combining queries. Jiang et al. [10,11] assumed that the last query was most important and all previous queries were of the same importance in a session, hence they assigned a higher weight to the last query while the same lower weights to all previous queries.

First vs. rest (FvR): [14] proposed to reward more to retrieval systems that retrieve more relevant documents in the earlier queries. This suggests higher importance of the first query. Thus, the first query is assigned a higher weight and the other queries including the last query share the same lower weights: $\lambda_i = \lambda_f$ if $i = 1$, otherwise $\lambda_i = 1$, where $\lambda_f > 1$.

Distance-based discounting (Dist.): In TREC Session 2012, [6] used a distance-based weight discounting scheme. They observed that influence of previous queries becomes weaker and weaker, while the last query, which is the most novel, is concerned the most by the user. Hence the last query receives the most weight. A monotonically decreasing function can be used to model the weight discounting: $\lambda_i = 1$ if $i = n$, otherwise $\lambda_i = \frac{\lambda_p}{n-i}$, where $\lambda_p < 1$ is a discount factor for the second last query.

Exponential: [7] implies an exponential discounting query aggregation. It considers session search as a Markov Decision Process (MDP) [21]. *Queries* are modeled as states, search engines and users are modeled as *agents* in this MDP. *Actions* are divided into *user actions* and *search engine actions*. User actions include keeping, adding, and/or removing query terms from the previous query q_{i-1}. Search engine actions include increasing, decreasing, and maintaining term weights in the scoring functions. The entire session search process can be viewed as a procedure that user actions and search engine actions influence each other iteratively until a search stops. Considering the whole session, the overall relevance is scored for document d to a session that starts at q_1 and ends at q_n as: $Score(session, d) = \sum_{i=1}^{n} \gamma^{n-i} Score(q_i, d)$, where $q_1, \cdots, q_i, \cdots, q_n$ are the queries in the session. $\gamma \in (0, 1)$ is the discount factor.

2.2 Implicit Query Aggregation

Implicit query aggregation schemes are also popular. For example, White et al. [22] observed that two adjacent queries in a session could be merged by a linear combination. Two queries in a pair were thus assigned complementary weights, less for the former. They assigned a weight with the form of $e^{-(p-1)}$ to a previous query, where p represented how far this query to the last query. Bennett et al. [2] chose a different base (0.95) in the above formula.

Liu *et al.* [19] also used query aggregation implicitly in their user behavior based retrieval model. They generated a term set from all queries. When a new query with m terms arrived, each term in the term set was assigned a initial uniform weight of $\frac{1}{m}$ and then merged into the term set, by decreasing weights of the terms already in the set. This procedure is equivalent to assigning earlier queries less weights.

Because of the complexity of session search, researchers have attempted to first classify sessions and then apply specific aggregation schemes to each class. For example, the CWI group [9] assumed two classes of users: "good" users and "bad" users. A "good" user learns from previous search results effectively so that the newer query expresses the information need more precisely. On the contrary, a "bad" user fails to learn from the search experience so as to adjust queries ineffectively, which ends up with random quality queries. The authors classified the users into "good users" and "bad users" based on the session length. They assumed the short session was typically issued by a "good user" and vice versa. A session submitted by a "good" user receives a discounted weighting scheme that accounts for lower weights for early queries than later queries in a session. The sessions issued by "bad" users received uniform query weights. It is a good idea to apply different aggregation schemes according to the search skill, but there is no strong evidence to justify that shorter sessions are from "better" users.

Xiang *et al.* [24] also classified sessions. They defined four session types: reformulation, specialization, generalization, and general association. For sessions of specialization and generalization, they discarded previous queries and only used the last query. For sessions of general association, uniform weights were assigned to each query. They did not apply query aggregation for other types of sessions. This classification of sessions is sensible. However, it is challenging to classify the queries into these types. Therefore, the authors sought for assistance from external knowledge such as Open Directory Project (ODP)[1]. This might hurt the system efficiency and the practical use of this method in real-time online search systems.

In this paper, we investigate various *explicit* aggregation schemes that are separated from the retrieval models. We report our findings in the following sections.

3   Problem Definition

In this paper, we present the whole session relevance score $Score(session, d)$ as a weighted linear combination of the relevance scores of queries in a session S. Let $Score(session, d)$ denotes the overall relevance score for a document d to a session that begins at q_1 and ends at q_n. The score can be written as:

$$Score(session, d) = \sum_{i=1}^{n} \lambda_i \cdot Score(q_i, d) \tag{1}$$

where λ_i represents the weight for each query $q_i \in S$.

By formulating λ_i differently, we can have different query aggregation schemes. It is worth noting that (1) allows us to choose aggregation schemes and retrieval models independently.

---

[1] http://www.dmoz.org

$Score(q_i, d)$ is the relevance score between document d and the ith query q_i in the session. $Score(q_i, d)$ can be calculated by a wide range of document retrieval models. The retrieval models used in this work include the state-of-the-art language modeling approach as well as a novel model which considers historical search query and results.

4   Experimental Setup

We use the TREC 2011 and TREC 2012 Session track [15,16] datasets in our evaluation. Table 1 lists the statistics of the TREC datasets.

TREC Session tracks emphasize on finding relevant search results for the last query in a session. This setting might not be ideal since it is not guaranteed that the last query well represents the information need for a whole session. For example, the last query in TREC 2012 session 27 (Table 3) is not good. After issuing the first two queries about *stock market* and *1998 world cup*, the user did not find any relevant documents and did not click any retrieved documents. In the last (the third) query, the user might be frustrated and just submitted a trivial query *french world cup 1998*, which missed an emphasized aspect *reaction* in the topic.

Table 3. An example (session 27) of TREC 2012 Session queries

Topic: *France won its first (and only) World Cup in*	queries
1998. Find information about the reaction of	q_1.stock market response to 1988 world cup
French people and institutions (such as stock	q_2.stock market response to 1998 world cup
markets), and studies about these reactions.	q_3.french world cup 1998

Nonetheless, we believe that most TREC sessions well represent common Web search behaviors. We have observed interesting patterns through experimenting with TREC datasets. Moreover, the ground truth provided by TREC Session tracks is valuable for evaluating aggregation schemes. We therefore employ TREC Session data and leave experiments over more popular Web search log datasets, such as the AOL query log and the Yahoo! Webscope query log, as future work. The corpus for retrieval used in our experiments is the ClueWeb09 CatB[2] collection. Spam documents whose Waterloo's "GroupX" spam score[3] is below 70 [4] are filtered out from the collection. TREC's official ground truth and evaluation scripts are used in the experiments. nDCG@10 is the main evaluation metric used in TREC Session tracks and also serves as the evaluation metric in our experiments.

As described in section 3, query aggregation schemes and retrieval models can be applied independently. Therefore, we experiment the aggregation schemes in combination with two retrieval models. The first retrieval model is the language model (LM). We modify the language model implementation in the Lemur search engine[4] to include query aggregation. The second retrieval model is the query change model (QCM)[7].

---

[2] http://lemurproject.org/clueweb09/
[3] http://durum0.uwaterloo.ca/clueweb09spam/
[4] http://www.lemurproject.org/, version 5.0

In the LM, the relevance score is calculated as in [20]:

$$Score(q_i, d) = \sum_{t \in q_i} \log P(t|d) \tag{2}$$

where the probability that t generates d (term weight) $P(t|d)$ is calculated based on multinomial query generation language model with Dirichlet smoothing [25]: $P(t|d) = \frac{\#(t,d) + \mu P(t|C)}{|d| + \mu}$, where $\#(t,d)$ denotes the number of occurrences of term t in document d, $P(t|C)$ is the Maximum Likelihood Estimation (MLE) of the probability that t appears in corpus C, $|d|$ is the document length, and μ is the Dirichlet smoothing parameter (set to 5000).

In the QCM, we modify (2) by adapting the adjustment for term weight in [7]:

$$Score(q_i, d) = \sum_{t \in q_i} w_t \log P(t|d) \tag{3}$$

where

$$w_t = \begin{cases} 1 + \alpha[1 - P(t|d_{i-1}^*)] & t \in q_{i-1} \text{ and } t \in q_i \\ -\beta P(t|d_{i-1}^*) + \epsilon idf(t) & t \in q_i \text{ but } t \notin q_{i-1} \\ -\delta P(t|d_{i-1}^*) & t \in q_{i-1} \text{ but } t \notin q_i \end{cases} \tag{4}$$

where $P(t|d_{i-1}^*)$ denotes the probability of term t occurring in SAT clicks [8], $idf(t)$ is the inverse document frequency of term t, α, β, ϵ, and δ are parameters.

5   The U-Shape Query Weight Curve

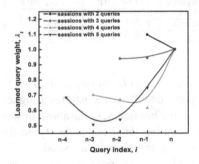
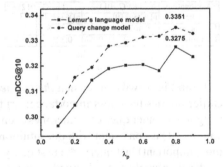

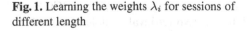

Fig. 1. Learning the weights λ_i for sessions of different length

Fig. 2. Tuning λ_p for the PvC scheme. nDCG@10 reaches the peak at $\lambda_p = 0.8$.

This section reports our findings of the U-shape query weight curve in session search. Initially, we aim to employ a supervised learning framework for ranking to obtain the query weights in a session. In this section, we plot the query weight curves learned from the training data, and then use those learned weights to aggregate the queries in a session for retrieval. However, surprisingly, the learned weights do not generate the best search accuracy as compared to other query aggregation schemes. This might be caused by overfitting. Nonetheless, we believe that we have learned the major trend of query importance in a session. In the next section, we describe a new query aggregation scheme that we derive from these discoveries. We employ SVMRank[5] to learn the query weights λ_i. SVMRank aims to optimize a ranking function [12]. The ranking function that SVMRank optimizes in our experiment is (1). We observe similar trends in learning results for the two retrieval models and thus only report one of them.

We build a training dataset by merging the ground truth data from both TREC 2011 and TREC 2012 Session tracks, which were provided after run submission [15,16]. Although it may be impractical to use ground truth in a real submission, the learning result can give us some inspiration about the importances of queries in a session.

The sessions are different in length. Table 2 lists the number of training instances for sessions in different lengths. We can see that most TREC search sessions contain two or three queries and on average the number of queries per session is 3.31. We group the training data by session length. For each group, we learn query weights λ_i by a 10-fold cross-validation. Few sessions are longer than five queries, hence we exclude them from the training data.

Fig. 1 plots the curves of query weight distribution over query position for sessions with lengths of 2, 3, 4, and 5, respectively. The x-axis displays the query position index and the y-axis shows the corresponding query weight. All learned query weights λ_i are normalized by λ_n, the weight for the last query q_n. For example, session 27 has three queries, i.e., $n = 3$, the query weights for q_1, q_2, and q_3 are 0.93, 0.94, and 1.

Table 4. nDCG@10 for query aggregation schemes for the LM. "↓" means decrement.

Aggregation	TREC 2011		TREC 2012	
Scheme	nDCG@10	↓	nDCG@10	↓
Exponential	0.4677	–	0.3288	–
Learning	0.4630	1.00%	0.3259	0.88%

Table 5. nDCG@10 for query aggregation schemes for the QCM. "↓" means decrement.

Aggregation	TREC 2011		TREC 2012	
Scheme	nDCG@10	↓	nDCG@10	↓
Exponential	0.4821	–	0.3368	–
Learning	0.4816	0.10%	0.3360	0.24%

From Fig. 1, we can see that *the learned curves are close to U-shape parabolas*: (1) earlier queries have less importance; (2) the first query usually demonstrates a higher weight than other queries, sometimes even higher than the last query. In the above observations, (1) is consistent with our intuition, while (2) implies that besides the (typically most important) last query, the first query shows a special importance in a session.

We then apply these learned query weights into (1) and compare with one of the top performing aggregation schemes, exponential discounting scheme. The nDCG@10 evaluation results are shown in Table 4 and 5 for the two retrieval models described in Session 3. We expect to observe a performance gain in nDCG@10 from the learned query weights as compared to the exponential scheme since the query weights are learned directly from the data. Surprisingly, we find that learned query weights experience a performance decrease. The undesirable performance of learned query weights

---

[5] http://svmlight.joachims.org/

is perhaps caused by overfitting. As we can see that the session lengths vary. When we chose a specific weight distribution for each session length, the training data is segmented and becomes more sparse. Moreover, learning and applying different weights for sessions with different lengths might not be infeasible in practice, because the system is not able to know the session length when a user is still issuing queries. Nonetheless, the learned query weight curve reveals interesting patterns and trends in query importance, which inspires us to propose a new query aggregation scheme in the next section.

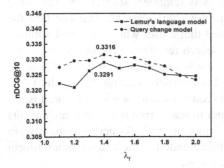 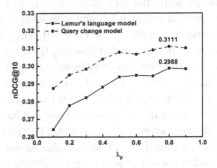

Fig. 3. Tuning λ_f for the FvR scheme. nDCG@10 reaches the peak at $\lambda_f = 1.4$.

Fig. 4. Tuning λ_p for the Dist. scheme. nDCG@10 reaches the peak at $\lambda_p = 0.8$.

6 Three-Step Query Aggregation

In this section, based upon this discoveries that we have made so far, we propose a smoothed version of the learned weights and yield a new three-step query aggregation scheme. The new scheme is one of the best query aggregation schemes in our experiments.

The U-shape query weight curves motivate us to treat the first, the current, and the middle queries in different ways. A three-step function seems a good choice. We thus propose a novel three-step aggregation scheme:

$$\lambda_i = \begin{cases} \lambda_f & i = 1 \\ \lambda_p & i = 2, \cdots, n-1 \\ 1 & i = n \end{cases} \tag{5}$$

where $\lambda_1 = \lambda_f$ denotes the weight of the first query, λ_p denotes the weight of middle queries; they satisfy $0 < \lambda_p < \lambda_f$.

It is worth noting that in most cases $\lambda_1 < \lambda_n$. However, the query weights are not only related to i, the position of the query, but also related to n, the session length. We observe that in Fig. 1 that the first query in a short session is of much higher importance than that in a long session. Moreover, the first query looks even more important than the last query in a session that contains two queries. In our opinion, a short session may be able to quickly satisfy the information need, which might be caused by starting with a highly relevant query so that the user no need to modify the query too much. In other words, the first query in a short session is of very high quality and represent the information need well. The higher the weights, the more important the queries, and the better quality of the queries. As a result, the first queries get higher query weights in short sessions than the first queries in long sessions. We explore the optimal values for λ_f and λ_p in section 7.2.

In addition, from Fig. 1, we can also see that shorter sessions have flatter weight curves while the weight curve of longer sessions is relatively steeper. The flat curve suggests a uniform-ish query weighting scheme for short sessions. This conflicts the assumption made by He et al. [9]. They assumed that a user who is satisfied within a short session is good at learning from previous search results and issuing good queries so that the most recently generated queries are most important than the earlier ones. Therefore, they propose to very different weights for individual queries in short sessions. Moreover, they consider that a user who requires a long session to search is not clear on the information need and is a bad learner to learn from previous search results and issue better queries sooner. Therefore, the importance of all queries in the session that are issued by a bad user should not be differentiated; which suggests a uniform distribution of the query weights for the long sessions.

We believe our observations are correct. Short queries usually demonstrate that the user is clearer about the search goal as compared to longer queries. Long queries imply users change their minds and try different queries during search. Therefore, the queries in a shorter session might show less "detour" in search and yield a flatter and higher valued curve for query weights than queries in longer sessions.

7   Evaluation

7.1   Aggregation Schemes under Comparison

We compare the following aggregation schemes in this evaluation. The search algorithm can be either the LM or the QCM.

- Uniform: All queries in a session share the same weight.
- Previous vs. current (PvC): All previous queries $q_1, ..., q_{n-1}$ share a lower weight than the last query.
- First vs. rest (FvR): The first query has a higher weight and the other queries including the last query share a lower and identical weight.
- Distance-based (Dist.): Query weights are discounted with how far the query is from the last query. The reciprocal function is used as the discounting function.
- Exponential (Exp.): A aggregation scheme proposed by this paper. It is derived from [7].
- Learning: The weights of queries are learned by SVMRank as described in section 5.

- Three-step: There are three levels in the query weighting function as defined in (5). The last query has the highest weight, the intermediate queries share the lowest weight, while the first query has a middle range weight between them.

In addition, the best results of the official TREC 2011 and TREC 2012 Session track (TREC best) [11], [19] are included for comparison and are used as the baseline. They both worked on the ClueWeb09 CatB corpus. Particularly, the system of [19] used an exponential function to discount the weight of query based on the distance between it and the last query. The system of [11] applied an aggregation scheme of the same as PvC, with assigning a weight of 0.6 to last query and 0.4 to the previous ones.

7.2 Parameter Settings

Query aggregation schemes presented in this paper all contain parameters except the uniform scheme (using 1 for all queries). Since the values of these parameters influence the effectiveness of query aggregation and search accuracy, we conduct parameter selection and present them in this section. All the tuning are done through 10-fold cross-validation. We plot the parameter settings for both LM and QCM. For the PvC scheme, we tune λ_p over a range of 0.1 to 0.9 to select the best value for λ_p. Fig. 2 indicates the trends of nDCG@10 values with λ_p. The curves show the same trends. The nDCG@10 values achieve peaks in both curves at around $\lambda_p = 0.8$. It implies that the aggregation scheme and retrieval model can work independently.

For the other aggregation schemes, we use the similar parameter sweeping method to find the best parameter values. Fig. 3, 4, 5, 6 illustrate the tuning procedures for FvR, distance-based, exponential, and three-step schemes. It is worth noting that Fig 5 suggests a fairly mild discount in exponential scheme, which means previous queries may be quite important as well.

7.3 Search Accuracy with Language Model

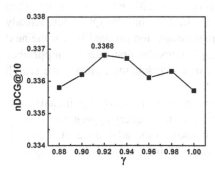
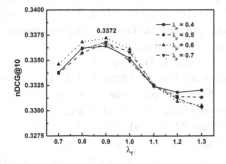

Fig. 5. Tuning γ for the exponential scheme. nDCG@10 reaches the peak at $\gamma = 0.9$.

Fig. 6. Tuning (λ_f, λ_p) for the three-step scheme. nDCG@10 peaks at (0.9, 0.6).

Table 6 compares the search accuracy under different aggregation schemes for the language modeling model [25], [20]. TREC participants usually provided high performance systems. Therefore, we use TREC best results as a strong baseline.

We adopt the parameters tuned in section 7.2 for PvC, FvR, Exponential, and the three-step aggregation schemes. The average learned query weights from section 5 are used in the Learning aggregation scheme.

From Table 6, we observe that PvC, FvR, exponential, learning, and three-step schemes outperform the TREC best runs. Furthermore, the exponential scheme performs the best in TREC 2011 while three-step scheme wins in TREC 2012.

The distance-based scheme performs the worst. In our opinion, the reciprocal function discounts the previous queries too much and hurts the search accuracy.

The proposed three-step scheme improves the search accuracy in TREC 2012. It implies that the first query may be more important than the middle queries because a user usually starts search from the topic words of his information need.

The three-step scheme is not the top in TREC 2011. We investigate the dataset differences between the TREC 2011 and TREC 2012. We find that 73 out of 98 sessions in TREC 2012 Session track contain the first query composed of only theme terms, while only 31 out of 76 in TREC 2011 Session track, which implies that the quality of the first queries in TREC 2012 may be better than that in TREC 2011. This may be the reason why the three-step scheme outperforms the exponential aggregation scheme in TREC 2012 but lose to it in TREC 2011 as shown in Table 6.

7.4   Search Accuracy with the Query Change Model

We compare the search accuracy for various aggregation schemes using the QCM. We observe similar trend as in the language modeling approach as well. The results are listed in Table 7.

By comparing Table 6 and Table 7, we find that the retrieval using two different models with query aggregation show similar trends for which aggregation schemes work the best. It again implies that query aggregation may be universally effective and independent of retrieval models.

There are some small differences in the search accuracy of the two retrieval models. First, FvR scheme is slightly better than PvC scheme in LM, while it is worse than PvC scheme in the QCM. The reason may lie in the fact that the QCM has already strengthened the first query by calculating the query transition probability for the next query. Therefore, the FvR scheme may over-emphasizes the first query's importance in the QCM. This may also be the reason why three-step scheme improve the search accuracy less significantly in the QCM than in LM.

Nonetheless, the threes-step query aggregation scheme statistically significantly outperforms the TREC best systems. It is also the top performing query aggregation scheme for the TREC 2012 Session dataset. Although it takes some advantage of using the ground truth for parameter tuning, it provides evidence that the importance of queries in a session may change non-monotonically.

Table 6. nDCG@10 for various aggregation schemes for Lemur's language model. TREC best serves as the baseline. † indicates a significant improvement over the baseline at $p <$ 0.05 (t-test, single-tailed).

Table 7. nDCG@10 for various aggregation schemes for the QCM. TREC best serves as the baseline. † indicates a significant improvement over the baseline at $p < 0.05$ (t-test, single-tailed).

Aggregation	TREC 2011		TREC 2012	
Scheme	nDCG@10	%chg	nDCG@10	%chg
TREC best	0.4540	0.00%	0.3221	0.00%
Uniform	0.4475	-1.43%	0.3033	-5.84%
PvC	0.4516	-0.53%	0.3275	1.68%
FvR	0.4390	-3.30%	0.3291	2.17%
Distance-based	0.4271	-5.93%	0.2988	-7.23%
Exp	**0.4677**	**3.02%**†	0.3288	2.08%
Learning	0.4630	1.98%	0.3259	1.18%
3-step	0.4552	0.26%	**0.3340**	**3.69%**†

Aggregation	TREC 2011		TREC 2012	
Scheme	nDCG@10	%chg	nDCG@10	%chg
TREC best	0.4540	0.00%	0.3221	0.00%
Uniform	0.4626	1.89%	0.3316	2.95%
PvC	0.4713	3.81%†	0.3351	4.04%†
FvR	0.4362	-3.92%	0.3316	2.95%
Distance-based	0.4431	-2.40%	0.3111	-3.42%
Exp	**0.4821**	**6.19%**†	0.3368	4.56%†
Learning	0.4816	6.08%†	0.3360	4.32%†
3-step	0.4781	5.31%†	**0.3372**	**4.69%**†

7.5 Analysis of the Query Weight Curves

To better understand the behavior of various query aggregation schemes and find out reasons for their different impacts on search accuracy for session search, we plot the query weights for all query aggregation schemes in Fig. 1. Our purpose is to lay out all the curves and look into the relationships among the query aggregation schemes.

The curve of the averaged learned query weights is the red solid line and is generated as follows. We average λ_i for previous queries over all the subsets with number of queries not greater than 5. For example, $\bar{\lambda}_1$ is averaged by the values of λ_1 trained on the subsets with number of queries of 2, 3, 4, and 5; while $\bar{\lambda}_2$ is averaged by the values of λ_2 trained on the subsets with number of queries of 3, 4, and 5 since λ_2 in the subset with query number of 2 is for the last query. The averaged curve of λ_i against query position is shown in Fig. 1 (red line with square symbols). It is thus used as an reference for all other curves. We understand that this learned weight curve did not generate the best search accuracy as we report in earlier section; however, it is directly learned from user data and should be close to real user behaviors. We therefore use it to help understand other aggregation schemes' search accuracy even itself does not directly generate the best performing search accuracy due to overfitting.

We find that the exponential scheme (indicated by the star symbol) aligns the best with the learned weights (the solid square symbols); whereas the distance-based discounting scheme the worst (the cross symbols).

On the other hand, since majority sessions have three or less queries, we focus more on the weights for the last three q_n, q_{n-1}, and q_{n-2}. We find that the exponential scheme aligns almost perfectly with the learned weights at the last two queries and only deviates a bit at q_{n-3}. Since most sessions have only 3 queries, this is a very good match between the learned red query weights for the first 3 queries and the weights generated by the exponential scheme. It might explain why the exponential scheme outperforms other aggregation schemes.

The three-step scheme (indicated by the circle symbol) aligns the learned curve well near the beginning of a session, i.e., the first query. the weight of earliest query, i.e., λ_1, increases again after the continuous decrease of the weights. This might indicate that the first query is also important to the whole session because users often starts with a query full of topic/theme terms, i.e., starting the search from general terms for the information need. The last query in a session receives high weight as well. In addition, it well represents the reduction of query importance for the middle queries. The weights decrease rapidly after q_{n-1}. This might imply that the unit of concept change. In other words, the user does not care about the queries $2 \sim 3$ iterations before when performing a session search. Therefore, in our opinion, this leads to the best performance of the three-step aggregation scheme in TREC 2012 dataset.

8   Conclusion

This paper studies the problem of query aggregation for session search. We first learn the optimal query weights using SVM ranking and discover a U-shape query weight distribution for session with various lengths. After observing the learning results, we propose a novel three-step aggregation scheme. Moreover, by comparing the new query aggregation schemes to the widely used ones such as uniform and distance-based, we conclude that the proposed scheme outperform the existing aggregation schemes. Specially, the three-step aggregation scheme works well for both TREC 2011 and TREC 2012 Session tracks, though it is outperformed by the exponential discounting query aggregation scheme over the TREC 2011 Session data. This suggests a dataset impact on query aggregation schemes.

Through the experiments, we find that the first and the last queries are of more importance to a session. Moreover, for sessions that starts with general theme terms for the sessions, the three-step query aggregation scheme is a better choice since these sessions explicitly require a higher weight to the first query.

The experiments also demonstrate that the query aggregation schemes can impact on the search accuracy independently from the retrieval model. This allows us to flexibly combine various query aggregation schemes and retrieval models in the more general whole session search framework.

References

1. Albakour, M.D., Kruschwitz, U.: University of essex at the trec 2012 session track. In: TREC 2012 (2012)
2. Bennett, P.N., White, R.W., Chu, W., Dumais, S.T., Bailey, P., Borisyuk, F., Cui, X.: Modeling the impact of short- and long-term behavior on search personalization. In: SIGIR 2012 (2012)
3. Carterette, B., Kanoulas, E., Yilmaz, E.: Simulating simple user behavior for system effectiveness evaluation. In: CIKM 2011 (2011)
4. Cormack, G.V., Smucker, M.D., Clarke, C.L.: Efficient and effective spam filtering and re-ranking for large web datasets. Inf. Retr. 14(5), 441–465 (2011)
5. Croft, B., Metzler, D., Strohman, T.: Search Engines Information Retrieval in Practice, 1st edn. Addison-Wesley, USA (2009)
6. Guan, D., Yang, H., Goharian, N.: Effective structured query formulation for session search. In: TREC 2012 (2012)

7. Guan, D., Zhang, S., Yang, H.: Utilizing query change for session search. In: SIGIR 2013 (2013)
8. Guo, Q., Agichtein, E.: Ready to buy or just browsing?: detecting web searcher goals from interaction data. In: SIGIR 2010 (2010)
9. He, J., Hollink, V., Bosscarino, C., Cornacchia, R., de Vries, A.: Cwi at trec 2011, session, web, and medical. In: TREC 2011 (2011)
10. Jiang, J., Han, S., Wu, J., He, D.: Pitt at trec 2011 session track. In: TREC 2011 (2011)
11. Jiang, J., He, D., Han, S.: Pitt at trec 2012 session track. In: TREC 2012 (2012)
12. Joachims, T.: Optimizing search engines using clickthrough data. In: KDD 2002 (2002)
13. Jones, R., Klinkner, K.L.: Beyond the session timeout: automatic hierarchical segmentation of search topics in query logs. In: CIKM 2008 (2008)
14. Kanoulas, E., Carterette, B., Clough, P.D., Sanderson, M.: Evaluating multi-query sessions. In: SIGIR 2011 (2011)
15. Kanoulas, E., Carterette, B., Hall, M., Clough, P., Sanderson, M.: Overview of the trec 2011 session track. In: TREC 2011 (2011)
16. Kanoulas, E., Carterette, B., Hall, M., Clough, P., Sanderson, M.: Overview of the trec 2012 session track. In: TREC 2012 (2012)
17. Kanoulas, E., Clough, P.D., Carterette, B., Sanderson, M.: Session track at trec 2010. In: TREC 2010 (2010)
18. Liu, J., Belkin, N.J.: Personalizing information retrieval for multi-session tasks: the roles of task stage and task type. In: SIGIR 2010 (2010)
19. Liu, T., Zhang, C., Gao, Y., Xiao, W., Huang, H.: BUPT_WILDCAT at trec 2011 session track. In: TREC 2011 (2011)
20. Metzler, D., Croft, W.B.: Combining the language model and inference network approaches to retrieval. Inf. Process. Manage. 40(5), 735–750 (2004)
21. Singh, S.P.: Learning to solve markovian decision processes. Tech. rep., Amherst, MA, USA (1993)
22. White, R.W., Bennett, P.N., Dumais, S.T.: Predicting short-term interests using activity-based search context. In: CIKM 2010 (2010)
23. White, R.W., Ruthven, I., Jose, J.M., Rijsbergen, C.J.V.: Evaluating implicit feedback models using searcher simulations. ACM Trans. Inf. Syst. 23(3), 325–361 (2005)
24. Xiang, B., Jiang, D., Pei, J., Sun, X., Chen, E., Li, H.: Context-aware ranking in web search. In: SIGIR 2010 (2010)
25. Zhai, C., Lafferty, J.: A study of smoothing methods for language models applied to information retrieval. ACM Trans. Inf. Syst. 22(2), 179–214 (2004)

A Comparative Evaluation of 2D And 3D Visual Exploration of Document Search Results

Rafael E. Banchs

Human Language Technology, Institute for Infocomm Research, Singapore
rembanchs@i2r.a-star.edu.sg

Abstract. This work presents and experimental comparison between 2D and 3D search and visualization platforms. The main objective of the study is two ex- plore the following two research questions: what method is most robust in terms of the success rate? And, what method is faster in terms of average search time? The obtained results show that, although successful rates and subject prefe- rences are higher for 3D search and visualization, search times are still lower for 2D search and visualization.

Keywords: Document Search, Ranking, Visual Exploration, Interface.

1 Introduction

Information retrieval applications and research have a long tradition as first automatic search systems were introduced back in the 1950's. The idea of automatically retriev- ing information from a digital collection can be traced back to Vannevar Bush 1945's article "As We May Think" [1], but the origin of modern information retrieval is mostly founded on the works of Gerard Salton and Sparck Jones [2-5].

Originally, the scope of information retrieval applications was restricted to arc- hives, libraries and other document collections. However, nowadays, with the explo- sion of information access provided by the World Wide Web, information retrieval has become a daily-life commodity for a huge proportion of the world's population.

Main current information retrieval systems, such as those provided by Google (www.google.com), Yahoo (www.yahoo.com), and Microsoft (www.bing.com), gen- erate a one-dimensional ranked list of results. The retrieved documents are organized in a list from the most relevant to the least relevant. Such lists, which can actually contain millions of documents, are presented in a set of pages, each of which contains a more reasonable number of documents that generally ranges from ten to a hundred. In these paginated lists, each document is represented by a clickable link (which al- lows the user to navigate to the corresponding document or website) and a snippet (a short segment of text aiming at providing a description of the document content).

This way of presenting the results of a search has two important problems. The first of these problems, and probably the most important one, is the fact that exploring the resulting document subset is a very complicated and uncomfortable task. Although most of the time, search engines claim to find a large amount of relevant

A. Jaafar et al. (Eds.): AIRS 2014, LNCS 8870, pp. 100–111, 2014.

documents, in practice, the user is able to explore only the first ten or twenty results. As a consequence, current search engines are designed to achieve very high precision (first ranked documents are actually relevant to the query) while recall is, most of the time, not taken into account (several relevant documents are lost in the long tail of results).

Some systems are already tackling with this major deficiency of traditional web-search engines by incorporating clustering algorithms which allows to group output results according to their similarities and semantic relationships. Some examples include search engines such as Yippy (http://search.yippy.com) and Carrot (http://search.carrot2.org), which, in addition to the conventional ranked list of documents, provide an automatically generated index of categories that allows for selecting specific subgroups of documents. Other search engines also incorporate more advanced natural language processing techniques for generating summaries of the retrieved information and classifying the outputs according to the credibility of the source. As example of these engines, we can mention Hakia (http://www.hakia.com) and SenseBot (http://www.sensebot.net). Finally, a more recent effort that must be mentioned is the case of Qwiki (http://www.qwiki.com), where main efforts are being invested in the compilation of retrieved information into a single coherent multimedia informative experience.

The second problem of the current paradigm of output representation, which is somehow related to the first one, is the low level of interactivity offered to the user for exploring the collection of retrieved documents. In our opinion, this problem is mainly due to two factors: a lack of immediate feedback at the visualization interface and a poor visualization scheme. Regarding the lack of immediate feedback, with the exception of the "remix" option offered by Yippy and the "more like this" modality offered by lucene-based search engines, user's relevance feedback in conventional search applications requires the user to modify the original query and conduct a new search.

Regarding the visualization scheme, a recent advance in this area, which has been implemented by the major web-search engines, includes the possibility of previewing a small image of the corresponding document when the cursor is located over the snippet. A similar strategy is implemented by Lycos (http://search.lycos.com) in a more standard and natural way. Other visualization modalities include the visual representation of clusters as sectors of a ring (as offered by Carrot), the use of tabs for showing and hiding categories of documents (as offered by Hakia) and the use of tag-clouds for presenting relevant terminology and concepts (as offered by SenseBot and Quintura http://www.quintura.com). Another interesting alternative, which is offered by SpaceTime 3D (http://search.spacetime.com) and Redz (http://redz.com), is the use of a slideshow of document images that the user can scan over in a simple manner.

The main objective of this paper is to conduct a comparative evaluation between two different strategies for visualizing document collections and exploring the outputs of an information retrieval system. The rest of the paper is structured as follows. In Section 2, a brief review of previous work related to document search result visualization in 2D and 3D is presented. Then, in section 3, the proposed comparative evaluation and the two methods to be compared are described. In section 4, the experimental evaluation and results are presented and discussed. Finally, in section 5, the main conclusions of our work are presented.

2   Visualizing Document Collections in 2D and 3D

The specific problem of visualizing document collections and large datasets is actually of larger scope than web-search applications. In this sense, we will also review here some available visualization technologies than can be applied in the context of the proposed technology.

Multidimensional scaling was one of the first techniques proposed for generating low dimensional maps from high dimensional data [6]. The idea of this technique is to generate an optimal low dimensional embedding (generally 2 or 3 dimensions) from a multidimensional dataset. The embedding is optimal in the sense that it minimizes a stress function that measures the difference between the distances in the generated embedding and the distances (or similarities) in the original space. The main purpose of such a dimensionality reduction is to be able to "visualize" the dataset structure.

More recent approaches to the same problem of computing low dimensional embeddings include the use of different artificial neural network architectures, such as, for instance, self-organized maps [7,8] and, more recently, auto-encoder neural networks [9]. Alternative procedures include the use of linear projection operators [10,11]. In general, such space reduction techniques, when applied to textual data, are generally referred to as Semantic Mapping [12].

Notice that for visualization purposes, the dimensionality reduction has to be conducted to dimensions as low as 2 or 3. The resulting maps can be presented as either an interconnected or unconnected graph of elements, where elements can be documents, concepts or categories (clusters of documents). Several works have addressed the use of this type of methods for exploring and mining document collections [13-17]. To the extent of our knowledge, the combination these visualization resources with a highly interactive interface has been only partially exploited in information retrieval applications such as Musicplasma (www.musicplasma.com), EyePlorer (http://eyePlorer.com) and Search-Cube (www.search-cube.com).

Two specific systems aiming at visualizing information retrieval results are the VIBE system (Visual Information Browsing Environment) [16], and the SPIRE system (Spatial Paradigm for Information Retrieval and Exploration) [17]. In the latter case, two specific visualization methods: Galaxies and Themescapes, are described.

In the case of the VIBE system, search results are commonly presented in a two-dimensional space, although some versions of VIBE interfaces allow for three-dimensional representations; such as, for instance, the VR-VIBE system [18]. In the generated representation space, some points of interest (POIs) are displayed along with the documents. Typically, the POIs are defined by the query terms the user has introduced for conducting the search. Each documents is then located over the geometrical simplex defined by the different combinations of POIs depending on the specific query terms contained in it. Although document retrieval is actually performed on a binary base, document placement over the representation space is conducted by using vector model representations of the retrieved documents. In the original method implementation [16], the specific location of documents within the map is computed by means of a spring-based model, but some other implementations have exploited the use of different physical metaphors for document location, as for example the Web-VIBE system [19], which implements a "magnetic force" mechanism. At the visualization stage, the obtained map can be interactively modified by adding, eliminating and/or moving around the different POIs.

In the case of the SPIRE system, it constitutes a method for visualization and analysis of textual information, which was developed under the MVAB (Multidimensional Visualization and Advanced Browsing) project [20]. As already mentioned, two specific visualization methods are provided. The first method, which is a document-oriented visualization method, is based on a metaphor of galaxies. According to this, a two-dimensional scatter plot of "docupoints" or "starfield" is used to represent documents and clusters, as well as their corresponding interrelations. Each "docupoints" in the resulting map can be interactively explored by the user.

The second method in SPIRE is a topic-oriented visualization method that is based on a landscape metaphor. In this case, relevant information is depicted in a three-dimensional abstract landscape of information called "themescapes", which aims at representing complex relationships among topics and themes in a data collection by means of hills and valleys. The main objective of this kind of visualization is to provide a global perspective of the most relevant topics and themes contained into a given data collection by revealing the interconnections among topics through visual spatial relationships within the constructed three-dimensional landscapes of information.

3   Selected Platforms and Proposed Evaluation

In this section we introduce the two searching and visualization platforms we have selected for our comparative analysis between 2D and 3D visual exploration of document search results, as well as the main objective of the proposed evaluation.

3.1   2D Document Search and Visualization Platform

For 2D document search and exploration, the publicly available search interface Search Point (www.searchpoint.com) was selected. This interface is illustrated in Fig. 1.

In the Search Point visualization interface, a ranked list of documents resulting from a query search is presented in a very similar way as other conventional search engines such as Google, Bing and Yahoo! do. For each document, a title, a snippet and a web link is provided. As there are typically much more documents than what can be presented in the page, a pagination system allows for moving forward into the tail of the ranked list.

The novel feature of Search Point is that it also presents a thematic map (see right hand side of Fig. 1), in which different keywords are arranged on a two-dimensional map. A red dot provides the current reference location in the map against which the current ranking has been performed. When the user moves the red dot over the different regions of the maps for "exploring" the resulting list of documents, the ranked list in the left hand side of the interface is updated accordingly.

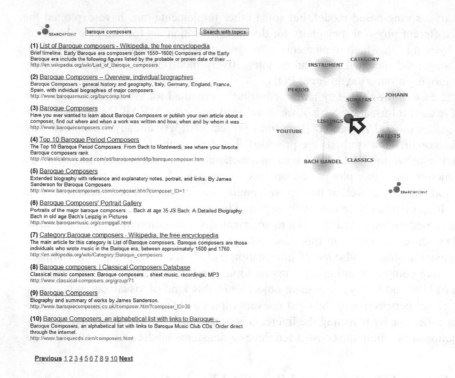

Fig. 1. Search point visualization interface

3.2   3D Document Search and Visualization Platform

For 3D document search and exploration, our in house developed 3D visualization interface, Document Planet, was used. This interface is illustrated in Fig 2.

In the Document Planet visualization interface, a two dimensional ranking of documents resulting from a query search is projected over the surface of a sphere. Each individual document is represented by a dot over the surface of the sphere, and the user can visualize the document's related information (title, snippet and web link) by placing the cursor over the corresponding dot in the sphere (see Fig. 2).

Similar to Search Point, this visualization interface also features a thematic map. However, different from Search Point, in this case the thematic map is embedded into the surface of the sphere in which the different keywords are spatially arranged over the surface where the documents are located. This allows to simultaneously visualizing documents and "thematic regions" over the same surface. The user can "explore" the resulting list of documents by navigating the surface of the sphere by means of different operations such as rotation, zoom in and zoom out.

As an additional feature of Document Planet, the thematic keywords are defined at three different resolution levels. At the lowest resolution level (the one displayed in Fig. 2) global or general category labels are presented. When the user zooms in into the sphere, in addition to the global category labels, a second set of keywords will appear that correspond to more "regional" category labels. Then, if the user continues zooming in, document titles will be displayed at each document location at the highest resolution level.

At any moment during the navigation process, the user is able to display at the bottom of the page the information (title, snippet and web link) corresponding to any document by just placing the cursor over it.

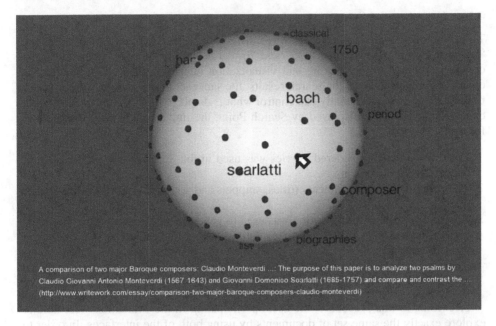

Fig. 2. Document planet visualization interface

3.3   Proposed Evaluation

As the main objective of the proposed evaluation is to compare the usefulness of both the ranking and visualization capabilities offered by each platform, similar retrieval performance is needed from both search engines in order to guarantee a fair comparative evaluation.

According to this, the experiment was designed so that the same subset of documents was displayed by both platforms for each query search result. This allowed the evaluation to focus on the specific problem of how the exploration of the resulting document list is conducted on each platform. Two main questions are addressed by the proposed comparative evaluation:

- What method is most robust in terms of the success rate on document search?
- What method is faster in terms of average search time on document search?

Different users were requested to complete some specific information search tasks over the document subset retrieved for a given predefined query. Both interfaces, Search Point and Document Planet, were used for completing the tasks.

4   Experiments and Results

In this section we describe the experimental setup and the obtained results for the comparative evaluation of 2D and 3D visual exploration of document search outputs.

4.1   Experimental Setup

To generate the evaluation datasets, three different and generic queries were defined: "baroque composers", "Italian food" and "travel deals". In order to guarantee a fair comparison between the ranking and visualization interfaces, as well as making the evaluation independent of the search results, the same set of documents were used for both interfaces. As we actually can control what is displayed by Document Planet, but cannot control what is displayed by Search Point, the implemented procedure was as follows:

1. Each of the three considered queries was used in the Search Point platform to retrieve a list of documents.
2. The resulting list of documents (titles, snippets and web links) were saved for each query.
3. The saved document information was used to generate the corresponding maps and extract keywords at the different resolutions levels to be used in the Document Planet platform.
4. The same search results from Search Point were displayed by the Document Planet interface for each of the three defined queries.

According to this procedure, the users participating in the evaluation were able to explore exactly the same set of documents by using both of the interfaces. In order to avoid possible bias resulting from "gaining experience" by using one interface before the other, half of the participants were requested to conduct the tasks first on Search Point and second on Document Planet, while the other half of the participants was requested to conduct the experiments in the reversed order.

The tasks were defined as simple questions that had to be answered by exploring the document lists resulting from the three predefined queries. The tasks were designed in such a way that the participants did not need to display the full document. The information contained in the available data for the documents: title, snippet and web link was enough to answer each of the posted questions.

Five questions were generated for each query-related document lists, so a total of 15 tasks were created. For defining the questions, five documents were randomly selected from each of the three query-related document lists and one question was defined for each document such that the answer was evident from the available information (title, snippet and web link)[1]. The 15 tasks designed for the evaluation are presented in Table 1.

---

[1]   Notice that while this procedure guarantees that there is an answer for each task proposed in the evaluation, it does not guarantee that the answer is unique. Indeed, for some of the defined tasks there is more than one document that provides a valid answer.

Table 1. The 15 tasks comprising the comparative evaluation

Query	Task
	Find the year in which JS Bach was born
	Find a website for downloading mp3s of baroque composers
Baroque	Find a website about renaissance, baroque and classical com-
composers	posers
	Find a Youtube video about baroque composers
	Find what Giulio Caccini is credited for inventing
	Find a website for buying Parmesan cheese online
	Find an Italian food blog
Italian food	Find a website containing recipes for risotto, pizza and tiramisu
	Find a website listing Italian restaurants in Westchester county
	Find an e-newsletter on food and wine
	Find hot travel deals from Yahoo! Singapore
	Find vacation packages to Nassau and Bahamas
Travel deals	Find the website link for cheap deals with Travelocity Travel
	Find deals and discount travels to Africa
	Find luxury hotels and 5-star resort vacations

For each task, each user was given a time limit of 60 seconds. If the participant was not able to accomplish the task, it was counted as a failure. On the other hand, if the participant was able to accomplish the task, the total amount of seconds required to complete the task was registered. Two specific metrics can be computed from this data:

- success rate = number of completed tasks / total number of tasks * 100%
- average time = summation of individual times for completed tasks / total number of completed tasks

In addition to the quantitative evaluation describe above, a subjective evaluation was also conducted by means of a brief survey. After completing all the proposed 15 tasks, each participant was asked about his/her preference between Search Planet and Document Planet (the option of not having any preference between both tools was also provided). Preferences were evaluated regarding the following issues:

- Which interface is easier to use?
- Which interface is more intuitive to use?
- Which interface allows finding the requested information faster?
- Which interface provides a better idea of the contents of the collection?
- Which interface organizes the information in a better way?
- Which interface is more interactive and dynamic?
- Which interface would you definitively prefer to use?

A total of 8 persons participated in the evaluation. All of them were familiar with search engines and computer interfaces. The population was composed of 3 researchers, 4 students and 1 engineer. Regarding gender, the population was composed by 2 female participants and 6 male participants.

4.2   Experimental Results

Table 2 presents aggregated results, over all eight participants, for the quantitative evaluation. The table presents resulting success rates and average times for each of the 15 considered tasks and both search and visualization platforms.

Table 2. Success rates and average times for each of the 15 considered tasks

Query	Task	2D-platform		3D-platform	
		success rate	average time	success rate	average time
Baroque Composers	1	87.50%	15.71	75.00%	14.17
	2	50.00%	31.00	87.50%	21.86
	3	75.00%	18.33	75.00%	28.17
	4	37.50%	13.67	62.50%	30.60
	5	12.50%	45.00	37.50%	25.33
Italian Food	1	37.50%	29.67	75.00%	39.00
	2	25.00%	20.50	50.00%	37.50
	3	87.50%	20.29	87.50%	30.43
	4	37.50%	22.33	100.00%	29.25
	5	25.00%	30.50	37.50%	34.33
Travel Deals	1	50.00%	26.25	75.00%	29.67
	2	0.00%	0.00	37.50%	33.33
	3	87.50%	27.00	37.50%	37.00
	4	62.50%	13.80	25.00%	52.50
	5	12.50%	58.00	75.00%	19.67
		45.83%	**24.80**	**62.50%**	**30.85**

As seen from Table 2, in the overall evaluation, Search Point demonstrated to be a faster search mechanism (as the average time for the accomplished task is 24.80 seconds, compared to 30.85 seconds in the case of Document Planet), while Document Planet demonstrated to be a more robust alternative (with a success rate of 62.50%, compared to 45.83% in the case of Search Point).

Regarding the subjective evaluation, Table 3 presents the corresponding aggregated results over the eight participants and the global "user satisfaction" that can be inferred from them, respectively. Notice from the table and the figure how, although the users preferred Search Point in some important aspects such as intuitiveness and information organization, in the overall appreciation assessments the Document Planet paradigm is preferred over the Search Point one. It is interesting to notice the inconsistency between the subjective evaluation (in which the users give preference to Document Planet regarding search speed) and the quantitative one, in which average times for accomplished tasks are lower for Search Point!

Table 3. Aggregated preferences for each evaluated subjective dimension

	2D-platform	3D-platform	Indifferent
easier to use	50.00%	37.50%	12.50%
more intuitive	37.50%	25.00%	37.50%
allows for faster search	25.00%	62.50%	12.50%
better idea of collection	25.00%	75.00%	0.00%
better organization	37.50%	25.00%	37.50%
more interactive	12.50%	87.50%	0.00%
preference of usage	0.00%	62.50%	37.50%
	26.79%	**53.57%**	**19.64%**

5   Discussion and Conclusions

The results of the conducted evaluation suggest that although the considered 3D search and visualization interface happened to achieve a higher success rate than 2D one, it does not constitute a more efficient and effective visualization strategy in terms of average search time.

Among the several facts that can explain this, we can mention the following two as the most important ones:

- users are much more familiar with 2-D interfaces than with 3-D interfaces, and
- image rendering in the current implementation of our 3D search and visualization interface is still laggy and slow.

One point of attention should be raised regarding the detected inconsistency between the objective evaluation, which revealed that average search times for accomplished tasks are lower in the 2D interface than in the 3D one, and the subjective evaluation, which revealed the participants perception about the 3D search and visualization method allowing for faster search than the 2D one.

One possible explanation of this inconsistency can be the fact that tasks were declared unsuccessful when they cannot be accomplished in a 60 second time interval. These time intervals of 60 seconds are not taken into account in the computation of average search times. On the other hand, as successful rates are higher for the 3D interface, the users might have had the perception of spending much more time on searches over the 2D one than over the 3D, so unconsciously they might be associating success rates to lower average search times.

One of the most important results of this evaluation are the potential improvements that can be incorporated into 3D search and visualization platforms by taking into account the feedback provided by the users. These feedbacks, most of which were provided in the form of open questions in the evaluation survey, include strategies such as adding colours to the sphere surface according to the clustering results, providing means for visualizing tags on the opposite side of the sphere, and improving the response of the graphic rendering during navigation, among others.

Acknowledgements. The author wants to thank the Institute for Infocomm Research for its support and permission for publishing this work.

References

1. Bush, V.: As We Think. Atlantic Monthly 176, 101–108 (1945)
2. Salton, G.: The SMART Retrieval System—Experiments in Automatic Document Retrieval. Prentice Hall Inc., Englewood Cliffs (1971)
3. Jones, K.S.: Automatic Keyword Classification for Information Retrieval, Butterworths, London (1971)
4. Sparck Jones, K.: A Statistical Interpretation of Term Specificity and its Application in Retrieval. Journal of Documentation 28, 11–21 (1972)
5. Salton, G., Wong, A., Yang, C.S.: A Vector Space Model for Information Retrieval. Communications of the ACM 18(11), 613–620 (1975)
6. Kruskal, J.B., Wish, M.: Multidimensional Scaling, Sage University Paper series on Quantitative Application in the Social Sciences, pp. 7–11. Sage Publications, Beverly Hills (1978)
7. Kohonen, T., Kaski, S., Lagus, K., Salojärvi, J., Honkela, J., Paatero, V., Saarela, A.: Self Organization of a Massive Document Collection. IEEE Transaction on Neural Networks 11(3), 574–585 (2000)
8. Lagus, K., Kaski, S., Kohonen, T.: Mining Massive Document Collections by the WEBSOM Method. Information Sciences 163(1-3), 135–156 (2004)
9. Hinton, G.E., Salakhutdinov, R.R.: Reducing the Dimensionality of Data with Neural Networks. Science 313, 504–507 (2006)
10. Jolliffe, I.T.: Principal Component Analysis, 2nd edn. Springer Series in Statistics (2002)
11. Deerwester, S., et al.: Improving Information Retrieval with Latent Semantic Indexing. In: Proceedings of the 51st Annual Meeting of the American Society for Information Science (1988)
12. Correa, R.F., Ludermir, T.B.: Dimensionality Reduction of Very Large Document Collections by Semantic Mapping. In: Proceedings of 6th Int. Workshop on Self-Organizing Maps (2007)
13. Feldman, R., Klosgen, W., Zilberstein, A.: Visualization Techniques to Explore Data Mining Results for Document Collections. In: Proceedings of the Third Annual Conference on Knowledge Discovery and Data Mining (KDD), Newport Beach (1997)
14. Newman, D., Baldwin, T., Cavedon, L., Huang, E., Karimi, S., Martinez, D., Scholer, F., Zobel, J.: Visualizing Search Results and Document Collections using Topic Maps. Web Semantics: Science, Services and Agents on the World Wide Web 8 (2010)
15. Kandogan, E.: Visualizing Multi-dimensional Clusters, Trends, and Outliers using Star Coordinates. In: Proceedings of the 7th ACM SIGKDD International Conference on Knowledge Discovery and Data Mining (KDD 2001), pp. 107–116 (2001)
16. Olsen, K.A., Korfhage, R.R., Sochats, K.M., Spring, M.B., Williams, J.G.: Visualization of a Document Collection: The Vibe System. Information Processing & Management 29(1), 69–81 (1993)
17. Wise, J.A., Thomas, J.J., Pennock, K.A., Lantrip, D.B., Pottier, M.C., Schur, A., Crow, V.: Visualizing the Non-visual: Spatial Analysis and Interaction with Information from Text Documents. In: Proceedings of the IEEE Symposium on Information Visualization (INFOVIS 1995). IEEE Computer Society, Washington, DC (1995)

18. Benford, S., Snowdown, D., Greenhalgh, C., Ingram, R., Knox, I., Brown, C.: VR-VIBE: A Visual Environment for Co-operative Information Retrieval. In: Eurographics 1995, pp. 349–360 (1995)
19. Morse, E.L., Lewis, M.: Why Information Retrieval Visualization Sometimes Fail. In: Proceedings of IEEE International Conference on Systems, Man and Cybernetics, pp. 1680–1685 (1997)
20. Crow, V., Pottier, M., Thomas, J., Lantrip, D., Struble, C., Pennock, K., Schur, A., Wise, J., Fiegel, T., York, J.: Multidimensional Visualization and Browsing for Intelligence Analysis. Technical Report, Pacific Northwest Lab, Richland, WA, United States (1994)

Multi-resolution Shape-Based Image Retrieval Using Ridgelet Transform

Mas Rina Mustaffa[1], Fatimah Ahmad[2], and Shyamala Doraisamy[1]

[1] Department of Multimedia, Faculty of Computer Science and Information Technology,
Universiti Putra Malaysia, 43400 Serdang, Selangor, Malaysia
{MasRina,Shyamala}@upm.edu.my
[2] Department of Computer Science, Faculty of Defence Science and Technology, Universiti
Pertahanan Nasional Malaysia, Sg. Besi Camp, 57000 Kuala Lumpur, Malaysia
Fatimah@upnm.edu.my

Abstract. Complicated shapes can be effectively characterized using multi-resolution descriptors. One popular method is the Ridgelet transform which has enjoyed very little exposure in describing shapes for Content-based Image Retrieval (CBIR). Many of the existing Ridgelet transforms are only applied on images of size $M{\times}M$. For $M{\times}N$ sized images, they need to be segmented into $M{\times}M$ sub-images prior to processing. A different number of orientations and cut-off points for the Radon transform parameters also need to be utilized according to the image size. This paper presents a new shape descriptor for CBIR based on Ridgelet transform which is able to handle images of various sizes. The utilization of the ellipse template for better image coverage and the normalization of the Ridgelet transform are introduced. For better retrieval, a template-option scheme is also introduced. Retrieval effectiveness obtained by the proposed method has shown to be higher compared to several previous descriptors.

Keywords: Multi-resolution, Ridgelet transform, Content-based Image Retrieval, Shape descriptor.

1 Introduction

Image retrieval has come a long way where it started off with text-based retrieval in the 1960's. Based on this concept, indexed keywords are used to retrieve image files. However, there are many problems associated with retrieving images based on text such as manual image annotations, differences in perceptions and interpretations, and language barriers where image annotations are usually presented in one language. Due to these reasons, researchers came up with CBIR where images are retrieved based on the information extracted from the content of the image instead of using image annotations or keywords.

One of the important components in a CBIR system is the feature extraction where significant information about the images are extracted based on low-level features (human vision related), middle-level features (objects related), or high-level features

A. Jaafar et al. (Eds.): AIRS 2014, LNCS 8870, pp. 112–123, 2014.

(semantic related). Some approaches have been carried out to bridge the semantic gap in CBIR such as involving human feedbacks, auto-annotation of images, and utilization of semantic templates and ontologies [1]. Most of these approaches are generally being paired with low-level features in order to retrieve more precise and relevant images. Thus, there is still a need of color, shape, texture, and spatial relationship image representations that are able to assist in bridging the semantic gap and retrieve the most relevant images required by a user.

Among these low-level features, shape is considered as one of the most important visual features used to describe the image content. This is because humans are likely to distinguish scenes as a composition of individual objects and these individual objects are indeed usually identified by their shape. There are many applications that rely on shape information like applications for trademarks or logos [2], shape classification [3], and medical imaging [4].

It has been observed that shapes can be well described through multiple resolutions representation [5]. Multi-resolution image analysis is an important aspect as it offers a hierarchical structure of image interpretation [6]. Therefore, this concept provides a richer and more in-depth description of the image at different scales, which lead to an improved accuracy in image analysis.

Ridgelet transform (RT) is one of the shape descriptors with multi-resolution property. However, many of the existing RTs mentioned in the literature are only applied to images of size $M \times M$ or the $M \times N$ images will need to be made $M \times M$ or segmented into several congruent blocks with fixed side-length ($M \times M$ sub-images) in order to process them (note that M and N represents the width and height of an image, respectively). The number of projection orientations and number of samples on each projection are also too little or too many which will either give us coarse representation or an increase in the computation time and complexity. The value for the projection parameters also varies according to the image size, which contributes to computational complexity. Therefore, the existing approaches put a huge limitation in describing shapes, as they are not flexible for images of various sizes. Another weakness of the existing RT is that they are usually defined on square images. According to Chen et al. [7], RT defined on square images is not suitable for extracting rotation-invariant features. Therefore, rotation-invariant RT defined on a circular disc containing the texture and pattern is proposed, instead of implementing the RT on a square template which is usually used by other researchers in the field. However, in order to achieve rotation-invariant RT which can suitably accommodate $M \times N$ images, using circular disc is not suitable either.

Therefore, this work aims to tackle the above-mentioned issues by introducing a shape descriptor based on RT that can handle images of various sizes. The invariant to rotation, scaling, and translation shape descriptor can then be applied in image retrieval applications. The proposed method will be tested on few different objective performance measurements to prove the stability of the method. The outline of this paper is as follows. Section 2 explains the related work followed by the explanation on the proposed Normalized Ridgelet-Fourier descriptor in Section 3. The extended version of the proposed Normalized Ridgelet-Fourier descriptor on the other hand is described in Section 4. Section 5 explains the framework for evaluation and analysis of results. Finally, the conclusion is presented in Section 6.

2   Related Work

One of the earliest shape descriptors with multi-resolution property is the discrete wavelet transform where it is based on the concept of multi-resolution analysis. Some of the previous works on wavelet descriptors in CBIR field can be found in the following references [8]. Shape descriptors based on wavelet transform are widely popular due to their many advantages such as they allow the coarse and fine details in a signal to be separated including discontinuities and sharp spikes while at the same time preserving the structure of the data. Despite having all these good traits, wavelets are not invariant to translation. In addition, wavelets are good at detecting and representing point singularities but not for line singularities (as in the case of 2D images) or more complex geometries which are usually present in an image. Separable wavelets can only capture limited directional information. Direction is an important factor as it allows for the transformation method to compute the discontinuities of images such as edges and contours more effectively with a fewer number of coefficients. These limitations of the multi-resolution wavelets in describing shapes indicate that more powerful representations are needed.

There are other multi-resolution representations that can capture the smoothness of edges as well as having good direction factor, which the traditional wavelet fails to capture such as Curvelet [9], Ridgelet [10], and Contourlet [11]. Of all these transforms, the factor of direction is said to be the most obvious in Ridgelet [12]. RT is introduced to deal effectively with line singularities for 2D instead of point singularities as in the case of wavelet. RT can be described as the application of 1D wavelet to the Radon slices of an image. The implementation of the RT helps to handle the line singularities directly present in the image and map them to point singularities. This will then allow the 1D wavelet transform to handle the converted line-to-point singularities in the Radon domain, which a wavelet is best at. Therefore, the RT combines advantages from both transforms that is the ability to detect lines from the Radon transform, and the ability of wavelet in handling point singularities as well as the multi-resolution property to analyze data at several levels of detail.

According to Candès and Donoho [10], the bivariate Ridgelet $\psi_{a,b,\theta} : R^2 \to R$ can be defined as:

$$\psi_{a,b,\theta} = a^{-1/2} \psi((x_1 \cos\theta + x_2 \sin\theta - b)/a), \tag{1}$$

Where $a > 0$ is the scaling parameter, $\theta \in [0, 2\pi)$ is the orientation parameters, $b \in R$ is the translation parameter, and $\psi(.)$ is a wavelet function. This function is constant along the lines $x_1 \cos\theta + x_2 \sin\theta$. Transverse to these ridges is a wavelet. Given an integrable bivariate image $f(x_1, x_2)$, its Ridgelet coefficients can be defined as:

$$R(a,b,\theta) = \int \psi_{a,b,\theta} f(x_1, x_2) dx_1 dx_2 \tag{2}$$

Equation (2) can be deduced into an application of 1D wavelet transform to the projections of the Radon transform where the Radon transform is denoted as:

$$RaT(\theta,t) = \int f(x_1,x_2)\delta(x_1\cos\theta + x_2\sin\theta - t)dx_1dx_2, \qquad (3)$$

where δ is the Dirac's delta function. Based on the formulations above, RT can be concluded as the application of a 1D wavelet transform to the slices of the Radon transform where the angular variable θ is constant and t is varying:

$$R(a,b,\theta) = \int \psi_{a,b}(t)RaT(\theta,t)dt \qquad (4)$$

RT has successfully been utilized for many applications such as for image authentication, pattern recognition and classification, image representation, and image denoising [7].

3   Normalized Ridgelet-Fourier Descriptor (NRF)

This research is an extension and improvement to the work done in [7] where the extended descriptor will now results in a rotation, scaling, and translation invariant RT for images of various sizes.

First of all, the   images will be made translation and scaling invariant. The translation invariant can be achieved by moving the centroid of the shape to the centre of the image through regular moments. Regular moments m_{pq} are defined as:

$$m_{pq} = \sum_{x=0}^{M-1}\sum_{y=0}^{N-1} x^p y^q f(x,y), \qquad (5)$$

where M and N represents the number of columns and rows, respectively while p and q represents the respective order moments. Initially, the m_{01}, m_{10}, and m_{00} are calculated using Equation (5) above. The value obtained for the respective regular moments will then be plugged into Equation (6) to obtain the centroid location, $\bar{x}$ and $\bar{y}$:

$$\bar{x} = \frac{m_{10}}{m_{00}}, \qquad \bar{y} = \frac{m_{01}}{m_{00}} \qquad (6)$$

By obtaining the centroid location $(\bar{x},\bar{y})$ using the equations above, the scaling invariant of an image can then be achieved using the following Equation (7):

$$a = \max\nolimits_{f(x,y)\neq 0} \sqrt{(x-\bar{x})^2 + (y-\bar{y})^2}, \qquad (7)$$

where a is the longest distance from the centroid location $(\bar{x},\bar{y})$ to a point (x,y) of the shape. Based on the values obtained from Equation (6) and Equation (7), the images can be normalized to be scaling and translation invariant through the representation $f\left(\dfrac{x}{a}+\overline{x}, \dfrac{y}{a}+\overline{y}\right)$, with $(\overline{x}, \overline{y})$ being the centroid of $f(x,y)$ and a as the suitable scaling factor.

Next, the pixels of the translation and scaling invariant image that fall outside of the ellipse template centered at $(M/2, N/2)$ will be ignored. An illustration of an ellipse template on an image can be found in Fig. 1.

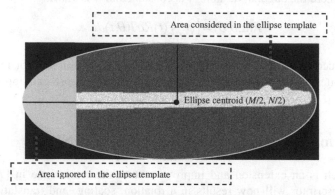

Fig. 1. Illustration of an ellipse template on an image

The Radon transform is then performed on the elliptical shape of the translation and scaling invariant images by summing the intensity values along the chosen radial line with the respective orientation. When discussing the Radon transform, there are two important parameters that need to be determined for this process where one is the theta (θ) and the other parameter is the rho (ρ). In order to make the framework suitable for $M \times N$ images, a solution for the θ is needed in such a way that it will no longer be a tedious process for $M \times N$ and the ρ will have to be in the form of 2^n to put up for $M \times N$ images and 1D discrete wavelet transform. Therefore, the Radon transform is computed using 128 points for both θ and ρ. In order to ease the calculation, the same number of θ and ρ is selected. More explanation on the ellipse template setting and the Radon transform normalization can be found in [13].

After performing the normalized Radon transform, the next step is to apply the 1D Daubechies-4 wavelet transform (Db4) on the normalized Radon transform coefficients where the angular variable is constant and the radial variable is varying to obtain the Ridgelet coefficients. Db4 is found to be one of the best to be used for shape representation [14]. Due to this reason, Db4 is utilized as the wavelet basis for the proposed shape descriptor. The 1D discrete wavelet transform is implemented up to four sub-bands with the total coefficients of 64, 32, 16, and 8 for each sub-band respectively. However, only sub-band 3 (16 coefficients) and sub-band 4 (8 coefficients) of the wavelet decomposition levels will be considered for the following steps. As mentioned in [7], the intermediate scale wavelet coefficients are usually preferred as the high frequency wavelet decomposition levels are very sensitive to noise and accumulation errors while the low frequency wavelet decomposition levels have lost important information of the original image. Therefore, the intermediate sub-band 3 and sub-band 4 are chosen for further computations.

In order to make the descriptor invariant to rotation, the 1D discrete Fourier transform is performed along the angular direction on the sub-band 3 and sub-band 4 of the wavelet decomposition levels. For simplicity, only 15 Fourier magnitude spectrums of each of the mentioned wavelet decomposition levels are captured to represent the shape. This makes the total coefficients for each image using the proposed NRF is 360, which is still a reasonable size for shape representation.

4   Extended Normalized Ridgelet-Fourier Descriptor (ENRF)

As mentioned in Section 2, one of the steps involved in the proposed NRF is to ignore the pixels of the translation and scaling invariant image that fall outside of the ellipse template centered at $(M/2, N/2)$. The Radon transform is then performed on the elliptical shape of the image. One of the main problems in utilizing an ellipse template is that it may not perform that well for images with object that is located too near towards the edge of the image area or when the object fully fills the image area. Some examples are shown in Fig. 2.

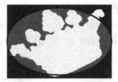 

Fig. 2. Example of shapes that are not fully covered by an ellipse template

In both of these cases, big portions of the shapes and patterns are not considered in the ellipse template compared to using the square template where the whole area of the image is being considered in the computation. This will definitely provide a better representation. However, most images are not in such nature and usually the shapes or patterns are located at the centre of the image area because the centre of the image area is known as the centre of attention. Furthermore, not many objects fully filled the entire image area. However, if all of the images are to be computed based on the Ridgelet method using only square template, this will cause unnecessary computations and hence, increasing the computation time and complexity. These findings have inspired the extension of the NRF to ENRF through the introduction of a template-option scheme. In this scheme, after the calculation using the ellipse template setting, the percentages of pixels that fall outside of the ellipse area are identified. A square template will be used if the percentage of pixels of the translation and scaling invariant image that fall outside of the ellipse area is more than the threshold value. Otherwise, the ellipse template will be utilized.

Based on a conducted empirical study, the most effective threshold value for this work is 4.3. This is calculated using the median approach which is widely used and known for computing threshold. Since the median approach is able to provide a sufficient result for this work, other approaches are not tested in obtaining the threshold value. However, more advanced approaches in determining the threshold value found in the following reference can also be considered [15].

5   Evaluation and Analysis of Results

In this section, the retrieval performance of the proposed NRF and ENRF are compared and tested. A series of experiments are conducted on an Intel Pentium Dual-Core 2.5 GHz desktop. The experiments are performed on the standard MPEG-7 CE-1 B dataset [16], which is usually used to test the overall robustness of the shape representations towards rotation, scaling, and translation invariant as well as similarity retrieval. It consists of 1400 shapes of 70 groups. There are 20 similar shapes in each group, which provide the ground truth. For the experiments, 50 classes from this dataset are considered which brings us to a total of 1000 images.

In order to show the robustness and stability of the proposed descriptors, the comparison and evaluation are done based on five different retrieval measurements which are the average 11 standard precision-recall [17], Average Retrieval Rate (ARR) [18], Average Normalized Modified Retrieval Rank (ANMRR) [18], average r-measure, and average p_1-measure [19].

To benchmark the retrieval performance, the result of the proposed NRF and the proposed ENRF are compared to that of Ridgelet-Fourier (RF) method [7] and the basic Ridgelet (R) descriptor. The parameters setting for each of the respective methods are shown in Table 1.

Table 1. Summary of the settings used by the four methods involved in the evaluation

Subject	Ridgelet Descriptor (R)	Ridgelet-Fourier (RF)	Normalized RF (NRF)	Extended NRF (ENRF)
Radon Transform Setting	θ : 128 ρ : 128	θ : π/M ρ : 64 where M is the shortest length of the image dimension	θ : 128 ρ : 128	θ : 128 ρ : 128
Template Setting	Square	Circle	Ellipse	Template Option: If Pixels_Outer_Ellipse>= threshold: Square template. Else : maintain Ellipse template
Rotation Invariant	Tensor Theory	1D Fourier transform	1D Fourier transform	1D Fourier transform
Total Coefficients	3072coefficients	180 coefficients	360 coefficients	360 coefficients

A total of three images from each image class are randomly selected as queries and retrievals are carried out. Overall, there will be up to 150 query images selected for the whole retrieval experiments. The Query-by Example (QBE) paradigm is employed. In QBE, the respective descriptor values are extracted from a query image and then matched to the corresponding descriptor values of images contained in the database. The distance (or dissimilarity) between two shapes is calculated using the L_1-norm distance metric.

A screen capture of the retrieval result according to the respective proposed methods and the benchmark methods can be found in Fig. 3. Given 'Comma-15.gif' as
the image query, it can be observed that the proposed ENRF has able to provide the
best result compared to the other methods by retrieving the correct similar images at
higher rank. The second best result is shown by the proposed NRF, followed by the
basic Ridgelet descriptor and lastly the Ridgelet-Fourier descriptor.

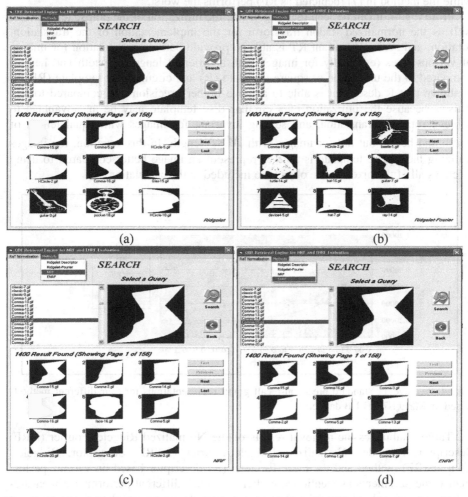

(a)   (b)

(c)   (d)

Fig. 3. Retrieval result based on (a) Ridgelet descriptor, (b) Ridgelet-Fourier descriptor,
(c) Normalized Ridgelet-Fourier descriptor, and (d) Extended Normalized Ridgelet-Fourier
descriptor

Fig. 4 shows the graph of the average 11 standard precision-recall of 150 queries
for MPEG-7 CE-1 B dataset for the proposed and comparable methods. The x-axis
of the graph represents the 11 standard recall levels while the y-axis represents the
average precision values at the 11 standard recall levels. From this figure, it can be
observed that the introduction of a template-option scheme which allows the method

to choose the suitable template between the square and ellipse for optimization purposes has further improved the precision rate to 61.36% compared to the NRF with only the ellipse template which obtains 57.24%. The proposed ENRF is not only able to obtain higher overall precision rate but it has also achieved higher precision rate at most of the 11 standard recall levels. The proposed NRF on the other hand comes in second followed by the basic Ridgelet descriptor (depicted as R) in the third place while the method in [7] (depicted as RF) performs the worst.

From Fig. 4, it can be seen that in general, the utilization of the ellipse template as well as the normalized Radon transform for the implementation of the translation, rotation, and scaling invariant RT is able to provide better representation for images of various sizes (especially for images with a different length of width and height) compared to the utilization of square template (R) and circular disc template (RF). It is shown that R descriptor is able to achieve higher precision rate compared to RF. This is because the utilization of a circular disc template may be an advantage to achieve rotation, translation, and scaling invariant for images with equal length of width and height but not for images with $M \times N$ length. In this situation, the images utilizing the square template is able to represent an image better compared to using circle as all of the pixels in the object are included in the calculation.

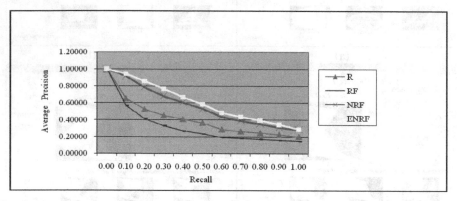

Fig. 4. Average 11 standard precision-recall graph representations for four different methods based on MPEG-7 CE-1 B dataset

Table 2 tabulates the retrieval results of the Normalized Ridgelet-Fourier (NRF) descriptor, Extended Normalized Ridgelet-Fourier (ENRF) descriptor, Ridgelet-Fourier (RF) method and the basic Ridgelet (R) descriptor based on various performance measurements as mentioned earlier. For each different performance measurement, the retrieval values of the method achieving better results than the rest are put in bold. From Table 2, we can see that the ENRF clearly outperforms the other methods in terms of all the performance measurements used. As we are aware, different evaluation criteria may have different priority e.g. precision-recall only focus on retrieving the relevant images without focusing on the retrieval rank, ARR focuses on retrieval rank but just the top retrieval, etc. So it is important to measure the performance of a method using various performance measurements to prove the stability.

The proposed ENRF and the proposed NRF are indeed stable methods as it has been shown that the proposed descriptors not only are able to retrieve most (if not all) of the correct images but it is also able to retrieve them at a much better (higher) rank compared to the RF method and basic Ridgelet descriptor.

Table 2. Retrieval results based on various performance measurements

Performance Measurement	Ridgelet Descriptor (R)	Ridgelet-Fourier (RF)	Normalized Ridgelet-Fourier (NRF)	Extended Normalized Ridgelet-Fourier (ENRF)
Average Precision-Recall (higher value is better)	0.42030	0.33291	0.57241	**0.6136**
ARR (higher value is better)	0.39133	0.33667	0.50533	**0.51933**
ANMRR (lower value is better)	0.65882	0.71723	0.53985	**0.50750**
r-measure (lower value is better)	1174	1261	389	**369**
Average r-measure (lower value is better)	7.82667	8.40667	2.59333	**2.46000**
p_1-measure (higher value is better)	28.45768	22.05528	42.19342	**42.53978**
Average p_1-measure (higher value is better)	0.18972	0.14704	0.28129	**0.28360**

A statistical comparison based on the two-tailed paired t-test has also been conducted to show the significant difference between the proposed NRF and ENRF with the comparable methods [20]. Let $Y_e, e \in \{\{R\}, \{RF\}, \{NRF\}, \{ENRF\}\}$ be the mean average precisions (retrieval accuracies) for each method. The null hypothesisis $H_0 : Y_e > 0.05$ and the alternative hypothesis is $H_1 : Y_e < 0.05$. The larger t-values is the more likely that the difference is significant. The statistical test result is as shown in Table 3 below. From the results, we can see that the proposed NRF and the proposed ENRF show a statistically significant improvement in retrieval performance when compared to the RF method and basic Ridgelet descriptor.

Table 3. Paired t-test at a significance level of 0.05. p-values less than 0.05 indicate significantly different results

Method	t-value	p-value	Null Hypothesis (H_0)	Remark
R vs. NRF	7.1407	1.6426E-10	Reject	NRF > R
RF vs. NRF	8.9436	2.3696E-14	Reject	NRF > RF
R vs. ENRF	8.9682	2.0959E-14	Reject	ENRF > R
RF vs. ENRF	10.4583	1.2280E-17	Reject	ENRF > RF
NRF vs. ENRF	6.2259	1.1922E-08	Reject	ENRF > NRF

Generally, the proposed shape descriptors are suitable for just any kind of shapes, especially those images where lines are relevant features. Examples of applications that these methods could contributed to are like trademarks and logos, building structures, paper defects, and nuts and bolts (car spare parts).

6   Conclusion

In this paper, two new invariant shape descriptors for images of various size based on the RT are proposed. The proposed Normalized Ridgelet-Fourier and the proposed Extended Normalized Ridgelet-Fourier have improved the common RT methods which usually relied on images that will need to be pre-segmented into several congruent blocks with a fixed length of $M \times M$. The proposed approaches have definitely overcome the huge limitation of most existing methods, as most of the images nowadays do not only come in one size.

The proposed methods are compared to that of Ridgelet-Fourier descriptor [7] and with the basic RT in terms of few performance measurements, namely average 11 standard precision-recall, ARR, ANMRR, average r-measure, average p_1-measure, and two-tailed paired t-test statistical method. Results indicate that the proposed methods have successfully achieved significant better results for all mentioned performance measurements compared to the other two previous methods, which indeed proves their superiority.

We believed that out methods are efficient and could support much larger scale of retrieval. However, the computation time and the scalability of the methods should be proven by conducting a proper testing in future.

References

1. Hare, J.S., Sinclair, P.A.S., Lewis, P.H., Martinez, K., Enser, P.G.B., Sandom, C.J.: Bridging the Semantic Gap in Multimedia Information Retrieval: Top-down and Bottom-up Approaches. In: 3rd Annual European Semantic Web Conference (2006)
2. Belongie, S., Malik, J., Puzicha, J.: Shape Matching and Object Recognition using Shape Contexts. IEEE Transactions on Pattern Analysis and Machine Intelligence 24(4), 509–522 (2002)
3. Wang, X., Feng, B., Bai, X., Liu, W., Latecki, L.J.: Bag of Contour Fragments for Robust Shape Classification. Pattern Recognition 47(6), 2116–2125 (2014)
4. Arslan, S., Ozyurek, E., Gunduz-Demir, C.: A Color and Shape-based Algorithm for Segmentation of White Blood Cells in Peripheral Blood and Bone Marrow Images. Cytometry Part A (2014)
5. Costa, L.D.F.D., Cesar Jr., R.M.: Shape Analysis and Classification: Theory and Practice. CRC Press LLC, Boca Raton (2001)
6. Koenderink, J.J.: The Structure of Images. Biological Cybernetics 50(5), 363–370 (1984)
7. Chen, G.Y., Bui, T.D., Krzyżak, A.: Rotation Invariant Feature Extraction using Ridgelet and Fourier Transforms. Pattern Analysis and Applications 9(1), 83–93 (2006)
8. Wang, X.R., Yang, Y.F.: Medical Image Retrieval based on Simplified Multi-Wavelet Transform and Shape Feature. Applied Mechanics and Materials 513, 2871–2875 (2014)
9. Candès, E.J., Donoho, D.L.: Curvelets - A Surprisingly Effective Non-adaptive Representation for Objects with Edges. In: Rabut, C., Cohen, A., Schumaker, L.L. (eds.) Curves and Surfaces, pp. 105–120. Vanderbilt University Press, Nashville (2000)
10. Candès, E.J., Donoho, D.L.: Ridgelets: A Key to Higher-dimensional Intermittency? Philosophical Transactions of the Royal Society of London. Series A: Mathematical, Physical and Engineering Sciences 357(1760), 2495–2509 (1999)

11. Do, M.N., Vetterli, M.: The Contourlet Transform: An Efficient Directional Multi-resolution Image Representation. IEEE Transactions on Image Processing 14(12), 2091–2106 (2005)
12. Huang, K., Aviyente, S.: Rotation Invariant Texture Classification with Ridgelet Transform and Fourier Transform. In: 2006 IEEE International Conference on Image Processing, pp. 2141–2144 (2006)
13. Mas Rina, M., Fatimah, A., Ramlan, M., Shyamala, C.D.: Generalized Ridgelet Fourier for M×N Images: Determining the Normalization Criteria. In: Ming, L.S. (ed.) IEEE International Conference on Signal and Image Processing Applications (ICSIPA), Kuala Lumpur, Malaysia, pp. 380–384. IEEE (2009)
14. Zhu, L.Q., Zhang, S.Y.: Multimodal Biometric Identification System based on Finger Geometry, Knuckle Print, and Palm Print. Pattern Recognition Letters 31(12), 1641–1649 (2010)
15. Mitchell, H.B.: Image Fusion: Theories, Techniques, and Applications. Springer, Heidelberg (2010)
16. Latecki, L.J., Lakamper, R., Eckhardt, T.: Shape Descriptors for nNon-rigid Shapes with a Single Closed Contour. In: IEEE Conference on Computer Vision and Pattern Recognition, pp. 424–429. IEEE (2000)
17. Salton, G., McGill, M.J.: Introduction to Modern Information Retrieval. McGraw-Hill, New York (1983)
18. Manjunath, B.S., Ohm, J.R., Vasudevan, V.V., Yamada, A.: Color and Texture Descriptors. IEEE Transactions on Circuits and Systems for Video Technology 11(6), 703–715 (2001)
19. Park, J., An, Y., Jeong, I., Kang, G., Pankoo, K.: Image Indexing using Spatial Multi-resolution Color Correlogram. In: IEEE International Workshop on Imaging Systems and Techniques, pp. 1–4. IEEE (2007)
20. Mann, P.S.: Introductory Statistics, 7th edn. John Wiley & Sons, Hoboken (2010)

Characteristics Classification of Durian Varieties Images for Knowledge Representation by Using Conceptual Graph

Nur Syafikah Ibrahim, Zainab Abu Bakar, and Nurazzah Abd Rahman

Department of Computer Science
Faculty of Computer and Mathematical Science,
Universiti Teknologi MARA, Shah Alam, Selangor, Malaysia
nsh.ibrahim89@gmail.com, {zainab,nurazzah}@tmsk.uitm.edu.my

Abstract. The importance and interest in agriculture field nowadays contributed to the rapid increasing of the deluge fruits images, for instance; durian images. With hundreds of durian varieties, it will be a challenging task to differentiate the images of this crop. Furthermore, with the existing of semantic gap, the current search engine unable to retrieve only the relevant varieties images to the user. Hence, applying semantic technology became the crucial thing in order to bridge the semantic gap. Thus, this paper will discuss about the durian varieties and its characteristics in order to differentiate and determine the images of a durian variety with other varieties. These characteristics then will be employed later in the Conceptual Graph to construct and semantically represent the knowledge regarding of durian varieties and its characteristics.

Keywords: Semantic Based Image Retrieval (SBIR), Knowledge Representation (KR), Conceptual Graph (CGs), Durian Varieties.

1   Introduction

In image retrieval field, there are three main approaches, which are Text Based Image Retrieval (TBIR), Content Based Image Retrieval (CBIR) and Semantic Based Image Retrieval (SBIR). According to [1], Text-Based Image Retrieval (TBIR) is a method to describe an image by using text related to the image. However, this approach faced with a problem which is difficult to specify the exact terms and phrases in describing the content of the image as the content is much richer than any set of keywords can express [2]. The second approach, Content-Based Image Retrieval (CBIR) is a technique which represents an image by extracting the low level features content of the image. The image would be indexed by its own visual content; color, texture and shapes. This type of approach also facing with limitation where the extracted contents always fail to meet the user perception. This is due to the low level features cannot describe the high level concept in user's mind [3]. The third approach, Semantic Based Image Retrieval (SBIR) or also referred to Concept Based Image Retrieval was firstly introduced in 2000s. This approach able to describe the image in an

A. Jaafar et al. (Eds.): AIRS 2014, LNCS 8870, pp. 124–135, 2014.

understandable way and promising ability to capture the conceptual thinking of human being.

The main limitation in the image retrieval field is the presenting of semantic gap, [4,5,6], the inconsistency of interpretation between natural language and programming language. Hence, applying semantic technology in SBIR is important in order to extract the cognitive concept of a human to map with the low level image features to the high level concept [3]. The word concept can be defined as an individual objects, classes or highly structured entities depending on the formalism used [7].

In SBIR, there is a technique called Knowledge Representation (KR) which is referring to the formalism of both syntax and semantic used to store knowledge in an architecture [8]. To represent the conceptual model of that knowledge, a formalism is needed. Conceptual Graph (CGs) is one of the KR formalism used in presenting the knowledge in a graph form.

The research in SBIR is conducted in various specific domains including inspiration [9], sports [10], medical [11], animal [12] and art [13]. However, in this paper the agriculture domain generally and durian domain specifically is chosen since the images of one variety with other varieties look almost the same and can be differentiated by specific characteristics. In this paper, the characteristics of durian varieties images will be discussed. These characteristics will act as the concepts to build and represent the knowledge by using the CGs formalism in the future work. 32 durian varieties that currently registered with the Department of Agriculture Malaysia (DOA) are chosen. By representing the knowledge using CGs, the specific characteristics of each variety could be determined.

2   Knowledge Representation (KR) and Conceptual Graph (CGs)

[14] defined KR as the scientific domain involve with the study of computational models which able to represent the knowledge explicitly by symbols and to process these symbols in order to produce new ones representing other pieces of knowledge. In the other word, KR is an association between related concepts which involve mathematical formulas or rules for natural language syntax to represent a simple facts or complex relationships. Conceptual graph, ontology, semantic networks, frame, description logics and fuzzy logic are the examples of "computer-friendly" formalism to represent the KR conceptual model [7].

Conceptual graph is a formalism of KR that was firstly introduced by Sowa in 1976 [15]. This CGs is considered as a bipartite graph and consists of two nodes; which are concept nodes and relation nodes. These two nodes are the most important components in the CGs vocabulary. The concept nodes represent the entities involved while the relation nodes represent the semantic role or the relationship for each concept in this graph. Nodes are labeled by types and a concept node with individual marker can be defined as a specific entity, otherwise it will call as unspecified entity [14]. Construction of the CGs for these durian varieties characteristics are based on these following steps:

(i)   Define the concepts – concepts which are denoting by nodes (rectangles shape represents the entities or objects of the durian description;

(ii) Define the relations – relations (denoting by ovals shape) represent the relationship between the concepts;

(iii) Define the signature – signature is an ordered list of the concept type which must be associated with the relation type;

(iv) Define the rules – determine how the concepts may be linked to the relations (representing the common sense knowledge); and

(v)   Define the individuals – an identifier which represents the specific entity.

Conceptual Graphs Graphical User Interface (CoGUI) was chosen as the tool for the construction of the CGs in this research. CoGUI is a graph-based visual tool for building CGs knowledge bases which offering data sharing and reasoning functions [16]. This tool allows a knowledge base (KB) to be created as well as edits and controls the structure and content of the created KB.

3   General Framework

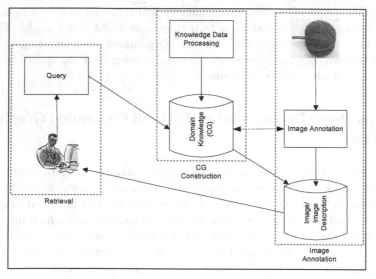

Fig. 1. General framework of the research

Fig. 1 above shows the general framework of the whole work. The processes can be explained as below:

(i)   CG construction -
      This process involves the construction of the CG to differentiate the durian varieties. The domain knowledge which is represented in CG form will be saved in COGXML format;

(ii) Image annotation -
    The durian image will be uploaded in the system. The annotation process will be done semi-automatically by selecting the suitable and relevant characteristics of that image from the dropdown menu. The listed characteristics are the concepts extracted from the CG. The system then will determine the variety of the durian image based on the image description by crossing check with the CG. The image and variety then will be saved in the database; and
(iii) Retrieval (query answering from the user) -
    User will submit a query. The query then will go through the CG to find the relevant variety. When the variety was determined, the system will search the durian images in the database. Finally, the relevance images will be retrieved to the user.

Although the propose work contains several processes, this paper will focus only on the first step, which will discuss the concepts of the chosen durian varieties domain in order to represent the knowledge in CG form.

4   Durian Varieties

Durian or botanically called as Durio Zibethinus L. is the king of the tropical fruits which is most popular among the Asians. In Malaysia, there are 197 varieties of durians that currently registered with the DOA [17,18]. These registered varieties are originally found in Malaysia and Thailand. However, all these varieties are currently planted and can be found in Malaysia. Durian variety is identified by a letter D followed with a unique numerical number. According to DOA, the first registered variety is D1 which is planted in Jalan Dusun Tua, Hulu Langat, Selangor [18].

Although currently there are many varieties were registered, but DOA recommends farmers to plant 10 varieties in a large scale due to their good performance. The performances are evaluated based on the fruit quality, fruit production, resistance ability of the disease and the ability towards the fruit retention [18]. The suggested varieties are D24, D99, D123, D145, D158, D159, D169, D188, D189 and D190. Table 1 shows the sample images of 32 durian varieties including the recommended 10 varieties.

5   Characterization Of Durian Varieties

There are some characteristics that can use to differentiate the durian varieties. DOA has briefly described the characteristics of the durian can be based on the fruits, aril (flesh), taste and spines (durian torn) [19] or based on fruits, aril and leaves [18]. Salma [17] described the durian based on the bark, bud, flower, fruits and seed. This paper will focus on the durian fruits images, so only fruit, spines and aril characteristics will be employed. Table 2 describes the fruit and spines characteristics while Table 3 describes the aril characteristics of durian observed from 32 durian varieties.

Table 1. Sample images of 32 durian varieties that currently registered in DOA

Varieties	Sample image	Varieties	Sample image	Varieties	Sample image
D2		D148		D190	
D7		D33		D197	
D140		D145		D98	
D141		D53		D99	
D142		D166		D123	
D143		D126		D159	
D8		D127		D169	
D24		D168		D158	
D29		D186		D6	
D109		D189		D149	
D113		D188			

Table 2. The fruit and spines characteristics observed from 32 durian varieties [17,18, 19,20]

Fruit		Spines			
Characteristic	Sub Characteristics	Characteristic	Sub Characteristics	Characteristic	Sub Characteristics
Length	Moderately long Long Short	Spines arrangement around the stalk	Soft spines Coarse spines Moderately coarse spines	Spines arrangement at the fruit base	Soft spines Coarse spines Spineless

Table 2. (*continued*)

Attribute	Value	Spines (locule)	Spines value	Color	Color value
Width	Moderately wide		Spineless		Small spines
	Wide		Joined		Short spines
Size	Medium		Short		Well spaced
	Large		Small base		Joined
	Small		Broad base		Disjoin
Shape	Ovoid		Moderately broad base		Clear base
	Round		Baseless		Small base
	Oblong	Spines type	Stouter than locule's spines		Broad base
	Flat	between the	Smaller than locule's		Baseless
		fruit locules	spines		
Upper	Round-pointed		Same as the locule's spines		Moderately broad base
side	Necked	Spines	Soft spines	Tip color	Brown
shape	Dent	shape at the	Coarse spines	Midst	Bonze green
	Pointed	fruit locule	Short spines	color	Yellowish-green
	Slightly flat		Moderately long spines		Greenish-brown
	Round		Long spines		Dark green
Bot-	Pointed		Small spines		Yellowish-brown
tom/base	Round		Medium-size spines		Brown
shape	Dent		Stout spines	Base	Bronze green
	Flat		Joined	color	Green
	Slightly dent		Wide base		Brownish-green
	Acuminate		Well spaced spines		Dark green
Fruit	"kop"		Ranges present		Greenish-brown
locules	Slightly "kop"		Small spines present be-		Yellowish-brown
shape			tween stout spines		
	No "kop" pre-	Spines	Straight		Brown
	sented	condition at			
The	Clear	the fruit	Attached		Greenish-yellow
clarify of	Quiet clear	locule	Concave		Yellowish-green
fruit	Unclear		Convex		
locules					
Stalk	Short		Slightly attached		
length	Moderately long		Detached		
	Long		Slightly concave		
Pericarp	Moderately thick		Slightly convex		
thickness	Thin		Soft spines present		
	Thick				

Table 3. The aril characteristics observed from 32 durian varieties [17,18, 19,20]

Aril					
Characteristic	Sub Characteristics	Characteristic	Sub Characteristics	Characteristic	Sub Characteristics
Color	Orange	Size	Medium	Firmness	Creamy
	Yellow		Large		Moderately firm
	Yellow-orange	Texture	Fine		Firm
	Pale yellow		Mild		Creamy and watery
	White		Rough		
	Yellowish white	Thickness	Thick		
	Pale orange		Moderately thick		
	Golden yellow				

6   Result and Discussion

To show the uniqueness of the discussed characteristics in Table 2 and Table 3, we tabulated the data of the 10 recommended durian varieties by DOA according to the fruit, aril and spines characteristics. For each characteristic, a variety may have none, one or more than one sub characteristics. Value 1 is given to the identified sub characteristics, else 0 value is given.

Table 4. The fruit characteristics of 10 recommended durian varieties

	Length		Width		Size		Shape			Upper side shape			Bottom/base shape				Fruit locules shape				The clarify of fruit locules			Stalk length			Pericarp thickness		
	Moderately long	Long	Moderately wide	Wide	Medium	Large	Ovoid	Round	Round-pointed	Dent	Pointed	Slightly flat	Pointed	Round	Dent	Flat	Slightly dent	"kop"	Slightly "kop"	No "kop" presented	Clear	Quiet clear	Unclear	Short	Moderately long	Long	Moderately thick	Thin	Thick
D24	1	0	1	0	1	0	0	1	1	0	0	0	0	1	0	0	0	0	0	1	0	1	0	0	1	0	1	0	0
D99	1	0	1	0	1	0	0	1	0	1	0	0	0	0	1	0	0	1	0	0	1	0	0	1	0	0	0	1	0
D123	1	0	1	0	0	1	1	0	0	0	1	0	1	0	0	0	0	1	0	0	1	0	0	0	0	1	1	0	0
D145	1	0	1	0	1	0	0	1	0	0	0	1	0	0	0	1	0	0	0	1	0	0	1	0	1	0	0	1	0
D158	1	0	1	0	1	0	1	0	0	0	0	1	0	0	0	0	1	1	0	0	1	0	0	0	0	1	0	1	0
D159	0	1	0	1	0	1	1	0	0	1	0	0	1	0	0	0	0	1	0	0	0	0	1	0	1	0	0	0	1
D169	1	0	1	0	1	0	1	0	0	0	0	1	0	1	0	0	0	0	1	0	0	1	0	0	1	0	1	0	0
D188	0	0	0	0	1	0	1	0	0	0	1	0	0	0	1	0	0	0	1	0	0	1	0	0	0	0	0	0	1
D189	1	0	1	0	1	0	1	0	0	1	0	0	0	0	1	0	0	0	1	0	0	1	0	0	1	0	0	1	0
D190	0	0	0	0	1	0	1	0	0	0	0	1	0	0	0	0	1	1	0	0	1	0	0	0	0	0	0	0	1
Total	7	1	7	1	8	2	7	3	1	3	3	3	3	1	3	1	2	5	3	2	3	5	2	1	5	2	3	4	3

Table 5. The spines characteristics of 10 recommended durian varieties

	Tip color	Midst color					Base color					Arrangement around the stalk			Arrangement at the fruit base							Shape at the fruit locule					Type between the fruit locules				Condition at the fruit locule						
	Brown	Bonze green	Yellowish-green	Greenish-brown	Dark green	Bronze green	Green	Brownish-green	Dark green	Greenish-brown	Yellowish-green	Soft spines	Coarse spine	Joined	Short	Small base	Soft spines	Coarse spines	Spineless	Short spines	Clear base	Soft spines	Coarse spines	Short spines	Moderately long spines	Long spines	Small spines present be-	Stouter than locule's spines	Smaller than locule's spines	Same as the locule's spines	Straight	Concave	Convex	Detached	Attached	Slightly concave	Slightly convex
D24	1	0	1	0	0	0	1	0	0	0	0	1	0	1	1	0	0	0	1	0	1	0	0	0	1	0	1	0	1	0	1	0	0	1	0	0	0
D99	1	0	0	1	0	0	0	1	0	0	0	0	1	1	0	0	1	0	0	1	0	1	0	1	0	1	0	0	0	1	0	0	1	0	0	1	0
D123	1	1	0	0	0	1	0	0	0	0	0	0	1	1	0	1	1	0	0	1	0	0	1	0	1	0	1	0	0	0	1	0	0	1	0	0	1
D145	1	0	0	0	1	0	0	0	1	0	0	0	1	0	0	0	1	0	0	0	0	1	0	0	0	0	1	0	0	1	0	0	1	0	0	1	1
D158	1	0	0	0	1	0	0	0	1	0	0	1	0	1	0	0	1	0	0	1	0	0	1	0	0	1	0	1	0	1	0	0	0	0	1	0	0
D159	1	0	0	1	0	0	0	0	0	1	0	1	0	1	0	0	1	0	0	1	0	0	1	0	0	1	1	0	0	0	1	0	0	0	0	1	1
D169	1	0	1	0	0	0	1	0	0	0	0	0	0	0	0	1	0	0	1	0	0	1	0	0	1	0	1	0	1	0	0	0	1	0	0	1	0
D188	0	0	0	0	0	0	0	0	0	0	1	0	0	0	0	0	0	0	0	0	0	0	0	0	0	0	0	0	0	0	0	0	0	0	1	0	0
D189	1	0	1	0	0	0	1	0	0	0	0	1	1	1	0	0	1	0	0	1	0	0	1	0	0	1	0	0	1	0	1	0	0	1	0	0	0
D190	0	0	0	0	0	0	0	0	0	1	0	0	0	0	0	0	0	0	0	0	0	0	0	0	0	0	0	0	0	0	0	0	0	0	0	0	0
Total	8	1	3	2	2	1	3	1	2	1	2	4	4	6	1	1	6	1	1	6	1	1	6	2	3	3	1	4	3	1	3	4	1	3	5	2	1

Table 4, Table 5 and Table 6 shows the tabulated data of the 10 recommended varieties of the fruit, spines and aril characteristics. The varieties are evaluated by using 10 main fruit characteristics with 36 sub characteristics, 8 main spines characteristics with 65 sub characteristics and 8 main aril characteristics with 15 sub characteristics. The results show that each of the varieties representing a unique sequence of 0 and 1 for fruit and spines. However, two varieties (D24 and D145) are sharing the same sequence of 0 and 1 for aril characteristic.

The result also can be concluded that for the fruit characteristics, most of the recommended varieties have moderately long and moderately wide fruit (70% each); medium size (80%); ovoid shape (70%); dent, pointed and slightly flat upper side shape (30% each); pointed and dent base shape (20%); "Kop" locules shape (50%);

quiet clear fruit locules (50%); moderately long stalk (50%); and thin pericarp thickness (40%).

Meanwhile, for the spines characteristics, most of the recommended varieties have brown tip color (80%); yellowish-green spine midst color (30%); green base color (30%); joined spines arrangement around the stalk (60%); soft and short spines arrangement at the fruit base (60% each); coarse spines shape at the fruit locule (60%); stouter than locule's spines (40%); and attached spines at the fruit locule.

At the meantime, for the aril characteristics, most of the recommended varieties have yellow aril color (50%); large aril size (60%); fine texture (50%); creamy aril firmness (50%); and thick aril (60%).

Table 6. The aril characteristics of 10 recommended durian varieties

	Color				Size		Texture			Firmness			Thickness	
	Yellow	Yellow-orange	Pale yellow	Golden yellow	Medium	Large	Fine	Mild	Rough	Creamy	Mod-erately Firm	Firm	Thick	Mod-erately thick
D24	1	0	0	0	1	0	1	0	0	1	0	0	0	1
D99	1	0	0	0	1	0	0	1	0	1	0	0	0	1
D123	0	1	0	0	0	1	0	1	0	1	0	0	0	1
D145	1	0	0	0	1	0	1	0	0	1	0	0	0	1
D158	1	0	0	0	1	0	1	0	0	1	0	0	1	0
D159	0	0	1	0	0	1	1	0	0	0	1	0	1	0
D169	0	0	1	0	0	1	0	0	1	0	1	0	1	0
D188	1	0	0	0	0	1	1	0	0	0	0	1	1	0
D189	0	1	0	0	0	1	0	1	0	0	0	1	1	0
D190	0	0	0	1	0	1	0	1	0	0	0	1	1	0
Total	5	2	2	1	4	6	5	4	1	5	2	3	6	4

Table 7. Characteristics tabulation result of 10 durian varieties in 0 and 1 representation

	Fruit	Spines	Aril
D24	1010100110000100001010010100	10100010000101100010100010101001000	10001010010001
D99	1010100101000010010010100100010	100100010000110010010101000100100 1000	10001001010001
D123	1010011000101000010010000 1100	11000100000011011001001010001001 00100	01000101010001
D145	1010100100010001000100101 0010	1000100010001000010000100100100110	10001010010001
D158	101010100001000011001000 01010	10001000100101000010010101000010100100	10001010010010
D159	010101100100100000100001010001	10010000010101001001001100010000010101	00100110001010
D169	1010101000101000001001001 0100	10100010000000010010010010101000100110	00100100101010
D188	0000101000100010001001000 00001	0000000001000000000000000000001000	10000110000110
D189	1010101001000010001001001 0010	101000100001110010010010010101001000000	01000101000110
D190	0000101000010000110001000 0001	0000000001000000000000000000000000	00010101000110

Table 7 indicates the summary of the characteristics tabulation result for 10 recommended varieties in 0 and 1 representation following the sub characteristics sequences in Table 4, Table 5 and Table 6. From the result, the fruit and spines characteristics of all 10 varieties have shown the uniqueness since the 0 and 1 representation for one variety is differ with other varieties. Hence, these characteristics alone are able to differentiate the varieties of durian. On the other hand, the aril alone cannot determine the durian variety since two of the varieties sharing the same aril characteristics. However, when all the three main characteristics are combined together, all the varieties show the unique 0 and 1 representation. From this result, observing the condition of the fruit, spines and aril characteristics are able to determine the durian variety.

Referable to the uniqueness of the discussed characteristics and sub characteristics in durian varieties differentiation make it relevant to be applied as the entity or concept types in CG. Fig. 2 shows the example of the concept types hierarchy and the graph representation of the concept types hierarchy for fruit characteristics in CoGUI interface.

To establish that the discussed characteristics are able to differentiate the durian varieties, a simple testing was done in CoGUI by providing a sample fruit characteristics query graph as indicated in Fig. 3. This query graph using the exact fruit data for variety D158 as tabulated in Table 4. 10 CG fact graphs which are representing 10 durian varieties recommended by DOA were constructed earlier by using data in Table 4, Table 5 and Table 6. The projection was expected to hit only on variety D158 fact graph. If the query graph projected to more than 1 fact graphs, it means that more than 1 varieties sharing the same fruit characteristics. As shown in Fig. 4, when the query was run by selecting all 10 fact graphs, only 1 projection was found which is hitting on D158 fact graph. This testing validate that the discussed characteristics are unique and able to differentiate the varieties of durian.

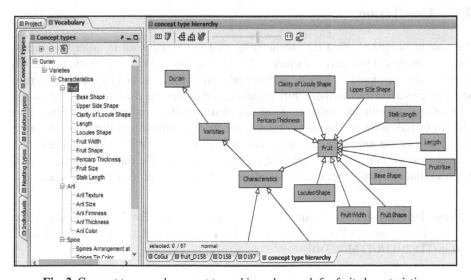

Fig. 2. Concept types and concept types hierarchy graph for fruit characteristics

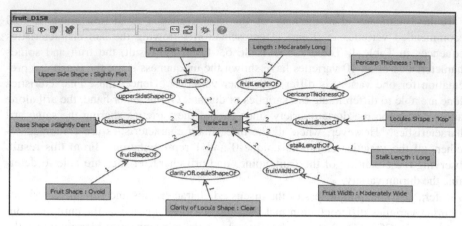

Fig. 3. Fruit characterisics query graph

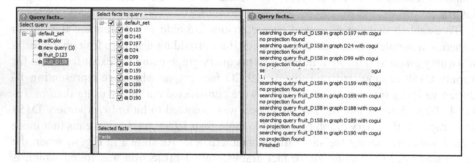

Fig. 4. The query facts projection result

7   Conclusion

This paper discussed about the characteristics of the durian fruit in order to differentiate the images of one durian variety with other varieties. From the study, the variety could be differentiated by looking at the condition of the fruit, aril and spines. Certain specific characteristics of these durian parts could determine the variety of the image. The testing authenticated that the discussed characteristics and sub characteristics are able to differentiate the durian varieties since the combination of these sub characteristics shown the unique binary representation of all the tested varieties. These characteristics are important to represent the knowledge of the durian varieties in CG form so that relevant images could be retrieved during the retrieval process later.

Acknowledgement. The research is sponsored by Malaysian Government and Universiti Teknologi MARA (UiTM) under the Large Rearch Grant Scheme (LRGS) LRGS/TD/2011/UITM/ICT/01.

References

1. Hernández-Gracidas, C.A., Sucar, L.E., Montes-y-Gómez, M.: Improving Image Retrieval by Using Spatial Relations. Multimedia Tools and Applications 62(2), 479–505 (2011)
2. Wang, H., Mohamad, D., Ismail, N.: Semantic Gap in Cbir: Automatic Objects Spatial Relationships Semantic Extraction and Representation. International Journal of Image... 4, 192–204 (2010)
3. Wang, H., Mohamad, D., Ismail, N.: Image Retrieval: Techniques, Challenge and Trend. In: Conference on Machine Vision, Image, pp. 718–720 (2009)
4. Qayyum, Z.U.: Image Retrieval Through Qualitative Representations Over Semantic Features. Multimedia Tools and Applications (2013)
5. Mylonas, P., Athanasiadis, T., Wallace, M., Avrithis, Y., Kollias, S.: Semantic Representation of Multimedia Content: Knowledge Representation and Semantic Indexing. Multimedia Tools and Applications 39(3), 293–327 (2007)
6. Hare, J.S., Lewis, P.H., Enser, P.G.B., Sandom, C.J.: Mind the Gap: Another Look at the Problem of the Semantic Gap in Image Retrieval, pp. 607309–607309 (2006)
7. Jakus, G., Milutinović, V., Omerović, S., Tomažič, S.: Concepts, Ontologies, and Knowledge Representation. Merrill 2000. Springer, New York (2013)
8. Definition of Knowledge Representation,
   http://ai.eecs.umich.edu/cogarch5/menu/props/kr
9. Fadzli, S.A., Setchi, R.: Semantic Approach to Image Retrieval Using Statistical Models Based on a Lexical Ontology, pp. 240–250 (2010)
10. Kong, H., Hwang, M., Kim, P.: The Study on the Semantic Image Retrieval based on the Personalized Ontology. International Journal of Information 12(2), 35–46 (2006)
11. Wei, W., Barnaghi, P.: Semantic Support for Medical Image Search and Retrieval. In: 2007: Proceedings of the 5th IASTED (2007)
12. Manzoor, U., Ejaz, N., Akhtar, N.: Ontology based Image Retrieval, pp. 288–293 (2012)
13. Jiang, S., Huang, T., Gao, W.: An Ontology-Based Approach to Retrieve Digitized Art Images. In: Proceedings of the 2004 IEEE/WIC/ACM, pp. 131–137 (2004)
14. Chein, M., Mugnier, M.: Graph-based Knowledge Representation. Advanced Information and Knowledge Processing (2009)
15. Van Harmelen, F., Lifschitz, V., Porter, B.: Handbook of Knowledge Representation, vol 1. Elsevier (2008)
16. CoGui - Cogui in a nutshell, http://www.lirmm.fr/cogui/nutshell.php
17. Idris, S.: Durio of Malaysia. Kuala Lumpur: Malaysian Agricultural Research and Development Institute, MARDI (2011)
18. Panduan pengesahan dan pencirian ketulenan anak pokok durian. Jabatan Pertanian Malaysia (2009)
19. Characteristics of Durian Varieties, Malaysia, Department of Agriculture (DOA), http://pvpbkkt.doa.gov.my/
20. Subhadrabandhu, S., Ketsa, S.: Durian King of Tropical Fruit. Daphne Brasell Associates Ltd, with Lincoln University Press and CABI Publishing (2001)

Integrating Semantic Term Relations into Information Retrieval Systems Based on Language Models

Mohannad ALMasri[1], KianLam Tan[1], Catherine Berrut[1],
Jean-Pierre Chevallet[2], and Philippe Mulhem[3]

[1] Université Joseph Fourier - Grenoble 1
{mohannad.almasri,kian-lam.tan,catherine.berrut}@imag.fr
[2] Université Pierre Mendès - Grenoble 2
jean-pierre.chevallet@imag.fr
[3] Centre National de la Recherche Scientifique
philippe.mulhem@imag.fr
LIG laboratory, MRIM group, Grenoble, France

Abstract. Most information retrieval systems rely on the strict equality of terms between document and query in order to retrieve relevant documents to a given query. The term mismatch problem appears when users and documents' authors use different terms to express the same meaning. Statistical translation models are proposed as an effective way to adapt language models in order to mitigate term mismatch problem by exploiting semantic relations between terms. However, translation probability estimation is shown as a crucial and a hard practice within statistical translation models. Therefore, we present an alternative approach to statistical translation models that formally incorporates semantic relations between indexing terms into language models. Experiments on different CLEF corpora from the medical domain show a statistically significant improvement over the ordinary language models, and mostly better than translation models in retrieval performance. The improvement is related to the rate of general terms and their distribution inside the queries.

1 Introduction

Classical retrieval models are primarily based on exact matching of terms between documents and queries, and are unable to capture relations between queries and documents terms. When users utilize different terms from those that are used in the index to express the same meaning, classical retrieval models suffer from term mismatch problem. Consequently, in order to overcome the term mismatch problem, we need a retrieval model that captures semantic relations between terms. Term relations are normally obtained from an external knowledge or resource[1]. The integration of term relations contributes to reduce the gap during the matching between a query representation and a document

---

[1] External knowledge with respect to queries and documents like thesaurus or ontology.

A. Jaafar et al. (Eds.): AIRS 2014, LNCS 8870, pp. 136–147, 2014.
© Springer International Publishing Switzerland 2014

index. Several types of semantic relations are identified between terms. We only focus on hierarchical relations or specific-generic relations.

Term specificity is a semantic property that can be applied to index terms: a term is more specific when its meaning is more detailed and precise. Term specificity may cause a mismatch when a user formulates her/his query using terms which are more general than those in the index. For instance, in the medical domain, the terms *"B-Cell"* and *"T-Cell"* are more specific than the term *"Lymphocyte"*. Moreover, *"B-Cell"* and *"T-Cell"* are types of *"Lymphocyte"* in the adaptive immune system. Therefore, when a user query contains the term *"Lymphocyte"*, then, a document talking about *"B-Cell"* or *"T-Cell"* is relevant to this query.

Term mismatch has been heavily studied in IR, and various approaches have been proposed to overcome it, generally through a pragmatic or an ad-hoc approach. However, a few of them have focused on formal integration of semantic term relations into retrieval models. Inside the family of language models for IR, the statistical translation models have been shown as an effective way to mitigate the term mismatch problem [3], [9], [20]. Statistical Translation models integrate semantic relations into language models to reduce the gap between documents and queries, but they require an estimation of the translation probabilities between words which is a crucial and hard point. We propose in this paper an alternative approach rather than statistical translation models to formally integrate semantic term relations into the framework of language models. Our approach propose to modify a document according to a given query and some knowledge about term relations. We then integrate the modified document into two smoothing methods from language models: Dirichlet and Jelinek-Mercer. In the rest of the paper, we refer by a term to an indexing term, which can be either: a word, a noun phrase, a n-gram, or a concept [5].

The paper is organized as follows: first, we present the term mismatch problem, and we discuss several approaches to solve this problem in Section 2 followed by our approach presented in Section 3. Our experimental set-up and the empirical results are presented in section 4; finally, section 5 concludes the paper and presents the future work.

2   Term Mismatch Problem

Several techniques have been proposed to tackle the term mismatch problem. Among these techniques: relevance feedback [11], [17], dimension reduction [2], [7,8], [10], [16], and integrating term similarity into retrieval models [3], [6], [9].

2.1   Relevance Feedback

Relevance feedback involves the user in the IR process in order to reformulate her/his query and to improve retrieval results. There are three types of relevance feedback: 1) explicit feedback, 2) implicit feedback and 3) pseudo or blind feedback [13]. Rocchio algorithm [17] is the classic algorithm for implementing explicit feedback which enables the user to select relevant documents in order to reformulate the original query. Query Reformulation is achieved by adding terms extracted from the selected documents into the original query.

Implicit feedback incorporates user behavior like clicks or the duration of time spent viewing a document, in order to predict relevant documents which are used to reformulate a user query. Blind feedback automates the manual part of the Rocchio algorithm without any consideration of the user interaction by assuming that the top k ranked documents are relevant. Lavrenko and Croft [11] propose a blind feedback approach to estimate a relevance model. The main problem in implicit and explicit feedback is that they may cause query drift[2] because not all documents in the feedback set may be relevant. Besides, documents in the feedback set, although containing relevant information, are sometimes partially related to the query topic.

2.2   Dimension Reduction

Dimension reduction is the process of reducing the chance that a query and a document use different terms for representing the same meaning. Among the techniques that are used for achieving this mission, we can mention: Stemming [10], [14], [16], Latent Semantic Indexing (LSI) [7], and Conceptual Indexing [2], [5], [12]. These techniques propose different strategies to reduce the chances that the query and the document refer to the same concept but using different terms.

Peng et al. [14] perform a stemming method according to the context of the query which helps to improve the accuracy and the performance of retrieval compared to the query independent stemmers such as Porter [16] and Krovetz [10]. Deerwester et al. [7] propose to solve the dimension reduction by representing queries and documents in a latent semantic space. In latent semantic space, each term is grouped with its similar terms. Similar terms in the space tend to be the terms that share the same context. The context is: a sentence, a paragraph, a window of successive words, etc..

Effectiveness of dimension reduction techniques essentially depend on the application domain and on the characteristics of the studied collection. Besides, dimension reduction may cause an oversimplification of the term space that may limit the expressiveness of the indexing language and could result in incorrect classification of unrelated terms [6].

2.3   Exploiting Term Similarity

We present, in this section, a class of retrieval models that attempt to solve the term mismatch problem by exploiting a partial or complete knowledge of term similarity. The use of term similarity enables to enhance classical retrieval by taking into account non-matching terms. We present two categories of models: Vector Space and Language Models.

---

[2] Query drift is the change in the query's topic to an unintended direction after query expansion.

Term Similarity in Vector Space Models. Crestani [6] proposes a general framework to exploit the term similarity into the matching process where $w_d(t)$ is the weight assigned to term t in the document d, and $w_q(t)$ is the weight assigned to term t in the query q, as shown below:

$$RSV(d,q) = \sum_{t \in q} w_d(t) \times w_q(t) \qquad (1)$$

In order to consider the non-matching terms from the query, Crestani exploits the term similarity by utilizing a similarity function Sim. If $t_i = t_j$, then $Sim(t_i, t_j) = 1$. If t_i and t_j are semantically related, then $0 < Sim(t_i, t_j) < 1$ and otherwise it is 0.

In fact, Crestani proposes to extend the previous RSV of Equation 1 in two ways. First, he extends the matching process, in case of mismatch: $t \in q$ and $t \notin d$ by determining the closest document term t^*, for which we have maximum value of similarity with the query term t. As a result, the extended RSV_{max} is defined:

$$RSV_{max}(d,q) = \sum_{t \in q} Sim(t, t^*) \times w_d(t^*) \times w_q(t) \qquad (2)$$

when $t = t^*$ then $Sim(t, t^*) = 1$, and we return back to the Equation 1.

Second, Crestani also extends RSV of Equation 1 by considering, not only the most similar term, but all the related terms from the document to a non-matched query term. As a result, the extended RSV_{tot} is:

$$RSV_{tot}(d,q) = \sum_{t \in q} [\sum_{t' \in d} Sim(t, t') \times w_d(t')] \times w_q(t) \qquad (3)$$

Crestani integrates term similarity into vector space model, which is an outdated model in information retrieval. We propose to integrate term similarity into language models which have been proven as very effective method for text retrieval [15], [21].

Term Similarity in Language Models. Statistical translation models are shown as an effective way to mitigate the term mismatch [3], [9], [20]. Statistical translation models incorporate semantic relations between terms into language models to reduce the gap between documents and queries. The idea is based on information theory where a translation model estimates the probability of translating a document to a user query according to the probability distribution $P(u|v)$, which gives the probability of translating a word v into a word u.

Statistical translation models [3], [9] are related to the second proposition of Crestani [6] where the idea is to consider the similarity between each query term and all document terms. The results obtained by statistical translation models show that integrating term similarity into language models is more effective than the existing approaches in information retrieval. However, Karimzadehgan and Zhai [9] noticed that the self-translation probabilities lead to non-optimal retrieval performance because it is possible that the value of $P(w|u)$ is higher than $P(w|w)$ for a word, w. In order to overcome this problem, Karimzadehgan and Zhai [9] defined a parameter to control the effect of the self-translation.

In a nutshell, we can remark that statistical translation models represent similarity between terms as a translation probability which may cause some problems: 1) the estimation of translation probabilities is not an easy practice, 2) the normalization of the mutual information is rather artificial and requires a parameter to control the effect of the self-translation, and 3) the regularization of the translation probabilities may look uncertain. Therefore, in the next section, we present an alternative approach that is based on a similarity measure between terms rather than translation probabilities. We believe that our approach is simpler and more efficient than statistical translation models.

3   Integrating Term Relations into Language Models

Referring to the different approaches which are presented in section 2, each approach has its strategy to reduce the potential gap that exists between queries and documents: Relevance feedback modifies the user query by adding some terms in order to shift it toward relevant documents. Dimension reduction represents documents and queries in a new space where the gap between queries and their relevant documents becomes smaller. Exploiting term similarity approaches integrate semantic relations between terms into retrieval models in order to reduce the gap between documents and queries.

We present, in this section, our approach that integrates semantic term relations into language models. Our approach modifies documents according to a given query and some knowledge about term relations. We then estimate the document language model according to the modified document in two smoothing methods of language models: Dirichlet and Jelinek-Mercer.

3.1   Query and Knowledge Dependent Document Model

Our aim is to reduce the gap between documents and queries by considering semantic relations between query and document terms. To do this, we propose to modify a document index according to the query and the external knowledge about term relations. Classical IR models compute the relevance value between a document d and a query q based on the coordination level, namely $d \cap q$. Instead of that, we here propose to compute the relevance value by considering also the *unmatched terms* of the query $t \in q \setminus d$, where $\setminus$ is the set difference operator. We therefore expand d by the query terms that are not in the document, but they are semantically related to at least one document term. In this way, we maximize the coordination level between the modified document and the query. As a result, we maximize the probability of retrieving relevant documents for a given query. We follow the first idea of Crestani presented in Equation2.

Fig. 1 illustrates how we expand d using the external knowledge, denoted by K, in order to maximize the coordination level between d and q. To put it more

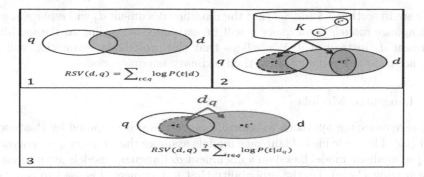

Fig. 1. Expand the document d using the knowledge K. We see that we expand d in order to maximize the coordination level between d and q.

formally, the modified document, denoted by d_q, is calculated as follows:

$$d_q = d \cup F(q \setminus d, K, d) \tag{4}$$

where $F(q \setminus d, K, d)$ is the transformation of $q \setminus d$ according to the knowledge K and the document d. The knowledge K provides a similarity function between terms $Sim(t, t')$ denoting the strength of the semantic similarity between the two terms t and t', see section 3.5. For each term in the query's unmatched terms $t \in q \setminus d$, we look for a document term t^* which is given by:

$$t^* = argmax_{t' \in d}Sim(t, t') \tag{5}$$

t^* is the most similar term of d for $t \in q \setminus d$. Then, the pseudo occurrences of a query term t in the modified document d_q rely on the occurrences of its most similar document term $\#(t^*; d)$, we define the pseudo occurrences of t as follows:

$$\#(t; d_q) = \#(t^*; d).Sim(t, t^*) \tag{6}$$

this pseudo occurrences of the term t are then included into the modified document d_q. Based on this definition, we now define the transformation function F which expands the document.

$$F(q \setminus d, K, d) = \{t | t \in q \setminus d, \exists t^* \in d, t^* = argmax_{t' \in d}Sim(t, t')\} \tag{7}$$

Not that, if t is not related to any document term, then we do not have a corresponding t^* for t. Then, the unmatched term $t \in q \setminus d$ will not expand d. Now, we replace the the transformation F with its value in the Equation 4 to obtain the modified document as follows:

$$d_q = d \cup \{t | t \in q \setminus d \wedge \exists t^* \in d : t^* = argmax_{t' \in d}Sim(t, t')\} \tag{8}$$

The length of the modified document $|d_q|$ is calculated as follows:

$$|d_q| = |d| + \sum_{t \in q \setminus d} \#(t^*; d).Sim(t, t^*) \tag{9}$$

We see in section 3.3 and 3.4 that the modified document d_q will replace d, and the language models for a query q will be estimated according to the modified document d_q instead of d. We believe that the probability estimation will be more accurate and more effective than ordinary language model.

3.2 Language Models

Language modeling approach to information retrieval is proposed by Ponte and Croft [15]. The basic idea of language models assumes that a query q is generated by a probabilistic model based on a document d. Language models are interested in estimating $P(d|q)$, i.e. the probability that a document d is used to generate query d. By applying Bayes' formula, we have:

$$P(d|q) \propto P(q|d).P(d) \tag{10}$$

$\propto$ means that the two sides give the same ranking. $P(q|d)$ the query likelihood for a given document d. $P(d)$ is often assumed to be uniform and thus can be discarded for ranking documents, then we can rewrite the formula after adding the *log* function as:

$$logP(d|q) = \sum_{t \in V} \#(t;q).logP(t|d) \tag{11}$$

where $\#(t;q)$ is the count of term t in the query q and V is the vocabulary set. Assuming a multinomial distribution, the simplest way to estimate $P(t|d)$ is the maximum likelihood estimator:

$$P_{ml}(t|d) = \frac{\#(t;d)}{|d|} \tag{12}$$

where $|d|$ is the document length. Due to the data spareness problem, the maximum likelihood estimator directly assign *null* to the unseen terms in a document. Smoothing is a technique to assign extra probability mass to the unseen terms in order to solve this problem.

3.3 Extended Dirichlet Smoothing

Dirichlet smoothing [21] is one of the smoothing technique based on adding an extra pseudo term frequency: $\mu P(t|C)$ as follows

$$P_\mu(t|d) = \frac{\#(t;d) + \mu P(t|C)}{|d| + \mu} \tag{13}$$

where C is the collection. The main idea of our proposal is to formally integrate term semantic relations into the current Dirichlet formula in order to solve the mismatch. As we mentioned in section 3.1, we assume the case of mismatch: $t \in q$, and $t \notin d$. There is a document term $t^* \in d$ semantically related to t that can play its role during the matching. More specifically, we consider that if t does not occur in the initial document d, it occurs in the *modified document* d_q, which is the result of expanding d according to the query q and some knowledge[3].

The probability of the term t is defined according to the modified document model d_q. Now, the extended Dirichlet smoothing leads to the following probability for a term $t \in d_q$, $P_\mu(t|d_q)$ which is defined as:

$$P_\mu(t|d_q) = \begin{cases} \frac{\#(t;d)+\mu P(t|C)}{|d_q|+\mu} & \text{if } t \in d \\ \\ \frac{\#(t^*;d).Sim(t,t^*)+\mu P(t|C)}{|d_q|+\mu} & \text{if } t \notin d \end{cases} \tag{14}$$

Note that in the special case where all the query terms occur in the document, we have $|d_q| = |d|$, and that leads to an equal probabilities $p_\mu(t|d) = p_\mu(t|d_q)$.

3.4   Extended Jelinek-Mercer Smoothing

Jelinek-Mercer smoothing [21] is another smoothing technique to add an extra pseudo term frequency: $\lambda P(t|C)$ to the unseen term as follows:

$$P_\lambda(t|d) = (1 - \lambda)P(t|d) + \lambda P(t|C) \tag{15}$$

The probability $P(t|d)$ is estimated using the maximum likelihood Equation 12. Similarly to the previous discussion for extending Dirichlet smoothing, we also refine the probability for a term $t \in d_q$, $P_\lambda(t|d_q)$ which is defined as:

$$P_\lambda(t|d_q) = \begin{cases} (1 - \lambda)\frac{\#(t;d)}{|d_q|} + \lambda P(t|C) & \text{if } t \in d \\ \\ (1 - \lambda)\frac{\#(t^*;d).Sim(t,t^*)}{|d_q|} + \lambda P(t|C) & \text{if } t \notin d \end{cases} \tag{16}$$

3.5   Term Similarity

We only focus, in this work, on the hierarchical relation or specific-generic relations between terms. We make the assumption that a term t is semantically related to a term t', iff t' is a descendant of t in the term hierarchy within an external knowledge K. Assume a query term t, t' refers to a document term, and the vocabulary V. We define the semantic similarity function $Sim(t, t')$ as follows, $Sim : V \times V \to [0, 1]$:

$$\forall t, t' \in V, 0 \leq Sim(t, t') \leq 1 \tag{17}$$

1. $Sim(t, t') = 0$, if t and t' are not semantically related, and $t \neq t'$.
2. $Sim(t, t') < 1$, if t' is a descendant of t in the term hierarchy in K, and $t \neq t'$.
3. $Sim(t, t') = 1$, if $t = t'$.

---

[3] The knowledge refers to the semantic similarity between terms.

The similarity *Sim* denotes the strength of the similarity between the two terms (the larger the value, the higher the similarity between these two terms). We propose to use a lightweight way to calculate the semantic similarity between terms. Our semantic similarity relies on a term hierarchy in an external knowledge. The similarity between two terms t and t' is the inverse of their distance, denoted $distance(t, t')$, between these two terms. We use the path length or the number of links in the hierarchy between two terms as distance [19].

The similarity score is inversely proportional to the number of nodes along the shortest path between the two terms. The shortest possible path occurs when the two terms are directly linked. Thus, the maximum similarity value is 1:

$$Sim(t, t') = \frac{1}{distance(t, t')}, distance(t, t') > 0 \qquad (18)$$

4 Experimental Setup

4.1 Documents and Queries

Conceptual indexing is the process of mapping text into concepts[4] of an *external resource*. Therefore, it needs a resource out of documents and queries which contains concepts, their relations, and other information about them. In our study, we use concepts as indexing terms i.e. documents and queries are represented by means of concepts rather than words.

Documents and queries are mapped into UMLS[5] concepts using MetaMap [1]. UMLS is a multi-source knowledge base in the medical domain, whereas, MetaMap is a tool for mapping text to UMLS concepts. Using concepts allows us to investigate the semantic relations between concepts, so it allows to build our concepts similarity values. We only consider, the hierarchical relations or specific-generic relations (ISA) between concepts from the different UMLS concept hierarchies. We define general concepts which are internal nodes in a concept hierarchy, or nodes which have at least one child. Returning to the example about term specificity in the introduction, the general concept *"Lymphocyte"* has two children *"B-Cell"* and *"T-Cell"*. Then, when a user query contains the term *"Lymphocyte"*, then, a document talking about *"B-Cell"* or *"T-Cell"* is retrieved using our approach. Therefore, general concepts have the potential to be linked, in the case of mismatch, to a descendant concept from a document using our extended matching model.

4.2 Corpora

Five corpora from CLEF[6] are used. Table 1 shows some statistics about them.

---

[4] "Concepts can be defined as human understandable unique abstract notions independent from any direct material support, independent from any language or information representation, and used to organize perception and knowledge [5]".

[5] Unified Medical Language System (http://www.nlm.nih.gov/research/umls/).

[6] www.clef-initiative.eu

- Image2010, Image2011, Image2012: contain short medical documents and queries.
- Case2011, Case2012: contain long medical documents and queries.

Table 1. Corpora statistics. *avdl* and *avql* are average length of documents and queries. Number of general concepts inside the queries.

Corpus	#d	#q	avdl (words)	avql (words)	Number of Concepts in the Queries	Number of General Concepts
Image2010	77495	16	62.12	3.81	186	109
Image2011	230088	30	44.83	4.0	374	198
Image2012	306530	22	47.16	3.55	204	132
Case2011	55634	10	2594.5	19.7	516	219
Case2012	74654	26	2570.72	24.35	1472	519

4.3   Results

All the experiments are conducted using the XIOTA engine [4]. The performance is measured by Mean Average Precision (MAP). The approaches used for experiments are as follows:

- DIR-BL (baseline): language model with Dirichlet smoothing.
- JM-BL (baseline): language model with Jelinek-Mercer smoothing.
- DIR-TM: translation model using Dirichlet smoothing [9].
- JM-TM: translation model using Jelinek-Mercer smoothing [9].
- DIR-CS: our extended Dirichlet smoothing after integrating the concept similarity.
- JM-CS: our extended Jelinek-Mercer smoothing after integrating the concept similarity.

Results of our extended language models are summarized in Table 2. We first observe a consistent performance improvement achieved over ordinary smoothing methods for our five target collections, which confirms our belief that integrating hierarchical relations from an external resource improves relevance model estimation. Second, the improvement occurs in the studied collection is independent to the length of documents and queries in these collections. It seems to be similar for both types of collection: 1) short documents and short queries, 2) long documents and long queries. Finally, the improvement in the two collections: Image2010 and Case2012 is not statistically significant because:

- Image2010: general concepts present in a limited number of queries and not well distributed overall the collection queries.
- Case2012: the rate of general concepts is not high enough comparing with other collections to significantly affect the improvement.

In nutshell, the improvement is related to the rate of general concepts and their distribution inside queries.

We now check how our extended models performs as comparing with the statistical translation models. Table 2 shows the results for (DIR-CS,JM-CS)

Table 2. MAP of Extended Dirichlet smoothing and Extended Jelinek-Mercer smoothing after integrating concept similarity. The gain is the improvement obtained by our approach over ordinary language models. † indicates a statistically significant improvement in over ordinary language models using Fishers Randomization test with $p < 0.05$.

Corpus	DIR-BL	DIR-TM	DIR-CS	Gain	JM-BL	JM-TM	JM-CS	Gain
Image2010	0.2571	0.2868	0.3049	+19%	0.2494	0.3008	0.3023	+21%
Image2011	0.1439	0.1550†	0.1559†	+7%	0.1641	0.1759	0.1757†	+7%
Image2012	0.1039	0.1188	0.1177	+12%	0.1068	0.1102	0.1186†	+11%
Case2011	0.1103	0.1212†	0.1192†	+8%	0.1480	0.1585†	0.1590†	+7%
Case2012	0.1788	0.1462	0.1861	+4%	0.1871	0.1873	0.1961	+5%

and (DIR-TM,JM-TM) methods. Comparing the columns (DIR-CS,JM-CS) and (DIR-TM,JM-TM) indicates that our extended models (DIR-CS,JM-CS) are, in most cases, better than statistical translation models (DIR-TM,JM-TM). Significant tests using Fishers Randomization [18] show that our extended models are statistically better than ordinary language models in five cases, whereas statistical translation models are statistically better in only three cases.

5   Conclusion and Future Work

We propose, in this paper, a model to exploit semantic relations between indexing terms in order to overcome the term mismatch problem. The proposed approach is based on modifying documents according to a given user query and some knowledge about semantic term relations. We extend the document by query terms which are not in the document but they are semantically related to at least one document term. We then integrate the modified document into two smoothing methods from language models: Dirichlet and Jelinek-Mercer. We only consider hierarchical relations between concepts in our similarity measure. Our experimental results indicate that our extended models are statistically better than exact match approaches, and in most cases better than translation models in retrieval performance. This improvement is independent of the length of documents and queries within the tested collections, but it is related to the rate of general terms and their distribution inside queries. We believe that our extension is suitable to integrate any other type of mutual information between indexing terms.

For future work, we plan to validate our extension using other types of relations between terms rather than hierarchical relations. In addition, we plan to apply our extension to other domains rather than the medical domain and other test collections like TREC.

References

1. Aronson, A.R.: Metamap: Mapping text to the umls metathesaurus (2006)
2. Bendersky, M., Croft, W.B.: Discovering key concepts in verbose queries. In: SIGIR 2008, pp. 491–498. ACM, New York (2008), http://doi.acm.org/10.1145/1390334.1390419

3. Berger, A., Lafferty, J.: Information retrieval as statistical translation. In: SIGIR 1999, pp. 222–229. ACM, New York (1999), http://doi.acm.org/10.1145/312624.312681
4. Chevallet, J.-P.: X-iota: An open xml framework for ir experimentation. In: Myaeng, S.-H., Zhou, M., Wong, K.-F., Zhang, H.-J. (eds.) AIRS 2004. LNCS, vol. 3411, pp. 263–280. Springer, Heidelberg (2005)
5. Chevallet, J.P., Lim, J.H., Le, D.T.H.: Domain knowledge conceptual inter-media indexing: Application to multilingual multimedia medical reports. In: CIKM 2007, pp. 495–504. ACM (2007), http://doi.acm.org/10.1145/1321440.1321511
6. Crestani, F.: Exploiting the similarity of non-matching terms at retrieval time. Journal of Information Retrieval 2, 25–45 (2000)
7. Deerwester, S., Dumais, S.T., Furnas, G.W., Landauer, T.K., Harshman, R.: Indexing by latent semantic analysis. Journal of the American Society for Information Science 41(6), 391–407 (1990)
8. Jing, Y., Croft, W.B.: An association thesaurus for information retrieval, pp. 146–160 (1994)
9. Karimzadehgan, M., Zhai, C.: Estimation of statistical translation models based on mutual information for ad hoc information retrieval. ACM (2010), http://doi.acm.org/10.1145/1835449.1835505
10. Krovetz, R.: Viewing morphology as an inference process, pp. 191–202. ACM Press (1993)
11. Lavrenko, V., Croft, W.B.: Relevance based language models. In: SIGIR 2001, pp. 120–127. ACM, New York (2001), http://doi.acm.org/10.1145/383952.383972
12. Lin, J., Demner-Fushman, D.: The role of knowledge in conceptual retrieval: A study in the domain of clinical medicine. In: SIGIR 2006 (2006), http://doi.acm.org/10.1145/1148170.1148191
13. Manning, C.D., Raghavan, P., Schütze, H.: Introduction to Information Retrieval. Cambridge University Press, New York (2008)
14. Peng, F., Ahmed, N., Li, X., Lu, Y.: Context sensitive stemming for web search. In: SIGIR 2007, pp. 639–646. ACM, New York (2007), http://doi.acm.org/10.1145/1277741.1277851
15. Ponte, J.M., Croft, W.B.: A language modeling approach to information retrieval. In: SIGIR 1998, pp. 275–281. ACM (1998), http://doi.acm.org/10.1145/290941.291008
16. Porter, M.F.: An algorithm for suffix stripping. In: Readings in Information Retrieval, pp. 313–316. Morgan Kaufmann Publishers Inc. (1997), http://dl.acm.org/citation.cfm?id=275537.275705
17. Salton, G. (ed.): The SMART Retrieval System - Experiments in Automatic Document Processing. Prentice Hall, Englewood (1971)
18. Smucker, M.D., Allan, J., Carterette, B.: A comparison of statistical significance tests for information retrieval evaluation. In: CIKM 2007. ACM (2007), http://doi.acm.org/10.1145/1321440.1321528
19. Widdows, D.: Geometry and Meaning. Center for the Study of Language and Inf. (November 2004), http://www.amazon.ca/exec/obidos/redirect?tag=citeulike04-20&path=ASIN/1575864487
20. Zhai, C.: Statistical Language Models for Information Retrieval. Now Publishers Inc., Hanover (2008)
21. Zhai, C., Lafferty, J.: A study of smoothing methods for language models applied to information retrieval 22(2), 179–214 (2004), http://doi.acm.org/10.1145/984321.984322

Towards Risk-Aware Resource Selection

Ilya Markov[1], Mark Carman[2], and Fabio Crestani[1]

[1] University of Lugano (USI),
Via G. Buffi 13, Lugano 6900, Switzerland
{ilya.markov,fabio.crestani}@usi.ch
[2] Monash University,
Victoria 3800, Australia
mark.carman@monash.edu

Abstract. When searching multiple sources of information it is crucial to select only relevant sources for a given query, thus filtering out non-relevant content. This task is known as resource selection and is used in many areas of information retrieval such as federated and aggregated search, blog distillation, etc. Resource selection often operates with limited and incomplete data and, therefore, is associated with a certain risk of selecting non-relevant sources due to the uncertainty in the produced source ranking. Despite the large volume of research on resource selection, the problem of risk within resource selection has been rarely addressed. In this work we propose a resource selection method based on document score distribution models that supports estimation of uncertainty of produced source scores and results in a novel risk-aware resource selection technique. We analyze two distributed retrieval scenarios and show that many queries are risk-sensitive and, because of that, the proposed risk-aware approach provides a basis for significant improvements in resource selection performance.

1 Introduction

In some cases, such as federated retrieval, aggregated search or blog search, it is necessary to perform retrieval over multiple sources of information, such as federated collections, verticals or blogs. For a given user's query often only few sources contain relevant information. Therefore, it is useful to filter out all non-relevant sources and search only those that are likely to contain relevant documents. The task of selecting such sources is referred to as *resource selection* and is usually performed by a centralized broker. Resource selection was introduced and extensively studied in the area of distributed information retrieval [1,2,3,4,5].

Due to operational constraints (e.g., sources do not provide direct access to their content) and for efficiency reasons resource selection is often performed based on incomplete samples of documents obtained from each federated source [6,7,8]. This introduces uncertainty into the selection process making it risky [9]. In this paper we approach the problem of risk-aware resource selection in the following way. First, we propose to perform resource selection based on the distribution of document scores in each federated source. Second, we derive a general formula of the variance of source scores, thus capturing their uncertainty.

A. Jaafar et al. (Eds.): AIRS 2014, LNCS 8870, pp. 148–159, 2014.

Third, following the risk-aware approach to IR [10], we incorporate the variance of source scores into the resource selection process and develop a risk-aware resource selection technique, where the amount of allowed risk is controlled by a risk-adjusting parameter.

We analyze two recently proposed distributed retrieval scenarios, namely federated Web search [11] and shard ranking [12], and show that many queries are risk-sensitive, i.e. require a risk-aware component when performing resource selection. We also show that the proposed risk-aware resource selection technique with appropriate values of a risk-adjusting parameter gives significant improvements of resource selection performance.

2   Related Work

Many resource selection techniques have been proposed in the literature. *Large-document* approaches (LD) represent each federated source as a concatenation of its documents and, given a user's query, rank these large documents using standard IR ranking functions, such as INQUERY in CORI [1] and language modelling in [13]. *Small-document* techniques (SD), instead, make use of a centralized index of documents sampled from federated sources (denoted as CSI for *centralized sample index*). These documents are ranked with respect to a user's query and sources are selected based on the number of documents they contribute to the top of such ranking [2,3,4,5], [12], [14]. SD techniques were shown to outperform LD methods [2,3], [5]. Therefore, we will follow the small-document idea in this paper. There is also a large volume of literature on efficient, supervised and theoretical methods for resource selection [8], but we do not describe them here as they are not directly related to the current work.

Despite many studies performed on resource selection, still little is understood about its uncertainty and the risk, associated with the selection process. Markov et al. [9] addressed the uncertainty in resource selection by perturbing various components of SD techniques, such as the document retrieval function, query and ranking of sampled documents. This approach managed to improve the performance of SD methods in some cases. However, this was done at the cost of performing resource selection multiple times, thus, hurting its efficiency. In this paper we propose a resource selection technique, which allows estimation of uncertainty, associated with source scores, using a single resource selection run. It then incorporates the estimated risk directly into the selection process, resulting in risk-aware resource selection.

Our method is based on the distribution of document scores, similarly to [15,16,17]. Baumgarten [16] models document scores using the Gamma distribution and estimates the parameters of the distribution assuming a particular retrieval model, namely probabilistic retrieval. The recently proposed Taily resource selection technique [15] infers score distributions from term statistics, cooperatively provided by federated sources, and also assumes a specific document retrieval function. Then both studies calculate source scores as the area under the right tail of the estimated score distribution. However, the approach in [16] is tied to a particular retrieval model and particular score distribution, while Taily requires certain cooperation from federated sources, which is rarely available in practice. Our approach, instead, is completely uncooperative and does not depend on a specific retrieval method and/or score distribution model. But the main novelty of our technique is that it considers the risk associated with source scores and incorporates it into the resource selection process.

3   Risk-Aware Resource Selection

In this section we first describe the idea of using score distributions for resource selection (called DSDE in this paper, which stands for Document Score Distribution Estimation). Then we show how the variance of source scores can be computed and incorporated into the selection process, resulting in a risk-aware resource selection (RA-DSDE). Finally, we instantiate our general approach using a normal distribution.

3.1   Score Distributions for Resource Selection

Small-document resource selection techniques aim at selecting those sources that contain the largest number of relevant documents for a given user's query. Since the actual relevant documents are not known, the top-ranked documents are used instead [4]. Thus, SD resource selection methods aim at selecting the sources that have the largest number of top-ranked documents for the query.

Following the SD approach, we first define a threshold τ and calculate the number of documents in a source R that have scores higher than τ (we consider these documents as high scoring):

$$count(R|q, \tau) = |d \in R : \ score(d|q) > \tau| \tag{1}$$

where d denotes a document and q denotes a query.

We assume that the distribution of document relevance scores in each source can be approximated by a probability distribution with a distribution function F and a density function f. The area under the density function to the right of the threshold τ is the approximate fraction of high scoring documents in R:

$$\frac{|d \in R : \ score(d|q) > \tau|}{|d \in R|} \approx P[score(d|q) > \tau] = \int_{\tau}^{\infty} f(t)dt = 1 - F(\tau) \tag{2}$$

By combining Equations 1 and 2 we can calculate the expected number of high scoring documents per source with a closed-form expression and use it as a score for ranking sources:

$$score(R|q, \tau) = \mathbb{E}[count(R|q, \tau)] = |R| \cdot (1 - F(\tau)) \tag{3}$$

where $|R| = |d \in R|$ is the number of documents in R and τ is the parameter of the DSDE approach, which can be used for tuning the algorithm according to user needs. Since relevance scores are comparable across different sources, the fitted models are also comparable and, therefore, we can use the same threshold τ for all sources. The value of τ used in our experiments is discussed in Section 4.

3.2 Expectation and Variance of Source Scores

Equation 3 gives an estimation of a score of a source R based on its distribution function $F(x)$. Since the exact function $F(x)$ is not known and has to be approximated for a given query, it becomes also a function of a set of parameters θ: $F = F(x; \theta)$.

The parameters θ are approximated based on the observed scores of documents sampled from R with the maximum likelihood estimation (MLE). Using the delta method, it can be shown that in this case the expectation and variance of the distribution function $F(\tau; \hat{\theta})$ are calculated as follows:

$$\mathbb{E}[F(\tau; \hat{\theta})] = F(\tau; \hat{\theta}) \tag{4}$$

$$Var[F(\tau; \hat{\theta})] = \frac{1}{n} \frac{\partial F}{\partial \theta^T}(\tau; \hat{\theta}) I(\hat{\theta})^{-1} \frac{\partial F}{\partial \theta}(\tau; \hat{\theta}) \tag{5}$$

where $I(\hat{\theta})$ is the Fisher information matrix and n is the number of documents sampled from R.

Based on the above discussion, Equation 3 can be rewritten as follows:

$$\widehat{score}(R|q) = |R| \cdot (1 - F(\tau; \hat{\theta})) \tag{6}$$

This means that $\widehat{score}(R|q)$ is just an approximation of the true $score(R|q)$. Combining this equation with Equations 4 and 5 we can calculate the expectation and variance of source score estimates:

$$\mathbb{E}[\widehat{score}(R|q)] = \mathbb{E}[|R| \cdot (1 - F(\tau; \hat{\theta}))] = |R| \cdot (1 - \mathbb{E}[F(\tau; \hat{\theta})])$$

$$= |R| \cdot (1 - F(\tau; \theta)) = score(R|q) \tag{7}$$

$$Var[\widehat{score}(R|q)] = Var[|R| \cdot (1 - F(\tau; \hat{\theta}))] = |R|^2 \cdot Var[F(\tau; \hat{\theta})]$$

$$= \frac{|R|^2}{n} \frac{\partial F}{\partial \theta^T}(\tau; \hat{\theta}) I(\hat{\theta})^{-1} \frac{\partial F}{\partial \theta}(\tau; \hat{\theta}) \tag{8}$$

In particular, Equation 7 means that the proposed source score estimate is unbiased and asymptotically converges to the true score.

3.3 Risk-Aware Resource Selection

Following the risk-aware approach to IR [10], we combine expectation and variance of source scores in the following way:

$$\widehat{score}(R|q) = \mathbb{E}[\widehat{score}(R|q)] - b \cdot Var[\widehat{score}(R|q)] \tag{9}$$

Here b is a risk-adjusting parameter, where $b > 0$ produces the risk-averse ranking and $b < 0$ gives the risk-inclined ranking of sources.

The final formula for calculating risk-aware source scores based on score distribution models is the following:

$$\widehat{score}(R|q) = |R| \cdot \left(1 - F - b \cdot \frac{|R|}{n} \cdot \frac{\partial F}{\partial \theta^T} I^{-1} \frac{\partial F}{\partial \theta} \right) \tag{10}$$

where the values of F, $\frac{\partial F}{\partial \theta}$ and I^{-1} are calculated at the point $(\tau; \hat{\theta})$. Note that this formula is generic with regards to a score distribution model F and any appropriate distribution can be used in practice.

3.4 Choosing a Score Distribution Model

Various combinations of probability distributions were proposed to model scores of relevant and non-relevant documents: two normal, two exponential, two Poisson, two Gamma and two log-normal distributions [18]. Also a number of mixtures were proposed, where the scores of non-relevant documents were modeled by an exponential or a Gamma distribution, while the scores of relevant documents were modeled with a normal, a Gamma or a mixture of normals [18]. However, the most widely used score distribution model is a mixture of an exponential and normal distributions [18,19]. Therefore, we use this model in our work.

Since our resource selection method is model-agnostic and does not necessarily require a mixture of distributions, we also use a number of single distributions to model document scores, because they have less parameters, are easier to estimate and simpler to work with. In particular, we use a Gamma, a normal and an exponential distributions. Preliminary experiments showed that the mixture, Gamma and normal models performed similarly to each other, while the exponential distribution performed significantly worse than others. This is because we model the scores of top-ranked documents and, therefore, the Gamma and normal provided better fit than the exponential model, while the mixture reduced to a single normal in most cases. Since most of the chosen models provide similar performance, we will use a normal distribution in this work, as it is the simplest to operate with. Note, however, that the following discussion is fully applicable to other models that provide a good fit of document scores.

3.5 Normal-Based Instantiation

The normal distribution is defined with a probability density function f and a distribution function F as follows:

$$f(x; \mu, \sigma^2) = \frac{1}{\sqrt{2\pi\sigma^2}} e^{\frac{-(x-\mu)^2}{2\sigma^2}}, \quad F(x; \mu, \sigma^2) = \frac{1}{2}\left[1 + \text{erf}\left(\frac{x-\mu}{\sqrt{2\sigma^2}}\right)\right] \quad (11)$$

where $\text{erf}(x) = \frac{2}{\sqrt{\pi}} \int_0^x e^{-t^2} dt$ is known as the *error function*. The MLE estimators of the mean μ and variance σ^2 for each source are the following:

$$\hat{\mu} = \frac{1}{n} \sum_{i=1}^n score(d_i|q), \quad \hat{\sigma}^2 = \frac{1}{n} \sum_{i=1}^n (score(d_i|q) - \hat{\mu})^2 \quad (12)$$

The Fisher information of a normal distribution and its inverse are given by the following matrices:

$$I = \begin{pmatrix} \frac{1}{\sigma^2} & 0 \\ 0 & \frac{1}{2\sigma^4} \end{pmatrix}, \quad I^{-1} = \begin{pmatrix} \sigma^2 & 0 \\ 0 & 2\sigma^4 \end{pmatrix} \quad (13)$$

Finally, the partial derivatives of the distribution function F with respect to the parameters μ and σ are the following:

$$\frac{\partial F}{\partial \mu}(x) = -f(x), \quad \frac{\partial F}{\partial \sigma}(x) = -\frac{x-\mu}{\sigma}f(x) \tag{14}$$

Substituting the generic expressions in Equation 10 with the above formulas for the normal distribution, we obtain the following equation for source scores:

$$\widetilde{score}(R|q) = |R|\left(1 - F(\tau) - b\frac{|R|}{n}f^2(\tau)\hat{\sigma}^2(1 + 2(\tau - \hat{\mu})^2)\right) \tag{15}$$

Below we evaluate the proposed risk-aware formula against its basic version ($b = 0$) and other state-of-the-art resource selection techniques.

4   Experimental Methodology

In this section we describe evaluation scenarios, testbeds, parameter values and the overall DIR setup used in our experiments.

Scenarios and Testbeds. We consider the following state-of-the-art cases, where resource selection has a direct application: federated Web search [11] and shard ranking [12].

In order to simulate these scenarios we adopt three testbeds, as in [20], which are the different splits of the TREC GOV2 dataset and contain about 22 million documents. The largest 1000 domains of GOV2 are used as 1000 Web search engines, constituting the gov2.1000 testbed. Since the GOV2 dataset is the crawl of the real Web, gov2.1000 can be used to simulate the federated Web search scenario. The domains of gov2.1000 are clustered into 250 partitions using the average-link agglomerative clustering (the gov2.250 testbed), making them more topically homogeneous. Therefore, gov2.250 can be seen as an intermediate scenario between federated Web search and shard ranking. Then gov2.1000 is also clustered into 30 partitions, creating the gov2.30 testbed. This testbed has topically homogeneous sources and, therefore, represents the shard ranking scenario. We use the titles of the TREC topics 701-850 from the Terabyte Track 2004-2006 as queries.

Parameter Settings. We compare the DSDE and RA-DSDE techniques to ReDDE [4] and CRCS [3], which were shown to be effective unsupervised SD resource selection methods [3], [5]. We consider the exponential and linear versions of CRCS denoted as CRCS(e) and CRCS(l) respectively. Based on our preliminary experiments, the original papers and recent resource selection studies, the parameters of the methods are set as follows: ReDDE considers the top 20 documents to be relevant, CRCS(e) uses $\beta = 0.28$, CRCS(l) considers $\gamma = 20$ documents to be relevant.

DSDE needs to estimate the distribution of document scores for each federated source. For this purpose we use the top 100 documents retrieved from a centralized sample index (CSI) for a given query for each source. The threshold τ is set to the score of the 10th document in a centralized ranking produced by CSI. The risk-adjusting parameter b of the RA-DSDE approach will be discussed in detail in Section 5.

DIR Setup. Both the federated Web search and shard ranking scenarios assume a low-cost (and sometimes uncooperative) environment, where the full centralized index of all documents is not available. In this case a number of documents are sampled from each federated source and stored in CSI. In cooperative scenarios, such as shard ranking for topically partitioned collections, a uniform sample of documents can be obtained [12]. In uncooperative environments the query-based sampling technique [21] can be used instead and we follow this approach here. Since the size of the three considered testbeds is the same, i.e. 22 million documents, we make their CSIs to be also of the same size, i.e. 300K documents for each testbed. This results in 300 sampled documents from each source of the gov2.1000 testbed, 1200 documents from each source of gov2.250 and 10000 documents from each source of gov2.30.

Since the actual size of sources may be unknown in uncooperative environments, we estimate it using the multiple capture-recapture algorithm with 80 queries [22]. The Terrier[1] implementation of BM25 is used as a document scoring function for CSI. After resource selection is performed, the query is sent to the selected sources and 100 documents are retrieved from each of them. The obtained results are merged using CORI [1] as presented in [23], because it showed the best performance in preliminary experiments. P@10 and MAP are used to evaluate the quality of merged results.

5   Results and Discussion

In this section we perform an empirical evaluation of the proposed risk-aware resource selection technique. We start by analyzing the optimal values of the risk-adjusting parameter b and studying the sensitivity of queries to risk. We then compare the performance of the RA-DSDE approach to basic DSDE and other state-of-the-art resource selection methods, namely ReDDE and CRCS.

5.1   Risk-Adjusting Parameter

Intuitively, the sensitivity to risk varies across queries: some queries tend to be risk-averse, i.e. require reducing the risk $(b > 0)$, while others are risk-inclined, i.e. take risks and gain performance improvement $(b < 0)$ [24]. Examples of different behaviors are given in Fig. 1. Here the improvement of p@10 is plotted against the values of b on a log-scale for the shard ranking scenario (the gov2.30 testbed).

Fig. 1 shows that the topic 819, "1890 Census", exhibits a risk-averse behavior and has higher p@10 when the uncertainty is reduced. On the other hand, the

---

[1] http://terrier.org

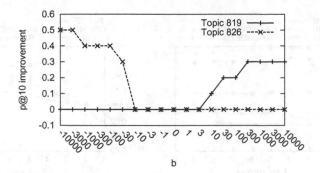

Fig. 1. Examples of risk-averse and risk-inclined topics for the shard ranking scenario (gov2.30)

Table 1. Query statistics for optimal values of b

Measure	Testbed	Number of queries		
		$b \neq 0$	$b > 0$ (%)	$b < 0$ (%)
p@10	gov2.1000	63	41 (65%)	22 (35%)
	gov2.250	75	44 (59%)	31 (41%)
	gov2.30	87	54 (62%)	33 (38%)
MAP	gov2.1000	97	52 (54%)	45 (46%)
	gov2.250	125	65 (52%)	60 (48%)
	gov2.30	133	71 (53%)	62 (47%)

topic 826, "Florida Seminole Indians", shows better performance for negative values of b. The differences in risk preferences can be attributed to the specificity of query terms and the overall difficulty of a query.

Table 1 presents the number of risk-sensitive queries, i.e. queries that benefit from a risk-aware component in terms of p@10 and MAP[2]. When considering p@10 as a performance measure, the federated Web search scenario (the gov2.1000 testbed) benefits from accounting for the risk in 63 cases out of 150 (42%). The intermediate scenario (the gov2.250 testbed) has half of queries being risk-sensitive, while in the shard ranking scenario (the gov2.30 testbed) 87 out of 150 queries (58%) benefit from a risk-aware component. Thus, when optimizing for p@10, on average half of the queries are risk-sensitive across various scenarios. The shard ranking scenario, having larger sources, tend to have more risk-sensitive queries then the federated Web search scenario. This is because larger sources contain more relevant documents and, therefore, are more sensitive to reranking.

Table 1 shows that more queries are risk-sensitive with respect to the MAP performance measure compared to p@10. 97 queries out of 150 (65%) benefit from a risk-aware component in terms of MAP for the federated Web search

---

[2] The total number of analyzed queries is 150.

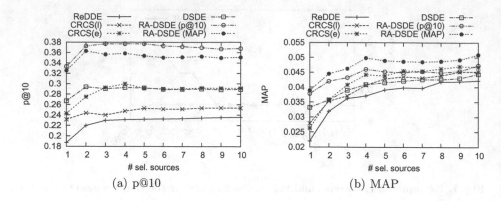

Fig. 2. P@10 and MAP for the federated Web search scenario (the gov2.1000 testbed)

scenario, 125 queries (83%) – for the intermediate case and 133 queries (89%) – for the shard ranking scenario. This behavior is intuitive, because even if accounting for risk does not affect precision at rank 10, it often improves precision at other ranks, thus improving MAP. This suggests that aggregate performance measures are more sensitive to risk and may benefit a lot from risk-aware resource selection. Also note that here, similar to p@10, the number of risk-sensitive queries increases for testbeds with larger sources.

The number of risk-averse ($b > 0$) and risk-inclined ($b < 0$) queries are also shown in Table 1. For p@10, on average, around 60% of risk-sensitive queries are risk-averse and 40% are risk-inclined. This means that more queries benefit from reducing the uncertainty in source ranking. Still there is a large portion of queries that improve performance by taking risks. For MAP these numbers are similar having slightly more risk-inclined queries. This can be explained by the aggregate nature of MAP: the risk-inclined behavior, even if hurting p@10, may improve precision at other ranks, thus improving MAP.

5.2   Retrieval Results

Resource selection performance is shown in Figs. 2 – 4. Here we plot p@10 and MAP against the number of selected sources. The performance of the RA-DSDE approach is given when optimized for p@10 and for MAP.

First, note that the basic DSDE approach ($b = 0$) outperforms the baseline methods for the shard ranking scenario in terms of p@10 in almost all cases (see Fig. 4). It also shows better p@10 when 1 and 2 sources are selected for the intermediate scenario (Fig. 3) and the federated Web search scenario (Fig. 2). However, the improvements are minor and not statistically significant.

On the other hand, as expected the optimized RA-DSDE technique significantly improves p@10 and MAP in all cases. This shows the potential of the risk-aware approach and the amount of improvement that can be achieved by

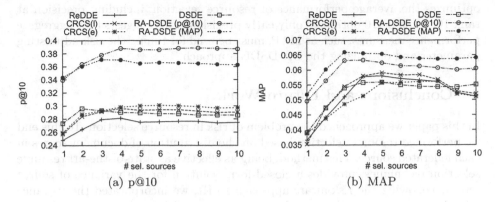

Fig. 3. P@10 and MAP for the intermediate scenario (the gov2.250 testbed)

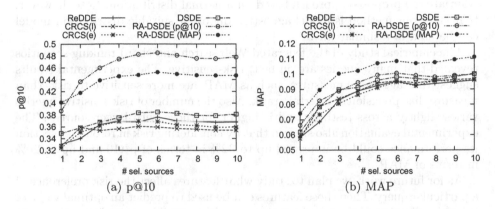

Fig. 4. P@10 and MAP for the shard ranking scenario (the gov2.30 testbed)

considering the risk in resource selection. In particular, the average improvement of RA-DSDE(p@10) over the basic DSDE method in terms of p@10 is 28% for the gov2.1000 testbed, 32% for gov2.250 and 24% for gov2.30. In terms of MAP, the RA-DSDE(MAP) method gives 17% improvement for the gov2.1000 testbed, 20% improvement for gov2.250 and 13% for gov2.30 over the DSDE baseline. These results show that both in the federated Web search and shard ranking scenarios significant improvements are possible by considering the risk-aware component during resource selection and optimizing the risk-adjusting parameter b.

Finally, note that RA-DSDE optimized for MAP also performs well in terms of p@10, although not as good as RA-DSDE(p@10). However, the opposite is not true, i.e. RA-DSDE(p@10) does not improve the performance of DSDE in terms of MAP in about half of the cases. These results are intuitive, as MAP optimizes the average performance of resource selection, including precision at rank 10, while p@10 optimizes only early precision. This suggests that aggregate performance measures, such as MAP, must be used for tuning the risk-adjunsting parameter and optimizing the RA-DSDE approach.

6   Conclusions and Future Work

In this paper we approached the problem of risk in resource selection. To this end we performed resource selection based on the distribution of document scores in each federated source. This method, being as effective as state-of-the-art resource selection techniques, provides a closed-form solution for the variance of source scores. Following the risk-aware approach to IR, we incorporated the variance into the source score estimates, thus, developing a risk-aware resource selection method. The amount of risk in this method is controlled by a risk-adjusting parameter that has to be set on a per query basis. Finally, we showed how to in- stantiate the proposed approach based on a normal distribution. Note, however, that since our method is model-agnostic, any other suitable distribution model can be used in a similar way.

The empirical study of the federated Web search and shard ranking scenarios revealed that many queries are, in fact, risk-sensitive. The experimental results suggest that aggregate measures, such as MAP, are more sensitive to risk, than measures like precision at a certain rank. Also the number of risk-sensitive queries varies slightly across testbeds and is higher for those with larger sources. The experimental evaluation also showed that by considering risk in resource selection its performance could be improved up to 32% in terms of p@10 and up to 20% in terms of MAP.

As for future work, we plan to study what features affect the risk preference of a particular query. Then those features can be used to predict an optimal value of the risk-adjusting parameter for a given user's query. The second direction is to apply portfolio theory to resource selection [25]. To this end, we plan to estimate the correlation between different sources and incorporate this correlation into the resource selection process.

References

1. Callan, J.P., Lu, Z., Croft, W.B.: Searching distributed collections with inference networks. In: Proceedings of SIGIR, pp. 21–28 (1995)
2. Paltoglou, G., Salampasis, M., Satratzemi, M.: Integral based source selection for uncooperative distributed information retrieval environments. In: Proceeding of workshop on LSDS for IR, pp. 67–74 (2008)
3. Shokouhi, M.: Central-rank-based collection selection in uncooperative distributed information retrieval. In: Proceedings of ECIR, pp. 160–172 (2007)
4. Si, L., Callan, J.: Relevant document distribution estimation method for resource selection. In: Proceedings of SIGIR, pp. 298–305 (2003)
5. Thomas, P., Shokouhi, M.: Sushi: scoring scaled samples for server selection. In: Proceedings of SIGIR, pp. 419–426 (2009)

6. Callan, J.: Distributed Information Retrieval. In: Advances in Information Retrieval, pp. 127–150. Kluwer Academic Publishers (2000)
7. Crestani, F., Markov, I.: Distributed information retrieval and applications. In: Proceedings of ECIR, pp. 865–868 (2013)
8. Shokouhi, M., Si, L.: Federated search. Foundations and Trends in Information Retrieval 5, 1–102 (2011)
9. Markov, I., Azzopardi, L., Crestani, F.: Reducing the uncertainty in resource selection. In: Proceedings of ECIR, pp. 507–519 (2013)
10. Zhu, J., Wang, J., Cox, I.J., Taylor, M.J.: Risky business: modeling and exploiting uncertainty in information retrieval. In: Proceedings of SIGIR, pp. 99–106 (2009)
11. Nguyen, D., Demeester, T., Trieschnigg, D., Hiemstra, D.: Federated search in the wild: the combined power of over a hundred search engines. In: Proceedings of CIKM, pp. 1874–1878 (2012)
12. Kulkarni, A., Tigelaar, A.S., Hiemstra, D., Callan, J.: Shard ranking and cutoff estimation for topically partitioned collections. In: Proceedings of CIKM, pp. 555–564 (2012)
13. Xu, J., Croft, W.B.: Cluster-based language models for distributed retrieval. In: Proceedings of SIGIR, pp. 254–261 (1999)
14. Markov, I., Crestani, F.: Theoretical, qualitative, and quantitative analyses of small-document approaches to resource selection. ACM Transactions on Information Systems 32(2), 9:1–9:37 (2014)
15. Aly, R., Hiemstra, D., Demeester, T.: Taily: shard selection using the tail of score distributions. In: Proceedings of SIGIR, pp. 673–682 (2013)
16. Baumgarten, C.: A probabilistic solution to the selection and fusion problem in distributed information retrieval. In: Proceedings of SIGIR, pp. 246–253 (1999)
17. Markov, I.: Modeling document scores for distributed information retrieval. In: Proceedings of SIGIR, pp. 1321–1322 (2011)
18. Arampatzis, A., Robertson, S.: Modeling score distributions in information retrieval. Information Retrieval 14(1), 26–46 (2011)
19. Manmatha, R., Rath, T., Feng, F.: Modeling score distributions for combining the outputs of search engines. In: Proceedings of SIGIR, pp. 267–275 (2001)
20. Arguello, J., Callan, J., Diaz, F.: Classification-based resource selection. In: Proceedings of CIKM, pp. 1277–1286 (2009)
21. Callan, J., Connell, M.: Query-based sampling of text databases. ACM Transactions on Information Systems 19(2), 97–130 (2001)
22. Shokouhi, M., Zobel, J., Scholer, F., Tahaghoghi, S.M.M.: Capturing collection size for distributed non-cooperative retrieval. In: Proceedings of SIGIR, pp. 316–323 (2006)
23. Markov, I., Arampatzis, A., Crestani, F.: On cori results merging. In: Proceedings of ECIR, pp. 752–755 (2013)
24. Zuccon, G., Azzopardi, L., van Rijsbergen, K.: Back to the roots: Mean-variance analysis of relevance estimations. In: Proceedings of ECIR, pp. 716–720 (2011)
25. Wang, J., Zhu, J.: Portfolio theory of information retrieval. In: Proceeding of SIGIR, pp. 115–122 (2009)

Personalizing Web Search Results Based on Subspace Projection

Jingfei Li[1], Dawei Song[1,2], Peng Zhang[1], Ji-Rong Wen[3], and Zhicheng Dou[4]

[1] School of Computer Sci & Tec, Tianjin University, Tianjin, China
[2] The Computing Department, The Open University, UK
[3] School of Information, Renmin University of China, Beijing, China
[4] Microsoft Research Asia
{dawei.song2010,darcyzzj,jirong.wen}@gmail.com,
jingfl@foxmail.com, zhichdou@microsoft.com

Abstract. Personalized search has recently attracted increasing attention. This paper focuses on utilizing click-through data to personalize the web search results, from a novel perspective based on subspace projection. Specifically, we represent a user profile as a vector subspace spanned by a basis generated from a word-correlation matrix, which is able to capture the dependencies between words in the "satisfied click" (SAT Click) documents. A personalized score for each document in the original result list returned by a search engine is computed by projecting the document (represented as a vector or another word-correlation subspace) onto the user profile subspace. The personalized scores are then used to re-rank the documents through the Borda' ranking fusion method. Empirical evaluation is carried out on a real user log data set collected from a prominent search engine (Bing). Experimental results demonstrate the effectiveness of our methods, especially for the queries with high click entropy.

Keywords: Personalization, User Profile, Subspace Projection.

1 Introduction

Over decades, modern search engines have transformed the way people access and interact with information. Users can easily search for relevant information by issuing simple queries to search engines. Despite the increasing popularity and convenience, search engines are facing some challenges. For example, given a query, a typical search engine usually returns a long list of URLs, usually displayed in a number of pages. We call the results list as *Original List*. However, the top ranked URLs may not always satisfy users' information needs well. Users may have to scroll down the current result page and even turn to the following pages to find desired information. This would affect the users' search experience and satisfaction. One way to tackle this problem is through search personalization based on an individual user's profile representing the user's personal preferences and interests.

A. Jaafar et al. (Eds.): AIRS 2014, LNCS 8870, pp. 160–171, 2014.
© Springer International Publishing Switzerland 2014

Personalized search has recently attracted much interest. Many personalized search strategies [5,6], [8], [10], [13] build on the users' click-through data, where it is assumed that the clicked URLs are relevant [8]. This assumption is not rigorous, because users often go back quickly after clicking an irrelevant result. Previous research indicated that the clicks with short dwell time ("quick backs") are unlikely to be relevant[10]. In this paper, we utilize the "SAT click" criteria [10] ([i] the user dwelled on the result page corresponding to the clicked URL for at least 30 seconds; [ii] the click was the last click in current query session) to judge the relevance of a clicked document. Only the "satisfied" click data (URLs and corresponding documents) are used to build a user profile. The "SAT click" data is also used as the ground truth when evaluating the proposed algorithms.

The classic Vector Space Model (VSM) has been a popular choice for user profile representation [21], in which the queries, documents and user profiles are all represented as vectors in a term space [12], [21]. Generally, the weight of each term (or keyword) in a user profile vector is calculated by its $TF \times IDF$ weight. However, representing user profiles as weighted keyword vectors has several inherent limitations. As the number of keywords increases, the vector representation becomes ambiguous. Moreover, the traditional bag of words models in IR, such as VSM and unigram language model, are based on the *term independence assumption*. This assumption simplifies the development and implementation of retrieval models, but ignores the fact that some words are dependent on each other. Intuitively, two co-occurring words can convey more semantic information than the single words individually. For example, when "Obama" and "Romney" co occur in a document, we may easily recognize that this document is about the American Election, but if we only observe one single word "Obama" or "Romney", the the topic of this document can be different. To address this issue, term dependencies need to be mined and incorporated into IR models to improve retrieval performance [1], [9], [21]. In this paper, we propose to represent a user profile as a vector subspace, and make use of term dependence information, in the form of a word-correlation matrix, to generate the user profile subspace.

Our method is inspired by the idea of using a vector space basis for modeling context, originally proposed by Melucci [15] , where each basis vector refers to a contextual property. In linear algebra, a vector can be generated by a basis. In this way, an information object (e.g., an information need) represented by a vector can be generated by the context modeled with the basis. Melucci [1] computed the probability that an information object has been materialized within a context. In this paper, we extend the idea to user profile representation. We systematically investigate and evaluate two novel algorithms based on the subspace projection for personalized re-ranking of Web search results. Specifically, we represent a user profile as a subspace spanned by a basis derived from a word-correlation matrix built from the user's SAT clicked web pages. The personalized score for a document can be computed by projecting the document (represented as a vector in the first algorithm or another word-correlation subspace in the second algorithm) onto the user profile subspace. Then we re-rank the original list returned by a prominent search engine (Bing) based on the Borda' rank fusion method [14].

2   Related Work

In this section, we briefly review the related work on two areas, including personalized information retrieval and the geometry underlying IR.

Personalized search aims to provide customized search results according to an individual user's interests. Various personalized search methods have been proposed in recent years [4], [5], [10]. They are based on either explicit relevance feedback or implicit feedback through various user interaction behaviors, such as clicks, scrollings, adding pages to favorites, and so on. For example, Bennett et al. [4] utilized the position information of users to influence search results. Sontag et al. [5] proposed a generative model to predict the relevance of a document for a specific user. Collins-Thompson et al. [20] took the reading level of the users into considerations to improve the effectiveness of retrieval. Xiang et al.[7] integrated various context information generated by user interaction into the learning to rank model to improve the IR performance. In [2], several personalization strategies were proposed. It came to a conclusion that personalized search can lead to a significant improvement on some queries but has little effect on other queries (e.g., queries with low click entropy).

In a seminal book about the geometry of IR [17], Hilbert's vector spaces were used to represent documents. Similarly, Melucci [15] proposed an idea of using a basis to model the context in IR. In [16], a geometric framework is proposed to utilize multiple sources of evidence presented in current interaction context (e.g., display time, document retention) to develop enhanced implicit feedback models personalized for each user and tailored for each search task. The models we develop in this paper are inspired by the subspace projection method investigated in [1], which, in our opinion, is a general and principled theoretical framework for incorporating word dependencies and provides a unified representation for both user profiles and documents.

3   The Subspace Theoretical Framework

3.1   Probability of a Vector Out of Subspace

Suppose $B = \{b_1, ..., b_k\}$ is a basis of a k-dimension subspace defined over R^n, where $b_i^T \cdot b_i = 1$ and b_i's are mutually orthogonal. $L(B)$ is the subspace spanned by B. $\mathbf{x}$ is a vector, and $L(\{\mathbf{x}\})$ is the set of vectors of the form $c\mathbf{x}$, where c is a scalar. The vector $\mathbf{x}$ may or may not be generated by B. If $\mathbf{x}$ is generated by B, there exists a set of weights $\{p_1, .., p_k\}$ such that $\mathbf{x} = p_1b_1 + ... + p_kb_k$. Note that every vector generated by B is entirely contained in $L(B)$. The vectors that cannot be generated by B is not contained in $L(B)$, but these vectors may be more or less close to $L(B)$. Intuitively, if a vector $\mathbf{x}$ is close to $L(B)$, the information object (e.g., a document) represented by $\mathbf{x}$ is likely within the context spanned by B. Similarly, the information object represented by a vector being far from $L(B)$ is unlikely to be generated by the context spanned by B. Based on the notions just illustrated, we can model a user profile as a basis and documents as vectors, then compute the inner product between a document vector and the projection of the vector onto the user profile subspace as the probability that the corresponding user is interested in the document, which formalized as Equation 1.

$$Pr[L(B)|L(\{\mathbf{x}\})] = x^{\mathrm{T}} \cdot P_B \cdot x \qquad (1)$$

where we restrict $x^{\mathrm{T}} \cdot x = 1$, P_B is the projector to $L(B)$, namely $P_B = B^{\mathrm{T}} \cdot B$, and $P_B \cdot x$ is the projection of x onto the subspace B. Each basis vector in the subspace can be considered as a concept of a user profile. The projection of a document vector onto the subspace can then be interpreted as the concept of user profile which is most related to the document. This formula is different from the traditional VSM modeling of user profile as a single vector, which may contain more irrelevant noises for current search topic.

3.2   Probability of a Subspace Out of another Subspace

In above theoretical framework, a document is represented as a normalized vector, which assumes that a document only contain one topic (corresponding to one basis vector). However the fact is that one document may have multiple topics, e.g., one document introduces both the beautiful scenery and the notability of one place. To address this gap, we extend the projection-based method in Section 3.1 to the projection from one subspace to another subspace. In the extension, we represent a document as a subspace instead of a vector, denoted as $L(O)$ spanned by a basis $O = \{x_1, ..., x_m\}$, where each dimension corresponds to a concept of the document. We then compute the probability of $L(O)$ out of $L(B)$ according to Luders's rule[1]:

$$Pr[L(B)|L(O)] = \frac{tr(P_O \cdot D \cdot P_O \cdot P_B)}{tr(D \cdot P_O)} \qquad (2)$$

where P_B, P_O are the projectors to L_B, L_O respectively, $tr(\cdot)$ is the trace of a matrix, and D is a density matrix (symmetric, positive definite and has trace one). In our work, the word correlation matrix built for user profile is regarded as the density matrix.

4   Personalized Web Search Re-ranking Algorithms

We now present our concrete algorithms that implement the subspace projection based theoretical framework described in the previous section. In this paper, a "query instance" refers to an information object that contains the user ID, query terms, query time stamp, original result list, clicked URL list, and so on. It is worth noting that different query instances may contain the same query terms. A user's search process is captured by the user's "query trace", which is a sequence of query instances sorted by query time stamp. A query trace is formalized as $q_1, ..., q_i, ..., q_{n-1}, q_n$, where $q_1, ..., q_i, ..., q_{n-1}$ are the historical query instances, and q_n is the current query instance (for which the original search results are to be re-ranked). For each q_i, we download the actual documents of the top 30 returned URLs from Bing search engine as the *original list*. When re-ranking the original list of q_n, we compute the personalized score for each URL using our personalized algorithms and obtain the *personalized ranked list* according to the personalized scores. After that, a *re-ranked list* is gained by combining the original list with personalized ranked list using the Borda' ranking fusion method [14].

4.1   Algorithm 1: Document Vector Projection onto User Profile Subspace Algorithm (V-S)

In this algorithm, we represent a user profile as a subspace that consists of the top K eigenvectors (corresponding to the top K eigenvalues) of a $N \times N$ word-correlation matrix, where N is the size of the vocabulary. Each eigenvector depicts a distribution of words corresponding to a concept of user's search interests. The top K eigenvectors constitute a basis of user profile subspace corresponding to the main aspects of user's search history. A document is represented as a N dimensional column vectors and can be generated from the user profile subspace with a probability. For example, if a document can be totally generated from this subspace, the probability is 1; conversely, the probability is 0. We can rank documents based on such probabilities to get a personalized ranked list for the current query instance.

Step1: Building the Word-Correlation Matrix for User Profile. In this work,.we build a document collection for each user, which are composed of all of the historical SAT clicked web pages. We preprocess each web page by segmenting it into a list of sentences. In this way, the document collection can be processed into a set of sentences, denoted as $S = \{s_k\}, k = 1, ..., M$. The word-correlation matrix for the user is built based on the sentence set. We denote the user profile matrix as M^P, each element of which is defined as:

$$M_{ij}^P = r(w_i, w_j) \times TFIDF(w_i) \times TFIDF(w_j) \qquad (3)$$

where M_{ij}^P is an element of M^P corresponding to the i_{th} row and the j_{th} column. w_i and w_j are two words, and $r(w_i, w_j)$ reflects the correlation between them. Equation 3 aims to not only capture the dependency relationship between words, but also reflect the importance of each word. $TFIDF(w_i)$ is the product of term frequency (TF) of w_i in the sentence set and its inverse document frequency (IDF) in a global document collection with 273298 web pages (not the user profile document collection). The mutual information (See Equation 4) between two variables is used to define the correlation between two words. Indeed, any other correlation measures can be applied here. A more systematic study of different correlation measurements will be carried out as future work.

$$r(w_i, w_j) = \begin{cases} I(X;Y), & \text{if } i \neq j \\ H(X), & \text{if } i = j \end{cases} \qquad (4)$$

$$I(X;Y) = \sum_{x \in X} \sum_{y \in Y} P(x,y) log \frac{P(x,y)}{P(x)P(y)} ; H(X) = - \sum_{x \in X} P(x) log P(x) \qquad (5)$$

where X and Y are two random variables which indicate the existence of w_i and w_j respectively. $P(x) = P\{X = x\}$, $P(y) = P\{Y = y\}$, $P(x,y) = P\{X = x, Y = y\}$, $x,y \in \{0,1\}$. Here, $P\{X = 1\}$ is the probability that w_i occurs in the sentence set, and $P\{X = 0\}$ is the probability that w_i does not occur in the sentence set. $P\{Y = 0\}$ and $P\{Y = 1\}$ have similar definition corresponding to w_j. $P(x,y)$ is the joint probability of X and Y. Note that, the Dirichlet smoothing method[19] has been used while estimating the word probability to avoid zero probability. $I(X;Y)$ is the mutual information of X and Y, which indicates the dependency relationship of the words. The diagonal elements of the matrix contains a factor, the self-information of X, which indicates the amount of information of X.

Step2: Computing the Personalized Score for each URL. The words-correlation matrix built in Step 1 is a $N \times N$ symmetric matrix. We can decompose it through the Singular Value Decomposition (SVD)[11] and get the top K eigenvectors as the basis $B_P = (v_1, ..., v_i, ..., v_K)_P$, where v_i is the i_{th} eigenvector of the user profile matrix corresponding to the i_{th} eigenvalue of the all eigenvalues in a descending order. Then the projector for the user profile (P_P) can be gained by the product of corresponding basis and its transposition, i.e., $P_P = B_P \cdot B_P^T$. In order to obtain the personalized score for each URL, we represent each document (URL) as a N dimensional vector (V^d) based on the vocabulary. We utilize the $TF \times IDF$ (denoted as $TFIDF$ here), after normalization, as the weight of each element in the document vector.

$$V_d = (\frac{TFIDF_1}{\sqrt{\sum_i TFIDF_i^2}}, ..., \frac{TFIDF_i}{\sqrt{\sum_i TFIDF_i^2}}, ..., \frac{TFIDF_N}{\sqrt{\sum_i TFIDF_i^2}})^T \qquad (6)$$

The personalized score of each URL can be obtained naturally by projecting the document vector onto the user profile subspace (also see Equation 1):

$$PScore(u) = V_d^T \cdot P_P \cdot V_d \qquad (7)$$

where $PScore(u)$ is the personalized score for a URL. After this step, we can get the personalized rank list according to $PScore(u)$.

Step 3: Re-Ranking the Query Instance. Since we cannot get the actual relevance score from the Bing search engine, we use the rank-based fusion method for re-ranking the original result list with the personalized ranked list. We denote the original result list of a query instance as τ_1 and the personalized ranked list gained in step 2 as τ_2. Then we combine the rankings in τ_1 and τ_2 using the Borda' ranking fusion method and sort the web pages with the combined rankings. Let u be one URL of the original result list of one query instance. Borda's method first assigns a score $B_i(u) = $ "the number of the URLs ranked below u in the rank τ_i", and then the total Borda' score $B(u)$ is defined as $\sum_{i=1}^{2} B_i(u)$ [14]. Finally, we re-rank the result list according to the Borda score $B(u)$ to get a re-ranked list τ. It should be noted that the different URLs may have the same

Borda' score in the actual experiment, which may lead to the uncertainty of ranking in the re-ranked list. To avoid this problem, we sort the URLs according to the relative order in τ_1 when the same Borda score occurs.

4.2 Algorithm 2: Document Subspace Projection onto User Profile Subspace (S-S)

This algorithm shares the same framework with the first algorithm described in Section 4.1, while the only difference is the method used for obtaining the personalized score for a URL. For this reason, we leave out the common parts of the two algorithm, and focus on how to get the personalized score. In this algorithm, the user profile subspace construction is the same as in Algorithm 1. Each document is also represented as a words-correlation matrix in the same way to build a user profile matrix. The document matrix is decomposed through SVD, so that the basis of the document subspace (B_d) is generated (also the selection of top K eigenvectors as the basis). From the basis, we get the projector for the document subspace $P_d = B_d \cdot B_d^{\mathrm{T}}$. The personalized score is derived by projecting the document subspace onto the user profile subspace as introduced in Section 3:

$$PScore(u) = tr(P_d \cdot M^P \cdot P_d \cdot P_P)/tr(D \cdot P_d) \qquad (8)$$

where M^P is the word-correlation matrix for user profile as a density matrix, P_P is the projector corresponding to the user profile subspace. The advantages of this algorithm compared with the first algorithm are that (i) the correlation between words is taken into account in the document representation; (ii) key concepts of a document with multiple topics are captured through SVD and considered in the document representation.

5   Empirical Evaluation

5.1   Baseline: Vector Space Model (VSM)

In this paper we set the VSM as a baseline algorithm to compare with our algorithms described above. In SVM, both user profile and documents are represented as vectors. The personalized score for a URL is the cosine similarity between the user profile vector V_P and the document vector V_d constructed with the same method as described in the first algorithm..

$$PScore(u) = \frac{V_P \cdot V_d}{\sqrt{V_P^{\mathrm{T}} \cdot V_P} \times \sqrt{V_d^{\mathrm{T}} \cdot V_d}} \qquad (9)$$

5.2   Experiment Settings

To test our personalized re-ranking algorithms, we conduct experiments on a real query log collection. In the experiments, we randomly sampled 107 users' query logs as the training and testing data from a global query log with 1166 users over a certain period of time. Table 1 shows the detailed information of the global query log and sampled query log, which indicates that they have some similar statistical properties. In addition, we store a global document collection with 273,298 web pages downloaded from the Internet based on the URLs in the selected query log. We have preprocessed the web pages by extracting the content data, segmenting them into sentences, removing stop words and stemming the words with Porter Stemmer [18].

We build a vocabulary for each user by selecting the top N words(we set $N = 1000$ in this paper) according to their TF-IDF weights in the SAT clicked document collection in the user's search history. The vocabulary is updated dynamically as user issuing new queries into the search engine. In the representation of user profile, K, the number of selected eigenvectors in the basis of the user profile subspace, is an important parameter which determines the number of the topics in the user profile used to personalize the web search results of the current query. We conduct systematic experiments to test the influence of different K on the algorithms' performance.

Table 1. Detailed information about the global query log and the selected query logs

Items	#users	#query	#distinct query	#Clicks	#SATClicks	#AverageActiveDays
Global Logs	1,166	541,065	221,165	475,624	357,279	20.963
Selected Logs	107	55,486	25,618	54,766	36,761	20.444

The Click Entropy is a concept proposed in [2], which is a direct indication of query click variation. It is computed based on all of the clicks for a distinct query (i.e., which is unique in the query log).

$$ClickEntropy(q) = \sum_{u \in U(q)} -P(u|q) \log_2 P(u|q) \tag{10}$$

where $U(q)$ is the collection of URLs that are clicked for the distinct query q, and $P(u|q)$ is the percentage of the clicks on the URL u among all the clicks for q. Dou et al.[2] pointed out that the smaller click entropy means that the majorities of users agree with each other on a small number of web pages for a query. It has been shown in the Literatures[2,3] that personalized search algorithms have different performance on query instances with different click entropies: generally speaking, the queries with low click entropy tend to have a less potential to benefit from personalization [2]. In this paper, we report the distribution of our experimental results over various different click entropy ranges. Note that, for statistical significance, we compute the click entropy for each distinct query based on a large scale global query log (see Table 1).

In the real scenario of searching, users may skip the first SERP (Search Engine Results Page) and turn to following pages. Intuitively, this phenomenon indicates that a user may dissatisfy the search results returned by the search engine. From this view, the percentage of turning pages (= number of query instances that users turn to next pages / total number of queries) can reflect the users' satisfaction with the search results to some extent. The larger the percentage is, the less the user's satisfaction tend to be. Fig.1 (a) shows that users have relatively high satisfaction with the search results for queries with lower click entropy and there is less need of re-ranking results for these queries. With this consideration, we focus on re-ranking the query instances with *relatively high* click entropy. This is a typical long tail task. Fig.1 (b) shows the distribution of the numbers queries over different click entropies for the test data.

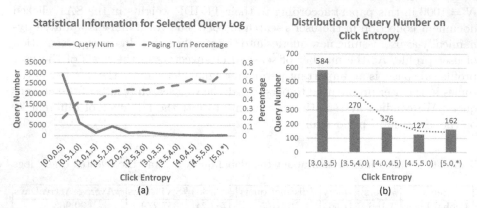

Fig. 1. (a) is the statistical information for selected query log; (b) is the histogram of query number distribution on click entropy for testing data set

5.3 Evaluation Metrics

We utilize the evaluation metric introduced in Dou et al. [2] to evaluate the quality of a ranked URLs list for query instances. It is called *Rank Scoring*, denoted as R_q for a query instance q. The average rank scoring for a set of query instances is denoted as $R_{average}$.

$$R_q = \sum_j \frac{\delta(q,j)}{2^{(j-1)/(\alpha-1)}}; R_{average} = 100 \frac{\sum_q R_q}{\sum_q R_q^{Max}} \tag{11}$$

where j is the rank of a URL in the list; $\delta(q,j)$ is 1 if URL j is relevant to user's information need in query instance q and 0 otherwise; and α is set to 5, which follows the setting in[2]. The R_q^{Max} is the obtained maximum possible rank scoring for a query instance when all relevant URLs appearing at the top of the ranked list. A larger rank scoring value indicates a better quality of the ranked URLs list. Moreover, the "SAT click" is used for relevance judgement of a URL. In our experiments, we evaluate the original result list given by Bing and the re-ranked list given by our algorithms in the same way. The performance of proposed algorithms can be measured by the *improvement percentage* of the re-ranked rank scoring compared with the Bing's original rank scoring. The positive value (improvement percentage>0) means that the performance is increased after re-ranking, while zero value means performance staying unchanged and the negative value means the performance decreased.

5.4 Experimental Results and Discussions

Fig.2 shows the re-ranking performance of our algorithms in comparison with the baseline algorithm (VSM). (A) and (B) show the improvement percentage of our algorithms with different parameter K distributed on different click entropy intervals. The results show that the re-ranking performance of both V-S and S-S reach their peaks at a specific K value. A too small K value, e.g., $K = 2$, implies that too few topics are selected to personalize the web search which may leave out some important information for the current query. A too large K value, e.g., $K = 20$, may introduce too much noise. Only a proper K value can result in the most improvement of re-ranking performance. The results also show that the re-ranking performance of our algorithms (V-S and S-S) is relative poor for the queries with lower click entropy (less than 5.0), and is relatively good for queries with higher click entropy. One reason is that the Bing search engine has returned relative good results to users in the former case and thus there is little potential to improve it. There may even be a risk to harm the users' search experience when we personalize the queries with lower click entropy.

The average best performance of algorithms V-S and S-S appears in $K = 7$ and $K = 17$ respectively. Table (C) compares the performance between VSM and our algorithms, namely S-S (K=17) and V-S (K=7). We observe that VSM demonstrates a better performance for lower click entropy queries ([3.0,3.5)); however, our two algorithms outperform VSM when the click entropy is large (> 4.0); especially, the S-S gain the best performance of a 35.20% improvement in click entropy interval [5.0,∞). Table (D) in Fig.2 shows the distribution of user

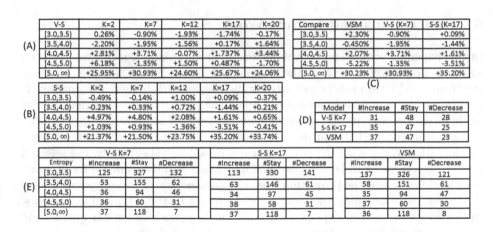

Fig. 2. The re-ranking performance evaluated from different angles. (A) and (B) show the improvement percentage of our algorithms with different parameter K distributed on click entropy intervals; (C) is the comparative results among VSM, S-S (K=17) and V-S (K=7); (D) is the distribution of user number on different re-ranking performance ('increase', 'stay' and 'decrease') for different algorithms; (E) is the distribution of query number on different click entropy intervals and different re-ranking performance ('increase', 'stay' and 'decrease') for different algorithms.

numbers over different re-ranking performance ('increase', 'stay' and 'decrease') for the 3 algorithms. This table indicates that the VSM helped slightly more users to improve the search results with the fewest harm (with the fewest number of users whose re-ranking performance is decreased) to user's search quality. (E) gives another statistical analysis of the experimental result, i.e., the distribution of query numbers over different click entropy intervals and different re-ranking performance ('increase', 'stay' and 'decrease') for different algorithms, showing that the VSM is more robust in lower click entropy intervals (less than 4.0) and the robustness in higher click entropy intervals for different algorithms is similar.

Overall, we find that our proposed algorithms are effective, especially, for the queries with higher click entropy (which are queries worthwhile to personalize [2]). The superiority of our methods are gained for four reasons: (i) we build word-correlation matrixes for user profile and documents, which not only captures the importance of single words, but also takes the correlation between words into consideration; (ii) we decompose the word-correlation matrix through SVD, and the dimensionality is reduced to a small value, so that the main aspects of the user search history can be used to personalize the new query; (iii) a document is represented as subspace spanned by the top K eigenvectors of the document word-correlation matrix, which captures the main topics of the documents and could serve as a denoising algorithm to some extent; (iv) the unified representation of the user profile and document as subspaces (or document as vector) well capture the geometrical features of the user profile and documents, and based on this representation, we incorporate the well-principled subspace projection theory into our personalization framework.

6   Conclusions and Future Work

In this paper we propose two novel personalized re-ranking algorithms, based on subspace projection, to re-rank the original web search results which outperform the traditional VSM model especially for the queries with higher click entropy. It is noting that, in our work, we did not select the most relevant historical queries for building the user profile, since we have utilized the subspace projection theoretical framework that can automatically detect the most relevant concepts (topics) when computing the personalized scores. More specifically, the selected top K eigenvectors can be seen as some important and different topics of user's search interests, and the projection from the document vector (subspace) to user profile subspace can map the most relevant topics to the retrieved documents. In the future, we will incorporate more information, such as similar queries and similar users, to further improve our model and algorithms.

Acknowledgments. This work is funded in part by the Chinese National Program on Key Basic Research Project (973 Program, grant no. 2013CB329304 and 2014CB744604), the Natural Science Foundation of China (grant no. 61272265), and the European Union Framework 7 Marie-Curie International Research Staff Exchange Programme (grant no. 247590).

References

1. Melucci, M.: A Basis for Information Retrieval in Context. ACM Transactions on Information Systems (TOIS) 26(3), 14 (2008)
2. Dou, Z., Song, R., Wen, J.R.: A large-scale Evaluation and Analysis of Personalized Search Strategies. In: WWW, pp. 581–590 (2007)
3. Teevan, J., Dumais, S.T., Horvitz, E.: Potential for Personalization. ACM Transactions on Computer-Human Interaction (TOCHI) 17(1), 4 (2010)
4. Bennett, P.N., Radlinski, F., White, R.W., Yilmaz, E.: Inferring and using Location Metadata to Personalize Web Search. In: SIGIR, pp. 135–144 (2011)
5. Sontag, D., Collins-Thompson, K., Bennett, P.N., White, R.W., Dumais, S., Billerbeck, B.: Probabilistic Models for Personalizing Web Search. In: WSDM, pp. 433–442 (2012)
6. White, R.W., Bennett, P.N., Dumais, S.T.: Predicting Short-term Interests using Activity-based Search Context. In: CIKM, pp. 1009–1018 (2010)
7. Xiang, B., Jiang, D., Pei, J., Sun, X., Chen, E., Li, H.: Context-aware Ranking in Web Search. In: SIGIR, pp. 451–458 (2010)
8. Agichtein, E., Brill, E., Dumais, S.: Improving Web Search Ranking by Incorporating User Behavior Information. In: SIGIR, pp. 19–26 (2006)
9. Zhang, S., Dong, N.: An Effective Combination of Different Order N-grams. In: Proceedings of O-COCOSDA, pp. 251–256 (2003)
10. Bennett, P.N., White, R.W., Chu, W., Dumais, S.T., Bailey, P., Borisyuk, F., Cui, X.: Modeling the Impact of Short-and Long-term Behavior on Search Personalization. In: SIGIR, pp. 185–194 (2012)
11. Golub, G., Loan, C.V.: Matrix Computation, 2nd edn. The Johns Hopkins University Press, Baltimore (1989)
12. Xu, S., Bao, S., Fei, B., Su, Z., Yu, Y.: Exploring Folksonomy for Personalized Search. In: SIGIR, pp. 155–162. ACM (2008)
13. Sun, J.T., Zeng, H.J., Liu, H., Lu, Y., Chen, Z.: CubeSVD: A Novel approach to Personalized Web Search, pp. 382–390 (2005)
14. Dwork, C., Kumar, R., Naor, M., Sivakumar, D.: Rank Aggregation Methods for the Web, pp. 613–622 (2001)
15. Melucci, M.: Context Modeling and Discovery using Vector Space Bases. In: CIKM, pp. 808–815 (2005)
16. Melucci, M., White, R.W.: Utilizing a Geometry of Context for Enhanced Implicit Feedback. In: CIKM, pp. 273–282 (2007)
17. Van, R., Cornelis, J.: The Geometry of Information Retrieval. The Cambridge University Press (2004)
18. Porter, M.F.: An Algorithm for Suffix Stripping, Program 14(3), 130–137 (1980)
19. Zhai, C., Lafferty, J.: A Study of Smoothing Methods for Language Models applied to ad hoc Information Retrieval. In: SIGIR, pp. 334–342 (2001)
20. Collins-Thompson, K., Bennett, P.N., White, R.W., de la Chica, S., Sontag, D.: Personalizing Web Search Results by Reading Level. In: CIKM, pp. 403–412 (2011)
21. Nanas, N., Vavalis, M., De Roeck, A.N.: A Network-based Model for High-dimensional Information Filtering. In: SIGIR, pp. 202–209 (2010)

Aggregating Results from Multiple Related Queries to Improve Web Search over Sessions

Ashraf Bah and Ben Carterette

Department of Computer Sciences, University of Delaware, Newark, DE, USA
{ashraf,carteret}@udel.edu

Abstract. Traditional information retrieval systems are evaluated with the assumption that each query is independent. However, during their interactions with search engines, many users find themselves reformulating their queries in order to satisfy their information need. In this paper, we investigate the impact of using ranking aggregation in the context of session information retrieval. First, we identify useful sources for terms to be used as related queries. For each query, we generate related queries from various sources and use those multiple representations of a query to obtain several rankings that we combine using simple rank aggregation methods. We compare the effects of using each source and show that some sources can provide up to 46% increase in nDCG@10 over our dirichlet-smoothed language model baseline and our best result is competitive with all TREC Session track systems for 2011 and 2012.

Keywords: Session Search, Ranking Aggregation, Relevance Feedback, Diversity Retrieval, Retrieval Models.

1 Introduction

The main goal of the TREC Session track search task is to improve the ranking of a current query given information about the previous interactions of a user in the same session. To that end, TREC Session track participants are provided with a set of query sessions, each of which contains a current query, one or more previous queries and a ranking list of documents (document Id, title, URL, snippets, clicked URLs and dwell time) for the previous queries [13,14]. Participants are asked to exploit that information to better rank ClueWeb09 results for the last query in the session.

We address the problem using CombMNZ and two other rank aggregation methods. Rank aggregation is concerned with combining the results of various rankings. Here the various rankings that we combine are the rankings for queries that we consider to be related to our main (current) query. Exploiting various useful pieces of information as related queries, and combining the rankings of the related queries using either one of the rank aggregation methods that we used, we are able to get significant improvements (up to 46% increase in some cases) over the baseline, especially when we exploit users' search history (i.e. session data). Improvements of the results are significant for both traditional measures and measures of diversity.

A. Jaafar et al. (Eds.): AIRS 2014, LNCS 8870, pp. 172–183, 2014.

2   Related Work

Session search is an important problem as it has been shown by Shokouhi et al, after analysis of Bing and Yandex search logs, that between 40% and 60% of sessions have two or more queries [19]. Query reformulations may be due to the difficulty, the ambiguity, the complexity or the broadness of a topic.

Zhang et al. approached the problem by proposing a relevance feedback model that utilizes query changes in a session [22]. In Zhang's work, when computing the relevance score between a current query and a document, terms' weights are increased or decreased depending on whether the term was added, retained or removed from previous queries in the session. In a similar approach [10], Guan et al. proposed to model sessions as Markov Decision Processes wherein the user agent's actions correspond to query changes, and the search agent's actions correspond to increasing or decreasing or maintaining term weights. Our work is similar to these two in the sense that we exploit the different formulations of the query, and in some instances we use relevance feedback. But our work differs in many points. First, in addition to exploiting previous queries, we identify and use various other useful pieces of information from previous ranking lists in a session. Secondly, we use those pieces of information in a different way, namely by considering them as related queries and aggregating over their results.

In another study closely related to ours, Raman et al. use related queries to diversify results while maintaining cohesion with the current query in order to satisfy the current query as well as future queries [17]. They do so using a two-level dynamic ranking where the user's interaction in the first level is used to infer her intent in order to provide a better ranking that includes second level rankings. The commonality between their approach and ours is that just like Raman et al. exploit intrinsic diversity (i.e. coverage of various aspects), we do the same, albeit we do so implicitly by relying on the aggregation algorithm to prefer documents that appeared in most previous ranking lists – and thus likely cover the most aspects. However, while we use previous session interactions to aid the performance for the current query, Raman et al. use a query to improve retrieval for a user's future session. Also, while Raman et al propose a re-ranking using an objective function that optimizes the selection of documents and queries, we on the other hand, identify pieces of information that can be used as related queries and aggregate over their results to select the best documents.

In yet another closely related work, Guan identifies text nuggets deemed interesting in each query and merges them to form a structured query (query aggregation) [9]. Notable approaches used by TREC participants include the work of [12] in which the authors combined Sequential Dependence Model features in both current queries and previous queries in the session for one system, and combined that method with pseudo-relevance feedback for other systems. Another notable approach is the use of anchor texts for query expansion proposed by [15] and adopted by others.

Previous studies of rank aggregation and data fusion techniques have shown that combining evidence from multiple query representations can be very useful for traditional ad-hoc retrieval tasks [2]. But, to the best of our knowledge, there hasn't been any previous attempt like ours to adapt such techniques to the context of session search.

3   Motivation and Hypotheses

The intuition behind using users' session data is that users may be reformulating their queries using pieces of information that were displayed to them during their previous interactions with the search engine [21], [8] and such pieces can give more insight about the user's actual intent, context or topic. In order to identify which pieces are more likely to hold added terms that are used in query reformulations, we inspect some sources of terms – snippets, titles and key-phrases – from documents in the ranking lists for previous queries. Key-phrases were obtained using AlchemyAPI [1] and Xtrak4Me [18]. The results shown in Table 1 suggest that in most cases, the new terms added by users in their reformulations come from snippets and key-phrases of documents from the ranking lists of previous queries. For instance, in the 2012 dataset, 41% of queries use new terms from previous interactions' snippets. This suggests that such sources contain other terms potentially useful for satisfying the session information need, if used as queries.

Armed with that finding, we conjecture that we can use terms from those useful sources in order to improve relevance for the session. Given the exploratory nature of many session queries, we further conjecture that we can achieve good results using a method that promotes documents that cover a myriad of relevant aspects. Thus, we naturally decided to use rank aggregation methods that exploit our useful sources of terms and that prefer documents that appeared in most previous ranking lists.

Table 1. Percentage of new terms from four sources in previous interactions

	Snippets	titles	Alchemy Keywords	Xtrak4Me Kewords
2011 dataset	38%	27%	52%	41%
2012 dataset	41%	33%	54%	47%

4   Methods

There are two components to our approach. First, we generate and select related queries which we submit to Indri [20], and then we aggregate the retrieved results for those queries.

4.1   Collecting Related Queries

Baselines: Language Model (LM) and Pseudo-Relevance Feedback
The first baseline we are comparing our results to is obtained using Indri's language model (LM) on each of the current query [20]. We filter baseline results and all other results using Waterloo's fusion spam classifier with a threshold of 0.75 [7].

For the second baseline, we use an adaptation of Lavrenko's *pseudo-relevance feedback* as implemented in Indri. We run the model with 6 different values for the number of documents used in the feedback: 10, 50, 100, 200, 300, 400 and 500. For each of the two datasets, we select the run with the maximum nDCG@10 as our second baseline. For 2011, the best feedback size is 50 documents with 0.3339 for nDCG@10 (and 0.2785 for ERR@10). For 2012, the best size is also 50 with 0.2317 for nDCG@10 (and 0.1626 for ERR@10).

Using Session-Dependent Data
The intuition behind using users' session data is that users may be reformulating their queries using pieces of information that were displayed to them during their previous interactions with the search engine [21], [8] and such pieces can give more insight about the user's actual intent, context or topic. We use pieces of information such as a user's own previous queries in the same session, document titles, document snippets (and important key-phrases) that appeared during a user's previous interactions in the same session. Specifically,

1. The previous queries in the user's session;
2. The titles of documents ranked for previous queries in the user's session;
3. Entire snippets (free of stop words) for the top 10 documents ranked for previous queries in the user's session;
4. Key phrases extracted from top-10 ranked documents for previous queries in the user's session. In this case we concatenate the top 5 key-phrases from each document into a single query;

Key-phrases were extracted using a model that exploits linguistic and statistical methods. The method uses statistical lexical analysis to determine the most significant single-word terms, and extracts those terms as well as their immediate context to form complex terms – using noun-chunks where applicable or n-grams. Then it proceeds by clustering similar complex terms – using Monge-Elkan distance as the string-similarity measure – and selecting a representative for each cluster to be a candidate key-phrase. For selecting a representative, a similarity maximization algorithm is used that prefers the key-phrase that resembles the remaining key-phrases most closely. Finally, all the candidates are analyzed in order to determine confidence scores for each in the context of the document in question. The confidence scores are obtained by combining the significance of cue tokens in the representing candidate, the scope, as determined by the distribution of the candidate cluster over the document, and number of words contained in the candidate.

Xtrak4Me [17] is an open-source library that performs this. We also use AlchemyAPI [1] to ensure that similar results can be obtained using other key-phrase extraction algorithms. And given the similarly good performances achieved by both the production-ready method and the academic open-source method, it is fair to conclude that decent key-phrase extraction algorithms can provide us with good enough key-phrases to be used as candidate related queries for the purpose of our experiment.

We submit the previous queries, titles, snippets, or keyphrases as queries to an Indri index of ClueWeb09 and aggregate results using the methods described below. Examples of related queries obtained from some documents in interaction 1 of session 7 in the 2011 dataset can be seen in Table 2 for Xtrak4Me method. The user's query for that interaction was "cosmetic laser treatment".

Table 2. Example of related queries obtained using Xtrak4Me method

Xtrak4Me (expanded) from doc at rank3	#weight(0.5 #combine(cosmetic laser treatment) 0.100 laser 0.100 skin 0.100 treatment 0.100 removal 0.100 acne)
Xtrak4Me from doc at rank 3	laser skin treatment removal acne
Xtrak4Me (expanded) from doc at rank6	#weight(0.5 #combine(cosmetic laser treatment) 0.100 cynosure 0.100 practitioner 0.100 inc 0.100 removal 0.100 skin)
Xtrak4Me from doc at rank 6	cynosure practitioner inc removal skin

Using Bing's Related Queries

In this method, we use Bing to obtain related queries for each current query. We provide queries using Bing API [3] and obtain related queries in response by the service. We submit them as queries and aggregate the results like in the previous case.

Using a combination of Bing related queries and session-dependent data

Here our aim is to observe what happens when we add Bing related queries to the set of related queries obtained from each source of session-dependent data.

4.2 Aggregation Algorithms

Previous research has shown that combining the evidence of multiple query reformulations helps improve results in information retrieval [2]. Two such methods are CombSUM and CombMNZ. For each query, CombSUM reranks documents based on their cumulative scores over all related queries. CombMNZ, on the other hand, uses the sum of similarity values times the number of non-zero similarity values [16]. Additionally, we propose another method, CombCAT with the purpose of experimenting what happens when we give precedence to documents that appear the most in our rankings. In CombCAT, for each query, we first group documents into different categories such that documents that appeared in n different rankings are put in the same category $category_n$. Then we proceed with our re-ranking by promoting documents that appear in the largest number of rankings. And within the same category, documents that have the largest sum take priority over others. Both CombMNZ and CombCAT explicitly reward documents that appear in the largest number of rankings – though in different ways. But since CombMNZ has been deeply analyzed in the literature [16], we use CombMNZ as the main aggregation in our paper for brevity. The results we obtained show very similar scores obtained using either of the three aggregation techniques. Most CombCAT and CombSUM results are left out due to space limitation. However, Fig. 1 and Fig. 2 show nDCG@10 and ERR@10 results for each of the three aggregation methods on the 2012 dataset.

5   Experiments and Results

5.1   Data

For our experiments, we use the TREC 2011 and 2012 Session track datasets [13,14]. In each, there are several sessions containing one or many interactions. The 2011 dataset contains 76 sessions while the 2012 dataset contains 98 sessions. A session is a sequence of query reformulations and interactions made by a user in order to satisfy an information need. A session consists of a current query and the previous interactions that led to the current query. In our datasets, an interaction more specifically consists of a query and a ranking list of documents for the query, titles, URLs and query-biased snippets (produced by Yahoo! BOSS) for each document. Also included are clicked documents and the time spent by the user reading a clicked document. *Note that only documents that exist in ClueWeb09 were retained.*

Session track participants must rank results for the *last query (current query)* in the session using their systems. The corpus on which the retrieval is performed for the 2011 and 2012 dataset is the category B subset of ClueWeb09. This was the same (sub)set used by the top TREC Session track systems.

The 2011 dataset includes subtopic judgments, making it possible to compute diversity measures for the 2011 dataset.

5.2   Evaluation Measures

For traditional measures, we opted for using two of the measures adopted by the TREC Session track organizers, namely the primary measure nDCG@10 and the second measure ERR@10 [5], [11]. Given that a user's information throughout a session might span several aspects of a topic, we deemed it necessary to use diversity measures to evaluate our methods. We used α-nDCG@10 and ERR-IA@10 [4], [6] as diversity measures.

5.3   Results

In the following tables, B is short for Bing, Q for Query, Alch for AlchemyAPI, Xtrak for Xtrak4Me and Snip for Snippets. For brevity, we left out ERR@10 and ERR-IA@10 results of some of our experiments. The best nDCG@10 is 0.432 for 2011 and 0.314 for 2012 which is on par with TREC Session track systems for 2011 and 2012. To put things in context, in 2012, our best run would be squeezed between the best run of the top group and the best run of the second-best team (which had nDCG@10 of 0.3221 and 0.3033 respectively). Similarly, in 2011, our best run would be squeezed between the best run of the second-best group and the best run of the third-best team (which had nDCG@10 of 0.4409 and 0.4307 respectively, and were dominated by the top team which reached 0.4540).

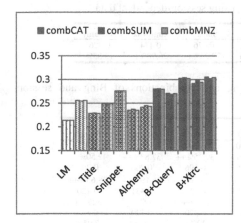 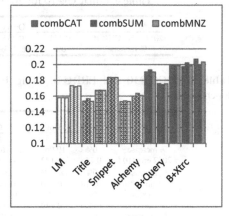

Fig. 1. nDCG@10 using CombCAT, CombSUM and CombMNZ on 2012 data

Fig. 2. ERR@10 using CombCAT, CombSUM and CombMNZ on 2012 data

Note: In our tables, + and ++ mean statistically significant at p<0.05 over the LM and pseudo-relevance feedback baselines respectively.

Table 3. nDCG@10 using session-dependent data

	LM	Query	Snippet	Xtrak4me	Alch
2012 ndcg@10	0.214	0.249	0.274	0.235	0.244
% increase	0%	16.49%	27.88%++	9.86%	13.87%
2011 ndcg@10	0.318	0.379	0.377	0.391	0.365
% increase	0%	19%	18%	23%+	15%

Using Bing's related queries only, we achieved a good improvement over the Indri baseline (19.06% nDCG@10 increase) for the 2012 dataset as shown in Table 5. The impact on the 2011 data using Bing only is more moderate (4% nDCG@10 increase). We get better improvements when we use session-dependent data. In particular, for 2012, we get a peak of 27.88% increase when we use snippets as related queries, and for 2011, we get a peak of 23% increase when we use Xtrak4Me key-phrases.
Combining Bing's related queries to session-dependent data gives even better results. For the 2012 data, using nDCG@10, we observe a peak of 42.5% increase when we use B+Alch and a low of 26.16% increase when we use B+Q. In fact for both 2011 and 2012 datasets, combing Bing and any session-dependent data produces a better result than using that session-dependent data alone. This may be because the combinations cover more aspects than the range of aspects covered by each source's queries alone. ERR@10 results follow the same trend as nDCG@10.

The 2011 session test set includes relevance judgments for subtopics as well. Using that, we were able to compute α- nDCG@10 and ERR-IA@10 diversity measures for the 2011 dataset. The trend is similar to that of traditional measures, with a peak of 44.72% increase for ERR-IA@10 (and 36.98% α-nDCG@10 increase) when combining Bing and XtraK4Me. These results were nothing but expected since we are exploiting intrinsic diversity in our methods.

Table 4. α-nDCG@10 for 2011 using session-dependent data

	LM	Query	Snippet	XtraK4me	Alchemy
2011 α-NDCG@10	0.374	0.435	0.476	0.474	0.426
% increase	0%	16.28%+	27.22%+	26.90%+	13.85%

Table 5. nDCG@10 and ERR@10 using Bing and combinations of Bing and session-dependent data

	LM	Bing	B+Q	B+Snip	B+Xtrak	B+alch
2012 ndcg@10	0.214	0.255	0.270	0.299	0.295	0.305
% increase	0%	19.06%	26.16%+	39.75%++	37.83%++	42.50%++
2012 err@10	0.158	0.172	0.175	0.196	0.200	0.203
% increase	0%	8.54%	10.88%	23.66%	26.19%++	28.65%++
2011 ndcg@10	0.318	0.330	0.378	0.431	0.431	0.420
% increase	0%	4%	19%++	36%++	36%++	32%++
2011 err@10	0.246	0.249	0.289	0.320	0.329	0.322
% increase	0%	1%	17%	30%+	34%++	31%+

Table 6. α-nDCG@10 and ERR-IA@10 using Bing and combinations Bing and session-dependent data

	LM	Bing	B+Query	B+Snip	B+Xtrk	B+alch
2011 α-nDCG@10	0.3737	0.391	0.440	0.510	0.512	0.493
% increase	0%	4.49%	17.46%++	36.27%++	36.98%++	31.85%++
2011 ERR-IA@10	0.3325	0.349	0.394	0.477	0.481	0.461
%increase	0%	4.97%	18.34%+	43.30%++	44.72%++	38.62%++

6 Analysis

In this section we show results for only some select cases simply for brevity.

Table 7. nDCG@10 for query expansion + CombMNZ

	B+AlchDoc 2012	B+XtrakDoc 2012	B+SnipDoc 2012	B+AlchDoc 2011	B+XtrakDoc 2011	B+SnipDoc 2011
ndcg@10	0.305	0.295	0.299	0.420	0.431	0.431
ndcg@10 w/ expansion	**0.314**	**0.313**	0.285	**0.422**	0.429	0.418

Effects of Query Expansion Prior to Aggregation:
In this experiment, instead of using each of the top 10 snippets retrieved by a query as related queries, we create 10 queries that contain the query text and expanded with the terms in the snippet. And we do so using keywords as well. The effect is insignificant: slight increase in three cases (Table 7 in bold font), but slight decrease in the other three cases.

Effects of the Number of Top Documents Used:
In general, increasing the number of top documents exploited from 5 to 10 causes an improvement of the results, albeit not significantly (see Table 8). This could be because most of the useful data is in the top 5 documents, and only little in the next 5. Further investigation would help determine the exact reasons.

Table 8. nDCG@10 for different cutoffs for top documents

	Snip 2012	XtrakDoc 2012	B+Alch 2012	B+AlchDoc 2012	Xtrak 2011	XtrakDoc 2011	B+Xtrak 2011	B+XtrakDoc 2011
Top 10 docs	0.274	0.282	0.305	0.314	0.391	0.411	0.431	0.429
Top 5 docs	0.255	0.273	0.300	0.313	0.338	0.419	0.421	0.420

Table 9. nDCG@10 for various ways of exploiting click data

	Snip 2012	Xtrak-Doc 2012	B+Alch 2012	B+AlchDoc 2012	Xtrak 2011	Xtrak-Doc 2011	B+Xtrak 2011	B+XtrakDoc 2011
no clicks	0.274	0.282	0.305	0.314	0.391	0.411	0.431	0.429
clicked only	0.182	0.210	0.291	0.291	0.265	0.345	0.353	0.362
boost clicked	0.280	0.284	0.305	0.314	0.391	0.416	0.425	0.432

Effects of Clicked Data:
Aggregating using data from clicked documents alone hurts the performance significantly. However when we include queries taken from clicked documents twice (instead of once, as per normal), we get slightly better results than when clicks are not

exploited at all (Table 9). That is, giving more voting rights to clicked documents improves performance. Determining by how much the voting rights must be increased is left for future work.

Table 10. 2011 Bing+XtractMe (Best of bing+session specific)

% of overlap	# of queries	ERR impact on queries			nDCG impact on queries		
		Incr	Same	Decr	Incr	Same	Decr
0%	41	22	7	12	19	7	15
10%	25	17	4	4	17	4	4
20%	6	2	0	4	3	0	3
30%	3	2	0	1	2	0	1
40%	1	0	0	1	0	0	1

We furthered our analyses to show that we are not merely rearranging, promoting and redisplaying documents that were shown in previous interactions of a given session. For that, we looked into document overlaps: for each session, there is only little or no overlap between our top 10 documents and the documents that are part of the previous interactions of the same session. For instance, as shown in Table 10, out of all 76 queries of the 2011 session dataset, 41 queries returned 10 top documents that do not overlap at all with the documents returned by the commercial engine for the previous interactions. Also, 21 out of the 41 queries witnessed an increase of ERR@10 over the baseline while only 12 witnessed a decrease and 7 remained with the same result. 25 returned 1 overlapping document out of 10. Only 1 query returned the maximum of 4 documents out of 10 that overlap with previous interaction documents. This suggests that we are not merely redisplaying the documents displayed to users in previous interactions when the session data was being collected.

For the 2012 session dataset, the topics are categorized under different types depending on their search goal (specific or amorphous goal) and their product type (factual or intellectual target). We evaluate our results for each task type and show in table 11 and 12 how the effects of our methods differ on each task type. In general, our methods achieve their biggest improvements on the intellectual session searches with a peak of 67.5% improvement over the baseline's nDCG@10 when using the combination of XtraK4Me keyphrases and Bing's related queries (B+Xtrk). Even when using session-dependent data only, we achieve a significant peak of 40.72% increase of the nDCG@10. Intellectual searches are more difficult than factual searches, so our systems perform better on the most difficult product type sessions. While the dirichlet-smoothed Language model gets 0.2215 for factual tasks and only 0.2129 for intellectual, B+Xtrk gets 0.2804 for factual and a very high 0.3408 for intellectual tasks comparatively. This may be because our system uncovers hidden interesting keywords that were not obvious from intellectual task topic description. However, it is noteworthy that our methods also get significant improvements on the other task types.

In a related effort, we strive to determine how many tokens introduced by our methods are not part of the main query, but are part of the topic description. Stop words are excluded from the lists of tokens. As can be seen in Fig. 4, Snip, Xtrak and Alch methods introduce a sizeable number of tokens that were not part of the *current-query* and would have hence been overlooked even though they are potentially important

Table 11. nDCG@10 per task type for 2012 session using session-dependent data for CombMNZ

	LM	Query	Snippet	XtraK	Alchemy
amorphous	0.2512	0.2707	0.2899	0.2659	0.2217
% change	0%	7.76%	15.41%	5.85%	-11.74%
factual	0.2215	0.2457	0.2631	0.2287	0.2526
% change	0%	10.93%	18.78%	3.25%	14.04%
intellectual	0.2129	0.2546	0.2996	0.247	0.2266
% change	0%	**19.59%**	**40.72%**	**16.02%**	6.43%
specific	0.1943	0.2318	0.2654	0.2112	0.2602
% change	0%	19.30%	36.59%	8.70%	**33.92%**

(since they are part of the topic description). In fact, Fig. 3 shows that our method is successful at promoting documents that cover two or more aspects of a topic. Out of the total 76 sessions, 35 witness Xtrak4Me doing better than the baseline in promoting documents that cover two or more aspects, 20 witness the inverse, and 21 witness no difference.

Table 12. nDCG@10 per task type for 2012 session using Bing alone and combinations of Bing and session-dependent data for CombMNZ. B is short for Bing

	LM	Bing	B+Query	B+Snip	B+Xtrk	B+alch
amorphous	0.2512	0.3064	0.3152	0.3255	0.3391	0.3242
% change	0%	21.97%	25.48%	29.58%	34.99%	29.06%
factual	0.2215	0.2309	0.252	0.2804	0.2595	0.2831
% change	0%	4.24%	13.77%	26.59%	17.16%	27.81%
intellectual	0.2129	0.301	0.3029	0.3408	0.3566	0.3426
% change	0%	**41.38%**	**42.27%**	**60.08%**	**67.50%**	**60.92%**
specific	0.1943	0.2165	0.2349	0.2836	0.259	0.2888
% change	0%	11.43%	20.90%	45.96%	33.30%	48.64%

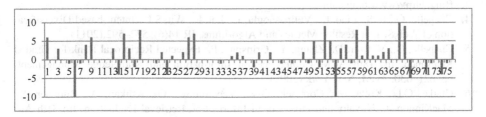

Fig. 3. Difference between Xtrak4Me and LM in terms of the number of documents that cover 2 or more aspects (y-axis) for all sessions, on the 2011 dataset

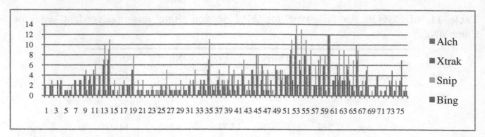

Fig. 4. Number of tokens introduced by Alch, Xtrak, Snip and Bing that are not part of the main query, but are part of the topic description on the 2011 dataset

7   Conclusion and Future Work

In this paper, we showed that using simple ranking aggregation methods over a good set of related queries helps improve results and we show which sources are useful for collecting good related queries. Bing's related queries are a good choice, and session-dependent data are even better. But we achieve even better results by combining Bing related queries to session-dependent queries. One possible future work idea would be to come up with a scheme to select only the more pertinent related queries pertaining to the actual topic to perform our aggregations in order to achieve even better performance. More efficient implementations are left for future work as well.

Acknowledgments. This work was supported in part by the National Science Foundation (NSF) under grant number IIS-1350799. Any opinions, findings and conclusions or recommendations expressed in this material are the author's and do not necessarily reflect those of the sponsor.

References

1. AlchemyAPI, http://www.alchemyapi.com
2. Belkin, N.J., Kantor, P., Fox, E.A., Shaw, J.A.: Combining the Evidence of Multiple Query Representations for Information Retrieval. IP&M 31(3), 431–448 (1995)
3. Bing, http://www.bing.com
4. Chapelle, O., Ji, S., Liao, C., Velipasaoglu, E., Lai, L., Wu, S.L.: Intent-based Diversification of Web Search Results: Metrics and Algorithms. IR 14(6), 572–592 (2011)
5. Chapelle, O., Metlzer, D., Zhang, Y., Grinspan, P.: Expected Reciprocal Rank for Graded Relevance. In: 18th ACM Conference on Information and Knowledge Management, pp. 621–630. ACM, New York (2009)
6. Clarke, C.L., Kolla, M., Cormack, G.V., Vechtomova, O., Ashkan, A., Büttcher, S., MacKinnon, I.: Novelty and Diversity in Information Retrieval Evaluation. In: 31th Annual International ACM SIGIR Conference on Reseearch and Development in Information Retrieval, pp. 659–666. ACM, New York (2008)
7. Cormack, G.V., Smucker, M.D., Clarke, C.L.: Efficient and Effective Spam Filtering and Re-ranking for Large Web Datasets. Information Retrieval 14(5), 441–465 (2011)

8. Dang, V., Croft, B.W.: Query Reformulation Using Anchor Text. In: 3rd ACM International Conference on Web Search and Data Mining, pp. 41–50. ACM (2010)
9. Guan, D.: Structured Query Formulation and Result Organization for Session Search. Dissertation, Georgetown University (2013)
10. Guan, D., Zhang, S., Yang, H.: Utilizing Query Change for Session Search. In: 36th International ACM SIGIR Conference on Research and Development in Information Retrieval, pp. 453–462. ACM, New York (2013)
11. Järvelin, K., Kekäläinen, J.: Cumulated Gain-based Evaluation of IR Techniques. Transaction on Information Systems 20(4), 422–446 (2002)
12. Jiang, J., He, D., Han, S.: On Duplicate Results in a Search Session. In: Proceedings of the 21th Text Retrieval Conference (2012)
13. Kanoulas, E., Carterette, B., Clough, P.D., Sanderson, M.: Overview of the trec 2011 session track. In: Proceedings of the 21st Text Retrieval Conference (2011)
14. Kanoulas, E., Carterette, B., Clough, P.D., Sanderson, M.: Overview of the trec 2012 session track. In: Proceedings of the 21st Text Retrieval Conference (2012)
15. Kruschwitz, U.: University of Essex at the TREC 2012 Session Track. In: Proceedings of the 21st Text Retrieval Conference (2012)
16. Lee, J.H.: Analyses of Multiple Evidence Combination. In: 20th Annual International ACM SIGIR Conference on Research and Development in Information Retrieval, pp. 267–276. ACM, New York (1997)
17. Raman, K., Bennett, P.N., Collins-Thompson, K.: Toward Whole-Session Relevance: Exploring Intrinsic Diversity in Web Search. In: 36th International ACM SIGIR Conference on Research and Development in Information Retrieval, pp. 463–472. ACM, New York (2013)
18. Schutz, A.T.: Keyphrase Extraction from Single Documents in the Open Domain Exploiting Linguistic and Statistical Methods. Dissertation, National University of Ireland (2008)
19. Shokouhi, M., White, R.W., Bennett, P., Radlinski, F.: Fighting Search Engine Amnesia: Reranking Repeated Results. In: 36th International ACM SIGIR Conference on Research and Development in Information Retrieval, pp. 273–282. ACM, New York (2013)
20. Strohman, T., Metzler, D., Turtle, H., Croft, W.: Indri: A Language Model-Based Search Engine for Complex Queries. In: Proceedings of the International Conference on Intelligence Analysis (2005)
21. Yue, Z., Jiang, J., Han, S., He, D.: Where Do the Query Terms Come From? An Analysis of Query Reformulation in Collaborative Web Search. In: 21st ACM International Conference on Information and Knowledge Management, pp. 2595–2598. ACM, New York (2012)
22. Zhang, S., Guan, D., Yang, H.: Query Change as Relevance Feedback in Session Search. In: 36th International ACM SIGIR Conference on Research and Development in Information Retrieval, pp. 821–824. ACM, New York (2013)

Modified Frequency-Based Term Weighting Scheme for Accurate Dark Web Content Classification

Thabit Sabbah and Ali Selamat

Faculty of Computing
Universiti Teknologi Malaysia (UTM)
81310 Skudai, Johor, Malaysia
sosthabit2@live.utm.my, aselamat@utm.my

Abstract. Security informatics and intelligence computation plays a vital role in detecting and classifying terrorism contents in the web. Accurate web content classification using the computational intelligence and security informatics will increase the opportunities of the early detection of the potential terrorist activities. In this paper, we propose a modified frequency-based term weighting scheme for accurate Dark Web content classification. The proposed term weighting scheme is compared to the common techniques used in text classification such as Term Frequency (TF), Term Frequency-Inverse Document Frequency (TF-IFD), and Term Frequency- Relative Frequency (tf.rf), on a dataset selected from Dark Web Portal Forum. The experimental results show that the classification accuracy and other evaluation measures based on the proposed scheme outperforms other term weighting techniques based classification.

Keywords: Term Frequency, Weighting, Text Classification, Dark Web.

1 Introduction

In the recent years, the Internet based technologies provides the world with a quick and easy access environment. Extremist groups are exploiting the latest Internet based technologies and their facilities such as anonymity, huge potential audience, and inexpensive development and maintenance broadcasting stations, to spread their propaganda, instructions, and to encourage others to join the extremism [1]. The September 11, 2001 (9/11) attacks motivated the information technology researchers to study, trace, and analyzing different types of online content, in order to prevent and reduce the potential terrorism around in the world. The hidden part of the web used by terrorist and extremist groups online is named to as the dark web (DW) [2]. As the non-dark web, the content of DW is categorized into text-based and multimedia types. Text-based content which is the large category in web data [3] and in DW collection [4] includes the static text-based files such as (.txt),(.doc), and (.pdf) files. On the other hand, multimedia contents consist of images, audio, and video files.

Over the recent years, many information security techniques are proposed to detect the terrorism on the web, since it was found that the group known as "Hamburg Cell" that was mainly responsible for the preparation of the September 11 attacks against

A. Jaafar et al. (Eds.): AIRS 2014, LNCS 8870, pp. 184–196, 2014.

the United States used Internet intensively [5]. Text analysis based-techniques has been used intensively in detecting potential terrorism on the web based on statistical methods [3]. Commonly, in statistical methods, the text is represented as vectors of weighted features (words). TF-IDF term weighting algorithm is the most commonly weighting scheme used to determine the significant words in the text [3]. In some other cases, text is represented statistically base on lexical, syntactic, domain specific bag of words, and n-grams [6-11] features. However, the inability of statistical methods to understand the semantic meanings of text written by human [3] cause the low performance of these methods in text classification. In general, the performance of TF-IDF and other statistical methods is not sufficient [3],[12],[13].

In this research we propose a modified frequency-based term weighting technique, and compare its performance as a feature selection methods to the common term weighting techniques such as Term Frequency Inverse Document Frequency (TF-IDF), Term Frequency (TF), Term Frequency-Relevance Frequency (tf.rf), Document Frequency (DF), Entropy, and Glasgow in dark web content classification.

The paper is organized as follows: Section 2 reviews the term weighting schemes used in this study, while Section 3 presents the proposed frequency-based term weighting scheme. Section 4 describes the datasets and experiment. Section 5 discusses the results, and finally, conclusions are drawn in Section 6.

2   Frequency-Based Term Weighting Techniques

In information retrieval and web-classification domain, the TF-IDF, Entropy [14], term-weighting techniques are used widely besides TF, DF, and IDF [12] and the Glasgow [15] techniques. The tf.rf scheme is one of the newest supervised term weighting schemes used in text classification [16,17]. However, there are many other term-weighting algorithms proposed and used in the domain [15],[18]. Here is the description of the techniques used for benchmarking in this study.

2.1   Term Frequency (TF)

TF is concerned with the normalized frequency of a certain term. More occurrences of a term indicate more significance of the term. $TF_{t,d}$ is defined as in equation (1) [19]:

$$TF_{t,d} = \frac{tf_{t,d}}{\sqrt{\sum_{t=1}^{n} tf_{t,d}^{2}}} \qquad (1)$$

where $tf_{t,d}$ is the number of occurrences of term t in document d, while the denominator is known as the Euclidean norm of the documents in which $tf_{t,d}$ is the frequency of tth term in document d, and n is the number of distinctive terms in document d.

2.2   Document Frequency (DF)

DF weight of a term t (denoted by DF_t) represents the number of documents within the collection in which the term t is found. *DF* is expressed by equation (2):

$$DF_t = \sum_{d=1}^{D} df_{t,d} \tag{2}$$

where D is the total number of documents in the collection, and $df_{t,d}$ is a function defined as in equation (3):

$$df_{t,d} = \begin{cases} 1 & t \in d \\ 0 & t \notin d \end{cases} \tag{3}$$

2.3   Inverse Document Frequency (IDF)

IDF is a very important statistical measure that supports the assumption that a more frequent term in the collection is considered less important. IDF is defined as in equation (4):

$$IDF_t = \log \frac{N}{DF_t} \tag{4}$$

where N is the total number of documents in the collection, DF_t is the number of documents within the collection in which the term is found. Since log is a monotonically increasing function, it can be safely used to make the factor less insensitive, and IDF is always positive because the denominator (DF_t) is always less than or equal to N.

In contrast to TF scheme, IDF is a global term weighting scheme, in which the term is weighted in respect to the collection and the term weight is the same in all documents. This case of weighting causes thousands of terms to have the same weight which make it difficult to select for example the top 50 or 100 terms as features for classification. In our experiments IDF measure will not be used, however it is mentioned here because of its importance to next weighting scheme.

2.4   Term Frequency-Inverse Document Frequency (TF-IDF)

TF-IDF is an ultimate ranking measure that represents the terms within the collection of documents that reflect the assumption that a less frequent term in the collection is the most significant term and vice versa. TF-IDF is used by many information-retrieval applications [20]. TF-IDF of a term t in document d, denoted by (TF-IDF$_{t,d}$), is the dot product of the Term Frequency (TF) and the Inverse Document Frequency (IDF) of the term, as in equation (5):

$$TF - IDF_{t,d} = TF_{t,d} \cdot IDF_t \tag{5}$$

2.5   Glasgow

Glasgow weighting scheme was proposed by [21]. The main aim of this weighting scheme is to prevent longer documents to be more favored because of the existence of many instances of insignificant terms in such documents. Glasgow term weight is defined as in equation (6):

$$w_{td} = \frac{\log(TF_{td} + 1)}{\log(length_d)} \times \log \left(N/DF_t \right) \tag{6}$$

where $length_d$ is the length of vector that represents the distinctive terms of document I. TF_{td} is the term frequency of tth term in d^{th} document, N is the total number of documents in the collection, and DF_t is document frequency of term t.

2.6   Entropy

Based on the probabilistic analysis of the text, Entropy technique considers that a more frequent term in the collection is the more important term [14] after removing the stop words. Entropy is defined as in equations (7)

$$w_{td} = L_{td} \times G_t \tag{7}$$

where G_t and L_{td} are known as the term's global weight and is the local weight of term t in document d, respectively. G_t and L_{td} are calculated using the equations 8 and 9

$$G_t = \frac{1 + \sum_{d=1}^{n} \frac{TF_{td}}{F_t} \log\left(\frac{TF_{td}}{F_t} + 1\right)}{\log N} \tag{8}$$

$$L_{td} = \begin{cases} 1 + \log TF_{td}, & TF_{td} > 0 \\ 0, & TF_{td} = 0 \end{cases} \tag{9}$$

2.7   Term Frequency-Relative Frequency (tf.rf)

tf.rf scheme is proposed by [16] as a supervised term weighting technique. In supervised weighting methods some prior statistical information such as χ^2 are involved in calculating the term weight [17]. In [16] the document distribution and the number of positive and negative documents containing the term to calculate the weight of term t in document d as in equation (10)

$$tf.rf_{td} = tf_{td}.\log\left(2 + \frac{a}{max(1, c)}\right) \tag{10}$$

where a is the number of documents in the positive category that contain this term t and c is the number of documents in the negative category that contain this term t.

3   Proposed Term Weighting Scheme

Our proposed term weighting scheme is extended from the standard TF formula. The main idea behind the proposed scheme is to include the proportion of the total number of term frequency in all collection's documents to the total number of distinctive terms in the collection. In addition the proportion of the length of the document to the total number of distinctive terms in the collection is considered in the normalization, when calculating the weight if term t in document d. the proposed scheme is named modified Term Frequency and denoted as $(mTF_{t,d})$. The formula is expressed as shown in equation (11).

$$mTF_{t,d} = \frac{tf_{t,d} \times \left(\frac{T_t}{T_c}\right)}{\log\left[\left(\sum_{t=1}^{n} tf_{t,d}^2\right) \times \left(\frac{length_d}{T_c}\right)\right]} \tag{11}$$

As in standard TF formula, $tf_{t,d}$ represents the number of occurrences of term t^{th} in the dth document in the collection. However, T_t stands for the total number of term frequency in all collection's documents which can be expressed as in equation (12), while T_c and $length_d$ are the total number of distinctive terms in the collection and the length of the dth document, respectively. The length of the document in this formula is defined as the number of distinctive terms in the documents.

$$T_t = \sum_{d=1}^{D} tf_{t,d} \qquad (12)$$

As mentioned in Section 2.1, the standard TF formula considers the more frequent term in the document as the more significant term. In the proposed mTF the proportion of the frequency of the term in the collection to the total number of distinctive terms in the collection is also considered, since the numeric value of the fraction $\left(\frac{T_t}{T_c}\right)$ will grow up by the increment of term frequency on the collection level. Moreover, mTF considers the proportion of the number of distinctive terms in the document to the number of distinctive terms in the collection in the normalization. The fraction $\left(\frac{length_d}{T_c}\right)$ reflects the number of missing terms if the documents relatively to the total number of terms in the collection, so that the length of the document here is considered as the number of the distinctive terms in the document.

Since the proposed formula is and extinction of the standard TF formula, the proposed formula can be used instead of the standard TF formula in TF-IDF weighting scheme discusses in section 2.4. The new form of the TF-IDF formula will be denoted as mTF-IDF and the its formula will be as in equations (13) and (14).

$$mTF - IDF_{t,d} = mTF_{t,d} \cdot IDF_t \qquad (13)$$

$$mTF - IDF_{t,d} = \frac{tf_{t,d} \times \left(\frac{T_t}{T_c}\right)}{\log\left[\left(\sum_{t=1}^{n} tf_{t,d}^2\right) \times \left(\frac{length_d}{T_c}\right)\right]} \times \log \frac{N}{DF_t} \qquad (14)$$

4   Experiments Setup and Performance Evaluation

4.1   Dataset

Many of existing works in DW classification and detection depend on the Dark Web Portal Forum (DWPF) as source of experimental datasets [22-28]. DWPF is the largest collection of crawled terrorist related documents, collected from 17 Arabic forums and many other English, German, French, and Russian forums [4]. Our dataset consists of 500 dark documents in addition to same number of non-dark documents. As in previous studies such as [13],[29] the dataset used is balanced dataset. In this research we focus on Arabic dark web content classification, so thousands of Arabic documents were downloaded from DWPF. Then, native Arabic experts examined the documents and labeled 500 documents as *Dark*. Finally, the non-Dark documents were imported from the *Open Source Arabic Corpora* (OSAC) text classification dataset[30]. OSAC dataset includes documents in many categories such as Economy, Education, Foods, Health, History, and Religion, as shown in Fig. 1.

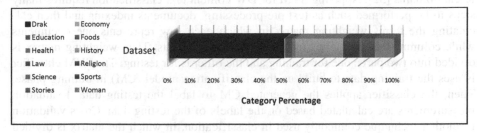

Fig. 1. Dataset documents categorical distribution

As in many of existing works, DW classification is binary classification, which concern in identifying the dark content, so the categories of non-dark documents are not important. However, the categories of the non-dark documents is mentioned to show the diversity of categories from which the dark content can be distinguished.

4.2 Experiments

Fig. 2 shows the framework of our experiments in which the SVM classifier is applied.

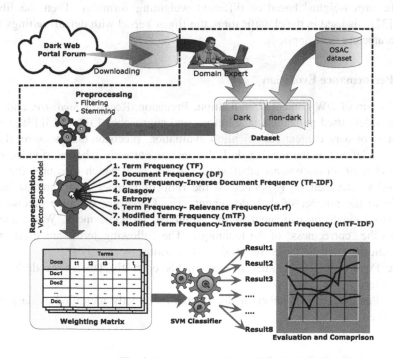

Fig. 2. Experimental framework

SVM classifier is proven to be superior in comparison with other classifiers such as C4.5 in the domain of DW analysis [8],[31]. Moreover, SVM has been shown to be one of the best performing and accurate classification approaches in many other different domains [32]. Applying SVM for DW content text classification requires many steps to be performed such as text pre-processing, documents indexing and then calculating the terms weighting matrix in which each row represents one documents while columns form the terms included by the documents. Then weighting matrix is divided into two parts: one for training and the other is for testing. The SVM classifier is uses the training data to build up the classification model (CM) in training phase. Then, the classifier applies the generated CM to label the testing data. Evaluation measurements are calculated based on the labels of the testing data. Cross validation is another technique commonly used in classification, in which the matrix is divided into k folds (10 folds is common), then $(k-1)$ folds are used as training data and the remaining fold is used for testing iteratively. In this research, classification in 10 fold cross validation approach is applied.

As shown in the experimental framework, the pre-processing step included filtering and stemming. Filtering in this research, stands for removing the meaningless word (also known as stop words), removing non-Arabic characters, removing numbers, symbols, and special characters such as punctuations, Arabic diacritics, and other characters [33-35]. However, stemming is the process of removing suffixes, prefixes, and infixes from the words [36].

In the indexing step, we use the Lucene 4.3 package[1] to index the documents and calculate term weights' based on different weighting formulas. Then the libSVM library [37]   is used in the classification, the linear kernel with default settings for all other parameters were applied.

4.3   Performance Evolution

In the domain of DW content classification, Precision, Recall, *f_measure*, and Accuracy are widely used in evaluating solutions and approaches [3],[4],[13],[38],[39]. In the context of dark content classification evaluation, precision that measures the "exactness" is defined as the number dark documents correctly labelled, divided by the total number of all documents labelled as dark. Recall, which measures the "completeness" of the method, is defined as the ratio of number of documents labelled correctly to the number of dark document. The *f_measure* combine precision and recall into a single measurement as the weighted harmonic mean. While accuracy evaluates the "correctness" of the technique. The following terms are used in DW classification to indicate the corresponding definitions:

- True Positive (TP): Number of documents correctly labeled as dark by the classifier.
- False Positive (FP): Number of documents incorrectly identified as dark by the classifier.

---

[1] http://lucene.apache.org/

- True Negative (TN): Number of documents correctly identified as non-dark by the classifier.
- False Negative (FN): Number of documents incorrectly identified as non-dark by the classifier.

The evaluation measures are calculated as in equations 15-18:

$$Precision(Dark) = \frac{|TP|}{|TP| + |FP|} \tag{15}$$

$$Recall(Dark) = \frac{|TP|}{|TP| + |FN|} \tag{16}$$

$$f_{measure} = 2 \times \frac{\text{Precision} \times \text{Recall}}{\text{Precision} + \text{Recall}} \tag{17}$$

$$Accuracy = \frac{|TP| + |TN|}{|TP| + |FP| + |FN| + |TN|} \tag{18}$$

5   Results and Discussions

Fig. 3 shows the precision evaluation measure, while Figs. 4, 5, and 6 show the recall, *f_measure* and accuracy results respectively.

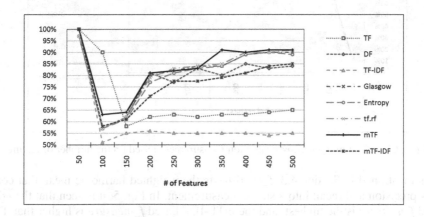

Fig. 1. Classification precision evaluation measurement based on the number of features

Fig. 3 shows that the precision measure based on the proposed term weighting scheme *mTF* is higher in general, and *m*TF-IDF based precision is also higher than the original TF and TF-IDF based classification precision. Moreover, it can be seen that the Entropy, Glasgow and tf.rf based precision are close to each other, however it is less than the *mTF* based classification precision. The higher *mTF* based precision in general means that a high number of dark documents are correctly labeled as dark by the classifier.

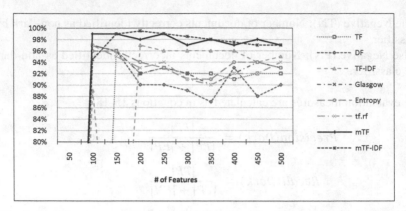

Fig. 2. Classification recall evaluation measurement based on the number of features

It can be seen in Fig. 4 that the classification recall based on the *mTF*-IDF weighting schemes is the highest. Moreover, the *mTF* based recall is also higher than other weighting formulas based recall. The highest classification recall measurements means the higher "completeness" of the solution.

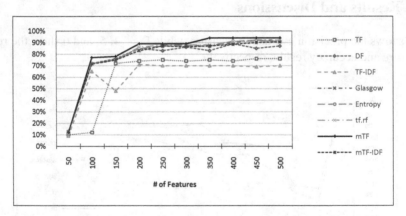

Fig. 3. Classification *f_measure* evaluation measurement based on the number of features

As mentioned in Section 4.3, *f_measure* is the weighted harmonic mean that combines precision and recall into a single measurement. In Fig. 5, it is seen that the *mTF* based *f_measure* is the highest, and the *m*TF-IDF based *f_measure* is higher than DF, TF, and TF-IDF based *f_measure*. High *m*TF based classification *f_measure* value indicates the high "effectiveness" of the formula.

Accuracy measure is used to evaluate the "correctness" of the technique. As it can be seen in Fig. 6, the classification accuracy based on the *m*TF formula is the highest among all schemes. The highest *m*TF based accuracy (94%) is achieved depending on at least 350 term as classification features. Moreover, it can be seen that the classification accuracy based on *m*TF-IDF also is higher than DF, TF, and TF-IDF based accuracy. Although, the accuracy based on Entropy, Glasgow, and tf.rf schemes are higher than the *m*TF-IDF based accuracy, the *m*TF-IDF accuracy is close to 90% based on 500 features.

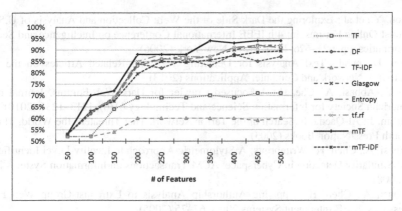

Fig. 6. Classification accuracy evaluation measurement based on the number of features

6   Conclusions

This paper proposed a modified frequency based term weighting scheme (mTF) extended from TF weighting formula. The proportion of sum number of occurrences over the collection and the length of the document to the total number of distinctive terms in the collection is involved in calculating the local term weight t in document d. Moreover, a new variant form of the standard TF-IDF formula is introduced by replacing the TF part by the proposed modified scheme. Both of proposed formulas were benchmarked with many different term weighting schemes used a dataset based on the DWPF and OSAC dataset. The experimental evaluation measurements results show that the proposed mTF consistently outperform other formulas in the classification accuracy, precision, and recall. Moreover, the proposed TF-IDF variant outperforms the original TF-IDF formula in all evaluation measurements. Our future work is focusing on testing and bench marking the proposed formula with standard text classification and categorization datasets in English such as 20 Newsgroups, Reuters, and Ohsumed corpora and in Arabic such as Watan, Khaleej, BBC, and CNN datasets.

Acknowledgment. The authors would like to thank the colleagues in the Software Engineering Research Group (SERG), Universiti Teknologi Malaysia who provided insight and expertise that greatly assisted the research. Moreover, this work is supported by the Research Management Centre (RMC) at the Universiti Teknologi Malaysia under Research University Grant (Vot 01G72) and the Ministry of Science, Technology & Innovations Malaysia under Science Fund (Vot 4S062).

References

1. Abbasi, A., Chen, H.: Affect Intensity Analysis of Dark Web Forums. In: IEEE International Conference on Intelligence and Security Informatics, pp. 282–288. IEEE Press, New York (2007)

2. Zhou, Y., et al.: Exploring the Dark Side of the Web: Collection and Analysis of U.S. Extremist Online Forums. In: 4th IEEE International Conference on Intelligence and Security Informatics, pp. 621–626. IEEE Press, New York (2006)
3. Choi, D., et al.: Text Analysis for Detecting Terrorism-Related Articles on the Web. Journal of Network and Computer Applications (2013)
4. Fu, T., Abbasi, A., Che, H.: A Focused Crawler for Dark Web Forums. Journal of the American Society for Information Science and Technology 61(6), 1213–1231 (2010)
5. Corbin, J.: Al-Qaeda: In Search of the Terror Network That Threatens the World. Thunder Mouth Press/Nation Books (2003)
6. Abbasi, A., Chen, H.: Writeprints: A Stylometric Approach to Identity-Level Identification and Similarity Detection in Cyberspace. ACM Transactions on Information Systems 26(2), 7 (2008)
7. Abbasi, A., Chen, H.: Applying Authorship Analysis to Extremist-Group Web Forum Messages. IEEE Intelligent Systems 20(5), 67–75 (2005)
8. Zheng, R., et al.: A Framework for Authorship Identification of Online Messages: Writing-style Features and Classification Techniques. Journal of the American Society for Information Science and Technology 57(3), 378–393 (2006)
9. Huang, C., Fu, T., Chen, H.: Text-Based Video Content Classification for Online Video-Sharing Sites. J. Am. Soc. Inf. Sci. Technol. 61(5), 891–906 (2010)
10. Tianjun, F., Chun-Neng, H., Hsinchun, C.: Identification of eExtremist Videos in Online Video Sharing Sites. In: IEEE International Conference on Intelligence and Security Informatics, pp. 179–181. IEEE Press, New York (2009)
11. Choi, D., et al.: Building Knowledge Domain n-gram Model for Mobile Devices. Information 14(11), 3583–3590 (2011)
12. Ran, L., Xianjiu, G.: An Improved Algorithm to Term Weighting in Text Classification. In: International Conference on Multimedia Technology, pp. 1–3. IEEE Press, New York (2010)
13. Greevy, E., Smeaton, A.F.: Classifying Racist Texts using a Support Vector Machine. In: 27th Annual International ACM SIGIR Conference on Research and Development in Information Rretrieval, pp. 468–469. ACM, New York (2004)
14. Selamat, A., Omatu, S.: Web Page Feature Selection and Classification using Neural Networks. Inf. Sci. Inf. Comput. Sci. 158(1), 69–88 (2004)
15. Crestani, F., et al.: Short Queries, Natural Language and Spoken Document Retrieval: Experiments at Glasgow University. In: Voorhees, E.M., Harman, D.K. (eds.) The Sixth Text Retrieval Conference (TREC-6), pp. 667–686. [NIST Special Publication 500–240], http://trec.nist.gov/pubs/trec6/papers/glasgow.ps.gz (accessed December 15, 2013)
16. Lan, M., Tan, C.-L., Low, H.-B.: Proposing a New Term Weighting Scheme for Text Categorization. In: 21st National Conference on Artificial Intelligence, pp. 763–768. AAAI Press, Boston (2006)
17. Man, L., et al.: Supervised and Traditional Term Weighting Methods for Automatic Text Categorization. Pattern Analysis and Machine Intelligence 31(4), 721–735 (2009)
18. Yang, Y., Pedersen, J.O.: A Comparative Study on Feature Selection in Text Categorization. In: 14th International Conference on Machine Learning, pp. 412–420. Morgan Kaufmann Publishers Inc. (1997)
19. Salton, G., Buckley, C.: Term-Weighting Approaches in Automatic Text Retrieval. Information Processing & Management 24(5), 513–523 (1988)
20. Chiang, D.-A., et al.: The Chinese Text Categorization System with Association Rule and Category Priority. Expert Systems with Applications 35(1-2), 102–110 (2008)

21. Sanderson, M., Ruthven, I.: Report on the Glasgow IR group (glair4) submission. In: The Fifth Text REtrieval Conference (TREC-5), Gaithersburg, Maryland, pp. 517–520 (1996)
22. Anwar, T., Abulaish, M.: Identifying Cliques in Dark Web Forums - An Agglomerative Clustering Approach. In: 10th IEEE International Conference on Intelligence and Security Informatics, pp. 171–173. IEEE Press, New York (2012)
23. Rios, S.A., Munoz, R.: Dark Web Portal Overlapping Community Detection based on Topic Models. In: ACM SIGKDD Workshop on Intelligence and Security Informatics, pp. 1–7. ACM, New York (2012)
24. Yang, C.C., Tang, X., Gong, X.: Identifying Dark Web Clusters with Temporal Coherence Analysis. In: IEEE International Conference on Intelligence and Security Informatics, pp. 167–172. IEEE Press, New York (2011)
25. L'Huillier, G., et al.: Topic-based Social Network Analysis for Virtual Communities of Interests in the Dark Web. In: ACM SIGKDD Workshop on Intelligence and Security Informatics, pp. 66–73. ACM, New York (2010)
26. Yang, C.C., Tang, X., Thuraisingham, B.M.: An Analysis of User Influence Ranking Algorithms on Dark Web Forums. In: ACM SIGKDD Workshop on Intelligence and Security Informatic, pp. 1–7. ACM, New York (2010)
27. Kramer, S.: Anomaly Detection in Extremist Web Forums using ADynamical Systems Approach. In: ACM SIGKDD Workshop on Intelligence and Security Informatics, pp. 1–10. ACM, New York (2010)
28. Sabbah, T., Selamat, A.: Revealing Terrorism Contents form Web Page Using Frequency Weighting Techniques. In: The International Conference on Artificial Life and Robotics (2014)
29. Aknine, S., Slodzian, A., Quenum, J.G.: Web personalisation for users protection: A multi-agent method. In: Mobasher, B., Anand, S.S. (eds.) ITWP 2003. LNCS (LNAI), vol. 3169, pp. 306–323. Springer, Heidelberg (2005)
30. Saad, M.K., Ashour, W.: OSAC.: Open Source Arabic Corpora. In: 6th International Symposium on Electrical and Electronics Engineering and Computer Science, Cyprus, pp. 118–123 (2010)
31. Chen, H.: Exploring extremism and terrorism on the web: The dark web project. In: Yang, C.C., et al. (eds.) PAISI 2007. LNCS, vol. 4430, pp. 1–20. Springer, Heidelberg (2007)
32. Lee, L., et al.: An Enhanced Support Vector Machine Classification Framework by Using Euclidean Distance Function for Text Document Categorization. Applied Intelligence 37(1), 80–99 (2012)
33. Chisholm, E., Kolda, T.G.: New Term Weighting Formulas for the Vector Space Method in Information Retrieval. Computer Science and Mathematics Division, Oak Ridge National Laboratory (1999)
34. Last, M., Markov, A., Kandel, A.: Multi-lingual detection of terrorist content on the web. In: Chen, H., Wang, F.-Y., Yang, C.C., Zeng, D., Chau, M., Chang, K. (eds.) WISI 2006. LNCS, vol. 3917, pp. 16–30. Springer, Heidelberg (2006)
35. Gohary, A.F.E., et al.: A Computational Approach for Analyzing and Detecting Emotions in Arabic Text. International Journal of Engineering Research and Applications (IJERA) 3(3), 100–107 (2013)
36. Ceri, S., et al.: An Introduction to Information Retrieval. In: Web Information Retrieval, pp. 3–11. Springer, Heidelberg (2013)
37. Chang, C.-C., Lin, C.-J.: LIBSVM: A Library for Support Vector Machines. ACM Trans. Intell. Syst. Technol. 2(3), 1–27 (2011)

38. Zimbra, D. and H. Chen.: Scalable Sentiment Classification Across Multiple Dark Web Forums. In: 10th IEEE International Conference on Intelligence and Security Informatics, PP. 78-83. IEEE Computer Society (2012)
39. Xianshan, Z., Guangzhu, Y.: Finding Criminal Suspects by Improving the Accuracy of Similarity Measurement. In: 9th International Conference on Fuzzy Systems and Knowledge Discovery, pp. 1145–1149. IEEE Press, New York (2012)

Online Social Network Profile Linkage

Haochen Zhang[1], Min-Yen Kan[2], Yiqun Liu[1], and Shaoping Ma[1]

[1] State Key Laboratory of Intelligent Technology and Systems,
Tsinghua National Laboratory for Information Science and Technology,
Department of Computer Science and Technology,
Tsinghua University, Beijing 100084, China
[2] Web, IR / NLP Group (WING)
Department of Computer Science, National University of Singapore, Singapore
zhang-hc10@mails.tsinghua.edu.cn

Abstract. Piecing together social signals from people in different online social networks is key for downstream analytics. However, users may have different usernames in different social networks, making the linkage task difficult. To enable this, we explore a probabilistic approach that uses a domain-specific prior knowledge to address this problem of online social network user profile linkage. At scale, linkage approaches that are based on a naïve pairwise comparisons that have quadratic complexity become prohibitively expensive. Our proposed threshold-based canopying framework – named OPL – reduces this pairwise comparisons, and guarantees a upper bound theoretic linear complexity with respect to the dataset size. We evaluate our approaches on real-world, large-scale datasets obtained from Twitter and Linkedin. Our probabilistic classifier integrating prior knowledge into Naïve Bayes performs at over 85% F_1-measure for pairwise linkage, comparable to state-of-the-art approaches.

Keywords: social media, user profiles, canopies, profile linkage.

1 Introduction

The Online Social Network (OSN) is a ubiquitous feature in modern daily life. People access social networks to share their stories and connect with their friends. Many netizens commonly participate in multipl social networks, to cover their social needs of reading, researching, sharing, commenting and complaining. There are a wealth of choices available to link their real-world social networks virtually, and to extend and enhance them online.

The variety of social networks are partially redundant but each has a niche focus that can provide different slants on an individual's virtual lifestyles. People may communicate with friends in Facebook, share their opinions in Twitter, exhibit artistic photographs in Flickr and maintain business relationships in LinkedIn. Rarely do individuals use a single OSN to cover all such facets. As such, studies that seek to understand the virtual netizen that capture a user's participation from only a single OSN will necessarily have a strong bias. To gain a holistic perspective, an understanding of an online individual is derivable from

A. Jaafar et al. (Eds.): AIRS 2014, LNCS 8870, pp. 197–208, 2014.
© Springer International Publishing Switzerland 2014

piecing together all of the myriad aspects of his online footprints. Furthermore, when the same users posts the same opinions in different OSNs, such *user linkage* is needed, to avoid double-counting and to accurately estimatef social signals.

Variants of this problem – commonly referred to as *record linkage* – have been investigated in the database community for decades. Relatively recent work has re-examined this problem in light of linkage within OSNs. Many works [4], [13], [15], [19] adapt standard supervised machine learning for linkage. These works focus on accuracy and rely on pairwise comparisons (i.e., Is profile x in OSN a the same as profile y in OSN b?). However these works are infeasible to apply to large-scale real-world datasets: as they do not address how to deal with the unbalanced ratio of positive to negative instances, and the enormous number of necessary pairwise comparisons. [12] carefully studies usernames and proposes a prior knowledge approach which significantly improves name-disambiguation performance in the user linkage task. [3] and [14] leverage the graphical structures of social networks and [20] identifies behavioral features extracted from usernames and user-generated content, both noting that external evidence can help in the linkage task. However, acquiring both forms of external evidence may be expensive, or even inaccessible. In summary, while the prior work we have surveyed here have introduced methods or features for the user linkage problem, few address the difficulties with the necessary quadratic complexity of pairwise comparison. None have reported their results on identifying individuals in real-world large-scale datasets.

In this paper, we address this problem of *large-scale online social network user profile linkage*. We investigate and optimally tune known techniques for record linkage, by applying them to the user profile linkage problem for the purpose of large-scale production use. The key contribution of our work is to link an individual user's user profiles together, exploiting the idiosyncrasies of the problem to achieve accurate, time-efficient and cost-sensitive linkage.

2   Related Work

2.1   Identifying Users across Social Networks

User profile linkage is a research area that has developed in parallel with the development online social networks. At its core, methods compare the similarity between two users' profiles (often, one from one social network and one from another) by carefully investigating their attributes [4], [13], [15], [19]. Vosecky *et al.* [19] and Carmagnola *et al.* [4] proposed linear threshold-based models, which combine each features with weights and determine whether they belong to one identity by comparing to the preset threshold. Malhotra *et al.* [13] and Nunes *et al.* [15] adopt supervised classification to decide on matching.

Aside from attribute comparison, Narayanan *et al.* [14] and Bartunov *et al.* [3] leverage a user's social connections to identify their OSN accounts. The former demonstrated that users can be de-anonymized without personal information, by exploiting the fact that users often have similar social connections in different

OSNs. Bartunov *et al.* similarly reported that modeling the user graph improves performance by re-identifying users with similar relationship structures.

Several works also aim to disambiguate users of the same name ("namesake users"), a subtask termed *name disambiguation* [1], [18]. Zafarani *et al.* [20] explored how the behavior features of how users express themselves and generate their usernames. Perito *et al.* [16] studied username choice discloses our identities to public, while Liu *et al.* [12] improves name disambiguation by modeling the commonality of usernames, to help better estimate the linkage likelihood.

2.2 Record Linkage and Entity Resolution

User profile linkage is similar to traditional record linkage (or *entity resolution*). Surveys [8,9]. review the various approaches, including named attributes computations [5], schema mapping [2], [17] and duplicate detection in hierarchical data[10], all which inform the construction of profile linkage techniques.

Both profile linkage and record linkage face the computational complexity problem. A key insight to reducing practical complexity is to note that many user profile pairs are highly disparate, and unnecessary to compare. Indexing techniques can then be used to find rough clusters for which expensive pairwise comparison can be applied [6]. Canopying [7] is one such techniques, setting up soft constraints to form overlapping clusters (canopies), and only comparing instances within each canopy.

3 Problem Definition

We first define the associated terminology and then formalize the problem of profile linkage:

Identity refers to a unique entity, usually identifiable in the real-world context. Identities usually correspond to individual people, but other physical and virtual entities – such as bands, companies and products – are also possible. The current U.S. president, Barack Obama, is an example of an identity.

Profile refers to a projection of an identity into a particular social network. A profile is a data structure, consisting of a set of **attributes** with values and implicitly belongs to its identity. Identities may participate in multiple social networks, and thus project a profile for each network. For example, currently, Barack Obama is `barackobama` on LinkedIn and Facebook, `BarackObama` on Twitter, and `+BarackObama` on Google Plus.

Intuitively, profiles that are projected from the same identity should have high similarity with each other. Returning to our example, We can see three of Barack Obama's profiles use the same user ID (ignoring capitalization). Profile linkage hinges on this assumption of similarity.

Profile linkage is thus the matching task of determining which profiles are projections of the same identity.

More formally, let $\mathcal{I} = \{I_i\}$ be set of identities, $\mathcal{R} = \{R_k\}$ be set of social networks and $\mathcal{P}_k$ denotes set of profiles in the online social network R_k. I_i has all his profiles $P_{k,i}$ in social network R_k where $P_{k,i} \subset \mathcal{P}_k$. Note that identities (I_i) are not observed, so we must infer whether its projections $\hat{I}_i$ in the observed online social networks are linked and represent it, where $\hat{I}_i = \bigcup_{\forall R_k \in \mathcal{R}} P_{k,i}$.

We define the *setwise profile linkage* problem as the task of fully recovering the set of $\hat{I}_i$ given online social networks $\mathcal{R}$ and profiles $\mathcal{P}_k$ of each social network k. At a smaller scale, the *pairwise profile linkage* problem is the task of determining whether two profiles are projected from the same identity.

By repeatedly solving the *pairwise profile linkage* problem for all profile pairs from any two social networks and resolving all transitivity conflicts, we solve the *setwise profile linkage task*. Notice that if there are only two social networks, *setwise profile linkage* reduces to *pairwise profile linkage*.

We address the *pairwise profile linkage* for the case of two social networks. For each query profile in OSN R_α, we retrieve a set of similar n target profiles from R_β, and determine (if any) of the P_β link; i.e., originate from the same identity i that generated the query profile P_α. In this paper, we additionally assume that each identity only projects at most a single profile per OSN.

4   Approach

Given the large-scale and reliance on external data, our OPL ("Online Profile Linkage") approach to profile linkage must consider computation cost at the core. OPL addresses the cost-sensitivity by controlling local computation by employing *canopies* to prune unnecessary pairwise comparisons.

OPL takes an indexing approach to accomplish setwise profile linkage. To avoid redundant comparisons, we sequentially traverse the two pending OSNs, by regarding one as a query profile source and the other as the target to be considered for linking. Our approach is symmetric, as either OSN can be treated as the query source.

4.1   Token-Based Canopies

To construct our canopies, we use tokens from usernames and names, as these are ubiquitous sources common in all OSNs. Then we index these profiles by corresponding tokens. Based on our observations, we find that 96.1% matched profiles share at least one token. By "token", we mean continuous letter or digit sequences segmented by intervening spaces or symbols. We make the implicit assumption that two matched profiles must share a common token.

Our detailed examination of tokens shows that they conform to a power law distribution very well (Zipf's Law). Thus, high-frequency tokens do not serve to distinguish truly linked profiles. As such tokens would create canopies of limited use that are large (or equivalently, costly), we filter out high-frequency tokens from consideration: tokens above a frequency threshold θ are discarded.

Canopy Complexity Analysis. We prove that token-based canopies yield a linear complexity in this section. Let the size of query profiles $\mathcal{Q}$ be $|Q|$, the size of target profiles $\mathcal{T}$ be $|T|$. Assuming that the set of all tokens is $\mathcal{M}$ and the frequency of token $m \in \mathcal{M}$ is N_m, then the set of tokens (after filtering) is regarded as $M = \{m|m \in \mathcal{M}, N_m \leq \theta\}$.

The total number of comparisons is the summation of each query's candidate profiles retrieved from the canopies:

$$C = \sum_{q \in Q} \sum_{m \in M_q} |D_m| \qquad (1)$$

where $M_q \subset M$ is the query profile q's token set, which is a subset of the tokens M. D_m denotes the set of target profiles indexed by specific token m and $|D_m|$ denotes its size.

Let the profile frequency of token m be $N_{m,Q}$ computed over Q and $N_{m,T}$ computed over $\mathcal{T}$. Notice that D_m equals to $N_{m,T}$, and that all candidates of m are retrieved $N_{m,Q}$ times and that $N_{m,Q} + N_{m,T} = N_m$. Therefore, we can compute the total number of comparisons C from a token perspective:

$$C = \sum_{m \in M} N_{m,Q} \times N_{m,T} \leq \sum_{m \in M} \frac{1}{4} \times N_m^2 \qquad (2)$$

Since the tokens' distribution follow a power law (Zipf's Law), we have:

$$N_m \approx H \times r_m^{-s} \qquad (3)$$

where s and H are parameters that characterize the distribution and r_m is the rank of m. Substituting Equation 3 into Equation 2, we derive:

$$C \leq \frac{1}{4} \sum_{m \in M} N_m^2 \approx \frac{H^2}{4} \int_{r_\theta}^{\infty} r^{-2s} \mathrm{d}r \qquad (4)$$

where r_θ is the rank of the token(s) with frequency θ, which equals to $(H/\theta)^{s^{-1}}$.

By employing linear regression, we estimate approximate value of s to be 1.053, which follows the empirical observations that $s \to 1$ and $H \propto (|Q| + |T|)$ when applied to human language [11]. We derive a final, concise relationship:

$$C \leq \zeta \times \theta \times (|Q| + |T|) \qquad (5)$$

where ζ is a constant to ensure equality. We can thus tune θ for a particular application scenario, knowing that we will have a complexity on the order of $O(|Q| + |T|)$, i.e. linear in size of Q and T.

4.2   Feature Selection

OPL uses a simple battery of features for linking in a supervised manner. We employ both local features extracted directly from profile attributes, and (optionally) external features acquired from the Web. All features are normalized to a range of $[0, 1]$ to simplify computation.

Local Features (5 Features). Username: Name comparison is a well-studied problem and many fuzzy matching approaches have been designed and evaluated for it. We adopt the Jaro Winker metric, as it been reported to be one of the best performing [5] metrics for name-like feature.

As many identities may have similar or even identical namesakes, the usernames alone are not sufficiently discriminative. When linking across the entire web dataset or treating person names with high namesake conflicts such as Chinese, name disambiguation techniques become more important.

Language: This attribute refers to the language(s) spoken by the user. This attribute is a set of enumerated types, taking on values from a fixed finite set. We employ the Jaccard similarity for this set attribute to compute the feature.

Description: The description is a free-form short text provided by the user, commonly mentioning their associations to organizations, their occupations and interests. We calculate the vector-space model cosine similarity with TF×IDF weighting, a commonly-used standard, for this feature.

URL: Some profile attribute values are URLs, while other URLs can be extracted from free text descriptions (e.g., `descriptions`). URLs pointing to specific pages (i.e., homepages, blogs) can be helpful. We split URLs into tokens, using cosine similarity with TF×IDF weighting of the tokens for comparison.

Popularity: We utilize the profile's friend or connection count. This value reflects the popularity and connectedness of the profile. OSNs often cap the total number of connections that are displayed; so to make two values comparable, we omit counts beyond this maximum limit. We adopt a normalized formula akin to Jaccard set similarity for popularity comparison:

$$F_{popularity} = \frac{|friend_q - friend_t|}{|friend_q + friend_t|} \tag{6}$$

where $friend_q$ ($friend_t$) is the count of friends for profile q (t).

External Features (2 Features) Location: Locations come in a variety of forms – detailed addresses, lat-long coordinates, or bare city names – such that standard string similarity fails here. We rely on the Google Maps API (GeoCode) to convert arbitrary locality strings into geographic coordinates, calculating spherical distance d in kilometers for comparison. We employ $e^{-\gamma d}$ to normalize the distance similarity within $[0, 1]$, where the scale parameter γ is assigned to be 0.001.

Avatar: is an image to represent the user, given as a URL in the profile. After downloading the image, we use a gray-scale χ^2 dissimilarity to compare the images. Our implementation is a bin-by-bin histogram difference based [21], which has been proved effective for texture and object categories classification, defined as:

$$F_{avatar} = \frac{1}{2} \sum_{i \in Bins} \frac{(H_{q,i} - H_{t,i})^2}{(H_{q,i} + H_{t,i})} \tag{7}$$

where $H_{q,i}$ and $H_{t,i}$ represent the ith bin of the query profile q and target profile t's image gray-scale histograms.

4.3   Probabilistic Classifier

As previously stated, the token type distribution obeys Zipf's law. This allows us to estimate the utility of a shared token for matching profiles based on its frequency within the collection. A shared rare token gives a larger probability of matching. We codify this evidence into a probablistic model.

To determine whether the query profile q and target profile t are from the same identity, we estimate its probability modeled as conditioned on the joint probabily of the similarity of the features and the set of shared tokens: $Pr(l_{q,t} = 1|F_{q,t}, M_{q,t})$ where $l_{q,t} = \{0,1\}$ denotes whether q and t are matched, $F_{q,t}$ denotes similarity features and $M_{q,t}$ denotes the shared tokens between q and t.

We make the assumption that the feature similarity and overlapping tokens are independent of each other, yielding:

$$Pr(l_{q,t}|F_{q,t}, M_{q,t}) = \frac{Pr(l_{q,t}|M_{q,t}) \times \prod_{f_k \in F_{q,t}} Pr(f_k|l_{q,t})}{\prod_{f_k \in F_{q,t}} Pr(f_k)} \tag{8}$$

where $Pr(l_{q,t}|M_{q,t})$ is the prior token distribution knowledge, and $Pr(f_k|l_{q,t})$ is the probability of observing feature k, conditioned on profile match or not.

Unfortunately, $Pr(l_{q,t}|M_{q,t})$ is difficult to measure in practice. We estimate it roughly as the fraction of profiles that have all observed tokens in q:

$$\hat{Pr}(l_{q,t} = 1|M_{q,t}) = \frac{1}{|\bigcap_{m \in M_{q,t}} D_m| + \beta} \tag{9}$$

where D_m is all corresponding profiles indexed by token m and β (empirically set to 0.5) is a smoothing factor that prevents $Pr(l_{q,t}|M_{q,t})$ from being 1. By applying the equality $Pr(l_{q,t} = 0|\cdot) + Pr(l_{q,t} = 1|\cdot) = 1$ to Equation 8, we derive:

$$p_{q,t} = Pr(l_{q,t} = 1|F_{q,t}, M_{q,t}) =$$
$$\frac{1}{1 + (|\bigcap_{m \in M_{q,t}} D_m| + \beta - 1) \times \prod_{f_k \in F_{q,t}} \frac{Pr(f_k|l_{q,t} = 0)}{Pr(f_k|l_{q,t} = 1)}} \tag{10}$$

where $\hat{Pr}(f_k|l_{q,t})$ is calculated over the training data. Since the feature counts are sparse, it is difficult to properly model their distribution, we employ the kernel density estimator to estimate the features' distributions. Given these estimates, we thus declare q to match t when $\hat{Pr}(l_{q,t} = 1|F_{q,t}, Mq, t) > 0.5$.

5   Experiment

We set up our experiments on linking over 150,000 users across two well-known social networks: Twitter and LinkedIn. We aim to answer the following questions: (1) How well does our approach perform on the real world large-scale dataset compared to other state-of-the-art approaches? (2) How does the setting of the canopy threshold θ practically impact performance and efficiency?

5.1 Dataset and Evaluation Metric

We describe our approach to construct a realistic dataset for the profile linkage problem. We consider the problem of linking user profiles from Twitter and LinkedIn. We first collected tweets from Twitter for one week, 9–16 October 2012. Then we sampled 152,294 Twitter users from these tweets and downloaded their profiles. LinkedIn users are randomly sampled from LinkedIn directory[1]. In total, we obtained 154,379 LinkedIn user profiles.

It is impossible to obtain the full ground truth for the dataset, short of asking each tweeter to disclose their LinkedIn profile. Instead we use public data already provided in third party websites, such as About.me and Google+, which encourages users to manually submit their OSN profiles' links. We assume that all social network accounts filled by one user belong to himself. We randomly crawl 180,000 Google+ profiles and extract this partial ground truth from the overlapping users of our dataset and the Google+ profiles.

The partial ground truth includes 4,779 matched Twitter–LinkedIn users, 3,339 isolated Twitter users and 1,632 isolated LinkedIn users, a total of 9,750 identities. We adopt this partial ground truth to estimate the performance.

We employ the standard IR evaluation metrics: Precision (Pre), recall (Rec) and F_1-measure (F_1) to evaluate the pairwise linkage. We also report the identity-based accuracy (I-Acc), which the accuracy of setwise linkage restricted to true positive matches (i.e., correctly identified identities divided by the total number of ground truth identities).

5.2 User Profile Linkage

We apply several approaches to link the Twitter–LinkedIn dataset using a canopy framework. To the best of our knowledge, no related work has attempted the linkage of complete OSN profiles on two real-world large-scale datasets. Both Bartunov el at. [3] and Vosecky el at. [19] executed experiments on a small-scale datasets. In related work, Liu el at. [12] focuses only on disambiguating profiles with identical username namesakes and Malhotra el at. [13] studied the linkage effectiveness on an artificial dataset. No works have yet to benchmark profile linkage on a real-world large scale dataset.

However, such studies are relevant as they describe comparable pairwise classifier to ours. [13] shows that with similar features, simple classifiers like C4.5, SVM and Naïve Bayes perform well in the artificial, balanced dataset scenario. [12] provides an improved model that combines SVM and username n-gram probability. We use these methods as comparative baselines. We use the WEKA3[2] library for its implementations of C4.5, SVM and Naïve Bayes classifiers. We re-implement Liu et al. (2013) approach following their work's description.

In our experiment, we set Twitter as the query dataset and LinkedIn as target dataset. For our canopy threshold, we set $\theta = 200$, as our parameter tuning

---

[1] http://www.linkedin.com/directory/people/a.html
[2] http://www.cs.waikato.ac.nz/ml/weka/

results. We randomly sampled 1,000 query instances from the ground truth, then retrieve all corresponding target instances by canopying to generate the training set.

Table 1. Linkage performance over our Twitter→LinkedIn dataset with all features

Method	Pre	Rec	F_1	I-Acc
C4.5	0.905	0.658	0.762	0.806
SVM	0.942	0.456	0.614	0.727
Naïve Bayes	0.934	0.625	0.748	0.801
Liu *et al.*	0.910	0.567	0.698	0.767
OPL	0.866	**0.846**	**0.856**	**0.865**

Table 1 shows the experimental results. Our approach achieves the best performance, in both F_1 and I-Acc. The standard Naïve Bayes classifier outperforms SVM. While not strictly comparable, our Naïve Bayes-based approach also betters Liu's SVM-based method [12]. This validates the same conclusion in [13]. We believe the reason for SVM's subpar performance is caused by missing features in a large proportion of the profiles, which we have described as quite significant an issue for profile linkage.

By reviewing the evaluation results, we observe that simple classifiers perform better in precision but underperform on recall. Although Malhotra *et al.* reports good performance on an artificially-balanced scenario, on real data, naïve classifiers prefer classifying instances as negative, as there is a much larger imbalance of negative instances. Both Liu *et al.* and our approach address this problem by employing prior knowledge about the rarity of tokens, that may carry stronger signals for matching. However, Liu's work adopts this prior in a simple linear way, while OPL embeds it directly within its probabilistic model.

5.3   Canopy Performance and Efficiency

Canopy settings affect both efficiency and linkage performance. Recall is reduced when θ is set too small, preventing correct potential profiles from being in the same canopy. Fig. 1–(a) illustrates the relationship between θ and missing pair. These missing pairs are indeed matched but at least one profile was pushed out of a matching canopy, as all of its tokens' frequencies are greater than the given θ. The miss percentage reaches a steady state when $\theta \geq 500$, and we feel is already insignificantly different when $\theta \geq 200$.

On the other hand, too large a setting of θ brings in noise that confuses classifiers. A large setting of θ also increases computational overhead (*cf* Section 4.1). Fig. 1(b) above illustrates the correlation between performance and θ on the full scale of our dataset. Fig. 1(b) shows that F_1-measure converges after $\theta \geq 200$, so we set $\theta = 200$ for our experiment.

While correct parameter setting primarily depends on the requirement of whether precision is more important than recall, θ's value also influences running time. The number of pairwise comparisons used by OPL over different scales of

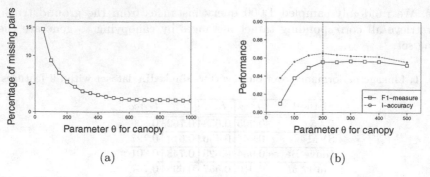

Fig. 1. Tuning parameter θ on the full dataset: (a) Missing pairs when varying θ, (b) Performance when varying θ

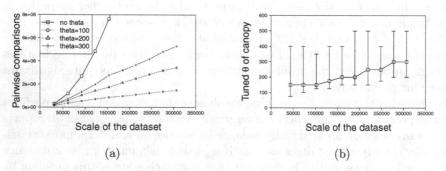

Fig. 2. Tuning OPL for scalability and efficiency: (a) Comparisons at different dataset scales, (b) Tuned θ for different dataset scales

θ is shown in the Fig. 2(a). We see that OPL using threshold-based canopies is approximately linear in computations to θ. As the computation complexity depends on θ, we also tune the performance against θ, at different dataset scales. Each square in Fig. 2(b) represents the θ with the best performance, and the respective vertical interval gives the acceptable range of θ values, for which the resultantq loss in F_1 is less than 0.5%. From these results, we can see that OPL is largely insensitive to dataset scale, a good signal that OPL adequately constrains the linkage task to an approximate linear complexity.

The reason why the optimal θ values show only a neglible increase when the dataset size is scaled up is due to our choice of canopying on username tokens. To avoid conflicts, we find that users prefer to select fairly unique usernames, that may incorporate rarer tokens whose frequencies are less than a most useful choices of θ.

6 Conclusion

We investigate the problem of real world large-scale profile linkage and propose OPL, a probabilistic classifier to address this. OPL caters to specific characteristics of this problem that differentiate it from toy linkage datasets: handling a) the unbalanced nature of the dataset and b) the largeness of the dataset scale. To link the hundreds of thousands of profiles, we employ threshold-based canopies, which directly manipulate and control the resultant linear complexity of the linkage task, allowing an operator a higher degree of flexibility and control over expected run times.

In our experimental results, we show effective performance with 85% F_1-measure and 86% I-accuracy, comparable to previous work. Our cost-sensitive framework also has the ability to prune unnecessary pairwise comparisons while keeping the loss in performance to an acceptable level.

In future work, we plan to improve OPL in two ways: first, to investigate more robust methods for linking OSNs when provided with other heterogeneous data. For example, linking an SNS user to a forum user, by way of the forum content. Second, to leverage the automatically identified set of users to build and test applications where the holistic user profile serves to better aggregate evidence for downstream applications, such as product sentiment estimation.

Acknowledgments. This work was supported by Natural Science Foundation of China (61073071). Part of the work was done at the Tsinghua-NUS NExT Search Centre, which is supported by the Singapore National Research Foundation & Interactive Digital Media R&D Program Office, under research grant R-252-300-001-490.

References

1. Anwar, T., Abulaish, M.: An MCL-Based Text Mining Approach for Namesake Disambiguation on the Web. In: Proceedings of the 2012 IEEE/WIC/ACM International Conference on Web Intelligence (2012)
2. Aumueller, D., Do, H.H., Massmann, S., Rahm, E.: Schema and Ontology Matching with Coma++. In: Proceedings of the 2005 ACM SIGMOD International Conference on Management of Data - SIGMOD 2005, p. 906. ACM Press (2005)
3. Bartunov, S., Korshunov, A., Park, S., Ryu, W., Lee, H.: Joint Link-Attribute User Identity Resolution in Online Social Networks. In: Proceedings of the 6th International Conference on Knowledge Discovery and Data Mining, Workshop on Social Network Mining and Analysis. ACM (2012)
4. Carmagnola, F., Cena, F.: User Identification for Cross-system Personalisation. Inf. Sci. 179(1-2) (2009)
5. Christen, P.: A Comparison of Personal Name Matching: Techniques and Practical Issues. In: Proceedings of the 6th IEEE International Conference on Data Mining Workshops, ICDM Workshops. IEEE (2006)
6. Christen, P.: A Survey of Indexing Techniques for Scalable Record Linkage and Deduplication. IEEE Transactions on Knowledge and Data Engineering 24(9) (2012)
7. Cohen, W.W., Richman, J.: Learning to Match and Cluster Large High-Dimensional Data Sets for Data Integration. In: Proceedings of the 8th International Conference on Knowledge Discovery and Data Mining, ACM (2002)

8. Elmagarmid, A.K., Ipeirotis, P.G., Verykios, V.S.: Duplicate Record Detection: A Survey. IEEE Trans. on Knowl. and Data Eng. 19(1), 1–16 (2007)
9. Köpcke, H., Rahm, E.: Frameworks for Entity Matching: A Comparison. Data Knowledge Engineering 69(2) (2010)
10. Leitão, L., Calado, P., Herschel, M.: Efficient and Effective Duplicate Detection in Hierarchical Data. IEEE Transactions on Knowledge and Data Engineering PP(99), 1 (2012)
11. Li, W.: Random Texts Exhibit Zipf's-law-like Word Frequency Distribution. IEEE Transactions on Information Theory, 1842–1845 (1992)
12. Liu, J., Zhang, F., Song, X., Song, Y.I., Lin, C.Y., Hon, H.W.: What's in A Name?: An Unsupervised Approach to Link Users Across Communities. In: Proceedings of the Sixth ACM International Conference on Web Search and Data Mining. ACM (2013)
13. Malhotra, A., Totti, L., Meira Jr, W., Kumaraguru, P., Almeida, V.: Studying User Footprints in Different Online Social Networks. In: International Workshop on Cybersecurity of Online Social Network (2012)
14. Narayanan, A., Shmatikov, V.: De-anonymizing Social Networks. In: Proceedings of the 2009 30th IEEE Symposium on Security and Privacy, IEEE (2009)
15. Nunes, A., Calado, P., Martins, B.: Resolving User Identities over Social Networks through Supervised Learning and Rich Similarity Features. In: Proceedings of the 27th Annual ACM Symposium on Applied Computing. ACM (2012)
16. Perito, D., Castelluccia, C., Kaafar, M.A., Manils, P.: How unique and traceable are usernames? In: Fischer-Hübner, S., Hopper, N. (eds.) PETS 2011. LNCS, vol. 6794, pp. 1–17. Springer, Heidelberg (2011)
17. Qian, L., Cafarella, M.J., Jagadish, H.V.: Sample-driven schema mapping. In: Proceedings of the 2012 International Conference on Management of Data - SIGMOD 2012, p. 73. ACM Press (2012)
18. Qian, Y., Hu, Y., Cui, J., Zheng, Q., Nie, Z.: Combining Machine Learning and Human Judgement in Author Disambiguation. In: Proceedings of the 20th ACM International Conference on Information and Knowledge Management. ACM (2011)
19. Vosecky, J., Hong, D., Shen, V.: User Identification Across Multiple Social Networks. In: Networked Digital Technologies. IEEE (2009)
20. Zafarani, R., Liu, H.: Connecting Users across Social Media Sites: A Behavioral-modeling Approach. In: Proceedings of the 19th ACM SIGKDD International Conference on Knowledge Discovery and Data Mining, pp. 41–49. ACM, New York (2013)
21. Zhang, J., Marszalek, M., Lazebnik, S., Schmid, C.: Local Features and Kernels for Classification of Texture and Object Categories: A Comprehensive Study. Int. J. Comput. Vision 73(2) (2007)

User Message Model: A New Approach to Scalable User Modeling on Microblog

Quan Wang[1], Jun Xu[2,*], and Hang Li[2]

[1] Institute of Information Engineering, Chinese Academy of Sciences, Beijing, China
quanwang1012@gmail.com
[2] Noah's Ark Lab, Huawei Technologies, Hong Kong
nkxujun@gmail.com, hangli.hl@huawei.com

Abstract. Modeling users' topical interests on microblog is an important but challenging task. In this paper, we propose User Message Model (UMM), a hierarchical topic model specially designed for user modeling on microblog. In UMM, users and their messages are modeled by a hierarchy of topics. Thus, it has the ability to 1) deal with both the data sparseness and the topic diversity problems which previous methods suffer from, and 2) jointly model users and messages in a unified framework. Furthermore, UMM can be easily distributed to handle large-scale datasets. Experimental results on both Sina Weibo and Twitter datasets show that UMM can effectively model users' interests on microblog. It can achieve better results than previous methods in topic discovery and message recommendation. Experimental results on a large-scale Twitter dataset, containing about 2 million users and 50 million messages, further demonstrate the scalability and efficiency of distributed UMM.

Keywords: microblog, user modeling, topic modeling.

1 Introduction

Microblogging systems such as Twitter and Sina Weibo[1] have become important communication and social networking tools. Recently, mining individual users' topical interests from their messages (tweets) attracts much attention. It has been demonstrated to be useful in many applications such as user clustering [9], friend recommendation [17], influential user detection [23], and user behavior prediction [2]. Various statistical topic modeling approaches have been applied to modeling users' interests on microblog [2], [17], [23], [25], [28]. However, it remains a non-trivial task with the following challenges.

1) *Data sparseness and topic diversity.* Microblog messages are short (restricted to 140 characters) and may not provide sufficient information. Therefore, taking each individual message as a short document and directly applying topic modeling approaches may not work well [9], [28]. That is, the data sparseness

---

* Jun Xu is currently affiliated with Institute of Computing Technology, Chinese Academy of Sciences.

[1] Sina Weibo (http://weibo.com) is a popular microblogging system in China.

A. Jaafar et al. (Eds.): AIRS 2014, LNCS 8870, pp. 209–220, 2014.

problem occurs. To tackle the problem, previous studies proposed to aggregate messages posted by each user into a "long" document and employ topic modeling approaches on aggregated documents [9], [17], [23]. However, such an aggregation strategy ignores the fact that topics discussed in different messages are usually different. Aggregating these topic-diverse messages into a single document and characterizing it with a unified topic distribution may be inaccurate. That is, the topic diversity problem occurs. We need to effectively deal with both problems.

2) *Joint modeling of users and messages.* In some applications (e.g., personalized message recommendation), not only users' topical interests but also messages' topic distributions need to be identified (e.g., to judge how much a user likes a message at semantic level). Therefore, modeling users and messages simultaneously is always preferred.

3) *Scalability and efficiency.* With the rapid growth of microblogging systems, more and more data is created every day. User modeling techniques which can efficiently handle large-scale datasets are sorely needed.

To address these challenges, we propose a novel user modeling approach, referred to as User Message Model (UMM). UMM is a hierarchical topic model in which users and their messages are modeled by a hierarchy of topics. Each user corresponds to a topic distribution, representing his/her topical interests. Each message posted by the user also corresponds to a topic distribution, with the user's topic distribution as the prior. Topics are represented as distributions over words. We further propose a distributed version of UMM which can efficiently handle large-scale datasets containing millions of users.

The advantages of UMM are as follows. 1) UMM can effectively deal with both the data sparseness problem and the topic diversity problem which previous methods suffer from. 2) UMM can jointly model users and messages in a unified framework. 3) UMM is easy to be implemented through distributed computing, and can efficiently handle large-scale datasets. To our knowledge, UMM is the first user modeling approach that can address all the challenges discussed above.

Experimental results on both Sina Weibo and Twitter datasets show that UMM can effectively model users' interests on microblog. It can achieve better results than previous methods in topic discovery and message recommendation. Experimental results on a large-scale Twitter dataset, containing about 2 million users and 50 million messages, demonstrate the efficiency and scalability of the distributed version of UMM.

2 Related Work

Mining users' topical interests from their messages (tweets) is a key problem in microblog analysis. A straightforward approach is to directly apply the Latent Dirichlet Allocation (LDA) [3] model on individual messages and simply represent each user by aggregating the topic distributions of his/her messages [22]. However, as messages on microblog are short, the data sparseness problem occurs. To tackle this problem, previous studies proposed to aggregate messages by user and then employ the LDA model on aggregated messages (user-level LDA) [7], [9].

Hong and Davison empirically demonstrated that user-level LDA can achieve better performance in user and message classification [9]. The effectiveness of user-level LDA in influential user detection and friend recommendation was further demonstrated in [17] and [23]. Ahmed *et al.* later proposed a time-varying user-level LDA model to capture the dynamics of users' topical interests [2]. Recently, Xu *et al.* employed a slightly modified Author-Topic Model (ATM) [20] to discover user interests on Twitter [25,26]. In fact, ATM is equivalent to user-level LDA when applied to microblog data [28]. Since different messages posted by the same user may discuss different topics, user-level LDA is plagued by the topic diversity problem. The proposed UMM can address both the data sparseness problem and the topic diversity problem.

Besides automatically discovered topics, users' interests can be represented in other forms, e.g., user specified tags [22], [24], ontology-based categories [15], and automatically extracted entities [1]. However, these methods rely on either external knowledge or data labeling, which is beyond the scope of this paper. There are also other studies on microblog topic modeling [5], [6], [11], [18,19], [27], but they do not focus on identifying users' interests.

3   User Message Model

3.1   Model

Suppose that we are given a set of microblog data consisting of U users, and each user u has M^u messages. Each message m (posted by user u) is represented as a sequence of N_m^u words, denoted by $\boldsymbol{w}_m^u = \{w_{mn}^u : n = 1, \cdots, N_m^u\}$. Each word w_{mn}^u comes from a vocabulary $\mathcal{V}$ with size W.

User Message Model (UMM) is a hierarchical topic model that characterizes users and messages in a unified framework, based on the following assumptions. 1) There exist K topics and each topic ϕ_k is a multinomial distribution over the vocabulary. 2) The first layer of the hierarchy consists of the users. Each user u is associated with a multinomial distribution π^u over the topics, representing his/her interests. 3) The second layer consists of the messages. Each message m is also associated with a multinomial distribution θ_m^u over the topics. The message's topic distribution θ_m^u is controlled by the user's topic distribution π^u. 4) The third layer consists of the words. Each word in message m is generated according to θ_m^u. Fig. 1 shows the graphical representation and the generative process. Note that θ_m^u is sampled from an asymmetric Dirichlet distribution with parameter $\lambda^u \pi^u$. Here, π^u is a K-dimensional vector, denoting the topic distribution of user u; λ^u is a scalar, controlling how a message's topic distribution might vary from the user's; $\lambda^u \pi^u$ means multiplying each dimension of π^u by λ^u.

UMM differs from Hierarchical Dirichlet Process (HDP) [21]. 1) UMM fully exploits the user-message-word hierarchy to perform better user modeling on microblog, particularly to address the data sparseness and topic diversity problems, while HDP is not specially designed for microblog data. 2) UMM keeps a fixed number of topics, while the topic number in HDP is flexible.

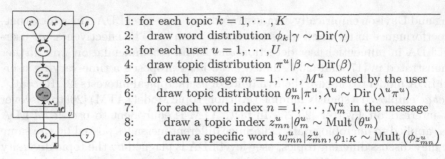

1: for each topic $k = 1, \cdots, K$
2:    draw word distribution $\phi_k | \gamma \sim \mathrm{Dir}(\gamma)$
3: for each user $u = 1, \cdots, U$
4:    draw topic distribution $\pi^u | \beta \sim \mathrm{Dir}(\beta)$
5:    for each message $m = 1, \cdots, M^u$ posted by the user
6:       draw topic distribution $\theta_m^u | \pi^u, \lambda^u \sim \mathrm{Dir}(\lambda^u \pi^u)$
7:       for each word index $n = 1, \cdots, N_m^u$ in the message
8:          draw a topic index $z_{mn}^u | \theta_m^u \sim \mathrm{Mult}(\theta_m^u)$
9:          draw a specific word $w_{mn}^u | z_{mn}^u, \phi_{1:K} \sim \mathrm{Mult}(\phi_{z_{mn}^u})$

Fig. 1. Graphical representations (left) and generative processes (right) of UMM

1: for each user $u = 1, \cdots, U$
2:    for each message $m = 1, \cdots, M^u$ posted by the user
3:       for each word index $n = 1, \cdots, N_m^u$ in the message
4:          $z_1 \leftarrow z_{mn}^u; \quad w \leftarrow w_{mn}^u$
5:          $N_{z_1|u} \leftarrow N_{z_1|u} - 1; \quad N_{z_1|m}^u \leftarrow N_{z_1|m}^u - 1; \quad N_{w|z_1} \leftarrow N_{w|z_1} - 1$
6:          sampling $(z_{mn}^u \leftarrow z_2) \propto \left(N_{z_2|m}^u + \lambda^u \frac{N_{z_2|u} + \beta}{N_{\cdot|u} + K\beta} \right) \frac{N_{w|z_2} + \gamma}{N_{\cdot|z_2} + W\gamma}$
7:          $N_{z_2|u} \leftarrow N_{z_2|u} + 1; \quad N_{z_2|m}^u \leftarrow N_{z_2|m}^u + 1; \quad N_{w|z_2} \leftarrow N_{w|z_2} + 1$

Fig. 2. One iteration of Gibbs sampling in UMM

3.2 Inference

We employ Gibbs sampling [8] to perform inference. Consider message m posted by user u. For the n-th word, the conditional posterior probability of its topic assignment z_{mn}^u can be calculated as:

$$P\left(z_{mn}^u = z \big| w_{mn}^u = w, \boldsymbol{w}_{-mn}^{-u}, \boldsymbol{z}_{-mn}^{-u}\right) \propto \left(\left(N_{z|m}^u\right)^{\neg z_{mn}^u} + \lambda^u \frac{(N_{z|u})^{\neg z_{mn}^u} + \beta}{(N_{\cdot|u})^{\neg z_{mn}^u} + K\beta} \right) \frac{(N_{w|z})^{\neg z_{mn}^u} + \gamma}{(N_{\cdot|z})^{\neg z_{mn}^u} + W\gamma}, \quad (1)$$

where $\boldsymbol{w}_{-mn}^{-u}$ is the set of all observed words except w_{mn}^u; $\boldsymbol{z}_{-mn}^{-u}$ the set of all topic assignments except z_{mn}^u; $N_{z|m}^u$ the number of times a word in message m has been assigned to topic z; $N_{z|u}$ the number of times a word generated by user u (no matter which message it comes from) has been assigned to topic z, and $N_{\cdot|u} = \sum_z N_{z|u}$; $N_{w|z}$ the number of times word w has been assigned to topic z, and $N_{\cdot|z} = \sum_w N_{w|z}$; $(\cdot)^{\neg z_{mn}^u}$ the count that does not include the current assignment of z_{mn}^u. Fig. 2 gives the pseudo code for a single Gibbs iteration.

After obtaining the topic assignments and the counts, π^u, θ_m^u, and ϕ_z can be estimated as:

$$\pi_z^u = \frac{N_{z|u} + \beta}{N_{\cdot|u} + K\beta}, \quad \theta_{m,z}^u = \frac{N_{z|m}^u + \lambda^u \pi_z^u}{N_{\cdot|m}^u + \lambda^u}, \quad \phi_{z,w} = \frac{N_{w|z} + \gamma}{N_{\cdot|z} + W\gamma}, \quad (2)$$

where π_z^u is the z-th dimension of π^u, $\theta_{m,z}^u$ the z-th dimension of θ_m^u, and $\phi_{z,w}$ the w-th dimension of ϕ_z.

Table 1. Complexities of MM, UM, UMM, and AD-UMM

Method	Time Complexity	Space Complexity
MM	$\mathcal{N}KT$	$3\mathcal{N} + KW$
UM	$\mathcal{N}KT$	$2\mathcal{N} + KW + KU$
UMM	$\mathcal{N}KT$	$3\mathcal{N} + KW + KU$
AD-UMM	$(\frac{\mathcal{N}K}{P} + KW \log P)T$	$\frac{3\mathcal{N}+KU}{P} + KW$

3.3   Advantages

We compare UMM with Message Model (MM), User Model (UM), and Author-Topic Model (ATM) [20], and demonstrate its advantages. MM is a message-level LDA model, where each individual message is treated as a document [22]. As messages on microblog are short, MM suffers from the data sparseness problem. UM is a user-level LDA model, where messages posted by the same user are aggregated into a single document [9], [17], [23]. As different messages may discuss different topics, UM suffers from the topic diversity problem. ATM is equivalent to UM when applied to microblog data, where each message belongs to a single user [28]. It also suffers from the topic diversity problem.

As opposed to the existing methods, UMM naturally models users and messages in a unified framework, and effectively deals with both the data sparseness and the topic diversity problems. Consider the Gibbs sampling procedure listed in Equation (1). The first term expresses the probability of picking a specific topic in a message, and the second the probability of picking a specific word from the selected topic. To pick a topic, one can rely on information either from the current message or from the current user. In the former case, a topic is picked with probability proportional to the number of times the other words in the current message have been assigned to the topic, i.e., $\left(N_{z|m}^u\right)^{\neg z_{mn}^u}$. In the latter case, a topic is picked with probability proportional to the number of times the other words generated by the current user have been assigned to the topic, i.e., $\left(N_{z|u}\right)^{\neg z_{mn}^u} + \beta$. Parameter λ^u makes a tradeoff between the two cases. In this way, UMM leverages the "specific but insufficient" message-level information and the "rich but diverse" user-level information, and can effectively address both problems. Table 1 further compares the time and space complexities of MM, UM, and UMM, where $\mathcal{N}$ is the number of words in the whole collection and T the number of Gibbs iterations. We can see that UMM is comparable with MM and UM in terms of both time and space complexities.

3.4   Scaling Up on Hadoop

To enhance the efficiency and scalability, we borrow the idea of AD-LDA [16] and design a distributed version of UMM, called Approximate Distributed UMM (AD-UMM). We implement AD-UMM on Hadoop[2], an open-source software framework that supports data-intensive distributed applications.

---

[2] http://hadoop.apache.org/

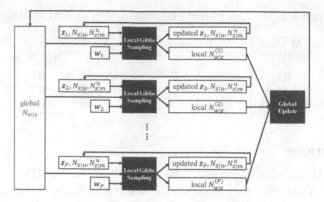

Fig. 3. One iteration of AD-UMM on Hadoop

AD-UMM distributes the U users over P machines, with $U_p = \frac{U}{P}$ users and their messages on each machine. Specifically, let $\boldsymbol{w} = \{w_{mn}^u\}$ denote the set of words in the whole collection, and $\boldsymbol{z} = \{z_{mn}^u\}$ the set of corresponding topic assignments. We partition $\boldsymbol{w}$ into $\{\boldsymbol{w}_1, \cdots, \boldsymbol{w}_P\}$ and $\boldsymbol{z}$ into $\{\boldsymbol{z}_1, \cdots, \boldsymbol{z}_P\}$, and distribute them over the P machines, ensuring that messages posted by the same user are shuffled to the same machine. User-specific counts $\{N_{z|u}\}$ and message-specific counts $\{N_{z|m}^u\}$ are likewise partitioned and distributed. Topic-specific counts $\{N_{w|z}\}$ and $\{N_{\cdot|z}\}$ are broadcasted to all the machines. Each machine p maintains its own copy, denoted by $N_{w|z}^{(p)}$ and $N_{\cdot|z}^{(p)}$.

In each iteration, AD-UMM first conducts local Gibbs sampling on each machine independently, and then performs a global update across all the machines. During the local Gibbs sampling step on machine p, for each message m shuffled to the machine, the topic assignment of word w_{mn}^u is sampled according to:

$$P\left(z_{mn}^u = z \middle| w_{mn}^u = w, \boldsymbol{w}_{-mn}^{-u}, \boldsymbol{z}_{p-mn}^{-u}\right) \propto \left(\left(N_{z|m}^u\right)^{\neg z_{mn}^u} + \lambda^u \frac{(N_{z|u})^{\neg z_{mn}^u} + \beta}{(N_{\cdot|u})^{\neg z_{mn}^u} + K\beta}\right) \frac{\left(N_{w|z}^{(p)}\right)^{\neg z_{mn}^u} + \gamma}{\left(N_{\cdot|z}^{(p)}\right)^{\neg z_{mn}^u} + W\gamma},$$
(3)

where $\boldsymbol{z}_{p-mn}^{-u} = \boldsymbol{z}_p \setminus \{z_{mn}^u\}$. After machine p reassigns $\boldsymbol{z}_p$, $\{N_{z|u}\}$, $\{N_{z|m}^u\}$, and $\{N_{w|z}^{(p)}\}$ are updated. To merge back to a single set of word-topic counts $\{N_{w|z}\}$, a global update is performed across all the machines:

$$N_{w|z} \leftarrow N_{w|z} + \sum_{p=1}^{P} \left(N_{w|z}^{(p)} - N_{w|z}\right), \quad N_{w|z}^{(p)} \leftarrow N_{w|z}.$$
(4)

The whole procedure is shown in Fig. 3.

Table 1 compares the time and space complexities of UMM and AD-UMM, where we have assumed that users and messages are almost evenly distributed. As the total number of words in the collection (i.e., $\mathcal{N}$) is usually much larger than the vocabulary size (i.e., W), it is clear that AD-UMM outperforms UMM in terms of both time and space complexities.

Table 2. Statistics of the datasets

Dataset	# Users	# Messages	Vocabulary Size
Weibo-I	1,900	343,888	109,447
Twitter-I	1,929	1,055,613	75,990
Weibo-II	1,204	32,091	53,084
Twitter-II	721	9,324	15,049
Twitter-III	2,076,807	48,264,986	944,035

4 Experiments

We have conducted three experiments. The first two tested the performance of UMM in topic discovery and message recommendation, and the third one tested the efficiency and scalability of AD-UMM.

4.1 Datasets

The first two experiments were conducted on two datasets: Weibo and Twitter. The Weibo dataset consists of 2,446 randomly sampled users and all the messages posted and re-posted by them in three months (Aug. 2012 – Oct. 2012). The messages are in Chinese. The Twitter dataset consists of 2,596 randomly sampled users and all the messages posted and re-posted by them in three months (Jul. 2009 – Sep. 2009). The messages are in English. For re-posted messages, only the original contents were retained. URLs, hash tags (#   #, #Twitter), and mentions (@   , @User) were further removed. For the Weibo dataset, the messages were segmented with the Stanford Chinese Word Segmenter[3]. For both datasets, stop words and words whose frequencies in the whole dataset are less than 5 were removed. Messages which contain less than 5 words and users who have less than 10 messages were further removed.

We split each dataset into two parts according to the time stamps: messages in the first two months were used for topic discovery (denoted as "Weibo-I" and "Twitter-I") and messages in the third month were used for message recommendation (denoted as "Weibo-II" and "Twitter-II"). Since in the recommendation task messages were further filtered by a five-minute-window (as described in Section 4.3), Weibo-II and Twitter-II have much fewer users and messages.

The third experiment was conducted on a large-scale Twitter dataset (denoted as "Twitter-III"), consisting of about 2 million randomly sampled users and the messages posted and re-posted by them in three months (Jul. 2009 – Sep. 2009). Twitter-III was preprocessed in a similar way, and finally we got about 50 million messages. Table 2 gives some statistics of the datasets.

4.2 Topic Discovery

The first experiment tested the performance of UMM in topic discovery, and made comparison with UM and MM. In the methods, K was set to 100, γ

---
[3] http://nlp.stanford.edu/software/segmenter.shtml

Table 3. Top-weighted topics of users generated by UMM, UM, and MM on Weibo-I

	User Bio	Top-weighted Topics			
UMM	(a real estate merchant)	(house price) (real estate) (land) (Beijing) (control)	(China) (society) (country) (freedom) (politics)	(life) (learn) (wisdom) (friends) (realm)	(economy) (enterprise) (market) (growth) (crisis)
	(best entertainment magazine in China)	(movie) (story) (director) (actor) (star)	(design) (fashion) (creativity) (clothes) (color)	(news) (media) (journalist) (news report) (Internet users)	(music) (voice) (song) (live) (concert)
UM	(a real estate merchant)	(life) (economy) (commerce) (entrepreneur) (enterprise)	(China) (country) (government) (America) (society)	(life) (world) (time) (problem) (society)	(house price) (real estate) (Beijing) (control) (city)
	(best entertainment magazine in China)	(movie) (Internet users) (media) (exposure) (a few days ago)	(life) (world) (time) (problem) (society)	(activity) (China) (Beijing) (time) (support)	(woman) (like) (man) (life) (happiness)
MM	(a real estate merchant)	(house price) (real estate) (house) (Beijing) (land)	(society) (China) (reform) (freedom) (politics)	(information) (users) (security) (website) (password)	(Apple) iPhone iPad (computer) (product)
	(best entertainment magazine in China)	(movie) (music) (voice) (song) (director)	(clothes) (fashion) (color) (hair) (pretty)	(man) (woman) (marry) (female) (love)	(news) (media) (journalist) (news report) (magazine)

(the Dirichlet prior on the topic-word distribution) was set to 0.01, and β (the Dirichlet prior on the user-topic/message-topic distribution) was set to $10/K$. In UMM, λ^u was set to 10 for all users.

Table 3 shows the top-weighted topical interests of two randomly selected users on Weibo-I, generated by UMM, UM, and MM. The user biographies are also shown for evaluation. From the results, we can see that 1) The readability of the UMM topics is better than or equal to that of the UM and MM topics.[4] Almost all the UMM topics are readable, while some of the UM and MM topics are hard to understand. For example, in the first UM topic for the first user, the word " (life)" is mixed with " (economy)" and " (commerce)". And in the first MM topic for the second user, the words " (movie)" and " (director)" are mixed with " (music)" and " (voice)". 2) UMM characterizes users' interests better than UM and MM. The top interests of the users discovered by UMM are quite representative. However, for the first user, the top interests discovered by MM are " (real estate)", " (society)", " (information security)", and " (electronic products)", where the last two seem less representative. And for the second user, the top interests discovered by UM are pretty vague and not so representative.

Table 4 further shows the top-weighted topics of two randomly selected messages generated by UMM on Weibo-I. The color of each word indicates the topic

---

[4] Topic readability refers to the coherence of top-weighted words in a topic.

Table 4. Top-weighted topics of messages generated by UMM on Weibo-I

Message	Top-weighted Topics			
(Beijing) (financial) (income) (growth) GDP (growth) , (cities and towns) (residents) (income) (growth)	(dollar) (growth) (profit) (income) (revenue)	(economy) (enterprise) (market) (growth) (crisis)	(government) (country) (department) (policy) (management)	(house price) (real estate) (land) (Beijing) (control)
(journalist) (truth) (story), (con-science) (responsibility), (authority) (supervise).	(China) (society) (country) (freedom) (politics)	(government) (country) (department) (policy) (management)	(news) (media) (journalist) (news report) (Internet users)	(literature) (Mo Yan) (Nobel) (writer) (novel)

from which it is supposed to be generated. From the results, we can see that UMM can also effectively capture the topics discussed in microblog messages, and the topic assignments of the words are also reasonable. We have conducted the same experiments on Twitter-I and observed similar phenomena.

4.3   Message Recommendation

The second experiment tested the performance of UMM in message recommendation. We formalize the recommendation task as a Learning to Rank problem [14]. In training, a ranking model is constructed with the data consisting of users, messages, and labels (whether the users have re-posted, i.e., have shown interests in the messages). In ranking, given a user, a list of candidate messages are sorted by using the ranking model.

The data in Weibo-II and Twitter-II were transformed for the ranking task, consisting of user-message pairs and their labels. The label is positive if the message has been re-posted by the user, and is negative if the message might have been seen by the user but has not been re-posted by him.[5] We randomly split each dataset into 5 parts by user and conducted 5-fold cross-validation.

Table 5 lists the features used in the ranking model. The seven basic features are suggested in [4] and [10]. To calculate the two term matching features, messages, user's historical posts, and their profile descriptions are represented as term frequency vectors. The topic matching features are calculated by UMM, UM, and MM models trained on Weibo-I and Twitter-I. Given user u and message m, the topic matching score is calculated as the dot product of their topic representations: $s(u, m) = \langle \pi^u, \theta^m \rangle$. We retain top 5 topics in π^u and θ^m, and truncate other topics. As UM/MM cannot directly output topic representations for messages/users, we calculate them using the learned topic assignments.

When training topic models, we set $K = 10, 20, 40, 60, 80, 100, 200, 400, 600, 800, 1000$. The other parameters were set in the same way as in Section 4.2. We employed Ranking SVM [13] to train the ranking model. Parameter c was set in $[0, 2]$ with interval of 0.1, and the other parameters were set to default values. We tested the settings of using the basic features only (denoted as "Basic"), the basic features plus the term matching features (denoted as "Basic+Term"), and the basic features, the term matching features, and one of the topic matching

---

[5] Messages posted within 5 minutes after a re-posted message are assumed to be seen by the user.

Table 5. Features used for message recommendation

Feature	Description	
Basic features	URL	Whether the message contains URLs
	Hash tag	Whether the message contains hash tags
	Length	Number of words in the message
	Verified publisher	Whether the author of the message is a verified account
	Follower/Followee ratio	Logarithm ratio of #follower and #followee of the author
	Mention	Whether the message mentions the user
	Historical forwarding	Times the user forwarded the author's posts in the past
Term matching	Historical post relevance	Cosine similarity between the message and the user's posts
	User profile relevance	Cosine similarity between the message and the user's profile
Topic matching	MM score	Topic matching score based on MM
	UM score	Topic matching score based on UM
	UMM score	Topic matching score based on UMM

Table 6. Recommendation accuracies on Weibo-II and Twitter-II

Method	Weibo-II			Twitter-II		
	NDCG@1	NDCG@3	NDCG@10	NDCG@1	NDCG@3	NDCG@10
Basic	0.5540	0.5668	0.6164	0.6962	0.7171	0.7661
Basic+Term	0.6412	0.6416	0.6828	0.7157	0.7377	0.7882
Basic+Term+MM	0.6860	0.6669	0.7037	0.7296	0.7439	0.7932
Basic+Term+UM	0.6736	0.6614	0.7010	0.7254	0.7405	0.7925
Basic+Term+UMM	**0.7143**	**0.6818**	**0.7164**	**0.7338**	**0.7440**	**0.7942**

features (denoted as "Basic+Term+UMM" for example). For evaluation, we employed a standard information retrieval metric of NDCG [12].

Table 6 reports the recommendation accuracies on Weibo-II and Twitter-II. The results indicate that 1) Topic matching features are useful in message recommendation. They can significantly (t-test, p-value < 0.05) improve the accuracies achieved by using only the basic and term matching features. 2) UMM performs the best among the three topic models. The improvements of UMM over MM and UM are statistically significant on Weibo-II (t-test, p-value < 0.05). 3) Content features (term matching and topic matching features) are more useful on Weibo-II than on Twitter-II, because more contents can be written in Chinese than in English with limited number of characters.

4.4   Scalability of AD-UMM

We first compared the efficiency of AD-UMM and UMM on Twitter-I. We built a 10-machine mini Hadoop cluster, each of which has a 2-core 2.5GHZ CPU and 2GB memory. In the cluster, 9 machines were used for distributed computing and 1 for scheduling and monitoring. AD-UMM was implemented on the Hadoop cluster, while UMM was implemented on a single machine. In UMM, with the limited 2GB memory, we set K in $\{50, 60, 70\}$. In AD-UMM, we set K in $\{50, 100, 200, 500\}$. The other parameters were set in the same way as in Section 4.2. Fig. 4 reports the average execution time per iteration (sec.) of UMM and AD-UMM on Twitter-I. The results indicate that AD-UMM is much more efficient than UMM, particularly when the number of topics gets large.

We further tested the scalability of AD-UMM on Twitter-III. Fig. 5 (left) shows the average execution time per iteration (min.) of AD-UMM when K

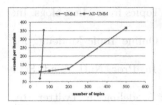

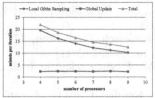

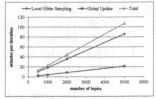

Fig. 4. Execution time on Twitter-I

Fig. 5. Execution time with various P (left) and K (right) values on Twitter-III

(number of topics) equals 500, with P (number of machines) varying from 4 to 9. Fig. 5 (right) shows the execution time when P equals 9, with K varying in $\{500, 1000, 2000, 5000\}$. Here, "Local Gibbs Sampling" and "Global Update" refer to the time costed in the local Gibbs sampling and global update steps respectively, and "Total" means the total time. The results indicate that 1) The execution time decreases linearly as the number of machines increases. 2) The execution time increases linearly as the number of topics increases. As a result, it is practical for AD-UMM to handle huge number of users, messages, and topics with an appropriate number of machines.

5 Conclusions

We have proposed a new approach to mining users' interests on microblog, called User Message Model (UMM). UMM works better than the existing methods, because it can 1) deal with the data sparseness and topic diversity problems, 2) jointly model users and messages in a unified framework, and 3) efficiently handle large-scale datasets. Experimental results show that 1) UMM indeed performs better in topic discovery and message recommendation, and 2) distributed UMM can efficiently handle large-scale datasets. As future work, we plan to apply UMM to various real-world applications and test its performances.

Acknowledgment. This work was done when the first author visited the Noah's Ark Lab of Huawei Technologies.

References

1. Abel, F., Gao, Q., Houben, G.-J., Tao, K.: Analyzing User Modeling on Twitter for Personalized News Recommendations. In: Konstan, J.A., Conejo, R., Marzo, J.L., Oliver, N. (eds.) UMAP 2011. LNCS, vol. 6787, pp. 1–12. Springer, Heidelberg (2011)
2. Ahmed, A., Low, Y., Aly, M., Josifovski, V., Smola, A.J.: Scalable Distributed Inference of Dynamic User Interests for Behavioral Targeting. In: SIGKDD, pp. 114–122 (2011)
3. Blei, D., Ng, Y., Jordan, I.: Latent Dirichlet Allocation. Mach. Learn. Res. (2003)
4. Chen, K., Chen, T., Zheng, G., Jin, O., Yao, E., Yu, Y.: Collaborative Personalized Tweet Recommendation. In: SIGIR, pp. 661–670 (2012)
5. Diao, Q., Jiang, J.: A Unified Model for Topics, Events and Users on Twitter. In: EMNLP (2013)

6. Diao, Q., Jiang, J., Zhu, F., Lim, E.P.: Finding Bursty Topics from Microblogs. In: ACL (2012)
7. Grant, C., George, C.P., Jenneisch, C., Wilson, J.N.: Online Topic Modeling for Real-time Twitter Search. In: TREC (2011)
8. Griffiths, T.L., Steyvers, M.: Finding scientific topics. In: Proc. Natl. Acad. Sci., USA (2004)
9. Hong, L., Davison, B.D.: Empirical Study of Topic Modeling in Twitter. In: SIGKDD Workshop, pp. 80–88 (2010)
10. Hong, L., Doumith, A.S., Davison, B.D.: Co-factorization Machines: Modeling User Interests and Predicting Individual Decisions in Twitter. In: WSDM, pp. 557–566 (2013)
11. Hu, Y., John, A., Wang, F., Kambhampati, S.: Et-lda: Joint Topic Modeling for Aligning Events and their Twitter Feedback. In: AAAI (2012)
12. Järvelin, K., Kekääinen, J.: Cumulated Gain-based Evaluation of IR Techniques. ACM Trans. Inf. Sys. (2002)
13. Joachims, T.: Optimizing Search Engines using Clickthrough Data. In: SIGKDD, pp. 133–142 (2002)
14. Li, H.: Learning to Rank for Information Retrieval and Natural Language Processing (2011)
15. Michelson, M., Macskassy, S.A.: Discovering Users Topics of Interest on Twitter: A First Look. In: CIKM Workshop, pp. 73–80 (2010)
16. Newman, D., Asuncion, A., Smyth, P., Welling, M.: Distributed Inference for Latent Dirichlet Allocation. In: NIPS (2007)
17. Pennacchiotti, M., Gurumurthy, S.: Investigating Topic Models for Social Media User Recommendation. In: WWW, pp. 101–102 (2011)
18. Ramage, D., Dumais, S.T., Liebling, D.J.: Characterizing Microblogs with Topic Models. In: AAAI (2010)
19. Ren, Z., Liang, S., Meij, E., de Rijke, M.: Personalized Time-aware Tweets Summarization. In: SIGIR, pp. 513–522 (2013)
20. Steyvers, M., Smyth, P., Rosen-Zvi, M., Griffiths, T.: Probabilistic Author-topic Models for Information Discovery. In: SIGKDD, pp. 306–315 (2004)
21. Teh, Y.W., Jordan, M.I., Beal, M.J., Blei, D.M.: Hierarchical Dirichlet Processes. J. Am. Stat. Assoc. (2006)
22. Wen, Z., Lin, C.Y.: On the Quality of Inferring Interests from Social Neighbors. In: SIGKDD, pp. 373–382 (2010)
23. Weng, J., Lim, E.P., Jiang, J., He, Q.: TwitterRank: Finding Topic-sensitive Influential Twitterers. In: WSDM, pp. 261–270 (2010)
24. Wu, W., Zhang, B., Ostendorf, M.: Automatic Generation of Personalized Annotation Tags for Twitter Users. In: NAACL-HLT, pp. 689–692 (2010)
25. Xu, Z., Lu, R., Xiang, L., Yang, Q.: Discovering User Interest on Twitter with a Modified Author-topic Model. In: WI-IAT, pp. 422–429 (2011)
26. Xu, Z., Zhang, Y., Wu, Y., Yang, Q.: Modeling User Posting Behavior on Social Media. In: SIGIR (2012)
27. Yuan, Q., Cong, G., Ma, Z., Sun, A., Magnenat-Thalmann, N.: Who, where, when and what: Discover Spatio-temporal Topics for Twitter Users. In: SIGKDD, pp. 605–613 (2013)
28. Zhao, W.X., Jiang, J., Weng, J., He, J., Lim, E.-P., Yan, H., Li, X.: Comparing Twitter and Traditional Media using Topic Models. In: Clough, P., Foley, C., Gurrin, C., Jones, G.J.F., Kraaij, W., Lee, H., Mudoch, V. (eds.) ECIR 2011. LNCS, vol. 6611, pp. 338–349. Springer, Heidelberg (2011)

Enhanced FastPFOR for Inverted Index Compression

S. Domnic[1] and V. Glory[2]

[1]Department of Computer Applications, National Institute of Technology, Tiruchirappalli,
Tamilnadu, India
domnic@nitt.edu
[2]Department of Computer Applications, National Institute of Technology, Tiruchirappalli,
Tamilnadu, India
glory.nitt@gmail.com

Abstract. Information Retrieval System is facing enormous performance challenges due to the rapid growth of the size of the data in information retrieval applications and the increasing number of users for these applications. The performance of IRS has been improved by compressing inverted index, which is commonly used data structure for indexing in IRS. Inverted index compression has focused on reducing the index size for fast interactive searching. Among many latest compression techniques, the performance of FastPFOR is significantly good in inverted index compression. However, its compression performance is still to be improved. In this paper, we propose a new compression technique, called Enhanced FastPFOR, to enhance the performance of FastPFOR. In the proposed method, the Predictive coding, Elias-Fano coding, Hybrid coding (Predictive + Elias - Fano), Golomb Coding and Gamma coding are used to compress the positional values of the exceptions to improve the compression performance of FastPFOR. For performance evaluations, we have used TREC data collections in our experiments and the results show that that the proposed method could improve the compression and decompression significantly.

Keywords: Data compression, Information Retrieval System, Inverted Index, Index compression, FastPFOR.

1   Introduction

Inverted Index data structure [1] is the main component of modern Information Retrieval System (IRS). Inverted index is simple and efficient data structure for keyword-based searching to find the particular term in the document collection. In a given set of N documents, each document is identified by a unique document identifier (docId). An inverted index file consists of 2 components: dictionary file (lexicon file) and inverted list (posting list). Dictionary file stores the distinct terms presented in the document collection and the total number of documents, in which a particular term appears i.e document frequency. Posting list for a term contains frequency value, the total number of documents in which the term appears, the identifiers of the documents (docids) and the positions of the term in the documents. DocIds in the posting list are usually sorted by increasing order and each docid is replaced with D-gap (difference between itself and its predecessor).

A. Jaafar et al. (Eds.): AIRS 2014, LNCS 8870, pp. 221–229, 2014.
© Springer International Publishing Switzerland 2014

In order to decrease the inverted index size and improve the query performance of IRS, highly optimized compression techniques are used. Depending on the attributes (in terms of bitwise, byte-aligned or word-aligned), Compression techniques are differentiated and classified into two, such as integer compression (compress every value individually) and integer list compression (group of values are compressed). Some of the integer compression techniques are Unary Code [2] (an integer n is represented as n-1 (0/1) bits and a (1/0) bit), Gamma Code [3] (represents n as the Unary representation of $|B(n)|$ (number of bits required to represent n) followed by the binary representation (or code) of n without its most significant bit ($\sim B(n)$)), Delta Code [3] (an integer n is coded by Gamma code of $|B(n)|$ followed by ($\sim B(n)$)), Golomb Code [4] (an integer n is divided by the divisor d, then the quotient value is coded by unary code and the remainder value is coded by binary code), Rice Code [5] (it same as Golomb code but the divisor should be a power of two to make efficient in implementation), Variable Byte Code [6] (represent an integer n as the sequence of bytes and in each byte the highest bit is used to indicate the next byte follows the current integer or not and lower 7 bits are the data represented by binary code), Fast Extended Golomb Code [7] (integer n is divided by the divisor d (d is always power of two) until quotient becomes zero. Each remainder is coded by binary code and the count of the divisions is coded by the unary code) and Reordered Fast Extended Golomb Code [8].

Among the integer compression techniques, Gamma, Delta, Golomb, Rice and Fast Extended Golomb Code is slower than Variable Byte code, But Variable Byte code is suited only for compressing the large range of integers. Compared to Variable Byte Code, Reordered Fast Extended Golomb Code gives better compression and decompression when the occurrence of middle and large range of integers are more in the data [8]. Some of the integer list compression techniques are Interpolative Code [9], Elias-Fano [10,11] (natural encoding of monotonically increasing sequence of integers), Simple Family [12], Frame-Of-Reference (FOR) [13,14] and Patched coding techniques (PFORDelta, NewPFD, OptPFD and FastPFOR) [15,16,17].

The works [12], [16] show that Interpolative coding is slower than Golomb coding. The compression performance of the interpolative coding is excellent among the integer list compression techniques, but its decoding speed is worst than other integer list compression techniques. The simple family techniques can perform well in compression than FOR and patched coding techniques. But, they are slow in general. From the paper [16], it was concluded that the decompression performance of FOR, PFORDelta (PFD), NewPFD and OptPFD is superior than integer compression techniques (Gamma, Delta, Rice, VBC) and other integer list compression techniques (interpolative coding and simple family) but their compression performance is not good when compared to other techniques.

The reason for the poor compression performance of FOR technique is that the existence of single large value will increase the minimum bit width (b) used to represent all other integers in the block to be compressed. To overcome the drawback of the FOR, PFOR or PFORDelta was proposed in the paper [15]. In this method, for every block of integers, a small bit width (b) is selected in such a way that most of the integers in the block can be represented by b. The integers in a range of greater than 2^b are treated as exceptions, which are represented by 32 bits.

To improve the compression performance of PFORDelta, H.Yan [16] et.al have proposed two methods: NewPFD and OptPFD. PFORDelta does not compress the exceptions where NewPFD and OptPFD compress the exceptions. NewPFD Techniques has two parts. In the first part, the normal values ($<2^b$) represented in b bits each and lower b bits of the exceptions ($\geq 2^b$) are stored. The positional values of the exceptions and the higher (32-b) bits are compressed using simple family technique and are stored in the second part. The OptPFD technique is same as NewPFD, but it selects b to optimize the compression ratio regardless of the number of exceptions. The compression performance of OptPFD is better than NewPFD. In order to achieve both the compression and decompression performances, FastPFOR (FastPFD) [17] was proposed. It gives better results both in compression and decompression than NewPFD, but it is inferior in compression than OptPFD. To enhance the performance of FastPFOR, we propose a new method called as Enhanced FastPFOR. The proposed method compresses the positional values of the exception using Predictive coding (new method in this paper) and Elias-Fano coding, Hybrid coding (Predictive code + Elias-Fano code), Golomb code and Gamma code to improve the compression performance of the FastPFOR. FastPFOR is discussed in detail in the next section. We have used TREC datasets to evaluate the performance of the proposed method. In this work, we have not considered the decompression speed of Rice, Gamma, Delta, VBC, Interpolative coding and Simple Family for comparison as these techniques are known to be relatively slow [16, 17, 18, 19].

The rest of the paper is organized as follows. Section 2 describes the FastPFOR techniques. Section 3 presents the proposed method. In section 4, experimental results are given. Finally, conclusions are derived in section 5.

2   FastPFOR

FastPFOR [17] technique which is similar to NewPFD and OptPFD design and it has attempted to offer better decoding speed and compression rate. In FastPFOR, the minimum bit width (b) is determined for every block of 128 integers by using the cost formula: $128 \times b + C \times (8 + \max b - b)$ where C is the number of exceptions ($\geq 2^b$) and max b is the number of bits required to represent largest value of the block. The cost formula is used here to optimize the number of exceptions, So that the number of bits required to compress the block can be minimized. FastPFOR has three parts in its storage structure. The first part is the header section, the second part is the normal data section and third part one is the exception section. The first two sections are maintained for every block of 128 integers. But, the exception section is maintained for every page of 2^{16} integers. The header section contains the sequence of bytes to store the following information.

- The bit width (b) – One byte
- Maximal bit width (max b) – One byte
- The Number of Exceptions (C) – One byte
- Location of the exceptions – C bytes.

The normal data section stores the normal values ($<2^b$) in b bits each and the lower b bits of the exceptions ($\geq 2^b$).

In exception section, the higher ($32-b$) bits of the exceptions are stored in one of 32 arrays. The difference between b and max b is used to locate the exceptions in these arrays (1 to 32). The decoding speed might be achieved in FastPFOR when encoding and decoding of the exceptions are done in bulk. The drawback of FastPFOR is the number of bytes used to store the location of the exceptions, which leads to a poor compression performance. In order to overcome this drawback, we have used predictive coding to compress the locations of the exceptions in our proposed method which is discussed in the next section. The storage structure used by FastPFOR is given below.

Header Section					Normal data Section (Storage array)			Exception data Section (32 storage arrays)		
Block 1			...	Block n	Block1	...	Block n			
b 8 bits	Max b 8 bits	C 8 bits	(C×8) bits	.. ...		Block Size * b bits	...	...	.. (Max b – b) bits	. ...

Fig. 1. Fast PFOR storage structure (used per page)

3   The Proposed Method

FastPFD scheme was proposed by D.Lemire et. al to achieve the compression like NewPFD with PFORDelta speed. However, FastPFOR does not give the better compression performance compared to OptPFD due to the storage requirements for the locations of the exceptions. Since, the location of each exception is stored in one byte; the number of exceptions will increase the number bytes, which will lead to a poor compression performance. To improve the compression performance of FastPFOR, we have used predictive coding to compress the locations of the exceptions. The storage structure of the proposed method is same as FastPFOR. The predictive coding is explained in the next sub section.

3.1   Predictive Coding

Predictive coding is proposed based on the idea that the number of bits required to represent n^{th} integer can be predicted from the number of bits required for $(n-1)^{th}$ integer. This prediction is possible when the sequence of the integers are sorted in descending order. Since the locations of the exceptions in the FastPFOR can be sorted in descending order, the proposed prediction method can be applied, So that, instead of storing the locations in fixed length bits (8 bits), they can be stored in variable length bits. Hence, the compression can be achieved. In the predictive coding, the first integer, saying n^{th} integer of the sequence is stored in 7 bits, the $(n+1)^{th}$ integer can be represented in Minimal Binary code of nth integer which needed only $|B(n^{th}$ integer$)|$ bits and $(n+2)^{th}$ integer in $|B(n+1)^{th}$ integer$)|$ bits and so on. The coding design for the block of 128 integers is given in Fig. 2.

n_1	n_2	n_3	n_4	n_5	...	n_{∞}
7	$|B(n_1)|$	$|B(n_2)|$	$|B(n_3)|$	$|B(n_4)|$	...	$|B(n_{n-1})|$

Fig. 2. Coding design for the proposed method

3.2 Illustration

The prediction coding is illustrated with an example.

Let a set of integers in the descending order be

$$< 120, 54, 43, 42, 30, 25, 20, 18, 10, 5, 2 >$$

The first integer value in the sequence will be coded using fixed length bits (8 or 16 or 32 bits). This can be decided based on the possibility of largest value in the sequence. In our example, the maximum value is 120; hence it is coded by 8 or 7 bits as given in Fig. 2. Then, the number of bits required to represent the next integer can be predicted from the previous integer. Since the value of the current integer to be coded is less than or equal to previous integer value (if the integers are sorted in descending order), the number of bits needed to represent the current integer should also be less than or equal to that of previous integer value. The number of bits required to represent each integer value of the descending order sequence (example set) is given in Fig. 3.

Integers	120	54	43	42	30	25	20	18	10	5	2
Bits	7	7	6	6	6	5	5	5	5	4	3

Fig. 3. Representation (bits) of integers in predictive coding

In our proposed method, we have used the predictive coding in FastPFOR to compress the locations of the exceptions in order to achieve low compression rate and we have also used Elias- Fano coding, Golomb coding and Gamma coding to compress the locations of the exceptions to test the compression performance of FastPFOR. The drawback of predictive coding is that, it does not achieve the compression when the occurrences of large values are more in the positional values list. Elias-Fano code can achieve better compression when there are more occurrences of integers within the given maximum limit of the integer values. Otherwise, it may not achieve good compression. On considering the advantages of predictive coding and Elias-Fano coding, we have used both, called as hybrid coding, to compress the positional values of the exceptions. In the hybrid coding, when the number of exceptions is less than or equal to 15 we have used the predictive coding otherwise, we have applied the Elias-Fano coding.

4 Experimental Results

We have implemented the proposed method and tested on TREC document collections such as Clueweb 09, Gov2 and Yandex to evaluate the performance of the compression techniques. The compression methods are evaluated based on compression rate and search time for all the document collections. We have used Intel Xeon processor machine equipped with 16 GB RAM and the OS is 64-bit version of windows 7 in our experiments. We have implemented our code in Java and used some of the source codes available as open source in [20].

In our experiment we have applied compression techniques to compress the document identifiers of the inverted lists which are constructed [18], [21] from TREC Web collections (Clueweb09, Gov2, Yandex). The GOV2 is a crawl of the .gov sites, which contains 25 million of HTML, text, and PDF documents. The Clueweb09 collection is a more realistic HTML collection of about 50 million crawled HTML documents, mostly in English. These collections statistics are given in Table 1.

Table 1. Data collections statistics

Collection	Documents#	Terms #	Encoded Integers
TREC GOV2	25205170	1365826	5396455619
Yandex	4578009	1204375	1299512662
Clueweb09	44233099	1000000	13723387410

The formula used to calculate compression rate (bits per integer) in our experiment is:

$$\textit{Compressio n (or Bit) Rate} = \frac{\textit{Compressed Size of Inverted List (docids)}}{\textit{Total number of Document Identifier s in the List}} \quad (1)$$

Table 2 shows the bit rates of the proposed method and other encoding methods. From the results, it is observed that the proposed method (Predictive coding) achieves the better compression rate for Gov2, Clueweb09 and Yandex collections except the hybrid coding (Predictive+Elias-Fano code) which gives the best results comparing all other methods. Table 3 shows the search performance of the coding methods and it is measured by using the equation (2). We generated a set of random queries for each collection to measure the search performance. Per query, approximately five thousand docid's (Inverted lists per query) are retrieved and decoded. We used 1000 random queries for each dataset to evaluate the search performance and it is measured by adding the time taken to retrieve the data from the disk and the time taken to decode the data.

$$\text{Search Time (ST)} = \text{Disk Access time (AT)} + \text{Decoding Time (DT)} \quad (2)$$

Table 2. Bit rate (bits per docid) for TREC data collections

Compression Techniques		Gov2	Clueweb	Yandex
Proposed Method	Predictive	**4.339**	**6.686**	**5.308**
	Elias-Fano	4.449	6.875	5.459
	Hybrid Coding	**4.300**	**6.616**	**5.250**
	Golomb	4.418	6.823	5.417
	Gamma	4.641	9.383	5.719
FastPFOR		4.661	6.871	5.460
New PFD		4.682	7.055	5.860
Opt PFD		4.509	6.708	5.384
Interpolative Coding		3.166	5.022	3.997
RFEGC		4.957	6.444	5.799
FEGC		4.957	6.444	5.799
VBC		8.631	9.23	9.23

Table 3. Search performance (data is retrieved from the disk and decompressed) time for TREC data collections

Compression Techniques	Gov2	Clueweb	Yandex
Proposed Method (Predictive)			
AT (μs)	**660**	**562**	**471**
DT (μs)	41980	29491	27190
ST (μs)	42640	30053	27661
Fast PFOR			
AT (μs)	756	662	670

Table 3. (*Continued*)

DT (μs)	41464	29247	29245
ST (μs)	42220	29909	29915
VBC			
AT (μs)	2946	2647	3020
DT (μs)	44682	44104	45099
ST (μs)	47628	46751	48119
RFEGC			
AT (μs)	1268	1189	1241
DT (μs)	54181	49089	49642
ST (μs)	55449	50278	50883
FEGC			
AT (μs)	1268	1189	1241
DT (μs)	87841	80188	80704
ST (μs)	89109	81377	81945

From Table 3, compared to other methods, the proposed method (Predictive coding) has given the better result in query processing time for Gov2, Yandex and competitive result for Clueweb 09 because it has the lower bit rate, so lesser time for accessing data from the disk. As a conclusion, our proposed method (Predictive coding) can give significant improvement both in compression and decompression.

5   Conclusion

In this paper, we have proposed a new patched coding, based on FastPFOR. In our method, we have used predictive coding (to represent the integers of the descending order sequence), Elias-Fano coding, Hybrid coding (predictive + Elias - Fano), Golomb coding and Gamma code to compress the positional values of the exceptions of FastPFOR. The experimental results show that the proposed method can achieve significant improvement both in compression and decompression.

References

1. Zobel, J., Moffat, A.: Inverted Files for Text Search Engines. ACM Computing Surveys 38(2), 1–56 (2006)
2. Salomon, D.: Variable-length Codes for Data Compression. Springer (2007)

3. Elias, P.: Universal Codeword Sets and Representations of the Integers. IEEE Trans. Inf. Theory 21(2), 194–203 (1975)
4. Golomb, S.W.: Run Length Encoding. IEEE Trans. Inf. Theory 12(3), 399–401 (1966)
5. Rice, R.F.: Some Practical Universal Noiseless Coding Techniques.Technical Report,pp. 79–22. JPL Publication Pasadena, CA: Jet Propulsion Laboratory (1979)
6. Salomon, D.: Variable-length Codes for Data Compression. Springer (2007)
7. Domnic, S., Glory, V.: Inverted File Compression using EGC and FEGC. In: Proc. ICCCS 2012, pp. 735–742 (2012)
8. Glory, V., Domnic, S.: Re-Ordered FEGC and Block Based FEGC for Inverted File Compression. Int. J. Inf. Retr. Research 3(1), 71–88 (2013)
9. Moffat, A., Stuiver, L.: Binary Interpolative Coding for Effective Index Compression. Inf. Retr. 3(1), 25–47 (2000)
10. Elias, P.: Efficient Storage and Retrieval by Content and Address of Static Files. J. ACM 21(2), 246–260 (1974)
11. Fano, R.M.: On the Number of Bits Required to Implement an Associative Memory. Memorandum 61. Computer Structures Group, MIT, Cambridge, MA (1971)
12. Anh, V.N., Moffat, A.: Inverted Index Compression using Word-Aligned Binary Codes. Inf. Retr. 8(1), 151–166 (2005)
13. Goldstein, J., Ramakrishnan, R., Shaft, U.: Compressing Relations and Indexes. In: Proc. ICDE 1998, pp. 370–379 (1998)
14. Ng, W.K., Ravishankar, C.V.: Block-oriented Compression Techniques for Large Statistical Databases. IEEE Trans. Knowledge and Data Engineering 9(2), 314–328 (1997)
15. Zukowski, M., Heman, S., Nes, N., Boncz, P.: Super-scalar RAM-CPU Cache Compression. In: Proc. ICDE 2006, pp. 59–71 (2006)
16. Yan, H., Ding, S., Suel, T.: Inverted Index Compression and Query Processing with Optimized Document Ordering. In: Proc. WWW 2009, pp. 401–410 (2009)
17. Lemire, D., Boystov, L.: Decoding Billions of Integers per Second through Vectorization. Software: Practice and Experience (2013)
18. Silvestri, F., Venturini, R.: VSEncoding: Efficient Coding and Fast Decoding of Integer Lists via Dynamic Programming. In: Proc. CIKM 2010, pp. 1219–1228 (2010)
19. Zhang, J., Long, X., Suel, T.: Performance of Compressed Inverted List Caching in Search Engines. In: Proc. WWW 2008, pp. 387–396 (2008)
20. FastPFOR Java Code (2013), https://github.com/lemire/JavaFastPFOR
21. Clueweb09 posting list data set,
    http://boytsov.info/datasets/clueweb09gap/

Linguistically Enhanced Collocate Words Model

Siaw Nyuk Hiong, Bali Ranaivo-Malançon, Narayanan Kulathuramaiyer,
and Jane Labadin

Faculty of Computer Science and Information Technology
University Malaysia Sarawak
Kuching, Malaysia
ftsm2006@yahoo.com, {mbranaivo,nara,ljane}@fit.unimas.my

Abstract. Bag-of-word (BOW) or fixed size window approach for word extraction in natural language text has ignored text structure and context information. Similarly, word co-occurrence based on linear word proximity has also ignored the linguistic criteria of words. This paper aims to propose a semantic window of word to address the needs to provide a context for capturing the structure and context of word in a sentence for analysis. The semantic window of word has linguistic elements which can be injected for collocate word identification. Selected data has been used as case studies. Quantitative analysis has been conducted as well. The proposed approach is evaluated and compared to sliding window which is the baseline. Semantic window is found to perform better than sliding window for linguistically enhanced collocate word extraction.

Keywords: Semantic dependency parsing, linguistic, collocation, semantic window.

1   Introduction

It has been reviewed that bag-of-word (BOW) approach ignores the context of occurrence of the word and association between words in documents [1]. A lot of text structure and context information are lost with BOW [2,3]. Similarly, the employment of a fixed size window in word co-occurrence identification [1], [4-9] is also lacking in capturing the semantic information of a text. Co-occurrence is a statistical view for related items identification [10]. This approach identified word co-occurrence based on linear word proximimity which actually has ignored the linguistic properties of the words [11]. The linguistically motivated view which defines items as syntactically related is called collocation [10]. Words extracted based on collocation can represent the content more accurately compared to isolated word extraction [12]. Padó and Lapata [13] shared similar view that the gist of a document can be better modeled by syntactically related co-occurrence than the surface co-occurrence of words. Many natural language processing (NLP) has applied collocation for research in text classification [14], topic segmentation [15], text summarization [16], machine translation [17,18], information retrieval [19] and word sense disambiguation [20,21,22]. According to Seretan [23], syntax-based approach has the advantage over

A. Jaafar et al. (Eds.): AIRS 2014, LNCS 8870, pp. 230–243, 2014.

the syntax-free approach for collocation identification since there is no limitations on the maximum distance that collocation components can be found. The main objective of this paper is to propose a semantic window of words to address the needs in providing a context to capture the structure and context of words in a sentence for analysis. The semantic window of words has linguistic elements which can be injected for collocate word identification.

2   Linguistic Motivated Collocation

The lexical-collocational layer of Firth's Model [24] plays an important role in providing the linguistic frame of reference for collocation identification. This is a simplified linguistic context structure used as a frame of reference for isolated words or sentences. A model could be built by combining this simplification with abstraction [25]. The lexical layer examines words in relationship to other words or word sequences. The sequence of subsequent words resulted in syntagmatic structure of a text. In syntagmatic context, the occurrences of two or more words are collocations. The collocation boundaries within a text can be determined by some syntactic preprocessing to obtain linguistic structure based on part-of-speech (POS) or phrasal elements [25,26]. This argument is based on the linguistic perspective that a linguistic expression has an underlying syntactic structure. The Firth's lexical-collocational layer has this property as it is on top of the syntactic layer.

Lexical co-occurrence is the most influential and widely use linguitic property of collocations. According to Firthian [24] and Neo-Firthian linguistics [27,28], collocations have some basic patterns of co-occurrence in relation to their constituent parts. The patterns can be used as the basis for lexical analysis of language. Many collocation extraction methods [29-35] have been carried out employing this property due to its quantitative and empirically verifiable nature.

Syntactic processing can be fed into semantic interpretation [25]. Such feature is provided through semantic dependency parsing. Predicate argument structure (PAS) obtained from the dependency parsing can be used as the linguistic structure to determine collocation boundaries. In this paper, a collocate word model based on these semantic boundaries (which will be called "semantic window of collocate words") is proposed. The following section describes the tasks employed for the model.

3   Semantic Dependency Parsing

Semantic dependency parsing is the process of obtaining a semantically labeled PAS for a predicate from a syntactic dependency tree [36]. Recent years' research have shown an increasing interest in employing parsers based on dependency structure to induce PAS for semantic dependency parsing. It is claimed that the dependency structure can provide a simple and transparent encoding of PAS [37-41].

The availability of PAS scheme corpora for semantic roles like FrameNet [42], PropBank [43], VerbNet [44] and NomBank [45] has enabled accurate and efficient semantic dependency parsers to be developed. A core task that has almost become a surrogate for semantic dependency parsing in recent year is semantic role lableing (SRL) [36]. The recent semantic dependency parsing researches have been fostered through CoNLL Shared Tasks 2006, 2007, 2008 [46,47,48] and CoNLL-X Shared Tasks 2009 [49]. Malt parser [50] and MST parser [47] have obtained state of the art performance in CoNLL Shared Tasks 2006 and 2007 while LTH parser [51] has the best performance in CoNLL Shared Tasks 2008. LTH parser is used for semantic dependency parsing in this research. The characteristic of CoNLL Shared Tasks 2008 and CoNLL-X Shared Tasks 2009 is the employment of an integrated syntactic and semantic approach for dependency parsing.

4   Semantic Window of Collocate Words

The different tasks employed in the proposed semantic window of collocate words identification are: (a) semantic dependency parsing, (b) semantic window of word, (c) collocate window, and (d) collocate words. These tasks are described below.

4.1   Semantic Dependency PAS

Based on semantic dependency PAS, the semantic event inherited the following properties:

> (a) Relative prominence relations among arguments via thematic hierarchy determined by the thematic properties of the predicate.
> (b) Continuous embedded projective dependency-syntactic structure for capturing nested event.

[52] has described nested event based on property (b). PAS 'frame' refers to the predicate and their arguments. It is the natural window that defines the boundary for thematically related word(s) or phrase(s) in the text. This window is exploited and used as the semantic window of word in this paper.

4.2   Semantic Window of Word

Nested event in dependency PAS resulted in many PAS 'frame'. Each PAS 'frame' has a predicate and its arguments. The predicate and arguments have thematic relationship in semantic dependency PAS. The boundary that defines predicate or arguments segmented the semantically related word(s) of a text into different chunks. These chunks represent the semantic window of words in this paper. Fig. 1 illustrates the semantic window of words formation.

Sentence	$w_1, w_2, w_3, w_4, w_5, w_6,$ ...., $w_{n-4}, w_{n-3}, w_{n-2}, w_{n-1}, w_n.$		
PAS	$[w_1, w_2, w_3]_{Arg} w_4, [w_5]_{Pred}, w_6,$ .... $[[[w_{n-4}]_{Pred}, [w_{n-3}]_{Arg}]_{Arg} [w_{n-2}]...[[w_{n-1}]_{Pred}, [w_n]_{Arg}]_{Arg}]_{Arg}$		
PAS 'frame'	Arg_1	Pred	Arg_2
1	$[w_1, w_2, w_3]$	$[w_5]$	$[w_{n-4}, w_{n-3}, w_{n-2}, w_{n-1}, w_n]$
2	$[w_{n-4}, w_{n-3}]$	$[w_{n-2}]$	$[w_{n-1}, w_n]$
3	$[w_{n-4}]$	$[w_{n-3}]$	
4		$[w_{n-1}]$	$[w_n]$
Semantic Window of Word	$[w_1, w_2, w_3]$ $[w_5]$ $[w_{n-4}, w_{n-3}, w_{n-2}, w_{n-1}, w_n]$ $[w_{n-2}]$ $[w_{n-4}, w_{n-3}]$ $[w_{n-1}, w_n]$ $[w_{n-4}]$ $[w_{n-3}]$ $[w_{n-1}]$ $[w_n]$		

Fig. 1. Semantic window of words

4.3 Collocate Window

Seretan [10] defines syntactically related items as collocation. In this paper, two semantically related windows are defined as collocate windows. The collocate windows have a predicate-argument relation. This collocation has been enhanced with linguistically injected elements in the form of thematically related predicate-argument. Words that exist within a semantic window are collocate words. Fig. 2 illustrates the formation of linguistically injected collocate window.

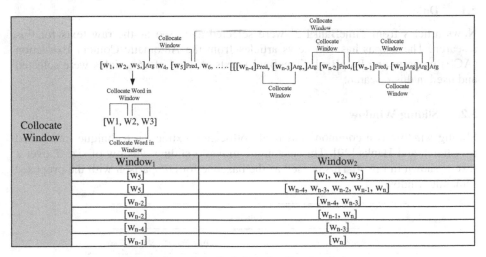

	Window₁	Window₂
	$[w_5]$	$[w_1, w_2, w_3]$
	$[w_5]$	$[w_{n-4}, w_{n-3}, w_{n-2}, w_{n-1}, w_n]$
Collocate Window	$[w_{n-2}]$	$[w_{n-4}, w_{n-3}]$
	$[w_{n-2}]$	$[w_{n-1}, w_n]$
	$[w_{n-4}]$	$[w_{n-3}]$
	$[w_{n-1}]$	$[w_n]$

Fig. 2. Linguistically injected collocate window

4.4 Collocate Words

From the prespective of linguistics, semantic compositionality and morpho-syntactic information are usually characterszed by collocation [10]. Based on this argument, the linguistically injected collocate window is used to identify collocate words in this research. Each word that exists in an argument is considered to collocate with the predicate and each word that exists in an argument is considered to collocate with other words in the same argument. Thus, the nested event of semantic dependency PAS results in the possibility of w_1 to collocate more than once with w_2. This recursively nested word-word binary collocation is an identification of complex collocations [10]. Fig. 3 illustrates the collocate words identified based on collocate window.

Collocate Window		Collocate Word
Window$_1$	Window$_2$	
[w$_5$]	[w$_1$, w$_2$, w$_3$]	{(w$_1$, w$_5$), (w$_2$, w$_5$), (w$_3$, w$_5$)}
[w$_5$]	[w$_{n-4}$, w$_{n-3}$, w$_{n-2}$, w$_{n-1}$, w$_n$]	{(w$_{n-4}$, w$_5$), (w$_{n-3}$, w$_5$), (w$_{n-2}$, w$_5$), (w$_{n-1}$, w$_5$), (w$_n$, w$_5$)}
[w$_{n-2}$]	[w$_{n-4}$, w$_{n-3}$]	{(w$_{n-4}$, w$_{n-2}$), (w$_{n-3}$, w$_{n-2}$)}
[w$_{n-2}$]	[w$_{n-1}$, w$_n$]	{(w$_{n-1}$, w$_{n-2}$), (w$_n$, w$_{n-2}$)}
[w$_{n-4}$]	[w$_{n-3}$]	{(w$_{n-4}$, w$_{n-3}$)}
[w$_{n-1}$]	[w$_n$]	{(w$_{n-1}$, w$_n$)}
Collocate Word in Window		
[w$_1$, w$_2$, w$_3$]		{(w$_1$, w$_2$), (w$_1$, w$_3$), (w$_2$, w$_3$)}
[w$_{n-4}$, w$_{n-3}$, w$_{n-2}$, w$_{n-1}$, w$_n$]		{(w$_{n-4}$, w$_{n-3}$), (w$_{n-4}$, w$_{n-2}$), (w$_{n-4}$, w$_{n-1}$), (w$_{n-4}$, w$_n$), (w$_{n-3}$, w$_{n-2}$), (w$_{n-3}$, w$_{n-1}$), (w$_{n-3}$, w$_n$), (w$_{n-2}$, w$_{n-1}$), (w$_{n-2}$, w$_n$), (w$_{n-1}$, w$_n$)}
[w$_{n-4}$, w$_{n-3}$]		{(w$_{n-4}$, w$_{n-3}$)}
[w$_{n-1}$, w$_n$]		{(w$_{n-1}$, w$_n$)}

Fig. 3. Collocate words

5   Semantic Window vs. Sliding Window : A Case Study

5.1   Data

News articles from TimeBank1.2[1] were selected and used as the raw texts for this research. The corpus has 183 news articles from the Automatic Content Extraction (ACE) program and PropBank (TreeBank) texts. A total of 66 articles were selected and used in this research.

5.2   Sliding Window

Sliding window is a common statistical collocation extraction technique introduced by Church and Hanks [29]. This technique moves a sliding window of size T over a text as shown in Fig. 4. This is used as the baseline for comparison with the proposed semantic window.

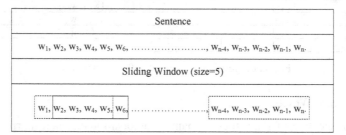

Fig. 4. Sliding Window of size 5

---

[1]   http://www.ldc.upenn.edu/Catalog/catalogEntry.jsp?catalogId=LDC2006T08

5.3   Method

In this research, each sentence is represented as a graph network consisting of linked collocate words. Co-occurrence frequency of collocate words constitute the weights of the link. The collocate words are identified based on the proposed semantic window of collocate words and sliding window is used as the baseline. The linked words resemble more to a neighbourhood network. Pagerank, a neighbourhood based centrality measure, is used to compute graph centrality scores.

Ranking words are computed using the graph centrality measure based on adjacency matrix prepared from sliding window and the semantic window of collocate words. A window span of five words is recommended for word extraction [10],[29] using sliding window. Besides, three experts are involved to annotate the same set of data to measure inter-rater agreement. Kappa coefficient (κ) is used to evaluate inter-method reliability and inter-rater agreement.

5.4   Relative Prominence of Semantic Role

SRL based semantic dependency PAS has been used in this research. Thematic role theories for SRL by Grimshaw [53] defined external argument as the most prominent in two hierarchies within lexical-semantic structure, which are given below:

> (Agent (Experiencer (Goal/Source/Location (Theme)))),
> (Cause (other (...))),

The parentheses reflect prominence and least embedded means most prominent, more deeply embedded means less prominent. For example, the verb *announce* has an external Agent and an internal Theme and Goal. Agent is more prominent than the other more embedded arguments. In the context of relative prominence to each other; the Goal is more prominent than the Theme.

> announce (AGENT (GOAL (THEME)))

5.5   Discussion

Based on the expert annotated data, a total of five sentences for inter-annotater agreement at a precision of 0.8 among all three annotaters are selected from the data for case studies. The relative prominence of verbal predicate for PAS of sentence *w_0019_0.txt* is *said((killed(watching)),emptied)*. The relative prominence of verbal predicate and the most frequently collocate content words would dictate the importance of words in a sentence based on semantic window of collocate words using Pagerank centrality measure. A summary for the case studies based on both semantic and sliding window in comparison with the three annotaters' top five content words is shown in Table 1.

Based on the analysis in Table 1, it is observed that semantic window of collocate words has better agreement with the annotators compared to sliding window. The overall precision is computed by comparing the top five content words obtained from Pagerank graph centrality measures with the three annotators' top five content words.

Table 1. Semantic window of collocate words vs. sliding window: case studies comparison with annotaters' top five ranking words

| Case Study | Semantic Window | | Sliding Window (top five ranking words) | Inter Annotater Agreement (precision=0.8 for top five ranking words) | semantic Window vs. Annotaters Accuracy | Sliding Window vs. Annotaters Accuracy |
	Relative Prominence of Verbal Predicate	Top Five Ranking Words				
w_0019_0.txt	said((killed(watching)),emptied)	said, robbers, pistol, emptied, Thursday	watching, store, police, woman, said	Brooklyn, killed, pistols, robbers	Average	Low
w_0201_5.txt	say(trying,eliminate,restore)	say, trying, Kosovo Liberation Army, order, eliminate	restore, say, order, trying, police	Police, eliminate, Kosovo Liberation Army, order	Average	Average
wsj_0745_3.txt	said(wrote(intends(wins)))	said, Jaguar, wrote, US, intends	wins, go, level, Jaguar, clearance	Jaguar, US, level, clearance	Average	Average
wsj_0027_9.txt	said(wants(resume))	said, wants, role, Mr. Stronach, resume	role, company, wants, Mr. Stronach, said	Mr. Stronach, resume, role, company, analysts	Average	Average
wsj_0675_2.txt	(expected, continue, launching)	funds, continue, program, launching, market	programs, expected, funds, market, index	funds, continue, programs, market	High	Average

Low=overall precision ≤ 1, Average= 2 ≤overall precision ≤ 3, High= overall precision ≥ 4

Semantic window of collocate words for case *wsj_0675_2.txt* and *w_0019_0.txt* have better agreement with the annotators compared to sliding window. The annotators have extracted verbal predicate and collocate content words similar to those extracted by semantic window of collocate words. Thus, a combination of relative prominence for verbal predicate and frequency of collocate content words has enabled semantic window of collocate words to model the extraction of top five content words very closely to the annotators.

Both semantic window of collocate words and sliding window have average precision for case *w_0201_5.txt*, *wsj_0745_3.txt* and *wsj_0027_9.txt* compared to the annotaters. This shows that semantic window of collocate words can perform equally well as the sliding window with semantic window having the advantage of generating lower number of windows (Fig. 5 shows an example). The efficiency of semantic window of collocate words is depended on the combination of relative prominence of

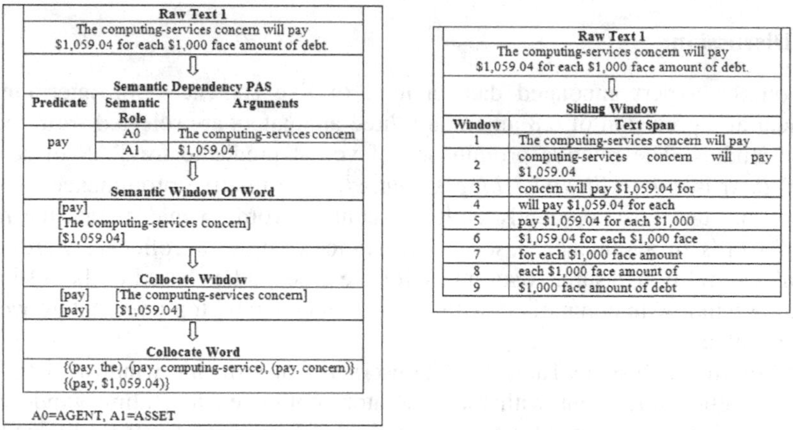

Fig. 5. Generated windows: semantic window of collocate words vs. sliding window

verbal predicate and collocate content words. This approach takes into consideration the structure and relationship between words in a sentence. One drawback of sliding window is that the linear word proximity approach actually has ignored the linguistic criteria of the words [11]. The value added features of the proposed semantic window of collocate words over sliding window are shown in Table 2.

Table 2. Value added features of semantic window of collocate words over sliding window

Features	Semantic Window of Collocate Words	Proof Of Claim
Generate a lower number of windows.	√	Fig. 5 as an example.
Capture linguistic structure of a text.	√	PAS structure of Nested Event Model [42].
Capture the semantic of a text.	√	PAS with thematic relation [42].
Linear word proximity.	×	Semantic window of word.

6   Semantic Window vs. Sliding Window: A Quantitative Analysis

This section will describe quantitative evaluation of word collocation extraction based on the semantic window of collocate words against sliding window. A total of 100 sentences were extracted from TimeBank1.2 corpus to be used as the raw text for data experimentation. From the sentences, 370 PAS are extracted. Weighted graphs that take into consideration the frequency and relative prominence of collocate words based on semantic window of collocate words are defined.

Definition 1
A relation that exists between w and w_i constitutes the edge of the graph. Frequency of co-occurrence constitutes the weight. The adjacency matrix $A = [a_{ij}] \in R^{n \times n}$ of the weighted collocate word graph G of order n is given by:

$$a_{ij} = \begin{cases} 1 & \text{if } (v_i, v_j) \in E \\ 0 & \text{otherwise} \end{cases}$$

where,
Vertices: $v_i \, \varepsilon \, V$
Edges: $a_{ij} = (v_i, v_j) \, \varepsilon \, E$

Definition 2
The structural information of PAS can be characterized by assigning different weight to the thematic relation for collocate words. The weight indicates the order of ranking in the thematic relation. The adjacency matrix $A = [a_{ij}] \in R^{n \times n}$ of the thematic relation weighted graph G of order n is given by:

$$a_{ij} = \begin{cases} 0.9, & \text{if}(v_i, v_j) \in E, E \in A0 \\ 0.6, & \text{if}(v_i, v_j) \in E, E \in A1 \\ 0.3, & \text{if}(v_i, v_j) \in E, E \subset A0 \text{ or } E \subset A1 \end{cases}$$

where,

        Vertices: $v_i \, \varepsilon \, V$
        Edges: $a_{ij} = (v_i, v_j) \, \varepsilon \, E$
        A0=AGENT
        A1=THEME

Definition 3

Weight for graph from definition 1 and 2 are compounded to represent collocate word and their thematic relations into a single graph. The adjacency matrix of the graph A = $[e_{ij}] \in R^{n \times n}$ for weighted graph G of order n is given by:

$$
w_{ij} = \begin{cases} w_1(v_i, v_j) * w_2(v_i, v_j) & \begin{array}{l} v_i, v_j \, \varepsilon \, E \\ w_1 = \varphi_1(e_{ij}) \\ \varphi_1 : E \to R \\ w_2 = \varphi_2(e_{ij}) \\ \varphi_2 : E \to R \\ otherwise \end{array} \\ 0 \end{cases}
$$

where,

        Vertices: $v_i \, \varepsilon \, V$
        Edges: $e_{ij} = (v_i, v_j) \, \varepsilon \, E$
        $w_{ij} = \varphi(e_{ij})$ is called a weight to an edge $e_{ij} = (v_i, v_j) \, \varepsilon \, E$, $\varphi : E \to R$ (R=real number)

The relative importance of nodes in a graph can be computed using centrality measures [54]. Three neighbourhood based centrality measures are used to compute centrality scores.

(a)   Eigenvector
(b)   Pagerank
(c)   Degree

Ranking words are computed using the three graph centrality meaures based on adjacency matrix prepared from the semantic window of collocate words and sliding window (baseline). A window span of $n=5$ is used for sliding window. Kappa coefficient (κ) is used to evaluate inter-method reliability. Fig. 6 shows an interpretation given by Green [55] for Kappa coefficient and strength of agreement.

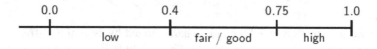

Fig. 6. Kappa coefficient and strength of agreement (Green [55])

The following terminology and notations are used for inter-method reliability calculation.

- $\{i \mid i \in I\}$: a set of items with cardinality i.
- $\{c \mid c \in C\}$: a set of categories with cardinality c.
- $\{r \mid r \in R\}$: a set of methods with cardinality r.

The category c for inter-method reliability used in this research is given by the following definition. Since top five ranking words are being compared, a precision at n P@n of ≥ 0.6 is used as the cut-off point to return matched cases.

$$c = \begin{cases} 1, & \text{if } n(A \cap B) \geq 3 \\ & A \in \text{top five content words of } \iota_A \\ & B \in \text{top five content words of } \iota_B \\ 0, & \text{otherwise} \end{cases}$$

7   Discussion and Conclusion

Comparing the three graph centrality measures for inter-method evaluation based on semantic window of collocate words, it is observed that the highest Kappa coefficients (κ) of ≥ 0.4 is give by Pagerank as the reference method. The results also indicate that a mark improvement in κ is obtained when a compound weight from graph definition 1 and 2 are used. The overall highest $\kappa \geq 0.6$ among all reference methods is given by Pagerank based on semantic window of collocate words. Even though different reference method gives different κ for either semantic window of collocate words or sliding window, the overall highest κ is given by semantic window of collocate words. The highest κ is obtained after thematic relation is included in the computation. This indicates that thematic relation can improve the score of κ. Analysis of inter-method's κ has provided the evidence that semantic window of collocate words has the potential to be a better alternative to induce and extract collocate words from a sentence. Table 3 shows the overall results of inter-method kappa coefficient.

Table 3. Overall results of inter-method Kappa coefficient

Reference Method	Inter-method	Kappa Coefficient	Standard Error (SE)
	Semantic Window		
Pagerank (F)	Degree vs. eigenvector(F)	0.4929	0.089
	Degree vs. eigenvector(F*T)	0.4453	0.098
Pagerank (F*T)	Degree vs. eigenvector(F)	0.6047	0.087
	Degree vs. eigenvector(F*T)	0.6173	0.087
Eigenvector (F)	Degree vs. Pagerank (F)	0.1506	0.1
	Degree vs. Pagerank (F*T)	0.2000	0.12
Eigenvector (F*T)	Degree vs. Pagerank (F)	-0.0059	0.13
	Degree vs. Pagerank (F*T)	0.1132	0.12
	Eigenvector (F) vs. Pagerank (F)	0.0623	0.13
Degree	Eigenvector (F) vs. Pagerank (F*T)	0.0511	0.15
	Eigenvector (F*T) vs. Pagerank (F)	-0.0386	0.14
	Eigenvector (F*T) vs. Pagerank (F*T)	-0.0199	0.17
	Sliding Window (baseline)		
Pagerank	Eigenvector vs. Degree	0.1545	0.0995
Eigenvector	Degree vs. Pagerank	0.439	0.096
Degree	Eigenvector vs Pagerank	0.174	0.099

F = frequency,   F*T = frequency * thematic relation

This paper has proposed and evaluated the semantic window of collocate words model. This model has many value-added features over the conventional sliding window for collocate word extraction. Case studies and quantitative evaluations have been carried out to compare the two approaches. It is observed that the proposed semantic window of collocate words performed better than sliding window. The objective of this research has been achieved. As a conclusion, the differences in experimental results between semantic window of collocate words and sliding window could be due to the different approach employed in extracting the collocate words.

Acknowlededegement. The sponsorship of this research is by the Education Sponsorship Division, Ministry of Education Malaysia.

References

1. Hassan, S., Mihalcea, R., Banea, C.: Random-Walk Term Weighting for Improved Text Classification. In: Semantic Computing, ICSC 2007, pp. 242–249 (2007)
2. Wang, W., Do, D.B., Lin, X.: Term Graph Model for Text Classification. In: Li, X., Wang, S., Dong, Z.Y. (eds.) ADMA 2005. LNCS (LNAI), vol. 3584, pp. 19–30. Springer, Heidelberg (2005)
3. Liu, J., Wang, J., Wang, C.: A Text Network Representation Model. In: Fifth International Conference on Fuzzy Systems and Knowledge Discovery, pp. 150–154 (2008)
4. Mihalcea, R., Tarau, P., Figa, E.: Pagerank on Semantic Networks, with Application to Word Sense Disambiguation. In: The 20th International Conference on Computational Linguistics (COLING 2004), Geneva, Switzerland, pp. 1126–1132 (2004)
5. Tomita, J., Nakawatase, H., Ishii, M.: Graph-based Text Database for Knowledge Discovery. In: 13th International World Wide Web Conference (WWW 2004), pp. 454–455 (2004)
6. Valle, K., Ozturk, P.: Graph-based Representations for Text Classification. India-Norway Workshop on Web Concepts and Technologies, Trondheim, Norway (2011)
7. Mihalcea, R., Tarau, P.: TextRank: Bringing Order into Texts. In: Proceedings of EMNLP, pp. 404–411 (2004)
8. Wan, X., Xiao, J.: Single Document Keyphrase Extraction using Neighborhood Knowledge. In: The Twenty-Third AAAI Conference on Artificial Intelligence, pp. 855–860 (2008)
9. Tsatsaronis, G., Varlamis, I., Nørvåg, K.: An Experimental Study on Unsupervised Graph-based Word Sense Disambiguation. In: Gelbukh, A. (ed.) CICLing 2010. LNCS, vol. 6008, pp. 184–198. Springer, Heidelberg (2010)
10. Seretan, V.: Syntax-based Collocation Extraction. Springer, New York (2011)
11. Seretan, V., Wehrli, E.: Multilingual Collocation Extraction with a Syntactic Parser. Language Resources and Evaluation 43(1), 71–85 (2007)
12. Yarowsky, D.: One Sense Per Collocation. In: Proceedings of ARPA Human Language Technology Workshop, pp. 266–271. Princeton (1993)
13. Padó, S., Lapata, M.: Dependency-based Construction of Semantic Space Models. Computational Linguistics, 161–199 (2007)
14. Williams, G.: In Search of Representativity in Specialised Corpora: Categorisation through Collocation. International Journal of Corpus Linguistics 7, 43–64 (2002)

15. Ferret, O.: Using Collocations for Topic Segmentation and Link Detection. In: Proceedings of the 19th International Conference on Computational linguistics (COLING 2002), pp. 260–266 (2002)
16. Seretan, V.: A Collocation-Driven Approach to Text Summarization. In: TALN 2011, pp. 9–14 (2011)
17. Wehrli, E., Seretan, V., Nerima, L., Russo, L.: Collocations in a Rule-Based MT System: A Case Study Evaluation of Their Translation Adequacy. In: The 13th Annual Conference of the EAMT, pp. 128–135 (2009)
18. Nerima, L., Wehrli, E., Seretan, V.: A Recursive Treatment of Collocations. In: Proceedings of the Seventh conference on International Language Resources and Evaluation (LREC 2010), pp. 634–638 (2010)
19. Arazy, O., Woo, C.: Enhancing Information Retrieval through Statistical Natural Language Processing: A Study of Collocation Indexing. MIS Quarterly 525–546 (2007)
20. Jin, P., Wu, Y., Yu, S.: SemEval-2007 Task 5: Multilingual Chinese-English Lexical Sample. In: Proceedings of the 4th International Workshop on Semantic Evaluations (SemEval 2007), pp. 19–23 (2007)
21. Li, W.: Chinese Collocation Extraction and its Application in Natural Language Processing. Doctor of Philosophy:The Hong Kong Polythenic University (2007)
22. Padó, S., Lapata, M.: Dependency-based Construction of Semantic Space Models. Computational Linguistics, 161–199 (2007)
23. Seretan, V.: Syntax-based Collocation Extraction. Springer, New York (2011)
24. Firth, J.R.: Papers in Linguistics 1934 - 1951. Oxford University Press, London (1957)
25. Wermter, J.: Collocation and Term Extraction Using Linguistically Enhanced Statistical Methods. Doctor of Philosophy: der Friedrich-Schiller-Universität Jena (2008)
26. Smadja, F.A.: Retrieving Collocations from Text: Xtract. Computational Linguistics 19(1), 143–177 (1993)
27. Halliday, M.A.: Lexis as Linguistic Level. In: Charles, E.B., John, C.C., Michael, A.K., Robbins, R.H. (eds.) Memory of F. R. Firth, pp. 148–162. Longman, Harlow (1966)
28. Sinclair, J.: Beginning the Study of Lexis. In: Charles, E., Bazell, J.C., Catford, H., Michael, A.K., Robbins, R.H. (eds.) Memory of F. R. Firth, Longman, London (1966)
29. Church, K., Hanks, P.: Word Association Norms, Mutual Information and Lexicography. Computational Linguistics 16, 22–29 (1990)
30. Church, K., Gale, W.A., Hanks, P., Hindle, D.: Using Statistics in Lexical Analysis. In: Uri, Z. (ed.) Lexical Acquisition. Using Online Resources to Build a Lexicon, pp. 115–164. Lawrence Erlbaum Associates, Hillsdale (1991)
31. Church, K.W.: One Term or Two? In: Fox, E.A., Ingwersen, P., Fidel, R. (eds.) Proceedings of the 18th Annual International ACM SIGIR Conference on Research and Development in Information Retrieval, SIGIR 1995, pp. 310–318. ACM Press, Seattle (1995)
32. Daille, B.: Study and Implementation of Combined Techniques for Automatic Extraction Of Terminology. In: Klavans, J.L., Resnik, P. (eds.) The Balancing Act: Combining Statistical and Symbolic Approaches to Language, pp. 49–66. MIT Press, Cambridge (1996)
33. Manning, C.D., Schutze, H.: Foundations of Statistical Natural Language Processing. Bradford Book & MIT Press, Cambridge (1999)
34. Evert, S., Krenn, B.: Methods for the Qualitative Evaluation of Lexical Association Measures. In: Proceedings of the 39th Annual Meeting of the Association for Computational Linguistics and the 10th Conference of the European Chapter of the Association for Computational Linguistics, pp. 188–195. Morgan Kaufmann, San Francisco (2001)

35. Evert, B.: The Statistics of Word Co-occurrences: Word Pairs and Collocations. University of Stuttgart, Doctor of Philosophy (2005)
36. Zhao, H., Zhang, X., Kit, C.: Integrative Semantic Dependency Parsing via Efficient Large-scale Feature Selection. Journal of Artificial Intelligence Research 46, 203–233 (2013)
37. Culotta, A., Sorensen, J.: Dependency Tree Kernels for Relation Extraction. In: Proceedings of the 42nd Annual Meeting of the Association for Computational Linguistics (ACL 2004), Barcelona, pp. 423–429 (2004)
38. Ding, Y., Palmer, M.: Synchronous Dependency Insertion Grammars: A Grammar Formalism for Syntax Based Statistical MT. In: Proceedings of the Workshop on Recent Advances in Dependency Grammar, Geneva, pp. 90–97 (2004)
39. Quirk, C., Menezes, A., Cherry, C.: Dependency Treelet Translation: Syntactically Informed Phrasal SMT. In: Proceedings of the 43rd Annual Meeting of the Association for Computational Linguistics (ACL 2005), Ann Arbor, MI, pp. 271–279 (2005)
40. Johansson, R., Nugues, P.: Dependency-based Semantic Role Labeling of PropBank. In: Proceedings of the 2008 Conference on Empirical Methods in Natural Language Processing, pp. 69–78. Association for Computational Linguistics, Honolulu (2008)
41. Nivre, J.: Dependency Parsing. Language and Linguistics Compass 4/3, 138–152 (2010)
42. Fillmore, C.J.: Frame Semantics and the Nature of Language. In: Annals of the New York Academy of Sciences: Conference on the Origin and Development of Language and Speech, pp. 20–32 (1976)
43. Palmer, M., Gildea, D., Kingsbury, P.: The Proposition Bank: An Annotated Corpus of Semantic Roles. Computational Linguistics, 71–105 (2005)
44. Kipper, K., Dang, H.T., Palmer, M.: Class-based Construction of a Verb Lexicon. In: AAAI/IAAI, pp. 691–696 (2000)
45. Meyers, A., Reeves, R., Macleod, C., Szekely, R., Zielinska, V., Young, B., et al.: The NomBank Project: An Interim Report. In: A.M. (ed.) HLT-NAACL 2004 Workshop:Frontiers in Corpus Annotation, Boston, MA, pp. 24–31 (2004)
46. Buchholz, S., Marsi, E., Dubey, A., Krymolowski, Y.: CoNLL-X Shared Task on Multilingual Dependency Parsing. In: Proceeding of the 10th Conference on Computational Natural Language Learning, CoNLL-2006 (2006)
47. Nivre, J., Hall, J., Nilsson, J., Chanev, A., Eryigit, G., Kübler, S., et al.: MaltParser: A Language-independent System for Data-driven Dependency Parsing. Natural Language Engineering 13(2), 95–135 (2007)
48. Surdeanu, M., Johansson, R., Meyers, A., Màrquez, L., Nivre, J.: The CoNLL-2008 Shared Task on Joint Parsing Of Syntactic And Semantic Dependencies. In: Proceedings of the 12th Conference on Computational Natural Language Learning (CoNLL-2008), Manchester, pp. 159–177 (2008)
49. Hajic, J., Ciaramita, M., Johansson, R., Kawahara, D., Marti, M.A., M'arquez, L., et al.: The CoNLL 2009 Shared Task: Syntactic and Semantic Dependencies inMultiple Languages. In: Proceedings of the 13th CoNLL-2009, Boulder, Colorado, USA, pp. 1–18 (2009)
50. McDonald, R., Crammer, K., Pereira, F.: Online Large-margin Training of Dependency Parsers. In: Proceedings of ACL-2005 (2005)
51. Johansson, R., Nugues, P.: The Effect of Syntactic Representation on Semantic Role Labeling. In: Proceedings of the 22nd International Conference on Computational Linguistics (COLING 2008), pp. 393–400 (2008)

52. Siaw, N.H., Narayanan, K., Bali, R.-M., Jane, L.: Nested Event Model. SoMet: The 13th International Conference on Intelligent Software Methodologies Tools and Techniques, Langkawi, Malaysia, September 22-24 (in press, 2014)
53. Grimshaw, J.: Argument Structure. MIT Press, Cambridge (1990)
54. Valle, K.: Graph-based Representations for Textual Case-Based Reasoning. Master Thesis. Norwegian University of Science and Technology (2011)
55. Green, A.: Kappa Statistics for Multiple Raters using Categorical Classifications. In: Proceedings of the 22 Annual SAS User Group International Conference, pp. 16–19 (1997)

Named Entity Extraction via Automatic Labeling and Tri-training: Comparison of Selection Methods

Chien-Lung Chou and Chia-Hui Chang

National Central University, Taoyuan, Taiwan
formatc@gmail.com, chia@csie.ncu.edu.tw

Abstract. Detecting named entities from documents is one of the most important tasks in knowledge engineering. Previous studies rely on annotated training data, which is quite expensive to obtain large training data sets, limiting the effectiveness of recognition. In this research, we propose a semi-supervised learning approach for named entity recognition (NER) via automatic labeling and tri-training which make use of unlabeled data and structured resources containing known named entities. By modifying tri-training for sequence labeling and deriving proper initialization, we can train a NER model for Web news articles automatically with satisfactory performance. In the task of Chinese personal name extraction from 8,672 news articles on the Web (with 364,685 sentences and 54,449 (11,856 distinct) person names), an F-measure of 90.4% can be achieved.

Keywords: Named entity extraction, co-labeling method, tri-training.

1   Introduction

Named entity extraction is a fundamental task for many knowledge engineering applications. Like many researches, this task relies on annotated training examples that require large amounts of manual labeling, leading to a limited number of training examples. While human-labelled training examples (L) have high quality, the cost is very high. Therefore, most tasks for NER are limited to several thousand sentences since the high cost of labeling. For example, the English dataset for the CoNLL 2003 shared task consists of 14,987 sentences for four entity categories, PER, LOC, ORG, and MISC. But it is unclear whether sufficient data is provided for training or the learning algorithms have reached their capacity. Thus the major concern in this paper is how to prepare training data for entity extraction on the Web.

The idea in this research is to make use of existing structured databases for automatically labeling known entities in documents. For examples, personal names, location names, and company names can be obtained from a Who's Who website, and accessible government data for registered organizations, respectively. Thus, we propose a semi-automated method to collect data that include known named entities and label answers automatically. While such training data may contain errors, self-testing can be applied to filter unreliable labeling with less confidence.

A. Jaafar et al. (Eds.): AIRS 2014, LNCS 8870, pp. 244–255, 2014.
© Springer International Publishing Switzerland 2014

On the other hand, the use of unlabeled training examples (U) has also been proved to be a promising technique for classification. For example, co-training [2] and tri-training [15] are two successful techniques that use examples with high-confidence as predicted by the other classifier or examples with consensus answers from the other two classifiers in order to prepare new labeled training data for learning. By estimating the error rate of each learned classifier, we can calculate the maximum number of new consensus answers to ensure the error rates are reduced.

While tri-training has shown to be successful in classification, the application to sequence labeling is not well explored. The challenge here is to obtain a common label sequence as a consensus answer from multiple models. Because of the k^d possible label sequences for an unlabeled example with length d and k labels, different mechanisms can be designed to select examples for training. Another key issue with tri-training is the assumption of the initial error rate (0.5), leading to a limited number of co-labeling examples for training and early termination for large data set training.

This paper extends our previous work on semi-supervised sequence labeling based on tri-training for Chinese person name extraction [4] and compares various selection methods to explore their effectiveness in tri-training. We give the complete algorithm for the estimation of initial error rate and the choice of a label sequence with the largest probability. In a test set of 8,672 news articles (364,685 sentences) containing 54,449 personal names (11,856 distinct names), the semi-automatic model built on CRF (conditional random field) with 7000 known celebrity names has a performance of 86.4% F-measure and is improved to 88.9% with self-testing. We show the proposed tri-training improves the performance through unlabeled data to 90.4% via random selection which outperform the S2A1D (Two Agree One Disagree) approach proposed by Chen et al [3].

2   Related Work

Entity extraction is the task of recognizing named entities from unstructured text documents, which is one of the information tasks to test how well a machine can understand the messages written in natural language and automate mundane tasks normally performed by human. The development of machine learning research from classification to sequence labeling such as the Hidden Markov Model (HMM) and the Conditional Random Field (CRF) [11] has been widely discussed in recent years. While supervised learning shows an impressive improvement over unsupervised learning, it requires large training data to be labeled with answers. Therefore, semi-supervised approaches are proposed as will be discussed next.

Semi-supervised learning refers to techniques that also make use of unlabeled data for training. Many approaches have been previously proposed for semi-supervised learning, including: generative models, self-learning, co-training, graph-based methods [14] and information-theoretic regularization [13]. In contrast, although a number of semi-supervised classifications have been proposed, semi-supervised learning for sequence segmentation has received considerably less attention and is designed according to a different philosophy.

Co-training and tri-training have been mainly discussed for classification tasks with relatively few labeled training examples. For example, the original co-training paper by Blum and Mitchell described experiments to classify web pages into two classes using only 12 labeled web pages as examples [2]. This co-training algorithm requires two views of the training data and learns a separate classifier for each view using labeled examples. Nigam and Ghani demonstrated that co-training performed better when the independent feature set assumption is valid [12]. For comparison, they conducted their experiments on the same (WebKB course) data set used by [2].

Goldman and Zhou relaxed the redundant and independent assumption and presented an algorithm that uses two different supervised learning algorithms to learn a separate classifier from the provided labeled data [4]. Empirical results demonstrated that two standard classifiers can be used to successfully label data for each other.

Tri-Training was an improvement of Co-Training, which use three classifiers and voting mechanism to solve the confidence issue of co-labeled answers by two classifiers. Based on three classifiers h_i, h_j and h_k ($i, j, k \in \{1,2,3\}$, $i \neq j \neq k$), Tri-training uses two classifiers h_j and h_k to label the common answers of each instance x in U. If the answer was not draw (equal answers) then we could trust the answer is correct and put the instance-answer pair to a collection L_i^t for the t-th iteration. Later we would use the union of the labeled training examples and obtained L_i^t from U, $L \cup L_i^t$ as training data to update classifier h_i in the next iteration.

While tri-training has been used in many classification tasks, the application in sequence labeling task is limited. In Chen et al.'s work [3], they considered only the most probable label sequence from each model and used the agreement measure as shown in Eq. (1) to select examples for h_i with the highest-agreement labeled sentences by h_j and h_k, and the lowest-agreement labeled sentences by h_i and h_j (S2A1D).

$$A_g(y_j, y_k) = \frac{\sum_{1 \leq d \leq n} I(y_{jd} = y_{kd})}{n} \tag{1}$$

where $y_j = \{y_{j1}, y_{j2}, y_{j3} \ldots y_{jn}\}$ is the label result by h_j with length $|y_j| = n$. The new training samples were chosen to be the one that is labeled by h_j, ignoring the label result by h_k. The process iterates until no more unlabeled examples are available. Thus, Chen et al.'s method does not ensure the PAC learning theory.

3   System Architecture

In this paper, we propose a semi-supervised learning model for named entity recognition (NER). The idea of semi-supervised training comes from two aspects: the first is annotating a large amount of training examples via automatic labeling of unlabeled data using existing entity names, and the second is making use of both labeled and unlabeled data during learning via tri-training. The framework is illustrated in Fig. 1.

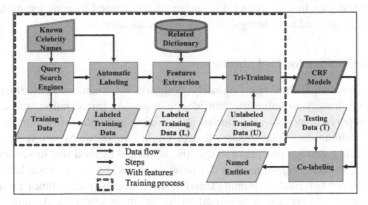

Fig. 1. Semi-supervised NER based on automatic labeling and tri-training

3.1   Tri-training for Sequence Labeling

Let L denote the labeled example set with size |L| and U denote the unlabeled example set with size |U|. In each round, t, tri-training uses two models, h_j and h_k to label the answer of each instance x from unlabeled training data U. If h_j and h_k give the same answer, then we could use x and the common answer pair as newly training example, i.e. $L_i^t = \{(x,y): x \in U, y = h_j^t(x) = h_k^t(x)\}$), for model h_i ($i, j, k \in \{1,2,3\}$, $i \neq j \neq k$). To ensure that the error rate is reduced through iterations, when re-train h_i, Eq. (2) must be satisfied,

$$e_i^t |L_i^t| < e_i^{t-1} |L_i^{t-1}| \tag{2}$$

where e_i^t denotes the error rate of model h_i in L_i^t, which is estimated by h_j and h_k in the t-th round using the labeled data L by dividing the number of incorrect labeled examples by h_j and h_k by the number of labeled examples by h_j and h_j made the same label, as shown in Eq. (3).[1]

$$e_i^t = \frac{|\{(x,y)\in L, h_j^t(x)=h_k^t(x) \neq y\}|}{|\{(x,y)\in L, h_j^t(x)=h_k^t(x)\}|} \tag{3}$$

If $|L_i^t|$ is too large, such that Eq. (2) is violated, it would be necessary to random select maximum u examples from L_i^t such that Eq. (2) can be satisfied.

$$u = \left\lceil \frac{e_i^{t-1}|L_i^{t-1}|}{e_i^t} - 1 \right\rceil \tag{4}$$

$$S_i^t = \begin{cases} Subsample(L_i^t, u) & violated\ Eq.\,(1) \\ L_i^t & otherwise \end{cases} \tag{5}$$

---

[1] Assuming that the unlabeled examples hold the same distribution as that held by the labeled ones.

For the last step in each round, the union of the labeled training examples L and S_i^t, i.e. $L \cup S_i^t$, is used as training data to re-train classifier h_i.

3.2   Modification for Co-Labeling

The tri-training algorithm was originally designed for traditional classification and used voting strategy to solve the confidence issue. At initialization, the classifiers recognition performance was low due to less training examples. Based on this reason, the added training data from unlabeled data might contain many wrong labeled data since the voting strategy compared to specific statistical method was lower accuracy.

For sequence labeling, we need to define what should be the common labels for the instance x when two models (training time) or three models (testing time) are involved.

In this study, we propose a new method for example selection. Assume that each model can output the m best labeled sequences labels with highest probability (m = 5). Let $P_i(y|x)$ denote the probability that an instance x has label y estimated by h_i. We select the common label with the largest probability sum, $P_j(y|x) + P_k(y|x)$, by the co-labeling method. In other words, we could use h_j and h_k to estimate possible labels, then chosen the common label y with the maximum probability sum to re-train h_i. Thus, the added set of examples, L_i^t, prepared for h_i in the t-th round is defined as follows:

$$L_i^t = \{(x,y): x \in U, max_y(P_j(y|x) + P_k(y|x)) \geq \theta * 2\} \tag{6}$$

where θ (default 0.5) is a threshold that controls the quality of the training examples provided to h_i.

During testing, the common label y for an instance x is determined by three models h_1, h_2 and h_3. We choose the final output with the largest probability sum from three models with a confidence $\theta * 3$ or $\theta * 2$. If the label with the largest probability sum from three models is not greater than $\theta * 3$, then we choose the one with the largest probability from single model with a maximum probability. That is to say, if the label with the largest probability sum from three models is not greater than $\theta * 3$, then we choose the one with the largest probability sum from two models with a confidence of $\theta * 2$. The last selection criterion is the label with the maximum probability estimated by the three models as shown in Eq. (7).

$$y = \max_y \begin{cases} max_y(P_1(y|x) + P_2(y|x) + P_3(y|x)) \geq \theta * 3 \\ max_y(P_i(y|x) + P_j(y|x)) \geq \theta * 2, i,j \in \{1,2,3\}, i \neq j \\ max_y(P_1(y|x), P_2(y|x), P_3(y|x)) \end{cases} \tag{7}$$

3.3   Modification for the Initialization

According to Eq. (2), the product of error rate and new training examples define an upper bound for the next iteration. Meanwhile, $|L_i^{t-1}|$ should satisfy Eq. (8) such that $|L_i^t|$ after subsampling, i.e., u, is still bigger than $|L_i^{t-1}|$.

$$|L_i^{t-1}| > \frac{e_i^t}{e_i^{t-1} - e_i^t} \tag{8}$$

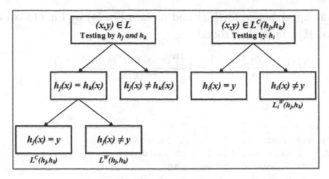

Fig. 2. The relationship among Eq. (10), (11), and (12)

In order to estimate the size of $|L_i^1|$, i.e., the number of new training examples for the first round, we need to estimate e_i^0, e_i^1, and $|L_i^0|$ first. Zhou et al. [15] assumed a 0.5 error rate for e_i^0, computed e_i^1 by h_j and h_k, and estimated the lower bound for $|L_i^0|$ by Eq. (9), thus:

$$|L_i^0| = \left\lfloor \frac{e_i^1}{e_i^0 - e_i^1} + 1 \right\rfloor = \left\lfloor \frac{e_i^1}{0.5 - e_i^1} + 1 \right\rfloor \qquad (9)$$

The problem with this initialization is that, for a larger dataset $|L|$, such an initialization will have no effect on retraining and will lead to an early stop for tri-training. For example, consider the case when the error rate e_i^1 is less than 0.4, then the value of $|L_i^0|$ will be no more than 5, leading to a small upper bound for $e_i^1|L_i^1|$ according to Eq. (2). That is to say, we can only sample a small subset $|S_i^1|$ from L_i^1 for training h_i based on Eq. (5). On the other hand, if e_i^1 is close to 0.5 such that the value of $|L_i^0|$ is greater than the original dataset $|L|$, it may completely alter the behavior of h_i.

To avoid this difficulty, we propose a new estimation for the product $e_i^0|L_i^0|$. Let $L^C(h_j, h_k)$ denote the set of labeled examples (from L) on which the classification made by h_j is the same as that made by h_k in the initial round, and $L^W(h_j, h_k)$ denote the set of examples from $L^C(h_j, h_k)$ on which both h_j and h_k make incorrect classification, as shown in Eq. (10) and (11). In addition, we define $L_i^W(h_j, h_k)$ to be the set of examples from $L^C(h_j, h_k)$ on which h_i makes incorrect classification in the initial round, as shown in Eq. (12). The relationship among $L^C(h_j, h_k)$, $L^W(h_j, h_k)$, and $L_i^W(h_j, h_k)$ is illustrated in Fig. 2.

$$L^C(h_j, h_k) = \{(x, y) \in L : h_j(x) = h_k(x)\} \qquad (10)$$

$$L^W(h_j, h_k) = \{(x, y) \in L^C(h_j, h_k) : h_j(x) \neq y\} \qquad (11)$$

$$L_i^W(h_j, h_k) = \{(x, y) \in L^C(h_j, h_k) : h_i(x) \neq y\} \qquad (12)$$

By replacing $e_i^0|L_i^0|$ with $|L_i^W(h_j, h_k)|$ and estimation of e_i^1 by $|L^W(h_j, h_k)|/|L^C(h_j, h_k)|$), we can estimate an upper bound for $|L_i^0|$ via Eq. (4). That is to say, we can compute an upper bound for $\left|L_i^0\right|$ and replace Eq. (4) by Eq. (13) to estimate the upper bound of $\left|L_i^1\right|$, in the first round.

$$\left|L_i^1\right| = \left\lceil\frac{e_i^0\left|L_i^0\right|}{e_i^1} - 1\right\rceil = \left\lceil\frac{\left|L_i^W(h_j,h_k)\right|*\left|L^C(h_j,h_k)\right|}{\left|L^W(h_j,h_k)\right|} - 1\right\rceil \tag{13}$$

```
Tri-Training4SeqLabeling(L, U, T, Learn)
01    Input: L: Original Labeled example set
02           U: Unlabeled example set
03           T: Testing data set
04           Learn: Learning algorithm
05           i,j,k ∈ {1,2,3}, i ≠ j ≠ k
06    for i ∈ {1..3} do
07        BSᵢ ← BootstrapSample(L); hᵢ ← Learn(BSᵢ); t ← 1
08    end of for
09    repeat until none of hᵢ(i ∈ {1..3}) changes
10        for i ∈ {1..3} do
11            Lᵢᵗ ← ∅; updateᵢ ← FALSE
12            eᵢᵗ ← MeasureError(hⱼ, hₖ) (j, k ≠ i)              // ref. Eq. (3)
13*           if (t == 1 or eᵢᵗ < eᵢᵗ⁻¹)                        // Eq. (2) is satisfied
14                then for every x ∈ U do
15*                   if (hⱼ(x) = hₖ(x))                          // co-labeling, ref. 3.2
16                        then Lᵢᵗ ← Lᵢᵗ ∪ {(x, hⱼ(x))}
17               end of for
18*               if (t == 1)                                     // first round
19*                   then u = ⌈ |L_i^W(hⱼ,hₖ)|*|L^C(hⱼ,hₖ)| / |L^W(hⱼ,hₖ)| − 1 ⌉   // ref. Eq. (13)
20*                   if (|Lᵢ¹| > u)
21*                        then Sᵢ¹ ← Subsample(Lᵢ¹, u)          // ref. Eq. (5)
22                   updateᵢ ← TRUE
23               else if (|Lᵢᵗ⁻¹| < |Lᵢᵗ|)                       // Eq. (2) is satisfied
24                   then if (eᵢᵗ|Lᵢᵗ| < eᵢᵗ⁻¹|Lᵢᵗ⁻¹|)            // Eq. (2) is satisfied
25                        then Sᵢᵗ ← Lᵢᵗ                          // ref. Eq. (5)
26                            updateᵢ ← TRUE
27                   else if (|Lᵢᵗ⁻¹| > eᵢᵗ / (eᵢᵗ⁻¹ − eᵢᵗ))      // ref. Eq. (8)
28                        then u = ⌈ eᵢᵗ⁻¹|Lᵢᵗ⁻¹| / eᵢᵗ − 1 ⌉      // ref. Eq. (4)
29                            Sᵢᵗ ← Subsample(Lᵢᵗ, u)             // ref. Eq. (5)
30                            updateᵢ ← TRUE
31        end of for
32        for i ∈ {1..3} do
33            if (updateᵢ == TRUE)
34                then hᵢ ← Learn(L ∪ Sᵢᵗ); eᵢᵗ⁻¹ ← eᵢᵗ; |Lᵢᵗ⁻¹| ← |Sᵢᵗ|
35            t ← t + 1
36        end of for
37    end of repeat
38*   Output: h(x) ← CoLabeling_Testing(x, hᵢ, hⱼ, hₖ), x ∈ T     // ref. Eq. (7)
```

Fig. 3. Pseudo Code of the proposed Tri-training for sequence labeling. Numbers with * are different from original tri-training.

The modified algorithm for tri-training is shown in Fig. 3, where line 13 and 18-21 are modified to support the new estimation of $|L_i^1|$, while line 15 and 38 are modified for sequence co-labeling as discussed above.

4   Experiments

We apply our proposed approach on Chinese personal name extraction on the Web. We use known celebrity names to query search engines from four news websites (including Liberty Times, Apple Daily, China Times, and United Daily News) and collect the top 10 search results for sentences that contain the query keyword. We then use all known celebrity names to match extraction targets via automatic labeling. Given different numbers of personal names, we prepare six datasets by automatically labeling and consider them as labeled training examples (L) (see Table 1).

We also crawl these four news websites from 2013/01/01 to 2013/03/31 and obtain 20,974 articles for unlabeled and testing data. To increase the possibility of containing person names, we select sentences that include common surname followed by some common first name to obtain 240,994 sentences as unlabeled data (U) (Table 1). Finally, we manually labeled 8,672 news articles, yielding a total of 364,685 sentences with 54,449 person names (11,856 distinct person names) as the testing data.

Fourteen features were used in the experiment including common surnames, first names, job titles, numeric tokens, alphabet tokens, punctuation symbol, and common characters in front or behind personal names. The predefined dictionaries contain 486 job titles, 224 surnames, 38,261 first names, and 107 symbols as well as 223 common words in front of and behind person names. For the tagging scheme, we used BIESO tagging to mark the named entities to be extracted. We use CRF++ [8] for the following experiments. With a template involving unigram macros and the previous three tokens and behind, a total of 195 features are produced. We define precision, recall and F-measure based on the number personal names.

4.1   Performance of Basic Model with Automatic Labeling and Self-testing

In this section, we report the performance of the basic model using D query keywords to collect and label the collected news articles with D celebrity names and six reporter name patterns. While this procedure does not ensure perfect training data, it provides acceptable labelled training for semi-supervised learning. The performance is illustrated in Fig. 4 with an F-measure of 0.768 for D1 and 0.864 for D6, showing large training data can greatly improve the performance.

Table 1. Labeled dataset (L) and unlabeled dataset (U) for Chinese person name extraction

	D1	D2	D3	D4	D5	D6	Unlabeled
#Names	500	1,000	2,000	3,000	5,000	7,053	--
Sentences	5,548	10,928	21,267	30,653	50,738	67,104	240,994
Characters	106,535	208,383	400,111	567,794	913,516	1,188,822	4,251,861

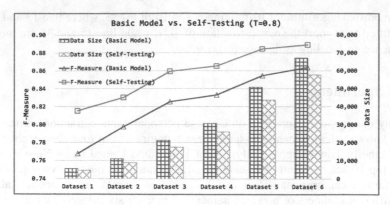

Fig. 4. Basic Model and Self-testing in testing set

Based on this basic model, we apply self-testing to filter examples with low confidence and retrain a new model with the set of high confidence examples. The performance is improved for all datasets with confidence levels from 0.5 to 0.9. An improved F-measure of 2.53% ~ 4.76% can be obtained, depending on the number of celebrity names we have (0.815 for D1 and 0.889 for D6).

4.2 Improvement of Modified Initialization for Tri-Training

Second, we show the effect of the modified initialization for tri-training (Fig. 5). With the new initialization by Eq. (13), the number of examples that can be sampled from unlabeled dataset $|L_i^1|$ is greatly increased. For dataset 1, the unlabeled data selected is five times the original data size (an increase from 4,637 to 25,234), leading to an improvement of 2.4% in F-measure (from 0.815 to 0.839). For dataset 2, the final data size is twice the original data size (from 8,881 to 26,173) with an F-measure improvement of 2.7% (from 0.830 to 0.857). For dataset 6, since $|L_i^1|$ is too large to be loaded for training with L, we only use 75% for experiment. The improvement in F-measure is 1.5% (from 0.889 to 0.904). Overall, an improvement of 1.2% ~ 2.7% can be obtained with this proposed tri-training algorithm for sequence labeling.

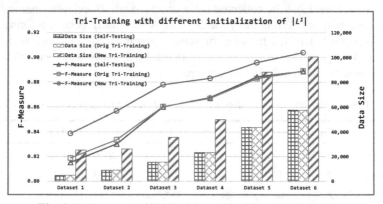

Fig. 5. Performance of Tri-Training with different initialization

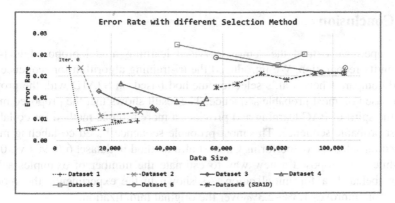

Fig. 6. Error rate in the training set

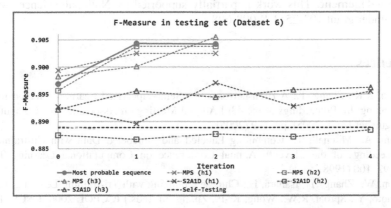

Fig. 7. F-measure in the testing set across iterations

4.3   Comparison of Selection Methods

Finally, we compare Chen's selection method with our proposed co-labeling method using error rate in the training set and F-Measure in the testing set. As shown in Fig. 6. , the proposed method based on most probable sequence stops (after 2 or 3 iterations) when the error rate increases for all datasets, while Chen' selection method (S2A1D) based on S2A1D continues execution as long as there are unlabeled training examples. Thus, the error rate fluctuates (i.e. it may increase or decrease) around 0.02. In other words, the modified tri-training by Chen et al. does not follow the PAC learning theory and there's no guarantee that the performance will increase or decrease in the testing set.

As shown in Fig. 7. , the F-Measure of the most probable sequence in testing set presents an upward trend and the three classifiers may outperform each other during different iterations. As for S2A1D, one of the classifier (h2) continues to be dominated by the other two classifiers and performs worse than the baseline (self-testing). It seems the final output does not take the advantage of the three classifiers and has similar result as the baseline (self-testing). On the contrary, the proposed method could combine opinions of three classifiers and output credible label via tri-training.

5 Conclusion

In this paper, we extend the semi-supervised learning model proposed in [4] for named entity recognition. We introduced the tri-training algorithm for sequence labeling and compare Chen et al.'s selection method based on S2A1D with the proposed method based on most probable sequence. The result shows that the proposed method retains the spirit of PAC learning and provides a more reliable method for co-labeling via most probable sequence. This most probable sequence based co-labeling method with random selection outperforms Chen et al.'s method in dataset 6 (0.904 vs. 0.890). Meanwhile, we proposed a new way to estimate the number of examples selected from unlabeled data for initialization. As shown in the experiments, the modified initialization improves 1.3%~2.3% over the original initialization.

Acknowlededgement. This work is partially supported by National Science Council, Taiwan under grant 102-2511-S-008-008.

References

1. Ando, R.K., Zhang, T.: A High-performance Semi-supervised Learning Method for Text Chunking. In: Proceedings of the 43rd Annual Meeting on Association for Computational Linguistics (ACL 2005), pp. 1–9 (2005)
2. Blum, A., Mitchell, T.: Combining Labeled and Unlabeled Data with Co-training. In: Proceedings of the Eleventh Annual Conference on Computational Learning Theory, pp. 92–100 (1998)
3. Chen, W., Zhang, Y., Isahara, H.: Chinese Chunking with Tri-training Learning. In: Matsumoto, Y., Sproat, R.W., Wong, K.-F., Zhang, M. (eds.) ICCPOL 2006. LNCS (LNAI), vol. 4285, pp. 466–473. Springer, Heidelberg (2006)
4. Chou, C.-L., Chang, C.-H., Wu, S.-Y.: Semi-supervised Sequence Labeling for Named Entity Extraction based on Tri-Training: Case Study on Chinese Person Name Extraction, Semantic Web and Information Extraction Workshop (SWAIE), In conjunction with COLING 2014, August 24, Dublin, Irland (2014)
5. Goldman, S.A., Zhou, Y.: Enhancing Supervised Learning with Unlabeled Data. In: Proceedings of the Seventeenth International Conference on Machine Learning (ICML 2000), pp. 327–334 (2000)
6. Grandvalet, Y., Bengio, Y.: Semi-supervised Learning by Entropy Minimization. In: CAP, pp. 281–296. PUG (2004)
7. Jiao, F., Wang, S., Lee, C.-H., Greiner, R., Schuurmans, D.: Semi-supervised Conditional Random Fields for Improved Sequence Segmentation and Labeling. In: Proceedings of the 21st International Conference on Computational Linguistics and the 44th Annual Meeting of the Association for Computational Linguistics (ACL-44), pp. 209–216 (2006)
8. CRF++: Yet Another CRF toolkit,
   http://crfpp.googlecode.com/svn/trunk/doc/index.html
9. Li, W., McCallum, A.: Semi-supervised Sequence Modeling with Syntactic Topic Models. In: Proceedings of the 20th National Conference on Artificial Intelligence (AAAI 2005), vol. 2, pp. 813–818 (2005)
10. Mann, G.S., McCallum, A.: Generalized Expectation Criteria for Semi-Supervised Learning with Weakly Labeled Data. J. Mach. Learn. Res. 11, 955–984 (2010)

11. McCallum, A., Li, W.: Early Results for Named Entity Recognition with Conditional Random Fields, Feature Induction and Web-enhanced Lexicons. In: Proceedings of the Seventh Conference on Natural Language Learning HLT-NAACL 2003 (CONLL 2003), vol. 4, pp. 188–191 (2003)

12. Nigam, K., Ghani, R.: Analyzing the Effectiveness and Applicability of Co-training. In: Proceedings of the Ninth International Conference on Information and Knowledge Management (CIKM 2000), pp. 86–93 (2000)

13. Zheng, L., Wang, S., Liu, Y., Lee, C.-H.: Information Theoretic Regularization for Semi-supervised Boosting. In: Proceedings of the 15th ACM SIGKDD International Conference on Knowledge Discovery and Data Mining (KDD 2009), pp. 1017–1026 (2009)

14. Zhou, D., Huang, J.: Schö, l., Bernhard: Learning from Labeled and Unlabeled Data on a Directed Graph. In: Proceedings of the 22nd International Conference on Machine Learning (ICML 2005), pp. 1036–1043. ACM (2005)

15. Zhou, Z.-H., Li, M.: Tri-Training: Exploiting Unlabeled Data Using Three Classifiers. IEEE Trans. on Knowl. and Data Eng. 17, 1529–1541 (2005)

Contrastive Max-Sum Opinion Summarization

Makbule Gülçin Özsoy and Ruket Çakıcı

Department of Computer Engineering
Middle East Technical University
Ankara, Turkey
{makbule.ozsoy,ruken}@ceng.metu.edu.tr

Abstract. People can reach all kinds of information online incuding reviews and comments on products, movies, holiday destinations and so on. However, one usually need to go through the reviews to have an objective opinion the positive and the negative aspects of the item reviewed. We aim to provie a method that will extract positive and negative opinions on a specific aspect and compare them in an attempt to ease on the information overflow. Contrastive opinion summarization (COS) aims to solve this issue. COS methods extract representative and comparative sentences in terms of specific aspects of a product. In this paper, we propose a new COS method, namely Contrastive Max-Sum Opinion Summarization (CMSOS). This method considers representativeness and contrastiveness at the same time. For the evaluation, we use an English dataset which was specifically created for COS studies. In addition, we created a new dataset in Turkish and shared it publicly. We provide the results on both datasets with our method.

Keywords: Contrastive opinion summarization, Representativeness, Contrastiveness.

1 Introduction

As the world wide web is becoming a more reliable and more easily available source of information people comment on products the had purchased, movies and locations they had seen, or they read the reviews such as these before they buy something. Today, a very big amount of opinionated text is available for the users. However, finding out the pros and cons of a product itself or a specific aspect of it is not trivial without having to read all the reviews to have an idea. A system which can extract positive and negative opinions on different aspects of a product and compare them is necessary.

Extraction of comparative sentences with contrasting opinions is a recently proposed problem in the literature. Kim and Zhai proposed this problem and named it as *contrastive opinion summarization (COS)* in [8] . In this study, the opinion labels of the sentences are given beforehand, and the system tries to select the most representative and comparable sentences accordingly.

In this paper, a new COS algorithm is proposed and evaluated. A new dataset in Turkish is created and the evaluation results for this new dataset are presented here. Our contributions are as follows: (1) A new algorithm, namely Contrastive Max-Sum Opinion Summarization (CMSOS), which extracts the most representative and comparable opinionated text in parallel. This algorithm gives better results on the dataset

A. Jaafar et al. (Eds.): AIRS 2014, LNCS 8870, pp. 256–267, 2014.

of [8] than the ones they report. (2) To our knowledge, there is no publicly available dataset in Turkish that gives aspects of items and opinion of users on these items. We created a new dataset that contains reviews and ratings of the users on movies and aspects that exists in the reviews[1]. (3) We also report the results of applying CMSOS to the newly created Turkish dataset in this paper. We conjecture that these results will aid in providing preliminary results for further studies.

In Section 2, information on related work is given. In Section 3, the proposed algorithm, namely Contrastive Max-Sum Opinion Summarization (CMSOS), is explained. In Sections 4 and 5 information on the datasets and evaluation results are given. Finally, Section 6 gives the conclusion.

2   Related Work

Opinion summarization techniques aim to find topics and classify the opinion attached to the topics. They sometimes do this taking into account different aspects of the topic in question. [4], [10], [12] are the representative works on opinion summarization, that apply data mining and heuristic methods. Heuristics used by these methods vary from word frequencies and noun phrase statistics to information from WordNet. However, these methods do not extract comparative sentences and/or documents.

There are studies that aim to collect comparative sentences, such as [5], [11], [15]. They detect contradiction in text and/or detect comparative sentences in the documents. They take several different approaches, such as searching words in the documents such as "than" [5], binary classification methods such as SVM [15] and graph representation based methods [11]. Although these methods aim to extract the comparative sentences, they do not aim to find the most representative chunks of text or comparative summaries.

Contrastive opinion summarization (COS) methods aim to collect not only the most representative sentences but also the contrastive ones from the input. This problem is introduced in the literature by [8]. They define COS as follows: "Given two sets of positively and negatively opinionated sentences which are often the output of an existing opinion summarizer, COS aims to extract comparable sentences from each set of opinions and generate a comparative summary containing a set of contrastive sentence pairs." They formulate the problem as an optimization problem and propose two methods each of which focuses on these two issues –representativeness and contrastiveness– in different orders, namely Representativeness First (RF) or Contrastiveness First (CF).

In RF approach, firstly, the input positive and negative sentence sets (X and Y respectively) are divided into sub-clusters using the representativeness measure. Then, the sentences from each cluster in X and Y are aligned using the representativeness and contrastiveness measures together. Even if multiple sentences in the same cluster have high scores, this approach collects a single sentence from each cluster. In CF approach, the contrastiveness of the sentences in X and Y are calculated first. After that, the pair with the highest contrastiveness is chosen as the first pair of the comparative summary. The other pairs are selected depending on the previously chosen pairs and

---

[1] The dataset will be made available to download at the following link.

http://www.ceng.metu.edu.tr/~e1395383/papers/airs2014/

representativeness and contrastiveness metrics. In this approach, if the first pair is not the optimal choice, the quality of the output comparative summary will be lower.

Paul *et al.* (2010) also aim to create contrastive summaries from the input set in [13]. They perform a two-stage approach. In the first step they extract multiple viewpoints from the text, and in the second stage they collect both representative and contrastive sentences. For the second stage, they propose Comparative LexRank method, which is based on random walk.

Lerman and McDonald (2009) also name their problem as contrastive summarization in [9]. However, their solution is different than the previous approaches. While previous studies aim to extract different viewpoints of a single product/aspect, this work aims to generate two different summaries on a pair of products. With this approach, the summaries highlight the differences of the products.

[14] focuses on constructing short and comparative summaries of product reviews. Unlike COS methods, they aim to compare two selected products. They produce aligned pairs of sentences related to products on different aspects. The aspects are also selected automatically by their method.

The literature related to opinion summarization in Turkish is limited as a result of the lack of datasets publicly available. Sentiment and/or emotion analysis can be considered as related to opinion summarization. The few works focused on sentiment and emotion analysis in Turkish belong to [1,2], [7]. None of these works focus on different aspects of the items and compare the sentiment results on aspects. A very recent work conducted by [6] provides results for feature based summarization of product reviews in Turkish. This study focuses on producing personalized review summaries on multiple products. Unlike our work, they do not return a list of comparative sentences on different aspects of a single product. They conduct their evaluation on a Turkish dataset that they created. Unfortunately, the dataset is not available publicly, to our knowledge.

3   Contrastive Max-Sum Opinion Summarization

Traditional opinion summarization techniques aim to select a set of the most representative opinionated text from an input set. Unlike them, contrastive opinion summarization (COS) methods aim to collect not only the most representative sentences but also the ones that have contrastive meaning. This helps users to become aware of the different opinions on different aspects of a chosen item/topic in order to have a better idea by making use of the created comparative summaries.

In this paper, we propose a COS method, namely Contrastive Max-Sum Opinion Summarization (CMSOS). The method creates a list of pairs of the most representative sentences related to a given aspect. Each pair contains a positive sentence and a negative sentence, that have contrastive meaning. For instance, assume that a user wants to find out what other users think about the design of a certain product. The system returns the pair of sentences *"it did an awesome job with the design."* as a positive sentence and *"but my biggest gripe is still the extremely ugly design."* as a negative one[2].

Contrastive Max-Sum Opinion Summarization (CMSOS) is adopted from Max-Sum Diversification method proposed in [3]. This algorithm is proposed as a solution to

---
[2] These example sentences are from the English dataset.

web-search and aims get the most relevant and novel document from the input set. In CMSOS, our aim is to get most representative and contrastive sentences. We used document similarity between sentences with the same labels (content similarity) to find out the representative sentences and document similarity between sentences with different labels (contrastive similarity) to find out the contrastive sentences.

The equation of CMSOS is written as in Equation 1. In the equation, S is the sentence set, u and v are the sentences in this set, $w(u)$ is the representativeness of the sentence u, $d(u,v)$ represents the contrast between sentences u and v, and λ is the parameter used for setting the trade-off between relevance and similarity. The aim is to maximize $f(S)$ in Equation 1.

$$f(S) = \sum (w(u) + w(v) + 2\lambda \sum_{u,v \in S} d(u,v)) \tag{1}$$

We calculate $w(u)$ using cosine similarity, Equation 2, which sums the similarity of the sentences to the other sentences and normalizes the result. We apply two different approaches to decide the cosine similarity. The first one is based on word frequencies. In Equation 3, $W(u,v)$ contains the common words in the sentences u and v. The $tf(u,i)$ represents the frequency of the word i in the sentence u. The second measurement is based on tf-idf values of the words in the sentence as shown in Equation 4. The only difference from the first version is that here we use the tf-idf values. Tf-idf is used commonly in information retrieval and text mining to reflect the importance of the word. The tf-idf value increases as the frequency of the word in the input sentence is high while the frequency of the word in the input dataset is low. We calculated the tf and the idf values using the input data. We observe that the input datasets contain repetitive sentences, so we applied the tf-idf version to observe the effect of these sentences on the performance.

$$w(u) = \frac{\sum_{v \in S \wedge u \neq v} cosSim(u,v)}{S-1} \tag{2}$$

$$cosSim_1(u,v) = \frac{\sum_{i \in W(u,v)} tf(u,i)tf(v,i)}{\sqrt{\sum_{i \in W(u,v)} tf(u,i)^2} \sqrt{\sum_{i \in W(u,v)} tf(v,i)^2}} \tag{3}$$

$$cosSim_2(u,v) = \frac{\sum_{i \in W(u,v)} tfIdf(u,i)tfIdf(v,i)}{\sqrt{\sum_{i \in W(u,v)} tfIdf(u,i)^2} \sqrt{\sum_{i \in W(u,v)} tfIdf(v,i)^2}} \tag{4}$$

In order to measure contrastive similarity we first remove the adjectives, that create the contrast. After the removal of adjectives, the cosine similarity between the sentences with different labels are calculated. The idea of the removal of sentiment related words is proposed in [8] in which sentiment related words are defined as negation words and adjectives. In Turkish, the negation is usually constructed by attaching the negation suffix to a verb or using the negation particle. In order to find out if a verb is in the negative form, one needs to apply morphological analysis. In this study, we did not apply any morphological analysis and considered it as a future work.

4 Evaluation Settings

4.1 Metrics

We use precision and aspect coverage as evaluation metrics, as suggested by [8]. Kim and Zhai in [8] explain that precision represents the contrastiveness of the sentence pairs and the aspect coverage indicates the representativeness of the summary. In all the calculations the responses of each human labeler are analysed separately before reporting the average value for the overall result. For some of the products, the human labelers labeled the sentences with different aspects (some aspects are not common). The uncommon aspects are combined under a new aspect with the name "other".

The precision is calculated by using Equation 5. In this equation, *#agreedPairs* is the number of times the found pairs and the human labels match and k is the total number of selected pairs. The k value is calculated by Equation 6, where $|X|$ and $|Y|$ are the number of positive or negative labeled sentences.

$$Precision = \frac{\#agreedPairs}{k} \qquad (5)$$

$$k = 1 + \log_2(|X| + |Y|) \qquad (6)$$

The aspect coverage is calculated by Equation 7. In this equation, the number of unique aspects collected in the summary is divided by the number of unique aspects labeled by human labelers.

$$AspectCov = \frac{\#uniqueAspects(Summary)}{\#uniqueAspects(LabelledManually)} \qquad (7)$$

4.2 Datasets

For evaluation, two datasets will be used: The dataset provided in [8][3] for English, and the newly created Turkish dataset[4] . In the following subsections, information on these datasets are given.

English Dataset. The English dataset [8] contains reviews on 13 different <product, aspect> sets, 12 of which are collected from Amazon website and 1 of which is a non-product-review text and is about aspartame. In the dataset, the sentences and their polarities are manually labeled by two human labelers. Additionally, a non-product-review is included to show the generality of their method. For this purpose they collected 50 positive and 50 negative sentences about Aspartame using Yahoo! search engine. The number of positive and negative sentences for each <product, aspect> tuple is given in Table 1.

---

[3] http://sifaka.cs.uiuc.edu/ir/data/cos/
[4] http://www.ceng.metu.edu.tr/~e1395383/papers/airs2014/

Table 1. Number of positive and negative sentences for the English dataset

Id	Product:Aspect Name	#Pos	#Neg
1	Apex AD2600 Progressive-scan DVD player:player	44	56
2	MicroMP3:batterylife	9	7
3	MicroMP3:design	8	6
4	MicroMP3:headphones	7	6
5	MicroMP3:software	7	9
6	Nokia 6600:battery-life	7	8
7	Creative Labs Nomad Jukebox Zen Xtra 40GB:navigation	9	8
8	Creative Labs Nomad Jukebox Zen Xtra 40GB:software	37	41
9	Creative Labs Nomad Jukebox Zen Xtra 40GB:size	15	11
10	Creative Labs Nomad Jukebox Zen Xtra 40GB:weight	7	7
11	Creative Labs Nomad Jukebox Zen Xtra 40GB:transfer	9	7
12	Hitachi router:adjustment	7	6
13	aspartame:safety	50	50

Turkish Dataset. To our knowledge, there is no publicly available dataset in Turkish with explicit information on the aspects of items, and the opinions and ratings of users on these items. We created a new dataset that contains reviews and ratings of the users on movies and on specific aspects of each movie that exist in the reviews.

Firstly, we collected the reviews and ratings of the users for the movies from a web-site, namely beyazperde[5]. On this website, users are asked to write reviews for movies and rate them in the range [1,5] with increments of 0.5. We considered the reviews with 3.5 or more points as positive and the rest as negative. We queried 1000 pages and collected only 107 of them since only these contain any review information.

Secondly, we asked two human labelers to label the reviews in terms of aspects. We created a form for the labelers with six different aspects; namely scenario, acting, music, visuals, director and general. The labelers are also allowed to write down their own aspects if they find any significant ones. Each labeler is assigned to different movies, so that the reviews of each movie are labeled by a single labeler. We could not use multiple labelers for each movie, since the time and the number of the labelers were limited.

Lastly, we removed movies whose positive or negative sentence counts were less than k, given in Equation 6. At the end, we obtained 31 movies with aspects, reviews and ratings in Turkish. The numbers of positive and negative sentences for each movie in this dataset are given in Table 2.

We share this dataset on our web-site and we conjecture that this new dataset will be useful to many researchers who needs data that contains aspect, rating and/or review information in Turkish.

5 Evaluation Results

We report results for cosine similarity and tf-idf usage on precision and aspect coverage metrics for both datasets. In Equation 1, λ is used for setting the trade-off between

---

[5] www.beyazperde.com

Table 2. Number of positive and negative sentences for the Turkish dataset

Id	Movie Name	#Pos	#Neg	Id	Movie Name	#Pos	#Neg
548	Yedinci Mühür	27	5	263	Paris, Texas	15	4
260	Otomatik Portakal	143	32	29	Serseri Aşıklar	16	8
305	Stranger Than Paradise	4	3	309	Yokedici	61	7
308	Taksi Şoförü	91	33	290	Siyam Balığı	26	5
297	Yedi Samuray	39	6	62	Yaratık	47	5
339	Gremlinler	22	5	337	Sekiz Buçuk	15	6
88	Annie Hall	25	8	363	Can Dostum	105	8
140	Birdy	20	5	142	Brazil	16	8
151	Köpekler	10	5	437	Hayalet Avcıları	19	6
188	Şeytanın Ölüsü	49	22	176	Dune	7	6
183	Eraserhead	21	12	180	Fil Adam	47	7
467	Enter The Dragon	15	4	462	Korku Burnu	41	11
448	Geleceğe Dönüş	162	9	505	13	20	10
226	Lolita	14	6	255	Nostalji	5	4
253	New York'tan Kaçış	10	5	248	Monty Python and the Holy Grail	9	7
243	Geceyarısı Ekspresi	21	39				

relevance and contrast, such that larger λ gives more importance to contrastiveness. In the experiments λ is set between 0 and 1 with 0.1 increments and the results for the datasets are presented in the following section.

5.1 Results for English Dataset

The precision and the aspect coverage results of CMSOS for the English dataset are given in Table 3 and Table 4. These values are obtained by taking the average of the results obtained for all <product,aspect> tuples.

Table 3. Results on precision of CMSOS for English dataset

lambda	Cosine similarity tf	Cosine similarity tf-idf
0.00	0.576	0.544
0.10	0.572	0.558
0.20	0.588	0.517
0.30	0.582	0.562
0.40	0.624	0.562
0.50	0.630	0.562
0.60	0.630	0.574
0.70	**0.649**	0.574
0.80	**0.649**	**0.594**
0.90	0.630	**0.594**
1.00	0.630	0.584

Table 4. Results on aspect coverage of CMSOS for English dataset

lambda	Cosine similarity tf	Cosine similarity tf-idf
0.00	0.910	**0.960**
0.10	0.901	0.877
0.20	0.918	0.935
0.30	0.910	0.935
0.40	**0.916**	0.935
0.50	0.897	0.928
0.60	0.897	0.928
0.70	0.897	0.941
0.80	0.887	0.941
0.90	0.895	0.941
1.00	0.895	0.941

The results in Table 3 show that in terms of precision, cosine similarity with tf performs better than cosine similarity with tf-idf. Actually cosine similarity with tf-idf is better for inputs where there are many repeated sentences. For example, we notice that the subject <aspartame, safety> includes sentences "asparteme is safe" and "asparteme is dangerous" several times. While using cosine similarity with tf, we observe that the resulting summary contains these sentences frequently. But when we use cosine similarity with tf-idf, we obtain better results which are not repetitive. The results obtained by our method using cosine similarity with tf or cosine similarity with tf-idf are given in Table 5 and Table 6 [6]. As expected, tf-idf usage inhibits the effects of repetitive terms, and can produce more informative summaries.

Table 4 shows that cosine similarity with tf and cosine similarity with tf-idf performs similarly as lambda value gets larger for aspect coverage. Aspect coverage results stay nearly balanced around 0.90-0.95 for different λ values.

Table 5. Outputs for <aspartame, safety> with cosine similarity

Id(+)	Sent.(+)	Id(−)	Sent.(−)
4	aspartame is safe	4	aspartame is dangerous
21	that aspartame is safe	20	that aspartame is dangerous
20	aspartame is safe	2	aspartame is dangerous
25	aspartame is safe	44	- aspartame is dangerous

We compare the results of our method to the results reported in [8], in Table 7. Two different methods proposed in [8], namely Representativeness First (RF) and Contrastiveness First (CF), are given with labels "Kim et al-RF" and "Kim et al-CF" respectively in the table. We also show the results of cosine similarity with tf-idf and cosine

---

[6] We removed punctuations and showed only the first four results.

Table 6. Outputs for <aspartame, safety> with tf-idf

Id(+)	Sent.(+)	Id(−)	Sent.(−)
21	that aspartame is safe	20	that aspartame is dangerous
37	conclusively determined that aspartame is safe	12	conclusively that aspartame is dangerous
29	aspartame is safe - scientists support aspartame safety	44	- aspartame is dangerous
46	can we tell if aspartame is safe	32	i can tell you from personal experience that aspartame is dangerous

similarity with tf results in the table. CMSOS configurations generally give the best results for precision and aspect coverage on this dataset. In CF if the initially chosen pair of sentences is not optimal this affects the quality of the output summary badly. CMSOS optimizes for representativeness and contrastiveness at the same time. It is able to choose multiple sentences from an aspect and it is not affected by any previously chosen sentence pairs.

Table 7. Comparison of results

Method	Prec.	AspectCov.
Kim et al-RF	0.503	0.737
Kim et al-CF	0.537	0.804
CMSOS(tf & λ=0.80)	**0.649**	0.887
CMSOS(tf-idf & λ=0.80)	0.594	**0.941**
CMSOS(tf & λ=0.10)	0.572	0.901
CMSOS(tf-idf & λ=0.10)	0.558	0.887

Our method gives the same priority to representativeness and contrastiveness, and it performs better than the methods that give precedence to one over the other. Cosine similarity with tf usage generally performs better than cosine similarity with tf-idf. However, for data with repeating sentences tf-idf usage is more helpful.

5.2   Results for Turkish Dataset

The average precision and aspect coverage results obtained for the Turkish dataset are given in Table 8 and Table 9, respectively.

In terms of precision, cosine similarity with tf and tf-idf perform similarly. The best precision result is 0.927 and 0.917 for tf and tf-idf metrics respectively. The best aspect coverage values are 0.928 and 0.901 for cosine similarity with tf and tf-idf metrics respectively.

Comparison of English and Turkish results show that the CMSOS algorithm performs equally well for both datasets, in terms of aspect coverage. However, in terms of precision the algorithm performs worse for the English dataset (about 0.650) than the Turkish dataset (about 0.920). This is the result of difference between the number of aspects labeled by users. The average number of aspects for the items in English dataset

Table 8. Results on precision of CMSOS for Turkish dataset

lambda	Cosine similarity tf	Cosine similarity tf-idf
0.00	0.913	0.862
0.10	**0.927**	0.875
0.20	0.890	0.894
0.30	0.924	0.896
0.40	0.911	0.891
0.50	0.911	0.908
0.60	0.904	0.916
0.70	0.899	0.905
0.80	0.893	0.905
0.90	0.893	0.905
1.00	0.893	**0.917**

Table 9. Results on aspect coverage of CMSOS for Turkish dataset

lambda	Cosine similarity tf	Cosine similarity tf-idf
0.00	0.923	0.899
0.10	**0.928**	0.896
0.20	0.923	**0.901**
0.30	0.919	**0.901**
0.40	0.927	**0.901**
0.50	0.926	**0.901**
0.60	0.926	**0.901**
0.70	0.926	**0.901**
0.80	0.918	0.891
0.90	0.926	0.891
1.00	0.926	0.891

is about 2.80, whereas, it is about 4.45 for the Turkish dataset. Therefore, it is easier to find an agreed pair for Turkish set than the English set.

We present the first results on the Turkish dataset. We conjecture that these results will be useful preliminary results for further research on this problem.

6 Conclusion

Traditional opinion summarization techniques do not output contrasting sentences as a feature. In order to deal with this problem a new kind of opinion summarization problem, namely contrastive opinion summarization (COS), is introduced in the literature. In this paper, we presented a new COS method, namely Contrastive Max-Sum Opinion Summarization(CMSOS), for this purpose. We considered representativeness and contrastiveness at the same time, and applied cosine similarity with tf and cosine similarity with tf-idf measures.

For the evaluation, we used a known English dataset, and we compared our results to the ones of [8], who have the initial results on this dataset. We obtained better results than their results. We observed that using cosine similarity with tf for calculations performed better than tf-idf usage. However, for data with a lot of repeated sentences we conjecture that tf-idf usage is more helpful. In addition, we created a new Turkish dataset for the COS purposes, which can also be used as data for further research that needs rating, review and/or aspect labeled data in Turkish. We evaluated the CMSOS method on the new Turkish dataset and reported the results in this paper.

Future work includes plans for increasing the size of the Turkish dataset, making the evaluation step automatic by automatic extraction of aspect names, and also applying CMSOS to the multiple product review summarization problem.

References

1. Boynukalın, Z., Karagöz, P.: Emotion analysis on Turkish texts. In: Gelenbe, E., Lent, R. (eds.) Information Sciences and Systems 2013. LNEE, vol. 264, pp. 159–168. Springer, Heidelberg (2013)
2. Eroğul, U.: Sentiment Analysis in Turkish. Master's thesis, Middle East Technical University, Turkey (2009)
3. Gollapudi, S., Sharma, A.: An axiomatic approach for result diversification. In: Proceedings of the 18th International Conference on World Wide Web, WWW 2009, pp. 381–390. ACM, New York (2009)
4. Hu, M., Liu, B.: Mining and summarizing customer reviews. In: Proceedings of the Tenth ACM SIGKDD International Conference on Knowledge Discovery and Data Mining, KDD 2004, pp. 168–177. ACM, New York (2004)
5. Jindal, N., Liu, B.: Identifying comparative sentences in text documents. In: Proceedings of the 29th Annual International ACM SIGIR Conference on Research and Development in Information Retrieval, SIGIR 2006, pp. 244–251. ACM, New York (2006)
6. Kavasoğlu, Z., Gündüz Öğüdücü, S.: Personalized summarization of customer reviews based on user's browsing history. International Journal on Computer Science and Information Systems 8, 147–158 (2013)
7. Kaya, M., Fidan, G., Toroslu, H.: Transfer learning using twitter data for improving sentiment classification of Turkish political news. In: Gelenbe, E., Lent, R. (eds.) Information Sciences and Systems 2013. LNEE, vol. 264, pp. 139–148. Springer, Heidelberg (2013)
8. Kim, H.D., Zhai, C.: Generating comparative summaries of contradictory opinions in text. In: Proceedings of the 18th ACM Conference on Information and Knowledge Management, CIKM 2009, pp. 385–394. ACM, New York (2009)
9. Lerman, K., McDonald, R.: Contrastive summarization: An experiment with consumer reviews. In: Proceedings of Human Language Technologies: The 2009 Annual Conference of the North American Chapter of the Association for Computational Linguistics, Companion Volume: Short Papers, NAACL-Short 2009, pp. 113–116. Association for Computational Linguistics, Stroudsburg (2009)
10. Liu, B., Hu, M., Cheng, J.: Opinion observer: Analyzing and comparing opinions on the web. In: Proceedings of the 14th International Conference on World Wide Web, WWW 2005, pp. 342–351. ACM, New York (2005)
11. Malouf, R., Mullen, T.: Taking sides: User classification for informal online political discourse. Internet Research (2008)

12. Mei, Q., Ling, X., Wondra, M., Su, H., Zhai, C.: Topic sentiment mixture: Modeling facets and opinions in weblogs. In: Proceedings of the 16th International Conference on World Wide Web, WWW 2007, pp. 171–180. ACM, New York (2007)
13. Paul, M.J., Zhai, C., Girju, R.: Summarizing contrastive viewpoints in opinionated text. In: Proceedings of the 2010 Conference on Empirical Methods in Natural Language Processing, EMNLP 2010, pp. 66–76. Association for Computational Linguistics, Stroudsburg (2010)
14. Sipos, R., Joachims, T.: Generating comparative summaries from reviews. In: CIKM, pp. 1853–1856 (2013)
15. Thomas, M., Pang, B., Lee, L.: Get out the vote: Determining support or opposition from congressional floor-debate transcripts. In: Proceedings of the 2006 Conference on Empirical Methods in Natural Language Processing, EMNLP 2006, pp. 327–335. Association for Computational Linguistics, Stroudsburg (2006)

Extracting Interest Tags from Twitter User Biographies

Ying Ding and Jing Jiang

School of Information Systems, Singapore Management University, Singapore
{ying.ding.2011,jingjiang}@smu.edu.sg

Abstract. Twitter, one of the most popular social media platforms, has been studied from different angles. One of the important sources of information in Twitter is users' biographies, which are short self-introductions written by users in free form. Biographies often describe users' background and interests. However, to the best of our knowledge, there has not been much work trying to extract information from Twitter biographies. In this work, we study how to extract information revealing users' personal interests from Twitter biographies. A sequential labeling model is trained with automatically constructed labeled data. The popular patterns expressing user interests are extracted and analyzed. We also study the connection between interest tags extracted from user biographies and tweet content, and find that there is a weak linkage between them, suggesting that biographies can potentially serve as a complimentary source of information to tweets.

1 Introduction

With a large percentage of the population, especially youngsters, using social media to communicate with families and friends nowadays, much personal information such as a user's gender, age and personal interests has been revealed online. Such personal information is of great value to both research and industry. For example, social scientists and psychologists can better study people's behaviors based on the tremendous amount of user information collected from social media [11], [16]. Companies can do targeted online advertising more accurately based on users' personal information. While personal information can be mined from various sources, an important source that has been largely neglected is users' biographies written by themselves in social media platforms. In this work we study how we can extract users' personal interests from Twitter user biographies.

In many social media platforms such as Twitter, users are given the opportunity to describe themselves using one or two sentences, which we refer to as biographies. Compared to structured user profiles in Facebook and LinkedIn, biographies are often written in free form, which is hard for computers to understand. However, because these biographies are written by users themselves, they are expected to reflect the users' background, interests and beliefs. For example, Table 1 shows a few example biographies from Twitter. We can see that in the first and the second biographies, there are phrases such as "Soccer fan" and "love video games" that clearly describe a user's interests. Phrases such as "Software Prof" shows a user's profession and "18 year old" shows a user's age. The third biography, on the other hand, is a popular quote "live life to its

A. Jaafar et al. (Eds.): AIRS 2014, LNCS 8870, pp. 268–279, 2014.

fullest," which reveals the user's attitude to life. A recent study based on a sample of users found that around 28% of Singapore Twitter users and over 50% of US Twitter users revealed personal interests in their biographies, which suggests the high value of mining Twitter biographies [4].

Table 1. Examples of user biographies on Twitter

User #1	Hyderabadi Ladka, Software Prof, Soccer fan
User #2	18 year old, theatre kid I love video games and cooking. Hmu on SnapChat (anonymaxx) Instagram @MaxxReginello
User #3	Young wild'n free... Hahaha, live life to the fullest with not regrets..

Intuitively, if we can automatically extract phrases such as "soccer" and "video games" from user biographies, these phrases serve as meaningful and informative tags for the respective users. We refer to this kind of words and phrases that describe users' personal interests as *interest tags*. In this paper, we try to automatically extract these interest tags. We also try to link the extracted interest tags to users' content (tweets) and study their correlations.

Extracting interest tags can be treated as a typical information extraction problem. A ready solution is to employ supervised sequence labeling algorithms such as CRF with labeled training data. However, manual annotation to obtain labeled data is labor-intensive. We observe that there are a few common syntactic patterns people use to describe their interests. We therefore first build a noisy training data set using a set of seed patterns and heuristic rules, and then train a CRF model on this labeled data set. With this approach, we are able to achieve an F1 score of 0.76 for interest tag extraction. We also show some top interest tags as well as pattern words found in our data set.

While a Twitter user may describe her interests in her biography, these interests may not be clearly reflected in her published tweets. To understand whether and which interest tags are likely to be represented by users' tweets, we further study the connection between interest tags and Twitter content.

The contributions of our work can be summarized as follows. We are the first to study how to extract interest tags from user biographies in social media. We show that with state-of-the-art information extraction techniques, we can achieve decent performance for this task. We also show that not all interest tags are reflected in users' tweets, which suggests that it is not sufficient to only consider tweets for finding user interests. We expect that interest tags extracted from user biographies can potentially be used for user profiling and many other applications.

The rest of the paper is organized as follows. We first review related work in Section 2. Then we present our observation about linguistic patterns of interest tags in Section 3. Our method and experiments will be presented in Section 4 and Section 5. We analyze and discuss the connection between interest tags and tweet content in Section 6. We conclude this work and give suggestions on future work in Section 7.

2 Related Work

Our work is related to a few different lines of work, which we briefly review below.

2.1 Psychological Studies on User Profiles

Biographies in social media have attracted much attention in the psychology community. Different questions have been studied in recent years. Counts and Stecher studied the creation process of profiles and found that people create profiles to match their self-representation profiles [3]. Lampe *et al.* study the relationship between profile structure and number of friends and discovered that some of the profile elements can predict friendship links [9]. Disclosure of user information in biographies is also an important problem to study in social media [14]. Profile information has also been used to do prediction in other applications, such as user need prediction [22] and sensational interest prediction [7]. However, studies in psychology do not focus on computational methods to automatically extract information from user biographies. In contrast, our work is about automatic extraction of user interests from biographies.

2.2 User Profile Construction

User profiling is an important research question, which aims at extracting and inferring attributes of a user from all his/her online behaviour. There has been a number of studies on user profile construction from different angles. Roshchina *et al.* built user profiles according to personality characteristics mined from review text [20]. They showed that based on a large number of reviews, it is possible to differentiate personality types and match users with reviews written by people with similar personality. Pennacchiotti and Popescu proposed a general framework to build user profiles [15]. Their work combines classification algorithms and label propagation in social network graphs. Their method shows encouraging results on three different tasks, which are identification of political affiliation, ethnicity and business affinity. Demographics information is one of the most important aspects in a user's profile. Gender and age prediction has also attracted much attention and has been studied in some recent work [2] ,[5], [12,13], [19].

User interest is also an important type of information for profiling a user. In this work, we extract users' interests from their biographies, which has not been done in existing work on user profile construction.

2.3 Information Extraction in Social Media

With the explosion of content generated in social media, information extraction, which aims at extracting structured, meaningful information from unstructured, noisy content edited by online users, becomes more necessary than ever before. Ritter *et al.* proposed an open domain event extraction approach, which leverages the large volume of Twitter messages and outperforms a supervised baseline [18]. Ritter *et al.* designed a new pipeline of named entity recognition adapted to Twitter corpus [17]. Benson *et al.* utilized a supervised principled model to extract events-related information from social media feeds [1]. A similar study was done by Imran *et al.* [8], which focuses more on valuable information of disasters.

Extracting tags to represent users' interests is very helpful to various applications such as online advertisement, friend recommendation. Wu *et al.* applied two standard methods (TF-IDF and TextRank) on tweets to generate personalized tags for users [21]. Liu *et al.* solved tag generation problem with a machine translation technique [10]. However, no work has systematically looked at information extraction from user biographies in social media.

3 Linguistic Patterns of Interest Tags

In order to design a suitable method to extract interest tags from user biographies, we need to first understand how users typically describe their interests in biographies. In this section, we show some typical linguistic patterns we found from a sample of Twitter biographies.

One author of this paper took a random sample of 500 biographies from our Twitter data (described in Section 5) and manually examined them carefully. First of all, the examination revealed that only 28.8% of biographies contain meaningful interest tags. The rest of the biographies often describes the user's attitude, belief or other demographic information. Among the biographies that do contain interest tags, the author found a set of common patterns as shown in Table 2. We can see that the majority of interest tags are expressed by the "Noun + Noun" pattern, where the first noun (or noun phrase) is the interest tag.

Table 2. Syntactic patterns describing user interests in Twitter biographies

Relative Frequency	Pattern	Example
66%	Noun + Noun	football fan
3%	Noun/Verb + Prep + Noun	obsessed with football / fan of football
5%	Verb + Noun	love football
26%	Others	reader / Beliebers should follow me. (Note: "Belieber" here means a fan of Justin Bieber.)

It is worth pointing out that in all these patterns, the interest itself is described by a noun or noun phrase such as "football" and "video games" and the rest of the pattern can be regarded as some kind of *trigger*. For example, words such as "fan" and "junkie" strongly indicate that there is a word or phrase nearby that describes an interest. This observation shows that contextual words are useful for identifying interest tags, which will guide our design of features when we apply supervised learning for tag extraction.

4 Extracting Interest Tags

Based on the analysis as described in the previous section, we design our solution in the following way. Our method eventually uses conditional random fields (CRFs), which represents the state of the art of information extraction. It defines the conditional probability of a sequence label $y_{1:N}$ given the observation sequence $x_{1:N}$ as

$$p(y_{1:N}|x_{1:N}) = \frac{1}{\mathbf{Z}}\exp(\sum_i \sum_k \lambda_k f_k(y_{i-1}, y_i, x_{1:N})), \qquad (1)$$

where $\mathbf{Z}$ is the normalization factor that can be calculated as

$$\mathbf{Z} = \sum_{y_{1:N}} \exp(\sum_i \sum_k \lambda_k f_k(y_{i-1}, y_i, x_{1:N})). \qquad (2)$$

Given a set of training data $\{\mathbf{x}, \mathbf{y}^*\}$, where $\mathbf{x}$ is the observation sequence and $\mathbf{y}^*$ is the correct sequence label, we can learn the model parameter $\Theta = \{\lambda_k\}_1^K$ as follows

$$\Theta = \arg\max_\Theta \sum_j \log p(\mathbf{y}_j^*|\mathbf{x}_j, \Theta) + \alpha \sum_k \lambda_k^2, \qquad (3)$$

where $\sum_k \lambda_k^2$ is a regularization term. After learning Θ, given an observation sequence $\mathbf{x}$, we can infer its sequence label $\hat{\mathbf{y}}$ as follows

$$\hat{\mathbf{y}} = \arg\max_{\mathbf{y}} p(\mathbf{y}|\mathbf{x}, \Theta). \qquad (4)$$

We model a biography as a sequence of words where each word has a hidden label. Following the common practice of using BIO notation in sequence labelling, each word in a sequence can be assigned one of the following labels: {B-INT, I-INT, O} where B-INT and I-INT indicate the beginning of and inside of an interest tag, respectively, and O indicates outside an interest tag. Fig. 1 shows an example sentence with the labels for each word.

Fig. 1. Example of a biography segment and the corresponding labels

In the rest of this section, we first describe how we obtain labeled data using seed patterns and heuristic rules. We then describe the features we use for CRF.

4.1 Generating Labeled Training Data

We build a noisy labeled data set here to avoid the time-consuming human annotation process. Our goal is to ensure high precision for such automatically generated labeled data. We first perform POS tagging on all sentences of biographies using Twitter-POS-Tagger [6][1]. As we only treat noun phrases as candidate interest tags, we need to identify noun phrases. We heuristically treat a consecutive sequence of nouns as a noun phrase. To get a set of labeled biographies, we start from a set of seed patterns and extract noun phrases inside these patterns. The seed patterns we use are "play + NP," "NP + fan" and "interested in + NP," where NP stands for a noun phrase. These seed patterns

---

[1] http://www.ark.cs.cmu.edu/TweetNLP/

are chosen manually based on our observations with the data. Although we observe that most of the time the noun phrases found in these patterns do indicate user interests, there are also cases when the noun phrases are not related to user interests, e.g. "life." To ensure high precision, we then focus on the more frequent noun phrases. All extracted noun phrases are ranked based on their numbers of appearances in the whole corpus and the top-100 ranked phrases are selected as our seed interest tags. We annotate all occurrences of these seed interest tags with "B-INT" and "I-INT" in the biographies we have, regardless of whether they co-occur with our seed patterns.

4.2 Sequence Labeling using CRF

Both lexical and POS tag features are used in the CRF model. We do not use syntactic and dependency features as Twitter biographies are usually short and many of them are not sentences but phrases. As our training data is generated using seed interest tags, to avoid over-fitting, we only use contextual features, i.e. features extracted from the surrounding tokens for each position. The feature set we use is shown in Table 3. Different combinations of word features and POS tag features are used in our experiments. These features are empirically selected to get the optimal performance on our test data.

Table 3. Features we use for the CRF model

Feature	Description
Word Features	w_{i-1}
	w_{i+1}
Bigrams	$w_{i-2} + w_{i-1}$
	$w_{i+1} + w_{i+2}$
PosTag	$POS_i + POS_{i+1}$
	$POS_{i-1} + POS_i$
PosTag+Word	$POS_i + w_{i+1}$
	$w_{i-1} + POS_i$

5   Experiments on Interest Tag Extraction

In this section, we present the empirical evaluation of the CRF-based method for interest tag extraction.

5.1   Data

We use a collection of 2,678,436 Twitter users' biographies, which are all written in English. We preprocess these biographies by splitting sentences, tokenizing text and removing all punctuation marks and URLs.

For evaluation purpose, we created an annotated data set as follows. Two graduate students were recruited as human annotators. The annotators were asked to choose words or phrases that describe a user's interest as interest tags. After discussion among the annotators, an annotation guideline about ambiguous cases was created and the annotators went through 500 randomly sampled biographies independently based on the guideline. Out of the 1190 sentences from the 500 biographies, only 10 sentences have different annotations. We discard these 10 sentences and use the remaining sentences as ground truth in the following experiments.

5.2   Experiment Setup

Creation of training data: As we have discussed in Section 4, to create our noisy training data, we first obtain a set of seed interest tags and then use them to obtain a set of positive training sentences, which each contain at least one of the seed interest tags. We also randomly select sentences that do not contain any seed interest tag as our negative training data. After experimenting with different ratios of the positive and negative training sentences, we find that a ratio of 10:1 (positive to negative) gives the best performance.

Using CRF: We use CRF++[2], which is a C++ implementation of CRF. We use the default parameters of this implementation as our preliminary experiment shows that the performance of our model does not change much under different parameter settings.

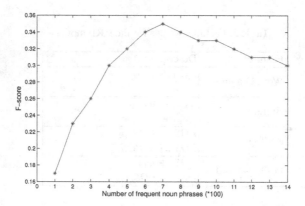

Fig. 2. F-score of baseline method over different number of frequent noun phrase

Baseline: As our task has not been studied before, there is no obvious baseline to compare against. We use two naive baselines for comparison. The first baseline, which is denoted by *Seed*, uses the seed pattern to extract interest tags directly. The second baseline first extracts all noun phrases from user biographies and then rank them by their numbers of appearances in the whole corpus. The top frequent noun phrases are selected and labeled as interest tags. As the performance of this baseline depends on the number of top frequent noun phrases we choose, we first conduct a preliminary experiments to choose the optimal number. Fig. 2 shows the performance in terms of F-score of using different numbers of top frequent noun phrases. The optimal value is 700. This method is denoted by *BL-700*.

---

[2] http://crfpp.googlecode.com/svn/trunk/doc/index.html

5.3   Results

Table 4 shows the performance of the trained CRF model and the baselines. While CRF have a comparable performance to *Seed*, it gets a much higher recall value. This shows that our seed patterns can only cover a small proportion of interest tags but a CRF classifier based on pseudo-labelled data generated by using seed patterns can extract more interest tags. We can also see that CRF outperforms *BL-700* substantially in all metrics, which shows the benefit of using supervised machine learning to perform the interest tag extraction task.

Table 4. Extraction performance of CRF and the baseline

	CRF	Seed	BL-700
Precision	0.91	0.92	0.22
Recall	0.65	0.03	0.76
F-score	0.76	0.06	0.35

Table 5 displays the top-10 frequent interest tags identified by CRF and BL-700. We can see that all interest tags extracted by CRF are meaningful words or phrases about users' interests, but many words found by BL-700 are not describing interests.

Table 5. Top 10 interest tags extracted by our method and BL-700

CRF	BL-700
music	life
food	instagram
twitter	love
travel	music
coffee	god
tv	world
web	girl
internet	people
beer	everything
social media	things

5.4   Frequent Patterns

In this section, we show the frequently used triggers that Twitter users tend to use to indicate their interests. We first extract the adjacent n-grams right before and after each interest tag extracted by our method in the same sentence. Table 6 shows the unigram patterns around interest tags in Twitter users' biographies. Words that can directly show interests are highlighted in bold font. We can see that Twitter users often use words such as "fanatic," "fan," "lover" and similar words to show their interests. In the list of unigram patterns right before interest tag, only "love" is a strong indicator. The other words are actually adjective words which are often used combined with words in the second

Table 6. N-gram patterns

Unigram		Bigram		Trigram	
Right Before	Right After	Right Before	Right After	Right Before	Right After
love	fanatic	I love	is my	to type with	is my life
Avid	fan	Subtly charming	glove on	I love one	happens for a
Wannabe	lover	Infuriatingly humble	is life	have a good	are my life
Extreme	enthusiast	type with	happens for	I am a	will be okay

column. For example, a user who is interested in football may describe himself as "extreme football fan" in his biography. Table 6 also shows patterns formed by bigrams and trigrams. We can see some clear patterns strongly indicating people's interests or preferences, such as "I love," "I like," "in love with" and "is my life."

6   Interest Tags and Tweets

One natural question to ask is what is the relationship between a user's interest tags in biography and her tweet content. In other words, are the interest tags extracted from biographies reflected in users' tweets? To study this problem, we treat interest tags as class labels and utilize tf-idf values of unigrams as features. For a given interest tag, we look at each user and predict whether or not this interest tag is relevant to her based on her tweets.

Tweets published by the users between September 2012 and August 2013 are collected. All conversational tweets that starts with "@"+username are removed. In each tweet, user names, retweet symbols, URLs and hashtags are also removed.

We extract the top-20 frequent interest tags and train a Logistic Regression classifier and an SVM classifier for each tag. The average accuracies based on 5-fold cross

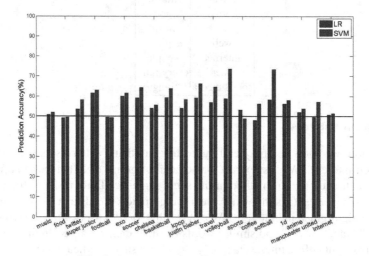

Fig. 3. Average accuracy for the top-20 tags.

validation are shown in Figure 3. The horizontal black line is the accuracy of random guess. We can see that the accuracy of most interest tags are just comparable to that of random guess and for some tags the performance is even worse than random guess. SVM classifier works better than LR for most tags. Both classifiers perform well in predicting tags such as "basketball", "soccer," "volleyball" and "softball", which are related to sports. This suggests that users with interest tags related to sports are more likely to tweet about things related to their interest tags. However, classifiers of those general interest tags, like "music", "sports" and "Internet", have very low accuracies, which indicates that these tags are harder to predict. One possible reason is that these tags are too general to be predicted.

We also consider another way to compare the interest tags extracted from biographies and users' tweets. Here we try to extract tags from tweets and compare them with those extracted from biographies. Tf-idf ranking, a method that has been used to generate personalized user tags [21], is used in this task. In this method, all posted tweets of a user are grouped together into a single document and then tf-idf scores of terms in the document are calculated. The top-N highly scored words are extracted as user tags. We apply tf-idf ranking on our data set and compare the generated tags with the interest tags extracted from users' biographies. For each user in the complete dataset, if we treat the interest tags from biographies as ground truth, we can calculate the recall of the tags extracted from tweets by tf-idf ranking. The results are shown in Table 7. We can see that the average recall of top-20 tags can only reach 7.2%, which is very low.

The above two experiments indicate that interest tags extracted from users' biographies are not necessarily reflected in a users' posted tweets. This suggests that using users' tweets alone may not be sufficient and interest tags extracted from biographies may provide supplementary information of a user.

Table 7. Recall of tags from tweets.

Number of selected phrases	Recall of TF-IDF
top-5	0.045
top-10	0.057
top-15	0.066
top-20	0.072

7   Conclusion

In this work, we study the interest tags hidden in user biographies in Twitter. We first design a strategy based on a set of seed syntactic patterns to get noisy labeled training data. Then a sequential labeling algorithm CRF is trained based on this training data set. Our experiments show that the trained model gets very good performance. We also study the popular expressions people use to indicate their interests in biographies. We discover that tweet content may not reliably reflect users' interest tags in biographies. Interest tags extracted from biographies provide supplementary information for users.

In the follow-up work, we are going to improve our sequential labelling model by introducing background knowledge to it, which could solve the low recall problem of the current model. Demographic and professional information are also valuable and extraction of such information will be studied in the future. Combining information in biographies and social networks is also an interesting topic that will be explored in our future work.

Acknowledgements. This research is partially supported by the Singapore National Research Foundation under its International Research Centre @ Singapore Funding Initiative and administered by the IDM Programme Office, Media Development Authority (MDA).

References

1. Benson, E., Haghighi, A., Barzilay, R.: Event discovery in social media feeds. In: Proceedings of the 49th Annual Meeting of the Association for Computational Linguistics: Human Language Technologies - Volume 1, pp. 389–398. Association for Computational Linguistics, Stroudsburg (2011)
2. Burger, J.D., Henderson, J., Kim, G., Zarrella, G.: Discriminating gender on Twitter. In: Proceedings of the Conference on Empirical Methods in Natural Language Processing, pp. 1301–1309. Association for Computational Linguistics, Stroudsburg (2011)
3. Counts, S., Stecher, K.B.: Self-presentation of personality during online profile creation. In: Proceedings of International AAAI Conference on Weblogs and Social Media, pp. 191–194. The AAAI Press, Dublin (2012)
4. Dong, W., Qiu, M., Zhu, F.: Who am i on Twitter?: A cross-country comparison. In: Proceedings of the Companion Publication of the 23rd International Conference on World Wide Web Companion, pp. 253–254 (2014)
5. Filippova, K.: User demographics and language in an implicit social network. In: Proceedings of the 2012 Joint Conference on Empirical Methods in Natural Language Processing and Computational Natural Language Learning, pp. 1478–1488. Association for Computational Linguistics, Stroudsburg (2012)
6. Gimpel, K., Schneider, N., O'Connor, B., Das, D., Mills, D., Eisenstein, J., Heilman, M., Yogatama, D., Flanigan, J., Smith, N.A.: Part-of-speech tagging for Twitter: annotation, features, and experiments. In: Proceedings of the 49th Annual Meeting of the Association for Computational Linguistics: Human Language Technologies: Short Papers - Volume 2, pp. 42–47. Association for Computational Linguistics, Stroudsburg (2011)
7. Hagger-Johnson, G., Egan, V., Stillwell, D.: Are social networking profiles reliable indicators of sensational interests? Journal of Research in Personality 45(1), 71–76 (2011)
8. Imran, M., Elbassuoni, S., Castillo, C., Diaz, F., Meier, P.: Practical extraction of disaster-relevant information from social media. In: Proceedings of the 22nd International Conference on World Wide Web Companion, pp. 1021–1024. International World Wide Web Conferences Steering Committee, Republic and Canton of Geneva, Switzerland (2013)
9. Lampe, C.A., Ellison, N., Steinfield, C.: A familiar face(book): Profile elements as signals in an online social network. In: Proceedings of the SIGCHI Conference on Human Factors in Computing Systems, pp. 435–444. ACM, New York (2007)
10. Liu, Z., Chen, X., Sun, M.: Mining the interests of Chinese microbloggers via keyword extraction. Frontiers of Computer Science, 76–87 (2012)
11. Marwick, A.E., et al.: I tweet honestly, I tweet passionately: Twitter users, context collapse, and the imagined audience. New Media & Society 13(1), 114–133 (2011)

12. Mukherjee, A., Liu, B.: Improving gender classification of blog authors. In: Proceedings of the 2010 Conference on Empirical Methods in Natural Language Processing, pp. 207–217. Association for Computational Linguistics, Stroudsburg (2010)

13. Nguyen, D., Smith, N.A., Rosé, C.P.: Author age prediction from text using linear regression. In: Proceedings of the 5th ACL-HLT Workshop on Language Technology for Cultural Heritage, Social Sciences, and Humanities, pp. 115–123. Association for Computational Linguistics, Stroudsburg (2011)

14. Nosko, A., Wood, E., Zivcakova, L., Molema, S., De Pasquale, D., Archer, K.: Disclosure and use of privacy settings in Facebook profiles: evaluating the impact of media context and gender. Social Networking, 1–8 (2013)

15. Pennacchiotti, M., Popescu, A.M.: Democrats, republicans and Starbucks afficionados: user classification in Twitter. In: Proceedings of the 17th ACM SIGKDD International Conference on Knowledge Discovery and Data Mining, pp. 430–438. ACM, New York (2011)

16. Qiu, L., Lin, H., Leung, A.K.Y.: Cultural differences and switching of in-group sharing behavior between an American (Facebook) and a Chinese (Renren) social networking site. Journal of Cross-Cultural Psychology 44(1), 106–121 (2013)

17. Ritter, A., Clark, S., Mausam, Etzioni, O.: Named entity recognition in tweets: an experimental study. In: Proceedings of the Conference on Empirical Methods in Natural Language Processing, pp. 1524–1534. Association for Computational Linguistics, Stroudsburg (2011)

18. Ritter, A., Mausam, E.O., Clark, S.: Open domain event extraction from Twitter. In: Proceedings of the 18th ACM SIGKDD International Conference on Knowledge Discovery and Data Mining, pp. 1104–1112. ACM, New York (2012)

19. Rosenthal, S., McKeown, K.: Age prediction in blogs: A study of style, content, and online behavior in pre- and post-social media generations. In: Proceedings of the 49th Annual Meeting of the Association for Computational Linguistics: Human Language Technologies, vol. 1, pp. 763–772. Association for Computational Linguistics, Stroudsburg (2011)

20. Roshchina, A., Cardiff, J., Rosso, P.: User profile construction in the twin personality-based recommender system. In: Proceedings of the Workshop on Sentiment Analysis where AI meets Psychology, pp. 73–79. Asian Federation of Natural Language Processing, Chiang Mai (2011)

21. Wu, W., Zhang, B., Ostendorf, M.: Automatic generation of personalized annotation tags for twitter users. In: Human Language Technologies: The 2010 Annual Conference of the North American Chapter of the Association for Computational Linguistics, pp. 689–692. Association for Computational Linguistics, Stroudsburg (2010)

22. Yang, H., Li, Y.: Identifying user needs from social media. IBM Research report (2013)

Named Entity Recognition in Crime
Using Machine Learning Approach

Hafedh Shabat, Nazlia Omar, and Khmael Rahem

Knowledge Technology Group, Center for AI Technology, Faculty of Information
Science and Technology, Universiti Kebangasaan Malaysia, 43600 Bangi, Selangor, Malaysia
h2005_ali@yahoo.com, nazlia@ukm.edu.my,
khm2006_rakem@yahoo.com

Abstract. Most of the crimes committed today are reported on the Internet by
news articles, blogs and social networking sites. With the increasing volume of
crime information available on the web, a means to retrieve and exploit them
and provide insight into the criminal behavior and networks must be determined
to fight crime more efficiently and effectively. We believe that an electronic
system must be designed for crime named entity recognition from the
newspaper articles. Thus, this study designs and develops a crime named entity
recognition based on machine learning approaches that extract nationalities,
weapons, and crime locations in online crime documents. This study also
collected a new corpus of crime and manually labeled them. A machine
learning classification framework is proposed based on Naïve Bayes and SVM
model in extracting nationalities, weapons, and crime location from online
crime documents. To evaluate our model, a manually annotated data set was
used, which was then validated by experiments. The results of the experiments
showed that the developed techniques are promising.

Keywords: Crime, Machine Learning, Named Entity Recognition, Support
Vector Machine, Naïve Bayes.

1   Introduction

With the rapid growth of the World Wide Web, the volume of crime information
available is growing exponentially. Media channels, especially print and broadcast
media, have been replete with reports of crime and violence. As a result, the process
of manually analyzing and processing the extensive data has become a difficult task.
The public, journalists, crime analysts, and policemen depend on resources reported
by media in investigating or monitoring crime. Finding relevant and timely
information from crime documents are crucial for many applications and can play a
central role in improving crime-fighting capabilities, enhancing public safety, and in
reducing future crimes. Useful and highly important information and entities, such as
the victims and their names, names of organizations, crime locations, used weapons,
and crime types, should be extracted. The crime domain has been chosen as an area in
this study because of its social importance. Named entity recognition system must be

A. Jaafar et al. (Eds.): AIRS 2014, LNCS 8870, pp. 280–288, 2014.

developed to process crime news and topics and detect new reports on a specific crime type. This system is beneficial to users, such as the public, in obtaining awareness on crimes committed in the past and at present.

This study aims to propose NER model that utilizes two techniques (Support Vector Machine (SVM) and Naïve Bayes(NB)) to extract data including weapons, crime locations, and nationalities of both the victim and the suspect. This model is targeted to be more effective than previously developed models.

2   Related Work

In the recent decade, several studies have been performed on crime data mining. The results are often used in developing new software applications for detecting and analyzing crime data. [1] designed neural network-based entity extraction techniques to recognize and classify useful entities from police narrative reports. The designed named entity recognition (NER) has five entity identifier types that crime investigators believe would be useful in their crime investigations. The five types are "person", "address", "vehicle", "narcotic drug", and "personal property". Result showed that the system achieved encouraging precision recall rates for person names and narcotic drugs, but did not perform well for addresses and personal properties. The limitation of this study is that only two named entities, namely, person name and drugs, were extracted, unlike the present study that will extract weapons, type of crime, location of crime, nationality of the victim, nationality of the suspect, and the association between the weapons and the type of crime.

[2] described a rule-based prototype for identifying types of crime in a text in the crime domain, which utilizes a list of keywords and a matching algorithm for classification. [3] had worked on addressing the crime pattern detection problem by using a clustering algorithm to help detect crime patterns and to hasten the process of solving crimes. The k-means clustering technique was employed with some improvements to support the process of identification of crime patterns in actual crime data acquired from the office of a sheriff. Result showed that the most important attribute in crime patterns are "race", "age", "gender", and "weapon". [4] combined IE and principles of the cognitive interview. The IE system combined a large crime-specific lexicon, several General Architecture for Text Engineering (GATE) modules, and an algorithm to recognize relevant entities. The cognitive interview is a psychological technique in which people recall information about an incident. Commonly extracted crime-related entities are race, gender, age, weapons, addresses, narcotic drugs, vehicles, and personal properties. In this paper, crime entities are combined to 15 categories, namely, "act/event", "scene", "people", "personal property", "vehicle", "weapon", "body part", "time", "drug", "shoes", "electronic", "physical feature", "physical condition", "hair", and "clothing". Result showed high precision recall for narrative types. [5] also created another similar system that recognized crime-related information besides the type of crime. The newer system has the capability to extract the nationalities of the victim and the

suspect as well as the location of the crime, aside from the crime type that can be extracted by the previous model. The system utilized an indicator in the Arabic language, which did not work correctly for English because the English language has its own multiple indicator terms. [6] suggested a model that relies on natural language processing methods and adopted the Semantic Inferential Model. The model utilized collaborative environments on the Internet. The system is called Wiki Crimes and can extract two main crime entities, namely, crime scene and crime type from online web sites. [7] developed an IE model that focused on the extraction of information specific to theft crimes, specifically the crime location (address), from newspaper articles. Theft information was extracted from newspaper articles in three different countries: New Zealand, Australia, and India. The model implemented entity recognition to reveal if the sentence indicated a crime location or not and the conditional random field approach, which is a machine learning method, to check whether or not a sentence shows the crime location.

3 Methodology

In Constructing a system for NER using a machine learning approach requires many computational steps, including data planning, pre-processing, feature extraction, classification, and evaluation. Fig. 1 shows the overall architecture of the method, which involves the following phases:
1. Language resource construction phase
2. Pre-processing phase
3. Feature extraction phase
4. Crime entity extraction and classification phase
5. Evaluation phase
The following subsection will describe each of the phases.

3.1   Language Resource Construction

The use of a supervised machine learning technique relies on the existence of annotated training data. Such data are usually created manually by humans or experts in a relevant field. The data used in this research were collected from the Malaysian National News Agency (BERNAMA). The weapons, locations, and nationalities mentioned in the documents were annotated manually. Each file consisted of an article by a journalist reporting on one or more crimes.

3.2   Pre-processing Phase

The pre-processing phase is a highly important phase in any system that uses a machine learning framework. Before extraction and classification, each document undergoes the pre-processing phase that has the following steps:

1. Tokenizing of words depending on the white space and punctuation marks
2. Stop word removal: Removing punctuation marks, diacritics, non-letters, and stop words.
3. Part of Speech (POS) disambiguation is the ability to computationally determine the POS of a word activated by its use in a particular context. In this step, each word is tagged using its unique POS tag. Fig. 2 shows a sample of a crime text annotated with POS tags.

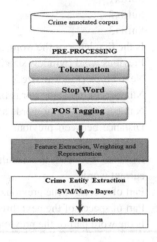

Fig. 1. The proposed crime entity extraction system architecture

On/IN	the/DT	first/JJ	count/NN		Nantha/NNP	Kumar/NNP	was/VBD
charged/VBN	with/IN		a/DT	few/JJ		others/NNS	who/WP
are/VBP	still/RB	at/IN	large/JJ	when/WRB		armed/VBN	with/IN
a/DT		knife/NN	to/TO	have/VB	robbed/VBN	R/NNP	
Victor/NNP	Ratnum/NNP		19/CD	of/IN	RM350/CD	a/DT	
handphone/NN	two/CD		gold/NN		rings/NNS	a/DT	silver/NN

Fig. 2. Sample of a crime text annotated with POS tags

3.3   Feature Extraction

Feature extraction is an important step in any classification system because it improves the efficiency of the classification tasks in terms of speed and effectiveness of learning. This phase aims to convert each word to a vector of feature values. This study defines a set of features for extracting information on nationalities, weapons, and crime locations from online crime documents. These features are grouped into three main feature sets: features based on POS tagging, features based on word affixes, and features based on the context. Table 1 details these feature sets. The word in the corpus is represented using the following feature vector.

Table1. Summary of the feature sets

Feature Set Name	Feature	Feature Name
Word affixes	F1	Prefix1
	F2	Prefix2
	F3	Prefix3
	F4	Suffix1
	F5	Suffix2
	F6	Suffix3
Context-based features	F7	Is the first letter of the word capitalized?
	F8	Previous word (window size 2)
	F9	Next words (window size 2)
	F10	Number of indicator words before (size of window 7)
	F11	Number of indicator words after (size of window 7)
	F12	Distance between previous indicator words and the current words
	F13	Distance between the resulting indicator words and the current words.
POS-based	F14	Part of speech of the previous three words
	F15	Part of speech of the next three words
	F16	Is the word part of the previous phrase?

3.4   Machine Learning and Classification

Most of the machine learning approaches has two phases in which training is first performed to generate a trained machine and then followed by a classification step. In this study, we will evaluate specific machine learning approaches. However, to extract the crime entities, namely, nationalities, weapons, and crime locations from online crime documents, the following machine learning classifiers are used:

SVM Classifier. Support vector machine (SVM) is an effective machine learning technique first introduced by [8]. SVMs are popular in the machine learning community because of their use of text categorization. The SVM classification method has been proven by many researchers as one of the most effective classification methods based on its performance on text classification and entities recognition [9-13]. Adopting the structural risk minimization principle from the computational learning theory, SVMs seek a decision surface to separate the training data points into two classes and to make decisions based on the support vectors selected as the only effective elements in the training set. Multiple variants of SVMs have been developed [10]. In this paper, our discussion is limited to linear SVMs because of their popularity and high performance. The optimization procedure of SVMs (dual form) is aimed to minimize the following:

$$\vec{\alpha} = argmin\{-\sum_{i=1}^{n}\alpha_i + \sum_{i=1}^{n}\sum_{j=1}^{n}\alpha_i\alpha_jy_iy_j\langle\vec{x_i},\vec{x_j}\rangle\} \tag{1}$$

$$Subjectto: \sum_{i=1}^{n}\alpha_iy_i = 0; \quad 0 \le \alpha_i \le C$$

Naive Bayes. The Naïve Bayes (NB) algorithm is a widely used algorithm for review classification. The main advantages of NB are that they are simple, easy to implement, and comprise better-performing algorithms. Given a feature vector table, the algorithm computes the posterior probability that the review belongs to different classes and assigns the review to the class that has the highest posterior probability. Two models (i.e., the multinomial model and the multivariate Bernoulli model) are commonly used in the application of the NB approach to text categorization. NB assumes a stochastic model of document generation and implements the Bayes' rule. To classify the most probable class c* for a new document d, NB computes:

$$c^* = \arg\max_c \; P(c\,/\,d) \tag{2}$$

The NB classifier calculates the posterior probability as follows:

$$p(c_j|d_i) = \frac{p(c_j)p(c_j|d_i)}{p(d_i)} \tag{3}$$

4   Performance Measures

The performance of the machine learning algorithms is measured on manually labeled crime corpus. The corpus contains 500 documents collected from the Malaysian National News Agency (BERNAMA). Each file consisted of an article by a journalist reporting on one or more crimes. The weapons, locations, and nationalities mentioned in the documents were annotated manually. Fig. 3 show a sample of the annotated of the used data set.

.... with a hold-up at a convenience store in Jalan\LOC-I Kuantan-Kemaman\ LOC–O yesterday ....The police recovered loot comprising RM2 500 homemade\WT-I pistol\WT-O two shotgun\WT-O pellets several knives\WT-O and a Perodua Myvi from the trio The suspects had taken away the car after robbing the store which was manned by two workers One of the suspects is believed to have supplied the gun\WT-O

Fig. 3. A Sample of the used dataset

All algorithms are evaluated using 10-fold cross-validation. The objective of this step-up is to filter the parameters and select the best methods for crime entity extraction. The performance measures used to evaluate the named entity recognition systems participating in the CoNLL-02, CoNLL-03, and JNLPBA-04 challenge tasks are precision, recall, and the weighted mean Fβ=1-score. Precision is the percentage of named entities found by the learning system as correct. Recall is the percentage of named entities present in the corpus that are found by the system. A named entity is correct only if an exact match of a corresponding entity in the data file, that is, the complete name of the entity, is identified. Definitions of the performance measures used are summarized below. The same performance measures are employed to evaluate the results of the baseline experiments.

$$Recall = \frac{\# \text{ of correctly classified entities}}{\# \text{ of entities in the corpus}} = \frac{tp}{tp + fn} \tag{4}$$

$$Precision = \frac{\# \text{ of correctly classified entities}}{\# \text{ of entities found by algorithm}} = \frac{tp}{tp + fp} \tag{5}$$

$$F_\beta = \frac{(1 + \beta^2) * (precision * recall)}{(\beta^2 * precision + recall)} \tag{6}$$

5   Results

In this experiment, the overall performance of each of two classifiers on crime entity extraction was examined. The two classifiers, NB and SVM, are applied on the entire feature space. Table 2 shows a summary of the experimental results using the NB and SVM classifiers in extracting the nationalities of the victim and the suspect, weapons, and crime locations.

Table. 2. Performance (the average F-measure for each class) of the NB and SVM classifiers on each crime entity

	SVM	NB
Weapons	91.08	86.73
Nationality	96. 25	94. 02
Location	89.28	87.66

As shown in Table 2, the highest performance on extracting weapons, nationalities, and crime locations from crime documents is exhibited by the SVM classifier. SVM uses a refined structure that acknowledges the relevance of most features. SVM also has the ability to handle large feature spaces. Therefore, probability is a good choice in the crime data set as the feature set cases of each example frequently occur.

The experiments in this study have generally shown highly promising results that clearly demonstrate the appropriateness of the application of machine learning algorithms for crime entity extraction. The promising result encourages the more comprehensive and comparative study of machine learning for all crime entity extraction techniques.

6   Conclusion

This paper presented a crime NER based on machine learning classification approaches, namely, NB and SVM, in extracting nationalities, weapons, and crime locations from online crime documents. This study collected a new corpus of crime and manually labeled them. A manually annotated crime dataset was used for the evaluation, which was then validated by experiments. Finally, the results demonstrated that the SVM classifier achieves the best performance and outperforms NB in extracting nationalities, weapons, and crime locations from online crime documents.

Future research may be targeted at developing a large crime corpus and designing a general framework for crime IE and analysis, which includes automatic classification of crime type, identification of weapons used in each crime, identification of nationalities of both victim and suspect, identification of crime location, and analysis on the association between the used weapons and the type of crime.

References

1. Chau, M., Xu, J.J., Chen, H.: Extracting Meaningful Entities from Police Narrative Reports. In: 2002 Proceedings of the 2002 Annual National Conference on Digital Government Research, pp. 1–5 (2002)
2. Alruily, M., Ayesh, A., Al-Marghilani, A.: Using Self Organizing Map to Cluster Arabic crime documents. In: Proceedings of the International Multiconference on Computer Science and Information Technology, IMCSIT, pp. 357–363 (2010)
3. Nath, S.V.: Crime Pattern Detection using Data Mining. In: 2006 IEEE/WIC/ACM International Conference on Web Intelligence and Intelligent Agent Technology Workshops, WI-IAT 2006 Workshops, pp. 41–44. IEEE (2006)
4. Chih Hao, K., Iriberri, A., Leroy, G.: Crime Information Extraction from Police and Witness Narrative Reports. In: Conference on Technologies for Homeland Security, pp. 193–198. IEEE (2008)
5. Alruily, M., Ayesh&, A., Zedan, H.: Automated Dictionary Construction from Arabic Corpus for Meaningful Crime Information Extraction and Document Classification, 137–142 (2010)
6. Pinheiro, V., Furtado, V., Pequeno, T., Nogueira, D.: Natural Language Processing based on Semantic Inferentialism for Extracting Crime Information from Text. In: IEEE International Conference on Intelligence and Security Informatics (ISI), pp. 19–24 (2010)
7. Arulanandam, R., Savarimuthu, B.T.R., Purvis, M.A.: Extracting Crime Information from Online Newspaper Articles. In: Proceedings of the Second Australasian Web Conference (2014)
8. Cortes, C., Vapnik, V.: Support-vector Networks. Machine Learning 20, 273–297 (1995)
9. Yang, Y., Pedersen, J.O.: A Comparative Study on Feature Selection in Text Categorization (1997)
10. Joachims, T.: The Maximum Margin Approach to Learning Text Classifiers: Methods,Theory, and Algorithms. PhD thesis, university Dortmund (2001)

11. Joachims, T.: Text Categorization With Support Vector Machines: Learning with Many Relevant Features. In: European Conference on Machine Learning, Chemnitz, Germany, pp. 137–142 (1998)
12. Isa, D., Lee, L.H., Kallimani, V.P., RajKumar, R.: Text Documents Preprocessing with the Bahes Formula for Classification using the Support Vector Machine. IEEE, TKDE 20(9), 1264–1272 (2008)
13. Saha, S., Ekbal, A.: Combining Multiple Classifiers using Vote based Classifier Ensemble Technique for Named Entity Recognition. Data& Knowledge Engineering, 85 (2013)

A New Combination Method Based on Adaptive Genetic Algorithm for Medical Image Retrieval

Karim Gasmi[1], Mouna Torjmen-Khemakhem[1], Lynda Tamine[2], and Maher Ben Jemaa[1]

[1] ReDCAD Laboratory, ENIS Soukra km 3,5, University of Sfax, TUNISIA
[2] IRIT Laboratory, University of Paul Sabatier, Toulouse
gasmikarim@yahoo.fr

Abstract. Medical image retrieval could be based on the text describing the image as the caption or the title. The use of text terms to retrieve images have several disadvantages such as term-disambiguation. Recent studies prove that representing text into semantic units (concepts) can improve the semantic representation of textual information. However, the use of conceptual representation has other problems as the miss or erroneous semantic relation between two concepts. Other studies show that combining textual and conceptual text representations leads to better accuracy. Popularly, a score for textual representation and a score for conceptual representation are computed and then a combination function is used to have one score. Although the existing of many combination methods of two scores, we propose in this paper a new combination method based on adaptive version of the genetic algorithm. Experiments are carried out on Medical Information Retrieval Task of the ImageCLEF 2009 and 2010. The results confirm that the combination of both textual and conceptual scores allows best accuracy. In addition, our approach outperforms the other combination methods.

Keywords: medical image retrieval, score combination, genetic algorithm, concept mapping.

1 Introduction

Traditional of information retrieval models uses the exact correspondence between the document terms and the query terms to select a document to return to the user. The problem of these models is that the meaning of a word can be expressed in different words, and one word can express different meanings in different contexts. This is due to the richness of the mechanisms of reflection and linguistic expression.

Some studies as [11], [26] have highlighted the inadequacy of document representation based on simple words [11], [26]. The authors in [8] showed that only 20% of Internet users use an application 100% accurately to their needs. Indeed, this wealth can be a source of ambiguity in natural language. To overcome the problem of term ambiguity, some research works proposed the use of

A. Jaafar et al. (Eds.): AIRS 2014, LNCS 8870, pp. 289–301, 2014.

relevance feedback. This technique allow to partially circumvent the problem of term synonymy, but it is not a satisfactory solution.

Recently, many approaches based on semantic indexing have been proposed [2], [6], [19]. The idea of the semantic indexing is to identify all the document terms, project them on an external resource [17](as ontologies) to extract concepts. The authors in [16] have shown that this technique does not cover all the meanings of words. Therefore, this approache needs a semantic resource with a rich terminology covers all terms addressed in the documents of the collection area. All areas require an aspect of optimization, including optimization algorithm we quote the genetic algorithm that is inspired by the genetic operations. Generally, GA is used either for optimization or for selection of parameters [18], [21]. In this paper, we focus on medical image retrieval using surrounding text as the annotation. We propose to compute two scores: the first based on the textual representation of the image annotation, and the second based on conceptual representation of the image annotation. Then, we adapt the genetic algorithm to combine these two scores. Wherein the two weights are two independent numbers. The rest of the paper is organized as follows. Some related work about the combination of two scores is described in Section 2. Following this, in section 3 we give the details of our approach about computing textual and conceptual scores for medical images. In section 4, we describe the genetic algorithm and how we adapt it to combine textual and conceptual scores to one medical image final score. Section 5 presents the corpus used in our experiments, the evaluation metrics and experimental results. Finally, we conclude in Section 6 with possible future work.

2   Related Work

Recently, many studies have highlighted the inadequate representation of documents (D) and requests (R) based on simple words [3], [26] and proposed to explore the semantics textual representation of D / R [19]. The idea of these approaches is to represent the D / R in the form of concepts extracted by projecting the text of the D / R to an external resource such as a semantic ontology. Thus, for a given text, only the words or recognized by the semantic resource sentences will be translated into concepts. We are talking about a conceptual representation or a conceptual indexing [5], [17], [19]. The disadvantage of this design is that indexing is based on the assumption that all the terms of the D / R exist in the semantic resource and therefore the passage of a textual representation to a conceptual representation will be well done. This hypothesis requires the use of a semantic resource with a rich terminology that covers the entire area covered in the documents of the collection. In its approach, Baziz [5] indicated that an ontology (e.g. Wordnet) does not cover all the vocabulary used in the collection. Therefore, Baziz [5] and Hinrich [14] proposed to combine two types of indexing: one using keywords and one using concepts. This idea allows to have significant results. One of the factors that influence performance is probably the quality of the ontology and especially its coverage of the vocabulary in the corpus.

Several methods are typically based on well known voting-based data fusion techniques [9] (e.g., CombMAX, CombLin, CombRank, etc.) that have been used to combine data from different information sources [4], [20], [24]. The existing methods of combination are manual methods, and do not cover the entire search space. In addition, these methods uses dependent weights, which minimizes the number of possible combinations. Table 1 depicts some voting techniques. They are grouped into two categories according to the source of evidence used.

Table 1. Voting techniques used for a multi-annotation

Category	Technique	Score
Rank-based	CombRank	$\alpha R_{text_i} + (1 - \alpha)R_{con_i}$
Score-based	CombMAX	$Max(S_{text_i}, S_{con_i})$
	CombMin	$Min(S_{text_i}, S_{con_i})$
	CombMed	$Median(S_{text_i}, S_{con_i})$
	CombLin	$score_i = \alpha S_{text_i} + (1 - \alpha)S_{con_i}$

3 Computing Textual and Conceptual Scores for Medical Image Retrieval

Four phases are the components of our attempt to develop a retrieval model for medical information. This model combines two different annotation methods: conceptual and textual. The first phase is the pre-processing. The second step is the step of indexing. For the textual indexing, we used Terrier IR platform, the open source search engine written in Java and developed at the School of Computing, University of Glasgow, and the conceptual indexing step is discrupted in the next section. The third phase is the calculation of the score for each image by both textual and conceptual model, using the vector space model. The last step is consists of searching the optimal weights of two scores from both textual and conceptual model, this step are based on the genetic algorithm. An overview of our model is done in Fig. 1.

3.1 Mapping Text to Concepts

The aim of this step is to map text into concepts. For this purpose, we start by preprocessing the collection and remove the stop word in order to keep only significant words. After the preprocessing step, we extract the concepts from the text, the switch of text to concepts is realized by an innate procedure system named MetaMap [3], followed by the U.S. National Library of Medicine. MetaMap scrutinized biomedical free-text and identified concepts that are derived from Unified Medical Language System (UMLS). MetaMap is broadly implemented in clinical NLP and IR. By means of MetaMap, the both queries and papers are transformed, [3] endow us with supplementary fine points of this course of action. The extraction of concepts step is a process which allows to highlight the most significant topics of the document by extracting the most relevant concepts. For example, the paradigm of *"brain cancer trial"* MetaMap

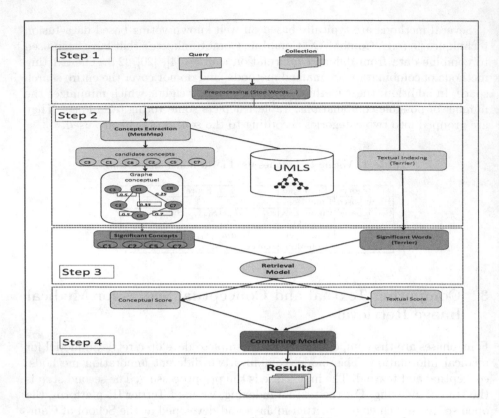

Fig. 1. Overview of our model of medical image retrieval

instrument engenders the concepts ID C0153633 and C0008976, which stand for correspondingly *"brain cancer"* from the semantic brand *"Neoplastic Process"* and *"Trial"* from the semantic brand *"Research Activity"*, as the paramount consequences amid the seven meta-nominees. After a thorough study on the UMLS ontology, we found that it suffers from several problems in relations between concepts such as erroneous relationship.

Authors in [7] reveale that a total of 17 022 (24.3%) of associations (parent-child) between UMLS notions can not be justified according to the semantic categories of concepts. Among several cases that can produce artificial relations, we cite:

- Cases where the semantic category of the child is very broad whereas the parent's semantic type is too specific;
- Situations where the parent-child relationship is erroneous;
- Cases where a parent-child relationship is lacking and have to be added to the UMLS semantic network;
- Conditions where the parent or the child is missing a semantic category;

In fact, these problems can lead to false conceptual annotations. It should, however, be noted those mistaken concepts may be chosen and hence the implicating of the article will be influenced. To surmount this problem, we use the method of enhancement concepts based on graph theory proposed by Gasmi [12], they put forward the computation of associations between concepts, and no more than associating concepts will be chosen.

Therefore, this method aims to select relevant concepts and to eliminate misconceptions. This method involves calculating distances between two types of concepts generated. Both distances are: one based on the arcs and another based on the information content of a concept. So, they have found as shown by a graph of concepts linked by arcs formed by the hybridization of two types of distances. Thereafter, the concepts which are not connected with other concepts will be deleted [12].

According to Fig. 1, D1 is a document presented by C1, C2, C3, C5, C7 and C8. After the weighting step, D1 is presented only by C1, C2, C5 and C7. C3 and C8 are removed because they do not have any relationship with other concepts.

3.2   Conceptual and Textual Score Fusion

To automate the combination of conceptual and textual results, we chose to implement the genetic algorithm to find the most optimal weight for each method, we followed the following equation:

$$score_i = \alpha score_{text_i} + \beta score_{con_i} \tag{1}$$

$score_{text_i}$:This is the score of the document i, obtained by the textual method
$score_{con_i}$:This is the score of the document i, obtained by the conceptual method
α ,β :are the weights of the two scores. Wherein the two weights are two independent numbers.

4   Score Combination Based on Adaptive Genetic Algorithm

Several researchers have used a genetic algorithm (GA) to find the most optimal solution in the retrieval information field. Including the use of this algorithm, the authors in [18], [21] use this algorithm to find the optimal combination of query. In its thesis, Yahya [1] proposed a method of combination of multiple similarity measures in the field of chemical information retrieval. This combination based on genetic algorithm can produce better results.

In genetic algorithms [13], the basic idea is to simulate the population evolution process. We start from a population of N solutions to the problem represented by individuals. The randomly selected population is called a relative population. The individual adaptation degree to the environment is expressed by the value of the cost function f (x), where x is the solution that the individual represents. It is declared that more an individual is better adapted to its environment, more the cost of the solution is lower.

For each problem to solve, a fitness function f should be provided. Its choice is crucial for the proper functioning of the algorithm. Given a chromosome, the fitness function must return a numeric value that represents its utility. This score will be used in the selection process of the parents, so that the fittest individuals will have a greater chance of being selected.

Within this population, a random selection of one or both parents is done, producing a new solution through genetic operators such as crossover and mutation. The new population, obtained by the choice of N individuals among parent and child populations is called next generation. By repeating this process, it produces a richer individuals that are better adapted to the population. Fig. 2 shows the procedure of the proposed GA weighting combining-annotation method as follows:

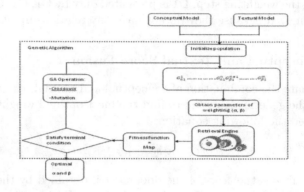

Fig. 2. Genetic algorithm process

Most operations require the Genetic Algorithm fitness function to calculate the adaptation of the individual. In the proposed approach, our fitness function depends on tow factors: (1) it depends on results returned by the retrieval model according to mean average precision (MAP), MAP is taken as a user who selected in each iteration the relevant documents found for calculated the Fitness for each chromosome; (2) the absolute value of subtraction between the two weights is added. The aim of the second part is to minimize the cost of any influence of annotations compared to the other on the Fitness function 2.

$$Fitness = MAP - \frac{1}{\|\alpha - \beta\|} \tag{2}$$

With:
$$MAP = \sum_{j=1}^{M} wq_i * AP_{qj} / M$$
where APq is the average precision of a query q, and M is the number of queries.

$$Precision = |relevantdocuments \cap retrievaldocuments| / |retrievaldocuments|$$

In our proposed method, we use the MAP measure, that is connected directly by the number of relevant documents found as he shows his formula, MAP is taken as a user who selected in each iteration the relevant documents found for calculated the Fitness for each chromosome.

- Step 1 : Encodes the chromosomes and the parameters representing the weighting indexing method as a binary string. Fig. 3 shows an example of a chromosome creation from two weights.

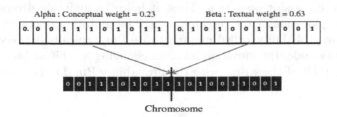

Alpha : Conceptual weight = 0.23   Beta : Textual weight = 0.63

Chromosome

Fig. 3. Coding of a Chromosome

- Step2 : Initializes the population and produces the initial population of chromosomes arbitrarily.
- Step3 : The fitness for each chromosome must be computed, this is related to the calculated results obtained by the fitness equation.
- Step 5 : The main feature is that the fitness value decreasing during the last M generation or N is reached as the maximum generation number.
- Step 6 : The iteration process stops only when the two criteria are achieved. Otherwise you have to move to step 5.
- Step 7 : To generate a offspring generation, genetic operations should be performed. The offspring generation has as components : crossover, mutation and tournoi reproduction.

4.1 *Crossover*

The main operator acting on the population of parents is the crossover, which is applied with a certain probability, called crossover rate Pc (typically close to unity). The crossing is to choose two individuals represented by their chains of genes randomly selected from the general population and define random or more crossing points. The new children are, then, created in inter changing different parts of each string.

Let G_α and G_β be two selected parent chromosomes, which are represented respectively as follows:

$$G_\psi = G_\psi^1, G_\psi^2, ... G_\psi^n$$
$$G_\omega = G_\omega^1, G_\omega^2, ... G_\omega^n$$
Then:

$$G_\xi = \begin{cases} G_\psi^i \; if \; 1 < i < k \\ G_\omega^i \; else \end{cases}$$
$$\text{With :}$$
$$k = random(1, n-1), 1 < k < n-1;$$

4.2 Mutation

This operation protects genetic algorithms premature loss of relevant information. It allows introducing some information in the population, which could be
lost during the crossing operation. Thus, it helps to maintain diversity, useful
for a good exploration of the research area. The mutation operator is applied
with a certain probability, called mutation rate Pm, typically between 0.05 and
0.10. In binary code, the mutation involves changing a 1 bit at bit 0, and vice
versa, for each bit of the string, with the probability Pm. Let G_α be the parent
chromosome,

$$G_\alpha = G_\alpha^1, G_\alpha^2, ... G_\alpha^n$$
$$\text{Then :} \; G_\alpha^k = 1 - G_\alpha^1$$
$$\text{With :} \; k = random(1, n-1), 1 < k < n-1;$$

5 Evaluation

5.1 Data Sets and Evaluation Metrics

To evaluate our approach, we use the 2009 and 2010 ImageCLEF collection
composed respectively of 74,902 and 77000 medical images and annotations associated with them. This collection contains images and captions from Radiology
and Radiographic, two Radiological Society of North America (RSNA) journals.
The number of queries is 25 from 2009 collection and 16 from 2010 collection.
They are queries selected by experts in information retrieval company to evaluate results by ImageCLEF collection. Table 2 contains the parameters used for
the genetic algorithm.

Table 2. Parameters of GA

GA property	Value/Method
Size of generation	100
Initial population size	30
Selection method	Tournoi
Number of crossover points	1
Crossover Probability	0.9
Mutation method	Uniform mutation
Mutation Probability	0.05

To evaluate our approach, we have used P@5, P@10 and Mean Average Precision MAP. To statistically validate our results, we used the signed-rank test of
the Wilcoxon test [27] which is the non-parametric equivalent of the paired sample test. This test consists in evaluating a value of significance $p \in [0, 1]$ which

estimates the probability that the difference between the two methods is due to chance. We can thereby conclude that two methods are statistically different when p$\leq \alpha$, where $\alpha \leq 0.05$ is commonly used [15]. More precisely, the more $p \to 0$, the more two methods are supposed to be different.

In our experiments, we consider that the difference between two methods is significant when p ≤ 0.1 , and it is very significant when p ≤ 0.05.

5.2   Retrieval Model

For both textual and conceptual representations, we have used the vector space model [22,23] to compute the similarity between documents and queries. Each dimension in this model represents a term or an ontology concept. Documents and queries are represented by a vector with n dimensions where n is the number of the terms or ontological concepts [25].

The value of system relevance is calculated using the similarity function $RSV(Q, d)$ (Retrieval Status Value) where Q is a query and D_j is a document. The RSV is calculated as follows:

$$RSV\left(Q, D_j\right) = \frac{\sum_{i=1}^{N} wq_i.w_{ij}}{\left(\sum_{i=1}^{N} wqi^2\right)^{\frac{1}{2}} . \left(\sum_{i=1}^{N} w_{ij}^2\right)^{\frac{1}{2}}} \tag{3}$$

– The term/concept frequency is:

$$w_{ij} = cf_{ij} * idf_{ij} \quad and \quad wq_i = cf_{qi} * idf_{qi} \tag{4}$$

where : cf_{ij}(respectively cf_{qi}) is the number of occurrences of the concept/term C_i in the document D_j (respectively the query q); And idf_{ij} that stands for the inverse document frequency, is equal to devide the number of documents containing the concept/term i, by the number of all documents in the collection.

5.3   Experimental Results

In this section, we present the different results obtained by different combination methods. Results according to P@5, P@10 and MAP measures for 2009 and 2010 data sets are presented in Table 3.

We note that our model results are better than conceptual and textual model. This observation affirms that the use of a combination solution improves the retrieval accuracy. Consequently, we can conclude that the use of both model conceptual and textual is a good solution, on the one hand to improve the outcome, and on the other to improve the semantic representation of the document.

Best results are obtained by our combination method for both data sets. Gains in MAP measure are presented in Table 4.

Symbol * after the gain indicates statistical significance using the Wilcoxon test at $p \leq 0.1$. Symbol ** after the gain indicates statistical significance using the Wilcoxon test at $p \leq 0.05$. Table 4 shows how our indexing approach is statistically significant and the improvements of our method compared to other

Table 3. Comparison between conceptual, textual, MaxComb, LinComb, RankComb and GentComb Methods

Category	P@5	P@10	MAP	Category	P@5	P@10	MAP
ImageClef 2010 Collection				ImageClef 2009 Collection			
Conceptual	0.362	0.293	0.208	Conceptual	0.480	0.450	0.264
Textual	0.399	0.393	0.298	Textual	0.620	0.600	0.386
MaxComb	0.333	0.3733	0.269	MaxComb	0.520	0.516	0.3451
LinComb	0.400	0.440	0.324	LinComb	0.640	0.600	0.390
RankComb	0.426	0.433	0.319	RankComb	0.640	0.584	0.381
GentComb	0.413	0.440	0.329	GentComb	0.660	0.630	0.398

Table 4. Gain between GentComb Method and the other Methods for 2009 and 2010 Collection

Category	P@5	P@10	MAP
ImageClef 2010 Collection			
GentComb /Conceptual	14% (*)	50% (**)	58.1% (**)
GentComb /Textual	3.5%	11.9% (*)	10% (*)
GentComb /CombMax	24.02% (**)	17.96% (*)	22.30% (**)
GentComb/CombLin	3.25%	0%	1.54%
GentComb/CombRank	-3.1%	1.61%	3.16%
ImageClef 2009 Collection			
GentComb/Conceptual	+37.5% (*)	+40% (**)	+50.75% (**)
GentComb/Textual	+6.45%	+5%	+3.1%
GentComb /CombMax	26.92% (**)	22.09% (**)	9.21% (**)
GentComb /CombLin	3.1%	5%	2%
GentComb Method/CombRank	3.1%	7.87%	4.46%

methods rates. We computed the Wilcoxon test between means of each ranking obtained by each indexing method. The Wilcoxon test validated our method for the 2010 query set ($p \leq 0.1$) compared to the textual baseline. Additionally, Table 4 shows that our proposed method (GENTComb) is statistically significant compared to the conceptual baseline ($p \leq 0.05$) for the 2010 and 2009 query set. Concerning the Map measure, our method outperforms every combination method rated at a result and on the other hand the proposed method uses two annotation-weight which are two automatic and separate numbers, unlike other method used an manually and dependent weight.

5.4 Comparison of Our Method with Official Submissions of Medical IMAGE CLEF 2009 and 2010

In this section, we compare our method with runs submitted for medical ImageCLEF 2009 and 2010. Only runs based on textual approaches are taken into account because our method is based only on textual annotation of images. For

Table 5. Comparison of our method with official runs of IMAGE CLEF 2009

	Rang	MAP	P5	P10
LIRIS maxMPTT extMPTT	1	0.43	0.70	0.66
Our Method (GentComb)	**2**	**0.398**	**0.660**	**0.630**
sinai CTM t	3	0.38	0.65	0.62
york.In expB2c1.0	4	0.37	0.61	0.60
ISSR text 1	5	0.35	0.58	0.56
ceb-essie2-automatic	6	0.35	0.65	0.62
deu run1 pivoted	7	0.34	0.58	0.52
clef2009	8	0.34	0.67	0.60
BiTeM EN	9	0.32	0.52	0.50
UNTtextrf1	10	0.26	0.53	0.44
OHSU SR1	11	0.18	0.59	0.54
MirEN	12	0.17	0.62	0.55
uwmTextOnly	13	0.13	0.44	0.40
Alicante-Run3	14	0.13	0.34	0.36

Table 6. Comparison of our method with official runs of IMAGE CLEF 2010

	Run Type	MAP	P5	P10
Our Method (GentComb)	Automatic	**0.329**	**0.440**	0.440
Information Processing Laboratory	Automatic	0.3235	0.3109	**0.4687**
OHSU	Automatic	0.3029	0.344	0.4313
UESTC	Automatic	0.2789	0.297	0.3125
ISSR	Automatic	0.2583	0.2667	0.3187
HES-SO VS	Automatic	0.2568	0.278	0.35
ITI	Automatic	0.188	0.2158	0.375
Bioingenium Research Group	Automatic	0.1005	0.1289	0.1875
XRCE	Feedback	0.2925	0.3027	0.4125
SINAI	Feedback	0.2672	0.2683	0.4125
XRCE	Not applicable	0.338	0.3828	0.5062

Medical IMAGE CLEF 2009, Table 5 compares our method (Gent-Comb) with the other official submissions.

For the best result of the IRIS team in 2009, the authors use a combination of two analysis tools, one with the MiniPar parser and the second with the TreeTagger tool. Then, they compare the combination of conceptual representation with the Kullback-Leiber divergence instead of the combination with likelihood function. Two RSV are used : one based on log-probability and the other based on divergence function. The best result is obtained with the log-probability method. This method is improved by using a relevance feedback extension of queries with the n first returned documents. Best results are obtained with n = 100. Using our proposition, we are ranked second. We recall that we do not use the relevance feedback.

For Medical IMAGE CLEF 2010, Table 6 compares our method (Gent-Comb) with the other official submissions.

Organisers consider the XRCE laboratory run is wrong and not applicable. Then, the best official result in 2010 is the one of Information Processing Laboratory team, the authors indexed the text usind Lucene framework. For the retrieval, first, the documents are expanded with the Mesh-terms, after that a combination of textual score and the score obtained by Mesh terms is released. To compute the fibal score of each medical image, a function proposed by Fang and Zhai [10] is used. Thanks to our proposed method, we are classified on first rank.

6 Conclusion and Future Works

The purpose of this paper is to better study the importance of combining two retrieval methods; textual and conceptual method. To do this, we used the UMLS as a specific ontology for the medical domain, which allowed us to extract concepts representative of each document. Our approach begins with extracting concepts by MetaMap tool, after words, it uses the graph theory to retain only the relevant concepts, and later to refine the results obtained we used the genetic algorithm to combine the two types of indexing: textual and conceptual. Our results showed that the combination method can on the one hand to improve the efficiency of our model and secondly to improve the semantic representation of the document.

References

1. Abderahman, Y.A.: Fusion of similarity measures using genetic algorithm for searching chemical database (2008)
2. Abdulahhad, K., Chevallet, J., Berrut, C.: Solving concept mismatch through bayesian framework by extending umls meta-thesaurus. In: Conference en Recherche d Infomations et Applications - CORIA 2011, pp. 311–326 (2011)
3. Aronson, A.R.: Effective mapping of biomedical text to the umls metathesaurus: the metamap program. In: Annual Symposium AMIA, pp. 17–21 (2001)
4. Aslam, J.A., Montague, M.: Models for metasearch. In: Proceedings of the 24th Annual International ACM SIGIR Conference on Research and Development in Information Retrieval, pp. 276–284 (2001)
5. Baziz, M.: Indexation conceptuelle guidée par ontologie pour la recherche d'information. In: Thesis, University Paul Sabatier, Toulouse, France (2005)
6. Chevallet, J., Lim, J., Le, D.T.H.: Domain knowledge conceptual inter-media indexing: application to multilingual multimedia medical reports. In: Proceedings of the sixteenth ACM conference on Conference on information and knowledge management, CIKM 2007, pp. 495–504 (2007)
7. Cimino, J.J., Min, H., Perl, Y.: Consistency across the hierarchies of the umls semantic network and metathesaurus. Journal of Biomedical Informatics 36(6), 450–461 (2003)
8. Crestani, F.: Exploiting the similarity of non-matching terms at retrieval time. Journal of Information Retrieval 2, 25–45 (1999)
9. Dinh, D., Tamine, L.: Combining global and local semantic contexts for improving biomedical information retrieval. In: Clough, P., Foley, C., Gurrin, C., Jones, G.J.F., Kraaij, W., Lee, H., Mudoch, V. (eds.) ECIR 2011. LNCS, vol. 6611, pp. 375–386. Springer, Heidelberg (2011)
10. Fang, H., Zhai, C.: An exploration of axiomatic approaches to information retrieval. In: Proceedings of the 28th Annual International ACM SIGIR Conference on Research and Development in Information Retrieval, SIGIR 2005, pp. 480–487 (2005)
11. Fieschi, M., Aronson, A.R., Morky, J.G., Gay, C.W., Humphrey, S.M., Rogers, W.J.: The nlm indexing initiative's medical text indexer. In: Proceedings of the 11th World Congress on Medical Informatics Demner-Fushman and Lin Answering Clinical Questions, pp. 268–272 (2004)

12. Gasmi, K., Khemakhem, M., Jemaa, M.B.: A conceptual model for word sense disambiguation in medical image retrieval. In: AIRS, pp. 296–307 (2013)
13. Goldberg, D.E.: Genetic Algorithms in Search, Optimization and Machine Learning, 1st edn. Addison-Wesley Longman Publishing Co., Inc. (1989)
14. Hinrich, J.O.P.: Information retrieval based on word senses (1995)
15. Hull, D.: Using statistical testing in the evaluation of retrieval experiments. In: Proceedings of the 16th Annual International ACM SIGIR Conference on Research and Development in Information Retrieval, SIGIR 1993, pp. 329–338 (1993)
16. Jimeno-Yepes, A.J., McInnes, B.T., Aronson, A.R.: Exploiting mesh indexing in medline to generate a data set for word sense disambiguation. BMC Bioinformatics 12, 223 (2011)
17. Khan, L., McLeod, D., Hovy, E.: Retrieval effectiveness of an ontology-based model for information selection. VLDB Journal, 71–85 (2004)
18. Lopez-Herrera, A., Herrera-Viedma, E., Herrera, F.: Applying multi-objective evolutionary algorithms to the automatic learning of extended boolean queries in fuzzy ordinal linguistic information retrieval systems. vol. 160, p. 2192–2205 (2009)
19. Mihalcea, R., Tarau, P., Figa, E.: Pagerank on semantic networks with application to word sense disambiguation. In: International Conference on Computational Linguistics (COLING), pp. 1126–1132 (2004)
20. Ogilvie, P., Callan, J.: Combining document representations for known-item search. In: Proceedings of the 26th Annual International ACM SIGIR Conference on Research and Development in Informaion Retrieval, SIGIR 2003, pp. 143–150 (2003)
21. Malo, P., Pyry Siitari, A.S.: Automated query learning with wikipedia and genetic programming 194, 86–110 (2013)
22. Salton, G.: The smart retricval system: Experiments in automatic document processing (1970)
23. Salton, G., McGill, M.: Introduction to modern information retrieval (1983)
24. Shaw, J.A., Fox, E.A., Shaw, J.A., Fox, E.A.: Combination of multiple searches. In: The Second Text REtrieval Conference (TREC-2), pp. 243–252 (1994)
25. Ventresque, A., Cazalens, S., Lamarre, P., Valduriez, P.: Improving interoperability using query interpretation in semantic vector spaces. In: Bechhofer, S., Hauswirth, M., Hoffmann, J., Koubarakis, M. (eds.) ESWC 2008. LNCS, vol. 5021, pp. 539–553. Springer, Heidelberg (2008)
26. Weeber, M., Mork, J., Aronson, A.: Developping a test collection for biomedical word senes disambiguation. In: Annual Symposium. AMIA Symposium, pp. 746–750 (2001)
27. Wilcoxon, F.: Individual Comparisons by Ranking Methods. Biometrics Bulletin pp. 80–83 (1945)

Leveraging Wikipedia and Context Features for Clinical Event Extraction from Mixed-Language Discharge Summary

Kwang-Yong Jeong[1], Wangjin Yi[2], Jae-Wook Seol[1], Jinwook Choi[3],
and Kyung-Soon Lee[1]

[1]Dept. of Computer Science & Engineering, CAIIT, Chonbuk National University, South Korea
{wodnr754,kyjeong0520,selfsolee}@chonbuk.ac.kr,
[2]Interdisciplinary Program of Bioengineering, Seoul National University, South Korea
[3]Dept. of Biomedical Engineering, College of Medicine,
Seoul National University, South Korea
{jinsamdol,jinchoi}@snu.ac.kr

Abstract. Unstructured clinical texts contain patients' disease related narratives, but it is required elaborate work to mine the kind of information. Especially for the classification of semantic types of a clinical term, implementations of domain knowledge from resources such as the Unified Medical Language System (UMLS) are essential. The UMLS has a limitation in dealing with other languages. In this paper, we leverage Wikipedia as well as UMLS for clinical event extraction, especially from clinical narratives written in mixed-language. Semantic features for clinical terms are extracted based on semantic networks of hierarchical categories in Wikipedia. Semantic types for Korean clinical terms are detected by using translation links and semantic networks in Wikipedia. An additional remarkable feature is a controlled vocabulary of clue words which can be contextual evidence to determine clinical semantic types of a word. The experimental result on 150 discharge summaries written in English and Korean showed 75.9% in F1-measure. This result shows that the proposed features are effective for clinical event extraction.

Keywords: Clinical event extraction, Semantic classification, Wikipedia, Mixture of language.

1 Introduction

Electronic Medical Record (EMR) systems can provide information rich environment to healthcare professionals[1]. Especially, a discharge summary is a clinical note describing a patient's clinical course and his/her clinical outcomes briefly. It contains abundant medical history. However, converting unstructured information into a structural form requires elaborative works. Nowadays the active implementation of language processing techniques in medical domain shows a lot of promising results [2]. We also envision the future in which the language techniques improve the quality of clinical practice eventually. Its applicability is on not only retrieving, but also a summarization or a visualization of clinical narratives.

A. Jaafar et al. (Eds.): AIRS 2014, LNCS 8870, pp. 302–313, 2014.

Our research is mainly focused on the feature extraction that is a key element in the clinical event extraction. This task is based on a visualization model proposed by [3]. The visualization model (V-Model) needs detection of description boundaries including a clinical event, and classification of their clinical semantic types, i.e., symptoms and medical signs, diagnostic tests, and medications.

To determine the semantic type of a clinical event, domain knowledge is required, and many researches use the UMLS (Unified Medical Language System) as a resource of the knowledge. It has two types of limitations. First, finding an entity in a thesaurus has a limitation in terms of the processing performance. Clinicians use jargons, abbreviations as frequently as standard terms. Moreover, some terms are from patients' words to describe their physical problems mostly which do not exist in the medical thesaurus in the form of layman's language. These kinds of errors occur because of a thesaurus can't cover all expressions in everyday expressions. The second limitation is an ambiguity problem occurring when an entry has several semantic types, for example, *PET* is classified as a diagnostic device (PET-CT) simultaneously with a companion animal in the UMLS.

Despite of its limitation, the UMLS provides rich domain knowledge as a standard thesaurus, and this paper mainly describes a method remedying their weak point for the clinical event extraction by leveraging both the Wikipedia as an additional thesaurus and a controlled vocabulary consisting of clue words. In addition, without any medical dictionary for Korean language, native technical terms are translated via the Wikipedia as if an English-Korean medical dictionary is employed.

To determine the semantic type of an event, these resources are imported as features and they are combined in conditional random fields (CRF) which can freely compose arbitrary features [4].

The rest of this paper is organized as follows. The related work section describes about recent clinical event extraction researches, feature selection from the Wikipedia, and recent researches for information retrieval in Korean EMR systems. In the section 3, we mainly describe our proposed features which are extracted from the Wikipedia and the UMLS, and collected clue word list. Results of our experiment are described in the Section 4, and the discussion and conclusion of our work are followed in Section 5 and 6.

2   Related Work

Past studies have adopted machine learning models or rule-based methods for the extraction of clinical events from clinical narratives written in English or a single language [5]. For example, i2b2 (informatics for integrating biology & bedside) has held shared tasks since 2007, and the recent tasks were identifying clinical concepts and their relationships [6], [10]. Most participants used rules or the CRF to identify clinical concepts.

Clinical events can be categorized as two or more various tags which are used in an application, such as medical problems, clinical actions, and/or results [6, 7, 8]. For instance, categories in the i2b2 challenges were 'medical problem', 'treatment', and 'diagnostic test'. The V-model for summarizing medical history subdivides them such as 'symptom and sign' (Sx), 'purpose of visit' (purpose), 'diagnostic test', 'finding', 'diagnosis' (Dx), 'operation', 'treatment' (Tx), 'medication' (Mx), 'place' (Visit), and 'event occurrence time' (TAP; time anchoring point). Previous studies on the semantic classifications mainly used the CRF to identify clinical events and classify them into a certain semantic type simultaneously.

The CRF allows arbitrary features and captures the dependencies among neighbor labels [9]. Commonly used features in the CRF are n-gram words, lexical features, morphological features, and POS tags [11]. In Medical Language Processing, medical thesauruses have been used to import domain knowledge such as UMLS, SNOMED-CT, MeSH [12,13,14].

Because of high usability of the CRF for the feature selection, researchers have proposed novel features improving the performance of their models. The Wikipedia is one of the novel resources in text processing. [15] imported a real-world knowledge derived from the Wikipedia to overcome the shortages of the bag-of-word approach.[11] presented a probabilistic model to integrate extraction and mining tasks on biographical texts from the Wikipedia. On the other hand, two features of the Wikipedia were utilized; first one is the category hierarchy of a term to be used in our semantic classification, and second one is their link between pages in both English and Korean Wikipedia which are used as a technical term translator.

In Korean medical language processing researches, [16] used the CRF to identify entities which were related to states of tumors in liver CT reports, and Jang et al proposed a method transforming a sequence into a single sequence combined with both an UMLS feature and clue words to be used in hidden Markov model. They applied the idea to extract patient's symptoms, clinical therapies, and performances.

In the following chapter, we introduce our method leveraging the Wikipedia and a controlled vocabulary to redeem the limitation of using the standard thesaurus only.

3   Leveraging Wikipedia and Context Feature

3.1   Clinical Event Extraction

Our research is based on the concept of the V-Model, which identifies descriptions related to clinical history and classifies semantic types of each clinical event. A description is a unit representing status of a key event, and it can be from a word to a phrase or wider boundary. For example, a symptom can be a word or a phrase such as 'azotemia' or 'prerenal azotemia', or wider boundary like 'prerenal azotemia 발생(occurred)'.

Following the tag set from [3], we defined our tag set consisting of Sx, Test, Finding, Dx, Tx, Mx, Purpose, Visit, and TAP as described in the previous chapter. The operation and treatment tags were merged because these tags had semantic similarity causing an ambiguity problem, and the operation tag rarely appeared in our corpus.

POS tags are imported because the clinical events were a member of a noun or an adjective phrase in our corpus, and they are used for the purpose of identifying boundaries of clinical events. Hierarchical tree structures of categories in thesauruses are utilized as a piece of evidence of the semantic classification. The thesauruses are the

UMLS as well as the Wikipedia. An additional feature is a list of deterministic clue words for certain semantic types. For the purpose of combining information which is derived from our observation, the features are transformed into feature vectors for each word in a text and CRF is trained with them to build an extraction model. It is implemented with MALLET [17].

By the nature of the CRF and the BIO tagging scheme [18], identifying clinical events can be performed simultaneously with classifying their semantic type. The BIO tagging scheme is a method tagging a semantic type of a token with 'B' or 'I' which 'B' means that the token is at the beginning of a boundary, and 'I' means that the token is in the middle or at the end of a boundary. For example, two tokens, 'lupus' and 'nephritis' in a subsequence "lupus nephritis", were tagged as 'lupus/B-Dx', 'nephritis/I-Dx'.

Fig. 1 represents our overall system. Discharge summaries were obtained from an EMR system of a University Hospital in Korea with Institutional Review Board approved. A POS tagging and an abbreviation resolution are performed for the preprocessing. The CRF is trained with general, dictionary, and contextual features.

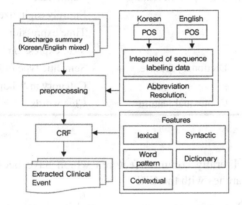

Fig. 1. Overall system flow diagram

The preprocessing is described in section 3.2, and our proposed features are presented in section 3.3.

3.2   Preprocessing

The POS tagging is performed separately according to the language of each token. To execute it separately, our preprocessor tokenizes words by whitespace first, and tokenizes a token into sub-tokens by the group of letters in the second step (e.g., "oxymetholone투여" to 'oxymetholone' and '투여'. '투여'means administration of a medication).The GENIA Tagger [19]is used for English POS tagging and the KLT(Korean Language Technology) [20]is used for Korean, then the results are integrated into one sequence.

The one of the most conspicuous problem in the clinical narratives was frequent abbreviations. Physicians frequently use abbreviations to describe clinical entities, and this is resolved by transforming them into the generic or full names found in a standardized clinical thesaurus. Medical abbreviations have been listed up in the referenced Wikipedia page. When a token in our clinical text corresponds with an entry in the list, the matched entry is used as the full name of the abbreviated word.

3.3   Feature Extraction

Features are categorized as general and semantic features as presented in Table 1. Semantic features are subdivided as dictionary and contextual features.

Table 1. Features for the clinical event extraction

Category		Feature
General feature	Lexical context feature	N-gram of tokens
	Syntactic context feature	POS tag
		Phrases of noun and adjective phrases
	Word pattern feature	Capitalized
		Entirely capitalized
		Time expression
		Visit expression
Semantic feature	Dictionary feature	Semantic type in UMLS
		Category in Wikipedia
	Contextual feature	Clue words

General feature

General features are literally common features which have been frequently used in entity extraction researches with the CRF.

- **N-gram:** The CRF is a linear chain model and it allows arbitrary features as we described above. We observed that neighbor words were effective to identify clinical events. To decide the size of N, the size was evaluated from 1 to 4, therefore, a bigram showed the best performance.
- **POS tag:** The results of the POS tagging modules are also used as features. Since Korean POS tags are different from English tags, "E_" is attached to English POS features and "K_" is attached to Korean POS features.
- **Phrase pattern:** We have observed that most clinical events were found in noun or adjective phrases of English from our texts. With the POS information of each token, this feature is exploited when a POS tag sequence is matched by a regular expression "JJ*NN+".
- **Capitalized:** This feature indicates whether the first letter is upper case alphabet in a token.
- **Entirely capitalized:** This feature indicates whether a token consists of all uppercase alphabets.

- **Time expression:** This feature indicates whether a token is matched to a word list or regular expressions of time expressions, e.g., "'?19[0-9]{2}\d?|'?20[0-9]{2}\d?|'?[0-9][0-9]\d?".
- **Visit expression:** Words corresponding to 'Visit' tag in discharge summaries were closed set and they were mostly written in Korean. Therefore, twelve correspond-ing words are collected such as "입원 (admission)", "외래 (visit outpatient de-partment)", "내원 (visit a hospital)", "본원 (our hospital)".

Semantic feature

Semantic features consist of semantic types in the UMLS as well as our proposed features. Our task-related semantic types are categorized and listed up from semantic type tree in the UMLS. The proposed features have been categorized into two groups, category information in the Wikipedia and our controlled vocabulary for contextual clue words. We call the feature on the UMLS as EF1, the feature on the Wikipedia as EF2, and the feature on our controlled vocabulary as EF3.

- **Semantic type in UMLS (EF1):** The UMLS is the integrated concept system link-ing multiple medical thesauruses. Its semantic network consists of 137 semantic types which are derived from member thesauruses. It means that each term has one or more semantic types from the multiple sources. To resolve this ambiguity, we calculated likelihoods of semantic types per each term and selected the most likely semantic type as a representative one for each term.

Table 2. Examples of categories and corresponding semantic types in the UMLS

Tag	Semantic type in UMLS
Sx	Sign or Symptom
	Injury or Poisoning
Dx	Disease or Syndrome
	Anatomical Abnormality
Tx	Therapeutic or Preventive Procedure
	Biomedical or Dental Material
Mx	Clinical Drug
	Antibiotic
Test	Medical Device
	Laboratory Procedure

Our method only uses predefined semantic types which correspond to our tag set. Table 2 shows examples of the categories which are grouped and listed upin the UMLS by our manual review.

- **Category in Wikipedia (EF2):**Wikipedia categories are leveraged inthe Wikipedia English sitefor the purpose ofimporting an additional realworld knowledge.Providing namespaces of entries by URI, the Wikipedia has utilizable semantic network among entries. The semantic networkis hierarchically structured categories. This characteristic is comparable with the relationship between a term and semantic types in the UMLS. Because a category have one or more parents in the Wikipedia, we manually reviewedhighly relavant categories to our tag set.Theyare presented in Table 3.

Table 3. Examples of highly relevant categories from Wikipedia with each semantic tag

Tag	Category in Wikipedia
Sx	Symptoms and sign
Dx	Diseases and disorders
	Medical diagnosis
Tx	Medical procedures
	Surgery
	Psychiatric treatments
	Alternative Medical treatments
	Cancer treatments
Mx	Pharmacology
	Drugs
Test	Medical tests
	Medical equipment

Fig. 2 is an example of a tree among parent categories and a word "Abdominal obesity". Among parents of the word,"Symptoms and sign" is highly relevant to the Symptom (Sx) tag.

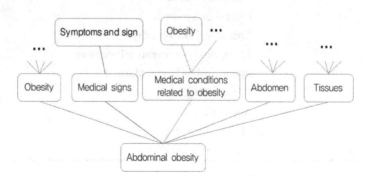

Fig. 2. An example of a hierarchical category for "Abdominal obesity" in the Wikipedia

The Wikipedia is also used as if an English-Korean medical dictionary during the extraction of this feature. Having given Korean medical dictionary showing low recall in our preliminary experiment, we evaluated our system without Korean medical vocabulary. Instead, the Wikipedia is utilized by providing a link between pages in both English and Korean site. Especially, when a certain clinical term has a Wikipedia page in their native language, its comparable English page exist in most cases. Given the page link, Korean clinical term is translated into English and the translated term is applied as a dictionary feature.

- **Clue word (EF3):**Classifying terms in a sentence may be required a consideration of the correlation how the neighbor words appear. Among neighbors, we observed highly deterministic neighbor words and patterns during data review, and they are listed up into a controlled vocabulary. Each entry has a form as (clue word or pattern, related semantic type)in the vocabulary. For example, in a sentence "퇴원 전 Pd 30 mg 로 증량 (Increased Pd to 30 mg before discharge)",readers can infer "Pd"represents a drug by some clues such as *'increase'*, *'mg'*. Our vocabulary for this feature contains 13entries.

4   Experiments

This section presents the results of our experiments performed on practical medical records to evaluate our suggestion. Experimental results are described in 4.1, and its results and performance for each feature are described in section 4.2.

4.1   Experimental Setup

We collected 150 cases of discharge summaries of patients diagnosed with systemic lupus erythematosus (SLE) in 2013. The patients were discharged from divisions of rheumatology and nephrology and the texts were from an EMR system in a university hospital in Korea. SLE is a chronic disease and leads to complications affecting various organs. For this reason, SLE patients often visit hospitals, and they have more clinical events than other patients.

Table 4. The number of events of each kind

Tag	Average per each text	The total number of tags
Sx	13.8	2,081
Dx	17.4	2,616
Test	5.2	789
Tx	3.5	539
Mx	15.5	2,325
Finding	15.0	2,255
TAP	21.2	3,189
Visit	6.6	998
Total	98.2	14,792

The experiments were evaluated by 5-fold cross validation in which 120 cases of discharge summaries were allocated to the training set and 30 cases were test set. Table 4 shows the average and total number of each tag in our corpus. *Test* and *Mx* tags appeared less than other tags.

4.2   Experimental Result

Table 5 shows our results of the clinical event extraction. Each method is how features are combined to confirm their contributions for the task. Our baseline used only general features and we denote it as (A) Baseline. Then, the results are listed by adding the features EF1 (semantic types in the UMLS), EF2 (categories in the Wikipedia), and EF3 (a list of clue words) respectively.

With measurements, we measured how each model identify correct boundaries and classify correct semantic types simultaneously. Scores are doubly presented by strict and lenient way. Strict matching means that the extracted boundary is exactly matched, and lenient matching means that we only consider core terms within the correct boundary.

Table 5. Results from feature contributions for the clinical event extraction task

Method	Strict (Lenient)		
	Precision	Recall	F measure
(A) Baseline	0.682 (0.759)	0.614 (0.683)	0.646 (0.719)
(B) A + EF1	0.695(0.762)	0.631 (0.716)	0.664 (0.738)
(C) A + EF2	0.704 (0.766)	0.626 (0.725)	0.662 (0.744)
(D) A + EF1 + EF2	0.710 (0.768)	0.634 (0.737)	0.669 (0.752)
(E) D + EF3	**0.723(0.775)**	**0.658(0.744)**	**0.688 (0.759)**

Our proposed features significantly improve its F-measureto4.2% from the baseline (A), and improve to 2.4% from general features and the UMLS (B)(p<0.01).

Table 6. Lenient results from every event for the clinical event extraction task

Method	Visit	Sx	Tx	Mx	Pur-	Finding	Dx	Test
(A) Baseline	0.771	0.720	0.534	0.734	0.786	**0.778**	0.751	0.697
(B) A + EF1	0.788	0.732	**0.557**	0.736	0.767	0.769	0.778	**0.708**
(C) A + EF2	**0.793**	**0.740**	0.553	**0.760**	**0.796**	0.777	**0.773**	0.706

Table 6 shows the F-measures for each tag, and Fig. 3 shows the distribution of Korean and English tokens from our corpus.

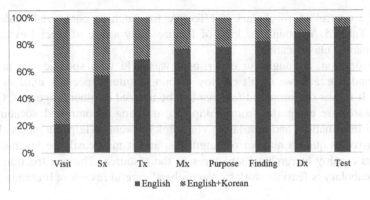

Fig. 3. The distribution of Korean and English words in our corpus

4.3   Error Analysis

We observed false positive errors which occurred when a semantic type in the UMLS covers multiple concepts and mismatches with our actual tagging, for instance, "hormone replacement" is a concept in a semantic type, "Therapeutic or Preventive procedure", and our annotation assigned the term as a Medication tag. However, the semantic type (Therapeutic or Preventive procedure) dominated the Treatment tag by probability distribution of words. Another type of errors came from insufficient training instances as our system achieved the lowest performance for the Tx tag.

5   Discussion

Our event extraction performance seemed low, but we think it may lead to further improvement when we consider the current status of similar tasks on Korean clinical texts. Our test set consists of entire sections in real clinical narratives and they are heterogeneous in terms of writing style (e.g., history of present illness, lab results, progression of hospital stay, and result of hospital stay). Moreover, our target descriptions are not only a word but also an expression therefore it is required more sophisticated language understanding processing. Compared with previous researches with Korean clinical texts, our performance is similar or higher. Jang et al reported 71% of recall for the extraction of problems, therapies, and results from a progression section in 300 texts. Oh et al reported 69% of F-measure for their extraction of tumor related entities from 100 CT reports of liver cancer patients.

We observed a tendency that the performance is improved with the Wikipedia feature when Korean/English ratio in a semantic tag is increased. Most semantic tags including more Korean tokens are reported the highest F-measure with the Wikipedia feature in Table 6 and Fig.3. In our opinion, translating Korean words via the page links in the Wikipedia positively affects the performance as if our system employs an English-Korean dictionary.

Using a controlled vocabulary is effective for catching contextual evidences as shown in Table 5. We think the kind of features play a role of crucial evidence for correct semantic classification.

In our opinion, although our experiment was held with specific two languages (English and Korean), we didn't employ certain features especially exist in Korean language. It means our proposed features can be utilized in other languages. Our proposed features are categories from Wikipedia, utilizing a controlled vocabulary for contextual information, and translating via a link between Wikipedia pages. The Wikipedia provides quite a number of languages, and it may easily be leveraged once researchers employ hierarchical structures in the resource. The construction of controlled vocabulary is feasible work by researchers' careful review of literatures.

6   Conclusion

Leveraging the Wikipedia and employing contextual information were significantly effective to the identification and classification of clinical events. In the process of identifying clinical events and classifying them from texts which were written in mixed languages, the Wikipedia was used as an additional thesaurus in clinical domain by its hierarchical category information, in addition, it played a role of an English-Korean medical dictionary with its page links which empowered the UMLS. Our controlled vocabulary was constructed to capture contextual information.

Our proposed method using these features can be utilized in other languages though we use a specific language, and researchers who use UMLS in other languages may redeem the limitation of the thesaurus by our approach leveraging the Wikipedia providing multi-language resources.

Acknowledgements. This research was supported by Microsoft Research. This work was also supported in part by Basic Science Research Program through the National Research Foundation of Korea(NRF) funded by the Ministry of Education, Science and Technology (NRF-2012R1A1A2044811), and the Brain Korea 21 PLUS Project, National Research Foundation of Korea.

References

1. Chaudhry, B., Wang, J., Wu, S., Maglione, M., Mojica, W., Roth, E., Shekelle, P.G.: Systematic review: impact of health information technology on quality, efficiency, and costs of medical care. Annals of Internal Medicine 144(10), 742–752 (2006)
2. Goodwin, T., Harabagiu, S.M.: The Impact of Belief Values on the Identification of Patient Cohorts. In: Forner, P., Müller, H., Paredes, R., Rosso, P., Stein, B. (eds.) CLEF 2013. LNCS, vol. 8138, pp. 155–166. Springer, Heidelberg (2013)
3. Park, H., Choi, J.: V-Model: A New Innovative Model to Chronologically Visualize Narrative Clinical Texts. In: Proceedings of the SIGCHI Conference on Human Factors in Computing Systems, pp. 453–462. ACM (2012)
4. Lafferty, J., McCallum, A., Pereira, F.C.: Conditional random fields: Probabilistic models for segmenting and labeling sequence data (2001)

5. Xu, Y., Hong, K., Tsujii, J., Eric, I., Chang, C.: Feature engineering combined with machine learning and rule-based methods for structured information extraction from narrative clinical discharge summaries. Journal of the American Medical Informatics Association 19(5), 824–832 (2012)
6. Sun, W., Rumshisky, A., Uzuner, O.: Evaluating temporal relations in clinical text: 2012 i2b2 Challenge. Journal of the American Medical Informatics Association 20(5), 806–813 (2013)
7. Uzuner, Ö., South, B.R., Shen, S., DuVall, S.L.: 2010 i2b2/VA challenge on concepts, assertions, and relations in clinical text. Journal of the American Medical Informatics Association 18(5), 552–556 (2011)
8. Jang, H., Song, S.-k., Myaeng, S.-H.: Text Mining for Medical Documents Using a Hidden Markov Model. In: Ng, H.T., Leong, M.-K., Kan, M.-Y., Ji, D. (eds.) AIRS 2006. LNCS, vol. 4182, pp. 553–559. Springer, Heidelberg (2006)
9. Kristjansson, T., Culotta, A., Viola, P., McCallum, A.: Interactive information extraction with constrained conditional random fields. In: AAAI, vol. 4, pp. 412–418 (2004)
10. Rink, B., Harabagiu, S., Roberts, K.: Automatic extraction of relations between medical concepts in clinical texts. Journal of the American Medical Informatics Association 18(5), 594–600 (2011)
11. Culotta, A., McCallum, A., Betz, J.: Integrating probabilistic extraction models and data mining to discover relations and patterns in text. In: Proceedings of the main conference on Human Language Technology Conference of the North American Chapter of the Association of Computational Linguistics, pp. 296–303. ACL (2006)
12. UMLS Knowledge Base, http://www.nlm.nih.gov/research/umls
13. MESH Knowledge Base, http://www.ncbi.nlm.nih.gov/mesh
14. SNOMED CT, http://www.ihtsdo.org/snomed-ct
15. Wang, P., Domeniconi, C.: Building semantic kernels for text classification using Wikipedia. In: Proceedings of the 14th ACM SIGKDD International Conference on Knowledge Discovery and Data Mining, pp. 713–721. ACM (2008)
16. Oh, H.S., Kim, J.B., Myaeng, S.H.: Extracting targets and attributes of medical findings from radiology reports in a mixture of languages. In: Proceedings of the 2nd ACM Conference on Bioinformatics, Computational Biology and Biomedicine, pp. 550–552. ACM (2011)
17. MALLET: A Machine Learning for Language Toolkit, http://mallet.cs.umass.edu
18. Ramshaw, L.A., Marcus, M.P.: Text chunking using transformation-based learning. In: Natural language processing using very large corpora. Text, Speech and Language Technology, vol. 11, pp. 157–176. Springer, Netherlands (1999)
19. GENIA Tagger, http://www.nactem.ac.uk/tsujii/GENIA/tagger/
20. KLT: Korean Language Technology, http://nlp.kookmin.ac.kr/

Impact of Stemmer on Arabic Text Retrieval

Jaffar Atwan[1], Masnizah Mohd[2], Ghassan Kanaan[3], and Qusay Bsoul[1]

[1] Faculty of Information Science and Technology,Universiti Kebangsaan Malaysia, Malaysia, Bangi
{jaffaratwan,masnizahm,qusaya068}@gmail.com
[2] School of Information Science, Japan Advanced Institute of Science and Technology, Japan
masnizahm@gmail.com
[3] Amman Arab University, Faculty of Computer Science and Informatics, Amman, Jordan
gkanaan@aau.edu.jo

Abstract. Stemming is a process of reducing inflected words to their stem, stem or root from a generally written word form. One of the high inflected words in the languages world is Arabic Language. Stemming improve the retrieval performance by reducing words variants, and in lcrease the similarity between related words. However, an Arabic Information Retrieval (AIR) can use stemming algorithms to retrieve a greater number of documents related to the users' query. Therefore, the aim of this paper is to evaluate the impact of three different Arabic stemmers (i.e. 'Information Science Research Institute" (ISRI), morphological and syntax based lemmatization "Educated Text Stemmer" (ETS), and Light10 stemmer) on the Arabic Information Retrieval performance for Arabic language, we used the Linguistic Data Consortium (LDC) Arabic Newswire data set as benchmark dataset. The evaluation of the three different stemmers ranked the best performance was achieved by light10 stemmer in term of mean average precision.

Keywords: Arabic language, Information Retrieval, Stemming, Educated Text Stemmer.

1   Introduction

Nowadays, hundreds of millions of people engages in information retrieval every day when they use a web search engine or search their email. [1] there are many search engine in the world, most of these search engine have same structure of the process derived from information retrieval ,"Information retrieval (IR) is finding material (usually documents) of an unstructured nature (usually text) that satisfies an information need from within large collections (usually stored on computers)". Any Information Retrieval IR should tackle many factors in response to the user request. These factors; retrieving the actual information required, user must be satisfied with the result, the retrieval effectiveness, and the speed of successful retrieval [2, 3].

Recently research work for Arabic language in IR had been developed and a good effort was spent. But, this work and efforts still not sufficient with what has been done in English language, where that, Arabic is an international language that is spoken in

A. Jaafar et al. (Eds.): AIRS 2014, LNCS 8870, pp. 314–326, 2014.

more than 20 countries. Arabic is also the language of the Holy Quran, the holy book of the Islamic world and is read and spoken by thousands of millions of Muslims across the globe [4, 5]. When subjected to morphological analysis, Arabic words are often ambiguous[6], so that, the problems in Arabic language are complex morphological and highly polysemous; in many situations we find it extremely necessary to disambiguate the word 'Term' senses [7].

Term conflation denotes when one term has different forms, known as linguistic variants, these variants in text occurrences conceptually share an original term. An IR system can use conflation methods to retrieve a greater number of documents related to the user query [8]. The term stemming refers to a conflation approach that attempts to find a common stem for a group of words that appear in a text, as illustrated in Table 1. In this approach, one stem for a group of words that are relevant in terms of having a related form can be found without the need to have a correct morphological root. For extract terms from words, there are four different approaches to Arabic, these approaches of stemming can be identified manually using constructed dictionaries, algorithmic light stemmers which remove prefixes and suffixes, morphological analyses which attempt to find roots, and statistical stemmers, which group word variants using clustering techniques [9].

Table 1. Many words are derived from the same root Ktb كتب

					Root(Stem)
Arabic Word	مكتب	كاتب	مكتبة	مكتوب	كتب
English Meaning	Office	Writer	Library	Written	Ktb

The research presents result of an experimental study of comparison of the three stemmers for Arabic language in information retrieval using the standard information retrieval evaluation as discussed later in section 4.2. Hence, the idea of comparing the three different Arabic stemmers is to shed the light on its effect in increase the information retrieval effectiveness for Arabic documents.

The remainder of this paper is organized as follows. Section 2 reviews previous work. Section 3, which is divided into three subsections, examines the process of Arabic document retrieval and describes our work. Section 4 is divided into three subsections: dataset used, performance evaluation and steps of experiment process, and an examination of performance measures. Section 5 presents the experimental results and discussions of these results. Finally, Section 6 presents the conclusions and future work.

2   Literature Review

The stemming of Arabic documents was performed manually prior to the Text Retrieval Conference (TREC) and only applied on small corpora. Later, many researchers, including both native and non-native Arabic speakers, created a considerable amount of Arabic stemming algorithms. Despite stemming errors, it has been empirically demonstrated that stemming improves retrieval in many languages, including

Arabic [10, 11]. It is noteworthy that Arabic is different from other Indo-European languages in terms of its syntax, morphology, and semantics. Since the morphological nature of the Arabic language is complex, there is a wide of body of research on this area that particularly focuses on the impact of Arabic morphology on Arabic IR (AIR).

Based on the required level of analysis, Arabic stemmers are categorized as either root-based[12] or stem-based [1], [13], [14]. In Arabic, the root is the original form of the word before any transformation process [5].However, a stem is a morpheme or a set of concatenated morphemes that can accept an affix [15], A wide body of research has been carried out in this particular of stemming domain. The focus of some re-searchers has been employed Khoja's stemmer, light stemmer, N-gram stemming, statistical stemmers, root-extraction stemmer and Lemmatization stemmer called the Educated Text Stemmer (ETS), to improve performance of Arabic IR (Table 2 illu-strate summery of some used stemmers techniques).

A superior root-based Arabic stemmer is Khoja's stemmer presented by[16]. The Khoja algorithm removes suffixes, infixes, and prefixes "as example shown in table 3" and uses pattern matching to extract the roots. However, the algorithm suffers from problems especially with names and nouns, on the other hand, there have been several proposed Arabic stem-based (light) algorithms [10, 17-20].The most widely used Arabic light stemmer is light10 developed by [18, 20]. Light stemming does not deal with patterns or infixes; it is simply a process of stripping off prefixes and/or suffixes. Unfortunately, the unguided removal of a fixed set of prefixes and suffixes causes many stemming errors especially where it is hard to distinguish between an extra letter and a root letter. Although light stemmers produce fewer errors than aggressive root-based stemmers, aggressive stemmers reduce the size of the corpus significantly. Both Arabic root-based and stem-based algorithms suffer from stemming errors. The main cause of this problem is the stemmer's lack of knowledge of the word's lexical category (e.g., noun, verb, and preposition).

Table 2. Summary of some used stemmers techniques

Refs	Datasets	Proposed	compared	domain	
[16]	Manual collected	Khoja's stemmer	-	NLP	
[10]	TREC 2001	light stemmer	[16]	IR	
[21]	Manual collected	N-gram stemming	Bag of words "without stemming"	TM	
[22, 23]	TREC 2001	N-gram stemming	Bag of words "with stemming"	IR	
[18], [20]	TREC 2001	light10, light8, light3, and light2.	[16]	IR	
[24]	TREC 2001	root-extraction stemmer (IRSI)	[16, 20]	IR	
[9]	Manual collected	Educated Text Stemmer (ETS),	[16]	IR	

[25]Shows that light stemming reduces over-stemming errors but increases under-stemming errors. On the other hand, heavy stemmers reduce under-stemming errors while increasing over-stemming errors. Since the Arabic language has more than 10,000 independent roots [26], it is time consuming and not sufficient to use a dictionary to recover wrongly stemmed words. The N-gram stemming technique is ineffective for Arabic text processing [21-23];The stem-based n-grams generally outperformed the word-based n-grams. however, Khoja's root-extraction stemmer [16] and Larkey's light stemmer [18, 20] are the two most effectual Arabic stemmers. Furthermore, [20] propose multiple light stemmers that depend on heuristics, which – along with statistical stemmers – would be able to handle all instances of co-occurrence in Arabic text retrieval.

Table 3. Example of suffix, infix and prefixes

suffix	infix	prefixes
	التحديات الإقليمية والدولية	
ها، ان، ات، ون، ين، يه، ية، ه، ة، ي	ت , ا , ل , و	ال، وال، بال، كال، فال، لل، و
التحدي الإقليم والدول	التحدات الإقليمية والدولية	تحديات إقليمية دولية
	تحد إقليم دول	

However, for cross-language retrieval, light stemmers are more effectual than morphological stemmers, which deal with the root of each word. Additionally, [27] investigates the impact of enhanced morphological analysis, particularly in terms of context-sensitive morphology, on monolingual AIR. Furthermore, comparative analysis of context-sensitive morphology and non-context-sensitive morphology found that the former is more effective in AIR than the latter; moreover, [24] state that employing a root-extraction stemmer for the Arabic language yields the same result as the Khoja stemmer (without using a root dictionary). Furthermore, the root-extraction stemmer is equal to light stemmers in monolingual document retrieval tasks. Nevertheless, (Khoja 2001)'s method, which initially removes the prefixes and suffixes of terms, later checks the root dictionary list. If a term is found in the list, it returns the root; if not, it returns the original word without modifying it.

It is noteworthy that paragraph in Arabic language contains morphology and syntactic structure, Arabic morphology in IR is aimed at finding words with identical or relevant meanings. Furthermore, it has been identified that by means of indexing Arabic text, the efficiency of retrieving words or stems can be substantially increased by using roots [28], on the anther side syntactic structure[17] introduces new stemming techniques that minimize stemming errors in light stemming, which improved retrieval results in some cases. He used a modified version of the light10 stemmer, developing three new versions: light11, light12 and light13. The modified version of light10 uses the grammatical and morphological rules of Arabic words to validate affixes. The three versions perform slightly better than the light10 stemmer, with light13 improving recall significantly when using relevance feedback over the TREC and Arabic GigaWord collections.

Lemmatization is an advanced stemming process that involves the usage of vocabulary and morphological analysis to reduce inflected (or sometimes derived) words to their stem, base, or root, generally from a written word form. Recently, [9] a new Arabic lemmatizer has been developed that has a high range of accuracy; it uses syntactical knowledge to make stemming decisions. [9] proposes an Arabic advance stemmer called the Educated Text Stemmer (ETS), which uses the [16] and [20] root-based stemmers. The Khoja method uses a root-base stemmer that removes suffixes, infixes, and prefixes (as mentioned above in Table 3) but also uses pattern matching to extract the roots, whereas Larkey's light10, a well-known Arabic light stemmer that does not deal with patterns or infixes, simply strips off prefixes and/or suffixes. The ETS lemmatizer tackles the Arabic word lexically, which is a drawback compared to other types of Arabic stemmers [9]. It uses a new and long list of affixes and short list of stopwords to distinguish between noun and verb. ETS consist of two main algorithms, initial algorithm which stems the word according to its previous stopword. Second one, stem the word by removing some affixes, and then use pattern matching to compare the result word to a group of similar words in terms of a common threshold. In general, the ETS is computationally expensive, its initial algorithm fail to improve IR due to long list of affixes and the lack of stopwords lists that can distinguish between verb and noun.

[29] introduce work similar to that of [9], which is also based on light10 [20], to handle the problem of the broken plural, which other stemmers are unable to do effectively. They propose a set of rules for detecting broken plural patterns and transforming these to their singular forms. Their method also uses a corpus to see whether the word resulting from the proposed transformation exists in the corpus or not. Moreover, the same process is also applied to remove certain prefixes and suffixes. At the end of the process, if the resulting word appears in the corpus, then this word is considered to be the stem. Their stemmer is applied to a corpus consisting of about one million tokens and is able to achieve high accuracy; however, it has not tested on an AIR system. The lemmatizers proposed by [20, 29] have not been tested against standard benchmarks or compared with each other. Furthermore, they use different rules in normalization and different stopwords lists. However, the results of their work indicate that, as stated earlier, a stemmer should tackle the word morphologically and be careful for the set of affixes to be removed from that word.

Table 4. The weakness of stemmers' techniques

Stemmers	Error type
Root base	Over-stemmer
Light, Root base	Under-stemmer
N-gram	Miss-stemmer

These stemming limitations can cause problems in applications that have strict word matching requirements. The goal of any new stemmer is to address stemming accuracy by avoiding over-stemming, under-stemming, and miss-stemming errors (as illustrated in table 4) without adding too much complexity to the stemming algorithm and without using any type of morphological analysis. In this research, we evaluate the impact of three different Arabic stemmers on document retrieval compared to raw data retrieval without stemming.

3   Arabic Document Retrieval

In this section discuss the process of document retrieval ranking which include: Pre-processing features weighting, Querying and IR model, where the preprocessing and features weighting will apply on dataset "documents" and query, then the cosine similarity will be used to rank documents relevant to query.

3.1   Preprocessing

Pre-processing phase is the first phase in each retrieval system. This phase, very important phase considering in document representation. Its concern to preprocess of the text in the corpus (collection) to select which terms to be indexed. During this phase other operations performed like, normalization, stopwords removal, and stemming.

3.1.1   Normalization and Tokenization

The corpus and queries were normalized according to the following steps, same normalization used by [20]:
- Remove punctuation, non-letters, diacritics (primarily weak vowels). Some entries contained weak vowels, removal made everything consistent.
- Replace إ ,أ, and آ with ا
- Replace final ى with ي
- Replace final ة with ه.

Tokenization is the process of split text into token. In this research after normalization and before stemming, the full word is considered a token and the white space its boundaries.

3.1.2   Stopwords Removal

Words that are frequently occurred in the documents are called stopwords, these words does not give any hint value to the content of their documents. The early elimination of stopwords during indexing will speed up the system processing and generally improve retrieval effectiveness [30]. There is no standard stopwords list to use in an IR experiment for the Arabic language. In this research we use a list included in Khoja for ISRI, [31] stopwords list for Light10, and for ETS its stopwords list.

3.1.3   Stemmers

3.1.3.1   ISRI

ISRI stemmer which is a rule based stemmer, stem the word according to specific rules to find its root similar to Khoja stemmer but without root dictionary. ISRI extract the trilateral and quadrilateral roots using 47 patterns comparing the remaining part of the word, after algorithm starting with normalization of word and with affixes removal.

3.1.3.2 ETS

This Arabic lemmatizer sharing features from two basic stemming process light and rule base stemmer with large number of patterns and affixes. This stemmer use different rules based on syntactic knowledge to determine the stemmed word is noun or verb. It depends on stopwords preceding verbs and nouns, the words start with "ال" are nouns, the word follows a verb is noun if it is not a stopwords, the un-flagged words are identified using noun and verb dictionaries as a lookup table. At the end the light stemming applied on nouns and Khoja root-based stemmer applied on verbs.

3.1.3.3 Light10

Light10 Arabic stemmer does not deal with patterns or infixes; it is simply the process of stripping off prefixes and/or suffixes, as shown in Table 5. Light10 stemmer is used in stemming process and we followed the same steps by Larkey's [20]:

- Remove "و" ("and") if the remainder of the word is 3 or more characters long.
- Remove any definite article (e.g. prefix) that leaves two or more characters.
- Go through the list of suffixes once in the (right to left), removing any that are found at the end of the word, if this leaves two or more characters.

Table 5. Suffixes and prefixes that are removed by Light10

Prefixes	Suffixes
ال، وال، بال، كال، فال، لل، و	ها، ان، ات، ون، ين، يه، ية، ه، ة، ي

The "prefixes" are actually definite articles and a conjunction. The light stemmers do not remove any strings that would be considered Arabic prefixes.

3.2 Querying and IR Model

Query processed same as document in preprocessing phase. IR model for ranking and finding similarity when searching documents. We use Vector Space (VS) model, VS is simple for implementing term weighting ranking and relevance feedback [30]. Cosine similarity is a similarity measure that is widely used in text document information retrieval [12]. Cosine similarity is used to measure the similarity between document and the query. For measuring two documents, the cosine similarity of $(\vec{t_a})$ and $(\vec{t_b})$ is determined by:

$$SIM_C(\vec{t_a}, \vec{t_b}) \; \frac{\vec{t_a} \cdot \vec{t_b}}{|\vec{t_a}| \times |\vec{t_b}|} \tag{1}$$

Where $\vec{t_a}$ and $\vec{t_b}$ are m-dimensional vectors within the term set T $\{t_1...t_m\}$. All the terms associated with their weight in the document correspond to a specific non-negative dimension. Consequently, the cosine similarity is non-negative and is enclosed in [0, 1]. In addition, the cosine similarity is independent of document length; this feature is considered as a vital property of cosine similarity. For example, to measure the cosine similarity between two identical copies of a document, measurements of d are combined to obtain a new pseudo document d_0. Hence, the cosine similarity between d and d_0 is 1, and therefore, the two documents are considered identical.

4   Experiments

This study explores the use of three Arabic stemmers in Arabic document retrieval, raw data, light 10, ETS and ISRI stemmer and their effects on AIR. We used the popular bag-of-words (BOW) methodology for document clustering because it is language independent. The BOW method does not depend on word meaning and performs well with noisy texts [34]. We also used a simple Boolean weighting method. In this method, 1 represents the presence of the term in the document and 0 represents its absence. (Term Frequency (TF) x Inverse Document Frequency (IDF)) (*TF x IDF*) weighting was used for the weighting process. In this approach, i denote the weight of the term and d represents the number of occurrences relative to proportional assignment. In the case of an inverse proportion, d is assigned as the number of documents in which the term occurs:

$$w_i = tf_i \cdot log\left(\frac{N}{df}\right) \tag{2}$$

Where N is the number of documents, tf_i is the number of term that belongs to document i and df is number of term appeared in all documents.

The study evaluates these stemmers using the standard recall and precision measures as the basis for comparison, In addition, we compare between three stemmers based on similarity. It answers the following questions:

a.   What is the effect of the stemmer on Arabic retrieval?
b.   How sensitive is retrieval to the use of stemmer?
c.   Which stemmers have high similarity?
d.   Which one of the stemmer, the light, the root based or the lemmatizer (i.e. advance stemmer) is superior to each other?

First, performance of term weighting scheme with elimination of stopwords was compared as baseline, and then with ISRI, ETS, and then the light stemmer respectively. The effectiveness of all stemmers with the stopwords list were evaluated to determine which one achieves the optimal performance for Arabic language retrieval.

4.1   Data Set

This research used the Arabic Newswire a corpus was created by[33]. It is composed of articles from the Agence France Presse(AFP) Arabic Newswire. The data is in 2,337 compressed Arabic text data files, with 383,872 documents containing 76 million tokens over approximately 666,094 unique words. The query set associated with the LDC corpus was created for TREC 2001[32]. There were 25 topics with relevance judgments, available in Arabic, French, and English, with Title, Description, and Narrative fields. We used the Arabic titles and descriptions as queries in our experiment.

4.2   Performance Evaluation

The retrieved document(s) is considered relevant or non-relevant based on the user (searcher) knowledge of the search topics. The following IR measures are used:
- Precision: The proportion of relevant documents to all documents retrieved.

$$Precision = \frac{number\ of\ relevant\ documents\ retrieved}{no\ of\ relevant\ documents} \tag{3}$$

- Recall: The proportions of relevant documents are retrieved, out of all available relevant documents.

$$Recall = \frac{number\ of\ relevant\ documents\ retrieved}{Total\ number\ of\ relevant\ documents\ in\ the\ collection} \tag{4}$$

- Mean Average Precision (MAP): The average of precision after each relevant document is retrieved, MAP is calculated after set of queries are executed.

$$MAP = \frac{\sum_{r=1}^{n}(p(r)\ x\ rel(r))}{no\ of\ relevant\ documents} \tag{5}$$

Where r is the rank, N the number retrieve documents, $rel\ (\ )$ binary function on the relevance of a given rank, and $p\ (\ )$ precision at a given cut-off rank.

4.3   Experiment Process

The data and the query set for the experiments were processed as following:
a.   The 383,872 files in the data set were converted from UTF-8 format to Windows.
b.   Title and description for each of the 25 queries were extracted from the original query set.
c.   The corpus and queries were Normalized and Tokenization as we mentioned in section 3.1.1.
d.   Stop words list are removed.
e.   Stemming using the three Arabic stemmers.
f.   Evaluation using standard TFIDF weighting schema, cosine similarity, precision and recall, and the mean average precision for the 25 queries for three stemmers.

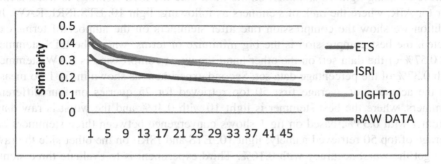

Fig. 1. Second experiment of average top 50 retrieved for 25 queries

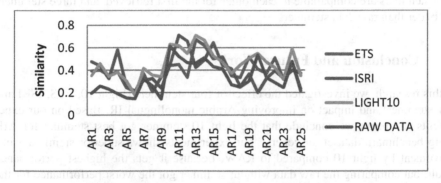

Fig. 2. Third experiment of first retrieved for 25 queries

5   Result and Discussion

This study involved three sets of experiments. First experiment is to retrieve the most related documents based on 25 queries for three stemmers and compare between them based on MAP accuracy, the second experiment is conducted to evaluate the average 25 queries with the top first 50 retrieved for three stemmers, the last experiments is to compare between three stemmers based on Similarity measure for the first retrieved from AIR.

Table 6. Mean Average Precision (MAP) and compression rate for the three runs

	RAW	ETS	ISRI	LIGHT10
MAP	0.162	0.21	**0.185**	**0.255**
Compression Rate	**0.37**	**0.57**	0.48	0.46

First experiment aims to impact three stemmers for benchmark Arabic dataset and their effect on retrieval effectiveness, and to measure the compression rate for three stemmers. So that, table 3 presented our experiment, the highest accuracy of AIR achieve by using light 10 stemmer, on the other side the ISRI stemmer is worst stemmer for AIR, where the rank of stemmers as following: light 10, ETS,ISRI, RAW. In addition we show the compression rate after stemmers on the number of terms extracted, the best compression is the big minimize of terms, where the ETS stemmer get 0.57% of the data set, on the other hand the worst compression is RAW stemmer with 0.37% of the percentage data set. Second experiment as shown in fig 1, to measure the accuracy of average first 50 top retrieved for 25 queries on four different stemmers, where the best stemmer is light 10 with 0.46% and the worst is raw data stemmer with 0.33%, based on fig 1 shows convergence between three stemmers on average of top 50 retrieved namely; light 10, ETS and ISRI, on the other side the raw data got the worst accuracy with 0.16%. Third experiment is to evaluate three stemmers based on first retrieved for each 25 queries, as shown in fig 2, light 10 ISRI and ETS stemmers are comparable to each other for the first retrieved, and three stemmers get better than raw data stemmer.

6   Conclusion and Future Work

In this research, we investigated the effect of four stemmers (Light 10, ETS, ISRI and raw stemmer) and impact on improving Arabic monolingual IR. Based on our experiments and result we conclude that the light 10 stemmer got best stemmer for AIR using benchmark dataset, in general, our experiments shows superior significant improvement by light 10 compared to RAW, because it gets the highest performance result, but comparing the raw data without stemmer got the worst performance for the four experiments. But without significant improvement between light10, ETS and ISRI stemmers.

We refute the reason of our result did not show significant between three stemmers because queries, the query is very short comparing with the documents retrieved and stemmers have challenge to detect the correct retrieved based on short query, also we concluded based on our knowledge earn from our applied AIR, stemmers not enough to enhance AIR, for that we suggest some future work based on our income, first, we suggest to apply Arabic Document Clustering to show the effect of stemmers on long query instead of short query, where the Document Clustering need to choose documents as a centroids for each clusters and that's will be enough long query to show the effect stemmers. Second, we suggestion to use Word Sense Disambiguation technique to increase the similarity between query and relevant retrieved. Third, we suggestion to use query expansion technique(s) to increase effect of retrieved.

Acknowledgment. We would like to thank linguistic Data Consortium (LDC) for providing us with LDC2001T55 Arabic Newswire Part 1 at no-cost, as one of the student recipients of the Fall 2012 LDC Data Scholarship program.

References

1. Manning, C.D., Raghavan, P., Schutze, H.: Introduction to Information Retrieval, vol. 1. Cambridge University Press, Cambridge (2008)
2. Blair, D.C.: The Data-document Distinction in Information Retrieval. Communications of the ACM 27(4), 369–374 (1984)
3. Blair, D.C.: The Data-document Distinction Revisited. ACM SIGMIS Database 37(1), 77–96 (2006)
4. Diab, M., Habash, N.: Arabic Dialect Processing Tutorial. In: Proceedings of the Human Language Technology Conference of the NAACL, Companion Volume, Tutorial Abstracts, Rochester, New York (2007)
5. Farghaly, A., Shaalan, K.: Arabic Natural Language Processing: Challenges and Solutions. ACM Transactions on Asian Language Information Processing (TALIP) 8(4), 14 (2009)
6. Al-Sughaiyer, I.A., Al-Kharashi, I.A.: Arabic Morphological Analysis Techniques: A Comprehensive Survey. Journal of the American Society for Information Science and Technology 55(3), 189–213 (2004)
7. Al-Shalabi, R., Mustafa, A., Nada, A.: Arabic Query Expansion using Interactive Word Sense Disambiguation. In: Proceedings of the Second International Conference on Arabic Language Resources and Tools, Cairo, Egypt (2009)
8. Galvez, C., de Moya-Anegón, F., Solana, V.H.: Term Conflation Methods in Information Retrieval: Non-linguistic and Linguistic Approaches. Journal of Documentation 61(4), 520–547 (2005)
9. Al-Shammari, E.T.: Lemmatizing, Stemming, and Query Expansion Method and System. Google Patents (2009)
10. Aljlayl, M., Frieder, O.: On Arabic Search: Improving the Retrieval Effectiveness via a Light Stemming Approach. In: Proceedings of the Eleventh International Conference on Information and Knowledge Management, pp. 340–347. ACM (2002)
11. Larkey, L., Connell, M.: Arabic Information Retrieval at UMass. In: TREC-10. NIST SPECIAL PUBLICATION SP, pp. 562-570 (2002)
12. Salton, G., Buckley, C.: Improving Retrieval Performance by Relevance Feedback. In: Information Retrieval, pp. 355–364 (1997)
13. Baeza-Yates, R., Ribeiro-Neto, B.: Modern Information Retrieval, vol. 463. ACM Press, New York (1999)
14. Llopis, F., Vicedo, J., Ferrández, A.: Passage Selection to Improve Question Answering. In: Proceedings of the 2002 Conference on Multilingual Summarization and Question Answering, vol. 19, pp. 1–6. Association for Computational Linguistics (2002)
15. Alqudsi, A., Omar, N., Shaker, K.: Arabic Machine Translation: A Survey. Artificial Intelligence Review, pp. 1-24 (2012)
16. Khoja, S.: APT: Arabic Part-of-speech tagger. In: Proceedings of the Student Workshop at NAACL, pp. 20–25 (2001)
17. Nwesri, A., Eng, M.: Effective Retrieval Techniques for Arabic Text. Doctor of Philosophy thesis. RMIT University (2008)
18. Larkey, S., Ballesteros, L., Connell, E.: Improving Stemming for Arabic Information Retrieval: Light Stemming and Co-occurrence Aanalysis. In: Proceedings of the 25th Annual International ACM SIGIR Conference on Research and Development in Information Retrieval. ACM, Finland (2002)
19. Al Ameed, H.K., Al Ketbi, S.O., Al-Kaabi, A.A., Al Shebli, K., Al Shamsi, N., Al Nuaimi, N., Al Muhairi, S.S.: Arabic Light Stemmer: A New Enhanced Approach (2005)

20. Larkey, L., Ballesteros, L., Connell, M.: Light Stemming for Arabic Information Retrieval. Arabic Computational Morphology, 221–243 (2007)
21. El-Kourdi, M., Bensaid, A., Rachidi, T.: Automatic Arabic Document Categorization based on the Naïve Bayes Algorithm, pp. 51 (2004)
22. Alshehri, A.M.: Optimization and Effectiveness of N-grams Approach for Indexing and Retrieval in Arabic Information Retrieval Systems. Ph.D. Dissertation. University of Pittsburgh, Pittsburgh, PA, USA (2002)
23. Xu, J., Fraser, A.: Weischedel R Empirical Studies in Strategies for Arabic Retrieval. In: Proceedings of the 25th Annual International ACM SIGIR Conference on Research and Development in Information Retrieval, pp. 269–274. ACM (2002)
24. Taghva, K., Elkhoury, R., Coombs, J.: Arabic Stemming without a Root Dictionary. In: ITCC International Conference on Information Technology: Coding and Computing, vol. 1, pp. 152–157 (2005)
25. Paice, C.: Method for Evaluation of Stemming Algorithms based on Error Counting. Journal of the American Society for Information Science 47(8), 632–649 (1996)
26. Al-Fadaghi, S., Al-Anzi, F.: A New Algorithm to Generate Arabic Root-pattern Forms. In: Proceedings of the 11th NCC, Dhahran, pp. 391–400 (1989)
27. Darwish, K.: Building a Shallow Arabic Morphological Analyzer in One Day. In: SEMITIC 2002 Proceedings of the ACL Workshop on Computational Approaches to Semitic Languages, pp. 1–8. Association for Computational Linguistics, Stroudsburg (2002)
28. Abu-Salem, H., Al-Omari, M.: Evens MW, Stemming Methodologies over Individual Query Words for an Arabic Information Retrieval System. Journal of the American Society for Information Science 50(6), 524–529 (1999)
29. El-Beltagy, S.R., Rafea, A.: An Accuracy-enhanced Light Stemmer for Arabic Text. ACM Transactions on Speech and Language Processing (TSLP) 7(2), 2 (2011)
30. Croft, W., Metzler, D., Strohman, T.: Search Engines: Information retrieval in practice, Addison-Wesley Reading (2010)
31. Atwan, J., Mohd, M., Kanaan, G.: Enhanced arabic information retrieval: Light stemming and stop words. In: Noah, S.A., Abdullah, A., Arshad, H., Abu Bakar, A., Othman, Z.A., Sahran, S., Omar, N., Othman, Z. (eds.) M-CAIT 2013. Communications in Computer and Information Science, vol. 378, pp. 219–228. Springer, Heidelberg (2013)
32. Technology NIoSa, Data-Non-English Relevance Judgements File List, http://trec.nist.gov/data/qrels_noneng/
33. Gey, F.C, Oard, D.W: The TREC-2001 Cross-language Information Retrieval Track: Searching Arabic using English, French or Arabic queries. In: TREC 2001, pp. 16–26 (2001)
34. Khreisat, L.: Arabic Text Classification using N-gram Frequency Statistics a Comparative Study. In: Proceedings of Data Mining, DMIN 2006, USA, pp. 78–82 (2006)

Distance Measures and Stemming Impact on Arabic Document Clustering

Qusay Bsoul[1], Eiman Al-Shamari[2], Masnizah Mohd[3], and Jaffar Atwan[1]

[1] Knowledge Technology Research Group, Universiti Kebangsaan Malaysia, Malaysia
{qusaya068,jaffaratwan}@gmail.com
[2] Faculty of Computer Engineering, Kuwait University, Kuwait
eiman.tamah@gmail.com
[3] School of Information Science, Japan Advanced Institute of Science and Technology, Japan
masnizah@jaist.jp

Abstract. Clustering of Arabic documents is considered as a vital aspect of obtaining optimal results from unsupervised learning. Its aim is to automatically group similar documents into a single cluster using different similarities or distance measures. However, diverse similarities and distance measures are available and their effectiveness in document clustering with a syntactic structure of the stemming is still not obvious. Therefore, this study aims to evaluate the impact of five similarity/distance measures (i.e., cosine similarity, the Jaccard coefficient, Pearson's correlation coefficient, Euclidean distance, and averaged Kullback-Leibler divergence) with two stemming algorithms (i.e., morphology- and syntax-based lemmatization; and morphology-based Information Science Research Institute (ISRI) stemming on clustering Arabic text dataset. We aim to identify the best performing similarity and distance measures and determine which measure is most suitable for Arabic document clustering. Our experimental method, which is based on syntactic structure and morphology, outperformed other stemming methods that use any of the five similarity/distance measures for Arabic document clustering. The best performing similarity/distance measures are cosine similarity and Euclidean distance, respectively.

Keywords: Similarity/distance measures, partitional clustering, lemmatization stemming, Arabic document clustering.

1 Introduction

The advent of information and communication technology and the rapid growth of the internet have significantly increased the need for highly effective information search and retrieval systems. These technological advancements have greatly benefited English language information search and retrieval. However, it is regrettable that Arabic language has not received significant attention in this field. Compared with other languages, insufficient effort has been made to advance Arabic language information search and retrieval.

A. Jaafar et al. (Eds.): AIRS 2014, LNCS 8870, pp. 327–339, 2014.

According to [1], the Arabic language is unique in terms of grammar, morphology, and semantics. Its complex morphology makes clustering extremely difficult. However, research into Arabic morphology and document clustering has recently been undertaken. Research on Arabic document clustering focuses on fusing Arabic words that convey similar meanings. [2] advocated that indexing Arabic text using roots rather than words or stems will potentially improve the effectiveness of retrieval.

It is pointed out that the process of stemming the words to their roots in Arabic is complex due to the complexity of the Arabic structure. It was also revealed that over-stemming, under-stemming, and mis-stemming are the common stemming errors encountered and suffered by stemmers [3]. However, it has been seen that the currently used approaches to Arabic stemming concentrate on the morphological structure and ignore the Arabic basic rules of syntax, thus, leading to errors in document clustering, automatic translation, text summarization, and Natural Language Processing (NLP). In general, document clustering can be categorized as unsupervised learning. It does not require predefined categories or labelled documents. Clustering is performed on the basis of maximal similarities within intragroup objects and low similarities within intergroup objects [4].

The remainder of this paper is organized as follows. Section 2 reviews previous work. Section 3, which is divided into three subsections, examines the process of Arabic document clustering and describes our work. Subsection 3.1 describes pre-process tokenization and normalization, and Subsection 3.2 describes a method for stemming data (lemmatization algorithm). Subsection 3.3 examines various similarity/distance measures. Section 4 is divided into two subsections: an explanation and discussion of clustering data using the K-means algorithm, and an examination of performance measures. Section 5 presents the experimental results and analysis of these results. Section 6 which presents the discussions and conclusions. Finally, future work presents in section 7.

2   Literature Review

Khoja's root-extraction stemmer [5] and Larkey's light stemmer [6] are two effective Arabic stemmers. However, [7] claims that derivational stemming is only effective for handling short queries. For long queries, the vagueness of search keys is increased. This induces greedy stemming, which affects the results. [8] states that conservative stemming is competent for identifying related materials for a long query. The application of stemmers for many languages has yielded very positive results, especially for English text retrieval (e.g., Lycos and Google). Stemmers have also been applied to other languages, including Indonesian [9], Malay [10], Slovakian [11], French [12], Dutch [13], modern Greek [14], Turkish [15], Arabic [6], Swedish [16], and German [17]. In evaluating the effect of four different similarity measure functions upon shared nearest neighbor (SNN) clustering approach, [18] employed similarity/distance measures on clustering. They carried subsequent comparison of the results, and based on the analysis of their results, they concluded that Euclidean function works best with SNN clustering approach in comparison to cosine, Jaccard, and correlation distance measures function. Similarly, [19] examined the effects of stemming and similarity/distance measures on clustering Arabic documents. It was identified that the cosine similarity and Jaccard coefficient similarity measures were more effective in partitional Arabic document clustering for identifying more coherent clusters by utilizing Information Science Research Institute (ISRI) stemming. In contrast, Pearson's correlation coefficient and averaged KL divergence did not yield good results.

Since stemming is expected to impact the other process in the system of Document Clustering, algorithm will be used to provide a definition of the rule of stemming. Such rule is based on the syntactic structure of word as a solution to overcome the morphological complexity and syntax by solving the three types of errors namely the mis-stemming, under-stemming and over-stemming [3].

In this study, we evaluate the impact of these five similarity/distance measures on document clustering using two stemming algorithms, i.e., morphology- and syntax-based Arabic lemmatization algorithm; morphology-based ISRI stemming and compare the results to raw data clustering 'without stemming'.

3   Process of Arabic Document Clustering

This section contains a discussion on the process of Arabic document clustering which include: Normalization and Tokenization, Lemmatization stemmer algorithm and last part is Similarity/ Distance measure.

3.1   Normalization and Tokenization

During this phase, the Arabic document is processed by popular Arabic tokenizing and normalizing methods. Normalization is advantageous to be conducted before carrying out the stemming task especially in the Arabic text. This is due to the text normalization which leads into reduction of the different forms of characters in Arabic languages to make one uniform character representing those characters. On another side, the text should be broken into discrete units separated by a space or other special marker which is inserted among them so that each unit corresponds to a word in the text; this entire task as previously stated is usually called or known as tokenization. Text pre-processing was performed as follows:

- •Step 1: Conversion of the text to Unicode.
- •Step2: Removal of digits, diacritics, and punctuation marks from the   text in the Arabic dataset.
- •Step 3: Filtering of non-Arabic words.
- •Step 4: Splitting text into tokens, usually consisting only of letters.
- •Step 5: Normalizing آ ,أ ,إ to (ا). In this case, removing the hamza does not affect the root.

3.2   Lemmatization Stemming Algorithm

Based on the lemmatization algorithm reported by Al-Shammari [3], Arabic stemmers have many common characters. However, these stemmers have a primary difference in their syntactic structure. Fig.1 shows the major steps of the Arabic lemmatization algorithm where syntactic structures such as syntactic knowledge are used to determine nouns and verbs as outlined by the following Rules:

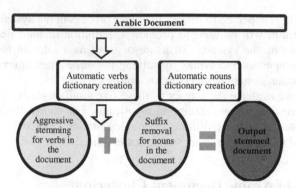

Fig. 1. Summary of lemmatization algorithm

R1.   List stop words proceeding verbs and nouns separately.

R2.   All words that start with definite articles, such as"ال," are identified as nouns.

R3.   Any word following a verb is identified as either a stop word or a noun. If this word is identified as a noun, it is added to the noun dictionary.

R4.   Using the noun and verb corpus as a lookup table will allow identification of un-flagged nouns.

These Rules were generated by Al-Shammari [3].

Table 1 shows examples of noun and verb identification according to these four Rules.

Table 1. Examples illustrating how syntactic structure identifies nouns and verbs

Example of lemmatization algorithm					
سعره	ازداد	المنتج	طلب	ازداد	كلما
the price	It increased	the product	order	increased	whenever
noun	verb	noun	noun	verb	useful word preceding verb
based on the R4	based on the R4	based on the R2	based on the R3	based on the R1	based on the R1

Table (2) shows the major steps of the Arabic lemmatization algorithm Al-Shammari [3].

Table 2. Arabic lemmatization stemming algorithm

Lemmatization

Input: Arabic documents.
Noun Dictionary. Verbs Dictionary.
V: Verb dictionary (one-dimensional array sorted alphabetically).
N: Noun dictionary (one-dimensional array sorted alphabetically).
NSW: Array of stop words proceeding nouns.
VSW: Array of stop words proceeding verbs.
SW: Array of stop words (including both NSW and VSW).
Step 1: Remove useless stop words.
Step 2: Locate words attached to definite articles and proceeded by NSW, and flag
         them as nouns.
Step 3: Add nouns to the noun dictionary N.
Step 4: Locate verbs proceeded by VSW. Flag verbs in the document.
Step 5: Add identified verbs to the verb dictionary V.
Step 6: Revisit the document searching for existing nouns and verbs.
Step 7: Tokens (words) with missing tags are treated as nouns.
Step 8: Remove the remaining stop words (useful stop words).
Step 9: Apply light stemming algorithm on nouns.
Step 10: Apply Khoja's root-based stemmer on verbs.
Output: Stemmed documents.

3.3   Similarity/Distance Measures

In this study, the similarity/distance measures evaluated are averaged KL divergence, Pearson's correlation coefficient, the Jaccard coefficient, Euclidean distance, and cosine similarity.

3.3.1   Averaged KL Divergence

In document clustering, which is derived from information theory, a document is recognized or identified as a probability in terms of distribution. The measured distance between two subsequent probability distributions that refers to the similarity of two documents is known as the KL divergence. Given two distributions P and Q, the KL divergence from distribution P to distribution Q is expressed as:

$$D_{KL}(P||Q) = P \, log(\frac{P}{Q}) \tag{1}$$

For such document circumstances, the discrepancy between two distributions of words is expressed as:

$$D_{KL}(\overrightarrow{t_a}||\overrightarrow{t_b}) = \sum_{t=1}^{m} w_{t,a} \times log(\frac{w_{t,a}}{w_{t,b}}) \tag{2}$$

However, the KL divergence is not symmetric, i.e., DKL (P∥Q) ≠ DKL (Q∥P). Consequently, it is not a true metric. Therefore, this study uses averaged KL divergence, which is defined as:

$$D_{AvgKL}(P||Q) = \pi_1 D_{KL}(P||M) + \pi_2 D_{KL}(Q||W) \tag{3}$$

Where π_1=P/ (P+Q), π_2=Q/ (Q+P), and M = π_1 P+π_2 Q for documents and the following formula illustrates the calculation of averaged KL divergence is expressed as:

$$D_{AvgKL}(\vec{t_a}||\vec{t_b}) = \sum_{t=1}^{m}(\pi_1 D_{KL}(w_{t,a}||w_t)\pi_2 D_{KL}(w_{t,b}||w_t)) \tag{4}$$

Where $\pi_1 = \frac{w_{t,a}}{w_{t,a}+w_{t,b}}, \pi_2 = \frac{w_{t,b}}{w_{t,b}+w_{t,a}}$ and w_t=$\pi_1 \times w_{t,a} + \pi_2 \times w_{t,b}$. It is evident that symmetry is guaranteed by the average weighting between two vectors. However, the divergence from document i to document j is symmetric to the divergence from document j to document i.

3.3.2   Pearson's Correlation Coefficient

Pearson's correlation coefficient is another similarity measure. It is prepared in different forms and gauges the degree of association between two vectors. Given the term set T= $\{t_1...t_m\}$, a commonly employed form can be expressed as:

$$SIM_P(\vec{t_a}, \vec{t_b}) = \frac{m\sum_{t=1}^{m} w_{t,a} - w_{t,b} - TF_a \times TF_b}{\sqrt{[m\sum_{t=1}^{m} w_{t,a}^2 - TF_a^2][m\sum_{t=1}^{m} w_{t,b}^2 - TF_b^2]}} \tag{5}$$

Where $TF_a=\sum_{t=1}^{m} w_{t,a}$ and $TF_b=\sum_{t=1}^{m} w_{t,b}$. Pearson's correlation coefficient differs from other similarity measures in that it ranges from −1 to +1. It is 1 when $\vec{t_a}=\vec{t_b}$. In subsequent experiments, the distance measure, D_p = 1-SIM_p, is utilized when $SIM_p \geq$ 0, and D_p=| SIM_p| is used when SIM_p< 0.

3.3.3   Jaccard Coefficient

The Jaccard coefficient, a similarity measure, gauges similarity between objects on the basis of the size of the intersection divided by the union of the objects. In text documents, the Jaccard coefficient is used to compare the total weight of shared terms with the total weight of the terms that are present in either of the two documents and are not shared terms. This can be expressed as follows:

$$SIM_J(\vec{t_a}, \vec{t_b}) = \frac{\vec{t_a}.\vec{t_b}}{|\vec{t_a}|^2 \times |\vec{t_b}|^2 - \vec{t_a}.\vec{t_b}} \tag{6}$$

The Jaccard coefficient similarity measure ranges between 0 and 1. It is 1 when $(\vec{t_a}) = (\vec{t_b})$ and 0 when $(\vec{t_a})$ and $(\vec{t_b})$ are incoherent. The resulting tance measure is shown as D_J =1-SIM_J and is used in our experiments.

3.3.4   Euclidean Distance

Euclidean distance is a measure used in clustering problems such as document clustering. This measure is also used to establish the default distance used by the K-means algorithm. For measuring the distance between text documents, d_a and d_b are represented by their term vectors $\vec{t_a}$ and $\vec{t_b}$, respectively. The Euclidean distance of these two documents is expressed as:

$$D_E(\vec{t_a}, \vec{t_b}) = \left(\sum_{i=1}^{m}|w_{t,a} - w_{t,b}|^2\right)^{1/2} \tag{7}$$

Based on the above equation, the term set is T {t₁...tₘ}, and as previously mentioned, the TFIDF value is used as term weight, i.e., $w_{t,a}$ = tfidf ($d_{a,t}$).

3.3.5   Cosine Similarity

Cosine similarity is a similarity measure that is widely used in text document information retrieval [20]and clustering applications [21]. For measuring two documents, the cosine similarity of $(\vec{t_a})$ and $(\vec{t_b})$ is determined by:

$$SIM_C(\vec{t_a}, \vec{t_b}) \frac{\vec{t_a}.\vec{t_b}}{|\vec{t_a}| \times |\vec{t_b}|} \tag{8}$$

Where $\vec{t_a}$ and $\vec{t_b}$ are m-dimensional vectors within the term set T {t₁...tₘ}. All the terms associated with their weight in the document correspond to a specific non-negative dimension. Consequently, the cosine similarity is non-negative and is enclosed in [0, 1]. In addition, the cosine similarity is independent of document length; this feature is considered as a vital property of cosine similarity. For example, to measure the cosine similarity between two identical copies of a document, measurements of *d* are combined to obtain a new pseudo document d_0. Hence, the cosine similarity between *d* and d_0 is *1*, and therefore, the two documents are considered identical.

However, none of the distance measures is a proper metric. To be qualified as a proper metric, a measure *d* must satisfy the following four conditions [22].

Let *x* and *y* be any two objects in a set, and d(*x*, *y*) be the distance between *x* and *y*.

- The distance between any two points must be non-negative, i.e., d(*x*, *y*) ≥ 0.
- The distance between two objects can be zero only if the two objects are identical, i.e., d(*x*, *y*) = 0 if and only if *x* = *y*.
- The distance must be symmetric, i.e., the distance from *x* to *y* equals the distance from *y* to *x*, i.e., d(*x*, *y*) = d(*y*, *x*).

The measure must satisfy triangle inequality, i.e., d(*x*, *z*) ≤ d(*x*, *y*) + d(*y*, *z*)

4   Experiments Settings

We used the popular bag-of-words (BOW) methodology for document clustering because it is language independent. The BOW method does not depend on word meaning and performs well with noisy texts [23]. We also used a simple Boolean weighting method. In this method, *1* represents the presence of the term in the document and *0* represents its absence. (Term frequency (tf) *x* inverse document frequency (idf)) (*TF x IDF*) weighting was used for the weighting process. In this approach, *1* denote the weight of the term and *d* represents the number of occurrences relative to proportional assignment. In the case of an inverse proportion, *d* is assigned as the number of documents in which the term occurs:

$$w_i = tf_i \cdot lo\, g\left(\frac{N}{df}\right) \tag{9}$$

Where N is the number of documents, tfi is the number of term that belongs to document i and df is number of term appeared in all documents.

For the testing dataset, we experimented with three similarities and two distance measures using Lemmatization stemming, morphology and syntactic structure from [3], comparing with result of [19], where they compared between ISRI stemming using morphological analyser from [24] and raw data "without stemming". The main differences being that Lemmatization does not have error rates, ISRI has over-stemming, and Raw Data "without stemming" has under-stemming [19].

4.1   Clustering

[25] state that cluster analysis is the process of grouping similar objects into clusters. Cluster analysis is used in various domains such as data mining, text mining, information retrieval, and pattern recognition. K-means is a popular partitional clustering method with linear time complexity [26]. It has been established that K-means is very efficient when used with distance measures aim at reducing intra-cluster distances.

The Euclidean distance and the averaged KL divergence are considered as distance measuring methods. Meanwhile, cosine similarity, Jaccard coefficient, and Pearson's coefficient, are similarity-measuring methods. This study uses a simple transformation to transform similarity measures to distance values. Because both cosine similarity and Jaccard coefficient are bounded in (0, 1) and monotonic $D = 1-SIM$ is used as the value of the corresponding distance. Pearson's correlation coefficient ranges from −1 to +1; therefore, $D=1-SIM$ is used when $SIM \geq 0$ and $D = |SIM|$ is used when $SIM < 0$.

4.2   Performance Measure and Datasets

This study employed an overall purity measure and an overall F-measure to assess external quality. These two measures are popular document clustering measures [21], [26]. The existence of higher overall purity and F-measures provides the best cluster.
Purity measures the degree of occurrence of documents from primarily one class in each cluster. For a specific cluster j of size nj, Where nji indicates the number of documents from class i assigned to cluster j.

The F-measure cluster validation metric combines precision and recall concepts from information retrieval. All the clusters are considered as the results of classes, and each class is assumed to be the desired set of documents for that classes. The F-measure value occurs at the interval (0, 1) and larger F-measure values correspond to higher clustering quality.

The tested dataset consisted of 1,680 documents, classified into four categories: art, economics, politics, and sports [27].

5   Analysis and Results

This study involved three sets of experiments. Each experiment was performed five times using various initial seed sets. The presented results are the averaged values from all five independent runs.

5.1   First Experiment

The first experiment aims to cluster documents under two different classes. Based on the results presented in Table 3, the highest value is obtained using the Cosine and Jaccard and the lowest value using the Pearson similarity with all methods stemming. The best value in Cosine and Jaccard similarities are 1 times better than Pearson similarity. Comparison between the same distances revealed that the highest value is obtained by using the Euclidean (0.85%) with Lemmatization method and the lowest value is found using Averaged KL divergence (0.75%) with the same method. In addition, the best value in Euclidean distance is 1 times better than it is found with Averaged KL divergence with lemmatization method, but with the ISRI and raw data methods, the best value in Averaged KL divergence (0.75%) is better than Euclidean (0.6%). The best value in Averaged KL divergence is 1 times better than Euclidean. And in comparing between the similarity and distance from our results, it is find that the similarity is 1.2 times better than the distance. Additionally, Clustering purity and F-measure using lemmatization outperformed those using ISRI and clustering raw data.

5.2   Second Experiment

The second experiment is conducted to cluster documents belonging to three classes. The results are presented in Table 4. In comparing between the values of the same similarities, the results displayed that the highest value is achieved with Jaccard with lemmatization method and the lowest value with Pearson with all methods of stemming. Moreover, the best value with Jaccard similarity is 1.4 times better than that with Pearson similarity. For the comparison conducted between the values of the same distances, it was found that the highest value (0.77%) is with Euclidean with lemmatization method and the lowest value (0.67%) is with Averaged KL divergence with same method of stemming.   The best value with Euclidean distance is 1.1 times better than that with Averaged KL divergence. But with ISRI and raw data method, the best value with Averaged KL divergence (0.6%) is better than that with Euclidean distance (0.43%) and it is estimated 1.2 times better than that with Euclidean distance. In comparing between the values of similarity and distance based on our results, the similarity value is 1.2 times better than the distance.

5.3   Third Experiment

The same experiments are performed but for four classes, Based on the results presented in Table 5, In comparing between the values of the same similarities, the results revealed that the highest value (0.7%) is achieved using Cosine, and the lowest value (0.2%) is with Pearson with without stemming method. The best value with Cosine is 1.5 times better than Pearson. For the values of the same distances, it was found that the highest value is obtained with Euclidean with all methods of stemming and the lowest value is with Averaged KL divergence with all methods of stemming. Thus, the best value with Euclidean is 1.5 times better than Averaged KL divergence.

For comparing between the values of similarity and distance measures, the results showed that the similarity is 1.6 times better than the distance. However, lemmatization showed better results than the ISRI and better than the raw data, where the best value is 70% for the cosine similarity and 65% for the Euclidean distance.

6   Conclusions and Future Work

Based on the experimental results, it can be concluded that similarity/distance measures are more effective in the lemmatization stemming of morphological and syntactically structured words than ISRI and raw data, that is expected where ISRI has over-stemming, and Raw Data "without stemming" has under-stemming.The findings also showed that for the similarity measure Cosine and Jaccard similarity achieved better result than Pearson similarity, and for the distance measure, Euclidean achieved better result than Averaged KL divergence when used on lemmatization stemmer.

Generally, based on the findings it was revealed that Cosine similarity is better than Euclidean distance and the rank of the similarity and distance depends on the size of the documents, where the rank for small number of documents was Jaccard. According to the small number of documents, they are ranked as follows: Cosine, Euclidean, Pearson and Averaged KL divergence. However, based on the big number of documents, the rank is found as follows: Cosine, Euclidean, Jaccard, Pearson and Averaged KL divergence.

One of the aims of our study was to determine the effectiveness of the three similarity and two distance measures using lemmatization stemming with a large number of documents. The characteristics of each cluster were investigated, and it was observed that sports and economics documents were wrongly clustered owing to the existence of many similar words, such as "said" (i.e. "said player" and "said economic research"). In contrast, with word meanings, identification of the various meanings of a word was possible owing to the variety of word meanings in different contexts. Table 6 shows the Arabic word (قلب), which has three meanings as a noun.

Table 3. Overall purity and F-measure evaluations for two-class clustering (art and economics)

Stemming	Evaluations	Similarity			Distance	
		Cosine	Jaccard	Pearson's	Euclidean	DAvg KL
Lemmatiza-	Purity	**0.9**	**0.9**	0.85	**0.85**	0.75
tion	F-measure	0.89	0.84	0.84	0.84	0.74
ISRI	Purity	0.7	0.65	0.6	0.6	0.7
	F-measure	0.67	0.6	0.58	0.52	0.69
Raw Data	Purity	0.7	0.6	0.45	0.6	0.75
	F-measure	0.67	0.52	0.37	0.52	0.74

*bold: highest value.

Table 4. Overall purity and F-measure evaluations for three-class clustering (art, economics, and politics)

Stemming	Evaluations	Similarity			Distance	
		Cosine	Jaccard	Pearson's	Euclidean	DAvg KL
Lemmatiza-	Purity	0.8	**0.83**	0.56	**0.77**	0.67
tion	F-measure	0.79	0.83	0.57	0.76	0.66
ISRI	Purity	0.6	0.6	0.53	0.47	0.6
	F-measure	0.57	0.58	0.52	0.39	0.62
Raw Data	Purity	0.6	0.6	0.4	0.43	0.57
	F-measure	0.55	0.51	0.38	0.37	0.59

*bold: highest value.

Table 5. Overall purity and F-measure evaluations for multi-class clustering (art, economics, politics, and sport)

Stemming	Evaluations	Similarity			Distance	
		Cosine	Jaccard	Pearson's	Euclidean	DAvg KL
Lemmatiza-	Purity	**0.7**	0.62	0.45	**0.65**	0.42
tion	F-measure	0.66	0.59	0.46	0.6	0.37
ISRI	Purity	0.57	0.57	0.2	0.42	0.2
	F-measure	0.52	0.54	0.29	0.38	0.28
Raw Data	Purity	0.5	0.55	0.2	0.42	0.2
	F-measure	0.49	0.49	0.21	0.35	0.28

*bold: highest value.

Table 6. One Arabic word has three meanings

Categories	Word Meaning	Sentence
Sport	Center/Middle	الكرة في قلب الملعب
Politic	Core	في قلب الاحداث
Economical	Main	ارتفاع أسعار النفط يصيب قلب الاقتصاد الأمريكي

Several suggestions for future research were made. First, it is recommended that the extensions of this work in the future can apply the same Lemmatization algorithm for other languages such as Malay and Turkish, etc... Since, they have a morphological and syntactic structure. Second, we propose the generation of a new stemming which can be based on the morphological, syntactic structure, and semantics such as Singular Value Decomposition (SVD) technique [28]. Third, we propose another similarity/distance measure [29] to merge between them to increase their effectiveness on document clustering.

References

1. Khoja, S.: APT: Arabic Part-Of-Speech Tagger. In: Proceedings of the Student Workshop at NAACL, pp. 20–25 (2001)
2. Hani, A., Mahmoud, A., Martha, W.: Stemming Methodologies Over Individual Query Words for an Arabic Information Retrieval System. J. Am. Soc. Inf. Sci. 50(6), 524–529 (1999)
3. Eiman A.: Patent Application Publication of Lemmatizing, Stemming, and Query Expansion Method and System, Pub.No.:US 2010/0082333 A1, Pub.Date: Apr.1 (2010), http://Www.Google.Com/Patents/US20100082333?Printsec=Abstrac t&Source=Gbs_Overview_R&Cad=0#V=Onepage&Q&F=False
4. Ozgür, A.: A Supervised and Unsupervised Machine Learning Techniques for Text Document Categorization, Master. Thesis. Bogazici University, Turkey (2004)
5. Khoja, S., Garside, R.: Stemming Arabic Text. In: Computing Department. Lancaster University, UK (1999), http://Www.Comp.Lancs.Ac.Uk/Computing/Users/Khoja/Stemmer.Ps
6. Larkey, S., Ballesteros, L., Connell, E.: Improving Stemming for Arabic Information Retrieval: Light Stemming and Co-Occurrence Analysis. In: Proceedings of the 25th Annual International ACM SIGIR Conference on Research and Development in Information Retrieval. ACM, Finland (2002)
7. Hull, D.: Stemming Algorithms: A Case Study for Detailed Evaluation. Journal of the American Society for Information Science 47(1), 70–84 (1996)
8. Korenius, T., Laurikkala, J., Järvelin, K., Juhola, M.: Stemming and Lemmatization in the Clustering of Finnish Text Documents. In: Proceedings of the Thirteenth ACM International Conference on Information and Knowledge Management CIKM, pp. 625–633 (2004)
9. Vinsensius, V., Stéphane, B.: Indexing The Indonesian Web: Language Identification and Miscellaneous Issues. In: Presented at Tenth International World Wide Web Conference, Hong Kong (2001)
10. Tai, Y., Ong, S., Abullah, A.: On Designing an Automated Malaysian Stemmer for the Malay Language. In: Proceedings of the Fifth International Workshop on Information Retrieval With Asian Languages, Hong Kong, pp. 207–208 (2000)
11. Popovi, M., Willett, P.: The Effectiveness of Stemming for Natural Language Access to Slovene Textual Data. Journal of the American Society for Information Science 43(5), 384–390 (1992)
12. Moulinier, I., Mcculloh, J., Lund, E.: West Group at CLEF: Non-English Monolingual Retrieval, Cross-Language Information Retrieval and Evaluation. In: Peters, C. (ed.) Proceedings of the CLEF 2000 Workshop, pp. 176–187. Springer (2001)
13. Kraaij, W., Pohlmann, R.: Viewing Stemming as Recall Enhancement. In: Proceedings of SIGIR, pp. 40–48. ACM, USA (1996)
14. Greengrass, M., Robertson, M., Schinke, R., Willett, P.: Processing Morphological Variants in Searches of Latin Text. Information Research News 6(4), 2–5 (1996)
15. Ekmekcioglu, C., Lynch, F., Willett, P.: Stemming and N-Gram Matching for Term Conflation in Turkish Texts. Information Research 2(2) (1996)
16. Carlberger, J., Dalianis, H., Hassel, M., Knutsson, O.: Improving Precision in Information Retrieval for Swedish Using Stemming. In: Proceedings of NODALIDA, pp. 21–22 (2001)
17. Monz, C., de Rijke, M.: Shallow Morphological Analysis in Monolingual Information Retrieval for Dutch, German, and Italian. In: Peters, C., Braschler, M., Gonzalo, J., Kluck, M. (eds.) CLEF 2001. LNCS, vol. 2406, pp. 262–277. Springer, Heidelberg (2002)

18. Anil, P., Jitendra, A., Nishchol, M.: Analysis of Different Similarity Measure Functions and their Impacts on Shared Nearest Neighbor Clustering Approach. International Journal of Computer Applications 40(16), 1–5 (2012)
19. Qusay, B., Masnizah, M.: Effect of IRSI Stemming on Similarity Measure for Arabic Document Clustering. In: Proceedings of the Seventh Asia Information Retrieval Societies Conference, pp. 584–593. Springer, Dubai (2011)
20. Baeza-Yates, R., And Ribeiro-Neto, B.: Modern Information Retrieval, vol. 463. ACM, New York (1999)
21. Larsen, B., Aone, C.: Fast and Effective Text Mining Using Linear-Time Document Clustering. In: Proceedings of the Fifth ACM SIGKDD International Conference on Knowledge Discovery and Data Mining KDD, pp. 16–22 (1999)
22. Froud, H., Benslimane, R., Lachkar, A., Ouatik, S.A.: Stemming And Similarity Measures For Arabic Documents Clustering. In: 5th International Symposium on I/V Communications and Mobile Network (ISVC), pp. 1–4 (2010)
23. Khreisat, L.: Arabic Text Classification Using N-Gram Frequency Statistics A Comparative Study. In: Proceedings of Data Mining DMIN, pp. 78–82 (2006)
24. Taghva, K., Elkhoury, R., Coombs, J.: Arabic Stemming Without A Root Dictionary. In: ITCC International Conference on Information Technology: Coding and Computing, vol. 1, pp. 152–157 (2005)
25. Jain, K., Dubes, C.: Algorithms for Clustering Data. Michigan State University (1988)
26. Steinbach, M., Karypis, G., Kumar, V.: A Comparison of Document Clustering Techniques. In: KDD Workshop on Text Mining, pp. 525–526 (2000)
27. Al-Salemi, B., Mohammad, A.: Statistical Bayesian Learning for Automatic Arabic Text Categorization. J. Comput. Sci. 7(1), 39–45 (2011)
28. Berry, W., Browne, M.: Understanding Search Engines: Mathematical Modeling and Text Retrieva. SIAM (1999) ISBN: 0898714370
29. Manning, D., Raghavan, P., Schütze, H.: Corporation.:Introduction to Information Retrieval, 1st edn. Cambridge University Press, Cambridge (2008)

Emotional Links between Structure and Content in Online Communications

Rafael E. Banchs[1] and Andreas Kaltenbrunner[2]

[1] Human Language Technology, Institute for Infocomm Research, Singapore
rembanchs@i2r.a-star.edu.sg
[2] Social Media and Interaction, Barcelona Media Innovation Centre, Barcelona
andreas.kaltenbrunner@barcelonamedia.org

Abstract. This papers aims at studying the existence of links between the structure of online communications and the contents they are composed of. The study is conducted over two datasets of similar online discussion platforms in different languages: English and Spanish. As a result of our analysis, it is concluded that there are significant trends in the variation patterns observed over the emotional load of user generated contents that are associated to the different types of communication structures existing in the datasets. Moreover, the observed trends are quite similar for both of the studied languages, suggesting that such kind of emotional links between structure and content in online communications are language independent in nature.

Keywords: online communications, structure, user generated content, emotions.

1 Introduction

Online communications has been extensively studied along the short history of the World Wide Web [15]. While several studies have paid attention to the structure of such communications [7],[10], other studies have focused on the analysis of the contents [6],[19]. Recently, a more comprehensive approach to the online communication problem has pointed out the necessity of taking both, structure and contents, into account, as well as exploring the possible relationships between these two dimensions of online communications [11],[18].

In this work, we focus our attention on exploring the possible existence of links of emotional nature between the structure and the contents of online communications. We based our assumption on the fact, described by [12], that the width (maximum number of responses at any level) and depth (largest chain of responses) in a given online discussion tree strongly depend on the specific forum category the discussion belongs to. Their empirical results, which are theoretically supported on deliberation theory [13,14], suggest that the level of engagement of participants in an online discussion is determinant to the evolution and final structure of the resulting discussion.

Although the level of engagement depends on a complex combination of several factors, emotions can be assumed to be a key player among these factors. In this work, we explore the possible relationship between emotions, as can be measured

A. Jaafar et al. (Eds.): AIRS 2014, LNCS 8870, pp. 340–347, 2014.

from the user generated content contained in the discussion, and the structure or topology of the corresponding discussion tread.

The rest of the paper is structured as follows. Section 2 gives a brief overview over previous research on online communication analysis and provides a detailed description on the two specific works on which this work is based. Section 3 describes both the datasets and the experimental analysis, as well as discusses the most relevant results derived from the analysis. Finally, section 4 presents the main conclusions and the proposed future research.

2   Related Work

In this section we first present a brief overview over previous research on online communication, followed by a detailed description of the works on which our research is based.

2.1   Research on Online Communications

As already mentioned, online communication has been an important topic of research for at least the last ten years or so. Pioneering research in this area can be traced back to work on computer mediated communication in distance learning applications [4].

More recently, the Web 2.0 phenomenon has called the attention of researches on the social network aspects of online communication [7],[10],[16,17],[23]; as well as on user generated content analysis [6],[8],[19],[22].

Another important body of research has been developed around the growing phenomenon of opinionated content analysis. This kind of research focuses more on the analysis of the subjective nature of user generated contents and aims at determining the specific sentiments and the polarity of the opinions conveyed in them [2],[3],[20].

2.2   Previous Related Research

This work, which aims at studying the existence of emotional links between the structure of online communications and the linguistic contents they are composed of, is mainly founded on two previous studies.

The first one [12] provides an empirical evidence about the possible dependence between the structural variables of a given online discussion and its topic. In that work, the authors operationalized the structural variables of depth and width for a discussion tree as follows: the depth corresponds to the maximum number of layers through which the discussion unfolds and the width corresponds to the maximum number of comments at any level of the tree.

They considered the depth and width of a discussion tree to be proxies to the deliberation theory variables of argumentation and representation, respectively. According to this, a given online discussion tree can be classified into one of four different types of communication depending on its location into the depth-width space, in a similar way political communications are categorized into the argumentation-representation space [1]. This notion is illustrated in Fig. 1.

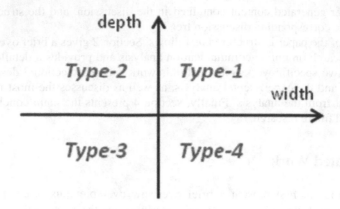

Fig. 1. The depth-width space and the four online communication type regions

As a result of their study, [12] demonstrated that the location of a given online discussion tree in the depth-width space was highly dependent on the specific category or topic being discussed. In such a way, those discussions belonging to political and other similar ideological categories tend to fall in the type-1 region, while discussions belonging to games, books and other similar categories tend to fall in the type-3 region.

The second previous related work [5] provides the empirical means for the direct estimation of the emotional load of a given document or segment of text. In that work the authors developed a human annotated lexicon denominated ANEW (Affective Norms for English Language Words).

The ANEW lexicon consists of about a thousand English frequently used words that have been individually scored along three different emotional dimensions: valence, arousal and dominance. Each of these three variables captures a different aspect of emotional load in a numerical scale that ranges from 1 (minimum degree) to 9 (maximum degree). While valence measures happiness, arousal measures anger, and dominance measures the feeling of assurance or confidence.

A similar lexicon has been also developed for the case of Spanish [21], which allows us to conduct the experimental analysis over Spanish online discussions too.

3   Empirical Analysis

In this section we describe in detail the empirical analysis that we conducted to study the differences in emotional trends between discussions of type-1 and type-3. First, we describe the datasets used for the analysis; afterwards we provide the details of the experimental analysis and present the experimental results.

3.1   Online Discussion Datasets

The empirical data collected and used for our analysis was extracted from the online discussion forum *Slashdot*(www.slashdot.com) and its Spanish version *Barrapunto*(www.barrapunto.com). These two sites are based on the same software platform, which provides a good source of experimental data as it allows for reliably reconstructing the discussion trees from the crawled html files [10].

The existence of these two (Spanish and English) online discussion forums, which are based on the same platform, also allows for the comparison of the experimental analyses in the two different languages. However, it is important to mention that the Spanish site has much less activity than the English one and, as a consequence, the volume of available data for the former case is much more restrictive.

A total of 10,012 discussion trees, compressing a little bit more than 2 million comments, were collected for the case of English, while a total of 6,252 discussion trees were collected for the case of Spanish. In both cases, the original collections were filtered by retaining only those discussion trees including at least 100 occurrences of words contained in the emotional lexicons. This should guarantee that reliable estimates of the emotional variables can be computed for each discussion tree.

Finally, type-1 and type-3 communications were identified by using a hyperbolic function centered on the median values of depth and width for each of the data collections. An adjustment factor was used to ensure that about 40%[1] of the discussions were selected as either type-1 or type-3.

The implemented hyperbolic function can be described by the following equation: $(d - d_{med}) \times (w - w_{med}) = f$; where d and w refers to depth and width, d_{med} and w_{med} refers to their corresponding median values in the considered data collection, and f is the adjustment factor. The depth and width median values observed in the case of *Slashdot* (English dataset) were $d_{med}= 8.00$ and $w_{med}= 4.07$; and the required adjustment factor for selecting 40% of the discussions as type-1 or type-3 was $f = 0.70$. In the case of *Barrapunto* (Spanish dataset), the parameters were as follows: $d_{med}= 7.00$, $w_{med}= 3.18$ and $f = 0.10$.

Fig. 2, illustrates the identification process for the case of the English dataset, and Table 1 summarizes the main characteristics of both online discussion datasets.

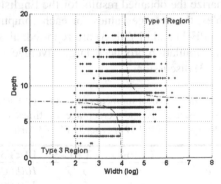

Fig. 2. Cross-plot of English discussions from *Slashdot* in the depth-width space and selected subsets of discussions within type-1 and type-3 categories

---

[1] Several experiments were conducted for different proportions by varying the adjustment factor. Similar results were always observed in those cases in which 60% or less of the discussions were selected. For proportions over 60%, the observed effects tended to fade away; and for proportions over 80%, most of the observed results were not statistically significant any more. In this work, we report those results corresponding to the 40% case.

Table 1. Main characteristics of English and Spanish online discussion datasets

Discussion Trees	English	Spanish
Originally collected	10012	6252
Filtered collection	9426	2744
Filtered type-1	1939	640
Filtered type-3	1831	556

3.2   Experimental Results

For evaluating the possible relations between structure and content, we studied the differences on the emotional variables between the two considered communications types (type-1 and type-3).More specifically, the four basic statistical moments (mean, variance, skewness and kurtosis) were computed at the discussion level for each of the three emotional dimensions (valence, arousal and dominance) according to the specific words occurring in the discussion which have been assigned emotional scores in the lexicons. Average values for each moment were finally computed over the subsets of type-1 discussions (TYPE-1) and type-3 discussions (TYPE-3).

The statistical significance of the observed differences was assessed by means of bootstrapping [9], a re-sampling method that allows for hypothesis testing. In our case, we were interested in estimating the degree of confidence with which the null hypothesis that both averaged emotional scores (for type-1 and type-3 discussions) belong to the same distribution can be rejected. In the implemented procedure, new discussion subsets were artificially generated from the original ones by using sampling with replacement. A total of 10,000 simulations were conducted in each case for confidence estimation purposes.

Table 2 and 3 summarize the obtained results for the English and Spanish datasets, respectively. In the tables, the average values for each computed moment over both types of discussions (TYPE-1) and (TYPE-3) are reported, along with the percentage of times each boot-strap simulation produced larger average values for either type-1 (T1>T3) or type-3 (T1<T3) discussions.

Table 2. Average values for the statistical moments of emotional variables estimated over both type-1 and type-3 English discussions and percentage of times each bootstrap simulation produced larger averages for type-1 (T1>T3) or type-3 (T1<T3) discussions

Average for	TYPE-1	TYPE-3	T1<T3	T1>T3
MEAN valence	*6.04*	*6.17*	*100.00*	*0.00*
MEAN arousal	*5.17*	*5.20*	*100.00*	*0.00*
MEAN dominance	*5.44*	*5.48*	*100.00*	*0.00*
VAR valence	*1.69*	*1.57*	*0.00*	*100.00*
VAR arousal	*0.92*	*0.90*	*0.00*	*100.00*
VAR dominance	*0.93*	*0.87*	*0.00*	*100.00*
SKW valence	*-0.96*	*-1.08*	*0.00*	*100.00*
SKW arousal	*0.12*	*0.05*	*0.00*	*100.00*
SKW dominance	-0.60	-0.61	40.02	59.98

Table 2. (*Continued*)

KURT valence	3.21	3.75	100.00	0.00
KURT arousal	2.82	2.87	99.98	0.02
KURT dominance	3.40	3.66	100.00	0.00

Table 3. Average values for the statistical moments of emotional variables estimated over both type-1 and type-3 Spanish discussions and percentage of times each bootstrap simulation produced larger averages for type-1 (T1>T3) or type-3 (T1<T3) discussions

Average for	TYPE-1	TYPE-3	T1<T3	T1>T3
MEAN valence	5.63	5.67	97.90	2.10
MEAN arousal	5.46	5.48	98.14	1.86
MEAN dominance	5.11	5.10	44.08	55.92
VAR valence	1.99	1.95	0.01	99.99
VAR arousal	0.95	0.93	0.04	99.96
VAR dominance	1.03	1.02	7.63	92.37
SKW valence	-0.63	-0.67	0.06	99.94
SKW arousal	-0.25	-0.26	34.14	65.86
SKW dominance	-0.27	-0.27	49.74	50.26
KURT valence	2.29	2.45	100.00	0.00
KURT arousal	2.47	2.50	96.01	3.99
KURT dominance	2.79	2.76	19.11	80.89

Several interesting observations can be drawn from Table 2 and 3. First of all, notice how for the case of the English dataset, with the exception of the skewness of dominance, all observed average differences can be regarded as statistically significant, while for the case of Spanish only three differences happen to be significant: the variance of valence and arousal and the kurtosis of the valence. This lack of statistically significant results in most of the Spanish cases can be explained by two factors: the less quantity of empirical data available for Spanish, and the richer morphology of Spanish with respect to English, which makes emotional estimation from a lemma-based lexicon a much more unreliable and noisier task. Nevertheless, it is interesting to observe that the general trends for both languages are quite similar.

From all observed differences in Table 2 and 3, the most important one in absolute terms is the drop in the kurtosis of the valence when we move from type-3 to type-1 discussions. This can be interpreted as an increment in the emotional polarization of the terms used in the discussion, which is also consistent with the observed increment in the variance of the valence. Notice that both results are statistically significant for the two languages.

4   Conclusions and Future Work

In this work, we focused our attention on exploring the possible existence of links of emotional nature between the structure and the contents of online communications. More specifically, the average variations of statistical moments for three different emotional variables were studied for two types of online discussion: type-1 (wide and deep trees) and type-3 (narrow and shallow trees).

We conducted the analysis over empirical data in both English and Spanish and observed similar and statistically significant trends for the cases of the kurtosis and the variance of the valence, being the drop in the kurtosis of the valence the most important one in absolute terms. This suggests an increment in the emotional polarization of the terms used in the discussion along this specific dimension, which measures the degree of happiness. This shows that the emotional load of the contents does actually affects the structure of the studied online communications.

As future research in this area we intend to extend our work to other languages, as well as to improve the emotional estimation in Spanish by morphologically enriching the current lemma-based lexicon.

Acknowledgements. The authors would like to thank their respective institutions: Institute for Infocomm Research and Barcelona Media Innovation Centre, for their support and permission for publishing this work.

References

1. Ackerman, B., Fishkin, J.: Deliberation Day. The Journal of Political Philosophy 10(2), 129–152 (2002)
2. Agarwal, A., Xie, B., Vovsha, I., Rambow, O., Passonneau, R.: Sentiment Analysis of Twitter Data. In: Proceedings of the Workshop on Language in Social Media, pp. 30–38. ACM, New York (2011)
3. Workshop on Computational Approaches to Subjectivity and Sentiment Analysis (WASSA), http://gplsi.dlsi.ua.es/congre-sos/wassa2011/
4. Berge, Z., Collins, M.: Computer Mediated Communication and the Online Classroom: Distance Learning. Hampton Press, Cresskill (1995)
5. Bradley, M., Lang, P.: Affective Norms for English Words (ANEW): Stimuli, Instruction manual and Effective Ratings. Technical report C-1, The Center for Research in Psychophysiology, University of Florida (1999)
6. Cassell, J., Tversky, D.: The Language of Online Intercultural Community Formation. Journal of Computer-Mediated Communication 10, 16–33 (2005)
7. Applying Social Network Analysis to Online Communications Networks. Leadership Learning Community,
   http://leadershiplearning.org/blog/nataliaca/2012-01-30/
   applying-social-network-analysis-online-communications-
   networks
8. Workshop on Content Analysis for the Web 2.0 (CAW2.0),
   http://caw2.barcelonamedia.org/
9. Davison, A., Hinkley, D.: Bootstrap Methods and their Applications. Cambridge Series in Statistical and Probabilistic Mathematics. Cambridge University Press (1997)
10. Gomez, V., Kaltenbrunner, A., Lopez, V.: Statistical Analysis of the Social Network and Discussion Threads in Slashdot. In: 17th International Conference on World Wide Web, pp. 645–654. ACM, New York (2008)

11. Gonzales, A., Hancock, J., Pennebaker, J.: Language Style Matching as a Predictor of Social Dynamics in Small Groups. Communication Research 37(1), 3–19 (2010)

12. Gonzalez-Bailon, S., Kaltenbrunner, A., Banchs, R.: The Structure of Political Discussion Networks: A Model for the Analysis of Online Deliberation. Journal of Information Technology, 1–14 (2010)

13. Habermas, J.: The theory of communicative action, I. Polity, Cambridge (1984)

14. Habermas, J.: The theory of communicative action, II. Polity, Cambridge (1987)

15. Herring, S.: Automating Analysis of Social Media Communication: Insights from CMDA. In: Proceedings of the Workshop on Language in Social Media, p. 1. ACM, New York (2011)

16. Kaltenbrunner, A., Bondia, E., Banchs, R.: Analyzing and Ranking the Spanish Speaking MySpaceC by their Contributions in Forums. In: 18th International World Wide Web Conference (2009)

17. Laniado, D., Tasso, R., Volkovich, Y., Kaltenbrunner, A.: When the WikipediansTalk: Network and Tree Structure of the Wikipedia Discussion Pages. In: 5th International AAAI Conference on Weblogs and Social Media (2011)

18. Workshop on Language in Social Media (LSM 2001),
    `http://research.microsoft.com/en-us/events/lsm2011/default.aspx`

19. Nguyen, D., Rose, C.: Language Use as a Reflection of Socialization in Online Communities. In: Proceedings of the Workshop on Language in Social Media, pp. 76–85. ACM, New York (2011)

20. Pang, B., Lee, L.: Opinion Mining and Sentiment Analysis. Foundations and Trends in Information Retrieval 2(1-2), 1–135 (2008)

21. Redondo, J., Fraga, I., Padron, I., Comesana, M.: The Spanish adaptation of ANEW (affective norms for English words). Journal of Behavior Research Methods 39(3), 600–605 (2007)

22. Rossler, P.: Content Analysis in Online Communication: AChallenge for Traditional Methodology. In: Hogrefe, Huber (eds.) Online Social Science, Cambridge (2002)

23. Szell, M., Lambiotte, R., Thurner, S.: Multirelational Organization of Large-Scale Social Networks in an On-line World. PNAS 107(31), 13636–13641 (2010)

Extraction of Semantic Features
from Transaction Dialogues

Aida Mustapha

Faculty of Computer Science and Information Technology
Universiti Tun Hussein Onn Malaysia
Parit Raja, 86400 Batu Pahat, Johor, Malaysia
aidam@uthm.edu.my

Abstract. Existing question and answering systems are mostly limited to answer queries in isolation, although the system's knowledge in determining whether a question is relevant to the previous interaction context is very important as supported in dialogue systems. Nonetheless, the problem with interpreting the input queries in both systems remains universal because utterances are typically short, single-sentenced, and may even be grammatically incorrect. This research presents a set of decision trees that form the rules in extracting semantic features encoded in dialogue utterances based on the Information Structure Theory. The extraction process is illustrated using a transaction dialogue corpus for a theater reservation system called SCHISMA. Because the basis of extraction is the informativeness in utterance within the domain knowledge, the proposed method may be used to improve research in QA systems by taking account the previous interaction context.

Keywords: Feature Extraction, Semantic, Topic and Focus, Dialogue Systems, Question-Answering Systems.

1 Introduction

Dialogue systems may be designed to be closed- or open-domain. While a closed-domain dialogue system is limited to particular field (i.e., theater, credit cards, medicine), an open-domain dialogue system is portable to cross fields with entirely different domain ontologies. At its lowest level, an open-domain dialogue system should behave like a question and answering (QA) system, whereby the system attempts to answer queries in natural language in an assortment of question types such as how, why, what [1]. However, most of the QA systems answer to queries in isolation. This is an obvious limitation because the system knowledge in determining whether a query is relevant to the previous interaction context is very important.

In many QA systems such as in [2,3,4,5,6,7], the answers to queries are usually ranked based on the standard precision and recall measurement. The rudimentary approach to such ranking ability lies in the way the utterances are interpreted in the first place, which is through terms extraction. This paper advocates

A. Jaafar et al. (Eds.): AIRS 2014, LNCS 8870, pp. 348–359, 2014.

for topical contributions in place of terms extraction to enhance the semantic understanding. This means, although utterances in a sequence of queries and answers may have the same topic as the common factor, the best answer will be based on how the topic relates to the context. For example, in a theater reservation system, the title of performance that serves as the topic may fall under different context; depending on whether it is extracted during the information-seeking or reservation activity.

To recognize the change of context in a series of question and answer exchange whether in a QA or dialogue systems, this research relies on focus of attention [8] to constrain the information that needs to be considered when judging the current context in relation to the previous interaction context. Because the context can be maintained through topics in utterances, focus of attention will bind the response to the current query that the system has to attend to. Nonetheless, system responses of similar topic may still not be answering to the same query, even when bounded with focus from the user utterance. The second level of discrimination warrant for the worth of knowledge itself that is encoded in each utterance. According to Maxim of Quantity (informativeness), a response must be as informative as is required with respect to current plan or goal [9]. This definition establishes constraints on magnitude of knowledge as whole, in addition to the contextual information.

Using a unified representation of semantic in utterances, the output of a natural language understanding (NLU) component is useful to both dialogue and question-answering systems. Natural language output consists of two elements, which are the communicative function (intention/speech acts) and the propositional content (semantics/topic and focus). They are commonly referred to input frame and are represented in the form of attribute-value pairs. Fig. 1 illustrates an example of input frame u of user input utterance U.

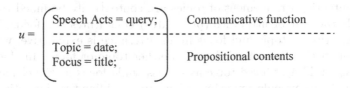

Fig. 1. Input frame for user input utterance

Extraction of semantic features in a query utterance depends on the structure of the utterances and how the information is packaged within the utterance according to the Information Structure Theory [10]. From the figure, this paper covers only formalization of the propositional contents in an utterance while the formalization of the communicative functions is beyond the scope of this paper. The remainder of this paper proceeds as follows. Section 2 presents the Information Structure Theory as the basis of semantic extraction in this work. Section 3 presents the extraction process as well as the dialogue corpus, SCHIMA.

Section 4 provides discussion before Section 5 concludes the research with some indications of the future works.

2 Information Structure Theory

Information structure refers to partitioning of utterance structure into semantic properties that could relate the utterance to discourse context. The semantics of utterances are modeled using two central notions in packaging the information structure, which are Topic and Focus from the theory of Information Structure [10]. According to this theory, topic is essentially what an utterance is about; it contains known information based on context of conversation. Focus, on the other hand, is new information that requires special attention. For example, in an utterance "When are the shows of King Lear?"; the topic is the date of performance as indicated by the keyword "When", and the focus is the title as indicated by keyword "King Lear".

In the literature, there are a number of overlapping distinctions of the term topic-focus, for instance given-new, background-focus, topic-comment, or theme-rheme. The concept of topic (theme, given) and focus (comment, theme) developed in this research follows relational view to topic and focus articulation in the sense that they are two complementary parts in a linguistic representation. Topic is given in relation to focus, and focus is new in relation to topic. Hence, distinguishing between topic and focus is performed through analysis of informational-structural pair in an utterance through linguistic structure or grammar. The correlations between topic-focus and discourse given-new are complicated, but Rats [11] provided a good discussion of the various dichotomies.

In linguistics, the study of topic and focus of sentences falls under the area topic-focus articulation (TFA). The linguistic structure approach to TFA is based on the intuition that topic is the subject and focus is the predicate. When assessment is syntactic, arrangement of topics are contextually bounded to the main verb, while the rest of utterance (predicates) constitutes the focus. Therefore, the identification of topic and focus in an utterance is exhaustive, whereby every element in the utterance belongs to either topic or focus. In this research, the analysis of TFA reduced topic as a class while focus as the elements in the class. Topic-focus articulation is imperative in providing the theoretical basis for semantic feature extractions in Section 3.

2.1 Information Structure

Because Information Structure Theory [10] adopted topic articulation as the first element in the sentence, topics are accessed depending on the mood of utterances such as assertives, imperatives, and interrogatives. Depending on the mood of utterances, the subject and verb also occupy different positions within the structure of utterance. Before going into details of the mood of utterances, a subject in a sentence refers to noun-phrase (NP), or phrases like gerund phrase, and subjects can be implied and omitted. A predicate in an a sentence refers

Table 1. Syntactic location for subjects

No.	Mood	Purpose	Subject Placement
1	Assertive	To make statement	Subject is placed before the verb
2	Imperative	To make demand/request	Subject is implied hence omitted
3	Interrogative	To request information	Subject is placed after the verb, or between helping verb and main verb

to a finite verb phrase (VP), which consists of a finite verb with zero or more objects, complements, or adverbials. Table 1 shows the syntactic location of subjects depending on sentence moods.

Grosz [12] proposed the use of focus of attention in tracking the entities as the discourse progresses. She defined two level of focus; (1) global focus, which is entity relevant to entire discourse, and (2) immediate focus, which is entity central to a particular utterance. While topic gets anchored to the common about, focus delivers the very information that the utterance is structured to convey.

2.2 Information Packaging

However, different utterance moods present different ways of information packaging. For example, left-dislocation or topicalization changes the structure, hence the object of the utterance. The purpose of topicalization is to highlight a piece of information that is important to a particular context. Consequently, this will lead to different topic and focus altogether. While information structure does not primarily affect the truth conditions of utterances, it does affect the packaging hence the emphasis of the utterances. Consider the following utterances that are realized in different packaging of the same information:

1. You can go to "Scherzo" played by Mini and Maxi in the period 9 March 1994 until 10 March 1994.
2. In the period 9 March 1994 until 10 March 1994, you can go to "Scherzo" played by Mini and Maxi.

Both utterances are assertion to state the date of a particular performance. However, after utterance (1) has been left-dislocated, the utterance structure changes into utterance (2). Although both utterances carry the same semantic meaning, focus and emphasis of the utterance has been changed from the *title* "Scherzo" as in utterance (1), to *date* "9 March 1994" in utterance (2). Consequently, the weight for information presented in both utterances is different in responding to an input utterance in a specific context. Similarly, such effects can also be observed in cleft vs. pseudo-cleft utterance and active vs. passive utterance.

2.3   Measuring Informativeness

Two important maxims related to measuring or assessing informativeness in utterances are the Maxim of Quantity and the Maxim of Relevance [9]. The first maxim states that contribution must be as informative as is required with respect to current plan or goal during the pair of utterance exchange, while the second maxim states that do not make contribution more informative than required. The central idea in preserving the previous interaction context in a QA system is to produce response or query answers that adheres to the maxim of quantity and relevance, by being informative with respect to the topic in hand. To illustrate the predicament in measuring the informativeness, consider the utterances as shown in Fig. 2. Although these utterances share the same topic, which is date of performance, there are different means to measure the value of informativeness in each utterance.

[1]	"Candide", played by Voltaire is to be seen on Wednesday 1 February 1995 in the Main Hall.
[2]	In the period 9 March 1994 until 10 March 1994, you can go to "Scherzo", played by Mini and Maxi.
[3]	Music shows are to be seen in the period 24 September 1993 until 29 April 1994.
[4]	No.
[5]	Show "Duifje Klok" by the group The National Theater has already been played.
[6]	Show "Under a blue roof" played by Mathilde Santing is to be seen on Friday 19 May 1995 in the Main Hall and starts at 20:00.
[7]	Sorry, I do not understand you!
[8]	The show of 3 May has these 10 cards still available.
[9]	Yes.
[10]	You can see "Under a blue roof" in the large hall on 19 May 1995.

Fig. 2. A list of dialogue utterances sharing the same topic; *date*

From the figure, all utterances in general contains domain knowledge in the form of domain attributes. For example, in utterance (1), "Candide" is a title of performance and "Voltaire" is a name of artist. One possible way to measuring informativeness is through frequency counts of domain attributes in each utterance. By count of frequencies, one utterance may deemed to be more informative to another. Nonetheless, frequency counts are not enough to distinguish between two different utterances. On the surface, utterance (6) and utterance (10) are similar in terms of content. However, if the informativeness score is solely based on the frequency of domain attributes, utterance (6) may carry more information as compared to utterance (10) because utterance (6) has one count for each domain attribute such as *title*, *artist*, *date*, *seat*, and *time*, while utterance (10) has similar counts for only three domain attributes.

Alas, informativeness based on frequency counts is just the face value of the utterances. Due to the insufficient representation of informativeness score as provided by the domain attributes, there is a need for a more suitable way to measure informativeness. This paper argues that the differential score lies in the contextual knowledge that an utterance carries, which is the value of the focus in utterance. As shown in Fig. 1, the propositional content in the input frame consists of topic and focus. While topic bears semantics for the utterance, focus is best used to measure the information within the utterances.

To illustrate the significant role of focus, utterances in (6) and (10) and compared. Even though both utterances are semantically equivalent on the surface, only one response utterance completely satisfy the need in the input utterance. Since the topic in utterance (6) is *title* while the topic in utterance (10) is *date*, utterance (10) is the best respond to the input query if and only if the focus of input utterance matches the topic, which is *date*. Similarly, focus of user utterances is important in measuring utterances that do not have domain attributes, for instance, response utterance (4), (7), and (9) because their frequency counts of domain attributes are zeroes. This shows that focus in utterances can be used to answer a query whether in a QA or dialogue system according to context, rather than answering in isolation.

3   Extraction of Semantic Features

According to Carberry [13], relevance issues are related to the topic of the conversation. In a dialogue system, an utterance is considered relevant only when it is aligned with the goals or sub-goals within the context of conversation. Similarly in a QA system, an answer can be related back to the previous interaction context by using topic and focus in an utterance. Basically, context is the global topic in a series of utterance exchange and topic is localized to a particular utterance with its corresponding focus of attention. Given the topic in an utterance, context can be derived from the abstraction of topic by keeping track the current value for topic. This is because at most of the time, dialogue between both user and system do not explicitly state whether they are moving from one context to another, for example from information-seeking to making reservation. To illustrate the extraction process for semantic features encoded in dialogue utterances, a transaction dialogue corpus for theater reservation system called SCHISMA is used.

3.1   SCHISMA Dialogue Corpus

SCHISMA is a theater information and booking system developed by the University of Twente [14]. It is chosen to demonstrate the semantic feature extraction process because the theater domain incorporates a variety of wide-ranging knowledge like *title* of performance, *date* and *time* of shows, names of *artists*, *authors*, *composers*, and *directors*. Because SCHISMA supports both information and reservation, it is a transaction dialogue where two dialogue participants negotiate to achieve a common goal [15]. In order to assist users to make reservation, SCHIMA demands the user to specify a unique title, an exact number of ticket, and additional information like the discount cards or preferred seats so the system could propose the ticket price accordingly. Although the interaction requires mutual commitment to achieve the discourse objective, which is theater

USER	Are there shows of opera?	(1)
SYSTEM	Yes.	(2)
USER	Which?	(3)
SYSTEM	You can go to the following opera performances: Der Vetter aus Dingsda, Der zigeunerbaron, Don Carlos, Eugen Onegin en Nabucco.	(4)
USER	When is the opera Eugen Onegin and Nabucco?	(5)
SYSTEM	Eugen Onegin, played by the national opera of Saint Petersburg is on 27 January 1994.	(6)
USER	Is this the only date of performance?	(7)
SYSTEM	Nabucco, played by Krakow Opera is on 15 April 1994.	(8)
USER	These are the only dates?	(9)
SYSTEM	Yes.	(10)
USER	Then I want 10 tickets for Nabucco, please.	(11)
SYSTEM	Valid reductions are CJP, JTK, and Senior Pass. Do you have a reduction card?	(12)
USER	no	(13)
SYSTEM	You can choose from ranks balcony 1 and main floor 1. Which rank do you want?	(14)
USER	1st balcony, please.	(15)
SYSTEM	The costs for these tickets are ff525.00.	(16)
SYSTEM	You have tickets for Nabucco, played by Krakow Opera on 15 April 1994. Commencement of show is 20:00. You are requested to collect these tickets minimum half an hour before commencement of the show.	(17)
USER	Are these then places in the centre of the row?	(18)
SYSTEM	With this information I can not find anything in the database.	(19)
USER	Okay	(20)
SYSTEM	With this information I can not find anything in the database.	(21)
USER	Can you then give seat numbers?	(22)
SYSTEM	I have no information on allocations of the auditorium. The places are given away in the most favorable way.	(23)
USER	I find the tickets somewhat too expensive, though	(24)
USER	can you exchange them with main floor tickets	(25)
SYSTEM	I request you to contact the counter with this question. I will give you the address.	(26)
SYSTEM	Name: Theater Twent, Address: Langestraat 49, Post code: 7511 HB, Place: Enschede, Tel: 053-858500, Information: 053-858500.	(27)
USER	But can you also arrange this?	(28)
SYSTEM	Sorry, I do not understand you, can you reformulate that?	(29)
USER	Can you not cancel the tickets and give me 10 floor tickets.	(30)
SYSTEM	Price does not matter. 10 floor cards are just as expensive such as 10 balcony cards.	(31)
USER	Okay	(32)
SYSTEM	Thanks for the effort and good-bye!	(33)

Fig. 3. A dialogue in SCHISMA

reservation, the user is also free to accept, reject or abandon any of his prior decisions. A dialogue excerpt from a theater information and booking system called SCHISMA is presented in Fig. 3.

From Fig. 3, utterances from line (1) to line (10) fall under performance context, whereby the user mainly inquires about details of performances. However, in line (11), the context has changed into reservation because user explicitly request for a reservation. Because informativeness is highly domain-specific, domain attributes play significant roles in determining the amount of information contained in a particular utterance. Domain attributes enable the measurement of informativeness in an utterance when used to represent the topic and focus.

3.2   Domain Attributes

Notice that example utterances in the previous section contain proper names, phrases, and dates like *Eugen Onegin*, *Krakow Opera*, *CJB*, or *27 January 1994*. This information corresponds to knowledge highly specific to the domain of SCHISMA. For example, *Eugen Onegin* is a title of performance, but *Krakow Opera* is the name of performing artist. This research adopts attribute-value pair formalism to represent information like <title–*Eugen Onegin*>and <artist–*Krakow Opera*>. With this regard, title and artist are known as domain attributes. The process to abstract out the domain knowledge is only a trivial task of searching and replacing the proper information into attribute forms. For example, the utterance (1) will be abstracted into the form of utterance (2).

1. The cost for *Nabucco* is ff23.00.
2. The cost for <title>is <cost>.

3.3   Topic and Focus

The extraction of topic of utterance is based on the Information Theory [10], whereby topics are assessed depending on mood of utterance i.e., assertive, imperative, or interrogative. According to this theory, the rule of thumb in determining the mood is that topic is always the subject and focus is the object in an utterance. The challenging task, however, is to access the subjects and objects because sentences vary in their structural form. The following are detailed descriptions for identifying the subjects and objects based on different classification of mood of utterance.

Assertive. Assertions are declarative utterances that are used to make a statement or to declare some facts. In declarative utterances, topic is the part of the proposition that is being talked about (predicated), which is the subject of utterance. This includes "Yes/No" answer that responds to a question [16], which in this case the utterance will inherit topic from question utterance. For example:

1. *Nabucco*, played by *Krakow Opera*, is to be seen on 15 April 1994.
2. I find the *Eugen Onegin* is very interesting.

Utterance (1) shows a straightforward example to capture topic of utterance, whereby *Nabucco* is the subject hence title is the topic. Utterance (2) however, has a noun *I* as the subject, hence the object title *Eugen Onegin* is the topic.

Imperative. Imperatives are command utterance, or utterance intended to instigate an action including an order, a request, an advice or a wish. Because the subject is often implied, topic corresponds to objects of utterance. For example:

1. I want 10 tickets, please!
2. In the date 27 January 1994, you can go to *Nabucco*.

In utterance (1), the subject is *I* and objects are ticket, thus topic is ticket. Utterance (2), however, is an example of left-dislocation in sentence. Although the original subject is title or *Nabucco*, date has been topicalized through left-dislocation and becomes new subject. Therefore, date is the topic of utterance (3), while title becomes the focus of attention.

Interrogative. Interrogative utterances are intended to elicit information from the listener, but not necessarily exists in question form. Topic is usually expressed as the object of the verb, unless the *wh*-phrase is direct object or an adjunct, then the topic corresponds to the subject of the verb. For example:

1. Do you have a *CJB* card?
2. When *Nabucco* will be performed by the *Krakow Opera*?

In utterance (1), the subject is you and object is *CJB*, a reduc. Since subject is a noun, both topic and focus will assume the value reduc. In utterance (2), title *Nabucco* is a direct object to "When". Although title is a subject, it is the topic of utterance and artist becomes the focus of attention. Other utterances that do not fall to either of this mood will be extracted as "other". This includes opening and closing utterances, as well as utterances that are not covered in the domain, for instance utterance "Can I pay with Mastercard?" or "What time the main floor opens?".

Once the subject and object in utterances have been assessed, the following decision tree is proposed to summarize the process of extracting the topic and focus in dialogue utterances as shown in Fig. 4.

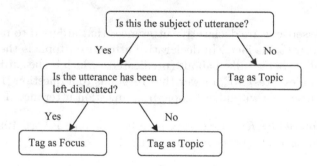

Fig. 4. Decision tree for *Topic* and *Focus*

3.4 Semantic Features Extracted

Finally, Table 2 shows the semantic features extracted from SCHISMA. The values such as *title*, *person*, and *reduc* were manually crafted using domain information. The two different contexts in SCHISMA shows that it is a transaction dialogue because information-seeking dialogue has only one context.

Table 2. Semantic features for SCHISMA

ID	Context	Topic/Focus	Topic User	Topic System	Focus User	Focus System
0	performance	title	103	124	200	219
1		genre	29	48	69	36
2		artist	42	59	57	32
3		time	32	18	11	22
4		date	91	64	58	84
5		review	56	50	18	8
6		person	30	26	12	9
7	reservation	reserve	150	74	91	80
8		ticket	80	55	75	84
9		cost	53	131	26	16
10		avail	14	12	11	28
11		reduc	73	87	116	68
12		seat	94	89	101	86
13		theater	12	24	12	20
14	other	other	61	59	63	128
			920	920	920	920

The entire of SCHISMA corpus is constituted by 64 dialogues of varied length. In total, there are 920 utterances belong to the user and 1,127 utterances belong to the system. Because SCHISMA is mixed-initiative, the distribution of contribution from both the user and the system is also balance. This is opposed to the single-initiative dialogue system such as the traditional QA system where one party does all the asking and one party does all the answering.

4   Discussions

In corpus-based dialogue studies, modeling general conversational behaviors in user utterances generally do not require any semantic information. Modeling negotiations in transaction dialogues, however, is constrained by the timing and semantic content [17]. The first constraint, timing refers to the negotiation phases within transaction dialogues, for example opening, information, proposal, confirmation, and closing. Timing in negotiation phases can only be determined with the aid of semantic interpretation of input utterances because the same communicative functions or intentions (refer Fig. 1) can occur in more than one negotiation phases (i.e., proposal vs. confirmation). Apart from semantic information, research in dialogue systems offer rich pragmatic information such as speech acts/intentions, grounding, and turn-taking. Conversational acts theory extended the account of speech acts by incorporating turn-taking, grounding, and discourse-level argumentation acts to describe conversation as a fully joint-action interaction [18]. In SCHISMA, the argumentation acts can be represented as phases during the negotiation such as proposal and confirmation.

While the semantic approach has been widely explored in the area of question answering (QA) and dialogue systems, the process of extracting the semantic within the sentence or utterance is also taking the standard natural language processing approach. In general, the steps involve tokenization to split the input utterance into a token of words, stemming to obtain the root words, and part-of-speech (POS) tagging to tag each root word with the POS component such as nouns, verbs, adjectives, adverbs, and others. The final process is extracting the nouns and assessing their semantics by checking against a dictionary or ontology of some sorts. This paper, on the contrary, attempts to provide an extraction process based on informativeness, which is basically the value of information that an utterance holds rather than based on keyword extractions.

It would be interesting to investigate whether the semantics from earlier exchange of question and answer in a QA system has any influence over its rate of precision and recall. The goal can be achieved by comparing the results based on the use of semantic features from previous n utterances. Rationally, the more topics from the previous interaction that a system holds, the more contextual knowledge it has, and consequently the better results of precision and recall. However, the results may also deteriorated as the time-span of dialogue increased, which in this case comes the question of the optimal value for n.

5   Conclusions and Future Works

This paper laid the theoretical foundation and presented decision trees that will form the rules in extracting semantic features from a natural language input. The decision trees are relevant to dialogue systems, QA systems as well as natural language interface (NLI) to ontologies. The extraction process was illustrated using a mixed-initiative, transaction corpus called SCHISMA. The process began by manually identifying a set of domain attributes in the corpus. From the domain attributes, semantic features such as the topic of utterance and focus of utterance were then extracted. In the future, the proposed decision trees will be applied in a question answering system to replace the traditional natural language processing approach such as keyword extraction in assessing the semantics. It is also hoped that this method could extend the capabilities in QA systems to answer queries within context rather than in isolation.

References

1. Road Maps for Question Answering and Summarization,
   http://www-nlpir.nist.gov/projects/duc/roadmapping.html
2. Ferret, O., Grau, B., Hurault-Plantet, M., Illouz, G., Jacquemin, C., Monceaux, L., Robba, I., Vilnat, A.: How NLP Can Improve Question Answering. Knowledge Organization 29(3-4), 135–155 (2002)
3. Tellex, S., Katz, B., Lin, J., Fernandes, A., Marton, G.: Quantitative Evaluation of Passage Retrieval Algorithms for Question Answering. In: 26th Annual International ACM SIGIR Conference on Research and Development in Information Retrieval, pp. 41–47. ACM (2003)

4. Harabagiu, S., Hickl, A.: Methods for Using Textual Entailment in Open-Domain Question Answering. In: 21st International Conference on Computational Linguistics and the 44th Annual Meeting of the Association for Computational Linguistics, pp. 905–912. Association for Computational Linguistics (2006)

5. Mustapha, A., Sulaiman, M.N., Mahmod, R., Selamat, M.H.: Classification-and-Ranking Architecture for Response Generation based on Intentions. International Journal of Computer Science and Network Security 8(12), 253–258 (2008)

6. Damljanovic, D., Agatonovic, M., Cunningham, H.: FREyA: An Interactive Way of Querying Linked Data using Natural Language. In: García-Castro, R., Fensel, D., Antoniou, G. (eds.) ESWC 2011. LNCS, vol. 7117, pp. 125–138. Springer, Heidelberg (2012)

7. Saany, S.I.A., Mamat, A., Mustapha, A., Affendey, L.S.: Incorporating User Modeling and Relevance Feedback in Question Analysis Model. In: 2nd IEEE Conference on Control, Systems and Industrial Informatics (ICCSII), Bandung, Indonesia, pp. 113–118 (2013)

8. McKeown, K.: Text Generation: Using Discourse Strategies and Focus Constraints to Generate Natural Language Text. Studies in Natural Language Processing. Cambridge University Press (1985)

9. Grice, H.P.: Studies in the Way of Words. Harvard University Press (1991)

10. Halliday, M.A.K.: Notes on Transitivity and Theme in English, Part 2. Journal of Linguistics 3(2), 199–244 (1967)

11. Rats, M.: Topic Management in Information Dialogues. Ph.D. thesis, Tilburg University, Netherlands (1996)

12. Grosz, B.: The Representation and Use of Focus in a System Understanding Dialogs. In: IJCAI 1977, pp. 67–76. Morgan Kauffman (1977)

13. Carberry, S.: Techniques for Plan Recognition. User Modeling and User-Adapted Interaction 11(1-2), 31–48 (2001)

14. van de Hoeven, G.F., Andernach, J.A., van de Burgt, S.P., Kruijff, G.-J., Nijholt, A., Schaake, J., de Jong, F.M.G.: SCHISMA: A Natural Language Accessible Theatre Information and Booking System. University of Twente (1994)

15. Hulstijn, J.: Dialogue models for inquiry and transaction. University of Twente (2000)

16. Whittaker, S., Stenton, P.: Cues and Control in Expert-Client Dialogues. In: 26th Annual Meeting on Association for Computational Linguistics, pp. 123–130. Association for Computational Linguistics (1998)

17. Traum, D.: Speech Acts for Dialogue Agents. In: Wooldride, M., Rao, A. (eds.) Foundations of Rational Agency, pp. 169–201. Kluwer (1999)

18. Traum, D., Hinkelman, E.: Conversation Acts in Task-oriented Spoken Dialogue. Computational Intelligence 8(3), 575–599 (1992)

Extracting Corpus-Specific Strings by Using Suffix Arrays Enhanced with Longest Common Prefix

Minoru Yoshida[1], Kazuyuki Matsumoto[1], Qingmei Xiao[2],
Xielifuguli Keranmu[1], Kenji Kita[1], and Hiroshi Nakagawa[3]

[1] Institute of Technology and Science, University of Tokushima
2-1, Minami-josanjima, Tokushima, 770-8506, Japan
{mino,matumoto,kita}@is.tokushima-u.ac.jp,
keranmu@iss.tokushima-u.ac.jp
[2] City Housing
3-8-1, Naka-josanjima, Tokushima, 770-0813, Japan
hanmay510122@gmail.com
[3] Information Technology Center, University of Tokyo
7-3-1, Hongo, Bunkyo-ku, Tokyo 113-0033, Japan
nakagawa@dl.itc.u-tokyo.ac.jp

Abstract. We propose a new term extraction algorithm that considers all of the substrings as term candidates. Our algorithm uses a suffix array as the data structure that emulates the suffix tree of the corpus. We use two scoring functions, one of which is used to detect good substring boundaries as linguistic chunks and the other is to find domain-specific phrases and combine them with a re-ranking approach. Experiments show that the proposed all-substring term extraction algorithm shows good performance for highly-frequent terms compared with the baseline algorithm that uses a morphological analyzer in the preprocessing step.

1 Introduction

In this paper, we propose a new algorithm for term extraction which considers all the substrings as term candidates. *Term extraction* is a task aimed at the extraction of phrases characterizing a given corpus. In our problem setting, we also use a *reference corpus* that is used to characterize the target corpus. Applications of such all-substring term extraction algorithms include finding the phrases that characterize some specific regions (such as the Western area in Japan compared to the Eastern area), some specific authors (such as young people), some specific topics (such as computer science), some time spans (such as in recent one year), etc. Typical term extraction algorithms use TF-IDF scores to rank phrases. Instead, we use a Bayesian probabilistic model for the scoring function because it is suitable in our situation where the task does not demand the extraction of *document-specific* phrases, but the extraction of *corpus-specific* phrases, which makes it difficult to use document frequency scores effectively.

A. Jaafar et al. (Eds.): AIRS 2014, LNCS 8870, pp. 360–370, 2014.

Previous term extraction systems for Asian languages make a set of candidate phrases by performing morphological analysis on the corpus, obtaining the term candidates by concatenating successive nouns, and ranking the extracted candidates. However, extracting candidates before considering the merit of each chunk as a corpus-specific phrase can miss numerous substrings that are document-specific phrases but cannot be extracted easily using heuristic candidate extraction rules.

In this paper, we propose an algorithm to use all the substrings of the given corpus as term candidates. Our algorithm extracts term candidates in a reasonable time by using suffix arrays and a scoring function that indicates the merits of substrings as linguistic chunks and can be calculated in a bottom-up manner.

2   Related Work

Several algorithms for term extraction have been proposed in literatures [1], [2], [5], [11]. Term extraction is typically performed by extracting a list of term candidates and then ranking them by a scoring function that represents the "termhood," which indicates how good each candidate term is as a term. The recent growth of electronic texts available on the Internet has resulted in many scoring functions using corpus statistics proposed in the past decade. They typically compare the frequency of the term in the corpus with the frequency outside (i.e., its frequency in the document other than the target corpus). TF-IDF is a well-known example of this approach. They usually extract term candidates by performing morphological analysis on the text and extracting the sequence of words with specific POS sequences. For languages with no word boundaries, e.g., Japanese, word segmentation is also performed in morphological analysis. To the best of our knowledge, no previous work has considered all substrings as term candidates.

Few researchers propose considering all the substrings as feature candidates for machine learning [4], [10]. The algorithm by Okanohara *et al.* [10] uses suffix arrays for data structure to enumerate all substrings efficiently.

3   Definitions

We assume that the input to our system is a pair of corpora $< C, C' >$. C is a *target corpus* from which we want to extract term-specific phrases. C' is a *reference corpus*, which is used to characterize the target corpus. Corpus C is assumed to be a string. For a set of documents, C is a result of concatenating those documents into one string. The output of the system is a list of substrings that are characteristic to corpus C compared with the reference corpus C'. Thus, C' should be relatively a set of unbiased texts compared to C. [1]

We denote the concatenation operation by a period. (e.g., $x.y$ means the substring by concatenating x and y).

---

[1] In our experiments in section 6, C is the "Wakamono Kotoba Corpus" and C' is the set of texts randomly collected from Twtter.

3.1   Suffix Arrays and LCP

A suffix tree [13] is a tree structure that is a modified trie for all suffixes of the given string (i.e., the corpus for our problem setting). The difference between a suffix tree and a trie is that all the nodes with only one branch are removed where the edge labels are concatenated. Because suffix trees are very space-consuming, we instead use the suffix arrays explained below for our implementation, which can emulate the search on suffix trees.

A suffix array [6] is a data structure that represents all the suffixes of a given string and is a sorted array of all suffixes of the string. Given the corpus C and C', after concatenating them into one corpus C'', we construct the suffix array $SA = <i_1, i_2, \cdots i_n>$, where i_k is the index of the k-th suffix of C'' when all suffixes of C'' are sorted in alphabetic order. Moreover, we assume that we have the *label array* $L = <l_1, l_2, \cdots l_n>$, where $l_k = 1, 0$ if the index i_k is in the target corpus and the reference corpus, respectively. By using the suffix array constructed on the corpus S, all the positions of s in S can be obtained quickly (in $P(logN)$ time, where N is the length of S) for any s. They require $4N$ bytes[2] of additional space in order to store indexes and even more space for construction. Here, we assume that both the corpus and the suffix array are in memory.

The longest common prefix (LCP) array is defined as the array that records the length of the longest string that is common in two consecutive suffixes in the suffix array, i.e., $LCP[i]$ is defined as the length of longest common prefix between $SA[i-1]$ and $SA[i]$.

We denote the frequency of s appearing in corpus C by $freq(s, C)$. We also define $freq(s) = freq(s, C) + freq(s, C')$, i.e., the number of appearance of string s in both C and C'.

4   Description-Length-Based String Extraction

We use a phrase score $SS(s)$ for string s defined as:

$$SS(s) = \frac{\alpha_1 + freq(s, C)}{\alpha_2 + freq(s, C) + freq(s, C')}. \tag{1}$$

This score can be seen as the Bayesian a posterior probability of s being in corpus C after observing $freq(s, C)$ and $freq(s, C')$. α_1 and α_2 are parameters that indicates "the confidence of the prior knowledge about the score." It can be regarded as assuming that we observed α_2 samples before observing actual samples. Currently, we set the number of these "virtual" samples as 10 and the prior ratio of observing s in C to C' is proportional to the ratio of the size of C to the size of C'. Therefore, α_2 is set to 10 and α_1 is set to $10 \cdot \frac{|C|}{|C|+|C'|}$ where $|C|$ is the length of the corpus C.

One of the main problems faced when performing the extraction of "any-length" strings is that there are many similar candidates with the same (or very

---

[2] If each index is represented by four bytes.

near) $SS(s)$ value, and the string with "best boundaries" should be selected from them. To achieve this goal, we define the following *edge scores* reflecting the merits of the string as linguistic chunks or the merits of the left and right boundary of string s, *i.e.*, string s starts and ends at the semantic boundary between words, phrases, sentences, etc.

The *edge score* of string s is defined as follows.

$$ES(s) = \frac{(freq(s) - 1) \cdot len(s)}{DL(s)} \tag{2}$$

where $DL(s)$, the description length of string s, is defined as the number of bits required to select the node in the suffix tree that has an edge label s. We define the *description length* of string s as the number of bits needed to select it in the suffix tree of corpus C. Note that the description length is calculated as $-\log p$, where p is the probability of s and defined as $p = \frac{freq(s)}{|C|+|C'|}$.

Intuitively, the $ES(s)$ score models the merits of the strings as linguistic chunks as the number of areas in the corpus divided by the description length for the string. This score is defined based on the assumption that "a string is likely to be a representative expression if it can cover the corpus with a short description length." The term -1 is added to $freq(s)$ to exclude one-frequency substrings because all of the one-frequency terms can be extended without increasing the value of $DL(s)$, which makes the corpus the best candidate among all one-frequency substrings.

As will be mentioned in section 5.2, if x' is the substring of x and $ES(x') < ES(x)$, x' is removed from chunk candidates. Consider the selection of the right boundary of string s.[3] Note that if only one character c can appear on the right of s, *i.e.*, $P(c|s) = 1.0$, obviously $ES(s.c) > ES(s)$ because $freq(s) = freq(s.c)$ and $DL(s) = DL(s.c)$. Thus, all the substrings corresponding to internal nodes with no branches in the suffix tree can be extended without reducing the $ES(s)$ value. Therefore, we only have to consider all the internal nodes in the suffix tree as candidate substrings. Similarly, edge selection with a small number of branches tends to proceed with an increase of $ES(s)$ scores, resulting in the preference for longer strings until we face a sudden increase in branch numbers.

4.1   Similarity to other Algorithms

Tanaka *et al.* [12] proposed Kiwi, an algorithm to find appropriate boundaries to extract common expressions starting with the given query string. The idea of Kiwi is to detect a sudden increase in the number of branches in tries, which tends to indicate semantic boundaries (i.e., to be a boundary of linguistic chunks). Our $ES(s)$ scoring function also tends to detect such sudden increases of branches as boundaries as mentioned above.

The Kiwi algorithm is designed in order to detect appropriate cutting points when *some queries are provided* and that the Kiwi score is for *one-direction string*

---

[3] The left boundary can be considered almost in the same manner.

searches where the query is given. This means that the Kiwi algorithm can find the right boundary of the phrase when the left boundary (i.e., starting point of the phrase) is given, or can find the left boundary when the right boundary is given, but it cannot find the left and right boundary *simultaneously* when no boundary information is provided first. (For example, it can find the phrase "Natural Language Processing" when the string "Nat" is given as a query, or when the string "ssing" is given as a query (for left direction search), but cannot find the phrase if such prefixes or suffixes are not given as queries.) This is because finding "increase of the number of branches" in the Kiwi algorithm needs the "previous number of branches" and the previous number of branches depend on the search direction and what queries are used first. In other words, boundary detection of the Kiwi algorithm require not only the statistics of the current string, but also the statistics of the *previous* string, and the previous string is changed according to the search direction and the query string. Thus, the Kiwi algorithm is not suitable for our purpose, i.e., finding the good chunk candidates from the corpus when no previous information about the boundaries is given.

However, our proposed score is able to extract all good chunks from the corpus when no queries are provided because the $ES(s)$ score is defined using only statistics of the current string s (i.e., $freq(s)$, $len(s)$, and $DL(s)$) designed to be high for chunks with the large number of branches as discussed in the previous section, and does not require the statistics of *previous* strings like the Kiwi algorithm. Therefore, our proposed score can be seen as the generalization of the Kiwi algorithm that provide a way to apply the idea of "detecting increase of the number of branches" to term extraction in a unified manner.

5   Calculation of Scores

As mentioned above, we only take the strings followed by two or more different characters and can ignore others including substrings with a frequency of 1. This means that we have only to calculate the score of phrases at all the branching nodes in the suffix tree; this calculation is emulated by the suffix array by using the LCP array as complementary information. The following section explains how to calculate scores for all internal nodes in the suffix tree. Scores for each node in the suffix tree are written in the position (in the suffix array) of the first (top) string that starts with the edge label of the node. Note that multiple nodes can thus be associated with the same entry. In such a case, the algorithm overwrites the scores. Thus, the value we find at each entry is the result for the node whose depth is the smallest among those processed so far.

5.1   Bottom-Up Calculation of Scores

We define the *summation array* S to record statistics of subregions. We also define the *end position array* E and *backlink array* B. S is used in STEP-2.

Figs. 2 (for STEP-1) and 3 (for STEP-2) show the algorithm, and Fig. 1 shows the example suffix array for explanation. $S_0[i]$ and $S_1[i]$ record the values for the region starting at the position i processed most recently. Note that we reuse these values for processing larger regions. For example, we can use the value $S_0[4]$ and $S_1[4]$ in the calculation of the values $S_0[0]$ and $S_1[0]$ because the value for the region starting at 4 and ending at 8 is already calculated and recorded at $S_0[4]$ and $S_1[4]$.

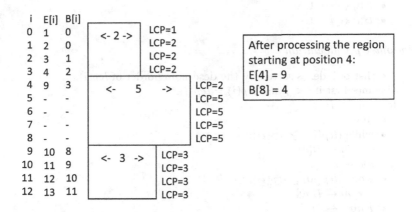

Fig. 1. Example suffix array for explanation of our algorithm

At each step, the algorithm calculates scores ($ES(s)$ in STEP-1 and $SS(s)$ in STEP-2) of the string and records them to the hash table. Note that the $SS(s)$ score in STEP-2 can be calculated in the following way:

$$SS(s) = \frac{\alpha_1 + freq(s, C)}{\alpha_2 + freq(s, C) + freq(s, C')} = \frac{\alpha_1 + sum_1}{\alpha_2 + sum_1 + sum_0}. \qquad (3)$$

5.2 Two-Stage Filtering Algorithm

We use a two-stage re-ranking approach for candidate extraction.

After STEP-1, the algorithm makes a list of candidate strings ranked in descending order of the ES score. Then, we keep the top N elements in the resulting list[4].

The extracted lists often contain redundant elements because they contain strings of any length. For example, "have to do" and "have to do it" can be in the same list. To remove such redundancy, we perform *list cleaning* on the resulting list. If the n-th element is a substring of the m-th element for $n < m$, the n-th element is removed from the list:

List Clearning If $rank(x) > rank(y)$ and x is contained by y, then x is removed from the list.

---

[4] We set $N = 30000$ in the experiments.

Notations

- $E[i]$: (the next to) the end point of the current region starting at i.
- $B[i]$: backlinks: the start point of the region ending at i.

Initialization

- for all i:
  - $E[i] \leftarrow i + 1$.
  - $B[i] \leftarrow i - 1$.

Bottom-Up Calculation

- $I \leftarrow$ list of indexes sorted by the descending order of $lcp(i)$.
  (i comes first if $i < j$ and $lcp(i) = lcp(j)$.)
- foreach $i \in I$:
  - $i0 \leftarrow i$.
  - while $(lcp(i0) \geq lcp(i))$:
    * $i0 \leftarrow B[i0]$.
  - $i00 \leftarrow i0$
  - while $(lcp(i0) \geq lcp(i))$:
    * $i0 \leftarrow E[i0]$
  - $E[i00] \leftarrow i0$.
  - $B[i0 - 1] \leftarrow i00$.
  - $s \leftarrow C''[(i00)..(i00 + lcp(i00))]$.
  - $Hashtable(s) \leftarrow ES(s)$.

Fig. 2. Candidate extraction algorithm (STEP-1)

We make a set K of elements remaining after the list cleaning.

In a similar way, after STEP-2, candidate strings are ranked in the descending order of the SS score. Note that we only consider the bottom-up score calculation, and only the substrings in the set K are included in the candidate list. We also perform *list cleaning* on the resulting list in order to obtain final results.

6   Experiments

We used the corpus called "Wakamono Kotoba Corpus"[7], which consists of "casual" sentences found on the Web. The sentences are provided with "casual words" tags, where "casual words" means new words, especially those used by young people.

Note that the corpus is constructed by collecting sentences by querying the words in "Wakamono Kotoba Dictionary" to the "Yahoo! blog search" system, thus each sentence in the corpus must include one or more "Wakamono Kotoba" terms. Thus, the experimental setting is somewhat "artificial" in the sense that the corpus is biased to contain more answer strings (i.e., strings to be extracted) than the corpus constructed not by such keyword search algorithms (e.g., the

Notations
- $E[i]$: (the next to) the end point of the current region starting at i.
- $S_0[i]$: the number of zeros in the current region starting at i.
- $S_1[i]$: the number of ones in the current region starting at i.
- $B[i]$: backlinks: the start point of the region ending at i.

Initialization

- for all i:
  - $S_0[i] \leftarrow 1$ if the label $L(i) = 0$.
  - $S_1[i] \leftarrow 1$ if the label $L(i) = 1$.
  - $E[i] \leftarrow i + 1$.
  - $B[i] \leftarrow i - 1$.

Bottom-Up Calculation

- $I \leftarrow$ list of indexes sorted by the descending order of $lcp(i)$.
  (i comes first if $i < j$ and $lcp(i) = lcp(j)$.)
- foreach $i \in I$:
  - $i0 \leftarrow i$.
  - while $(lcp(i0) \geq lcp(i))$:
    * $i0 \leftarrow B[i0]$.
  - $i00 \leftarrow i0$
  - $sum_0 \leftarrow 0$, $sum_1 \leftarrow 0$.
  - while $(lcp(i0) \geq lcp(i))$:
    * $sum_0 \leftarrow sum_0 + S_0[i0]$
    * $sum_1 \leftarrow sum_1 + S_1[i0]$
    * $i0 \leftarrow E[i0]$
  - $S_0[i00] \leftarrow sum_0$
  - $S_1[i00] \leftarrow sum_1$
  - $E[i00] \leftarrow i0$.
  - $B[i0 - 1] \leftarrow i00$.
  - $s \leftarrow C''[(i00)..(i00 + lcp(i00))]$.
  - $Hashtable(s) \leftarrow SS(s)$.

Fig. 3. Candidate extraction algorithm (STEP-2)

corpus constructed by collecting all articles including specific tags in the metadata.)

As a reference corpus C', we collected texts from Twitter by the random sampling function provided by TwitterAPI because Twitter texts are also casual texts written by relatively young people.

Existing term extraction algorithms for Asian languages, e.g., Japanese, typically make a set of candidate terms by performing morphological analysis on the corpus and then extracting nouns or two or more consecutive nouns, as candidates [9]. Moreover, typical *unknown-word extraction* systems extract "undefined" tag sequences as candidates of unknown words [8]. Thus, as a baseline, we used Gomoku[5], a Japanese morphological analyzer implemented as Java classes[6]. Candidate strings are extracted as one or more consecutive nouns[7], which are then ranked in order of $SS(s)$ that is the score used in our proposed algorithm. By comparing our algorithm and the baseline, we can investigate the effect of using all substrings as term candidates.

6.1 Evaluation Metrics

We used *average precision* [3] for our performance evaluation. This is the value defined in the ranked list of some elements where the list includes some *correct elements* that are the elements included in some *set of answers*. Given a list of extracted terms $\langle c_1, c_2, \cdots c_n \rangle$ ranked by the score, and a set of answers (i.e., the set of "Wakamono Kotoba") $S = \{s_1, s_2, \cdots\}$, the average precision of the result list is calculated as

$$\frac{1}{|S|} \sum_{1 \leq k \leq n} r_k \cdot precision(k), \qquad (4)$$

where $precision(k)$ is the accuracy (i.e., the ratio of correct answers to all answers) of the top k candidates, and r_k represents whether the k-th document is relevant (1) or not (0) (in other words, $r_k = 1$ if $c_k \in S$, and $r_k = 0$ otherwise). We calculated the average precision in several settings by changing the threshold value for the set of answers. When using the threshold β, only the answers a whose frequency $f(a) \geq \beta$ are considered.

Table 1. Experimental results

Average Precision			
Answer frequency threshold	# of answers	Baseline	Proposed
100	102	48.68	74.59
50	140	43.05	69.81
10	331	36.28	39.14
5	498	28.07	26.14
2	887	18.37	15.17
1	2231	8.836	6.171

7 Discussion

Table 1 shows the results. We observed that the proposed algorithm outperformed the baseline algorithm for highly-frequent terms, such as the average precision for the terms with frequency values equal or more than 100 and 50.

---

[5] https://github.com/sile/gomoku

[6] Note that the Kiwi algorithm was not used as the baseline because it cannot be used in our task as mentioned in section 4.1.

[7] Gomoku does not output "undefined" tags, but instead "noun" tags in many cases.

Examples of the terms that were extracted by our algorithm but not by the baseline algorithm include phrases that contain two kinds of parts of speech (like a sequence of an adjective and a noun, or a sequence of a noun, preposition, and noun, etc.), and terms that contain no Kanji (Chinese characters). These terms are difficult to extract as candidates by using ordinary morphological analyzers, whereas our algorithm can extract them due to the character-based candidate enumeration approach.

However, for the average precision for all the terms, including those whose frequency is 1, neither of the two algorithms showed a good performance. Thus, we need some method to combine these two algorithms by, for example, merging the results by looking at the frequency of each extracted term.

8   Conclusions and Future Work

This paper proposed a new term extraction algorithm that considers all of the substrings as term candidates. We proposed a suffix-array based algorithm for the efficient calculation of scores, and a two-stage re-ranking approach to combine two scoring functions. Experimental results showed that our algorithm works well, especially for high-frequency terms. However, because the proposed algorithm does not work well for low-frequency terms, we need to improve our algorithm by, for example, merging the results from our algorithm and other algorithms looking at the frequency of the extracted terms. Comparing our algorithm with algorithms using unknown word extraction algorithms as preprocessing is also interesting future work.

Acknowledgement. This work was supported by JSPS KAKENHI Grant Number 24500162.

References

1. COMPUTERM 1998 First Workshop on Computational Terminology (1998)
2. COMPUTERM 2002 Second Workshop on Computational Terminology (2002)
3. Chakrabarti, S.: Mining the Web: Discovering Knowledge from Hypertext Data. Morgan-Kaufmann Publishers (2002)
4. Ifrim, G., Bakir, G.H., Weikum, G.: Fast logistic regression for text categorization with variable-length n-grams. In: Proceedings of KDD 2008, pp. 354–362 (2008)
5. Kageura, K., Umino, B.: Methods of automatic term recognition: A review. Terminology 3(2), 259–289 (1996)
6. Manber, U., Myers, G.: Suffix arrays: A new method for on-line string searches. In: Proceedings of the First ACM-SIAM Symposium on Discrete Algorithms, pp. 319–327 (1990)
7. Matsumoto, K., Sayama, H., Konishi, Y., Ren, F.: Analysis of wakamono kotoba emotion corpus and its application in emotion estimation. International Journal of Advanced Intelligence (IJAI) 3(1), 1–24 (2011)

8. Murawaki, Y., Kurohashi, S.: Online acquisition of japanese unknown morphemes using morphological constraints. In: Proceedings of the 2008 Conference on Empirical Methods in Natural Language Processing (EMNLP 2008), pp. 429–437 (2008)
9. Nakagawa, H., Mori, T.: A simple but powerful automatic term extraction method. In: Proceedings of Computerm2: 2nd International Workshop on Computational Terminology, COLING 2002 Workshop, pp. 29–35 (2002)
10. Okanohara, D., Tsujii, J.: Text categorization with all substring features. In: Proceedings of SDM 2009, pp. 838–846 (2009)
11. da Silva Conrado, M., Felippo, A.D., Pardo, T.A.S., Rezende, S.O.: A survey of automatic term extraction for brazilian portuguese. Journal of the Brazilian Computer Society 20(12) (2014)
12. Tanaka-Ishii, K., Nakagawa, H.: A multilingual usage consultation tool based on internet searching —more than search engine, less than qa. In: Proceedings of the 14th International World Wide Web Conference (WWW 2005), pp. 363–371 (2005)
13. Weiner, P.: Linear pattern matching algorithms. In: Proceedings of the 14th Annual IEEE Symposium on Switching and Automata Theory, pp. 1–11 (1973)

Feasibility Study Concerning the Use of Reasoning Technique in Semantic Reasoners

Mary Ting[1], Rabiah Abdul Kadir[2], Tengku Mohd Tengku Sembok[3], Fatimah Ahmad[3], and Azreen Azman[1]

[1] Faculty of Computer Science and Information Technology, Universiti Putra Malaysia, Serdang, Selangor 43400, Malaysia
gigimtty.mt@gmail.com, azreenazman@upm.edu.my
[2] Institute of Visual Informatic, Universiti Kebangsaan Malaysia
43600 UKM Bangi, Selangor Malaysia
bieupm69@yahoo.com
[3] Department of Computer Science, Faculty of Defence Science and Technology National Defence University of Malaysia,
Kem Sungai Besi, 57000, Kuala Lumpur Malaysia
{tmts,Fatimah}@upnm.edu.my

Abstract. Inference engine plays an important role in knowledge-based system, where it is used to perform reasoning when queries are entered. There is a need to incorporate a semantic reasoner in the engine, in order for it to perform reasoning. With the growth of Semantic Web and increasing number of ontology implemented recently, several semantic reasoner have been design and implemented to cater the need of the current ontology-based systems. Since there are various numbers of available semantic reasoners in the market for general knowledge-based system or ontology-based system, developers are required to choose an appropriate reasoner that met the system requirements when developing the engine. This paper will review six different ontology reasoners, which have been widely applied previously in ontology based system. By studying the strength and weaknesses of the techniques and algorithms implemented, developer able to select an appropriate reasoner that will work efficiently according to system requirements.

Keywords: reasoning technique, reasoning algorithm, tableau algorithm, rule-based reasoner, description logic.

1   Introduction

Inference engine plays an important role in knowledge-based system where it is used to access to the knowledge encoded in the knowledge base for reasoning when queries are entered. Incorporation of the engine in the system will enable it to perform reasoning on the existing knowledge base. The reasoner has the ability to derive new logical conclusion about the environment using the existing set of fact reside in the knowledge base instead of just extracting the existing facts stored previously.

A. Jaafar et al. (Eds.): AIRS 2014, LNCS 8870, pp. 371–381, 2014.

This information is the logical consequences deduce from manipulating a set of asserted facts or axioms. For an example, an existing fact in the knowledge base stated that white-collar employee did not work on public holiday. When "John is a white-collar employee" fact is asserted into the knowledge base. A new proposition stated that John did not work on public holiday can be derived from the manipulating the existing facts. From the example, implicit information is deduced since the engine is not able to directly return the result based on the existing facts.

The growth of the semantic web technology has increased the need of a semantic reasoner. Due to this, several forms of formalisms of knowledge representation are used to store knowledge. Currently, most of the users or developers are following the RDF/XML and OWL standard. Since the knowledge is encoded in either RDF/XML or OWL, the need to a reasoner has become the key component in retrieving relevant information from Ontology. The engine is used to discover new relationships between resources according to the vocabulary or rule set. Since most of the knowledge stored in the ontology might not be explicit, thus queries must be passed to a reasoner in order to retrieve relevant information from an OWL Ontology. The reasoner has the ability to deduce the implicit knowledge from the existing triples that are not expressed in the ontology by analyzing and managing these triples. [1] The ontology reasoner should have the abilities to check on consistency of the term used, computing entailments, query processing, reasoning with rules and handling XML data types [2].

In order to derive relevant information from a repository such as ontology or knowledge base, developer needs to choose one of the available reasoners in the market to meet the system requirements. The research will study six different reasoners that are commonly used in ontology development.

2   Inference Techniques

Many inference techniques have been introduced to perform reasoning from available knowledge. Generally, reasoning can be categories into deductive reasoning or inductive reasoning. Majority of the systems has implemented deductive reasoning technique in the inference engine, where the drawn conclusion will be true if the premises are true. For example, premises state that "if someone is a something and this something is a sub class of something else, then someone is a something else as well". This form of reasoning technique works well on any type of formalisms. [3] introduce a forward reasoning engine known as FreeEnCal, which has the ability to perform deductive, inductive and abductive reasoning on various forms of logic system. The engine has been very useful for those knowledge-based systems, since it has the ability to deal with creation, prediction and discover. Table 1 in the below shows the application of deductive reasoning in different type of knowledge representation. Same conclusions are drawn when the same premises and reasoning technique are used even though it appears in different formalism.

Table 1. Deductive reasoning application in rule-base, predicate logic and triple

Formalism	Premises	Conclusion
Rule-base	Mohammad is a student.	Mohammad is a person.
	Student sub class of person.	
Predicate logic	isA(Mohammad, student).	isA(Mohammad, person).
	subClassOf(student, person).	
Triple	(Mohammad, isA, student)	(Mohammad, isA, person)
	(student, subClassOf, person)	

Basically, there are two principal ways of deciding which rule to execute when searching through the knowledge base during the reasoning process; forward chaining and backward chaining. The forward chaining (data driven) involves in applying inference rules to the existing facts in order to generate new facts. These rules also can be used to generate new facts when it is reapplied on the combination of original facts and inferred facts. The process is iterative and continuous until no more new facts could be produced. The strategy can be seen in the Table 1, where the existing information (two existing premises) is used as a starting point used before the new information can be derived.

As for the backward chaining (goal driven), it involves with by proving the existing facts or examine the rules when queries are entered. It is also an iterative process, which will terminate when the all relevant rules have been examined or no solution can be found. Using back the same example in the Table 1; an input such as "Mohammad is a person" is checked and see if the premises for this conclusion exist or agreed. This input can only be successfully asserted if the premises are true.

Most of the current inference engines implement both forward and backward chaining strategies together in order to handle all kind of situation. The technique is known as a hybrid strategy where knowledge engineer does not have to decide on which strategies is suitable for the engine. Usually, the basic mechanism for the engine is backward chaining as the technique is easier to implement than a pure forward chaining. The process can be done by re-writing each backward chaining rule into a new form. For example, a backward rule: isA(Someone, P) :- isA(Someone, S), subClassOf(S, P) will become r:- not(isA(Someone, P)), isA(Someone, S), subClassOf(S, P), asserta(isA(Someone, P)).

2.1   Ontology Reasoning

Web Ontology Language (OWL) can be classified as OWL lite, OWL DL and OWL full. OWL DL itself is rooted in description logic (DL), which able to maximize the expressiveness while retaining computational completeness and decidability. [4] DL is a subset of first-order logic where it can be used to model the concepts, roles and individuals. It also has been identified for decidable reasoning. [5] The semantic of DL are defined by interpreting concepts as a set of individual and roles as a set of order pairs of individual.

A general knowledge base consists of two main components, TBox (terminological) that is used to describe the existing concepts and ABox (assertional), which is used to describe the facts. Both terms can also use to describe two different types of statements in ontology. In the ontology, TBox describes the controlled vocabularies such as class, properties and constraint whereas ABox is used to describe the individual properties or instances. A descriptive logic (DL) knowledge base can be defined as K, which is a pair of <T,A> where T is used to represent TBox and A is used to represent ABox. Description logic check against the consistency of ABox instances with TBox concepts to ensure that ABox met all the restrictions. DL also checks the ABox instances to ensure that the concepts have been defined by TBox. Other than that, DL also help to check whether a class is a subsumes of another class [6].

Even though OWL is rooted in DL, first-order logic terms use for ontology development. Thus, in OWL terms such as class is used in place of a concept, object in place of an individual and property in place of a role. In the ontology, the reasoning can be performed by setting the constraints of the class such as restriction, DisjointClassess, someValueFrom and intersectionOf. [5] Other than setting the constraints, application of distribution rules such as existential and universal quantification can be considered as well. OWL DL implements monotonic logic to perform reasoning, where addition of new explicit statement into the ontology may extend the inferred closure. Figure 1 in the following shows some of the constraints use to declare the knowledge with OWL DL. From the figure, the first sample stated that sugar is different from salt, and pepper is different from salt and sugar. In the second sample, it states that rice is a subclass of food but not fruit. And finally, in the third sample, it states a person can have pets, but one of the pets must be a cat.

Sample 1:   <ingredient rdf:ID="salt">
              <ingredient rdf:ID="sugar">
              <owl:differentFrom rdf:resource="#salt"/>
              </ingredient>
              <ingredient rdf:ID="pepper">
              <owl:differentFrom rdf:resource="#salt"/>
              <owl:differentFrom rdf:resource="#sugar"/>
              </ingredient >

Sample 2:   <owl:Class rdf:ID="rice">
              <rdfs:subClassOf rdf:resource="#food" />
              <owl:disjointWith rdf:resource="#fruit" />
              </owl:Class>

sample 3:   <owl:Restriction>
              <owl:onProperty rdf:resource="#hasPet" />
              <owl:someValuesFrom rdf:resource="#Cat" />
              </owl:Restriction>

Fig. 1. OWL DL constraints

Non-monotonic reasoning has been commonly applied in both ontology-based and knowledge-based systems. The technique has successfully captured several forms of common sense and database reasoning, where it has the ability to invalidate the existing conclusion when new information is added. When updating the knowledge reside in the ontology might cause the changes in the existing knowledge. In a situation where the information at hand is complete, monotonic reasoning is more appropriate since new information will not invalidate the existing conclusion. F-OWL implemented to handle frame logic in the ontology supports non-monotonic reasoning [2].

2.2   Reasoning Algorithm

Many reasoning algorithms have been design and deploy to cater the need of conducting semantic reasoning. These algorithms play the major role in the inference engine to ensure the accuracy of the information retrieved or derived when a query entered by the user. One of the most famous algorithms that have been implemented to work on Semantic Web is the description logic, which integrates with the OWL or tableau algorithm. As for the reasoning algorithm implemented in the knowledge-based system, RETE algorithm that has been successfully implemented a number of production rule systems. The algorithm has also been tested in several ontology developments. [7,8]

Tableau algorithm

Tableau algorithm is design to check the knowledge consistency in a knowledge base. The algorithm is used to ensure that at least one individual is an instance of that class through constructing a knowledge base model. Model constructed are a sequence of ABoxes ($A_0, A_1, \ldots A_n$) to model the knowledge base, K. Incorporated inference rules will make implicit information in the axioms of R and explicit information in T. The algorithm will search the model through a process of completion starting with constructing an initial completion graph from the ABox.[9] The algorithm will terminate when no more inference rules are applicable or there is a contradiction among ABoxes. [10,11]. Fig. 2 shows the derivation rules that are commonly used in DL tableau calculi.

$\sqcup$-rule: Given $(C_1 \sqcup C_2)(s)$, derive either $C_1(s)$ or $C_2(s)$.

$\sqcap$-rule: Given $(C_1 \sqcap C_2)(s)$, derive $C_1(s)$ and $C_2(s)$.

$\exists$-rule: Given $(\exists R.C)(s)$, derive $R(s,t)$ and $C(t)$ for t a fresh individual.

$\forall$-rule: Given $(\forall R.C)(s)$ and $R(s,t)$, derive $C(t)$.

$\sqsubseteq$-rule: Given a GCI $C \sqsubseteq D$ and an individual s, derive $(\neg C \sqcup D)(s)$.

Fig. 2. Derivation rules used in DL tableau calculi

RETE algorithm

The RETE algorithm has been design to cater large scales of rules and facts with pattern matching. The process will match the new or existing facts against the rules defined. The algorithm works very well in matching the fact and rules, which work repetitively in matching the fact against each rule in the ruleset. During each cycle, a list of fact will be modified either by retracting or adding to/from the list. The algorithm will take a pool of the common components from those similar rules, so that these common components will not be computed again. At the same time, it will reduce or eliminate the redundancy of repeating the matching process again. [7]

Each cycle consists of three phrases; match, select and execute. During the matching phrase, the conditions of the rules are matched against the facts in order to determine which rules are to be executed. These rules will be stored in a list called "Agenda" for execution. Among this list, one of the rules will be triggered or executed according to the priority, recency of usage and etc. When the rule is executed, new facts might be asserted or existing facts might be retracted through the use of a decision table engine [12].

3   Reasoning Techniques and Their Applications in Ontology Based Retrieval Systems.

A semantic reasoner is design to infer logical results from a set of claim facts or input query. Various numbers of semantic ontology reasoners have been implemented to manipulate the ontologies. Each of the reasoner applied different methods and strategies in order to derive an accurate result when the knowledge is stored implicitly or due to the complexity of the developed ontology. Some of the widely used ontology reasoners are Jena, Pellet, OWLIM , RACER, FaCT++ and HermiT. Protégé able to support all these reasoners except Jena which is a framework itself and OWLIM is integrated with Sesame engine.

3.1   JENA

Jena is a Semantic Web framework that provides support of OWL by providing an API for RDF. The framework consists of various internal reasoners such as SPARQL query engine and rule-based inference engine. The rule base reasoner provides three reasoning strategies; forward chaining, backward chaining and hybrid execution model. The reasoner are made of two rule engines; a forward chaining RETE engine that implements the use of RETE algorithm and a tabled backward-chaining that implements the tabled datalog engine. The reasoner also has the ability to combine inferencing for RDFS/OWL over its own Jena rules. [13] The forward rules are expressed by "->" and backward rules are expressed by "<-" whereas the hybrid rules consist of one or more backward chaining rules in the head of a forward chaining rule. Fig. 3 shows the hybrid model allows the execution of forward, backward and hybrid rules [14].

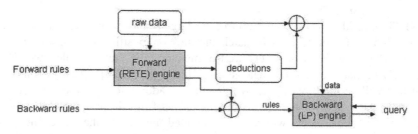

Fig. 3. Hybrid reasoning

3.2   PELLET

Pellet is one of the first reasoners that able to support all of the expressiveness of OWL DL reasoning. The reasoner provides programmatic access to the reasoning functions such as validation, checking the consistency, classification and entailment. Pellet consists of Datalog rules that are used to handle datatype reasoning. The rules are encoded in Semantic Web Rule Language (SWRL). The reasoner is integrated with tableaux algorithm to deal with expressiveness of the description logic. [9] The algorithm has the ability to perform the abilities of the description logic function such as of consistency checking, concepts satisfiability, classification and realization. [15] The axioms about the classes are put into the TBox component and assertions about the individual are stored in the ABox component. TBox axioms will be fed into the tableaux reasoner.

3.3   OWLIM

OWLIM is a scalable semantic repository and reasoner which support the semantic for RDFS, OWL Horst and OWL 2RL. It is a triple-based rule reasoner that uses Triple reasoning and rule entailment engine (TRREE) to perform reasoning using forward chaining strategy. Other than that, the reasoner also offers configurable reasoning support and performance. [16] research states that the reasoning process and query evaluation are performed in the main memory. [17] works on the repository integrated with Storage and inference layer (SAIL) for Sesame RDF database.

3.4   RACER

Renamed ABoxes and Concept Expression Reasoner (Racer) reasoner implements the description logic SHIQ for TBox and ABox using tableaux algorithm. It is one of the first OWL DL reasoner that able to support rules and partial Semantic Web Rule Language (SWRL). The reasoner is able to support new optimization techniques as well as the existing FaCT optimization techniques when dealing with the number restrictions and ABoxes [18]. [19] research working on using the Racer reasoner to perform ontology syntactic evaluation to validate the consistency of the knowledge reside in the ontology.

3.5   FaCT++

Fast Classification of Terminologies (FaCT) uses a new ToDo list architecture to control the rule expansion. The reasoner is designed as a platform to handle SHOIQ description logic through incorporation of Tableaux algorithm decision procedure and optimisation technique. The platform is used to investigate new optimisation techniques and handle expressiveness of description logic. The tableaux algorithm decision procedure implemented in the reasoner has the ability to handle TBoxes and incomplete support for ABoxes.[20] The reasoner, extends the features and optimisation techniques of FaCT; therefore able to support OWL DL and OWL 2 DL partially. Since it only supports OWL 2 DL partially, thus it does not support the keys and only work on certain datatype such as literal, string, boolean, float and etc. [21] The reasoning process in FaCT++ starts with several optimisation techniques. Once completed the pre-processing of the input. The process will continue with classification by choosing the concepts using satisfiability checker.

3.6   HermiT

HermiT reasoner is implemented based on hypertableau calculus algorithm and incorporates the "anywhere blocking" strategy to reduce the number of possible models, which must be considered. It is a theorem prover for description logic that has the ability to handle DL SHIQ. The reasoner has the ability to check the ontology consistency and also subsumption relationships among concepts. Other than that, the reasoner also has the ability to handle class and property classification as well as a description graph. [11],[22] Hypertableau calculus reside in the reasoner is used to handle ontology consistency. The reasoning component will be used to arrange class, object and data properties into hierarchies during the classification process. It also used to compute the set of instances for each class and property during the realisation process [22].

Among these six ontology reasoners, all of them support OWL DL formalism and rule reasoning except FaCT++, which does not work with rules. Majority of the ontology reasoners applied tableau algorithm to handle the ontology consistency. Each reasoner has the choice of defining and using own custom rule language or uses the standard rule language defined by semantic web, which is known as SWRL. Table 2 shows the comparison of these six different ontology reasoners, which have been commonly deployed in ontology development.

Table 2. Semantic ontology reasoners comparison

Type	Jena	Pellet	OWLIM	Racer	FaCT++	HermiT
Rule support	Yes	Yes	Yes	Yes	No	Yes
Support language	OWL	OWL-DL	OWL	OWL-DL	OWL-DL	OWL-DL
Logic	Rule based	DL	Rule entailment	DL	DL	DL
Language rules	Jena	SWRL	Owl Horst	SWRL (partly)	No	SWRL
Methodology	Rete Algorithm	Tableau based	SAIL, TRREE	Tableau based	Tableau based	Hypertableau based
Protégé	Not applicable	Yes	No	Yes	Yes	Yes
Consistency check	Yes	Yes	Yes	No	Yes	Yes
Classification	Yes	Yes	Yes	Yes	Yes	Yes
ABox reasoning	Yes	Yes	Yes	Yes	Yes	Yes

Based on the experiments carried out in the researches done previously by [8], [9], [11],[17],[16], [23] and [24]. Due to different number of TBoxes and ABoxes defined in the ontology as well as the complexity of the ontology design, each reasoner will perform differently on each ontology. One reasoner can perform exceeding well in one ontology but worst in another. Thus different reasoner will perform differently in each ontology based system. These reasoners have been tested against the ontology consistency, ontology classification, and subsumption relationship among the concepts and also query processing time.

HermiT reasoner generally performs better than other reasoners in the situation where the ontology is easy to handle due to the smaller size and simple structure. Pellet reasoner performs better than FaCT++ and Racer during the consistency checking. Racer does not perform well in consistency checking because the reasoner requires a higher initial preparation to build index structure for performance of ensuring the ontology consistency. As for the classification, HermiT will not be able to perform efficiently in the situation where the ontology is complicated and large in size. Normally, Pellet reasoner is more efficient than OWLIM, FaCT++ and Racer reasoners. Racer will only be more efficient when it is used to handle TBox reasoning. FaCT++ outperforms others in checking the subsumption relationship among the concepts. Pellet reasoner comes up in the second and follows by racer and hermit reasoners. And lastly, the OWLIM is the most efficient reasoner when dealing with query processing. Jena is quite efficient when compare to Pellet reasoner.

4   Conclusion

Different ontology reasoner will yield different results when it is applied on the same ontology. This is due to different technique and strategy applied into it. Choosing an appropriate reasoner to deploy will be depending on the ontology designed. HermiT reasoner will be a suitable choice, if the ontology implemented is simple and small in size. For a large scale of ontology, OWLIM will be a better choice as it able to retrieve the relevant information in the shortest time. Generally, Pellet reasoner has shown a good performance in ensuring the consistency, classification and subsumption while managing the ontology. Jena framework work very well without the need to applying a tableau algorithm. The engine incorporates 3 reasoning strategies to deduce the result when query is inputted. Implementation of RETE algorithm in Jena has increased the query processing speed through pattern matching.

If the available reasoners do not meet the system requirements, a new reasoner will be implemented accordingly. Reasoning techniques or strategy and any other algorithm implemented will depend on the system criteria. Selecting an appropriate technique or algorithm will greatly improve the processing performance and the accuracy of the information retrieved. For example, forward chaining will use a lot of memory and loading time if the knowledge base is very large. Thus, this technique might not be advisable for large knowledge base. Backward chaining will not be an appropriate strategy, if the design of the knowledge base is complicated. Sometime it is useful to implement a hybrid strategy, since it combines both strategies together. The strategy able to perform basic inference using backward chaining and using forward chaining when establish a new fact.

Acknowledgement. The work presented in this paper has been supported by the Long Term Research Grant Scheme (LRGS) project funded by the Ministry of Higher Education (MoHE), Malaysia under Grants No. LRGS/TD/2011/UiTM/ICT/03.

References

1. Sowa, J.F.: Future Directions For Semantic System. In: Tolk, A., Jain, L.C. (eds.) Intelligence-Based Systems Engineering. ISRL, vol. 10, pp. 23–47. Springer, Heidelberg (2011)
2. Zou, Y., Finin, T.W., Chen, H.: F-Owl: An Inference Engine For The Semantic Web 1. In: Hinchey, M.G., Rash, J.L., Truszkowski, W.F., Rouff, C.A. (eds.) FAABS 2004. LNCS (LNAI), vol. 3228, pp. 238–248. Springer, Heidelberg (2004)
3. Cheng, J., Nara, S., Goto, Y.: Freeencal: A Forward Reasoning Engine With General-Purpose. In: Apolloni, B., Howlett, R.J., Jain, L. (eds.) KES 2007, Part II. LNCS (LNAI), vol. 4693, pp. 444–452. Springer, Heidelberg (2007)
4. Knowledge Representation Technologies in The Semantic Web, http://stexx.files.wordpress.com/2010/07/termpaper.pdf
5. Rif Rdf and Owl Compatibility, http://www.w3.org/TR/rif-rdf-owl/
6. Dalwadi, N., Nagar, B., Makwana, A.: Semantic Web And Comparative Analysis of Inference Engines. Int. J. of Computer Science and Information Technologies 3(3), 3843–3847 (2012)
7. Rezk, M., Nutt, W.: Combining Production Systems and Ontologies. In: Rudolph, S., Gutierrez, C. (eds.) RR 2011. LNCS, vol. 6902, pp. 287–293. Springer, Heidelberg (2011)
8. Meditskos And, G., Bassiliades, N.: Dlejena: A Practical Forward-Chaining Owl 2 Rl Reasoner Combining Jena and Pellet. Web Semant. Sci. Serv. Agents World Wide Web 8(1), 89–94 (2010)
9. Sirin, E., Parsia, B., Grau, B.C., Kalyanpur, A., Katz, Y.: Pellet: A Practical Owl-Dl Reasoner. Web Semant. Sci. Serv. Agents World Wide Web 5(2), 51–53 (2007)
10. Motik, B.: Hypertableau Reasoning For Description Logics. J. of Artificial Intelligence Research 36, 165–227 (2009)
11. Hermit: A Highly-Efficient Owl Reasoner, http://sunsite.informatik.rwth-aachen.de/Publications/CEUR-WS/Vol-432/owled2008eu_submission_12.pdf
12. Introduction to the Rete Algorithm Applies To, http://www.sdn.sap.com/irj/scn/go/portal/prtroot/docs/library/uuid/10dea1d3-fbef-2d10-0e89-a7447f95bc0e?QuickLink=index&overridelayout=true&49868865442396
13. Rattanasawad, T., Saikaew, K.R., Buranarach, M., Supnithi, T.: A Review and Comparison of Rule Languages and Rule-Based Inference Engines for the Semantic Web. In: International Computer Science and Engineering Conference, pp. 1–6. IEEE Press, New York (2013)
14. Apache Jena - Reasoners and Rule Engines: Jena Inference Support, http://Jena.Apache.Org/Documentation/Inference/
15. Sirin, E., Parsia, B., Cuenca, B., Grau, K.A., Katz, Y.: Pellet: A Practical OWL-DL Reasoner. J. Web Semantics 5(2), 51–53 (2007)
16. Haase, P., Ji, Q., Volz, R.: Benchmarking Owl Reasoners. In: Workshop on Advancing Reasoning on the Web: Scalability and Commonsense (2008)

17. Shi, H., Maly, K., Zeil, S., Zubair, M.: Comparison Of Ontology Reasoning Systems Using Custom Rules. In: International Conference on Web Intelligent, Mining and Semantics, p. 1. ACM, New York (2011)
18. Haarslev, V., Möller, R.: Racer System Description. In: Goré, R., Leitsch, A., Nipkow, T. (eds.) IJCAR 2001. LNCS (LNAI), vol. 2083, pp. 701–705. Springer, Heidelberg (2001)
19. Zouaq, A., Nkambou, R.: Building Domain Ontologies From Text For Educational Purposes. IEEE Transaction on Learning Technologies, 49–62 (2008)
20. Abburu, S.: A Survey on Ontology Reasoners and Comparison. Int. J. of Computer Applications. 57(17), 33–39 (2012)
21. Tsarkov, D., Horrocks, I.: Fact ++ Description Logic Reasoner: System Description. In: Furbach, U., Shankar, N. (eds.) IJCAR 2006. LNCS (LNAI), vol. 4130, pp. 292–297. Springer, Heidelberg (2006)
22. Glimm, B., Horrocks, I., Giorgos, M., Zhe, S.: Hermit: An Owl 2 Reasoner. J. of Automated Reasoning 1, 1–25 (2014)
23. Cuenca, B.: Comparison Of Reasoners for Large Ontologies in The Owl 2 El Profile. J. Semantic Web. 2(2), 1–5 (2011)
24. Stoilos, G., Cuenca Grau, B., Motik, B., Horrocks, I.: Repairing Ontologies For Incomplete Reasoners. In: Aroyo, L., Welty, C., Alani, H., Taylor, J., Bernstein, A., Kagal, L., Noy, N., Blomqvist, E. (eds.) ISWC 2011, Part I. LNCS, vol. 7031, pp. 681–696. Springer, Heidelberg (2011)

Nature Inspired Data Mining Algorithm for Document Clustering in Information Retrieval

Athraa Jasim Mohammed[1,2], Yuhanis Yusof [1], and Husniza Husni[1]

[1] School of Computing, College of Arts and Sciences, Universiti Utara Malaysia,
06010 Sintok, Kedah, Malaysia
s94734@student.uum.edu.my, {yuhanis,husniza}@uum.edu.my
[2] Information and Communication Technology Center, University of Technology,
Baghdad, Iraq
autoathraa@yahoo.com

Abstract. Document clustering is an important technique that has been widely employed in Information Retrieval (IR). Various clustering techniques have been reported, but the effectiveness of most techniques relies on the initial value of k clusters. Such an approach may not be suitable as we may not have prior knowledge on the collection of documents. To date, there are various swarm based clustering techniques proposed to address such problem, including this paper that explores the adaptation of Firefly Algorithm (FA) in document clustering. We extend the work on Gravitation Firefly Algorithm (GFA) by introducing a relocate mechanism that relocates assigned documents, if necessary. The newly proposed clustering algorithm, known as GFA_R, is then tested on a benchmark dataset obtained from the *20Newsgroups*. Experimental results on external and relative quality metrics for the GFA_R is compared against the one obtained using the standard GFA and Bisect K-means. It is learned that by extending GFA to becoming GFA_R, a better quality clustering is obtained.

Keywords: Firefly algorithm, text clustering, document clustering.

1 Introduction

Document clustering plays an essential role in Information Retrieval (IR) as it is capable to increase the precision and recall [1] values. This is due to having a better structure in accessing the required information. Document clustering includes techniques that automatically partition a collection of documents into meaningful groups, formally known as clusters [2]. Based on literature, document clustering techniques can be categorized into two approaches; Partitional and Hierarchical clustering techniques [3, 4].Partitional clustering can be used to classify a set of documents into a number of clusters and represent them into a flat level [5]. K-means is an example of this approach [6] where the clusters are constructed by minimizing the distance between center and objects. Because of its simplicity and efficiency for large dataset, it has been used in many applications and proved to be successful.

A. Jaafar et al. (Eds.): AIRS 2014, LNCS 8870, pp. 382–393, 2014.

However, the main drawback of the algorithm is that it is highly dependent on the initialization of k number of clusters [6].

On the other hand, Hierarchical clustering builds multi levels of clusters by utilizing one of the two widely used approaches; divisive approach(top down) or agglomerative approach (bottom up) [7]. The divisive approach divides a dataset into smaller groups and organizes clusters in a hierarchy form [8]. An example of this approach is the Bisect K-means [9, 20], where, at each level, the algorithm chooses cluster to classify into two clusters by selecting two centers and assigning the objects to similar center. The operation of identifying a cluster to be split is based on some criterion such as minimum intra cluster or maximum average distance. On the other hand, the agglomerative approach merges two clusters into one cluster based on some criterion such as single link, complete link or average link [20]. One popular algorithm of such approach is the UPGMA [10].

The goal of document clustering algorithms is to obtain natural clusters without the utilization of prior knowledge. Nevertheless, most clustering algorithm requires the initialization of k value, which is usually unknown to the user. This problem can be treated as an optimization problem. Based on literature, there are two approaches to identify the optimal k value: first, using the swarm based approach that mimics the capability of swarm insects such as ants, flocks, bees, etc. [11]. Swarm based approach utilize swarm like agents to group data directly without the need to define the number of clusters. An example is the Dynamic FClust that is based on bird flocks of agents [12]. The other approach obtains the actual k value using performance metrics in estimation the clustering. Using this approach, initially, we need to define the range of k values; minimum and maximum value of k. Then, execute the clustering method with different k clusters and measure the performance. The maximum/minimum value of performance metrics can be chosen to represent the best obtained clusters [1].

In this paper, the Firefly Algorithm (FA), which was introduced by Yang (2010) [16, 17, 18], is utilized for text clustering. In particular, we extend the work of Gravitation Firefly Algorithm GFA [19], by introducing a re-locate mechanism that aims to improve the clustering result by enhancing the purity of produced clusters. A benchmark dataset obtained from the *20Newsgroups* is used to realize the proposed mechanism. The paper is organized as follows; Section 2 provides the related work in text clustering while section 3 includes description on GFA clustering algorithm [19]. Section 4containselaboration on the proposed GFA_R and the results are presented in section 5. Finally, conclusion of the work is made in section 6.

2   Related Works

This section provides a review on several algorithms commonly used in text clustering, and this includes K-means and Bisect K-means. Furthermore, it also contains discussions on swarm algorithms such as PSO and Firefly Algorithm.

2.1   K-means

K-means is an example of partitional clustering algorithm that has been widely used in many domains. It is easily implemented, efficient in execution and simple [6]. K-means initially selects k number of clusters. This is followed by assigning objects in a dataset to the nearest center (The similarity is determined by Euclidean distance). The center of each cluster is calculated by identifying the mean. The process of assigning objects and recalculates continue until the stopping condition is reached. Fig. 1 illustrates the process of K-means.

Step1: Randomly choose K cluster centers.
Step2: Assign each object to closest center.
Step3: Recalculate the centers.
Step4: Repeat step1 and step2 until stop condition is reached.

Fig. 1. Steps in K-means [6]

K-means has been widely utilized in text clustering [21], [27]. The work presented in [27] solves the problem of random initial centers in k-means by using a prior knowledge of documents in the collection and employs Euclidean distance of K-means. The results outperformed the standard K-means. On the other hand, in [21], researchers proposed a variant of K-means, known as Bisect K-means. It generates better document clusters compared to K-means according to entropy performance metric and overall similarity metric.

2.2   Bisect K-means

Bisect K-means is an example of algorithm for divisive hierarchical approach and was proposed by Steinbach et al. in 2000 [21]. The algorithm classifies collection of objects into smaller groups and organizes clusters in a hierarchy. At each level,it randomly chooses two centers and assigns objects to a similar center. The operation of choosing a cluster to be split is based on some criterion such as minimum intra cluster or maximum average distance [9], [20]. The process of Bisect K-means is illustrated in Fig. 2.

Step1: Randomly choose two cluster centers.
Step2: Clustering using K-means method.
Step3: If not reach number of clusters.
Step4: Choose the cluster that has smallest intra similarity,
       Repeat step1 until reach number of clusters.

Fig. 2. The process of Bisect K-means [20, 21]

There has been work[9] that proposed a cooperative approach between Bisect K-means and K-means, where, the cooperative approach combines the output results of Bisect K-means and K-means utilizing cooperative and merging matrices. Similarly, in [20], a hybrid between Bisect K-means and UPGMA is proposed where Bisect

K-means generates higher than K number of cluster and use UPGMA to combine clusters to produce better clusters. We learn from these two works that a refinement step is important to change the misplaced document.

2.3   Particle Swarm Optimization PSO

As discussed in section one, various work can be seen in utilizing swarm based approaches in addressing problem faced by the K-means algorithm. One example of Meta-heuristic optimization algorithm includes the Particle Swarm Optimization (PSO) which was invented by Kennedy and Eberhart(1995). The basic idea of PSO comes from the flock and foraging behavior where each solution has n dimensions search space. The birds did not have search space, so it is called "Particles". Each particle has a fitness function value that can be computed using a velocity of particles flight direction and distance. The process of basic PSO clustering [15] is illustrated in Fig. 3.

Step1: Each particle, randomly choose K cluster centers.
Step2: For each Particle.
Step3: Assign each document to closest center.
Step4: Compute the fitness value based on average distance between documents and center (ADDC).
Step5: Update the velocity and position of particle.
Step6: Repeat step2 until one of stop conditions is reached; the maximum number is reached or the average change in center is less than threshold (predefined value).

Fig. 3. The process of basic PSO clustering algorithm [15]

In [15], empirical work on the integration of PSO and K-means has been presented to solve the problem of local optima in K-means. Such an approach has later motivated the utilization of extended Jaccard coefficient as objective function in PSO [28]. The results demonstrated that a better performance was obtained compared to the K-means [6], Bisect K-means [9], agglomerative [20] and graph based.

2.4   Standard Firefly Algorithm

Another swarm based algorithm is the Firefly algorithm (FA). It has ability to identify global optimal solution efficiency [29]. The idea of Firefly algorithm is based on two important factors; the light intensity and the attractiveness between fireflies. The light intensity of a firefly is related with the objective function $f(x)$. The objective function can be a maximization or minimization problem. The attractiveness, β, between fireflies is related with light intensity and changes based on the distance between two fireflies. The process of Firefly algorithm is shown in Fig. 4 [16], [18].

In this paper, we present a variant of the FA to be employed in document clustering, the Gravitation Firefly Algorithm (GFA) [19]. Our earlier work GFA is extended to include a relocating mechanism that can be utilized upon the completion of clusters creation. In the following section, we present the GFA while a newly proposed variant of FA is included in section 4.

Step1: Generate Initial population of firefly randomly xi (i=1, 2,.., n),Light Intensity I at xi
       is determine by Objective function f(xi).

Step2: Define light absorption coefficient γ.

Step3: While (t < Max Generation)

Step4: For i=1 to N (N all fireflies)

Step5: For j=1 to N

Step6: If (Ii<Ij) { $X^i = X^i + \beta_0 exp^{(-\gamma r_{ij}^2)} * (X^j - X^i) + \alpha \varepsilon_i$ }

Step7: $\beta = \beta_0 exp^{(-\gamma r_{ij}^2)}$

Step8: Evaluate new solutions and update light intensity.

Fig. 4. The process of Firefly Algorithm [16]

3   Gravitation Firefly Algorithm (GFA)

Gravitation Firefly algorithm [19] was introduced as a variant of FA in text clustering. It contains two parts; obtain centers and construct clusters. In [19], to obtain the centers, each firefly is represented by a single document and the initial brightness, I, of the firefly is presented by the force between each document and an identified center of cluster. The document that has high force is selected to represent the centroid. The GFA [19] structure is as shown in Fig. 5.

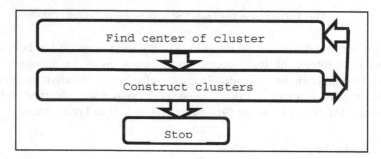

Fig. 5. Structure of GFA [19]

The 'construct clusters' phase starts after a center is found. Initially, two clusters are constructed; the first includes documents that have high similarity with the identified center (centroid), and the second cluster contains documents with lower similarity values. The process of finding a centroid and its cluster continues for the second cluster and repeats until all documents are grouped accordingly. Such an approach may produce a large number of clusters and hence may jeopardize the performance of a retrieval system. Furthermore, the assignment of a document to a cluster is permanent as it is based on a pre-defined threshold value. This means that documents that are similar to the first identified centroid are assigned to the first cluster. However, there is a possibility that these documents are more similar to any of the upcoming centroids. Such a situation will lead to poor purity. Hence, it is proposed that the GFA allows the re-location of an assigned document.

4   Gravitation Firefly Algorithm with Relocate Mechanism (GFA_R)

In this paper, we introduced another variant of FA that is termed as Gravitation Firefly Algorithm with Relocate (GFA_R). The GFA_R operates when a new cluster, in GFA [19], is constructed. This algorithm calculates the similarity between the newly identified centroid (center of new cluster) and documents that have been assigned to other (previous) clusters. If the similarity value is higher, then the document is moved (re-locate) from the original cluster to the newly created cluster. Fig. 6 illustrates the pseudo code of the proposed GFA_R.

```
Step1: Initial m=number of clusters.
Step2: If m>=2
Step3: For K=1 to (m-1)
Step4: If length (current cluster (K))>1
Step5: For Z=1 to length (current cluster(K))
Step6: If document (Z) not equal center(K)
Step7: If similarity (center(m),document(Z)) greater than similarity (center(K),
        document (Z))
Step8: Move (Z) from current cluster to recent cluster (m).
Step9: end for
Step10: end for
```

Fig. 6. Pseudo code of GFA_R

5   Experimental Results

In order to study the effectiveness of introducing a re-locate mechanism in GFA, an experiment was conducted on the 20Newsgroups [22]. Table 1 illustrates a brief description of the utilized dataset.

Table 1. Description of data

Dataset Topics	No. of Documents	Classes	Total No. of Documents	Total No. of Classes	No. of Terms
Comp.sys.mac.hardware	100	1			
Rec.sport.baseball	100	1	300	3	2275
Sci.electronic	100	1			

This evaluation is performed by comparing the proposed GFA_R with the standard GFA [19] and also Bisect K-means [20]. Two types of performance indices are used; Relative indices such as Davis Bouldin Index (DBI) and Dunn's Index (DI), and External indices such as Purity, F-measure and Entropy. Further, a statistical analysis of paired samples t-test is performed on the differences between the pairs of GFA and GFA_R, and GFA_R and Bisect K-means. All experiments were carried out in Matlabon windows 8 with a 2000 MHz processor and 4 GB memory. We execute GFA [19], GFA_R, and Bisect K-means [20] for ten (10)times with different number of iterations and compute the average value for each validity indices.

5.1   Comparison of GFA_R with GFA and Bisect K-means

Table 2 tabularizes the experimental results of Purity, F-measure, Entropy, DBI and DI for three algorithms, the proposed GFA_R, GFA and Bisect K-means. As can be seen from Table 2, the DBI value for GFA [19] is less than the GFA_R and Bisect K-means in all iteration, while, the DI value of GFA_R is higher than GFA in iteration 1, 2 and 10 compare against GFA and higher than Bisect K-means in all iteration. Based on literature, the high value of DI and smallest value of DBI is best quality algorithm [26].

Table 2. Results: GFA_R vs. GFA vs. Bisect K-means

Validity Indices		Algorithms	Iterations				
			1	2	5	10	20
Relative Indices	DBI	GFA	1.5189	1.5426	1.5702	1.6212	1.6155
		GFA_R	1.6342	1.6527	1.6632	1.6488	1.6501
		Bisect K-means	7.005	6.4493	6.6672	6.7440	6.8225
	DI	GFA	0.8783	0.8597	0.8646	0.8453	0.8561
		GFA_R	0.9108	0.8945	0.8590	0.8584	0.8540
		Bisect K-means	0.1640	0.2053	0.1769	0.1864	0.1873
External Indices	Purity	GFA	0.7557	0.6910	0.6803	0.6857	0.6833
		GFA_R	0.8723	0.8807	0.8593	0.8640	0.8567
		Bisect K-means	0.4006	0.4137	0.4480	0.4297	0.4950
	F-measure	GFA	0.5323	0.4705	0.4647	0.4717	0.4821
		GFA_R	0.4622	0.4526	0.4602	0.4889	0.4804
		Bisect K-means	0.4245	0.4375	0.4486	0.4391	0.4855
	Entropy	GFA	0.7816	0.9679	0.9595	0.9411	0.9353
		GFA_R	0.5011	0.4798	0.5134	0.5118	0.5319
		Bisect K-means	1.5413	1.5316	1.4759	1.5057	1.4071

Further, it is noted from Table II that the purity of GFA$_R$ outperformed the GFA and Bisect K-means in all iterations where the best purity value (0.8807) generates by GFA$_R$ in iteration 2 while the best for Bisect K-means is (0.4950) generated in iteration 20 and the best purity value for GFA is (0.7557) generated in iteration 1. In addition, the GFA$_R$ has best Entropy against GFA and Bisect K-means also in all iteration, where the best value of GFA$_R$ is (0.4798) produced in iteration 2, while Bisect K-means generates best value (1.4071) in iteration 20 and GFA generates best value (0.7816) in iteration 1. Despite of GFA$_R$ has the highest F-measure against Bisect K-means in most iterations (refer to iterations 1, 2, 5 and 10), where the best value (0.4889) is obtained in iteration 10, but it fails in F-measure quality against GFA, where GFA performs well. It is learned from the literature, that high value of purity and F-measure (approaching to 1) and lower Entropy (approaching to 0) leads to good quality clusters [8, 20].

Fig. 7 shows the graphical results of the relative indices among GFA, GFA$_R$ and Bisect K-means.

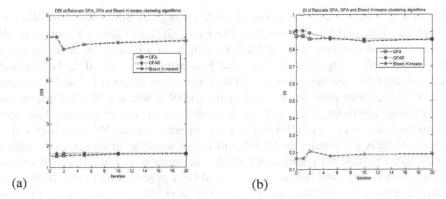

Fig. 7. Graphical results of relative indices among three algorithms; GFA, GFA$_R$ and Bisect K-means algorithms. (a) DBI and (b) DI.

In Fig. 7(a), it can be observed that the curve of DBI in GFA is smallest than GFA$_R$ and Bisect K-means. According to [26] the better clustering solution has smallest value of DBI. This means the relocating algorithm not enhance the DBI metric in GFA. In Figure 7(b), we can see the curve of DI in GFA$_R$ is highest value than Bisect K-means in all iteration and is highest than GFA in iteration 1, 2, 10 and 20 excluding iteration 5 which GFA has highest value than GFA$_R$. According to [26] the better clustering solution has highest value of DI. This means the relocating algorithm effect on DI metric in GFA.

Fig. 8 displays the graphical results of the external indices among GFA, Relocating GFA$_R$ algorithms and Bisect K-means.

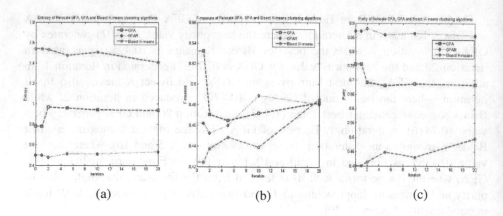

(a)   (b)   (c)

Fig. 8. Graphical results of external indices among three algorithms; GFA, GFA_R and Bisect K-means algorithms. (a) Purity, (b) F-measure and (c) Entropy

Fig. 8(a) illustrates the Purity curve of GFA, GFA_R and Bisect K-means. We can see that the curve of GFA_R higher than the curve GFA and Bisect K-means in all iteration. We can conclude that the GFA running with a relocate mechanism has a higher purity effect. Fig. 8(b) includes the F-measure curve of GFA, GFA_R and Bisect K-means. We see that the curve of GFA increase in iteration 1, 2 and 5 than the curve of GFA_R which generates the best value 0.4889 in iteration 10. This means that the relocating algorithm affect few on F-measure quality performance. Fig. 8(c) presents the Entropy curve of GFA, GFA_R and Bisect K-means. We can observe that the curve of GFA_R is smaller than GFA and Bisect K-means in all iterations, where the best value is (0.4798) produced by GFA_R in iteration 2, while Bisect K-means generates best value (1.4071) in iteration 20 and GFA generates best value (0.7816) in iteration 1. Lesson learned from this result is that the GFA_R produces better Entropy values.

5.2   Statistical Result

The statistical analysis of paired samples t-test is performed on the differences between the pairs GFA and GFA_R, and also Bisect K-means and GFA_R. We suppose the null hypotheses and the alternative hypotheses as shown below:

H_0: There is no difference between the mean of two algorithms.
H_1: There is a difference between the mean of two algorithms.

Table 3 illustrates the p-value using the samples of purity metric GFA_R, GFA and Bisect K-means. As can be seen in the table, i.e Table 3, the p-value between GFA_R and GFA and GFA_R and Bisect K-means is less than (0.05). This means the re-locate mechanism affects the purity of GFA. Therefore, we reject the null hypotheses and conclude that there is sufficient evidence to accept the alternative hypotheses.

Table 3. The p-value between GFA & GFA$_R$ and Bisect K-means &GFA$_R$

iteration	Purity	
	GFA &GFA$_R$	Bisect K-means &GFA$_R$
1	2.2403E-4	6.7699E-11
2	7.7829E-6	1.23628E-9
5	6.8930E-7	3.40578E-9
10	1.2662E-8	7.62733E-9
20	-	2.43039E-7

Note: In iteration 20, the value cannot be computed because the standard error of the difference is 0.

6   Conclusion

In this paper, we present a GFA that includes a relocate mechanism and this new variant of FA is introduced as Gravitation Firefly Algorithm with Relocate (GFA$_R$). The GFA$_R$ offers the ability to change the location of any assigned document(s) from a cluster to a newly created cluster. Such an approach is taken to improve the clustering result (in particular the purity value) produced by the standard GFA [19]. The proposed GFA$_R$ is realized in a benchmark dataset obtained from *20Newsgroups*. The obtained results indicate that the proposed GFA$_R$ outperformed GFA in Purity, Entropy and DI. Additionally, it is also a better approach as compared to the Bisect K-means. Hence, indicating that it can become a competitive method in the area of swarm based clustering.

Acknowledgement. Authors would like to thank the Ministry of Education for providing the financial support under the Fundamental Research Grant Scheme (s/o: 12894).

References

1. Sayed, A., Hacid, H., Zighed, D.: Exploring Validity Indices for Clustering Textual Data. In: Zighed, D.A., Tsumoto, S., Ras, Z.W., Hacid, H. (eds.) Mining Complex Data. SCI, vol. 165, pp. 281–300. Springer, Heidelberg (2009)
2. Miner, G., Elder, J., Fast, A., Hill, T., Nisbet, R., Delen, D.: Practical Text Mining and Statistical Analysis for Non-structured Text Data Applications, 1st edn. Elsevier (2012)
3. Jain, A.K., Murty, M.N., Flynn, P.J.: Data Clustering: A review. ACM Comput. Surv. 31(3), 264–323 (1999)
4. Aliguliyev, R.M.: Clustering of Document Collection-A Weighted Approach. Expert Systems with Applications 36(4), 7904–7916 (2009)
5. Luo, C., Li, Y., Chung, S.M.: Text Document Clustering based on Neighbors. Data and Knowledge Engineering 68(11), 1271–1288 (2009)
6. Jain, A.K.: Data Clustering: 50 years beyond K-means. Pattern Recognition Letters 31(8), 651–666 (2010)
7. Gil-Garicia, R., Pons-Porrata, A.: Dynamic Hierarchical Algorithms for Document Clustering. Pattern Recognition Letters 31(6), 469–477 (2010)

8. Forsati, R., Mahdavi, M., Shamsfard, M., Meybodi, M.R.: Efficient Stochastic Algorithms for Document Clustering. Information Sciences 220, 269–291 (2013)
9. Kashef, R., Kamel, M.S.: Enhanced Bisecting K-means Clustering using Intermediate Cooperation. Pattern Recognition 42(11), 2557–2569 (2009)
10. Yujian, L., Liye, X.: Unweighted Multiple Group Method with Arithmetic Mean. In: The IEEE Fifth International Conference on Bio-Inspired Computing: Theories and Applications (BIC-TA), pp. 830–834 (2010)
11. Tan, S.C., Ting, K.M., Teng, S.W.: A general stochastic clustering method for automatic cluster discovery. Pattern Recognition 44(10-11), 2786–2799 (2011)
12. Saka, E., Nasraoui, O.: On Dynamic Data Clustering and Visualization using Swarm Intelligence. In: 2010 IEEE The 26th International Conference on Data Engineering Workshops (ICDEW), pp. 337–340 (2010)
13. He, Y., Hui, S.C., Sim, Y.: A Novel Ant-Based Clustering Approach for Document Clustering. In: Ng, H.T., Leong, M.-K., Kan, M.-Y., Ji, D. (eds.) AIRS 2006. LNCS, vol. 4182, pp. 537–544. Springer, Heidelberg (2006)
14. Zaw, M.M., Mon, E.E.: Web Document Clustering Using Cuckoo Clustering Algorithm based on Levy Flight. International Journal of Innovation and Applied Studies 4(1), 182–188 (2013)
15. Cui, X., Potok, T.E., Palathingal, P.: Document Clustering using Particle Swarm Optimization. In: Proceedings of the 2005 IEEE Swarm Intelligence Symposium, SIS 2005, pp. 185–191 (2005)
16. Yang, X.S.: Nature-inspired Metaheuristic Algorithms, 2nd edn. Luniver Press, United Kingdom (2010)
17. Yang, X.S.: Firefly Algorithm, Stochastic Test Functions and Design Optimization. Int. J. Bio-Inspired Computation 2(2), 78–84 (2010)
18. Yang, X.S., He, X.: Firefly Algorithm: Recent Advances and Applications. Int. J. Swarm Intelligence 1(1), 36–50 (2013)
19. Mohammed, A.J., Yusof, Y., Husni, H.: A Newton's Universal Gravitation Inspired Firefly Algorithm for Document Clustering. In: Jeong, H.Y., Obaidat, M.S., Yen, N.Y., Park, J.J. (eds.) Advanced in Computer Science and Its Applications. LNEE, vol. 279, pp. 1259–1264. Springer, Heidelberg (2014)
20. Murugesan, K., Zhang, J.: Hybrid Bisect K-means Clustering Algorithm. In: IEEE International Conference on Business Computing and Global Informatization (BCGIN), pp. 216–219. IEEE (2011)
21. Steinbach, M., Karypis, G., Kumar, V.: A comparison of document clustering techniques. In: Proc. KDD Workshop on Text Mining, Boston (2000)
22. 20 Newsgroup Data Set, http://people.csail.mit.edu/20Newsgroup/
23. Manning, C.D., Raghavan, P., Schütze, H.: Introduction to Information Retrieval, 1 ed. Cambridge University Press (2008)
24. Shannon, C.E.: A Mathematical theory of communication. Bell System Technical Journal 27, 379–423, 623–656 (1948)
25. Das, S., Abraham, A., Konar, A.: Metaheuristic Clustering. Springer, Heidelberg (2009)
26. Youssef, S.M.: A New Hybrid Evolutionary-based Data Clustering Using Fuzzy Particle Swarm Optimization. In: The 23rd IEEE International Conference on Tools with Artificial Intelligence, pp. 717–724 (2011)
27. Hu, G., Zhou, S., Guan, J., Hu, X.: Towards Effective Document Clustering: A Constrained K-means Based Approach. Information Processing & Management 44(4), 1397–1409 (2008)

28. Lu, Y., Wang, S., Li, S., Zhou, C.: Text Clustering via Particle Swarm Optimization. In: The Swarm Intelligence Symposium, pp. 45–51. IEEE (2009)
29. Tang, R., Fong, S., Yang, X.S., Deb, S.: Integrating Nature-Inspired Optimization Algorithms to K-means Clustering. In: Proceedings of the 7th International Conference on Digital Information Management (ICDIM), pp. 116–123. IEEE, Macau (2012)

Enhancing Machine-Learning Methods for Sentiment Classification of Web Data

Zhaoxia Wang[1], Victor Joo Chuan Tong[1], and Hoong Chor Chin[2]

[1] Social and Cognitive Computing Department
Institute of High Performance Computing (IHPC),
Agency for Science, Technology and Research (A*STAR), Singapore, 138632
{wangz,tongjc}@ihpc.a-star.edu.sg
[2] Department of Civil & Environmental Engineering,
National University of Singapore, Singapore, 117578
chin.hc@nus.edu.sg

Abstract. With advances in Web technologies, more and more people are turning to popular social media platforms such as Twitter to express their feelings and opinions on a variety of topics and current issues online. Sentiment analysis of Web data is becoming a fast and effective way of evaluating public opinion and sentiment for use in marketing and social behavioral studies. This research investigates the enhancement techniques in machine-learning methods for sentiment classification of Web data. Feature selection, negation dealing, and emoticon handling are studied in this paper for their ability to improve the performance of machine-learning methods. The range of enhancement techniques is tested using different text data sets, such as tweets and movie reviews. The results show that different enhancement methods can improve classification efficacy and accuracy differently.

Keywords: Emoticon handling, negation dealing, feature selection, hybrid method, machine learning, sentiment classification, Twitter, Web data.

1 Introduction

With the advent of social media, the ways in which people communicate their comments, feedback and critiques have changed dramatically. They can now post reviews and opinions on discussion topics, products, services, policies and other issues through blogs, social networks and social media such as Twitter. Twitter is a micro-blogging service that allows its users to publish status known as "tweets" which are limited to 140 characters in length. The service boasts over 140 million active users and over 340 million tweets per day [1].

"Tweets" as one of popular Web data reflects users' emotions and attitudes on almost every topic for which they can find readers and listeners [2]. As a result, sentiment analysis has emerged as a powerful tool for using tweet data to extract useful information for public organizations and governments, as well as private organizations and citizen's groups [1].

A. Jaafar et al. (Eds.): AIRS 2014, LNCS 8870, pp. 394–405, 2014.

Sentiment analysis can be used to characterize a user's attitude towards a topic or issue of interest based on the identification of patterns of reactions that can be discovered within text-based data that is posted and made available for collection [3,4,5]. Sentiment patterns hidden within comments, feedback and critiques often provide useful information that can be leveraged for different purposes [1]. One example is to obtain the data shared by Internet users reflecting their sentiments toward services or products to help improve product or service quality.

Sentiment patterns can be categorized into various types, for example, positive, negative, neutral and ambivalent (mixed) or into more detailed categories, such as very good, good, satisfactory, bad, and very bad [6]. Sentiment pattern analysis can be thought of as a pattern-detection and classification task in which each category takes on the form of a sentiment pattern [3].

Sentiment-classification methods can be broadly categorized into two main classes: lexicon-based and machine-learning-based methods. The lexicon-based method derives the dominant polarity of a text (i.e., positive or negative) by searching for opinion and emotion indicators based on lexicons [7,8]. It derives the sentiment of the entire text based on handling the use of these words or phrases that appear in the lexicons. However, the accuracy of the existing lexicon-based approach is limited by semantic ambiguity.

The other class is a learning-based approach that derives the relationship between features of the text segment. Models based upon such machine-learning-based methods typically require a large training database. This approach can achieve better classification results compared to simple lexicon-based approaches and is widely used [9,10]. However, it is difficult to improve the performance of such machine-learning methods even there are enough training datasets [11]. Therefore, how to increase the classification accuracy of machine-learning-based methods through improved knowledge and design has been a key concern for many researchers [11].

Several enhancements, i.e., feature selection [12,13,14], negation dealing [10],[15] and emoticon handling [16,17] are used to handle the sentiment classification problem. While these enhancements have been employed previously, how they perform alongside the different machine-learning methods has not been well researched. Therefore, from this paper, we seek to demonstrate how these enhancement techniques can improve the efficacy and accuracy in sentiment classification of Web data for the machine-learning methods studied. Among the many existing machine-learning-based methods, the methods of naïve Bayes (NB) [18,19] Maximum Entropy (MaxEnt) [20] and support vector machine (SVM) [21,22] are chosen for investigation in this paper, because these have been commonly applied in text data analysis.

2   Web Data Collections and Preparations

The Internet has long been recognized as an accessible, inexpensive and effective channel within which to collect all kinds of cross-sectional data. Web data can be downloaded directly from the web or collected by using various application programming interfaces (APIs) and web crawlers that are provided by third parties.

We made use of two types of dataset: (1) data downloaded directly from third parties and (2) data collected using an API.

For the first type of dataset, we downloaded the data from a "twitter-sentiment-analyzer" website which contained 1.6 million pre-classified tweets prepared as part of a research effort [23]. We downloaded ds_10k, ds_20k, ds_40k, ds_200k, ds_400k and ds_1400k which consisted of 10k, 20k, 40k, 200k, 400k and 1.4m pre-classified tweets respectively.

We also downloaded movie-review data [24] for use in sentiment-analysis experiments. This is a collection of 1000 positive and 1000 negative processed movie-review documents labeled with respect to their overall sentiment polarity.

Twitter provides an API that allows easy access to tweets. Using the GET search/tweets resource, we could search for tweets on a specific topic or keyword and limited to a specific geographical region and also to a specific language.

Sentiment patterns derived from public domain social media data may be indicators of changes that can have negative and potentially serious consequences, as is the case with worsening social sentiment related to public transportation, the degradation of air and water quality, and other issues that affect land and livability issues [25]. Therefore, the second type of data was collected through Twitter API by using the keyword "MRT" (for "Mass Rapid Transit") in Singapore. We used location-constraining geo codes to ensure that the tweets originated from Singapore. The collection and analysis of such data can help government agencies and other organizations to understand public attitudes toward urban transportation services through sentiment analysis.

Since a training data set or a set of pre-classified data was necessary for machine-learning-based methods, the collected data needed to be pre-classified to obtain training data if the data had not been annotated or labeled. To analyze the tweets on Singapore's MRT service from citizens and residents, two social scientists with domain expertise in MRT performance were tasked to extract relevant tweets. Eight assistants with different backgrounds (e.g. students and researchers from the National University of Singapore, students from high schools and scientists from Social and Cognitive Computing group) worked as annotators to classify the tweets manually. They performed the classification tasks independently.

We compared and analyzed the classifications of the eight annotators and found that the coincident percentages among them were between 80.1% and 86.8%. Different people have different understandings for the same tweet. We selected the tweets that the annotators gave the same classifications and excluded the ones that different annotators give different classifications to form a human annotated dataset. The obtained human annotated datasets (HA data) together with the downloaded pre-classified data were both used to test the enhancement of the classifiers.

We separated each type of dataset obtained into a training set and a testing set, containing three-quarters and one-quarter of the entities respectively.

3   Methods and Enhancements

Sentiment classification can be described as a process in which a classification algorithm determines the target cluster to which some data belongs. There is a wide variety of machine-learning-based methods, such as naïve Bayes (NB) classifier, Maximum Entropy (MaxEnt) classifier and support vector machine (SVM), etc.

Naïve Bayes classifier is a probabilistic classifier that assumes the statistical independence of each feature (or word) and is a conditional model based on Bayes' formula [18,19]:

$$P(c_i|d)=P(c_i). P(d \mid c_i) \ /P(d) \tag{1}$$

where $P(c_i|d)$ is the posterior probability of instance d being in class c_i , $P(c_i)$ is prior probability of occurrence of class c_i. It can be calculated by $P(c_i)$ $=N_i/N$, where N_i is the number of textual data assigned to class $P(c_i)$, and N is the number of total textual data. $P(d \mid c_i)$ is the probability of generating instance d given class c_i, and $P(d)$ is the prior probability of instance d occurring.

For a textual data $d = (d_1,d_2,...,d_n)$, with the independence assumption, a Bayes classifier, is a function defined as follows [18,19]:

$$Classifying \ (d,c_i) = argmax \ P(c_i) . P(d_1|c_i) . P(d_2|c_i) \ ... \ P(d_n|c_i) \tag{2}$$

MaxEnt is another probabilistic classifier and uses a multinomial logistic regression model [20]. It is closely related to Naive Bayes classifier, but the model uses search-based optimization to find weights for the features that maximize the likelihood of the training data.

For each feature d_i and class c_i, a joint feature $g(d_i,c_j)=m$ is defined, where m is the number of times that d_i occurs in a document in class c_i.   Via iterative optimization, a weight γ is assigned to each of the joint feature $g(d_i,c_j)$, so as to maximize the log-likelihood of the training data. The probability of class c_i given a document d and weights γ :

$$P(c_i|d,\gamma) = \frac{exp \sum_i \gamma_i g_i(c_j,d)}{\sum_j exp \sum_i \gamma_i g_i(c_j,d)} \tag{3}$$

The difference between these two probabilistic classifiers, Naïve Bayes and MaxEnt classifier, can be seen from Eqn. 1 and 3.

SVM is a non-probabilistic classifier that works by constructing a decision surface on a high-dimensional space [21,22]. The principle of the SVM algorithm is to find a decision surface, named hyperplane that optimally splits the training set. The training data are mapped to a very high-dimensional space. Then, the algorithm finds the hyperplane in this space with the largest margin, separating the data to different groups [21] .

The decision function is defined as follows:

$$f(x) = sign \ (\sum_i \alpha_i K(x_i^p,x) + b) \tag{4}$$

where α_i is Lagrange multipliers determined during SVM training. Parameter b determines the shift of the hyperplane, and it is determined during SVM training. $K(x_i^v, x)$ is kernel function [26]. Parameter selection is a pivotal step to decide the performance of SVM [21], [26]. We have tested different parameters and found that for this problem, the best parameter selection is when svm_type is "C-SVC" (multi-class classification) and kernel_type is "LINEAR".

In this paper we explore these three machine-learning methods, and integrate feature selection, negation dealing, and emoticon-handling techniques to test and compare the conformance of the machine-learning methods.

We started with a basic implementation of each of these machine-learning classifiers. After analyzing their performance, we improved them by integrating different enhancement techniques, including feature selection [12,13,14] negation dealing [10] and emoticon handling [16,17].

3.1   Feature Selection

The main difficulties of the implementation of the machine-learning classifiers are the learning speed and effectiveness [12].   Without super computers, it is difficult to perform the task using machine-learning methods when dealing with high dimension data, especially with huge training datasets. In this paper, *Chi Square* feature selection is leveraged to reduce the number of data dimensions to improve the performance classifiers. *Chi Square* feature selection not only reduces the number of data dimensions, it also removes irrelevant, redundant, and noisy data [13].

Chi Square feature selection can be described as following:

$$\kappa^2 (c, f) = N (AI\text{-}BH) / [(A+H) (B+H) (A+B) (H+I)] \qquad (5)$$

where N is the total number of the training datasets. A is the number of data that contain the feature, f, and also belong category, c. B is the number of data that contain the feature, f, but do not belong to category, c. H is the number of data that do not contain the feature, f, but belong to category, c. I is the number of data that do not contain the feature, f, and do not belong to category, c.

The priority of each feature is calculated by *Chi Square* feature selection equation (Eqn. 1) and only top n features were selected.

3.2   Negation Dealing

During human comprehension of a sentence, negative words/phrases such as 'do not', 'never', 'seldom' can be one of the indicators for judging the orientation of the sentence [10]. For example, 'love' is a positive word, but it does not make the sentence positive in "I do not love this". Two ways of dealing with negation words are considered in this paper.   (1) Appending a NEGATE to the word directly after the negation word (NEGdword) and (2) appending a NEGATE to all words after the negation word until reaching a punctuation mark (NEGall).

3.3   Emoticon Handling

Analyzing the collected tweets, it was observed that emoticons were very often used by the Twitter user and presented the orientation of the sentiment of the tweets [17]. So by making use of emoticons, we considered the variants of positive and negative emoticons as shown in Table 1. We considered only these emoticons because they are widely used and have no ambiguous meaning. Analyzing the data collected, we found that there were sometimes negative emoticons in positive comments. Typing errors (e.g. typing a frowning face instead of a smiling face) could account for these. We assumed that the chance of mistyping an emoticon was low.

Table 1. Emoticon list

Positive Emoticons						Negative Emoticons		
:P	(:	;-)	(~:	[;	:d	:(	)':	)':
;P	(;	(-:	(~;	=]	;d	;(	=(	=(
:))	=)	(-;	:]	[=	:D	):	)=	)=
:)	(=	:~)	;]	;)	;D	);	={	={
:p	:-)	;~)	[:	;))	((;	:'(	}=	}=
;p	:3	;3	:-3	;-3	((:	T_T	Y_Y	Y.Y
^_^	^-^	<3	xD	XD		v.v	V_V	

4   Performance Evaluation

We trained each classifier using the training set and tested its accuracy using the testing set. The following performance metrics are used to evaluate the classification results: precision, recall, F-measure, and accuracy [9] [27]. These metrics are computed based on the values of true positive (*Tp*), false positive (*Fp*), true negative (*Tn*) and false negative (*Fn*) assigned classes.

Tp refers to the number of correctly identified positive. *Fp* is refers to the number of incorrectly identified positive. Similarly, *Tn* refers to the number of correctly identified negative. *Fn* is refers to the number of incorrectly identified negative.

Precision is the number of true positive out of all positively assigned documents, and it is given by:

$$\text{Precision} = Tp / (Tp + Fp) \tag{6}$$

Recall is the number of true positive out of the actual positive documents, and it is given by:

$$\text{Recall} = Tp / (Tp + Fn) \tag{7}$$

F-measure is a weighted method of precision and recall, and it is obtained as:

$$\text{F-measure} = 2 * \text{Precision} * \text{Recall} / (\text{Precision} + \text{Recall}) \tag{8}$$

Accuracy is calculated using the following formulae:

$$\text{Accuracy} = (Tp+Tn) / (Tp+Tn+Fp+Fn) \tag{9}$$

One or more of those items are selected by different research groups to discuss the performance [9], [27]. For real-world data analysis, the accuracy of the algorithm is one of the most important issues that concern managers or decision makers. In this paper, the discussion is focused on the accuracy of the classifiers.

5   Performance Results with Discussions on Different Enhancements

5.1   Basic Implementation of Machine-Learning Methods

Table 2 shows the results obtained by the basic implementation of each of these classifiers. The standard packages are used as basic implementation of the classifiers without leveraging any enhancement. There is no feature selection, negation dealing, and emoticon handling enhancements involved in this basic implementation.

Table 2. Classification accuracy of the basic implementation of the classifiers

Dataset	Accuracy of the classifiers (%)		
	SVM	*NB*	*MaxEnt*
ds_10k	70.12%	70.36%	70.20%
ds_20k	69.92%	70.40%	70.58%

The results show that the accuracies of these machine-learning methods are similar at about 70%.

The results of other larger datasets are not listed here because they cannot be computed for some classifiers (e.g. SVM faced "out of memory", and training time was long for other classifiers, such as MaxEnt).

5.2   Machine-Learning Methods with Feature Selection and Negation Dealing

In order to enhance the efficiency of the basic classifiers developed in Section A, only the top n features were selected. This selection ensured more common or high-frequency words were selected. As shown in Table 3, the selection enabled the classifier to use larger datasets, but when using larger datasets to train SVM, we still ran into memory limits, which we mark as "-" in the tables.

Table 4 and Table 5 show the results obtained by using NEGdword and NEGall techniques respectively.

Comparing Table 4 and Table 5, the accuracy of SVM is 74.17% using NEGd-word, higher than the 73.65% obtained by using NEGall, when using ds_40k dataset. The results of other larger datasets are not available for SVM since it faced "out of memory" problems.

Table 3. Classification accuracy of the classifiers with Top *n* feature selected

Dataset	Accuracy of the classifiers (%)			
	n	*SVM*	*NB*	*MaxEnt*
ds_40k	8000	73.98%	72.51%	72.89%
ds_200k	10000	-	74.91%	75.11%
ds_400k	10000	-	74.47%	74.60%
ds_1400k	12000	-	76.83%	76.84%

Table 4. Classification accuracy of the classifiers with Top *n* feature selected and NEGdword

Dataset	Accuracy of the classifiers (%)			
	n	*SVM*	*NB*	*MaxEnt*
ds_40k	8000	74.17%	72.90%	73.38%
ds_200k	10000	-	75.23%	75.40%
ds_400k	10000	-	74.93%	75.05%
ds_1400k	12000	-	77.30%	77.29%

Table 5. Classification accuracy of the classifiers with Top *n* feature selected and NEGall

Dataset	Accuracy of the classifiers (%)			
	n	*SVM*	*NB*	*MaxEnt*
ds_40k	8000	73.65%	72.97%	73.45%
ds_200k	10000	-	75.27%	75.46%
ds_400k	10000	-	74.88%	75.00%
ds_1400k	12000	-	77.28%	77.28%

For NB and MaxEnt classifiers, the accuracy fluctuated between 72.90% and 77.30% when integrating NEGword for classifying different dataset, while, the accuracy fluctuated between 72.97% and 77.28% when integrating NEGall. The results in Table 4 and Table 5 indicate that using NEGdword and NEGall have similar results when classifying the Tweet data. These similarities may be due to the simpler and shorter sentence structures that tweets have.

In order to further investigate the effect of the two negation-dealing techniques, we tested both the NEGdword and NEGall design for classifying more complicated and longer data, such as movie-review data.

The tweet data was simpler and shorter than the movie-review data since Twitter permits only 140 characters (letters) in a single tweet [28,29], while each movie review included about 3,000 characters   or several paragraphs, of around 700 words [27].

The results for classifying movie-review data are shown in Table 6. For these more complicated data, using NEGall was better than NEGdword for SVM and NB, while different for MaxEnt.

Overall both NEGall and NEGdword showed similar improved performance of the classifier when dealing with simpler and shorter sentence structure data, such as tweets. But, for more complicated data, NEGall and NEGdword could work differently.

Table 6. Classification accuracy of the classifiers with Top *n*   feature selected and two ways of dealing with negation

Movie dataset	Accuracy of the classifiers (%)			
	n	*SVM*	*NB*	*MaxEnt*
Without Negation Dealing	8000	82.8%	81.2%	81.8%
NEGdword	8000	82.80%	81.20%	81.80%
NEGall	8000	84.00%	81.60%	81.20%

5.3   Machine-Learning Methods with Feature Selection and Emoticon Handling

The pre-classified dataset we downloaded from the web does not include emoticons. As mentioned in Section 3, tweets were extracted using the Twitter API, which were then identified to be related to MRT service by the two domain experts and further classified by eight annotators into positive and negative tweets with and without consideration of the text emoticons. The accuracy of the different classifications is shown in Table 7.

Table 7. Classification accuracy of the classifiers with emoticon handling

Dataset	Accuracy of the classifiers (%)		
	SVM	*NB*	*MaxEnt*
Without Emoticon handling	61.11%	66.67%	72.22%
With Emoticon handling	75.00%	69.44%	75.00%

It is observed from Table 7 that the accuracy of SVM classifiers increased from 61.11% to 75.00%.   The accuracy of NB classifiers increased from 66.67% to 69.44% and for MaxEnt increased from 72.22% to 75.00%. Thus, emoticon handling has improved the performance of all the classifiers.

5.4   Further Discussions on the Enhancement of Machine-Learning Methods

Comparing the results for classifying these two types of data (tweets and movie reviews), the accuracy of the three classifiers was different, with higher accuracy when classifying movie reviews and lower accuracy when classifying tweets, as shown in Table 4. When we used the tweet data to train the classifier and tested the classifier with the movie-review data, the accuracy was rather low. These results are consistent with our previous experience that machine-learning classifiers are domain specific [12]. It is not easy to create a domain-independent machine-learning classifier while training the classifiers on a domain-mixed set of data [8].

It is well known that besides domain dependency, there are other disadvantages and challenges for machine-learning-based methods [22], such as labeling the documents or obtaining the training set, achieving high accuracy (higher than 80%), selecting the appropriate machine-learning method, modifying and dealing with unbalanced datasets. Despite these disadvantages and challenges, machine-learning methods are very useful and popular tools for classification tasks.

Currently, we are also working on lexicon-based sentiment-classification methods, hybrid methods (combining lexicon and machine learning), ruled-based methods, and emotion-pattern methods to develop more powerful tools for sentiment classification. Our experience shows that the crucial problem is the accuracy of the classifiers.

With increasing popularity in microblogging, there will be greater interest among netizens to express their opinions online. This is a rich source of data for analyzing and understanding social sentiments. Therefore, it is important that a system of enhancement and classification methods be established to do the work accurately and reliably.

6   Conclusion and Future Work

This research explores and improves on current machine-learning-based classification methods by integrating several enhancement designs in the classification process.

Selection of the most informative features is a crucial addition that greatly increases memory efficiency and shortens training time. In dealing with negation, NEGone and NEGall produce similar performance when dealing with tweet data, but give different results when dealing other types of data. Emoticon handling is very useful for classifying tweets with emoticons. In general, both these enhancements improve the performance of the classifiers. Our analysis results indicate that in dealing with tweet datasets, of the three machine-learning methods, NB and MaxEnt are the best choices for classifying Web text data with higher accuracy. NB needs a small memory resource, while SVM is able to achieve competitive accuracies but requires a large memory footprint.

This paper demonstrates the viability and applicability of using enhancements for various machine learning-based methods. Investigations into lexicon-based sentiment classification methods including the use of colloquial words and other local characteristics are in progress.

Acknowledgements. The work is supported by A*STAR Joint Council Office Development Programme "Social Technologies plus Programme". The authors would like to thank Dr. Rick GOH, Dr. Yinping YANG and Dr. Xiuju FU for their valuable discussions and comments. The authors would also like to thank Mr Siyu QIU from NUS high school of Mathematics and Science and Xuefeng BAI from National University of Singapore for their assistance and invaluable help in conducting this study.

References

1. Kontopoulos, E., Berberidis, C., Dergiades, T., Bassiliades, N.: Ontology-based Sentiment Analysis of Twitter Posts. Expert Systems with Applications 40(10), 4065–4074 (2013)
2. Go, A., Bhayani, R., Huang, L.: Twitter Sentiment Classification using Distant Supervision.CS224N Project Report, Stanford 1–12 (2009)
3. Ghiassi, M., Skinner, J., Zimbra, D.: Twitter Brand Sentiment Analysis: A Hybrid System using N-gram Analysis and Dynamic Artificial Neural Network. Expert Systems with Applications 40(16), 6266–6282 (2013)
4. Montoyo, A., Martínez-Barco, P., Balahur, A.: Subjectivity and Sentiment Analysis: An Overview of the Current State of the Area and Envisaged Developments. Decision Support Systems 53(4), 675–679 (2012)
5. Trilla, A., Alías, F.: Sentence-based Sentiment Analysis for Expressive Text-to-speech. IEEE Transactions on Audio, Speech, and Language Processing 21(2), 223–233 (2013)
6. Chung, W., Tseng, T.-L.(B.): Discovering Business Intelligence from Online Product Reviews: A Rule-induction Framework. Expert Systems with Applications 39(15), 11870–11879 (2012)
7. Maks, I., Vossen, P.: A Lexicon Model for Deep Sentiment Analysis and Opinion Mining Applications. Decision Support Systems 53(4), 680–688 (2012)
8. Boiy, E., Moens, M.-F.: A Machine Learning Approach to Sentiment Analysis in Multilingual Web texts. Information Retrieval 12(5), 526–558 (2008)
9. Haddi, E., Liu, X., Shi, Y.: The Role of Text Pre-processing in Sentiment Analysis. Procedia Computer Science 17, 26–32 (2013)
10. Pang, B., Lee, L., Vaithyanathan, S.: Thumbs up? Sentiment Classification using Machine Learning Techniques. In: Proceedings of the ACL-02 Conference on Empirical Methods in Natural Language processing, vol. 10, pp. 79–86. Association for Computational Linguistics (2002)
11. Pan, S.J., Ni, X., Sun, J.-T., Yang, Q., Chen, Z.: Cross-domain Sentiment Classification via Spectral Feature Alignment. In: Proceedings of the 19th international conference on World wide web, pp. 751–760. ACM (2010)
12. Duric, A., Song, F.: Feature Selection for Sentiment Analysis based on Content and Syntax Models. Decision Support Systems 53(40), 704–711 (2012)
13. Alshalabi, H., Tiun, S., Omar, N., Albared, M.: Experiments on the Use of Feature Selection and Machine Learning Methods in Automatic Malay Text Categorization. Procedia Technology 11, 748–754 (2013)
14. Li, S., Xia, R., Zong, C., Huang, C.-R.: A Framework of Feature Selection Methods for Text Categorization. In: Proceedings of the Joint Conference of the 47th Annual Meeting of the ACL and the 4th International Joint Conference on Natural Language Processing of the AFNLP, pp. 692–700 (2009)
15. Li, S., Yat, S., Lee, M., Chen, Y., Guodong, C.-R.H.: Sentiment Classification and Polarity Shifting. In: Proceedings of the 23rd International Conference on Computational Linguistics, Association for Computational Linguistics, pp. 635–643 (2010)

16. Hogenboom, A., Bal, D., Frasincar, F., Bal, M., de Jong, F., Kaymak, U.: Exploiting Emoticons in Sentiment Analysis. In: Proceedings of the 28th Annual ACM Symposium on Applied Computing - SAC 2013, p. 703 (2013)
17. Davidov, D., Tsur, O., Rappoport, A.: Enhanced Sentiment Learning Using Twitter Hashtags and Smileys. In: Proceedings of the 23rd International Conference on Computational Linguistics: Posters, Association for Computational Linguistics, pp. 241–249 (2010)
18. Ortigosa-Hernández, J., Rodríguez, J.D., Alzate, L., Lucania, M., Inza, I., Lozano, J.A.: Approaching Sentiment Analysis by using Semi-supervised Learning of Multi-dimensional Classifiers. Neurocomputing 92, 98–115 (2012)
19. Glorot, X., Bordes, A., Bengio, Y.: Domain Adaptation for Large-scale Sentiment Classification: A Deep Learning Approach. In: Proceedings of the 28th International Conference on Machine Learning (ICML-2011), pp. 513–520 (2011)
20. Ji, H., Deng, H., Han, J.: Uncertainty Reduction for Knowledge Discovery and Information Extraction on the World Wide Web. Proceedings of the IEEE 100(9), 2658–2674 (2012)
21. Chang, C.-C., Lin, C.-J.: LIBSVM: A Library for Support Vector Machines.Software pp. 1-39 (2013), http://www.csie.ntu.edu.tw/~cjlin/libsvm
22. Wilson, T., Wiebe, J., Hoffmann, P.: Recognizing Contextual Polarity: An Exploration of Features for Phrase-level Sentiment Analysis. Computational linguistics 35(3) (2009)
23. Twitter-sentiment-analyzer Data, https://github.com/ravikiranj/twitter-sentiment-analyzer/tree/master/data
24. Movie Review data, http://www.cs.cornell.edu/people/pabo/movie-review-data/
25. Wang, F.-Y., Zeng, D., Carley, K.M., Mao, W.: Social Computing: From Social Informatics to Social Intelligence. IEEE Intelligence Systems 22(2), 79–83 (2007)
26. Byvatov, E., Fechner, U., Sadowski, J., Schneider, G.: Comparison of Support Vector Machine and Artificial Neural Network Systems for Drug/nondrug Classification. Journal of Chemical Information and Computer Sciences 43(6), 1882–1889 (2003)
27. Na, J.-C., Khoo, C.S.G.: Aspect-based Sentiment Analysis of Movie Reviews on Discussion Boards. Journal of Information Science 36(6), 823–848 (2010)
28. Bae, Y., Lee, H.: Sentiment Analysis of Twitter Audiences: Measuring the Positive or Negative Influence of Popular Twitterers. Journal of the American Society for Information Science and Technology 36(12), 2521–2535 (2012)
29. Gunter, B., Koteyko, N., Atanasova, D.: Sentiment Analysis: A Market-relevant and Reliable Measure of Public Feeling? International Journal of Market Research 56(2), 231 (2014)

Name Disambiguation by Collective Classification

Zhongxiang Chen, Jiafeng Guo, Yanyan Lan, Lei Cao, and Xueqi Cheng

Institute of Computing Technology, CAS, Beijing, China 100190
{chenzhongxiang,leicao}@software.ict.ac.cn,
{guojiafeng,lanyanyan,cxq}@ict.ac.cn

Abstract. Disambiguating person names in a set of documents (e.g. research papers or Web pages) is a critical problem in many knowledge management applications. The phenomenon of ambiguity will deteriorate the quality of service, such as the scholar searching and expert finding. Despite years of research, this problem remains largely unsolved, where the unknown number of persons with the same name and the information scarcity in documents pose many difficulties and challenges. In this paper, we formalize name disambiguation as a collective classification problem and solve it using a simple yet effective iterative classification algorithm, referred as ICAND (i.e. Iterative Classification Algorithm for Name Disambiguation). Experimental results on researcher dataset show that the proposed approach can significantly outperform several baseline methods.

Keywords: Name Disambiguation, Collective Classification, Digital Library.

1 Introduction

Name ambiguity is a challenging problem in many domains, where one person can be referenced by multiple name variations in different situations or even share the same name with other persons. For example, in digital libraries (like DBLP or CiteSeer), a very common Chinese name "Lei Zhang" can be shared by tens of authors, and may be written in abbreviation like "L. Zhang". The phenomenon of ambiguity will deteriorate the quality of service such as the scholar searching or expert finding. Therefore, it is necessary to study how to solve it effectively. Despite years of research, this problem remains largely unsolved.

Most previous approaches directly take name disambiguation as a clustering problem [4], [7], [18]. Unfortunately, it is unclear how to determine the number of clusters. In [1], Beckkerman and McCallum tried to address this problem by Agglomerative/Conglomerative Double Clustering (A/CDC). However, it still relies on some predefined threshold to control the clustering process, which is unknown in different applications. Tang *et al.* [14] employed Bayesian Information Criterion (BIC) to select the cluster number. However, their approach tends to find a small cluster number, which may fail when the actual number of persons is large [17].

A. Jaafar et al. (Eds.): AIRS 2014, LNCS 8870, pp. 406–417, 2014.
© Springer International Publishing Switzerland 2014

To avoid the decision of the cluster number, some approaches formalize the problem in a classification manner[4], [17]. However, these methods may suffer from the information scarcity problem. Information scarcity refers to the common phenomenon that a single document may have very sparse attributes for disambiguation [3], [12]. Therefore, it would be quite difficult to classify one document or a pair of documents only relying on their intrinsic features.

To address these above problems, in this paper, we introduce a novel classification method for name disambiguation. The motivation of our approach stems from observations on how human beings disambiguate names. When disambiguating person names in a set of documents, people would like to check whether two documents belong to a same person. The disambiguation process usually works in an iterative process: (1) Most obvious and confident pairs would be settled down first; (2) All the information from the predicted results will also help to disambiguate the remaining "difficult" data; (3) The previous decisions may be adjusted along with the process until a stable result is obtained.

Inspired by the above observations, we formalize name disambiguation as a collective classification problem and use an iterative approach to imitate the above process. Specifically, for each test name, we introduce a relational pairwise graph where each node represents a document pair sharing the same name, and there is an edge between two nodes if they share one same document. The task is then to predict whether each pair of documents on the graph belongs to a same person or not. The key idea of the collective classification is that, when predicting the label of a node, one leverages the relational (extrinsic) features from predicted neighbors as well as the intrinsic features of that node. We propose to employ a simple yet effective iterative classification algorithm (ICA) [13] to solve this problem, referred as ICAND (i.e. Iterative Classification Algorithm for Name Disambiguation). In training, a local classifier is learned based on the labeled data. In this work, we develop a novel sampling strategy for better training the local classifier. In testing, an iterative classification process is conducted on the relational pairwise graph by exploiting both intrinsic and relational features.

Our approach enjoys the following merits: (1) The number of distinct persons can be automatically determined after the classification process; (2) It is flexible to incorporate various intrinsic and relational features to help prediction; (3) A collective inference algorithm is employed to exploit dependencies between documents to well address the information scarcity problem.

To verify the effectiveness of our method, we conduct empirical experiments on an academic dataset collected from an online scholar system SocialScholar[1]. The dataset contains 4,429 publications of 75 different author names[2]. The experimental results show that our method can reach a performance of 89.2% (by F1-score), significantly outperforming the baseline methods.

The rest of our paper is organized as follows. Section 2 presents some related work. In section 3, we formalize name disambiguation problem in the relational pairwise graph. In section 4, we give a detailed description of our iterative

---

[1] http://soscholar.com
[2] http://static.soscholar.com/pub/dataset.html

approach called ICAND. In section 5, several experiments are conducted to empirically prove the effectiveness of our approach. Finally, we conclude and discuss future work in section 6.

2   Related Work

In this section, we first review techniques developed in literature on name disambiguation, and then review some related work on collective classification.

2.1   Name Disambiguation

Name disambiguation has been studied for several years, and in general previous approaches can be categorized into two folds: clustering, and classification.

In clustering approaches, the problem of name disambiguation is directly formalized as partitioning documents into different clusters, where each cluster corresponds to a distinct person. For example, in [5], Han *et al.* proposed an unsupervised approach using K-way spectral clustering method in which they took use of three citation attributes for name disambiguation. Wang *et al.* [16] investigated an approach for finding atomic clusters to improve the performance of clustering based algorithms. In [7], Huang *et al.* proposed a two steps framework for name disambiguation. They first trained a distance function between papers using LASVM, and then applied the distance function to DBSCAN clustering process to get results.However, most clustering methods need the number of clusters as a preliminary, which is usually not available.

To avoid the decision of the cluster number, several approaches formalize the problem of name disambiguation in a classification manner. For example, Wang *et al.* [17] tried to predict whether two documents belong to a same person based on a pairwise factor graph, and employed active learning to improve disambiguation performance. However, these methods usually classify one document or a pair of documents only relying on their intrinsic features, which may suffer from the information scarcity problem when documents have very sparse attributes. Our approach falls into this classification category, and exploits relational features as well as intrinsic features to alleviate the information scarcity problem.

2.2   Collective Classification

Collective classification is a method for jointly classifying relational data. Collective classification methods employ a collective inference algorithm that exploits dependencies between instances, enabling them to often attain higher accuracies than traditional methods when instances are interrelated [8], [11], [15], [13]. Even though exact methods such as junction trees [6] or variable elimination [2], [19] can be applied for collective inference, these methods may be prohibitively expensive to use in practice. As a consequence, most research in collective classification has been devoted to the development of *approximate inference algorithms*.

There are two primary types of approximate collective inference algorithms, i.e. *local classifier-based methods* and *global formulation-based methods* [13]. For local classifier-based methods, the collective inference is an iterative process where a local classifier predicts labels for each instance using both intrinsic features and relational features (derived from the current label predictions). Two types of most commonly used approximate inference algorithms following this approach are the *iterative classification algorithm* (ICA) and *gibbs sampling*.

3   Problem Formalization

We consider the name disambiguation problem in digital library scenario where the targets are author names. given an author name, we denote papers containing the author name a as $P^a = \{p_1, p_2, \ldots, p_n\}$. Suppose in these papers there are actually K distinct authors $\Pi = \{\pi_1, \pi_2, \ldots, \pi_K\}$ sharing the same name. The task of the problem is to find the number of distinct authors K, and associate each paper $p_i \in P$ to the right author $\pi_k \in \Pi$.

First of all, we view the name disambiguation task in a classification way. That is, we aim to predict whether each pair of papers (p_i, p_j) containing the same name a belongs to a same author or not. If we can correctly predict all the document pairs, we can automatically find the real author number K, and meanwhile associate each paper to the right author.

For formal definition, we first introduce the relational pairwise graph. Given an author name, we denote a relational pairwise graph over the paper collection sharing the author name as $G = (V, E, X, Y)$, where V is a set of nodes with $v_{i,j} \in V$ representing paper pairs (p_i, p_j), E is a set of undirected edges; each node $v_{i,j} \in V$ has a feature vector $x_{i,j} \in X$ which is a concatenation of the intrinsic feature vector $x_{i,j}^{int}$ and relational feature vector $x_{i,j}^{rel}$, and an unknown label $y_{i,j} \in Y$; there is an edge between two nodes if they share a common paper, e.g. node $v_{i,k}$ is connected with node $v_{j,k}$ as they share the paper p_k. An example relational pairwise graph over a list of papers $P = \{p_1, p_2, p_3, p_4\}$ containing a same author name is shown in Fig. 1.

The author name disambiguation task is then formalized as the following collective classification problem. Given a relational pairwise graph $G = (V, E, X, Y)$ for an author name, one needs to predict the label $y_{i,j} \in \{-1, +1\}$ for each node $v_{i,j} \in V$, representing whether the pair of papers (p_i, p_j) belong to a same author $(y_{i,j} = +1)$ or not $(y_{i,j} = -1)$.

4   Our Approach

We propose using an iterative algorithm to solve this collective classification problem. As aforementioned, the key idea of using such an iterative process comes from the observation on how human beings disambiguate names.

When disambiguating author names in a set of papers, people would like to check whether two papers belong to a same author in an iterative process. Those

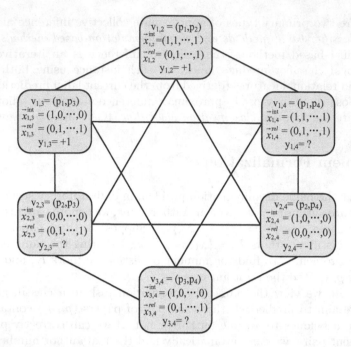

Fig. 1. Relational pairwise graph for 4 papers all sharing an identical author name a

paper pairs with strong signals (e.g. paper p_1 and p_2 appear on a same home-page) would be considered as from a same author with high confidence first, while those with weak and scarce signals (e.g. paper p_3 cites p_2) would be difficult to predict at first and leave for latter decision. Once a pair of papers are taken as from a same author, one will naturally leverage one paper's attributes to enrich the other and help latter prediction.

We employ an iterative classification algorithm, referred as ICAND, to imitate the above process and solve the collective classification problem. The overview of our algorithm is as follows. In the initial step, we predict the label $y_{i,j}$ of each node $v_{i,j} \in V$ using a local classifier f based on intrinsic features $x_{i,j}^{int}$ constructed from the attributes of the paper pairs on $v_{i,j}$. This step is a "bootstrap" step since none of the nodes' labels are known. After the bootstrap step, all labels of the nodes are predicted. Then in the following iteration step, for each node ICAND selects confidently predicted positive neighbors as observed labels, compute the relational features $x_{i,j}^{rel}$ based on these neighbors, and then re-predict the labels using the local classifier based on both intrinsic and relational features. This step iterates until convergence or the iteration count exceeds some predefined threshold. Finally, a post-aggregation step is conducted to generate the paper clusters, each corresponding to a distinct author. The pseudo-code of our algorithm is summarized in Algorithm 1.

Algorithm 1. Iterative classification algorithm for Name disambiguation

---

Input: graph $G = (V, E, X, Y)$ for a given author name where Y is unknown initially, local
classifier f, max iteration steps T
Output: paper clusters, each representing a distinct author
1 $step \leftarrow 0$
2 **for** *each node* $v_{i,j} \in V$ **do**
3      $y_{i,j}^{(0)} \leftarrow f\left(x_{i,j}^{(0)}\right)$ \\ bootstrap step
   end
4 **repeat**
5   **for** *each node* $v_{i,j} \in V$ **do**
6   sort and select confidently predicted neighbors $v_{k,l} \in Neighbor(v_{i,j})$ with
             $y_{k,l}^{(step)} = +1$
7   re-compute the feature vector $x_{i,j}^{(step+1)}$ with the selected neighbors' labels observed
8          $y_{i,j}^{(step+1)} \leftarrow f\left(x_{i,j}^{(step+1)}\right)$
       end
9      $step \leftarrow step + 1$
   until $Y^{(step+1)} = Y^{(step)}$ *or* $step \geq T$;
10 post-aggregation based on final predictions Y to get paper clusters
11 **return** *paper clusters*

4.1 Intrinsic and Relational Features

Intrinsic features are static features extracted from the node which describe how likely two papers in that node are from a same author. The value of the feature could either be binary or real value. In this paper, we define 10 features for our disambiguation task, including author-based, venue-based, citation-based, and content-based features. The specific description of each feature is listed in Table 1. As most of the features are quite intuitive, The feature CoConcept may need more explanation. In our work, we build a concept dictionary based on all the key words from papers in the academic dateset.

Table 1. Description of features for a paper pair (p_i, p_j) given the Author Name a

Name	Description	Type
CoAuthor	paper p_i and p_j have at least one same author except a	binary
CoOrganization	the organization of author a in p_i and p_j are the same	binary
CoOrgOccur	the organization of author a in p_i appears in content of p_j, or vice versa	binary
CoHomepage	paper p_i and p_j appear on a same author's homepage	binary
CoVenue	paper p_i and p_j are published on the same journal or conference	binary
CoRefCite	paper p_i and p_j cite or are cited by at least one same paper	binary
Citation	paper p_i cites p_j, or vice versa	binary
TitleSim	title similarity between paper p_i and p_j (cosine similarity based on tf-idf word vector)	real
AbstractSim	abstract similarity between paper p_i and p_j (cosine similarity based on tf-idf word vector)	real
CoConcept	paper p_i and p_j hit at least one same concept in title or abstract	binary

Different from intrinsic features, relational features are dynamic features derived from neighborhood and are re-calculated in each iteration step. As aforementioned, relational features are constructed based on the neighbors with positive labels. Going back to the example shown in Fig. 1, if the paper pair (p_1, p_2)

has already been labeled as positive confidently, we can then leverage the attributes of p_1 to help disambiguate (p_2, p_3), and extract relational features based on papers p_1 and p_3. Note that the specific definition of relational features are exactly the same as that of intrinsic features; in other words, there are 10 relational features.

When there are multiple neighbors with positive labels, we need to use an aggregation operator to generate a fixed-length relational feature vector. Past research has used a variety of aggregation operators such as minimum, maximum, and count [13]. The choice of the aggregation method depends on the specific application and the definition of relational features. In our work, we define a max operator to aggregate the relational features. The purpose of this max operator is to obtain the strongest signals from neighborhoods. Specifically, the l-th relational feature of node $v_{i,j} \in V$ is defined as

$$\boldsymbol{x}_{i,j}^{rel}[l] = \max_{v_{i,k}, v_{k,j} \in S^+} \{\boldsymbol{x}_{i,k}^{int}[l], \boldsymbol{x}_{k,j}^{int}[l]\} \qquad (1)$$

where S^+ denotes the set of neighbors of node $v_{i,j}$ with positive labels in prediction.

4.2   Local Classifier

We can use anything ranging from SVM to decision tree as the local classifier. In our work, we choose to use SVM with linear kernel. The local classifier is trained on the labeled ground truth. Specifically, the ground truth dataset for author name disambiguation usually consists of a set of M author names $A = \{a_1, \ldots, a_M\}$, where for each name $a_m \in A$, the number of distinct authors are known and a set of papers containing that name are associated to the right author (i.e. cluster). In the training process, for each name $a_m \in A$, we construct the corresponding relational pairwise graph $G^{a_m} = \{V^{a_m}, E^{a_m}, X^{a_m}, Y^{a_m}\}$, where the features for each node are extracted based on the node attributes and ground truth labels of neighbors. The local classifier is then trained based on the training data $(\boldsymbol{x}_{i,j}^{a_m}, y_{i,j}^{a_m})_{a_m \in A}$.

Note that when calculating the relational features for constructing the training data, there might be multiple strategies on the usage of ground truth labels. In previous work, the local classifier is usually trained on full-label assumption, i.e. for each node, the labels of all the neighbors are available. However, the classifier trained under this strategy may not work well when very few labels can be leveraged in the early stages of the iterative process in testing. Therefore, in this paper, we propose a novel sampling strategy on label usage, i.e. for each node, only partial labels of neighbors are available.In our experiments, we find that the classifier learned under this strategy can achieve better performance.

4.3   Collective Inference

The collective inference algorithm is the central part of a collective classification approach. In our work, we employ a local classifier-based method, i.e. the iterative classification algorithm, to conduct approximate collective inference. This algorithm has been shown to be simple yet effective as compared with other local and global methods [13].

The iterative algorithm exploits positive label predictions to help inference in each iteration, as shown in Algorithm 1. One major issue we need to address is how to select confident label prediction for next inference. In our work, we take some cautious strategies for label selection [9,10]. Specifically, in each iteration, the predicted positive labels are ordered by confidence value (i.e. predicted score) and only top confident labels are used for inference. The proportion of top confident positive labels in usage could be fixed (i.e. using predefined proportion like 10%) or dynamic (e.g. increasing the proportion per iteration from 0%, 10%, ..., up to 100%). In our experiments, we empirically compared different strategies in label selection and show how these strategies affect the performance.

4.4 Post-aggregation Step

For the goal of the name disambiguation task, we need to find out the actual K distinct authors (K is unknown in our case) sharing the same name and associate each paper to the right author (i.e. dividing the papers into K clusters). Therefore, we take a simple post-aggregation step to obtain the final K clusters, i.e. the step 9 in Algorithm 1. The aggregation is in a agglomerative clustering manner. At the beginning, each paper forms a cluster. If a paper pair has been predicted with positive label and the two papers come from two different clusters, then the two clusters are merged together. This process iterates until no further merging can take place. As we can see, the final author number K can be automatically determined after the post-aggregation step.

One thing need to mention in the post-aggregation process is the triplet violation problem. Specifically, suppose both of the pairs (p_1, p_2) and (p_1, p_3) have already been labeled as "+1", the label of pair (p_2, p_3) should be also assigned as "+1", otherwise it will lead to triplet violation problem.

However, since in our iterative classification process there is no constraint to avoid this problem, it is possible that there are triplet violation in the final classification results. Fortunately, such violation can be naturally solved in the agglomerative clustering process described above naturally. Nevertheless, it would be interesting to investigate how to add constraints into the collective classification process to avoid such problem in the future work.

5   Experiments

In this section, we conduct experiments to empirically evaluate the effectiveness and efficiency of our proposed approach.

5.1   Experimental Setting

Dataset. To evaluation our proposed method, we create an academic dataset from SocialScholar system. SocialScholar has collected and combined papers from DBLP, IEEE, ACM and CiteSeer, and formed a publication dataset of $8,014,742$ papers and $24,303,153$ citation relationships. For evaluation, we employed three graduate student in computer science to manually labeled $4,429$ papers for 75 author names. For each author name, a paper containing that name was labeled with a number indicating the actual author. For disagreements in the annotation, we applied majority voting for decision.

Baselines. For evaluation, we consider both clustering and classification methods as our baselines. For the clustering methods, several existing methods for name disambiguation, including hierarchical agglomerative clustering method (HAC), K-Means, and SA-Cluster [20], are taken as baselines. In the first two method, we try to take all features defined in our method. In SA-Cluster method, we consider organization and venue of each paper as attribute features, and simply treat others features as edges. In all these clustering methods, the real number of persons K is preliminarily provided.

For the classification methods, we take the Pairwise Classification (PC) method as the baseline. The PC method can be viewed a simplified version of our ICAND method, which drops the relations between nodes in our relational pairwise graph, and conducts training and prediction only based on intrinsic feature. A same post-aggregation process is employed to get final K Clusters. The PC method also employs SVM with linear kernel as the base classifier.

In our experiments, for the supervised methods where a classifier need to be trained first, we divide the dataset into five folds and conducted five-fold cross validation for evaluation. For our method, we set the max iteration number as 10 since we found that in most cases the iterative process converges quickly.

5.2   Evaluation Measures

We employ the widely used pairwise measures [14], [16,17] to evaluate our approach and compare with baseline methods. The pairwise measures evaluate the performance of disambiguation based on the paper pairs assigned with the same label. For some special author names, there is only one paper corresponds to each distinct author. Since these above measures only consider paper pairs assigned with same label, they cannot well evaluate the results on such names. Therefore,we employ *pairwise_accuracy* as supplementary measure. The definitions of these measures are shown as follows.

$$pairwise\_precison = \frac{\#PairsCorrectlyPredicted2SameAuthor}{\#PairsPredicted2SameAuthor}$$

$$pairwise\_recall = \frac{\#PairsCorrectlyPredicted2SameAuthor}{\#TotalPairs2SameAuthor}$$

$$pairwie\_F1 = \frac{2*pairwise\_precison*pairwise\_recall}{pairwise\_precison+pairwise\_recall}$$

$$pairwise\_accuracy = \frac{\#PairsCorrectlyPredicted}{\#TotalPairs}$$

5.3   Strategy Analysis

We conduct experiments to study how different strategies used in the training and testing process in ICAND affect the disambiguation performance.

Training Label Selection. Here we first compare the strategy on the usage of ground truth labels in training process, and show how different training strategies affect the final performance. For comparison, two strategies are taken into account. One is the conventional full-label strategy, i.e. when computing relational features for each node, all the ground truth labels of neighbors are available. The other is the proposed sampling strategy, i.e. when computing relational features for each node, only partial ground truth labels of neighbors are available. Specifically, for each node, we vary the proportions of available labels in neighbors from 0% to 100% with step length 10%. For each proportion, we sample the labels of neighbors for each node, compute the relational features as well as intrinsic features, and obtain the corresponding training data. The final training dataset is constructed by merging all the data generated under different label proportions with the duplication removed.

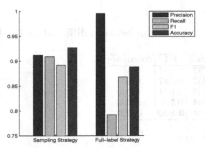

Fig. 2. Performance comparison on name disambiguation using different strategies on training data construction

Table 2. Performance comparison on name disambiguation using different label selection strategies in collective inference

Type		Precision	Recall	F1	Accuracy
fixed	10%	1	0.167	0.253	0.559
	20%	1	0.293	0.425	0.631
	30%	1	0.451	0.596	0.713
	40%	0.997	0.573	0.703	0.781
	50%	0.990	0.660	0.775	0.825
	60%	0.976	0.724	0.816	0.856
	70%	0.968	0.806	0.866	0.898
	80%	0.944	0.852	0.881	0.911
	90%	0.912	0.909	**0.892**	**0.927**
	100%	0.835	0.944	0.853	0.897
dynamic	+5%	0.847	0.941	0.862	0.907
	+10%	0.847	0.942	0.862	0.908

As shown in Fig. 2, the disambiguation performance under the sampling strategy is better than that of full-label strategy in terms of average recall, F1 and accuracy. The average F1 scores are 0.892 and 0.853 under sampling strategy and full-label strategy, respectively. The major reason is that the full-label strategy tends to obtain a strict local classifier with high precision. As a result, the final performance achieve high precision but low recall. In contrast, the sampling strategy builds a more diverse dataset, which captures different scenarios of the classifier may face during the iterative process. Therefore, the local classifier learned under this strategy become more robust with better balance between recall and precision, and thus obtain better disambiguation performance.

Inference Label Selection. We further compare the label selection strategy in the collective inference process. For the fixed proportion strategy, we vary the predefined proportion at different levels (i.e. 10%, 20%, ..., or 100%). For the dynamic proportion strategy, we increase the fraction from 0% to 100% with constant step length (i.e. 5% or 10%).

The disambiguation performance comparison among these label selection strategies is shown in Table 2. We can see that for fixed proportion strategy, a low proportion leads to high precision but low recall in final performance. This is natural since we only trust those very confident positive label predictions. With the increase of the proportion, we obtain higher recall but lower precision gradually. The best performance is achieved at the proportion of 90%. If one simply trust all the positive predictions, the precision become low since there might be many incorrect positive predictions selected in the process making the error propagate. For the dynamic proportion strategy, there is almost no difference between the two different step lengths. However, the precision is not high for dynamic strategy, which might be caused by the selection of incorrect positive predictions when the confidence proportion becomes larger and larger.

In the following experiments, we use the ICAND approach with the local classifier trained under the sampling strategy, and a fixed proportion (i.e. 90%) label selection strategy for the collective inference process.

Table 3. Performance comparison on name disambiguation between different methods

Method	Precision	Recall	F1	Accuracy
HAC	0.838	0.787	0.801	0.859
K-Means	0.763	0.461	0.547	0.694
SA-Cluster	0.669	0.588	0.611	0.766
PC	0.728	0.904	0.720	0.696
ICAND	**0.912**	**0.909**	**0.892**	**0.927**

5.4   Disambiguation Performance

We now compare the disambiguation performance of our approach with the baseline methods. As shown in Table 3, on average, our method can achieve a precision of 91.2%, recall 90.9%, F1 89.2% and accuracy 92.7%. We can see that our approach can clearly outperform all the baseline methods in terms of all the evaluation measures (+9.1% over HAC, +34.5% over K-Means, +28.1 % over SA-Cluster, and +17.2% over PC by F1 score). All the improvements are statistically significant (p-value< 0.01). The results demonstrate that by using the collective inference approach which exploits various intrinsic as well as relational features, we can better address the name disambiguation problem.

6   Conclusion

In this paper, we address name disambiguation by formalizing it as a collective classification problem. We then employ an iterative algorithm to solve this collective classification problem, referred as ICAND. Our approach can automatically determine the number of distinct persons for a given name after the classification process. Moreover, the collective inference algorithm employed in our approach exploits relational features based on label prediction, which can well address the information scarcity problem. We conducted extensive experiments on an academic dataset to demonstrate the effectiveness of our approach.

Acknowledgments. This research work was funded by the National Grand Fundamental Research 973 Program of China under Grant No. 2014CB340401, the National High-tech R&D Program of China under Grant No. 2012AA011003, the National Natural Science Foundation of China under Grant No. 61232010, Grant No. 61173064 and Grant No. 61203298, and the National Key Technology R&D Program of China under Grant No. 2012BAH39B04 and Grant No. 2012BAH39B02.

References

1. Bekkerman, R., McCallum, A.: Disambiguating Web appearances of people in a social network. In: WWW, p. 463. ACM Press (2005)
2. Dechter, R.: Bucket elimination: A unifying framework for probabilistic inference. In: UAI, pp. 211–219 (1996)
3. Fan, X., Wang, J., Pu, X., Zhou, L., Lv, B.: On Graph-Based Name Disambiguation. JDIQ 2(2), 1–23 (2011)
4. Han, H., Giles, L., Zha, H., Li, C., Tsioutsiouliklis, K.: Two supervised learning approaches for name disambiguation in author citations. In: JCDL (2004)
5. Han, H., Zha, H., Giles, C.L.: Name disambiguation in author citations using a K-way spectral clustering method. In: JCDL (2005)
6. Huang, C., Darwiche, A.: Inference in belief networks: A procedural guide. IJAR 11(1), 158 (1994)
7. Huang, J., Ertekin, S., Giles, C.L.: Efficient Name Disambiguation for Large-Scale Databases. In: PKDD, pp. 536–544 (2006)
8. Jensen, D., Neville, J., Gallagher, B.: Why collective inference improves relational classification. In: SIGKDD, pp. 593–598 (2004)
9. McDowell, L., Gupta, K., Aha, D.: Meta-prediction for collective classification. In: Proceedings of the 23rd International FLAIRS Conference (2010)
10. Mcdowell, L.K.: Cautious Collective Classification. JMLR (2009)
11. Neville, J., Jensen, D.: Iterative classification in relational data. In: Proc. AAAI-2000 Workshop on Learning Statistical Models from Relational Data (2000)
12. Qian, Y., Hu, Y., Cui, J., Zheng, Q., Nie, Z.: Combining Machine Learning and Human Judgment in Author Disambiguation. In: CIKM (2011)
13. Sen, P., Namata, G., Bilgic, M., Getoor, L., Galligher, B., Eliassi-Rad, T.: Collective classification in network data. AI magazine (2008)
14. Tang, J., Fong, A.C.M., Wang, B., Zhang, J.: A Unified Probabilistic Framework for Name Disambiguation in Digital Library. TKDE 24, 975–987 (2012)
15. Taskar, B., Abbeel, P., Koller, D.: Discriminative probabilistic models for relational data. In: UAI, pp. 485–492 (2002)
16. Wang, F., Li, J., Tang, J., Zhang, J., Wang, K.: Name Disambiguation Using Atomic Clusters. In: WIAM, pp. 357–364. IEEE (July 2008)
17. Wang, X., Tang, J., Cheng, H., Yu, P.S.: ADANA: Active Name Disambiguation. In: ICDE, pp. 794–803. IEEE (December 2011)
18. Yin, X., Han, J., Yu, P.S.: Object Distinction: Distinguishing Objects with Identical Names. In: ICDE, pp. 1242–1246 (2007)
19. Zhang, N.L., Poole, D.: A simple approach to bayesian network computations. In: Canadian Conference on Artificial Intelligence (1994)
20. Zhou, Y., Cheng, H., Yu, J.X.: Graph Clustering Based on Structural / Attribute Similarities. In: VLDB (2009)

Hierarchical Dirichlet Process Topic Modeling for Large Number of Answer Types Classification in Open domain Question Answering

Seonyeong Park, Donghyeon Lee, Junhwi Choi, Seonghan Ryu, Yonghee Kim, Soonchoul Kown, Byungsoo Kim, and Gary Geunbae Lee

Department of Computer science and Engineering,
Pohang University of Science and Technology, Pohang, Gyungbuk, South Korea
{sypark322,semko,chasunee,ryush,ttti07,theincluder,
bsmail90,gblee}@postech.ac.kr

Abstract. We propose a new method that uses the Hierarchical Dirichlet Process (HDP) to classify a large number of answer types for a question posed using natural language. We used the HDP model to build a classifier that assigns test questions to certain clusters, then computes similarity among the questions within the same cluster. Our answer-type classifier finds the n-best similar training questions to the test questions and classifies the test question's answer type as the majority of the n-best training question's answer type. The proposed method achieved similar accuracy and lower sensitivity to the presence of a large number of answer types than existing methods that use classification algorithms with same features. Also, we can guarantee that appropriate answer type can be among the ranked answer types with high recall.

Keywords: Answer-type classifier, HDP, Cosine-similarity measurement, UIUC data, Yahoo! answers data.

1 Introduction

The purpose of question answering systems is to provide answers to user questions by analyzing huge natural language corpora [1,2]. Previous search engines such as Google and Baidu just return documents related to the answer, but question-answering systems return short phrase answers that the user seeks [3]. In the big data era, this property of question answering is much required. Question answering typically consists of three steps: question processing, candidate answer searching and answer selection [4,5]. During the question processing, keywords and answer types are extracted to be used in the search for candidate answers or texts related to them [4,5].

Answer type is the type of the information that a user wants to find; it sets a boundary of search space by mapping a question to a predefined category that specifies the type of entity of the expected answer [5]. Finding an answer accurately requires first filtering out a wide range of candidates based on some categorization of answers. Many researchers combine pattern-matching and rule-based approaches with a

A. Jaafar et al. (Eds.): AIRS 2014, LNCS 8870, pp. 418–428, 2014.
© Springer International Publishing Switzerland 2014

statistical model to classify answer types. For example, SiteQ [6] uses lexical-semantic patterns (LSP). It constructs an LSP such as "(%who)(%be)(@person) →
PERSON", maps the LSP to a user's question like "Who was president Cleveland's
wife?" and classifies the answer type as "PERSON". But this LSP approach is based
on hand-crafted rules, and the number of rules is limited; if a case does not correspond to a rule, SiteQ cannot detect an answer type. To avoid this weakness of the
rule-based approach, many researchers use supervised learning algorithms such as
Support Vector Machines (SVMs) [7] and Maximum Entropy (ME) [8]. Previously
many answer type classification approaches use lexical and syntactic features like
word n-gram, surface form, chunk, and part-of-speech tags. Numerous recent studies
use semantic features like headwords, hypernyms and question categories such as
"what" and "which". In many cases, answer type is usually implicit. So, finding the
answer type is difficult when only lexical or syntactic features are used. However,
some research with semantic features achieved > 90% accuracy for a small set of
answer type training data when classifying the answer type [8,9,10].

University of Illinois at Urban Champaign (UIUC) data [11] are standard for answer type classification task. However these data were collected for academic use.
IBM Watson showed some new approaches that generate a candidate answer without
an answer type, and applied a weak-type coercion method to candidate answers because they must cover extremely large answer types for the Jeopardy! Show [12].
However, to save time and effort, search space must be reduced using pre-computed
answer types while retaining a large number of answer types; this is the motivation of
our model based on the Hierarchical Dirichlet Process (HDP) [13]. Many open-
domain question-answering systems use a large number of answer types [12,13,14].
Previous classification-based answer type computing methods were sensitive to the
large scale and variety of answer types, because previous answer type classifier mainly work for a small set of pre-defined answer types, so when the number of answer
types increases or if the answer type is not predefined, the classification accuracy of
methods decreases greatly [7-11]. In this paper, we propose a model that uses HDP
which is widely-used for topic modeling to overcome the large scale and undefined
answer type problem. Our new method works reasonably well with UIUC data and is
specifically superior to the state-of-the-art method for large-scale Yahoo! Answers
data.

2   Method

2.1   Unsupervised Model: Hierarchical Dirichlet Process

We propose a model that uses HDP [13], which is widely-used for topic modeling to
overcome large scale and the problem of undefined answer types. A topic is a multinomial distribution that represents a coherent concept of text. We assume that a question has only one answer type, just as a sentence has only one topic. HDP is widely
used for document clustering. We adapted HDP to sentence clustering.

HDP is a probabilistic generative model that assumes that an answer type generates
a question. The feature vector represents a single user's questions. We extract features

that are useful for answer-type classification in each sentence. Feature vectors are generated from an unlimited number of cluster states; in this case, the cluster state is the answer type. The answer-type generates feature vectors that represent each user question. Unlike Latent Dirichlet Allocation (LDA), HDP does not need the pre-defined number of possible answer types.

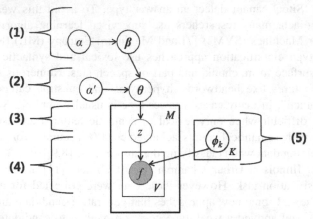

Fig. 1. HDP model for answer-type clustering: symbols and processes are described in the text

Our model consists of five processes, numbered (1) to (5) (Fig.1). Process (1) uses a Griffiths-Engen-McCloskey distribution with hyperparameter α to generate a base distribution β. Process (2) uses Dirichlet processing of hyerparameter α' and a base distribution β to generate a base distribution θ. Process (3) uses the multi-nomial distribution of θ to generate cluster ID z. Process (4) generates questions, represented as a feature vector f by each answer type z that represents the state of the cluster, i.e., cluster ID, which is the most important step in the model. Process (5) uses ϕ_k which is the   multinomial distribution of feature vector distribution of each cluster k to generate emission probabilities that govern the distribution of the observed variable at a certain cluster ID. In the HDP, feature vectors are the only observed data. HDP clustering is used to assign questions to the same cluster if they have the same answer type.

2.2   Similarity Measurement

Similarity is computed to detect which feature vectors are similar. We used the Cosine similarity (1):

$$Cosine\ similarity(\theta) = \frac{A \cdot B}{\|A\|\|B\|}$$

$$= \frac{\sum_{i=1}^{n} A_i \times B_i}{\sqrt{\sum_{i=1}^{n}(A_i)^2} \times \sqrt{\sum_{i=1}^{n}(B_i)^2}},\tag{1}$$

where A and B are feature vectors of each question , $\cdot$ is inner product, $\|\cdot\|$ is length of the vector, n is the size of each feature vector and, i and j are indexes of each feature value in the feature vectors.

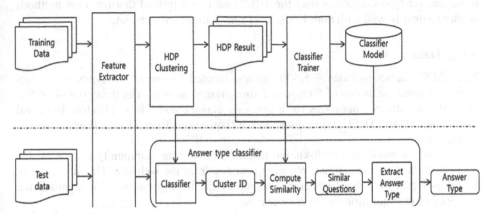

Fig. 2. Overall architecture of the proposed method: processes are described in the text

We combined the HDP and the computed similarity to build a new answer-type classifier (Fig. 2). We represent each question in a corpus as a feature vector: the features in this vector are similar to those used in previous work and we added a new focus feature. We divided the model into a training classifier part (Fig. 2, above dotted line) and a testing answer-type classifier (Fig. 2, below dotted line).

In the training part, the goal is to use HDP clustering to develop a classifier. We input feature vectors into HDP clustering. After clustering, each feature vector receives a cluster ID tag, i.e., answer type. We applied the HDP result to ME classifier training. After classifier training, a classifier model was generated. For example, if we input feature vectors, we get their cluster ID such as "2".

We used the classifier model to classify unknown test data. The classifier outputs the cluster ID of each feature vector. We computed the similarity between each data's feature vector and the training data's feature vector which had been tagged with the same cluster ID in the HDP clustering step. We extracted the n-best similar questions to the test data and classified the test data's answer type as the one that was the majority of these n-best answer types.

We use these methods to classify answer type because combining a generative model HDP with computation of similarity is helpful to increase the number of classes. Also, we can use unlabeled large-scale web data to train an answer-type classification model. Most classifiers that use a discriminative model are not good to classify a large number of classes. However our model is relatively not sensitive to the number of classes.

3   Experiment

We compared our answer-type classifier to an existing answer-type classifier that uses a discriminative model and to a method uses similarity only, to prove that HDP modeling is more efficient and adaptive than computing only similarity in this answer-type classification problem. We use both the UIUC data which is standard data in this field, and Yahoo! answers data which is more familiar than UIUC data and has more answer-type categories than the UIUC data. We proved that our new methods work reasonably well with both UIUC data and Yahoo! answers data.

3.1   Data

The UIUC dataset includes ~ 5,500 entries, labeled as one of six types of coarse-grained answer, or as one of 50 types of fine-grained answer. The data consist of 500 manually-constructed questions for a few rare classes, 894 TREC (Textual Retrieval Conference) 8 and TREC 9 questions, and 500 questions from TREC 10 which serves as a test set.

"Yahoo! answers" is a well-known question-answering community site on which users post their own questions. We used user log from the web site. This dataset provided as a part of Yahoo! research consists of millions questions. We regarded the category of user questions as an answer type.

3.1.1   Features

- *Main verb:* We used Clearnlp[1] to extract the main verb from the question, because this verb usually shows the main intention of the user questions.
- *Question type*: Classifying the question type such as "what" or "which" is important. We extracted both the question type word and other words immediately before and after it.
- *Graph based Reduction Feature*: Graph-based reduction reduces the parse tree by applying predefined reduction rules. For example, "What's the shape of a camel's spine?" can be reduced to "What's shape camel's spine".
- *Semantic role label Feature*: We extracted semantic role in the each question by using Clearnlp. We extracted argument of predicate in the question. For example, in the question " What is the birthstone of October?" , we extracted semantic role label "birthstone" and "what". Also, their pos, WP and NP and extracted dependency label between main verb and them, What – attr – is, is – nsubj-birthstone.
- *Word form of noun and verb:* Nouns and verbs usually have important roles and key meanings in the questions, so we extracted those features.
- *Focus:* We extracted the focus which is the head of the question type.
- *Lexical Answer Type (LAT):* We define LAT as the type of answer. We can define LAT using the words in the user question.
- Ex) What is the longest river in New South Wales? LAT: river
- Sometimes the LAT in a sentence is difficult to detect.
  Ex) What did Bruce Carver die from?
  The answer type is maybe death cause or something else, so the exact LAT is difficult to find. In this case, we did not extracted LAT. We extracted LAT based on rule based approach. It can be further improved.

---

[1] `http://clearnlp.wikispaces.com/`

3.1.2   Evaluation

We trained ~5,500 training questions and tested over the 500 test questions for UIUC data, and we used ~25,000 Yahoo! answers questions data. The number of main categories is 28, and the number of sub categories is 235. We used five-fold cross-validation to reduce the problem of over-fitting to training data and to solve the relative lack of training data compared to the number of labels. We provide only the clustering evaluation and final result (i.e., accuracy and recall of answer-type classification).

3.2   Data Flow

We first obtained features from the vectors by analyzing the user questions, then obtained the cluster IDs after HDP/LDA clustering. We used cluster ID-tagged data to train a Maximum Entropy (ME) model. When the user question input our answer type, our ME model return the cluster ID of the question. In the last step, we computed similarity among clusters and finally classified the user question as the n-best similar questions' human-tagged answer type. We found n which achieved highest accuracy by greedy approach. The shaded part represents data and un-shaded part represents module (Fig. 3).

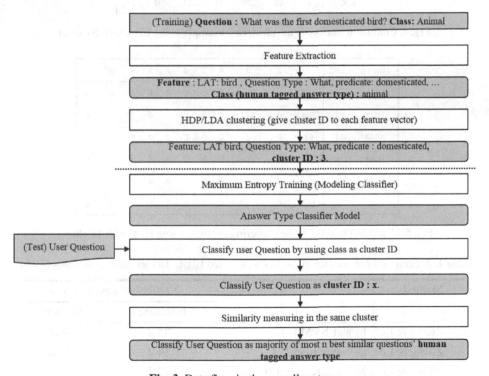

Fig. 3. Data flow in the overall system

3.3 Experimental Result

In our HDP model, the hyperparameters were manually set to $\alpha =1$, $\alpha'= 0.1$ and $\phi_k=0.1$. These values are temporary (not optimal). To perform inference, we used Gibbs sampling, a stochastic procedure that produces samples from the posterior distributions. The clustering results were obtained after 500 iterations.

Clustering results were obtained using different models, features and different data. Basically, we clustered using unigram features as same as other approaches. We added a confusion matrix using same features, unigram features and use two type of algorithm: HDP and LDA (Fig. 4 and Fig. 5).

Label(H)	L₩C	1	2	3	4	5	6
DESC	1	480	280	151	87	115	49
ENTY	2	379	138	92	168	245	228
ABBR	3	83	2	0	0	1	0
HUM	4	93	63	24	411	104	528
NUM	5	41	77	433	217	97	31
LOC	6	66	120	15	114	481	39

Fig. 4. Confusion matrix for the clustering example using LDA with 6 cluster

Label(H)	L₩C	1	2	3	4	5	6	7	8	9	10	11
DESC	1	950	0	212	0	0	0	0	0	0	0	0
ENTY	2	708	0	542	0	0	0	0	0	0	0	0
ABBR	3	84	0	2	0	0	0	0	0	0	0	0
HUM	4	207	0	1016	0	0	0	0	0	0	0	0
NUM	5	593	0	303	0	0	0	0	0	0	0	0
LOC	6	519	0	316	0	0	0	0	0	0	0	0

Fig. 5. Confusion matrix for the clustering example using HDP with 11 cluster

Table 1. Accuracy (%) of question classifiers which used UIUC data set and bag of words feature

Methods	Number of answer types	
	6 (coarse)	50 (fine)
Zhang & Lee, Linear SVM [7]	85.4	80.2
Zhang & Lee, Decision tree[7]	84.2	77.0
Zhang & Lee, Naïve Bayesian [7]	77.4	58.4
LDA + cosine similarity	73.6	61.6
HDP + cosine similarity	84.2	76.2

Table 2. Accuracy (%) of question classifiers which used UIUC data set and new feature

Methods	Number of answer types	
	6 (coarse)	50 (fine)
Zhang & Lee, Linear SVM [7]	87.4	79.2
Vijay et al., SVM + CRF [10]	93.4	86.2
Huang et al ., ME [8]	93.6	89.0
HDP + cosine similarity	**88.4**	**82.7**

We used UIUC Answers data with various answer type categories. As the number of answer types increased, the accuracy decreased in the ME model and the SVM model and other classification algorithms which were commonly used in previous work (Table 1 and Table 2). We used the clustering results of HDP and LDA as training data of ME. The number of clusters is as same as the number of classes of ME. During the running time, the user question is classified as certain class (i.e., exact cluster number, e.g. 3). We must return their natural language answer type (e.g. human). We calculated similarity among questions (run time) and training data questions in the cluster to which the question belongs. In the training data, natural language answer type was annotated, so we can extract the natural language answer type. We used class-annotated data. Our purpose of using HDP is to reduce the number of classes required for ME training, because HDP can perform clustering without determining the number of classes. After clustering, the final number of clusters was determined. Number of clusters can be different from the real number of classes (e.g. number of clusters: 20, number of real classes: 100). We can train ME with this reduced number of classes. Also, most of the questions can find their answer type in the cluster. The recall is almost 1.

The previous work used UIUC data, as we do. We used the same features as did those methods (Table 1) because our model achieved accuracy that was independent of the number of features. This small difference between the accuracy when using coarse-grained answer types and fine-grained number answer types is due to use of our HDP model, because other features are the same as those used in other methods. The accuracy of our methods was relatively not affected by the number of answer types.

When we used UIUC data, we compared the accuracy of our method with existing methods to show that our method works reasonably well compared to the state-of-the art methods when the number of answer types is small (Table 2). Some results with high accuracy used semantic features but we did not use in this experiment. We used similar features to those in [7], but attained higher accuracy than that method. Previous research [7–11] showed that accuracy differed among experiments that used the six coarse classes and the 50 fine classes. [10] used SVM and CRF; compared to [10] their accuracy was better in the six coarse classes but inferior in the 50 fine classes. All other methods usually showed decreasing accuracy as the number of classes increased, but the accuracy of our model was relatively independent of the number of classes.

Even though our accuracy of question classifiers which used Yahoo Data set is not much higher than that of ME, our method is useful enough in real question answering systems (Table 3). Also, using only similarity achieved poor accuracy. Computing similarity within the same cluster provided much better accuracy than using only similarity; this means that HDP clustering was effective. We present only the result of Yahoo data using unigram feature. Because the question set data are so varied, extracted by the NLP tool (clear NLP) features can have many errors.

Table 3. Accuracy (%) of question classifiers which used yahoo data set and new feature

Methods	Number of answer types	
	28	235
Cosine Similarity	0.4	0.1
ME	17.2	10.8
HDP+ cosine Similarity	29.2	20.6

4   Discussion

We showed that the proposed method using HDP topic modeling is more accurate than other methods, especially when the number of answer types is large. Our method was 9.8 % more accurate than the ME classifier in 235 Yahoo! answer types, because the ME classifier is sensitive to the number of answer types (Table 3).

Using HDP topic modeling, we devised a classifier model that needs neither a list of answer types nor the number of them. For this reason, we can reduce the number of answer types to classify, because we first automatically classify an answer type as a cluster ID i.e., a general answer type first, and then use computed similarity to classify a real answer type. The accuracy of the proposed method is almost independent of the number of answer types. However, training the HDP model takes longer than training previous classifier models. The answer types required in Question Answering systems are becoming increasingly complex [12], [14], so the number of answer types to classify is increasing. However, many other methods have low accuracy when classifying a large number of answer types. Using the proposed method we solve this problem.

5   Conclusion and Future Work

We showed a novel approach to find answer type by applying an HDP topic model to an answer-type classifier. For clustering, we used the HDP model that exploits training data that include neither the answer types nor the number of them. But our training data still needs answer-type tagging to provide answer types by computing n-best similarity in the same clusters. We used Yahoo! answers data to generate answer type training data. Using cluster ID as answer type seems reasonable because our features are adapted to extract answer types. Currently, we do not use all features that other methods use; instead, we focused on meaningful features, and proved that our method achieves reasonable accuracy in a small set of answer type compared to previous methods. Also, previous approaches determined answer type and found the appropriate answer for user question in real time. However, when an extremely large answer type is needed, our method can be a valid alternative to the existing methods. IBM Watson showed some new approaches that generate a candidate answer without an answer type, and applied a weak-type coercion method to candidate answers. To save time and effort, search space must be reduced using pre-computed answer types while retaining a large number of answer types; our clustering result can be an alternative method when the number of answer types is large. However, finding n requires high time complexity; to eliminate this problem, we have must improve the method of finding appropriate n.

In future work, we will develop an alternative similarity-computing method that uses training data without answer-type tags to develop an answer-type classifier that has the same accuracy as the one that uses tagged training data.

Acknowledgements. This work was partly supported by the ICT R&D program of MSIP/IITP [10044508, Development of Non-Symbolic Approach-based Human-Like-Self-Taught Learning Intelligence Technology] and National Research Foundation of Korean (NRF) [NRF-2014R1A2A1A01003041, Development of multi-party anticipatory knowledge-intensive natural language dialog system].

References

1. Harabagiu, S.M., Maiorano, S.J., Pasca, M.A.: Open-Domain Textual Question Answering Techniques. Natural Language Engineering 9, 231–267 (2003),
   http://journals.cambridge.org/abstract_S1351324903003176
2. Kolomiyets, O., Moens, M.F.: A Survey on Question Answering Technology from an Information Retrieval Perspective, Information Science (2009),
   http://hmi.ucsd.edu/pdf/HMI_2009_
3. Ntoulas, A., Cho, J.H., Olston, C.: What's New on the Web? The Evolution of the Web from a Search Engine Perspective. In: Proceedings of the 13th International Conference on World Wide Web (2004)
4. Moldovan, D., Harabagiu, S., Pasca, M., Mihalcea, R., Goodrum, R., Girju, R., Rus, V.: Lasso: A Tool for Surfing the Answer net. In: 8th Text REtrieval Conference (1999)
5. Harabagiu, S., Moldovan, D., Pasca, M., Mihalcea, R., Surdeanu, M., Bunescu, R., Girju, R., Rus, V., Morarescu, P.: Falcon: Boosting knowledge for Answer Engines. In: 9th Text Retrieval Conference (2000)
6. Lee, G.G., Seo, J.Y., Lee, S.W., Jung, H.M., Cho, B.Y., Lee, C.K., Kwak, B.K., Cha, J.W., Kim, D.S., An, J.H., Kim, H.S., Kim, K.S.: SiteQ: Engineering High performance QA System using Lexico-Semantic Pattern matching and shallow NLP. In: 10th Text Retrieval Conference (2001)
7. Zhang, D.,, W.: S Lee.: Question Classification using Support Vector Machine, SIGIR (2003)
8. Huang, Z., Thint, M., Celiylimaz, A.: Investigation of Question Classification in Question Answering, ACL and AFNLP (2009)

9. Babak, L., Gijs, V.T., Pascal, W., Tax, D., Marco, L.: Question Classification by Weighted Combination of Lexical, Syntactic and Semantic Features, Text-Speech and Dialogue (2011)
10. K.Vijay, D. Sujatha and C. Soumen.: Enhanced Answer Type Inference from Questions Using Sequential Models. In: Proceedings of the conference on Human Language Technology and Empirical Methods in Natural Language Processing, Association for Computational Linguistics (2005)
11. Xin, L., Dan, R.: Learning Question Classifier. In: Proceedings of the 19th International Conference on Computational Linguistics, vol. 1 (2002)
12. Murdock, J.W., Kalyanpur, A., Welty, C., Fan, J., Ferrucci, D.A., Gondek, D.C., Zhang, L., Kanayama, H.: Typing Candidate Answers Using Type Coercion. IBM Journal (2012)
13. Teh, Y.W., Jordan, M.I., Beal, M.J., Blei, D.M.: Hierarchical Dirichlet Process. Journal of the American Statistical Association (2006)
14. Schlaefer, N., Ko, J., Betteridge, J., Sautter, G., Pathak, M., Nyberg, E.: Semantic Extensions of the Ephyra QA system for TREC 2007. In: 16th Text Retrieval Conference (2007)

A Comparative Study of Feature Selection and Machine Learning Algorithms for Arabic Sentiment Classification

Nazlia Omar, Mohammed Albared, Tareq Al-Moslmi, and Adel Al-Shabi

School of Computer Science, Faculty of Information Science and Technology,
Universiti Kebangsaan Malaysia, 43600 Bangi, Selangor, Malaysia
nazlia@ukm.edu.my, mohammed_albared@yahoo.com,
{tareq.almoslmi,Adel.alshabi}@gmail.com

Abstract. Sentiment analysis is a very challenging and important task that involves natural language processing, web mining, and machine learning. Sentiment analysis in the Arabic language is a more challenging task than in other languages due to the morphological complexity of the Arabic and the large variation of its dialects. This paper presents an empirical comparison of seven feature selection methods (Information Gain, Principal Components Analysis, Relief-F, Gini Index, Uncertainty, Chi-squared, and Support Vector Machines (SVMs)), and three machine learning classifiers (SVM, Naive Bayes, and K-nearest neighbor) for Arabic sentiment classification. A wide range of comparative experiments are conducted on an opinion corpus for Arabic (OCA). This paper demonstrates that feature selection does improve the performance of Arabic sentiment-based classification, but the result depends on the method used and the number of features selected. The experimental results demonstrate that feature reduction methods are found to improve the classifier performance. Moreover, the experimental results indicate that SVM-based feature selection yields the best performance for feature selection and that the SVM classifier outperforms the other techniques for Arabic sentiment-based classification. Finally, the experiments indicate that the SVM classifier with the SVM-based feature selection method yields the best classification method, with an accuracy of 92.4%.

Keywords: Arabic Sentiment Analysis, Opinion Mining, Machine Learning, Feature Selection.

1   Introduction

The web has become the most important place for expressing sentiments, evaluations, and reviews about products, services, and policies. A large number of people freely participate in and exchange their opinions through online community-based social media, such as web forums, shopping sites, and blogs. The explosive growth of the user-generated content of "What other people think□" represents an extremely important source of information for many special groups. Identifying and analyzing helpful reviews efficiently and accurately to satisfy both current and potential customer needs have become a critical challenge for market-driven product design. Recently, there

A. Jaafar et al. (Eds.): AIRS 2014, LNCS 8870, pp. 429–443, 2014.

have been many interests in the natural language processing and data mining communities to develop text mining techniques with the capability of accurately extracting people's opinions from large volumes of unstructured review text.

Sentiment classification is a key issue in a special type of text classification that focuses on classifying reviews of overall sentiment polarity into positive or negative categories. There is a diversity of methods and approaches for sentiment classification and opinion mining. The majority of techniques fall into two main methodologies: supervised and unsupervised learning approaches. In the supervised machine learning approach, sentiment corpora are used to train classifiers[1, 2].

The unsupervised approaches, or semantic orientation (SO) approaches, utilize lexical resources, such as SentiWordNet, to measure the polarity orientation of the words to classify the reviews [3].Both approaches have their own advantages and drawbacks. For example, a high-quality supervised machine learning approach critically depends on the availability of labeled data sets (training data), which are often impossible or difficult to find, partially due to the novelty of the task. In contrast, the SO strategy requires a large amount of linguistic resources, the availability of which typically depends on the language [1].

Most of the studies on sentiment classification consider only English reviews, perhaps due to the lack of resources in other languages. Work on other languages is still growing, including German, Chinese, Spanish, and Arabic [1, 4, 5]. Despite the fact that Arabic is currently among the top 10 languages used most frequently on the Internet according to the Internet World State rankings, there are very few resources and tools for sentiment or opinion classification in the Arabic language. However, people typically use their own language to express their experiences, opinions, and points of view. Consequently, the need for constructing resources and tools for subjectivity and sentiment analysis in languages other than English is growing. The work presented in this paper is mainly motivated by the need to develop sentiment classification systems in languages other than English, and the paper specifically focuses on Arabic sentiment classification.

In this paper, we have designed several sentiment classification models for Arabic sentiment analysis. We present an empirical comparison of seven feature selection methods (information gain (IG), principal components analysis (PCA), Relief-F, Gini Index, uncertainty, Chi-square, and support vector machines (SVMs)). The classification performance of the feature selection methods (FSMs) is investigated by using three machine learning classifiers (SVM, Naive Bayes (NB), and K-nearest neighbor (KNN)). All of the models are evaluated on an opinion corpus for Arabic (OCA) that was collected from a variety of web pages about movie reviews in the Arabic language[6].

The remainder of this paper is organized as follows. Section 2 reviews related work in the area of sentiment analysis. The methodology and the different key techniques and approaches are described in Section 3. In Section 4, we present the experiment setup and discuss the experimental results. Finally, we conclude our work and discuss future directions of research in Section 5.

2   Related Work

The research literature includes some comprehensive reviews related to sentiment analysis [7, 8] that describe different techniques used for sentiment analysis in text documents. Many of the research studies on sentiment and subjectivity analysis have been applied to English, but work on other languages is still growing, including German, Chinese, Spanish, and Arabic [1], [4], [5]. Most of the existing sentiment analysis work focuses on determining the sentiment orientations at one of three levels: the document level [9, 10], the sentence level [11-14], or the feature level [15-19].

In document-level sentiment analysis, reviews are classified into positive, negative, or neutral according to the overall sentiments expressed in the reviews. A number of machine learning techniques have been employed in several sentiment classification research studies. Traditional classification methods, such as NB [3], [20], SVMs [7], [21], decision tree [22, 23], and KNN [24] have been applied to sentiment classification.

However, the success of these methods depends on the domain, topic, and time period represented by the training data. A study on the effectiveness of machine learning techniques has been conducted by Pang et al. [25, 26], who apply three traditional supervised classification methods to sentiment classification. The experiments indicate that standard machine learning techniques definitively outperform human-produced baselines.

In addition, the semantic orientation approach or unsupervised learning method is also used in sentiment classification. The semantic orientation approach does not require any prior training. Instead, it uses lexical resources to calculate how far a word is positively or negatively inclined. Kamps et al. [27] use lexical relations in sentiment classification. Esuli and Sebastiani[28] propose a semi-supervised learning method using WordNet as a lexical resource. Their method starts by expanding an initial seed set from WordNet. Their basic assumption is that terms that have similar orientations tend to have similar sentiments. These authors use a statistical technique to determine an expanded seed term's semantic orientation through classification of the word sentiments. Finally, transfer learning approaches are also employed, particularly when there are no labels on the data [29, 30]. The transfer-based approaches aim to utilize data from other domains or time periods to help the current learning task. Recently, transfer learning has drawn increasing attention as an important research field in machine learning [31].

Most of the other Arabic sentiment analysis papers [32, 33] have used supervised approaches but have not included any comparison of FSMs and machine learning methods. Some of the FSMs mentioned above have been studied individually. Accordingly, the performance of different types of FSMs must be compared and analyzed when used with different machine learning techniques. In addition, those FSMs that have not yet been applied to any Arabic text classification tasks (including sentiment classifications such as SVM-based and PCA) must be investigated, and their effect on the performance of state-of-the-art machine learning algorithms must be compared with those of other FSMs.

3   Methodology

The methodology used in our sentiment classification system is shown in Fig. 1. First, preprocessing tasks are used to eliminate the incomplete noisy and inconsistent data. Data must be preprocessed to perform any further data mining functionality. Then, we apply FSMs to identify discriminating terms for training and classification. Finally, a machine learning method is used to classify sentiments into positive and negative classes.

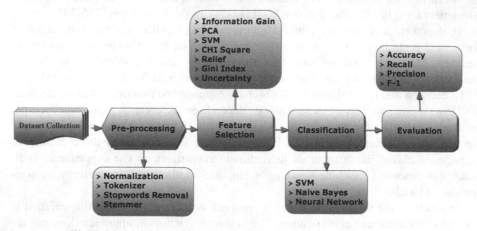

Fig. 1. Methodology used in the Arabic sentiment classification system

3.1   Pre-processing

Data preprocessing comprises three steps: 1) tokenization, 2) normalization, and 3) stop word removal. All of the reviews involve a preprocessing stage. In the normalization process, diacritics, repeated characters, and social media tags are removed. Second, in this phase, we remove certain stop words that are common in all of the reviews to avoid misclassifying the reviews. Finally, a stemming process is conducted to exclude the root forms of the words.

3.2   Feature Selection Methods

A FSM is an important component for an effective sentiment classification system. An FSM improves the performance for text classification tasks in terms of their learning speed and effectiveness. A FSM also reduces the number of data dimensions and removes irrelevant, redundant, and noisy data [34]. Our selection of the FSM metrics is influenced by the data size and data consistency [35]. In addition, our selection is also influenced by the need to investigate the most efficient FSMs, such as SVM-based, Relief, and PCA; these methods have not yet been applied to any Arabic text classification tasks, including sentiment classification. We compare their performance with other common FSM metrics, particularly those that have been proven effective in Arabic text classification tasks, such as Chi-squared [36]. The performance of these feature selection algorithms will be studied with three state-of-the-art machine learning algorithms.

In this section, we provide a brief introduction to seven effective FSMs: IG, PCA, Relief, Gini Index, uncertainty, Chi-squared, and SVM-based methods. These seven methods compute a score for each individual feature and then select a predefined size for the feature set.

Information Gain. IG is a well-known algorithm for feature selection. It has been used as a term goodness measure in the field of machine learning [37]. IG measures how much information the presence or absence of a feature contributes to make the correct classification decision on any class.

$$IG(t) = -\sum_{i=1}^{|c|} p(c_i) \log p(c_i) + p(t) \sum_{i=1}^{|c|} p(c_i|t) \log p(c_i|t) + p(\bar{t}) \sum_{i=1}^{|c|} p(c_i|\bar{t}) \log p(c_i|\bar{t})$$

(1)

where $p(c_i)$ denotes the probability that class c_i occurs; $p(t)$ denotes the probability that word t occurs; and $p(\bar{t})$ denotes the probability that word $\bar{t}$ does not occur.

Principal Components Analysis. The purpose of PCA [38] is to derive new variables that are linear combinations of the original variables and are uncorrelated. Geometrically, PCA can be thought of as a rotation of the axes of the original coordinate system to a new set of orthogonal axes that are ordered in terms of the amount of variation in the original data for which they account.

Let x be the original D-dimensional observation vector that represents a review and let ξ be a new multi-dimensional extracted vector obtained by a linear transformation:

$$\xi = A'x$$

(2)

The coefficients of the D × d matrix A can be found as follows. Let Σ be the covariance matrix of x. This matrix has D eigenvalues:

$$\lambda_1 \geq \lambda_2 \geq .... \geq \lambda_D \geq 0$$

(3)

It can be deduced that matrix A is composed of d D eigenvectors that correspond to the d largest eigenvalues $\lambda_i, D \geq i \geq 1$. Every eigenvector is a column of the matrix A. Additional details about the PCA as a feature selection algorithm can be found in [38, 39].

SVM-Based Feature Selection. In this study, the SVM linear kernel is used. The data instances are described by the vectors xi = (xi1,...,xid), where d represents the number of distinct features in the model. In general, the class predictor trained by SVM has the form

$$Prediction(x) = sgn[b + \sum_i \alpha_i K(x, x_i)] \tag{4}$$

However, in the case of a linear kernel $K(x, z) = xTz$, this statement can be rewritten as

$$sgn[b + wTx] \quad \text{for } w = \sum_i \alpha_i x_i \tag{5}$$

where the vector of weights $w = (w1,...,wd)$ can be computed and accessed directly. Geometrically, the predictor uses a hyperplane to separate the positive from negative instances, and w is the normal to this hyperplane. The linear classifier categorizes new data instances by testing whether the linear combination $w_1 x_1 + ... + w_d x_d$ of the components of vector $x = (x1,...,xd)$ is above or below a given threshold. For a feature selection approach, the absolute value |wj| is used as the weight of a feature j. Only the features for which the value of |wj| exceeds the threshold value are retained.

The idea here is that one can consider a feature important if it significantly influences the width of the margin of the resulting hyperplane; this margin is inversely proportional to ||w||, the length of w. Because $w = \sum_i \alpha_i x_i$ for a linear SVM model, one can regard $\left\| w \right\|^2$ as a function of the training vectors $x_1,...,x_l$, where $x_i = (x_{i1},..., x_{id})$; thus, we can evaluate the influence of feature j on $\left\| w \right\|^2$ by considering the absolute values of the partial derivatives of $\left\| w \right\|^2$ with respect to x_{ij}.

Relief. Relief-f [40, 41] is a commonly used metric for feature ranking that estimates the relevance of features according to how well its values distinguish the sampled instance from its nearest hit (instance of the same class) and nearest miss (opposite class). The Relief feature selection algorithm selects feature instances randomly from the training data. For each sampled instance, the nearest hit and nearest miss are found. A high weight is assigned to a feature if it differentiates between instances from different classes and has the same value for instances of the same class. Specifically, it attempts to find the best estimate of W_x from the following probabilities to allocate that value as the weight for each term feature f [42]:

$$W_x = (\textit{different value of } f \textit{ / } \text{nearest instances from different class}) - $$
$$(\textit{different value of } f \textit{ / } \text{nearest instances from same class})$$

$$\tag{6}$$

Chi-Squared Statistic (χ^2). The χ^2 statistic is one of the most commonly-used feature selection algorithms. The χ^2 statistic measures the lack of independence between the term and category [43] and is defined as follows:

$$\chi^2(c,t) = \frac{N \times (\text{AD-BC})}{(A+C)(B+C)(A+B)(C+D)} \tag{7}$$

$$\chi^2 \max(t) = \max_i \left(CHI\left(t,c_i\right)\right) \tag{8}$$

where A is the number of times that t and c co-occur, B is the number of times that t occurs without c, C is the number of times that c occurs without t, D is the number of times that neither c nor t occurs, and N is the total number of documents.

Gini Index. A novel Gini Index algorithm, introduced by Wenqian Shang et al. [44], is based on the Gini Index theory. The original form of this algorithm was used to measure the impurity of attributes toward classification and to find the best split of attributes in decision trees. The quality of the attribute improves with decreasing impurity size.

$$Gini(\text{t}) = \sum_{i=1}^{|c|} p(\text{w}|c_i)^2 p(\text{w}|c_i)^2 \tag{9}$$

In this formula, if the feature t appears in every document of classc_i, then the maximum value, $Gini(\text{t}) = 1$, is obtained.

Uncertainty-Based Term Selection. This operator calculates the relevance of the attributes of the given training set by measuring the symmetrical uncertainty with respect to the class. The relevance is calculated by the following formula:

$$Relevance\ (t)\ = \frac{2 * \left(P(C) - P(C|t)\right)}{P(C) + P(t)} \tag{10}$$

3.3   Classification Methods

In this study, three classifier methods are used in Arabic sentiment classification; the NB, SVM, and KNN methods are used due to their simplicity, effectiveness, and accuracy. Brief descriptions of these methods are provided below.

SVM Classifier. A SVM is a relatively new class of machine learning techniques that was first introduced by [45]. SVMs are a very popular technique for text categorization used in the machine learning community. They are considered to be one of the most effective classification methods according to their performance on text classification, as proven by many researchers [46, 47]

Based on the structural risk minimization principle from computational learning theory, SVMs seek a decision surface to separate the training data points into two classes and to make decisions based on the support vectors that are selected as the only effective elements in the training set.

Multiple variants of SVMs have been developed [48]. In this paper, our discussion is limited to linear SVMs due to their popularity and high performance in text categorization [37]. The optimization procedure of SVMs (dual form) is to minimize the following:

$$\vec{\alpha} = \arg\min\left\{-\sum_{i=1}^{n}\alpha_i + \sum_{i=1}^{n}\sum_{j=1}^{n}\alpha_i\alpha_j y_i y_j\left\langle\vec{x_i},\vec{x_j}\right\rangle\right\}$$
(11)

$$subject\ to: \sum_{i=1}^{n}\alpha_i y_i = 0;\ 0 \leq \alpha_i \leq C$$

Naive Bayes. The NB algorithm is a widely used algorithm for review classification. Given a feature vector table, the algorithm computes the posterior probability that the review belongs to different classes and assigns it to the class that has the highest posterior probability. There are two commonly used models (i.e., the multinomial model and multi-variate Bernoulli model) for applying the NB approach to text categorization. NB assumes a stochastic model of document generation and uses Bayes' rule. To classify the most probable class c* for a new document d, NB computes

$$c* = \arg\max c\ P(c/d)$$
(12)

The NB classifier calculates the posterior probability as follows:

$$pcjdi = p(cj)pcjdip(di)$$
(13)

K-Nearest Neighbor Classifier. The KNN is a well-known example-based classifier. The KNN has been called lazy learners because it defers its decision on how to generalize beyond the training data until each new query instance is encountered. To categorize a review, the KNN classifier ranks the review's neighbors among the training reviews. Then, the KNN uses the class labels of the K most similar neighbors.

Given a test review d, the system finds the K nearest neighbors among the training reviews. The similarity score of each nearest neighbor review to the test review is used as the weight of the classes of the neighbor review. The weighted sum in KNN classification can be written as follows:

$$score(\mathrm{d}, \mathrm{t}_i) = \sum_{d_j = KNN(d)} sim(\mathrm{d}, \mathrm{d}_j)\delta(\mathrm{d}_j, \mathrm{c}_i)$$
(14)

Where $KNN(d)$ indicates the set of K nearest neighbors of review d. If d_j belongs to c_i, then $\delta(d_j, c_i)$ equals one; otherwise, it is zero. For test review d, it should belong to the class that has the highest resulting weighted sum.

3.4   Experimental Setup

We conduct several experiments to evaluate our model. First, we evaluate the performance of the classification algorithms. We measure the performance of these classification algorithms on an OCA. The corpus contains 500 movie reviews collected from different web pages and blogs in Arabic; 250 of them are considered positive reviews, and the other 250 are considered negative.

All of the algorithms are evaluated using K-fold cross-validation. The objective of this step is to tune the parameters and select the best methods for Arabic sentiment analysis. To measure the performance of these classification methods, experimental results are sorted into the following: True Positive (TP) is the set of reviews that is correctly assigned to the given category, False Positive (FP) is the set of reviews that is incorrectly assigned to the category, False Negative (FN) is the set of reviews that is incorrectly not assigned to the category, and True Negative (TN) is the set of the set of reviews that is correctly not assigned to the category. However, we use the F1 and Macro-F1 measures. The following describes these metrics:

$$\text{Precision} = \frac{\text{TP}}{(\text{TP} + \text{FP})}$$

$$\text{Recall} = \frac{\text{TP}}{(\text{TP} + \text{FN})} \tag{15}$$

$$F_1 = \frac{2 * \text{Recall} * \text{Precision}}{(\text{Recall} + \text{Precision})}$$

$$F_1^{macro} = \frac{1}{m} \sum_{i=1}^{m} F_1(i)$$

4   Experimental Results

To examine the classifiers' overall performance on Arabic sentiment analysis without feature reduction, NB, SVM, and KNN classifiers are initially applied on the entire document-term feature space. The experimental results using the NB, SVM, and KNN classifiers are summarized in Table 1. In applications made without using any feature reduction method, the highest performance is obtained with the SVM classifier, and the worst performance is obtained with the NB classifier. Next, the seven FSMs (IG, PCA, SVM, Relief, Chi, Gini, and uncertainty) are applied to select the feature spaces. In this phase, the effects of the individual feature ranking methods on classifier performance are examined.

The macro-averaging F-measure results for the NB classifier with the seven FSM selection methods at different feature subset sizes, as it presented in Table 2. The seven FSMs (IG, PCA, SVM, Relief, Chi, Gini, and uncertainty) perform better than the original classifier. The SVM-based and IG FSMs typically yield the best performance in terms of the macro-averaging F-measure (see the average row in Table 2). According to Table 2, the highest performance (90.58) of the NB classifier is obtained when using 100 of the weighted features from the SVM-based methods.

Table 1. Performance (the average value of Macro-F1 and the F-measure for each class) of the NB, SVM, and KNN classifiers

	Macro F-MEASURE	F1 Measure For the Positive Class	F1 Measure For the Negative Class
NB	80.52	81.61	79.44
KNN	82.36	83.12	81.59
SVM	83.16	82.39	83.93

Table 2. Macro-averaging precision values for the NB classifier with the seven FSMs with different sizes of feature sets

NB							
	SVM	PCA	IG	CHI	RE	GI	CER
100	90.58	77.60	85.36	84.74	83.79	84.97	84.35
200	89.18	82.78	85.74	83.93	84.96	85.33	84.73
300	88.96	82.74	86.96	84.52	83.76	86.74	83.47
400	88.36	83.30	86.35	85.10	83.32	85.12	84.12
500	87.56	84.31	86.72	83.89	84.91	86.93	84.29
600	86.74	81.89	86.74	85.32	83.90	86.74	84.72
Average	**88.56**	**82.10**	**86.31**	**84.58**	**84.11**	**85.97**	**84.28**

The macro-averaging F-measure results for the SVM classifier with the seven FSM selection methods at different feature subset sizes, as it presented in Table 2. Four of the seven FSMs (SVM, IG, CHI, and GINI) perform better than the original classifier. SVM-based and IG tend to yield the highest performance in terms of macro-averaging the F-measure (see the average row in Table 3). According to Table 3, the highest performance (92.38) of the SVM classifier is obtained when using 300 of the weighted features by the SVM-based method.

Table 3. Macro-averaging precision values for the SVM classier with the seven FSMs with different sizes of feature sets

SVM							
	SVM	PCA	IG	CHI	RE	GI	CER
100	84.92	77.53	85.51	85.71	86.77	84.67	80.71
200	88.11	82.31	84.62	83.57	81.83	85.22	82.51
300	92.38	78.57	88.17	81.21	81.75	86.94	82.26
400	90.56	89.57	86.54	83.20	80.22	85.51	83.20
500	88.12	80.03	86.34	84.03	81.35	85.10	80.91
600	87.31	82.19	86.33	81.79	82.42	85.31	82.16
Average	**88.57**	**81.70**	**86.25**	**83.25**	**82.39**	**85.46**	**81.96**

For the KNN classifier with the seven FSM selection methods at different feature subset sizes, the macro-averaging F-measure results showed in Table 4. Three of the seven FSMs (SVM, IG, and GINI) perform slightly better than the original classifier. GINI performs best in terms of macro- averaging the F-measure (see the average row in Table 4). According to Table 4, the highest performance (88.00) of the KNN classifier is obtained when using 100 of the weighted features from the Relief method.

Table 4. Macro-averaging precision values for the KNN classier with the seven FSMs with different sizes of feature sets

	KNN						
	SVM	PCA	IG	CHI	RE	GI	CER
100	85.33	81.59	84.55	84.73	88.00	84.13	81.04
200	86.37	81.38	81.40	82.06	80.50	79.94	75.56
300	82.72	82.40	87.60	78.51	78.08	86.19	80.59
400	77.87	84.20	87.38	78.88	79.26	87.77	78.53
500	76.61	84.40	84.15	79.76	73.21	86.16	77.39
600	87.80	79.00	76.52	82.59	77.60	74.96	75.65
Average	**82.78**	**82.16**	**83.60**	**81.09**	**79.44**	**83.19**	**78.13**

Comparing the classifier performances (Tables 2, 3, and 4), the SVM algorithm outperforms the NB and KNN algorithms. Furthermore, the highest accuracies are obtained when the feature selection operations are made by the SVM-based method. In general, using FSMs positively contributed to the performance of all classifiers (Tables 1, 2, 3, and 4) in an affirmative manner.

Comparing the behaviors of the three classifiers in terms of the macro-averaging F-measure results with each FSM, using different sizes of feature sets as shown in Fig. 2, the results reveal that the classification performances of the three classifiers with one FSM vary when using different numbers of features. In addition, there is no superior classifier for all feature selection algorithms. As shown in Figure 2, the NB classifier outperforms the SVM and KNN classifiers when the Relief, Chi, and uncertainty FSMs are used, whereas the SVM classifier outperforms the NB and KNN classifiers when the SVM and PCA FSMs are used and the KNN classifier outperforms the NB and SVM classifiers when the GINI FSM is used. However, when the IG FSM is used, the three classifiers have almost equal performance. Thus, both the number of features and the FSMs are key factors in determining the suitable classification method.

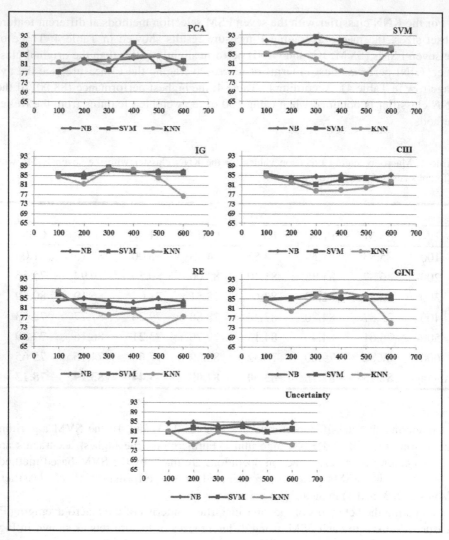

Fig. 2. Comparisons of the performance of the NB, SVM, and KNN approaches with each FSM for different sizes of feature sets

5   Conclusions

This paper presented an extensive comparative study of seven FSM methods and three selections for Arabic sentiment classification tasks. The main contribution of this work is the investigation of the performance of different feature selection and machine learning methods in terms of the macro-F measure. The results indicate that there is no superior classifier for all feature selection algorithms and that there is no superior FSM method for all dataset sizes. The results also demonstrate that the use of the best seven FSMs yields improved results compared to those obtained using the original classifier, particularly with the NB and SVM classifiers. Finally, the results demonstrate that the SVM-based FSM performs the best among the sentiment FSMs and that the SVM classifier demonstrates the best performance for the Arabic sentiment classification with an accuracy of 92.4%, whereas NB classifier yields better results when used with the other FSMs considered.

Our future efforts will be targeted at developing Arabic SentiWordNet and an Arabic large sentiment corpus, investigating the implementation of Semantic orientation approaches, and investigating the implementation of some optimization algorithms to address the feature selection problem for Arabic sentiment classification.

References

1. Martín-Valdivia, M.-T., et al.: Sentiment Polarity Detection in Spanish Reviews Combining Supervised and Unsupervised Approaches. Expert Systems with Applications 40(10), 3934–3942 (2013)
2. Prabowo, R., Thelwall, M.: Sentiment Analysis: A Combined Approach. Journal of Informetrics 3(2), 143–157 (2009)
3. Kang, H., Yoo, S.J., Han, D.: Senti-lexicon and Improved Naïve Bayes Algorithms for Sentiment Analysis of Restaurant Reviews. Expert Systems with Applications 39(5), 6000–6010 (2012)
4. Banea, C., Mihalcea, R., Wiebe, J.: Multilingual Sentiment and Subjectivity Analysis. Multilingual Natural Language Processing (2011)
5. Tan, S., Zhang, J.: An Empirical Study of Sentiment Analysis for Chinese Documents. Expert Syst. Appl. 34(4), 2622–2629 (2008)
6. Rushdi-Saleh, M., et al.: OCA: Opinion Corpus for Arabic. Journal of the American Society for Information Science and Technology 62(10), 2045–2054 (2011)
7. Vinodhini, G., Chandrasekaran, R.: Sentiment Analysis and Opinion Mining: A Survey. International Journal 2(6) (2012)
8. Tang, H., Tan, S., Cheng, X.: A Survey on Sentiment Detection of Reviews. Expert Systems with Applications 36(7), 10760–10773 (2009)
9. Moraes, R., Valiati, J.F., Gavião Neto, W.P.: Document-level Sentiment Classification: An Empirical Comparison between SVM and ANN. Expert Systems with Applications 40, 621–633 (2013)
10. Missen, M.M.S., Boughanem, M., Cabanac, G.: Opinion Mining: Reviewed from Word to Document Level. Social Network Analysis and Mining 3(1), 107–125 (2013)
11. He, Y.: Bayesian Models for Sentence-Level Subjectivity Detection. Technical report kmi-10-02, Knowledge Media Institute, The Open University (2010)
12. Fu, G., Wang, X.: Chinese sentence-level sentiment classification based on fuzzy sets. In: Proceedings of the 23rd International Conference on Computational Linguistics: Posters, Association for Computational Linguistics (2010)
13. Albornoz, J.C.D., Plaza, L., Gervás, P.: A Hybrid Approach to Emotional Sentence Polarity and Intensity Classification, pp. 153-161 (2010)
14. Varma, V.: Language Independent Sentence-Level Subjectivity Analysis with Feature Selection. In: 26th Pacific Asia Conference on Language,Information and Computation 2012, pp. 171–180 (2012)
15. Duric, A., Song, F.: Feature Selection for Sentiment Analysis based on Content and Syntax Models. Decision Support Systems 53, 704–711 (2012)

16. Shi, L., MingYu, J.: A dfm Model of Mining Product Features from Customer Reviews. In: 2011 International Conference on Control, Automation and Systems Engineering (CASE). IEEE (2011)
17. Wilson, T., Wiebe, J., Hoffmann, P.: Recognizing Contextual Polarity: An Exploration of Features for Phrase-level Sentiment Analysis. Computational linguistics 35(3), 399–433 (2009)
18. Popescu, A.-M., Etzioni, O.: Extracting Product Features and Opinions from Reviews. In: Natural Language Processing and Text Mining, pp. 9-28. Springer (2007)
19. Hu, M., Liu, B.: Mining Opinion Features in Customer Reviews. In: Proceedings of the National Conference on Artificial Intelligence, AAAI Press; MIT Press, Menlo Park, Cambridge (2004)
20. Melville, P., Gryc, W., Lawrence, R.D.: Sentiment Analysis of Blogs by Combining Lexical Knowledge with Text Classification. In: Proceedings of the 15th ACM SIGKDD International Conference on Knowledge Discovery and Data Mining. ACM (2009)
21. Mountassir, A., Benbrahim, H., Berrada, I.: An Empirical Study to Address the Problem of Unbalanced Data Sets in Sentiment Classification. In: 2012 IEEE International Conference on Systems, Man, and Cybernetics (SMC), pp. 3298–3303 (2012)
22. Jia, L., Yu, C., Meng, W.: The Effect of Negation on Sentiment Analysis and Retrieval Effectiveness. In: Proceedings of the 18th ACM Conference on Information and Knowledge Management. ACM (2009)
23. Annett, M., Kondrak, G.: A Comparison of Sentiment Analysis Techniques: Polarizing movie blogs. Advances in Artificial Intelligence, pp. 25–35 (2008)
24. Tan, S., Zhang, J.: An Empirical Study of Sentiment Analysis for Chinese Documents. Expert Systems with Applications 34(4), 2622–2629 (2008)
25. Pang, B.: Automatic Analysis of Document Sentiment, Cornell University (2006)
26. Pang, B., Lee, L.: Opinion Mining and Sentiment Analysis. Foundations and Trends® in Information Retrieval 2, 1–135 (2008)
27. Kamps, J., et al.: Using Wordnet to Measure Semantic Orientations of Adjectives (2004)
28. Esuli, A., Sebastiani, F.: Determining the Semantic Orientation of Terms through Gloss Classification. In: Proceedings of the 14th ACM International Conference on Information and Knowledge Management. ACM (2005)
29. Brooke, J.: Cross-Linguistic Sentiment Analysis: From English to Spanish. In: RANLP, pp. 50–54 (2009)
30. Dubois, D.: Sentiment Analysis: Transferring Knowledge Across Domains. The University of New Brunswick (2012)
31. Pan, S.J., Yang, Q.: A Survey on Transfer Learning. IEEE Transactions on Knowledge and Data Engineering 22(10), 1345–1359 (2010)
32. Korayem, M., Crandall, D., Abdul-Mageed, M.: Subjectivity and Sentiment Analysis of Arabic: A Survey, pp. 1-10 (2012) http://cs.indiana.edu
33. Omar, N., Albared, M., Al-Shabi, A., Al-Moslmi, T.: Ensemble of Classification Algorithms for Subjectivity and Sentiment Analysis of Arabic Customers' Reviews. International Journal of Advancements in Computing Technology 14(5), 77–85 (2013)
34. Sebastiani, F.: Machine Learning in Automated Text Categorization. ACM Computing Surveys 34, 1–47 (2001)
35. Dash, M., Liu, H.: Feature Selection for Classification. Intelligent Data Analysis 1(1-4), 131–156 (1997)
36. Mesleh, A.M.: Feature Sub-set Selection Metrics for Arabic Text Classification. Pattern Recognition Letters 32(14), 1922–1929 (2011)

37. Yang, Y., Pedersen, J.O.: A Comparative Study on Feature Selection in Text Categorization. In: Machine Learning-International Workshop Then Conference, Morgan Kaufmann Publishers, Inc. (1997)
38. Fengxi, S., Zhongwei, G., Dayong, M.: Feature Selection Using Principal Component Analysis. In: 2010 International Conference on System Science, Engineering Design and Manufacturing Informatization, ICSEM (2010)
39. Lu, Y., et al.: Feature Selection using Principal Feature Analysis. In: Proceedings of the 15th International Conference on Multimedia. ACM (2007)
40. Kira, K., Rendell, L.A.: A Practical Approach to Feature Selection. In: Proceedings of the Ninth International Workshop on Machine Learning 1992, pp. 249–256. Morgan Kaufmann Publishers Inc., Aberdeen (1992)
41. Bergadano, F., De Raedt, L. (eds.): ECML 1994. LNCS, vol. 784. Springer, Heidelberg (1994)
42. Sharma, A., Dey, S.: A Comparative Study of Feature Selection and Machine Learning Techniques for Sentiment Analysis. In: Proceedings of the 2012 ACM Research in Applied Computation Symposium, ACM (2012)
43. Galavotti, L., Sebastiani, F., Simi, M.: Experiments on the use of feature selection and negative evidence in automated text categorization. In: Borbinha, J.L., Baker, T. (eds.) ECDL 2000. LNCS, vol. 1923, pp. 59–68. Springer, Heidelberg (2000)
44. Wenqian, S., et al.: Research on the Algorithm of Feature Selection Based on Gini Index for Text Categorization. Journal of Computer Research and Development 10, 001 (2006)
45. Cortes, C., Vapnik, V.: Support-vector Networks. Machine learning 20(3), 273–297 (1995)
46. Joachims, T.: A Statistical Learning Model of Text Classification for Support Vector Machines. SIGIR Forum (ACM Special Interest Group on Information Retrieval), 128-136 (2001)
47. Isa, D., et al.: Text Document Preprocessing with the Bayes Formula for Classification using the Support Vector Machine. IEEE Transactions on Knowledge and Data Engineering 20(9), 1264–1272 (2008)
48. Joachims, T.: Text Categorization with Support Vector Machines: Learning with many relevant features Machine Learning: ECML-98. In: Nédellec, C., Rouveirol, C. (eds.) ECML 1998. LNCS, vol. 1398, pp. 137–142. Springer, Heidelberg (1998)

Undersampling Techniques to Re-balance Training Data for Large Scale Learning-to-Rank

Muhammad Ibrahim and Mark Carman

Faculty of Information Technology,
Monash University, VIC 3800, Australia
muhammad.ibrahim@monash.edu, mark.carman@monash.edu

Abstract. Learning-to-rank (LtR) algorithms for information retrieval use the supervised learning framework to learn a ranking function from a training set consisting of query-document pairs. In this study we investigate the imbalanced nature of LtR training sets, which generally contain very few relevant documents as compared to the number of irrelevant documents. The need to include as many relevant documents as possible in the training set is well-known, but we ask the question as to how many irrelevant documents are needed in order to learn a good ranking function. We employ both random and deterministic undersampling techniques to reduce the number of irrelevant documents. Minimizing the training set size reduces the training time which is an important factor in large scale LtR. Extensive experiments on Letor benchmark datasets reveal that the performance of a LtR algorithm trained on a much smaller training set remains similar to that of the original training set. Thus this study suggests that for large scale LtR tasks, we can leverage undersampling techniques to reduce training time with negligible effect on performance.

Keywords: Learning-to-rank, undersampling, scalability, imbalanced data.

1 Introduction

Ranking a set of documents based on their relevance with respect to a given query is a central problem of information retrieval. Traditionally people have been using (unsupervised) scoring functions like BM25, Language Models, etc. to accomplish this task. In recent years researchers have started to use supervised learning framework to learn a ranking function where a training example is a query-document pair, the corresponding label is the relevance judgement, and the features are measurements of various base rankers (eg. cosine similarity using tf-idf document vectors). The task of learning a ranking function from this training set is called learning to rank (LtR). LtR algorithms have been studied extensively over the past few years [14].

Most of the existing work in LtR has aimed at developing better algorithms for learning a ranking function given a training set, while relatively little research has been devoted to *out-of-the-box* engineering topics such as how to improve the quality of the training data, or how to tackle the scalability issue for large scale LtR.

The task of developing an LtR-based IR system can be viewed as a two stage process [5], [16]. The first stage involves the following steps:

A. Jaafar et al. (Eds.): AIRS 2014, LNCS 8870, pp. 444–457, 2014.

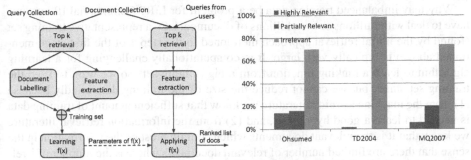

Fig. 1. LtR based IR system

Fig. 2. Relevance level distribution for three different datasets

1. *Top k retrieval.* An *initial retrieval approach* is used to retrieve k documents from the whole collection for each query according to one or more base rankers.
2. *Human labelling and feature extraction.* Relevance judgements for the selected k documents are collected usually from human [1], [18]. Also, features are extracted for each of these query-document pairs. These features along with relevance labels given by human judges constitute the training set.

The following steps are then performed in the second stage:

3. *Learning.* An LtR algorithm is used to learn a ranking function $f(x)$ from the training set.

Once the system has been trained, the following steps are performed during real time evaluation:

1. *Top k Retrieval.* For a query given by the user, the same top-k retrieval is used.
2. *Feature Extraction.* Features are extracted for the retrieved documents with respect to the query.
3. *Application of the Learned Model.* A relevance score for each document is generated using the learned model. Then the documents are ranked using those scores, and the ranked list is returned to the user.

Fig. 1 depicts the complete scenario.

Some studies have been performed on the first stage which will be discussed in the next section. That is, how to develop a better initial retrieval approach. But we are interested in yet another aspect which lies somewhere between the first and second stages. One of the characteristics of LtR training data is, after applying the initial approach to retrieve the top k documents from the entire document collection, the training data is usually highly imbalanced in the sense that there are very few relevant documents for a query as compared to the number of irrelevant ones. This aspect is shown in Fig. 2 for some datasets of the most prominent publicly available benchmark LtR dataset collection[1] [19].

---

[1] http://research.microsoft.com/en-us/um/beijing/projects/letor//

Why may imbalanced training data be a problem for LtR? Commercial IR systems have to deal with millions or even billions of documents. So a representative training set (found by the initial retrieval approach mentioned in the step 1 of the first stage mentioned above) is typically very large. It is computationally challenging for a learning algorithm to learn a ranking function from a big training set. So we want to keep the training set small, but we cannot reduce the size of the training data blindly because (1) from the machine learning literature we know that sufficient amount of training data is needed to learn a good hypothesis, and (2) from the information retrieval literature we know that it is the relevant documents which contain most of the information in the sense that there are limited number of relevant documents whereas the number of irrelevant documents for a particular query is very large. So intuitively, we should retain all the relevant documents because otherwise we could miss important information (about the relevant documents). Hence we pose the following question: are all the irrelevant documents which are currently being used necessary for learning a good ranking function? That is, is a smaller subset of irrelevant documents sufficient for learning a good ranking function which can distinguish between relevant and irrelevant documents? If we find that we can use a much smaller subset from these large number of irrelevant documents without compromising the accuracy of the learning algorithm, the training time complexity in large scale LtR problem (which is an important issue [4], [13, Ch. 7], [14, Ch. 20]) will be significantly reduced.

2 Related Work

Aslam *et al.* [1] investigate different methods for top-k retrieval from a large corpus. That is, they studied techniques for generating a good training set from the original large document collection. To complement their work, our work is in yet another area: all of their methods have the characteristics that the selected document collection (to be used as training set) is usually still highly imbalanced. We, therefore, want to explore whether or not the techniques to deal with imbalanced nature of training data can have any positive effect.

McDonald *et al.* [16] focus on the properties of a good training set through extensive empirical study on some large datasets. They consider the size of the sample to be used in the top k retrieval stage in their experiment (i.e., different values of k), and empirically search for the optimal values of k for different tasks and datasets. They use a single base ranker as the initial retrieval method, and experimented with some values of k which are selected based on previous studies and rules of thumb. Their conclusions include: retrieval performance in general increases with increasing size of training sample (i.e., the values of k) up to a certain point, after which it saturates. It can be noted here that if our experiments can establish that the training set size can be significantly reduced by discarding many of the irrelevant documents found by top k retrieval, then the need for research on which is the optimal value for k becomes less significant because we can use large enough k, and after that we can reduce the training set size by discarding many of the irrelevant documents.

Dang *et al.* [5] develop an improved initial retrieval method in the sense that it retrieves more relevant documents than existing methods like mere BM25. Their method uses some advanced features like proximity based features [2]. Note that the goal of depth-k pooling approach for initial retrieval is also the same as the goal of their paper, i.e., to increase the number of relevant documents.

We note that although one of the goals of the methods used in top k retrieval stage is to retrieve as many relevant documents as possible, it turns out that the disparity between the number of relevant and irrelevant documents is still high [3].

Long *et al.* [15] propose an Active Learning framework which selects the example which minimizes expected DCG loss over a training set. The main motivation of active learning is to reduce the large cost associated with manually labelling documents. Some other works such as Donmez *et al.* [6], Yu [21] also try to find the examples which, if added to a training set, increase the quality of the learned ranking function. This category of works which try to improve the quality of the training set while keeping its size small do not differentiate between relevant and irrelevant documents, whereas our work is specifically concerned with the importance of irrelevant documents. That is, the training set found after applying their methods may still be highly imbalanced, and thus eligible for applying the techniques proposed in our work.

From the discussion above, we see that although there are various studies on how to improve the quality of the training data while limiting its size, none of them is primarily concerned with the irrelevant documents, in other words, none of them is concerned with the imbalanced nature of the training data. Since our re-balancing techniques can be applied after applying those methods (and before the learning phase), this work is distinctive from and complementary to the existing works.

3 Approach

Our goal is to reduce the number of irrelevant documents which comprise the vast majority of the training set, and then to examine the effect of learning from the reduced training set on evaluation metrics while testing on a separate (non-reduced) test set. In order to achieve this goal we can utilize the concept of undersampling techniques for imbalanced data from the machine learning literature [10]. Undersampling techniques aim at making the training set more balanced in terms of the number of instances from each class. In this paper we report findings from two approaches: (1) random undersampling, and (2) simple deterministic undersampling. The application of more advanced techniques such as Synthetic Minority Oversampling [9] is left to future work.

Since the LtR data are divided by queries, we perform undersampling at the query level. That is, for each query, we retain all the relevant documents, and select a subset of irrelevant documents according to some criteria (either randomly or based on a particular feature value) for inclusion in the training set. We then evaluate performance on a (non-reduced) test set to compare performance at different amounts of training data.

The working strategy of random undersampling is simple – we randomly select a subset of irrelevant documents. For deterministic undersmapling, our goal is to retain the most *informative* irrelevant instances (i.e., query-document pairs) so that the learning algorithm can effectively learn to distinguish between relevant and irrelevant documents with fewer irrelevant documents in the training set. One approach to identifying informative irrelevant documents is to use an informative feature from the training set itself, such as the BM25 score. We assume that the lower the BM25 score of an irrelevant document with respect to a particular query, the more highly informative it is as an irrelevant document. The reason is, most of the relevant/irrelevant documents have higher/lower BM25 scores respectively. So the irrelevant documents with lower BM25 scores should represent the "true characteristics" of the "irrelevant nature" of a document. However, there do exist some irrelevant documents with high BM25 scores and also some relevant documents with low BM25 scores (simply because BM25 is not a panacea to the ranking problem).

4 Experiments

4.1 Experimental Setup

As rank learners we used two algorithms: (1) an updated version of the RankSVM algorithm[2] [12], which is a popular pairwise LtR algorithm that formalizes LtR as a problem of binary classification on instance pairs, and solves the problem using Support Vector Machines, and (2) LambdaMart algorithm [20] which is a listwise LtR algorithm using Gradient Boosting framework [7]. We use three widely used evaluation metrics, namely, NDCG (normalized discounted cumulative gain), precision, and MAP (mean average precision)[3]. We use nine different datasets[4] from a variety of search-related tasks: domain-specific search (Ohsumed), topic distillation (TD2003 and TD2004), homepage finding (HP2003 and HP2004), named page finding (NP2003 and NP2004), and general web search (MQ2007 and MQ2008). We make use of the evaluation scripts provided by the Letor website[5]. At first we explain the results found using RankSVM algorithm. Later we talk about the LambdaMart.

4.2 Random Undersampling

The results of random undersampling technique are shown in Fig. 3. For each dataset, we plot several performance metrics, namely, NDCG@10, precision@10, MAP, and average of NDCGs (and precisions) from k=1 up to 10, against the percentage of the original training set used. Each plot starts with a training set which includes all the relevant documents and one irrelevant document per query. Subsequent training sets (whose percentages are indicated along the x-axis) contain increasing numbers of irrelevant documents. To prevent random fluctuations due to sampling effects, we perform 10 independent runs of each experiment, and report the average result.

---

[2] http://research.microsoft.com/en-us/um/beijing/projects/letor/ Baselines/RankSVM-Primal.html. Please note that performance of this updated version is better than the original RankSVM – for details, please see http://research.microsoft.com/en-us/um/beijing/projects/ letor/letor3baseline.aspx

[3] To know details of these metrics, one useful study is [11].

[4] For details of these datasets, please see the Letor website http:/research.microsoft.com/en-us/um/beijing/projects/letor/

[5] http:/research.microsoft.com/en-us/um/beijing/projects/letor/

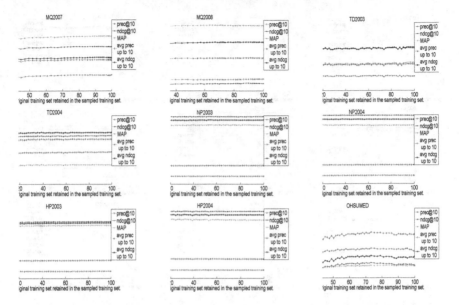

Fig. 3. Results for random subsampling across the nine datasets; Five different metrics shown on each graph. Each point corresponds to the average value of the performance metric over 10 distinct sampling runs

In Fig. 3 we observe that initially (with very few irrelevant documents) performance is poor, as expected. As the number of irrelevant document increases so does the performance. In general, after the initial increase, relatively minor improvements in performance are observed with increases in the number of irrelevant document (note the restricted interval on the y-axis).

It appears that performance profiles are task or corpus dependent since similar patterns are observed for MQ2007 and MQ2008, for TD2003 and TD2004, for NP2003 and NP2004 etc. A close inspection of the graphs also reveals that for most of the datasets even better performance can sometimes be achieved using a subset of the training data rather than the entire dataset.

4.3 Subset Selection Based On Feature Values

The second approach performs a deterministic selection of the irrelevant document subsets. It works as follows: for every query, we, as before, add all relevant documents to the training set. We then sort the irrelevant documents in ascending order based on a particular feature value. We then take only the first irrelevant document (with the minimum feature value) and add it to the training set for that query. For subsequent iterations, additional irrelevant documents are added in order of the feature value. Here we also perform the same procedure but with descending order of feature values in order to validate the motivation behind using the standard (ascending) one.

Figs. 4 and 5 show performance plots across the nine datasets for the feature-based ordering in *descending* and *ascending* order respectively. For the datasets TD, HP, NP

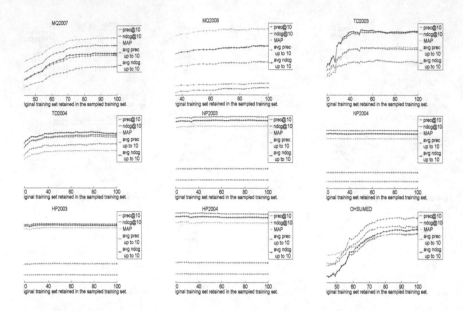

Fig. 4. Results for descending feature-based subset selection across the nine datasets

and OHSUMED, BM25 is used to sort the documents. The dataset provider does not disclose the features of MQ2007 and MQ2008, so we simply select the first feature for sorting.

We conjecture that the higher the BM25 score (or any other particularly informative feature) of an irrelevant document, the less information this document is likely to contain about the "irrelevance nature" of the documents.

For *descending* (Fig. 4) approach, we see the curves initially have very low performance values, because the first irrelevant documents being added are those that have high BM25 scores and are thus the least informative as far as the learning algorithm is concerned. The curves of all nine datasets then start to rise quickly as the training set size increases, because more informative irrelevant documents (with lower BM25 scores) are starting to be included in the training set, and thus it becomes easier for the learning algorithm to learn patterns of the irrelevant documents thereby yielding better performance on test set. After including enough[6] irrelevant documents, the performance appears to saturate, such that including additional irrelevant documents after that point does not improve performance significantly. Finally, one exceptional pattern is witnessed in Ohsumed where the performance first goes down.

We gain even further improvement in terms of training time if we use *ascending* order of sorting as shown in Fig. 5. Using the same argument mentioned above, we expect a sharp rise (may not be noticeable in the plots unless we magnify the y-axis), and then a roughly flat curve. The reason is, in the early training sets, only the irrelevant documents with very low BM25 scores will be included which are mostly very

---

[6] Admittedly, the amount of *enough* documents is currently not known to us, we intend to work on it in future.

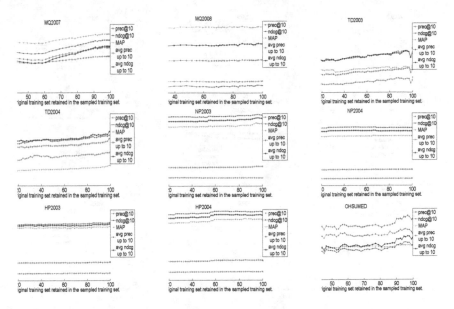

Fig. 5. Results for ascending feature-based subset selection across the nine datasets

distinctive irrelevant document (because BM25 is a good base ranker), so adding highly informative irrelevant documents helps the learning algorithm to learn (and thereby to distinguish) the patterns of relevant and irrelevant ones thereby yielding better performance in test time. After that, when we continue to include comparatively larger BM25 scores, the performance should still continue to increase slightly because even though BM25 is a good ranker, it does not win all the time. So there do exist some irrelevant documents which have high BM25 scores. Including these documents in the training set helps the learning algorithm to learn these patterns in addition to the normal patterns (i.e., low BM25 scores) of the irrelevant documents. The Fig. 5 shows that our analysis holds for most of the datasets with an exception in MQ2007.

Thus the findings of these two experiments show that indeed the ascending approach has some advantage over descending one in terms of minimum percentage of training set required to achieve good performance.

4.4 Direct Comparison between Subsampling Approaches

Now we compare performance in terms of MAP and NDCG@10 of the different approaches to subsampling in Figs. 6 and 7 respectively across the nine datasets. As shown previously, the sorting approach in descending order performs poorly in comparison with the other approaches. Then comes the sorting approach in ascending order. The random undersampling wins almost consistently over the others. We conclude that in the training set the importance of irrelevant documents with low BM25 scores is (generally) more than those with high BM25 scores, but that low BM25 scores alone cannot yield the best performance, rather some high BM25 scores are also necessary due the

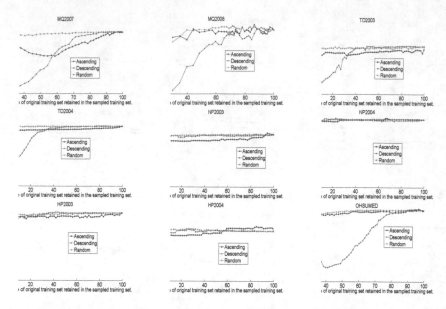

Fig. 6. Performance comparison for ascending, descending and random sampling on the nine different datasets in terms of MAP

fact that some irrelevant document at test time do indeed also have high BM25 scores. So a next natural approach would be to systematically include some low BM25 and a few high BM25 irrelevant documents after sorting the scores in order to achieve even better performance than random approach. We expect better performance because (1) including only high BM25 scores in the training set does not do well (cf. initial stage of the plots of descending sorting approach), (2) even though random approach includes some of these *less informative* (i.e., having high BM25 scores) irrelevant documents drawn from a uniform distribution in the training set, their performance is the best, (3) low BM25 scores are good (cf. initial stages of the plots of acending sorting approach). So why not systematically including more low than high in the training set? We leave this to future work.

In Table 1 we analyze the minimum percentage of training set needed to achieve 90%, 95% and 98% performance (in terms of Average NDCG up to rank 10) of original training set. A question may arise here that why we do not use standard statistical significant tests? The answer is, statistical significant tests are meant to use to reject a null hypothesis, they cannot be used to prove the null hypothesis. So it will not be appropriate if we, in the context of our experiments, say that *since we cannot reject the null hypothesis (that the baseline and some earlier configuration of our experiments having less training set are the same), the null hypothesis is proved,* because it may happen that we simply do not have enough evidence to reject the the null hypothesis.

We see from Table 1 that the percentage of the original training set needed to have similar performance to that of the baseline (100% of the training data) varies from task

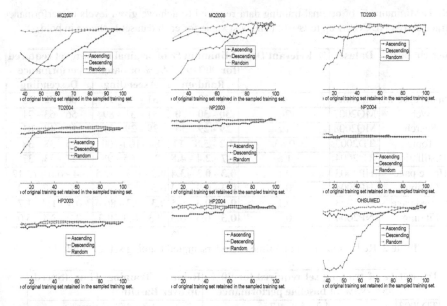

Fig. 7. Performance comparison for ascending, descending and random sampling on the nine different datasets in terms of NDCG@10

to task. As was seen also in Fig. 6, this table confirms that the random undersampling strategy is the most reliable, followed by the ascending ordering approach.

We note that our results are not directly comparable with that of existing methods (as explained in the Related Work Section) since we investigate sub-sampling of only irrelevant documents in post-labelling phase whereas existing works focus on (1) sampling both relevant and irrelevant documents, and (2) before labelling.

4.5   Training Time

We have so far discussed the importance of reducing the training set size in order to decrease the time required to learn a ranking function, but have not thus far reported on such time improvements. In Table 2 we show the time taken to train the models for the TD, NP and HP datasets (where the positive effect of reduction in training set size is apparent). We see consistent speed-ups in the range of 3 to 5 times faster learning as a result of reductions in the number of irrelevant documents present in the training set, indicating the efficacy of our approach. Fig. 8 shows that the training time increases linearly with increasing training set size. The minor fluctuations are possibly because we ran these experiments in a desktop computer where we also run other experiments simultaneously.

4.6   Using LambdaMart Algorithm

The above results and analyses are based on the results found by running RankSVM algorithm. To be certain about the findings, we run another algorithm called LambdaMart

Table 1. Minimum % of original training data required to achieve given levels of performance (average across NDCG@1 up to @10). (The best value for each dataset is shown in bold)

Search Task	Dataset	% Relevant Docs	Minimum % of original training set required for 90%-95%-98% of baseline performance		
			Random	Ascending	Descending
Domain specific	Ohsumed	30	**31 - 33 - 41**	**31 - 31 - 90**	68 - 72 - 75
Web	MQ2007	26	**30 - 30 - 30**	31 - 31 - 89	56 - 63 - 71
Search	MQ2008	19	**29 - 29 - 34**	**29 - 29 - 39**	29 - 48 - 81
Topic	TD2003	0.83	**4.2 - 5.8 - 17**	84 -100-100	35 - 38 - 38
Distillation	TD2004	1.5	**1.7 - 2.4 - 4.8**	2.1 - 65 - 98	27 - 33 - 37
Home page	HP2003	0.1	**0.3 - 0.3 - 3.4**	0.3 - 0.3 - 59.5	3.4 - 6.6 - 13.12
Finding	HP2004	0.3	**0.3 - 0.9 - 3.3**	0.3 - 0.3 - 56.4	1.7 - 1.7 - **3.3**
Named page	NP2003	0.1	**0.3 - 0.3 - 6.5**	0.3 - 0.3 - 86.6	0.9 - 1.7 - **1.7**
Finding	NP2004	0.1	**0.3 - 0.3 - 0.3**	0.3 - 0.3 - 0.3	0.9 - 3.4 - 5.0

Table 2. Reduction in training time of undersampled training set (cf. Table 1)

Dataset	% of training set required for 90%-95%-98% of baseline performance	Relative Training Time (Speed-up over Baseline)
TD2003	4.2 - 5.8 - 17	4.3 - 4.3 - 3 times
TD2004	1.7 - 2.4 - 4.8	5 - 5 - 4.5 times
HP2003	0.3 - 0.3 - 3.4	4.5 - 4.5 - 4 times
HP2004	0.3 - 0.9 - 3.3	5 - 4.5 - 4.5 times
NP2003	0.3 - 0.3 - 6.5	4.5 - 4.5 - 3 times
NP2004	0.3 - 0.3 - 0.3	4 - 4 - 4 times

[20] which is a state-of-the-art listwise algorithm. We used an open source implementation[7] of it mentioned in [8]. Plots of three datasets are shown in Fig. 9. Since the plots are similar to the ones found from RankSVM, we do not repeat the result analysis.

5   Discussion

Training time of the LtR algorithms in large scale LtR task is considered to be an important issue [4], [13, Ch. 7], [14, Ch. 20]. Undersampling techniques decreases the training set size thereby decreasing training time. Also, smaller training set requires smaller feature computation time, and some features are computationally costly to calculate [4], [16,17].

Our work is distinct from and complementary to the existing works on using a better initial retrieval approach (top k retrieval as mentioned in Section 2) and on selecting informative samples in the sense that our work is applicable *after* using these methods. The existing works focus on the quality of the training set, whereas we primarily focus on the training set size in the context of necessity of including large number of irrelevant documents. Moreover, our methods can also be extended to focus on the quality of the

---

[7] https://code.google.com/p/jforests/

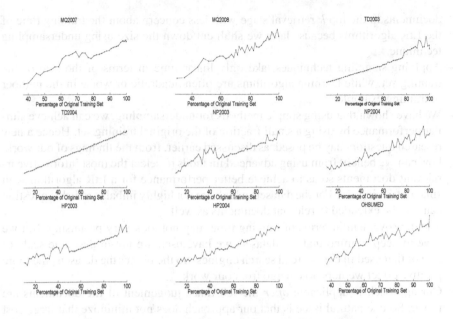

Fig. 8. Training time versus percentage of original training set

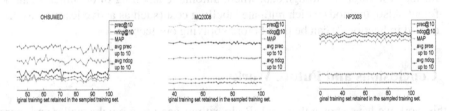

Fig. 9. Results for random subsampling using three datasets using LambdaMart Algorithm, Five different metrics shown; Each point corresponds to the performance metric of one run

training set because we can think of using more advanced methods to select an effective subset of **irrelevant** documents to include in the training set.

Based on our experiments, the following conclusions can be drawn.

- Our findings suggest that in many cases much less training data (in some cases as little as 0.3-4% of the training set (for TD, NP and HP datasets)) can be used without significant degradation of performance. Thus our methods are more applicable for these kind of tasks where the data are highly imbalanced.
- Research on determining the most effective value of k for initial top-k retrieval for LtR algorithms is still preliminary [16]. If we can reduce the training set size *after* top k retrieval, the need to optimise this value may be reduced, and instead a "sufficiently large" value could be chosen, after which we can drop off many of the documents by using undersampling techniques, but still retaining the same level of test performance of the LtR algorithms. Put differently, we can fetch enough

documents in the top k retrieval stage with less concern about the training time of the LtR algorithms because later we shall cut down the size using undersampling technique.

- Applying sampling techniques take only linear time in terms of the size of the training set, while learning algorithms are often quadratic or worse in the number of training examples.
- We have shown that using simple methods for undersampling, we can achieve similar performance by using a small fraction of the original training set. Hence a new research question may be posed, as discussed earlier, from the findings of our work: how can we benefit from using advanced methods to select the most informative irrelevant documents so as to achieve better performance for a LtR algorithm with smaller training set? For the datasets which are not highly imbalanced, this question can also be extended to relevant documents as well.
- The improvement in terms of training time may not look very promising. But we have to keep in mind that the datasets we have used are not in the same scale of size of that used in commercial search engines. So the bigger the datasets, the more positive effect we hope to emerge from our work.
- Our approach is applicable *after* the relevance judgement of the documents are found. So one natural issue is that our approach does not minimize that large cost associated with human labelling. The answer is, our techniques are more useful for the case of click-through data where automatic labelling of documents can be found. Also, methods which mitigate labelling cost (such as active learning as discussed in Section 2) can be used before applying our techniques.

6   Conclusions and Future Work

In this work we have shown that the LtR algorithms can use a much smaller and more balanced training set than the existing practice – balanced in the sense that we can retain only a fraction of the available irrelevant documents (which comprise the vast majority) from the original training set produced by an initial retrieval approach. In doing so, we can reduce the training time for the LtR algorithms which is an important factor for large scale learning to rank task.

There is scope to work with advanced undersampling techniques so as to achieve better performance with smaller training set. Also, it may be worth to investigate why there is more fluctuation in the performances of some datasets than others. That is, to find out some *elite* group of irrelevant documents (if any) in reasonable computational time which, if included in the training set, causes the performance to be better.

References

1. Aslam, J.A., Kanoulas, E., Pavlu, V., Savev, S., Yilmaz, E.: Document selection methodologies for efficient and effective learning-to-rank. In: Proc. of the 32nd International ACM SIGIR Conf. on Research and Development in Information Retrieval, pp. 468–475. ACM (2009)

2. Bendersky, M., Metzler, D., Croft, W.B.: Learning concept importance using a weighted dependence model. In: Proc. of 3rd ACM Intl. Conf. on Web Search and Data Mining, pp. 31–40. ACM (2010)
3. Chapelle, O., Chang, Y.: Yahoo! learning to rank challenge overview. Journal of Machine Learning Research-Proceedings Track 14, 1–24 (2011)
4. Chapelle, O., Chang, Y., Liu, T.Y.: Future directions in learning to rank. In: JMLR Workshop and Conference Proceedings, vol. 14, pp. 91–100 (2011)
5. Dang, V., Bendersky, M., Croft, W.B.: Two-stage learning to rank for information retrieval. In: Serdyukov, P., Braslavski, P., Kuznetsov, S.O., Kamps, J., Rüger, S., Agichtein, E., Segalovich, I., Yilmaz, E. (eds.) ECIR 2013. LNCS, vol. 7814, pp. 423–434. Springer, Heidelberg (2013)
6. Donmez, P., Carbonell, J.G.: Optimizing estimated loss reduction for active sampling in rank learning. In: Proc. of 25th International Conf. on Machine Learning, pp. 248–255 (2008)
7. Friedman, J.H.: Greedy function approximation: a gradient boosting machine. Ann. Statist 29(5), 1189–1232 (2001) (english summary)
8. Ganjisaffar, Y., Caruana, R., Lopes, C.V.: Bagging gradient-boosted trees for high precision, low variance ranking models. In: Proceedings of the 34th international ACM SIGIR Conference on Research and development in Information Retrieval, pp. 85–94. ACM (2011)
9. Han, H., Wang, W.-Y., Mao, B.-H.: Borderline-SMOTE: A new over-sampling method in imbalanced data sets learning. In: Huang, D.-S., Zhang, X.-P., Huang, G.-B. (eds.) ICIC 2005. LNCS, vol. 3644, pp. 878–887. Springer, Heidelberg (2005)
10. He, H., Garcia, E.A.: Learning from imbalanced data. IEEE Transactions on Knowledge and Data Engineering 21(9), 1263–1284 (2009)
11. Järvelin, K., Kekäläinen, J.: Ir evaluation methods for retrieving highly relevant documents. In: Proceedings of the 23rd Annual International ACM SIGIR Conference on Research and Development in Information Retrieval, pp. 41–48. ACM (2000)
12. Joachims, T.: Optimizing search engines using clickthrough data. In: Proc. of 8th ACM SIGKDD Intl. Conf. on Knowledge Discovery and Data Mining, pp. 133–142. ACM (2002)
13. Li, H.: Learning to rank for information retrieval and natural language processing. Synthesis Lectures on Human Language Technologies 4(1), 1–113 (2011)
14. Liu, T.Y.: Learning to rank for information retrieval. Springer, Heidelberg (2011)
15. Long, B., Chapelle, O., Zhang, Y., Chang, Y., Zheng, Z., Tseng, B.: Active learning for ranking through expected loss optimization. In: Proceedings of the 33rd International ACM SIGIR Conf. on Research and Development in Information Retrieval, pp. 267–274. ACM (2010)
16. Macdonald, C., Santos, R.L., Ounis, I.: The whens and hows of learning to rank for web search. Information Retrieval, 1–45 (2012)
17. Pan, F., Converse, T., Ahn, D., Salvetti, F., Donato, G.: Feature selection for ranking using boosted trees. In: Proceedings of the 18th ACM Conference on Information and Knowledge Management, pp. 2025–2028. ACM (2009)
18. Pavlu, V.: Large scale ir evaluation. ProQuest LLC (2008)
19. Qin, T., Liu, T.-Y., Xu, J., Li, H.: Letor: A benchmark collection for research on learning to rank for information retrieval. information Retrieval 13(4), 346–374 (2010)
20. Wu, Q., Burges, C.J., Svore, K.M., Gao, J.: Adapting boosting for information retrieval measures. Information Retrieval 13(3), 254–270 (2010)
21. Yu, H.: Svm selective sampling for ranking with application to data retrieval. In: Proceedings of the Eleventh ACM SIGKDD International Conference on Knowledge Discovery in Data Mining, pp. 354–363. ACM (2005)

Nurturing Filled Pause Detection for Spontaneous Speech Retrieval

Raseeda Hamzah[1], Nursuriati Jamil[1,2], and Noraini Seman[1,2]

[1] Computer Science Department, Faculty of Computer & Mathematical Sciences
[2] Digital Image, Audio and Speech Technology (DIAST) Research Group,
Advanced Computing and Communication Communities of Research,
Universiti Teknologi MARA (UiTM), 40450 Shah Alam,
Selangor Darul Ehsan, Malaysia
{aini,liza}@tmsk.uitm.edu.my

Abstract. In this paper we investigate methods to adapt a system for filled pause (FP) disfluency removal to different data properties. A gradient descent algorithm for parameter optimization is presented which achieves 80.6% recall and 87.7% precision on the FP dataset and 46.5% recall and 79.6% precision on the FPElo dataset. This compares to the results produced with hand-optimization on the test set. Furthermore we investigated the impact of cross-validation and training set selection on recognizer output in order to improve the speech retrieval system.

Keywords: Speech Retrieval, Disfluency, Cross-validation, Gradient Descent, Multi-layer Perceptron.

1 Introduction

Efficient organization, retrieval and convenient browsing of multimedia content are an attractive application today. A large proportion of multimedia documents involve speech such as news broadcasts, meetings, interviews, technical presentations, movies and lectures. With the increasing importance of human-machine interaction, speech, as the most natural way of human communication, has become the core of many Natural Language Processing (NLP) applications. The retrieval of multimedia documents using the spoken audio parts is commonly referred to as *spoken document retrieval* (SDR) or alternatively, *speech retrieval*. Research in SDR is concerned with the re-presentation of spoken audio in video and/or audio documents using speech recognition techniques, for application in information retrieval (IR). The goal in SDR is to gain access to the information that is "encoded" in the speech by "decoding" the speech signal to a suitable format typically words, that can be used as a searchable representation of such documents. Nowadays, finding for such spoken documents will be an integral part of the browsing interface, facilitating search, indexing and retrieval. Without doubt, speech retrieval has generated a lot of interest lately. Strictly speaking, in this area, the focus of SDR is not on spoken documents but on the spoken audio contained in multimedia documents. A lot of useful information can be found in

A. Jaafar et al. (Eds.): AIRS 2014, LNCS 8870, pp. 458–469, 2014.

the spoken audio contained in a multimedia document and by deploying the state-of-the-art in current speech recognition technology, a considerable part of information can successfully be recovered.

Within the context of international benchmarks and collection specific projects, much work on SDR has been done in recent years. In 2000 the issue of automatic speech recognition (ASR) for spoken document retrieval was declared *solved* for the broadcast news domain. Many collections however, are not in this domain and ASR for these collections may contain spontaneous speech yielded specific new challenges to SDR. Transcripts of speech obtained through ASR contain recognition errors, which can be as high as 40% for spontaneous speech [1]. Unlike written languages, spoken documents are less well formed linguistically, e.g., they contain a variety of speech disfluencies such as lexicalized or non-lexicalized pauses, repetitions, and false starts. This has impact in several natural language processing tasks such as part-of-speech tagging, audio segmentation, capitalization, punctuation, summarization, speech translation, etc. Thus, disfluencies which can be removed in order to retrieve the originally intended fluent utterance. Disfluency removal makes sentences shorter, less ill-formed and thus facilitates the downstream processing by natural language understanding components such as machine translation or summarization. Initial results on disfluency remover into a speech-to-speech translation system show very promising results. Although the ASR system has to account for all the disfluent categories (filled pauses, prolongations, repetitions, deletions, substitutions, fragments, editing expressions, insertions, and complex sequences), the focus of the present study is on the detection of filled pauses. Filled pauses (FP) are amongst the most frequent disfluent types produced, where it is a vocalized pause that is usually used by speakers to prevent interruption from others while planning their utterances [1]. In many cases of ASR, filled pause is commonly grouped with word elongations as they have similar acoustical features [2,3,4].

However, word elongation has semantic content in a speech sentence and grouping it with FPs may affect meaning of a sentence. Previous researches of detecting and managing filled pauses in spontaneous speech were done by using two approaches. The first approach is by using a FP corpus to give prior knowledge to the speech recognizer [5]. On the other hand, the second approach detects and deletes FPs prior to recognition [6]. In the first approach, both elongation and FP are classified in the same class, therefore FP detection is less a problem. The second approach detects and removes FP using acoustical features before speech recognition is done. This approach poses a problem as both elongation and FP have stable formant frequencies, flat pitch, constant energy and longer duration [7,8]. Therefore, elongation is confused as FP and consequently removed.

In order to improve FP and elongation classification rate, modelling technique such as Hidden Markov Model has been used and has shown promising results [7]. Garg and Ward attempted FP and elongation classification for Mandarin language and achieved 80.6% precision and 92.59 recall rates. In ASR, well-known classifiers such as Hidden Markov Model (HMM), Gaussian Mixture Model (GMM), Support Vector Machine (SVM) and Artificial Neural Network (ANN) have been utilized. Among these classifiers, ANN is proven to be the most efficient in speech recognition [9]. The generalization ability of ANN allows the hidden part of the population to be understood even if the sample data contains noisy information [10]. ANN has also been used for disfluency detection [5]. However, FP and elongation are grouped as disfluency and no distinct classification is made. In this research, we present and compared two training algorithms of ANN to classify elongation and FP in spontaneous speech.

The direction of this work is composed into several sections. Section 2 provides an overview of the data collection. The details of the methods and implementation are described in Section 3. Section 4 describes the experimental and performance evaluation of the speech recognizer and retrieval. In Section 5, the experimental results are reported and discussed. Finally, the conclusion is drawn in Section 6.

2   Speech Data Collection

The speech data used in this research is gathered from *hansard* documents of Malaysian Parliament's debate sessions of 2008. It comprises Malay language spontaneous speeches spoken by male and female speakers of Malay, Chinese and Indian ethnics. Since the speech data was recorded live, it is surrounded with background noise, interruptions, and various speaking style (low, medium and high intonation). A total of 1348 sentences are selected from the speech data for our experiment. There are 148 sentences contained FPs alone which is defined as *FP dataset* and the remaining sentences (1200) contained both FPs and elongated words and defined as *FPElo dataset*, when all 1328 sentences were annotated manually. Further analysis shows that 440 FPs and 1,241 normal words of different duration and multi-speakers are then gathered from these sentences. We subsequently extracted 129 elongated words from FPElo dataset and define it as ELO_dataset for testing purposes. In English language, ELO is described as the extension at the end of the utterances as a replacement of FP [11]. Malay words are agglutinative alphabetic-syllabic that are based on four distinct syllable structures, i.e. V, VC, CV and CVC [12]. Based on our data analysis, we described our ELO as the last syllable of an utterance. The selection of the elongated data is based on the most common uttered words in ELO_dataset. The example of words is tabulated in Table 1.

Table 1. List of words

Word	Structure	Word	Structure
Ada	V+CV	*Maka*	CV+ CV
Bahawa	CV+CV+CV	*Mereka*	CV+CV+CV
Berapa	CV+CV+CV	*Negara*	CV+CV+CV
Bila	CV+CV	*Nya*	CCV
Cuma	C+VC	*Pada*	CV+CV
Tua	C+VV	*Paksa*	CVC+CV
Dua	C+VV	*Pertama*	CVC+CV+CV
Harga	CVC+CV	*Peserta*	CV+CVC+CV
Juga	CV+CV	*Saya*	CV+CV
Kata	CV+CV	*Secara*	CV+CV+CV
Kerana	CV+CV+CV	*Tanya*	CV+CCV
Kira	CV+CV	*Warna*	CVC+CV

3   Methods and Implementation

The general idea towards this work is to classified two spontaneous speech disfluencies that are FP and ELO. For this purpose, FP and FPElo datasets are used in the experiments. Both datasets are divided in a training set, a testing set and a development test set for cross-validation.   Since only little data is available, the entire test set and ELO dataset were used for testing and tuning the system and facilitate the removal of FPs automatically. Pre-processing operations such as framing, windowing and filtering are subsequently applied to the datasets.

As mentioned earlier elongation word is normally confused as FP and consequently removed, thus affect the semantic contents and meaning of the sentences. Having generated the transcripts for the speech corpus, an information retrieval engine indexes the transcripts for retrieval. In order to improve speech retrieval process of spoken documents transcriptions, the first stage is to automatically segment the boundary of filled pause and the elongation words into syllables by using Voice Activity Detection (VAD) method. The aim is to determine exact representation of both data before acoustical features are extracted. Boundary detection of FP and elongated words, classification, recognition and indexing are all conducted offline as illustrated in Fig. 1 below.

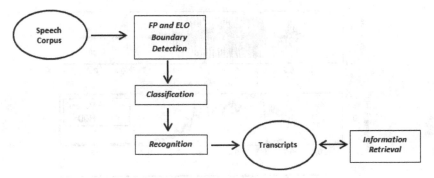

Fig. 1. The speech retrieval process diagram

3.1   FP and ELO Boundary Detection

In ASR, there is a need to process the utterance consisting of speech, silence and other background noise. The detection of the presence of speech embedded in the various types of non-speech events and background noise is called end point detection, speech detection or voice activity detection (VAD). In our research, we integrate Volume and First Order Differences (VFOD) for voice activity detection. The key parameter in volume-based VAD is a volume threshold, Vol_{Thr} computed as follows:

$$Vol_{Thr} = \frac{Vol_{max} - Vol_{min}}{V_c} \tag{1}$$

where, Vol_{max} and Vol_{min} is the maximum and minimum volume vector of the speech and V_c is the coefficient that is set to 10^{19}. Volume vector is further calculated by using the following formula.

$$V_i = \sum_{n=Ki_L}^{Ki_F} |x(n)| \tag{2}$$

where Ki_F and Ki_L is the first and the last sample of the speech utterances and i is the number of frames. FOD is based on first-order differences of a given signal as characteristics in time domain and is defined as:

$$H_i = \sum_{Ki_L}^{Ki_F} \left| \frac{\Delta^j x(n)}{\Delta n^j} \right| \tag{3}$$

where i represents number of time frames used to compute H_i and j is the order of the differences. Fig. 2 illustrates an example of VFOD's result for the word /ADA/. From this result, it can be seen that the duration of the last syllable /DA/ is 500ms. Thus, it can be confirmed that the segmented of last syllable of normal words can be confused as FP if it reached more than 200ms duration [2].

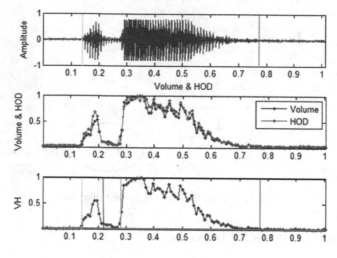

Fig. 2. VFOD syllable detection for word /ADA/

3.2   Classifier

For classification, we use the noisy-channel approach, a concept which is borrowed from statistical machine translation [13]. The basic idea is that a fluent string C is passed through a channel that adds noise (in form of disfluencies) to this string. We can only observe the noisy, i.e. the FP disfluent string N which is above than 200ms can be considered as FP [2]. The goal of FP removal is to recover the string $\hat{C}$ that is most likely to be the fluent input string given the noisy output string. In statistical machine translation the fluent string is associated with the target language, the disfluent string with the source language. Thus, this problem can be reformulated as the translation of the disfluent string into a fluent one as adopted from [14]. In Equation (4), the problem is expressed in mathematical terms and reformulated using Bayes rule. C denotes the fluent string, N the disfluent string.

$$C = \arg \max_{C} P(C \mid N) = \arg \max_{C} \{P(N \mid C).P(C)\} \qquad (4)$$

The probability $P(C)$ with an n-gram language model trained on fluent speech is modeled. The probability $P(N \mid C)$ can be decomposed as in Equation (5), which is simplified from translation model [4].

$$P(N \mid C) = P_{I,J}(m) \cdot \prod_{j=1}^{J} P_w(n_j) \qquad (5)$$

The probability $P_{I,J}(m)$ models the number m of contiguous word sequences which can be deleted in N to obtain C. $P_w(n_j)$ is the probability that word n_j of the string N is FP disfluent. I denotes the length of the fluent sentence C and J length of the disfluent sentence N. Each of the probabilities $P_w(n_j)$ is finally composed of weighted sum over two models, where (M1) models the position of FP and (M2) models the position of ELO as shown in Equation (6).

$$P_w(n_j) = \frac{\sum_{k=1}^{2} \lambda_k P_{Mk}(n_j)}{\sum_{k=1}^{2} \lambda_k} \qquad (6)$$

where $P_{Mk}(n_j)$ is the contribution of model Mk and λ_k is the weighting factor for model Mk. Using Equation (4) until Equation (6) will transform the result into negative log space, the search criterion becomes:

$$\hat{C} = \arg \min_{C} S(C \mid N) = \arg \min_{C} \gamma S(C) + (1 - \gamma) S(N \mid C) \qquad (7)$$

with

$$S(N \mid C) = S_{J,I}(m) - \sum_{j=1}^{J} \log \left(\sum_{k=1}^{2} \frac{\lambda_k P_{Mk}(n_j)}{\sum_{k=1}^{2} \lambda_k} \right) \qquad (8)$$

The factor γ represents a weighting factor that controls the influence of the language model over the translation model. While all probabilities can be learned from the training data, the weighting factors γ and λ_k have to be determined separately. Iterative gradient descent procedure which maximizes the average probability

$P(C \mid N)$ for given pairs (C, N) of the training data.

Starting with a set of initial parameters ($\lambda^{(0)}$, $\lambda_k^{(0)}$, for each pair (C, N) new parameters values are calculated using the following updates rules:

$$\gamma^{(1+1)} = \gamma^l + \Delta\gamma^{(l)} \qquad\qquad \lambda_k^{(l+1)} = \lambda_k^{(1)} + \Delta\lambda_k^{(l)} \qquad\qquad (9)$$

The update quantities $\Delta\gamma^{(l)}$ and $\Delta\lambda_k^{(l)}$ are calculated as follows:

$$\Delta\gamma^{(l)} = -\eta \frac{\partial S^{(l)}(C \mid N)}{\partial \gamma} + \alpha\Delta\gamma^{(l-1)} \qquad\qquad (10)$$

$$\Delta\lambda_k^{(l)} = -\eta \frac{\partial S^{(l)}(C \mid N)}{\partial \lambda_k} + \alpha\Delta\lambda_k^{(l-1)} \qquad\qquad (11)$$

The factor η is the learning rate, α is a momentum term, which includes previous update directions to the current update direction and thus influences the effective learning rate. This procedure is continued until the difference between the average value of $S(C \mid N)$ of previous and the current epoch (one epoch is one complete iteration through the training set) falls below a given threshold. The final parameter set is taken from the epoch, in which the average value of $S(C \mid N)$ over the pairs $(N_{\chi v}, C_{\chi v})$ of development test set is minimal.

4   Evaluation Measures

For the known-item speech retrieval evaluation, a set of 1348 sentences from *hansard documents* were collected and manually transcribed on the word level. Manually segmented hand annotated temporal FPs boundaries were given three types of FPs (uhm, eer and aaa) and were further interpreted as query aiming at the retrieval of the respective sentences. The retrieval task was to find for every query, the target sentences which include FPs and elogated words. For evaluating speech recognition performance we used the standard word error rate (WER) as our metric over manual hand annotated transcription.

We define, N_r as the total words in the reference transcription, $N\alpha$ as the total words in the automatic transcription, S as the number of substituted words in the automatic transcription, D as the number of words from the reference deleted in the automatic transcription, I as the number of words inserted in the automatic transcription not appearing in the reference, and H as the number of correctly recognized words. The word error rate is defined as:

$$WER = \frac{S + D + I}{N_r} \qquad (12)$$

While this measure is most commonly used as an error rate, it is also often quoted as the *word recognition rate*,

$$WRR = 1 - WER = \frac{H - I}{N_r} \qquad (13)$$

On the other hand, we used precision and recall evaluation measures with respect to manual transcription to evaluate the retrieval performance. Precision and recall can be calculated for each word v_i of the given sentences. To calculate the measures instead over the entire vocabulary, we may take either the *micro-average* or the *macro-average* [11]. The micro-average (denoted by subscript μ) weighs each individual information unit (word occurrence) equally, as:

$$\rho_\mu = \frac{\sum_i^l R_i \cap A_i|}{\sum_i^l R_i |} \text{, and} \qquad (14)$$

$$\pi_\mu = \frac{\sum_i^l R_i \cap A_i|}{\sum_i^l A_i |} \qquad (15)$$

while the macro-average (denoted by subscript M) instead weights each query (vocabulary word) equally:

$$\rho_M = \frac{1}{|V_r|} \sum_i \rho_i \text{, and} \qquad (16)$$

$$\pi_M = \frac{1}{|V\alpha|} \sum_i \pi_i \qquad (17)$$

where V_r is the subset of words in V that are present in the reference transcription, $V\alpha$ is the subset of word in V occurring in the automatic transcription and where in all cases the summation is only over terms i where the corresponding word-based measures are defined.

A major difference between the information retrieval framework and the string edit framework of the WER is the way in which word substitution errors are handled. In our proposed framework there are fundamentally only two types of errors, insertions (false alarms) and deletions (false rejections). We view a substitution error as a construct describing the case when these co-occur. In terms of information content, a substitution error represents both a loss of relevant information as well the retrieval of erroneous information, and thus is considered as both a deletion and an insertion error. While the "common sense" view in ASR considers that counting substitutions twice is unfair, it is evident that this should be the case if we consider properly the information content of the words in the context of an end application. Of course, it is feasible that the substitution of one particular word by another may be allowable for a given application as it incurs no cost in terms of system usability. Such cases can be catered for in the information retrieval framework by applying a text normalization process (e.g. stemming, synonym-matching, homophone-matching) prior to calculating evaluation measures, with this in mind, relating the information retrieval framework to standard error types encountered in speech recognition, the word recognition rate is given by (from Equation 12):

$$WRR = \frac{\sum_i (|\ R_i \cap A_i\ |) - I}{\sum_i |\ R_i\ |} = \rho_\mu - \frac{I}{N_r} \qquad (18)$$

which is a difficult quantity to interpret. This equation highlights the fact that the word recognition rate can be negative and that interpreting values depends on the relative sizes of the relevant sets and the total number of insertions. In this study, it can be considered that WRR as the micro-averaged recall penalized by including insertion errors in the numerator. In the information retrieval perspective presented here, there is no basis or clear interpretation for such a measure. The micro-averaged recall can be written as,

$$\rho_\mu = \frac{\sum_i (|\ R_i \cap A_i\ |)}{\sum_i |\ R_i\ |} = \frac{H}{N_r} \qquad (19)$$

which is equivalent to the word correct rate (WCR), and the micro-averaged precision can be expressed as,

$$\pi_\mu = \frac{H}{N_\alpha} \qquad (20)$$

From this we see that the WRR is essentially equivalent to the WCR (recall) penalized to also include insertion errors. A more consistent way of evaluating the rate of insertion errors is to instead define the corresponding precision measure, and use principled combinations, such as the F-measure [15], whenever a single measure is required.

5   Results and Discussion

This section compares the results obtained from using the gradient descent procedure to results from hand-optimizing the parameters on the test data as given in Table 2 below.

Table 2. Results for gradient descent compared to hand tuning on FP and FPElo datasets

Setup	Dataset	WER	Recall	Precision
Hand optimized	FP	10.02%	76.56%	86.60%
	FPElo	18.02%	48.06%	78.54%
Gradient descent	FP	12.44%	80.60%	87.05%
	FPElo	20.80%	46.50%	79.06%

As can be seen, the parameter set resulting from the gradient descent procedure achieves the same as the hand tuned parameter set. These results are very encouraging since the hand optimization was performed on the test data and therefore defines a kind of golden standard. These results hold for both datasets, and indicate that the gradient descent procedure generalizes well. We conclude that the gradient descent procedure is an appropriate method for rapid system development that makes hand tuning obsolete. According to several experiments, hand tuning requires tremendous manual and computational effort and expertise, since the whole system has to be run for several parameter combinations and the results have to be evaluated carefully, in order to find a good parameter set.

The above result was performed on manual transcriptions. Table 3 represents the experiments on applying FPElo dataset to FPs removal system of recognized speech. We investigated the following training and cross-validation setups: (S1) Training on manual transcriptions, cross-validation on recognizer output, (S2) training and cross-validation on recognizer output, (S3) training and cross-validation on manual transcriptions, and (S4) training and cross-validation on a combination of manual transcriptions and recognizer output. Parameters for each setup were optimized using the gradient descent procedure. The FP and ELO in recognized speech were annotated by aligning the recognizer output with the annotated manual transcriptions using the minimal editing distance. Results of the experiments for the different setups are given in below.

Table 3. Results on recognizer output for different setups

Setup	WER	Recall	Precision
S1	18.02%	69.60%	80.02%
S2	26.02%	58.86%	78.04%
S3	12.44%	70.08%	80.05%
S4	20.80%	66.50%	80.06%

As expected, the removal system suffers a significant degradation when tested on recognition output rather than manual transcriptions. The lower recall may result from the fact that words tagged as disfluent are not deleted by the system, since they are falsely recognized and thus perceived as fluent by the system in the given context. Furthermore, due to recognition errors, sequences which are tagged as repetitions no longer exist as sequences of repeated words. The lower precision can be explained by the fact that wrongly recognized words appear to be FPs in their context although the original word is fluent.

The setup (S1) achieves the best results with respect to the F1 score. This indicates that introducing noise in form of recognition errors during training does not help to improve performance on noisy test data. The decrease of recall in the other setups is mostly due to the performance in deletions of short words (such as *"Tua"*, *"Nya"*). Using (S2) for training, due to recognition errors these words occur less frequently in contexts in which they are deleted. Precision increases for experiments with setup (S2) because a system trained on recognized speech can cope better with the problem of ill-formed and ungrammatical sentences in a test set that is based on recognized speech as well. Therefore, a smaller number of false positives are produced, since some ill-formed constructions are tolerated. The results produced with setup (S3) are almost as good as the results produced with setup (S1). This indicates that training on manually transcribed speech produces better results overall, however for tuning the model weights a cross-validation set based on recognized speech seems more appropriate. The combination of manually transcribed and recognized speech in (S4) does not improve the results. This means that a simple combination does not profit from the gains seen in (S2) and (S3).

6   Conclusions

In this paper we presented two approaches to automatically detected and removed FPs in transcription of spoken documents retrieval system. We implemented a gradient descent method to automatically optimizing the parameter weights. The resulting system is as good as the golden standard which was set by hand optimizing the parameters on the test data. These results are very encouraging since they allow for a rapid deployment of the disfluency removal system in new domains or languages. Second, we extended our experiments to recognizer output. We achieved best results when we trained the models on manually transcribed data and optimized the model weights on recognizer output data.

Acknowledgements. Due acknowledgement is accorded to the the Research Management Institute (RMI), Universiti Teknologi MARA for the funding received through the Cluster Grant, 600-RMI/DANA 5/3/CG (5/2012).

References

1. Goto, M., Itou, K., Hayamizu, S.: A Real-Time Filled Pause Detection System. In: ESCApp., pp. 227–230 (1999)
2. Audhkhasi, K.: Formant-Based Technique for Automatic Filled-Pause Detection in Spontaneous Spoken English. In: IEEE Trans, Acoustics, Speech and Signal Processing Proc. (2009)
3. Kaushik, M.: Automatic Detection and Removal of Disfluencies from Spontaneous Speech. In: 13th Australasian Int. Conf. on Speech Science and Technology Melbourne, pp. 98–101 (2010)
4. Veiga, A., Candeias, S.: Carla, L., Fernando, P.: Characterization of Hesitations Using Acoustic Models. In: ICPhS XVII (2011)
5. Stouten, F., Martens, J.P.: A Feature-Based Filled Pause Detection System for Dutch. In: IEEE, pp. 2–7. ASRU (2003)
6. Ogata, J., Goto, M., Itou, K.: The Use of Acoustically Detected Filled and Silent Pauses in Spontaneous Speech Recognition National Institute of Advanced Industrial Science and Technology (AIST) (2), 4305–4308 (2009)
7. Garg, G., Ward, N.: Detecting Filled Pauses in Tutorial Dialogs 0415150, 1–9 (2006)
8. Xiong, L.Y.: A Novel Detection Method of Filled Pause in Mandarin Spontaneous Speech. In: IEEE Trans, Computer and Information Science Proc. (2008)

9. Majeed, S.A., Husain, H., Samad, S.A., Hussain, A.: Hierarchical K-Means Algorithm Applied on Isolated Malay Digit Speech Recognition. In: ICSEM 2012, vol. 34, pp. 33–37 (2012)
10. Zhang, G.P.: Neural networks for classification: a survey. IEEE 30(4), 451–462 (2000)
11. Kitayama, K., Goto, M., Itou, K., Kobayashi, T.: Speech Starter: Noise-Robust Endpoint Detection by Using Filled Pauses, pp. 1237–1240 (2003)
12. Lee, L.W., Low, H.M., Mohamed, A.R.: A Comparative Analysis of Word Structures in Malay and English Children's Stories. Social Sciences & Humanities 21(1), 67–84 (2013)
13. Wang, Y., Waibel, A.: Decoding Algorithm in Statistical Machine Translation. In: Proceedings of the 35th Annual Meeting of the ACL (1997)
14. Honal, M., Schultz, T.: Automatic Disfluency Removal on Recognized Spontaneous Speech - Rapid Adaptation to Speaker-Dependent Disfluencies. In: Proceedings of the International Conference on Acoustics, Speech, and Signal Processing (ICASSP), pp. 969–972 (2005)
15. Baeza-Yates, R., Ribeiro-Neto, B.: Modern Information Retrieval. Addison Wesley (2012)

Analysis of Japanese Wikipedia Category
for Constructing Wikipedia Ontology
and Semantic Similarity Measure

Masaharu Yoshioka

Graduate School of Information Science and Technology, Hokkaido University
N-14 W-9, Kita-ku, Sapporo 060-0814, Japan
yoshioka@ist.hokudai.ac.jp

Abstract. Wikipedia is a free encyclopedia on the Internet that contains millions of articles. Wikipedia ontologies (e.g., YAGO2 and the Japanese Wikipedia ontology) have been constructed to utilize the semantic information in this encyclopedia; in these ontologies, the category information from each article is used to construct concept hierarchies. However, Wikipedia categories were originally designed for navigation, to help users find appropriate articles, and they are not equivalent to concept hierarchies in Wikipedia ontologies. In this study, we briefly review the definition of a category in Wikipedia and exhaustively investigate the category structure in the Japanese Wikipedia. We also discuss how category structure information can be utilized to construct an ontology and to calculate a semantic similarity measure.

1 Introduction

Wikipedia[1] is a free, Wiki-based encyclopedia that anyone can edit, and it contains a huge number of articles (4,465,757 articles in the English version and 898,433 articles in the Japanese version; 2014/3/6). Wikipedia ontologies (e.g., YAGO2 [2] and the Japanese Wikipedia ontology [5]) have been constructed to utilize the semantic information in Wikipedia. In each of these ontologies, a concept hierarchy has been constructed based on information from the Wikipedia category structure. In addition, several approaches have been used to calculate the semantic similarity based on the category structure [3,4], [6].

However, the Wikipedia category structure was originally designed for navigation, to help users find appropriate articles, and it is not equivalent to the concept hierarchy in Wikipedia ontologies. In this study, we briefly review the definition of a Wikipedia category and its structure based on the information provided in Wikipedia. Using this definition, we exhaustively investigate the category structure of the Japanese Wikipedia (not by random sampling) and discuss the types of parent–child category pairs in this category structure based on syntactic patterns. We also discuss how category structure information can be utilized to construct an ontology and to calculate a semantic similarity measure.

---

[1] http://www.wikipedia.org/

A. Jaafar et al. (Eds.): AIRS 2014, LNCS 8870, pp. 470–481, 2014.

2   Information in Wikipedia for Ontology Construction

Each Wikipedia article (or "page") is about some named entity or concept. These articles are organized into categories that aim to group together pages on similar subjects [2]. The categories are in turn organized as overlapping "trees" using parent–child category pairs.

In this section, we briefly review the definition of a Wikipedia article and category, and discuss how Wikipedia ontologies can be constructed based on the information provided in Wikipedia. We use boxes to reference sentences found in Wikipedia.

2.1   Articles

The definition of a Wikipedia article is as follows.

> "A Wikipedia article, or entry, is a page that has encyclopedic information on it" [a].
>
> ---
> [a] http://en.wikipedia.org/wiki/Help:Article

Most articles contain information about a particular named entity or concept and they include the following types of information.

- Title: a string that represents the particular named entity or concept (target) described in the article.
- Description: a summary that represents the target.
- Infobox: structured information about the target in a tabular format.
- Text: a detailed description of the target, which is organized into sections.
- Category: an index used to characterize the target.

Fig. 1 shows an example of an article.

DBpedia [1] extracts structured information, mainly from infoboxes, and organizes this information into a database. A DBpedia ontology has also been constructed manually, and it contains 590 concepts for classes (DBpedia Ontology 3.9) that maintain the class–instance relationships between concepts and articles. YAGO2 [2] is a huge semantic knowledge base derived from Wikipedia, WordNet, and GeoNames. In addition to the structural information extracted from DBpedia, an information concept hierarchy has also been constructed, containing more than 350,000 classes from WordNet and the category structure of Wikipedia. In these classes, most of the Wikipedia category names are used as class labels, and the class–instance relationships are maintained using category and article relationships.

The Japanese Wikipedia ontology [5] also uses infoboxes to extract structural information, in which the category names are used as class labels, and the relationships between articles and categories are employed as class–instance relationships. However, Wikipedia categories were originally designed to facilitate navigation by Wikipedia users, and several categories are not appropriate for representation using a concept hierarchy in a Wikipedia ontology.

---
[2] http://en.wikipedia.org/wiki/Help:Category

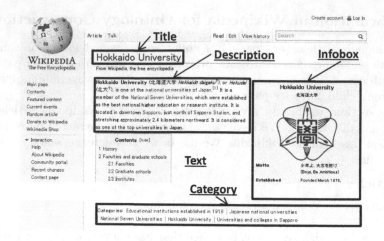

Fig. 1. Example of a Wikipedia article

2.2 Wikipedia Categories

In Wikipedia, a category and a category tree structure are defined as follows.

> "Categories are used in Wikipedia to link articles under a common topic" [a]. "Categories are organized as overlapping "trees", formed by creating links between inter-related categories (in mathematics or computer science this structure is called a lattice or a partially ordered set). Any category may contain (or "branch into") subcategories, and it is possible for a category to be a child category of more than one "parent" category. (A is said to be a parent category of B when B is a child category of A). There are following two main kinds of category.
>
> – Topic categories: are named after a topic (usually sharing a name with the Wikipedia article on that topic). For example, Category:France contains articles relating to the topic France.
> – Set categories: are named after a class (usually in the plural). For example, Category: Cities in France contains articles whose subjects are cities in France.
>
> Sometimes, for convenience the two types can be combined, to create a set-and-topic category (such as Category:Voivodeships of Poland, which contains articles about particular Voivodeships as well as articles relating to Voivodeships in general)" [b].

---

[a] http://en.wikipedia.org/wiki/Help:Categories
[b] http://en.wikipedia.org/wiki/Wikipedia:Categorization#Category_tree_organization

Based on this definition, it is appropriate to use set categories as class definitions in the concept structure. However, it is necessary to consider the appropriateness of using topic categories and set-and-topic categories as class definitions.

3 Analysis of Japanese Wikipedia Categories

3.1 Syntactic Patterns for Category Analysis

The discussion in the previous section shows that it is essential to clarify the types of categories used to construct the concept structure based on the Wikipedia category tree structure.

In order to understand the types of categories employed in Wikipedia, we analyzed the categories and category tree structures in the Japanese Wikipedia.

We obtained all the Japanese Wikipedia category information from a data dump on 2013/8/18, which comprised 121,346 categories. From these categories, we excluded the categories related to Wikipedia maintenance (e.g., H elp, stub, and template) and those with year information (e.g., "1975(movies from 1975)"), which yielded 99,902 categories for the analysis. These categories included 208,999 parent–child category pairs.

In the analysis, we classified the categories using syntactic patterns. Based on a preliminary analysis of the categories, we found that most of the categories could be represented by the following elements (Fig. 2).

- Noun: represents a topic term (e.g., "(Japan)", " (Company)").
- Verb phrase: represents a relationship between nouns (e.g., " (featured)", "(based on)").
- Japanese particles: represent a relationship between nouns and verb phrases (e.g., "(ga: a case marker that represents a subject)" and "(no: a case marker that represents possession)").
- Conjunction: represents a relationship between nouns and verb phrases (e.g., "(and)").
- Additional information: represents information that facilitates disambiguation (e.g., "() (novels)" and "() (by company)").
- Modifier: represents additional information about a term (e.g., "(defunct)").

defunct	Japanese		company	(by industry)
かつて存在した	日本	の	企業	(業種別)
Modifier	Noun	Particles	Noun	Additional information

Fig. 2. Syntactic elements of a category label

Additional information and modifiers were not important for the detailed analysis, so we excluded this information from the labels in the subsequent analysis.

Table 1 shows the numbers of syntactic expression patterns for different category labels. In this analysis, we used MeCab for morphological analysis, except for specific types of proper nouns. For example, the Japanese animation movie " (Castle in the Sky)" belongs to the pattern *Noun (" (sky)") + "(no)" + Noun ("(rapyuta: castle)")* according to the MeCab results. We checked the proper nouns manually and categorized them as *Noun only*.

Table 1. Classification of Wikipedia categories based on syntactic expression patterns

Expression pattern	Count
Noun only	39,584
"(Japan)" "(Utada Hikaru)"	(39.6%)
Noun + "(no)" + Noun	56,938
" (Japanese baseball player)"	(57.0%)
Noun + "(wo)" + Verb phrase + Noun	1,468
" (rail transport in fiction)"	(1.5%)
Noun + "(no)" + Noun+ "(no)" + Noun	1,122
"(images of shrines in Kyoto)	(1.1%)
Noun + "(ni)" + Verb phrase + Noun	584
"(department related to commerce)"	(0.58%)
Other	206

3.2   Analysis of Category Labels

The analysis in Section 3.1 showed that the *Noun only* and *Noun + "(no)" + Noun* patterns were the two most common patterns (96.6% in total), and thus we focused on a detailed analysis of these two patterns.

The *Noun only* patterns included proper nouns and common nouns. However, most of the *Noun + "(no)" + Noun* patterns constructed from nouns were *Noun only*.

It is not easy to discuss the characteristics of labels for *Noun only* patterns, so we used *Noun + "(no)" + Noun* patterns to analyze different types of nouns. In this analysis, the labels of the first and last nouns were N_a and N_b, respectively $(N_a + "(no)" + N_b)$.

For N_a, there were 18,449 unique nouns, and Table 2 shows the most frequent ones. For N_b, there were 5,525 unique nouns, and Table 3 shows the most frequent ones.

Table 2. Frequently used nouns for N_a

Nouns	Count
(Japan)	2,951
(USA)	1,003
(By nation)	690
(England)	642
(France)	600

Table 3. Frequently used nouns for N_b

Nouns	Count
(Person)	3,697
(Image)	2,460
(Player)	2,314
(Teacher)	1,939
(Music)	1,777

When we checked the frequently used nouns, we found many proper nouns for N_b, but few proper nouns for N_a. Therefore, in many cases, N_a + "(no)" + N_b patterns were constructed using topic terms for N_a and set terms for N_b. This information was useful for identifying the type of noun in *Noun only* patterns.

3.3   Analysis of Parent–Child Category Pairs

Among the 208,999 parent–child category pairs, we used 192,601 (92.2%) *Noun only* and *Noun + "(no)" + Noun* pairs in this analysis. These pairs were categorized into four types (Table 4).

Table 4. Parent–child category pairs

		Parent category	
		Noun only	*Noun + "(no)" + Noun*
Child category	*Noun only*	43,349	29,980
	Noun + "(no)" + Noun	29,528	89,744

First, we analyzed the *Noun + "(no)" + Noun* and *Noun + "(no)" + Noun* pairs. Most of these pairs shared common nouns in the parent and child categories. These relationships comprised four types. Table 5 shows examples of the category pairs and their frequencies.

Table 5. *Noun + "(no)" + Noun* and *Noun + "(no)" + Noun* pairs

Parent category	Child category	Count
N_a + "(no)" + N_b (Ex: (people by nationality))	N_a + "(no)" + N_b (Ex:() (people by occupation and nationality))	555 (0.62%)
N_a + "(no)" + N_b (Ex: (Japanese baseball))	N_a + "(no)" + N_b' (Ex: (Japanese baseball player))	34,617 (38.7%)
N_a + "(no)" + N_b (Ex: (geography by nation))	N_a' + "(no)" + N_b (Ex: (Japanese geography))	39,267 (43.8%)
N_a + "(no)" + N_b (Ex: (University of Hokkaido))	N_a' + "(no)" + N_b' (Ex: (professors at Sapporo City University))	15,305 (17.1%)

The first type shared both nouns (N_a + "(no)" + N_b → N_a + "(no)" + N_b), and these pairs included additional information used mostly for disambiguation.
The second type shared the first noun (N_a + "(no)" + N_b → N_a + "(no)" + N_b'). Table 6 shows common examples of these pairs, which included concept hierarchy pairs (e.g., "(sportsperson)") and related terms (e.g., " (geography)").
The third type shared the last noun (N_a + "(no)" + N_b → N_a' + "(no)" + N_b). Table 7 shows common examples of these pairs, which included class–instance

Table 6. Frequent pairs for N_a + "(no)" + N_b → N_a + "(no)" + N_b'

Pairs of N_b and N_b'	Count
(Sportsperson)→(Football player)	177
(Sportsperson)→(Olympic competitors)	165
(Sportsperson)→ (Athlete (track and field))	137
...	...
(Geography)→(Cities)	214
(Geography)→(Landforms)	189
...	...

Table 7. Frequent pairs for N_a + "(no)" + N_b → N_a' + "(no)" + N_b

Pairs of N_a and N_a'	Count
(by nation)→(Japan)	595
(by nation)→(USA)	505
(by nation)→(England)	406
...	...
(Japan)→(Hokkaido)	50
(Japan)→(Tokyo-to)	38
...	...

pairs (e.g., "(by nation)") and "geographically-part-of" relationship terms (e.g., "(Japan)").

Table 8 shows pairs for ("(by nation)"). It was easy to extract class–instance pairs by identifying common pairs, but the low-frequency terms contained several errors in some cases.

The last type did not share nouns (N_a + "(no)" + N_b → N_a' + "(no)" + N_b'). Typical pairs of this type related to universities and professors are shown in Table 5. In this case, it would be better to have an intermediate category " (Sapporo City University)" to maintain the consistency among parent–child category pairs. This is true for several universities with multiple categories (e.g., " (University of Tokyo)"), but Wikipedia guidelines may not allow the production of intermediate categories with only one child category.

Table 9 shows three *Noun* and *Noun* + " (no)" + *Noun* patterns. For the first two patterns, most of the set-and-topic categories had set and topic categories as parent categories. It is appropriate to use N_b → N_a + "(no)" + N_b patterns (set → set-and-topic) in the concept hierarchy, but N_a → N_a + "(no)" + N_b patterns (topic → set-and-topic) may not be suitable for concept hierarchy construction. Thus, related terms (e.g., "(age)" and "(long life)") could be extracted to analyze the latter patterns.

Table 10 shows the patterns for the *Noun* + "(no)" + *Noun* and *Noun* pairs. Sixteen exceptions shared nouns, but all of these cases were related to additional information provided for disambiguation. The remaining pairs had three types of relationships: class–instance relationships between N_b and N_c (examples are shown in Table 10); class–subclass relationships between N_b and N_c, such as

Table 8. Pairs for $N_a \rightarrow N_a'$ for "(by nation)"

(Japan)	595
(USA)	55
(UK)	406
(France)	401
(Germany)	379
...	...
(Ancient orient)	2
(Antarctic)	2
(Somaliland)	2
...	...
(North America)	1
(Japan Maritime self defense force)	1
Thailand)	1
...	...

Table 9. *Noun* and *Noun* + *"(no)"* + *Noun* pairs

Parent category	Child category	Count
N_a	N_a + "(no)" + N_b	16,582
(Ex:(Geography))	(Ex:(Japanese geography))	(18.9%)
N_b	N_a + "(no)" + N_b	5,563
(Ex:(Japanese temples))	(Temples by prefecture))	(0.04%)
N_c	N_a + "(no)" + N_b	7,383
(Ex:(History of Hokkaido))	(Hokkaido (Age of Ryou-sei)))	(0.02%)

Table 10. *Noun* and *Noun* + *"(no)"* + *Noun* patterns

Parent category	Child category	Count
N_a + "(no)" + N_b	N_b (Ex: ()	11
(Ex:(Japanese temples))	(Temples by prefecture))	(0.04%)
N_a + "(no)" + N_b	N_b (Ex: ()	6
(Ex:(History of Hokkaido))	(Hokkaido (Age of Ryou-sei)))	(0.02%)
N_a + "(no)" + N_b	N_c (Ex:	29,963
(Ex:(University in Osaka))	(Osaka University))	(99.9%)

"(Japanese) (no) (song)" → "(Enka: Japanese music genre)"; and geographically-part-of relationships between N_a and N_c, such as "(Hyogo) (no) (municipalities)" → " (Kobe City)."

To evaluate the distributions of the relationship types for the parent–child category pairs, we manually constructed a database to classify the parent–child category pairs using category information.

As shown in Tables 6–8, it was not difficult to classify the highly frequent pairs with *Noun* + " (no)" + *Noun* and *Noun* + "(no)" + *Noun* patterns. However, because the irregular pairs included some low-frequency pairs with different characteristics, we investigated these pairs and excluded irregular pairs from the final dataset.

We also used pairs with *Noun (N$_a$)* + " *(no)*" + *Noun (N$_b$)* and *Noun (N$_c$)* patterns to extract class–instance and geographically-part-of relationships. Table 11 shows the number of manually classified relationship pairs in the database for each relationship type. The manual construction process required approximately 30 hours using a single assessor.

Table 11. Construction of the database to classify parent–child category pairs

Relation type	count
Class-Instance (Ex:(Artist)→(Hikaru Utada)	17,348
Class-Subclass (Ex:(Sports)→(Baseball))	18,153
Geographically part of (Ex:(Hokkaido)→(Sapporo))	5,244

Table 12 shows the distribution of the relationship types for nouns among the *Noun (N$_a$)* + "*(no)*" + *Noun (N$_b$)* → *Noun (N$_a$)* + "*(no)*" + *Noun (N$_b$)* pairs in the database. The results show that many instances belonged to the type N_a, but very few instances belonged to N_b. In addition, many cases had "instance–instance" relationships linking $N_a \to N_a'$. "(Japanese) (no) (train)" → " (JR East) (no) (train)" is a typical example of this type of relationship, which shows that "(JR East)" is a company in "(Japan)." Most of these relationships represented attribute value relationships, which was also the case for "instance–other" relationships. However, "other–instance" relationships included various types of relationships, and it was necessary to investigate them in more detail.

The number of nouns categorized as "other" for $N_b \to N_b'$ was higher than that for $N_a \to N_a'$ because many cases used abstract keywords that represented specific domains (e.g., "(culture)," "(history)," and "(geography)") for N_b. For example, "(Asian) (no) (culture)" → "(Asian) (no) (language)" might not be class–subclass or class–instance relationships.

Table 12. Relationship types of parent–child category pairs with *Noun (N$_a$)* + "*(no)*" + *Noun (N$_b$)* → *Noun (N$_a$)* + "*(no)*" + *Noun (N$_b$)* patterns

Relationship type	$N_a \to N_a'$ (share of N_b: 39,267)	$N_b \to N_b'$ (share of N_a: 34,617)
Class–subclass	430 (1.1%)	20,669 (59.8%)
Class–instance	20,163 (51.3%)	51 (0.15%)
Geographically-part-of	9,884 (25.2%)	0 (0%)
Instance–instance	3,907 (12.5%)	0 (0%)
Instance–other	1,646 (4.2%)	76 (0.22%)
Other–instance	1,615 (4.1%)	46 (0.13%)
Other	1,622 (4.1%)	13,775 (39.8%)

Table 13 shows the distribution of the relationship types for nouns in *Noun (N$_a$)* + "*(no)*" + *Noun (N$_b$)* → *Noun (N$_c$)* pairs in the database. These results show that the relationships $N_a \to N_c$ and $N_b \to N_c$ had similar characteristics to $N_a \to N_a'$ and $N_b \to N_b'$ in Table 12, respectively. Table 14 shows the distribution of the relationship types for nouns in *Noun* $(N_a) \to$ *Noun* (N_b) pairs in the database. These results show that the more than half of relationship are categorized by the manually constructed data 12, respectively.

Table 13. Relationship types for parent–child category pairs with *Noun* (N_a) + *"(no)"* + *Noun* $(N_b) \to$ *Noun* (N_c) patterns

Relationship type	$N_a \to N_c$ (29,964)	$N_b \to N_c$ (29,964)
Class–subclass	541 (1.8%)	4,654 (15.5%)
Class–instance	246 (0.82%)	10,137 (33.8%)
Geographically-part-of	4,249 (14.2%)	0 (0%)
Instance–instance	12,021 (40.1%)	89 (0.30%)
Instance–other	5,901 (19.7%)	35 (0.12%)
Other–instance	3,096 (10.3%)	9,118 (30.4%)
Other	3,968 (13.2%)	5,989 (20.0%)

Table 14. Relationship types for parent–child category pairs with *Noun* $(N_a) \to$ *Noun* (N_b) patterns

Relationship type	$N_a \to N_b$ (43,349)
Class–subclass	9,455 (21.8%)
Class–instance	1,801 (4.2%)
Geographically-part-of	308 (0.71%)
Instance–instance	5,147 (11.9%)
Instance–other	3,573 (8.2%)
Other–instance	4,936 (11.4%)
Other	18,129 (41.8%)

3.4   Discussion

In this study, we conducted an exhaustive analysis of parent–child category pairs in the Japanese Wikipedia. Using a manually constructed dataset, we characterized parent–child category pairs with specific syntactic patterns. The results of this analysis are summarized as follows.

- Most Japanese Wikipedia categories use *Noun only* (39.6%) or *Noun* + *"(no)"* + *Noun* (57.0%) patterns.
- The pattern *Noun* (N_a) + *"(no)"* + *Noun* (N_b) is used to represent set-and-topic categories. It is rare for instance keywords to use the pattern N_b, and thus it is better to treat N_b as keywords for sets and N_a as keywords for topics. However, it is not always the case that *Noun* (N_a) + *" (no)"* + *Noun* (N_b) has a parent category of *Noun* (N_a) or *Noun* (N_b).

- It is useful to employ syntactic patterns to extract "class–subclass" relationships (the number of "class–subclass" relationships extracted for "*Noun only* → *Noun only*" (9,455) was smaller than that in the manually constructed dataset (18,153)).
- It is difficult to generate rules to extract class–subclass relationships using syntactic patterns alone. However, the simple aggregation of data can support the manual construction of a dataset. However, further analysis is required to increase the coverage of this type of extraction support.
- Parent–child category pairs include various relationships (e.g., class–subclass, class–instance, geographically-part-of, and attribute), and thus it is better to select the relationship types to calculate the similarity between categories.

Based on this analysis, we propose the following guidelines for utilizing Wikipedia category structures in ontology construction and for calculating semantic similarity measures.

Ontology Construction. It is necessary to exclude information related to instances to utilize a general concept hierarchy based on Wikipedia category information. In order to identify the names of instances, we can use highly frequent nouns and their child category names to support a manual instance name-construction process. This operation facilitates the more precise utilization of the concept hierarchy.

Semantic Similarity Measure Calculation. It is preferable to use a general concept hierarchy to perform semantic similarity measure calculations. Attribute information may also be helpful for this purpose. For example, two songs that belong to "(Japanese) (no) (composition and recording)" may be more similar than one from "(Japanese) (no) (composition and recording)" and one from "(French) (no) (composition and recording)." However, the depth of this type of attribute-based category depends on the number of articles in Wikipedia, and there is a lack of consistency among similar categories. The following are examples of the shortest paths for parent–child category pairs.

- "(Tokyo) (no) (university)" → " (University of Tokyo)" → "(University of Tokyo) (no) (people)" → "(University of Tokyo) (no) (professors)"
  No direct link from " (University of Tokyo)" → " (University of Tokyo) (no) (professors)"
- " (Hokkaido) (no) (university)" → " (Hokkaido University)" → "(Hokkaido University) (no) (professors)"
- " (Hokkaido) (no) (university)" → " (Sapporo City University) (no) (professors)"
  No category for "(Sapporo City University)"

Two methods can be used to normalize these differences: normalizing categories by extracting set categories only from set-and-topic categories, or generating similar category structures for the same set category. For example, all set-and-topic categories should have set and topic categories for their parent categories, and all university categories should have "(people)" and "(professors)" hierarchical categories. The use of the latter approach can also support the construction of set-and-topic categories with SPARQL queries based on the infobox information extracted by DBpedia.

4 Summary

In this study, we performed an exhaustive analysis of the category structure in the Japanese Wikipedia to facilitate the use of this structure as a concept hierarchy in Wikipedia ontologies. We confirmed that various types of parent–child category relationships were present in the structure. We also found that it was not easy to construct syntactic patterns to allow the automatic classification of parent–child category relationships. However, frequency-based analysis may be helpful for constructing a noun-to-noun relationships database, including class–instance, class–subclass, and geographically-part-of patterns. Finally, we suggested guidelines about how to use the category structure for ontology construction and for calculating semantic similarity measures.

In future research, we plan to construct a large noun-to-noun relationships database based on the category structure, and we will also consider the irregular types of parent–child category pairs. This database may provide a basis for constructing a Japanese Wikipedia ontology.

References

1. Bizer, C., Lehmann, J., Kobilarov, G., Auer, S., Becker, C., Cyganiak, R., Hellmann, S.: Dbpedia a crystallization point for the web of data. Web Semantics: Science, Services and Agents on the World Wide Web 7(3), 154–165 (2009)
2. Hoffart, J., Suchanek, F.M., Berberich, K., Weikum, G.: A spatially and temporally enhanced knowledge base from wikipedia. Artificial Intelligence 194(0), 28–61 (2013)
3. Ponzetto, S.P., Strube, M.: Knowledge derived from wikipedia for computing semantic relatedness. J. Artif. Int. Res. 30(1), 181–212 (2007)
4. Taieb, M.A.H., Aouicha, M.B., Hamadou, A.B.: Computing semantic relatedness using wikipedia features. Knowledge Based Systems 50(0), 260–278 (2013)
5. Tamagawa, S., Sakurai, S., Tejima, T., Morita, T., Izumi, N., Yamaguchi, T.: Learning a large scale of ontology from japanese wikipedia. Journal of Japanese Society of Artificial Intelligence 25(5), 623–636 (2010) (in Japanese)
6. Yan, P., Jin, W.: Mining semantic relationships between concepts across documents incorporating wikipedia knowledge. In: Perner, P. (ed.) ICDM 2013. LNCS, vol. 7987, pp. 70–84. Springer, Heidelberg (2013)

Correlation-Based Feature Selection for Association Rule Mining in Semantic Annotation of Mammographic Medical Images

Nirase Fathima Abubacker[1], Azreen Azman[1], Shyamala Doraisamy[1],
Masrah Azrifah Azmi Murad[1], Mohamed Eltahir Makki Elmanna[2],
and Rekha Saravanan[3]

[1] Faculty of Computer Science & Information Technology, University Putra Malaysia,
Serdang, Malaysia
[2] Biomedical Engineering Department, Cairo University, Giza, Egypt
[3] Department of Computer Science, R. D. Govt Arts College, India
gs32867@mutiara.upm.edu.my

Abstract. Mining of high dimension data for mammogram image classification is highly challenging. Feature reduction using subset selection plays enormous significance in the field of image mining to reduce the complexity of image mining process. This paper aims at investigating an improved image mining technique to enhance the automatic and semi-automatic semantic image annotation of mammography images using multivariate filters, which is the Correlation-based Feature Selection (CFS). This feature selection method is then applied onto two association rules mining methods, the Apriori and a modified genetic association rule mining technique, the GARM, to classify mammography images into their pathological labels. The findings show that the classification accuracy is improved with the use of CFS in both Apriori and GARM mining techniques.

Keywords: Correlation-based feature selection, multivariate filters, association rule mining, mammographic image classification, and semantic annotation.

1 Introduction

The advancement in medical imaging has resulted in many breakthroughs in the medical field. The use of digital images is essential in the diagnosis and also research, especially by the radiographers. As huge number of digital images is being created, it becomes problematic for storage and retrieval. In addition, the semantic gap problem, which is the difference in the representation of digital images and the actual keyword query from the user, increases the difficulty for effective retrieval of those medical images. Furthermore, the use of image as a query such as in the case of query by example (QBE) to overcome the semantic gap problem may not be practical in this context.

A. Jaafar et al. (Eds.): AIRS 2014, LNCS 8870, pp. 482–493, 2014.

Fortunately, recent technology in medical imaging allows for metadata being associated with the images. Those metadata can facilitate for text-based retrieval, in which those images are indexed based on their metadata or annotations and the keyword-based query submitted by the user will be matched to the indexed metadata for retrieval. Due to limited information stored as metadata for each image, such a system will not be effective for robust retrieval of medical images. Therefore, the performance of such a retrieval system can be significantly improved by adding semantic annotation onto the images for indexing.

Automatic and semi-automatic image annotation can be accomplished through classification of images according to label of concepts. Such labels will be considered as potential query terms, and are used to annotate those images for indexing. Fortunately, the set of label of concepts has been established in the medical field for manual indexing of resources, such as ICD10 [1] etc. The labels usually represent the pathological description of certain diseases. As such, this paper investigates the problem of annotating mammography images into *normal*, *benign* or *malignant* classes that represent the stages of breast cancer.

Association rules (AR) mining gain popularity as the classification technique for semantic annotation. Generally, this approach will generate many rules based on the frequent itemset generated for all features. Instead, a condition is set such that the consequence of the rules must be the class categories, *normal*, *benign* or *malignant*. As such, there will be many rules generated for each of the classes. Similar to other data mining approaches, the performance of AR depends largely of the features used for the mining task. A huge number of features used may enhance the classification accuracy, but will affect the efficiency of AR through the generation of too many itemset as well as rules. The number of features can be reduced through the process of feature selection to improve the efficiency and to maintain or improve the accuracy of the classification. As such, this paper investigates the effect of using Correlation-based Feature Selection (CFS) for association rules mining in the context of mammography image classification.

The remaining of this paper is ordered as follows. Related work is presented in Section 2. In Section 3, a detailed discussion on Correlation-based Feature Selection approach is presented. The experimental setup and analysis is given in Section 4. Section 5 describes the conclusion and future work.

2   Related Work

The quality of decision for automatic diagnosis in the medical field depends on the quality data. The elimination of redundant features reduces the data size. Integrating feature selection reduces number of features, removes noisy or irrelevant data, thus speeding up the mining process. Hence, mining on a reduced set of data helps to make the association rule pattern to be discovered easily and to improve its predictive accuracy. There are two types of data reduction methods, which are wrapper and filter methods. Even though wrapper methods can produce better result, they are expensive for the large dimensional database. On the other hand filter method is computationally simple and fast and precedes the actual association rule generation process. Filter methods use some properties of the data to select the feature. An intrinsic property such as entropy has been used as a filter method for feature selection. In [2], Lei Yu *et al.* proposed a selection method using a correlation measure that identifies redundant features. Many popular search procedures like particle swarm optimization, sequential forward selection, sequential backward selection, genetic search, etc. have been proposed in many researches. Genetic Algorithms are effectively applied to a variety of problems like feature selection problems [3], data mining problems [4], scheduling problems [5], machine learning problems [6,7], multiple objective problems [8,9], and traveling salesman problems [10]. Since the univariate filters does not justify for interactions between features multivariate filter correlation based feature selection (CFS) can be used to overcome the drawback of the univariate filter for determining the best feature subset.

Numerous authors have proposed many algorithms in recent years for mining association rules such as Genetic Algorithm (GA). Manish Saggar *et al.* [11] have used the GA to optimize the rules generated by the Apriori algorithm. The rule based classification systems can even predict negative rules with the improvements applied to GAs. Ashish Ghosh et al. [12] solved the multi-objective rule mining problems by representing the rules as chromosomes using Michigan approach. Virendra Kumar et.al [13] extracted interesting association rules using an optimized GA using the measures like interestingness, completeness, support and confidence. Nikhil Jain et.al [14] used a genetic algorithm for the whole process of optimization of the rule set to find a reduction of Negative and Positive Association Rule Mining. Amy et.al [15] proposed Hybrid genetic algorithm for mining workflow best practices, using correlation measures instead of traditional support and confidence. Peter et.al [16] used a genetic algorithm for a structured method to find the unknown facts in large data sets. Jesmin Nahar et al. [17] proposed Association rule mining for the detection of sick and healthy heart disease factors, using the UCI Cleveland dataset, a biological database. Sufal et.al [18] proposed a method of utilizing linkage among feature selections using Multi-objective Genetic Algorithm for data quality mining. Dong Gyu Lee et al [19] used Genetic algorithm for generating association rules related to hypertension and diabetes in discovering medical knowledge for young adults with acute myocardial infarction. Ramesh Kumar et.al [20] proposed a novel genetic algorithm for the prioritization of association rules produced by the Apriori algorithm and tested for the four different data sets. Basheer et.al [21] proposed a multi-objective genetic algorithm for generating association rules in discovering interesting association rules. J. Malar Vizhi et al. [22] proposed a genetic algorithm using multi-objective evolutionary framework for the Primary - tumor dataset to generate high quality association rules. Tournament selection and multipoint crossover methods were used for a large number of attributes in the database for flexibility. The approach has been tested for only numerical and categorical valued attributes. Bettahally et.al [23] compared conventional mining algorithm, i.e. Apriori algorithm with the proposed genetic algorithm in local search for privacy preserving over distributed databases. In the Apriori algorithm population is formed in only single recursion, but in genetic algorithm population is formed in every new production. To overcome the disadvantages of Apriori algorithm, Genetic algorithm can be used for association rule mining. Above research gap helps to improve the Apriori algorithm as well as an existing Genetic algorithm, which can further be improved.

3   Correlation-Based Feature Selection (CFS)

In general, several features are usually used to describe the character of an object. The characteristic features that are used to classify the normal and abnormal lesions can be represented as mathematical descriptions. Feature extraction methodology analyses mammogram images to extract the most prominent features that represent various classes of the images. Unlike the complicated process of a human observer to identify a mass, the machine makes decisions with only limited features. In this paper, the statistical texture features such as contrast, coefficient, entropy, energy, homogeneity and a few other Haralick [24] and Soh [25] features that efficiently classify the benign and malignant mammograms are extracted with the distance between the pixel of interest and its neighbor equal to 1 and the angle of 0 .Let p(i,j) be the (i,j)th entry in a normalized Gray Level Co-occurrence Matrix (GLCM).μ and are the mean and standard deviation for the rows and columns of the matrix.

   The representation and quality of data may have an effect on a given task in machine learning. Theoretically, the more discriminating power can be achieved by having more features, but current machine learning toolkits are not sufficient to deal with up to date datasets [26]. Many of the features extracted during the training phase are either partially or completely irrelevant to an object that has no effect on the target concept. The feature selection process helps to remove redundant and irrelevant features, thus reducing the feature space. This minimizes the computation time and helps in improving the prediction accuracy [27]. Data reduction methods are of two types, wrapper and filter methods. On the other hand filter approach measures the feature subset relevance and is independent of learning algorithm. Since the univariate filters does not justify for interactions between features we use multivariate filter correlation based feature selection (CFS) to determine the best feature subset. Correlation based Feature Selection involves heuristic search to evaluate the subset of features. This is a simple filter algorithm based on correlation heuristic function. This function evaluates the subsets that are highly correlated and uncorrelated with each other and class. The features are accepted depending on its level of extent in predicting its class. The features that did not influence the class will be ignored as irrelevant features. The stages of CFS are shown in combination with data discretization in Fig. 1.

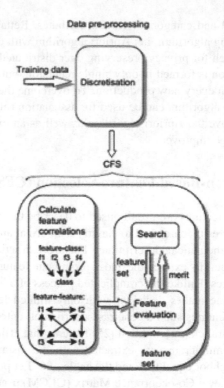

Fig. 1. The components of CFS

The mammogram training data are discretized first and then passed to CFS. For the prediction of class labels, this CFS considers the efficacy of individual features and its inter-correlation. If given the inter-correlation between each pair of features and the correlation between each of the features and its class, then the correlation between a subset of features selected for evaluation can be predicted from the formula

$$cr_{zc} = \frac{f\,\overline{cr_{zi}}}{\sqrt{f + f(f-1)\overline{cr_{ii}}}}$$

where cr_{zc} = heuristic merit of a feature subset for f number of features, $c\,\overline{r_{zi}}$ the = average of the correlations between the class and the features, $c\,\overline{r_{ii}}$ = average inter-correlation between feature pairs [28]. The subset with the highest cr_{zc} value is used to reduce the data dimensionality.

The feature selection process together with CFS undergoes some search procedure. This paper uses Weka GA as a search method with CFS as a subset evaluating mechanism. Genetic algorithm (GAs) is modeled based on the process of natural selection. At every iteration new populations are generated from old ones in each iteration. They are actually binary encoded strings. Every string is evaluated to measure its fitness value for the problem. Likewise the entire generation of new strings can be computed using the genetic operators, on an initially random population. This operative way of discovering large search space is essential for feature selection. The individual fitness can be decided by the correlation between the features. Based on the correlation coefficient the individuals will be assigned a rank by the fitness function. The features that have the lower correlation coefficients and with higher fitness value will be appropriate for crossover operations.

3.1 Dataset and Selection of ROI

The data set used in this experiment is taken from the digital database for mammography from the University of South Florida [29], which is DDSM. All images are digitized using LUMISYS Scanner at a resolution of 50 microns, and at 12 bit grayscale levels. The dataset consists of 240 images that include three categories of which 80 are normal, 80 are benign and 80 are malignant. Then, the region of interest (ROI) is isolated within those images as the preprocessing step. We use the contour supplied together with the images in the DDSM dataset to extract ROIs of size 256 x 256 pixels.

A total of 242 ROIs are extracted with the mass centered in a window of size 256×256 pixels, where 162 are abnormal ROIs (circumscribed masses, speculated masses, ill-defined masses and architectural distortion) and 80 are normal ROIs.

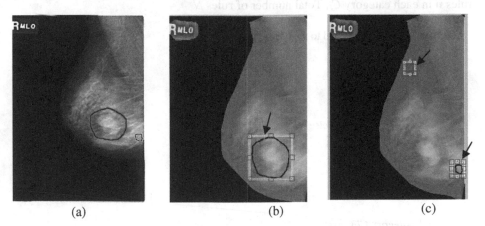

(a)   (b)   (c)

Fig. 2. Example of ROI for (a) original image, abnormal (b) and normal cases (c)

3.2 Association Rules Mining

For each image, the selected discretized features are stored in such a way that n columns represent n features while the last column represent a class (eg. *normal, benign* and *malignant*). Two association rules mining techniques are used to discover the frequent itemset and eventually to generate the rules, which are the classical Apriori algorithm and also a modified genetic algorithm based association rule mining, GARM. The Apriori algorithm tends to produce a huge number of rules, that is redundant and may not be efficient. On the other hand, genetic algorithm (GA), such as

GARM can generate good rules by performing a global search with better attribute interactions thus can improve the effectiveness of association rule mining. For each category in the database, the GA is applied separately to construct sets of rules. For each rule the fitness value is calculated and the rule that has the highest fitness value in each population will be stored as the global best rule. Then, the best rules from each category are pooled to form rule set. New population can be computed using the genetic operators like reproduction, crossover, and mutation to extract the best local rules.

3.3   Classification

The extracted set of rules represents the actual classifier. It classifies a new image to its category. When a new image is provided, a feature vector is extracted and it searches in the rules for matching classes. Then, the number of matched rules for each class is calculated. Based on the matched rules in each class, the average *confidence* score is calculated. The class for the new image is identified based on the highest average *confidence* score in the class and the number of rules matched. The algorithm describes the classification of a new image.

Input: Number of category C, list of training rules for each category C_i, Number of rules **n** in each category C_j, Total number of rules N

Output: Category attached to the new image

for each category Ci
   for each rule R do
    If R matches I then
          MC++
              else
        NMC++

      end if
   end for
end for

for each category Ci subset
   find P= $\dfrac{MC}{n}$ the percentage of set of rules that match I
   find average confidence Q of rules
end   for

Put the new image in the category Ci that has the highest average confidence and higher percentage of matching

3.4   Experimental Results

In order to evaluate the performance of the CFS feature selection method, the 10-fold cross validation is used. Ten equal groups with an equal number of images from each class is formed. One group is selected as the test images and the remaining nine groups are used to generate the rules. In the classification stage, the class for each image in the test group is identified and average accuracy measure (AC) of the classification is measured as follows:

$$AC= [(nc_1+ nc_2 +nc_3)/N_T] * 100 \tag{1}$$

where nc_1, nc_2 and nc_3 are the number of correctly classified images in class C_1, C_2 and C_3, respectively, while N_T is the total number of images in the test group.

Table 1. The average accuracy measures (AC) for CFS with different AR algorithms

Group	Apriori		GARM	
	w/o CFS	with CFS	w/o CFS	with CFS
1	79.9	82.6	81.7	87.9
2	83.4	85.7	84.4	89.4
3	78.6	81.8	80.9	88.6
4	85.2	85.6	86.8	92.6
5	82.8	83.6	82.1	85.4
6	83.9	86.9	84.9	87.2
7	79.6	83.2	79.7	87.9
8	80.4	82.8	83.5	86.3
9	82.5	84.7	82.3	85.7
10	84.3	87.4	85.1	90.2
Average AC	**82.06**	**84.43 (+2.9%)**	**83.13**	**88.12 (+6%)**

The average accuracy measure (AC) for CFS with Apriori and GARM algorithms is a depicted in Table 1. The result shows that a marginal performance improvement can be achieved when CFS is used before the application of both AR algorithms, with an improvement of 2.9% and 6% for the average AC on Apriori and GARM algorithm, respectively. This finding indicates that the feature selection process can potentially improve the effectiveness of AR based classification on mammography images. It is also learnt that CFS can have a bigger impact on the performance of genetic algorithm based association rules mining as compared to the classical Apriori algorithm.

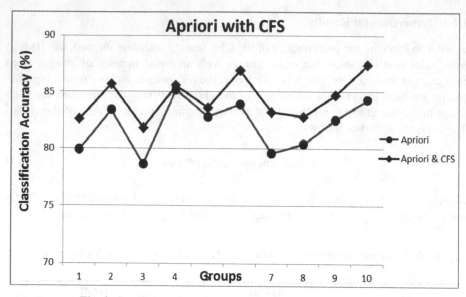

Fig. 3. Comparison of AC for Apriori algorithm based on group

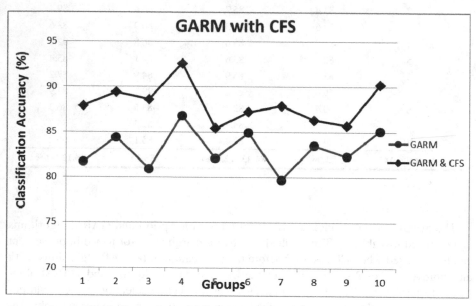

Fig. 4. Comparison of AC for GARM algorithm based on group

Fig. 3 & Fig. 4 show the comparison of AC for different algorithms in each group. Based on the figure, it clearly shows that the classification has more effective as the CFS consistently shown better performance in all groups as compared to not using CFS for both AR algorithms. An interesting findings show that genetic algorithm based association rules without CFS does not have a significant impact on the classification performance as compared to the classical Apriori algorithm without CFS which is only 1.7% difference, despite being more efficient. It also learnt that the difference in performance for both classical Apriori algorithm and genetic algorithm can be enlarged with the use of CFS with 4.4% difference.

4   Conclusion

This paper investigates the effect of using feature selection process, CFS, on two AR algorithms, the classical Apriori algorithm and a genetic algorithm based AR algorithm, GARM, for the mammography image classification problem. The result is promising, where the algorithms are able to achieve 88% correct classification using GARM with CFS compared to [30] without any feature selection. In addition, the use of feature selection, CFS, can improve the classification performance of both AR algorithms. However, the benefit of using an efficient GARM algorithm does not necessarily improve the classification accuracy. Our further work will be on GA for optimization of Association Rule Mining to improve the classification accuracy for an automatic diagnosis and suggestions of possible pathological terms.

Acknowledgements. This work is supported in part by the Universiti Putra Malaysia under the GP-IPS Grant (GP-IPS/2014/9431600).

References

1. http://www.icd10data.com/ICD10CM/Codes/Z00-Z99/Z00-Z13/Z12-/Z12
2. Yu, L., Liu, H.: Feature Selection for High Dimensional Data: A Fast Correlation-based Filter Solution. In: Proceedings of the twentieth International Conference on Machine Learning, pp. 856–863 (2003)
3. Holland, J.: Adaptation in Nature and Artificial Systems. MIT Press Cambridge (1992)
4. Goldberg, D.E.: Genetic Algorithms in Search, Optimization, and Machine Learning. Addison-Wesley Professional, Reading (1989)
5. Hou, E.S.H., Ansari, N., Ren, H.: A Genetic Algorithm for Multiprocessor Schedul-ing. IEEE Trans. Parallel Distrib. Syst. 5, 113–120 (1994)
6. Davis, L.: Hybrid Genetic Algorithms for Machine Learning. Mach. Learn. 117, 9/1-9/3 (1990)
7. Vafaie, H., De Jong, K.: Genetic Algorithms as a Tool for Feature Selection in Ma-chine Learning. In: Proc. 4th Int. Conf. on Tools with Artificial Intelligence, pp. 200–203 (1992)
8. Deb, K., Pratap, A., Agrawal, S., Meyarivan, T.: A Fast Elitist Non-dominated Sorting Genetic Algorithm for Multi-objective Optimization: NSGA-II. IEEE Trans. Evol. Comput. 6, 182–197 (2002)
9. Dias, H.F., de Vasconcelos, J.A.: Multiobjective Genetic Algorithms Applied to Solve Optimization Problems. IEEE Trans. Magn. 38, 1133–1136 (2002)
10. Tsai, F., Tsai, C.W., Chen, C.P., Lin, F.C.: A Multiple-searching Approach to Genetic Algorithms for Solving Traveling Salesman Problem. Proc. of Joint Conf. on Information Sciences 3, 362–366 (2002)

11. Saggar, M., Agrawal, A.K., Lad, A.: Optimization of Association Rule Mining using Improved Genetic Algorithms. In: IEEE International Conference on Systems, Man and Cybernatics, pp. 3725–3729 (2004)

12. Ghosh, A., Nath, B.: Multi-objective Rule Mining Using Genetic Algorithms. Information Sciences 163, 123–133 (2004)

13. Shrivastava, V.K., Kumar, P., Pardasani, K.R.: Extraction of Interesting Association Rules using GA Optimization. Global Journal of Computer Science and Technology 10(5), 81–84 (2010)

14. Jain, N., Sharma, V., Malviya, M.: Reduction of Negative and Positive Association Rule Mining and Maintain Superiority of Rule Using Modified Genetic Algorithm. International Journal of Advanced Computer Research 4(6), 2277–7970 (2012), ISSN (print): 2249-7277

15. Lim, A.H.L., Lee, C.-S., Raman, M.: Hybrid Genetic Algorithm and Association Rules for Mining Workflow Best Practices. Expert Systems with Applications 39, 10544–10551 (2012)

16. Wakabi–Waiswa, P.P.: Venansius Baryamureeba and Karunakaran Sarukesi.: Optimized Association Rule Mining with Genetic Algorithms. In: 7th International Conference on Natural Computation (2011)

17. Nahar, J., Imam, T., Tickle, K.S., Chen, Y.-P.P.: Association Rule Mining to Detect Factors which Contribute to Heart Disease in Males and Females. Expert Systems with Applications 40, 1086–1093 (2013)

18. Das, S., Saha, B.: Data Quality Mining using Genetic Algorithm. In: International Journal of Computer Science and Security (IJCSS), vol. 3

19. Lee, D.G., Ryu, K.S., Bashir, M., Bae, J.-W., Ryu, K.H.: Discovering Medical Knowledge using Association Rule Mining in Young Adults with Acute Myocardial Infarction. Journal of Medical Systems 37(2) (2013)

20. Ramesh Kumar, M., Iyakutti, K.: Genetic Algorithms for the Prioritization of Association Rules. IJCA Special Issue on "Artificial Intelligence Techniques - Novel Approaches & Practical Applications" AIT, 35–38 (2011)

21. Al-Maqaleh, B.M.: Discovering Interesting Association Rules: A Multi-objective Genetic Algorithm Approach. International Journal of Applied Information Systems 5(3), 47–52 (2013)

22. Malar Vizhi, J., Bhuvaneswari, T.: Data Quality Measurement with Threshold Using Genetic Algorithm. International Journal of Engineering Research and Applications 2(4), 1197–1203 (2012)

23. Keshavamurthy, B.N., Khan, A.M., Toshniwal, D.: Privacy Preserving Association Rule Mining over Distributed Databases using Genetic Algorithm. Neural Computing and Applications (2013)

24. Haralick, R.M., Shanmugam, K., Dinstein, I.: Texture Features for Image Classification. IEEE Trans. Syst. Man. Cybern. 8(6), 610–621 (1973)

25. Soh, L., Tsatsoulis, C.: Texture Analysis of Sar Sea Ice Imagery using Gray Level Co-occurrence Matrices. IEEE Transactions on Geoscience and Remote Sensing 37(2), 780–795 (1999)

26. Liu, H., Motoda, H.: Feature Selection for Knowledge Discovery and Data Mining. The Springer International Series in Engineering and Computer Science, vol. 454

27. Liu, H., Motoda, H.: Computational Methods of Feature Selection Chapman & Hall/CRC Data Mining and Knowledge Discovery Series (2007) ISBN-10:1584888784, ISBN-13:978-1584888789

28. Hall, M.A.: Correlation-based Feature Selection for Machine Learning, Dept of Computer Science, University of Waikato

29. Heath, M., Bowyer, K., Kopans, D., Moore, R., Kegelmeyer, W.P.: The Digital Database for Screening Mammography. In: Yaffe, M.J. (ed.) Proceedings of the 5th International Workshop on Digital Mammography, pp. 212–218. Medical Physics Publishing (2001) ISBN 1-930524-00-5
30. Thangavel, K., Kaja Mohideen, A.: Classification of Microcalcifications Using Multi-Dimensional Genetic Association Rule Miner. International Journal of Recent Trends in Engineering 2(2), 233–235 (2009)

Content Quality of Clustered Latent Dirichlet Allocation Short Summaries

Muthukkaruppan Annamalai[1,2] and Siti Farah Nasehah Mukhlis[1]

[1] Faculty of Computer and Mathematical Sciences
[2] Applied Ontologies Research Group (AORG),
Advanced Computing and Communication Communities of Research,
Universiti Teknologi MARA (UiTM), 40450 Shah Alam,
Selangor, Malaysia
mk@tmsk.uitm.edu.my, seha.aries@yahoo.com

Abstract. Latent Dirichlet Allocation (LDA) is a commonly used topic model based summarisation method. However, the generated summaries contain words that are somewhat general and unrelated to the topic. Since the summary depends on word distribution in the input documents and, because the topic signature feature values are averaged across all documents, we think clustering can help to overcome this problem. Therefore, this work sets out to investigate whether clustering the input documents beforehand *(clusLDA)* can help to improve the content quality of the generated summaries. The words in a LDA summary are weighted and a short summary of 0.67% of the input text size is constituted using significant words proportionally drawn from the clustered summaries. The divergence probabilities of the resulting summaries are compared against the summary produced by LDA without clustering *(UnclusLDA)*. The results are validated using input of various text sizes and different clustering techniques. And, our findings indicate that clustering does not necessarily help to improve the content quality of short summaries.

Keywords: Latent Dirichlet Allocation, Clustering, Summarisation, Keyword Extraction, Content Quality.

1   Introduction

Latent Dirichlet Allocation (LDA) is a popular model used to summarise textual documents. In LDA, the documents being processed are viewed as a mixture of various topics. Consequently, LDA summarises the documents into sets of words that can serve as the constituent topics covered by these documents [1]. However, one weakness of LDA is that the summary generated from the input documents contains general and what appears to be unrelated to the topic [2]. The gravity of this matter is more apparent in short summaries constituted from weighty words in LDA summaries. For example, Table 1 shows the first four topics and their corresponding sets of words for a collection of documents on *Durian*. Each topic is assigned a topic weight by LDA (shown in the brackets beneath the topic labels). The set of words that constitute a

A. Jaafar et al. (Eds.): AIRS 2014, LNCS 8870, pp. 494–504, 2014.
© Springer International Publishing Switzerland 2014

topic is shown on the right hand side column. Each word of a topic is assigned a word weight by LDA (shown in the brackets next to the words). The words are sorted based on their LDA word weights. It can be seen that weighty topical words like *page*, *edit* and *www* are not quite related to the subject are present. There are also redundant words such as *fruit* and *tree* in the summary.

First, LDA extracts co-occurring words in documents to form topics. As such, the summary depends much on the word distribution in the documents [3]. A topic is drawn from the topic-specific words as well as their background words in the input documents. Second, even though, the topics in LDA are not equi-probable (i.e., some topics are assumed to have higher absolute probability value than others) [4], the topic signature feature values are averaged across all input documents. Third, while the weighty LDA words distinguish the high-content words in the documents, there is still the need to restrict the number of words in order to filter out the less important words in order to form a 'good' short summary.

Table 1. The first four topics in a LDA summary about *Durian* fruit

Topic	Weighted Words
0 (0.15765)	fruits(51.167) fruit(49.167) durian(20.167) maturity(17.167) storage(15.167) page(15.167) mature(15.167) harvested(14.167) cultivars(13.167) harvesting(11.167) anthesis(9.167) life(9.167) abscission(8.167) market(7.167) ripe(7.167) stage(7.167) good(7.167) time(7.167) dehiscence(6.167) ...
1 (0.13409)	durian(167.167) fruit(55.167) tree(47.167) durians(34.167) fruits(31.167) trees(31.167) season(26.167) years(15.167) back(15.167) good(12.167) smell(12.167) news(11.167) strong(10.167) part(10.167) edit(10.167) consumers(10.167) production(10.167) ripen(9.167) photo(9.167) ...
2 (0.10159)	durian(28.167) mg(27.167) fruit(27.167) vitamin(15.167) flesh(15.167) nutrition(13.167) seeds(13.167) malaysia(10.167) fruits(9.167) cm(8.167) body(6.167) popular(6.167) durio(6.167) cooked(5.167) source(5.167) back(5.167) health(5.167) species(5.167) hotels(5.167) ...
3 (0.08468)	chang(15.167) durians(13.167) history(11.167) penang(10.167) varieties(9.167) taste(9.167) red(7.167) bak(7.167) ang(7.167) pulau(7.167) rm(7.167) found(7.167) sheng(6.167) bao(6.167) experience(6.167) portal(6.167) creamy(6.167) wet(5.167) www(5.167) ...

Clustering is a collection of data that is grouped together because of their similarities. In a sense, it is a type of classification [5]. Since documents about similar topics tend to contain similar words, they can be grouped using clustering. For instance, similar documents grouped by clustering tend to be relevant to the same user queries, and so document clustering is used to improve information retrieval [6].

Therefore, we regard document clustering can be a useful technique to overcome the limitations of LDA stated in the second paragraph. We hypothesise that if the input documents can be clustered according to their similarity content before applying to LDA, the resulting short summary constituted from weighty words that are proportionately drawn from each cluster will signify a higher quality of the summary.

2   Tools and Techniques

2.1   Latent Dirichlet Allocation

LDA is a generative unsupervised probabilistic model that is popularly applied in topic modelling [1] (c.f. text summarisation). In LDA, the data is in the form of a collection of documents, where each document is considered as a collection of words. LDA attempts to provide a brief description of the words in the documents by preserving the essential statistical relationships between the words. For this, LDA assumes that each document is represented as a mixture of latent topics, and each topic is represented as a mixture over words. These mixture distributions are further assumed to be Dirichlet-distributed random variables, which must be inferred from the data itself. The generative process is outlined as follows:

1. For each topic, sample a distribution over words from a Dirichlet prior
2. For each document, sample a distribution over topics from a Dirichlet prior
3. For each word in the document
   - Sample a topic from the document's topic distribution
   - Sample a word from the topic's word distribution
   - Observe the word

2.2   Document Clustering

Basically, there are two common types of document clustering techniques, i.e., hierarchical and partitional clustering [5],[7].

Hierarchical clustering produces a nested sequence of partitions, with one inclusive cluster at the top and singleton clusters of documents at the bottom. Each in-between level is like combining two clusters from the next lower level. The result can be viewed as a tree, also known as a dendogram. While the method scales linearly, it is sensitive to the order of the documents in the collection. For example, Qlango [8] is a clustering tool that uses the Hierarchical Agglomerative Clustering (HAC) approach to cluster documents.

Partitional clustering creates a flat partition of the documents. If k is the desired number of clusters, then it will compute a k-way clustering directly or via a sequence of repeated bisections. A direct k-way clustering will find all k clusters at once. A k-way partitioning via repeated bisections recursively applies 2-way partitional clustering. While the method is relatively efficient, we need to specify the number of clusters, i.e., the k value in advance. For example, Data Ninja [9] is a Partitional document clustering tool.

2.3   Summary Evaluation

When evaluating summaries, there are two measures that are often considered: Retention ratio and Compression ratio [10].

Retention Ratio shows how much of the central information is retained, i.e., how much of the information from the full text (documents) is retained in the summary as described by Equation (1).

$$Retention\ ratio, RR = \frac{information\ in\ summary}{information\ in\ full\ text} \tag{1}$$

A high RR means the much of the relevant information in text is preserved in the summary information, and vice versa. The retention can be evaluated by considering the similarities and differences between full text and summary. In this regards, Jensen-Shannon Divergence Probability (JSD) [11], Kullback Leibler Divergence (KLD) [12] and similarity measures (such as Cosine Similarity [13]) are few methods that are utilised to evaluate the effect of summarisation.

KLD is used to evaluate the value of summary information by comparing the entropies or information theoretical divergence of priori distribution P from posteriori distribution Q. In text summarisation, KLD is used to evaluate the divergence between probability distributions of the words in the full text and in the summary. However, KLD is a non-symmetric measure.

JSD is a symmetrical measure defined in terms KLD. JSD incorporates the idea that the distance between two distributions cannot be very different from the average of distances from their mean distribution. A lesser divergence indicates that the deviation of the probability value is small. As a result, a lower divergence probability value signifies a higher retention quality of the summary, i.e., the distribution of the topical words in the summary closely relate to the distribution of the words in the document collection.

Equation (2) defines the JSD measure J, where P and Q are two probability distribution; D refers to KLD measure between probability distributions R and S (see Equation (3)); and A is the mean distribution of P and Q (i.e., A = [P + Q] / 2).

$$J(P \parallel Q) = \frac{1}{2}[D(P \parallel A) + D(Q \parallel A)] \tag{2}$$

$$D(R \parallel S) = \sum_i ln\left(\frac{R_i}{S_i}\right) R_i \tag{3}$$

Cosine Similarity calculates the similarity between two documents: A and B. The measure calculates the cosine of the angle θ between them, which is done by calculating the dot product for the cosine θ, which is shown by Equation (4).

$$Similarity(A, B) = cos\ \theta = \frac{A \cdot B}{\|A\| \|B\|} \tag{4}$$

However, when compared to KLD and Cosine Similarity, JSD outperforms the former methods in measuring the content quality of summaries [14]. JSD is said to provide a reasonably good measure for summarisation tasks that do not rely on the use of model summaries for comparison purposes [15]. Consequently, we used JSD in place of RR. In a way, JSD assesses the retention of relevant text information in the summary by measuring the 'closeness' between probability models of the collection of documents and the content of their summary. Consequently, the Summary Input similarity Metrics (SIMetrix) tool [14] is used to calculate the JSD values of the summaries.

Compression Ratio is the ratio of the length of the compressed text (summary) to the length of the full text [16]. It is represented by Equation (5) as shown below.

$$Compression\ Ratio, CR = \frac{length\ of\ summary}{length\ of\ full\ text} \tag{5}$$

The shorter a summary, the higher is its CR. However, a high CR means less information is retained, which suggests that relevant text information may have been discarded.

Therefore, it is obvious that retention and compression are inversely proportional to each other. The strategy is to find a balance when considering both these properties of a summary. In this study, the CR is fixed at 0.67% of the input text size; that way, we can objectively measure the content quality of the short summaries based on JSP measures alone.

3   The Proposed Clustered-LDA Method

We propose a Clustered-LDA (*ClusLDA*) that adopts the LDA approach to summarise text documents, with the inclusion of a priori clustering process. The conceptual framework of the proposed method is shown in Fig. 1. The idea is that a collection of text documents d, will be clustered into n groups using a clustering technique. Each of these clustered documents, d_C, are separately summarised by LDA, which will result in n topical word summaries (one for each cluster), w_C. Finally, the topical words with higher probabilities (weights) in each summary will be extracted to form the representative summary of the whole collection, sw.

4   Experiment

The purpose of the research is to test the hypothesis that clustering can help to improve the quality of short summaries of LDA. We follow an empirical research approach.

4.1   Sample Documents

The sample documents are extracted from forty-two (42) websites on crops describing events during the agriculture life cycle: *Durian* (14 websites), *Banana* (6), *Corn* (6), *Okra* (5), *Pineapple* (3), *Oil Palm* (4), and *Rambutan* (4). Fig. 2 shows a partial list of web bookmarks that link to the document sources used in this research.

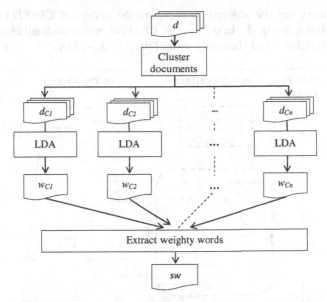

Fig. 1. Conceptual framework of *ClusLDA*

```
1   http://en.wikipedia.org/wiki/Durian
2   http://gallery.durianss2.com/
3   http://raubdurianorchard.blogspot.com/
4   http://gsndev.org/archives/webs/durian/nftree.html
5   http://gsndev.org/archives/webs/durian/nfdisease.html
6   http://gsndev.org/archives/webs/durian/nfcommunity.html
7   http://gsndev.org/archives/webs/durian/nfproduction.html
8   http://gsndev.org/archives/webs/durian/nfnewsmore.html
```

Fig. 2. A list of bookmarks describing the links to document sources

Since we are only interested in text summarisation, the website contents are converted into text format in the experiment. The content from each website is treated as a single document.

4.2   Text Processing Tools

The LDA analysis is performed using the MALLET toolkit [17]. For sake of validation, two clustering techniques, which are supported by their corresponding tools, i.e., Qlango [8] and DataNinja [9] are used to cluster the documents.

4.3   Experiment Design

First, the collection of documents is clustered in k-ways, producing k clusters. In our case, the collection of documents is clustered using Data Ninja's heuristic measure, which determines the k value based on the input text size.

Next, we carry out the analysis to compare the results of *ClusLDA* against *Un-ClusLDA* as shown in Fig. 3. In the case of *ClusLDA*, we considered clustering using DataNinja (DN+LDA), and clustering using Qlango (QL+LDA).

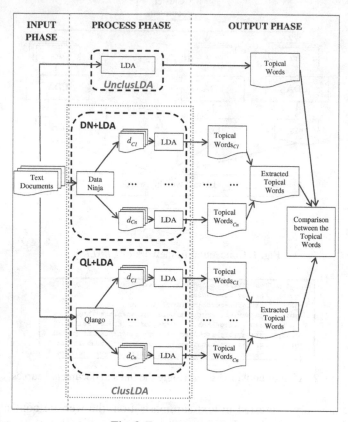

Fig. 3. Experiment design

The three experiments involving *ClusLDA* (DN+LDA and QL+LDA) and *Un-clusLDA* are conducted on three datasets of varying text sizes: Small (14 documents; ≈ 15,000 words), Medium (20 documents; ≈ 30,000 words) and Large (42 documents; ≈ 60,000 words). Therefore, in total nine cases are analysed. The numbers of clusters, k for the three datasets are heuristically determined by DataNinja as 3, 4 and 5, respectively.

In order to produce the representative summary for a collection, we first set the number of top n topics to consider based on the LDA topic weights (tw)[1]. We combine the redundant words and their corresponding word weights (ww)[2]; thus, leaving only unique candidate words of each topic. Next, we select the top 20 words based on their word weights in each topic, which are regarded as good representative

---

[1]   The LDA topic weights are shown beneath the topic labels in the first column of Table 1.
[2]   The word weights are shown next to the words of a topic in the second column of Table 1.

candidates of the topic. For example, the number of topics, n considered for Small dataset using *UnclusLDA* is 5. Since each topic consists of 20 unique weighty candidate words, the number of words in the representative summary of *UnclusLDA* for the Small dataset, m is 100. Note that m is approximately 0.67% of the input text size, i.e., the predetermined compression ratio, *CR*.

While the *UnclusLDA* outputs a single summary of words based on a single cluster, the *ClusLDA* (DN+LDA and QL+LDA) outputs a summary for each cluster, which means there are three or more summaries to consider in the case of latter. For example, in the case of Small dataset, the m value is still 100; however, the n value for each of the three clusters in the *ClusLDA* is 5, which means there are 15 * 20 = 300 candidate words to consider. So, we sort the candidate words of all n topics of each cluster based on their topic and word weights (*tw* * *ww*) and extract the candidate words from each cluster that is proportionate to the size of the cluster in order to form a representative summary of the collection of size m words.

Table 2 describes the information about the three experiment datasets. Note that the n and m values are doubled and quadrupled corresponding to the text sizes of the Medium and the Large datasets, respectively; thus, maintaining the *CR* at 0.67% of the input text size.

Table 2. The three experiment datasets

Factor	Dataset		
	Small	Medium	Large
No. of words in documents	15,049	30,009	60,035
No. of clusters	3	4	5
No. of LDA topics, n	5	10	20
No. of words in summary, m	100	200	400

5   Experiment Results

We evaluated the content quality of the summaries of *UnclusLDA* and *ClusLDA* (DN+LDA and QL+LDA) using JSD and CR. The results of the Small, Medium and Large datasets are shown in Tables 3, 4 and 5, respectively. A lower JSD value signifies a higher quality of the summary. Because the *CR* value is fixed, we can objectively measure and compare the content qualities of the summaries of different text sizes.

Table 3. Content quality of summaries of the Small dataset

System	No. of Docs	No. of Clusters	JSD	No. of Words in Dataset	No. of Words in Summary	CR	JSD*CR
UnclusLDA			0.3907				0.0026
DN+LDA	14	3	0.3905	15,049	100	0.0066	0.0026
QL+LDA			0.3888				0.0026

Table 4. Content quality of summaries of the Medium dataset

System	No. of Docs	No. of Clusters	JSD	No. of Words in Dataset	No. of Words in Summary	CR	JSD*CR
UnclusLDA			0.3467				0.0023
DN+LDA	20	4	0.3720	30,009	200	0.0067	0.0025
QL+LDA			0.3748				0.0025

Table 5. Content quality of summaries of the Large dataset

System	No. of Docs	No. of Clusters	JSD	No. of Words in Dataset	No. of Words in Summary	CR	JSD*CR
UnclusLDA			0.3183				0.0021
DN+LDA	42	5	0.3359	60,035	400	0.0067	0.0022
QL+LDA			0.3337				0.0022

For the Small dataset, the JSD value for the *ClusLDA* using QLango, i.e., QL+LDA is the smallest at 0.3888. In fact, both DataNinja and QLango clustered-LDA (i.e., DN+LDA and QL+LDA) have a smaller JSD value than *UnclusLDA* for this dataset. This means that there is an improvement in the quality of the summary when clustering is applied. However, the improvement is not very significant. For DN+LDA, the JSD measure has improved by only 0.1%, while for QL+LDA, the improvement is 0.5%.

For the Medium and the Large datasets, the JSD value of *UnclusLDA* is the smallest, i.e., 0.3467 and 0.3183, respectively. The quality of the summary of the *UnclusLDA* appears to be better than that of *ClusLDA* in these two cases. The result shows a decline in the quality of the summary by 7.3% and 8.1% for the Medium dataset, and a decline of 5.5% and 4.8% for the Large dataset, when using the Data-Ninja and Qlango, respectively.

6   Conclusion

The study tests the hypothesis that if the input documents can be clustered according to their similarity content before applying to LDA, the resulting summary constituted from weighty words that are proportionately drawn from each clusters will signify a higher quality of the summary. For sake of validation, inputs of various text sizes are considered and checked the results using two clustering techniques, i.e., agglomerative and partitional clustering using Qlango (QL) and DataNinja (DN) tools, respectively. The experiments are conducted using three datasets classified as Small, Medium and Large. The content quality of the summaries of *UnclusLDA* and *ClusLDA* (DN+LDA and QL+LDA) are evaluated using JSD (c.f. RR) and CR.

The results show that the quality of the summaries generated by *ClusLDA* is (insignificantly) better compared to the summaries produced by *UnclusLDA* when summarising small datasets. However, the latter outperforms the former by a slight margin when summarising larger datasets. Therefore it appears that clustering does not necessarily help to improve the content quality of short summaries.

The current work has several limitations. First, only two clustering techniques are tested. Additional clustering techniques can be considered in future work for better comparison of the results. Second, the size of the Large dataset can be increased. If the documents are from mixed subjects, and are much larger, the comparison might produce a more pronounced result. Third, a more defined method can be applied to determine the number of clusters. The use of heuristics based on text size is rather simplistic. Forth, future work can study the effect of increasing the CR from the present 0.67% of the input text size.

Acknowledgement. This project is supported by the Universiti Teknologi MARA's Cluster Grant No. 600-RMI/DANA 5/3/CG (12/2012).

References

1. Blei, D., Ng, A., Jordan, M.: Latent Dirichlet Allocation. Journal of Machine Learning Research 3, 993–1022 (2003)
2. Jamaludin, N.A., Annamalai, M., Jamil, N., Bakar, Z.A.: A Model for Keyword Profile Creation using Extracted Keywords and Terminological Ontology. In: IEEE Conference on e-Learning, e-Management and e-Services, Kuching, Malaysia, pp. 136–141 (2013)
3. Kang, Y., Ma, J., Liu, Y.: Transfer Topic Modeling with Ease and Scalability. In: Twelfth SIAM International Conference on Data Mining, Anaheim, CA, USA, pp. 564–575 (2012)
4. Arora, R., Ravindran, B.: Latent Dirichlet Allocation based Multi-Document Summarization. In: Second Workshop on Analytics for Noisy Unstructured Text Data, Singapore, pp. 91–97 (2008)
5. Konchady, M.: Clustering Documents. In: Text Mining Application Programming, ch. 8. Charles River Media, Boston (2006)
6. Yoo, I., Hu, X.: A Comprehensive Comparison Study of Document Clustering for a Biomedical Digital Library MEDLINE. In: Sixth ACM/IEEE-CS Joint Conference on Digital Libraries, pp. 220–229. Chapel Hill, NC (2006)
7. Steinbach, M., Karypis, G., Kumar, V.: A Comparison of Document Clustering Techniques. In: KDD Workshop on Text Mining, Boston, MA, USA, pp. 109–111 (2000)
8. Qlango, http://semanticsearchart.com
9. Data Ninja, http://sourceforge.net/projects/dataninja
10. Hassel, M.: Evaluation of Automatic Text Summarization: A Practical Implementation. Licentiate Thesis, University of Stockholm, Sweden (2004)
11. Lin, J.: Divergence Measures based on the Shannon Entropy. IEEE Transactions on Information Theory 37(1), 145–151 (1991)
12. Kullback, S., Leibler, R.A.: On Information and Sufficiency. Annals of Mathematical Statistics 22(1), 79–86 (1951)
13. Perone, C.S.: Machine Learning: Cosine Similarity for Vector Space Models (Part III). Pyevolve, http://pyevolve.sourceforge.net/wordpress/?cat=213
14. Louis, A., Nenkova, A.: Automatically Evaluating Content Selection in Summarization Without Human Models. In: Conference on Empirical Methods in Natural Language Processing, Singapore, pp. 306–314 (2009)
15. Torres-Moreno, J.-M., Saggion, H., da Cunha, I., Velázquez-Morales, P., SanJuan, E.: Summary Evaluation With and Without References. Polibitis: Research Journal on Computer science and Computer Engineering with Applications 42, 13–19 (2010)

16. Hobson, S.F.: Text Summarization Evaluation: Correlation Human Performance on an Extrinsic Task with Automatic Intrinsic Metrics. Doctoral Thesis, University of Mary-land, College Park (2007)
17. MALLET: MAchine Learning for LanguagE Toolkit, http://mallet.cs.umass.edu

Author Index